Oor Wedding

Wedding Invitation

Dear Reader,

You and yours are invited to the wedding o' oor

The reception will be in the Co-operative Hall and winna be an early feenish. Mind and tak' yer dancin' shoes and we look forward tae hae'in a birl roond the flair wi' you.

C and Paw Broon

R.S.V.P

The Broons
10 Glebe Street

(If you dinna hae an invite you can aye jist pay at the door) I'M JOKIN'!!

If you are struggling for a weddin' present idea then let me mention that last time we were at Maggie and Dave's new hoose, their carpets, Granpaw and me had tae share a soup spoon at denner time.

1. **Maggie May** TMK Stewart/Quittenton-
Rod Stewart/EMI April Music Inc/EMI Music
Publishing Ltd/EMI Full Keel Music

2. **Beautiful Sunday** TMK McQueen/Boone
Emi Music Publishing Ltd

3. **Scottish Waltz** Ceilidh-M

4. **Broon's Reel (Dashing White Sergeant)** Ceilidh-M

5. **Gay Gordons** Ceilidh-M

6. **The Road and The Miles To Dundee**
The Munros Featuring Cailean McLean

7. **Jigs** Stevie Lawrence

8. **Strip The Willow** Ceilidh-M

9. **Scots Wha Hae**
The Munros Featuring Cailean McLean

10. **Loch Lomond (Accordion Version)**
Billy McIntyre And His Ceilidh Band

11. **Brown Eyed Girl** TMK Morrison Web IV Music Inc/
Universal Music Publishing International Ltd/
Universal Music Publishing Ltd

12. **Dancing Queen** TMK Andersson/Anderson/Ulvaeus
Universal/Union Songs Musikforlag Ab Bocu Music Ltd
Bocu (Abba) Music

13. **I'm In The Mood For Dancing** TMK Findon/
Myers/Puzey Emi Music Publishing Ltd

14. **Night Fever** TMK Gibb/Gibb/Gibb Gibb Brothers
Music/Universal Music Publ International MGB Ltd/
Universal Music Publishing International Ltd/
Universal Music Publishing MGB Ltd

15. **Save Your Kisses For Me** TMK Hiller/Lee/
Sheridan Emi Music Publishing Ltd

16. **Sweet Caroline** TMK Diamond Stonebridge-
Music Inc/Sony-ATV Tunes Llc/Sony/ATV Music
Publishing Llc/Sony/ATV Music Publishing Llc

17. **The Locomotion** TMK Goffin/King
Screen Gems-Emi Music Ltd

18. **Tie A Yellow Ribbon** TMK Brown/Levine
Irwin Levine Music/Spirit One Music/Spirit Music
Publishing Ltd/Peermusic III Ltd

19. **Pipe Band Medley** Oban High School Pipe
Band Trad

20. **Auld Lang Syne (Bagpipes Version)**
The Munros

Traditional arrangements are published by DC Thomson & Co Ltd.
Pipe Band Medley performed by and permission of Oban High School
Pipe Band
Packaging © DC Thomson & Co, Ltd 2012 The Broons © DC Thomson &
Co. Ltd 2012.
Mastered at The Music Kitchen Ltd, for DC Thomson & Co Ltd.

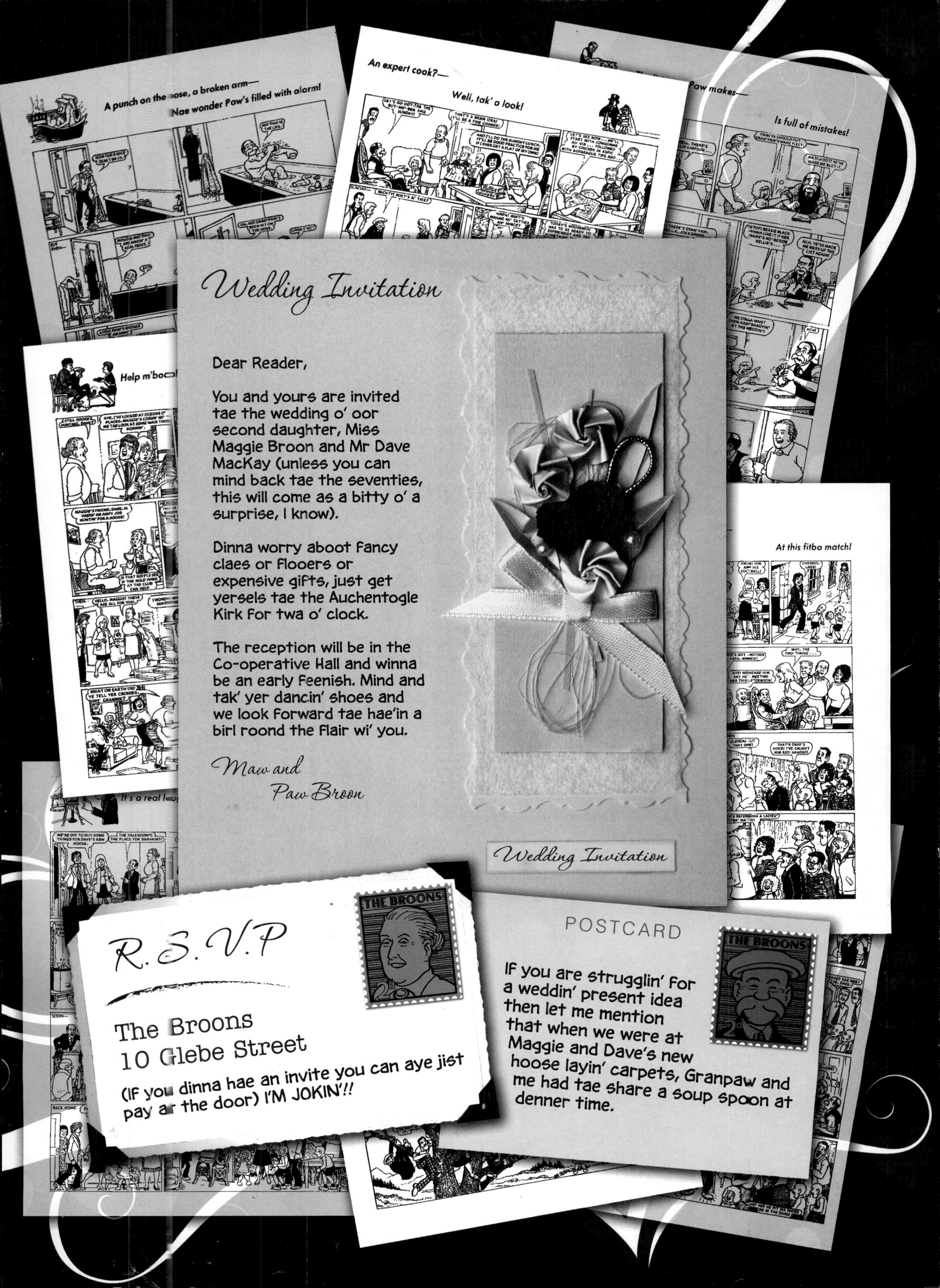
A punch on the nose, a broken arm—
Nae wonder Paw's filled with alarm!
An expert cook?—
Well, tak' a look!
Paw makes—
Is full of mistakes!
At this fitba match!
Wedding Invitation
Dear Reader,
You and yours are invited tae the wedding o' oor second daughter, Miss Maggie Broon and Mr Dave MacKay (unless you can mind back tae the seventies, this will come as a bitty o' a surprise, I know).
Dinna worry aboot fancy claes or flooers or expensive gifts, just get yersels tae the Auchentogle Kirk for twa o' clock.
The reception will be in the Co-operative Hall and winna be an early feenish. Mind and tak' yer dancin' shoes and we look forward tae hae'in a birl roond the flair wi' you.
Maw and
Paw Broon
Wedding Invitation
THE BROONS
R.S.V.P
The Broons
10 Glebe Street
(If you dinna hae an invite you can aye jist pay at the door) I'M JOKIN'!!
POSTCARD
THE BROONS
If you are strugglin' for a weddin' present idea then let me mention that when we were at Maggie and Dave's new hoose layin' carpets, Granpaw and me had tae share a soup spoon at denner time.

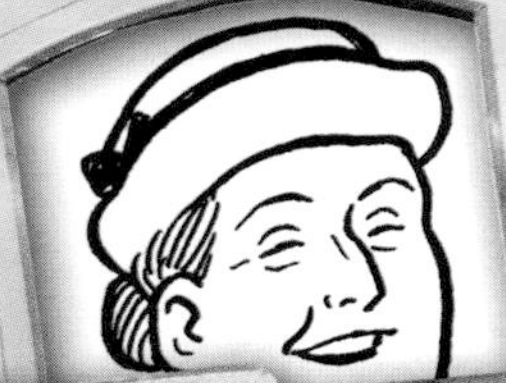

In This Book

The romance between Maggie Broon and Dave McKay started in 1977. Readers of The Sunday Post saw Dave for the first time in March of that year when he was invited to spend the weekend with the family at the But an' Ben. The romance continued in the weekly Broons strips through 1977, 1978 and into 1979. This was a serious romance and the couple got engaged to be married. Together they bought a house and a wedding date was set.

The Broons and Oor Wullie strips had a very distinctive look during this period in the seventies, this was down to a new artist, Tom Lavery. Tom was the first regular artist to illustrate the strips since the death of the legendary Dudley D Watkins who had designed the characters in 1936 and drew their weekly exploits continuously for 33 years. So, the wedding was planned, a house bought, Paw Broon even practised walking Maggie down the aisle. But would there be a son-in-law for Maw Broon? Will you ever see this photo?

Read on, dear reader, all will be revealed...

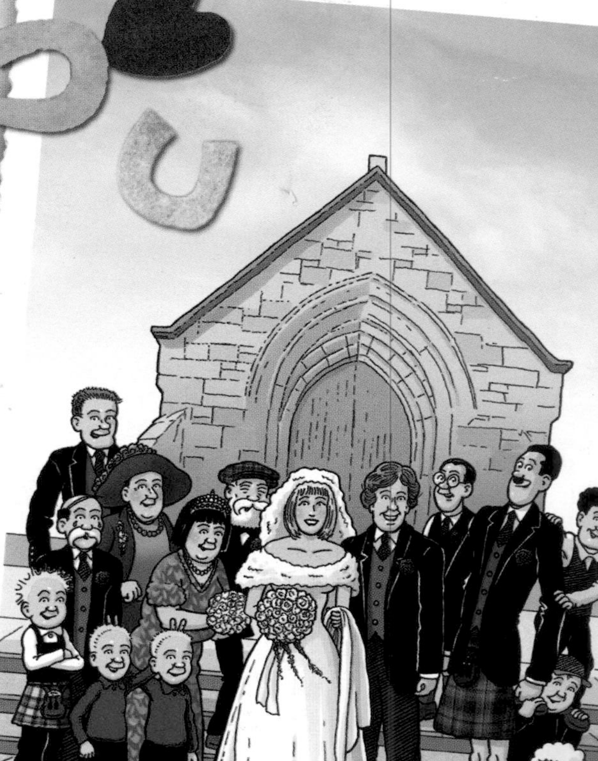

Well, well, well! Did you ever see—

Such a funny-looking family tree?

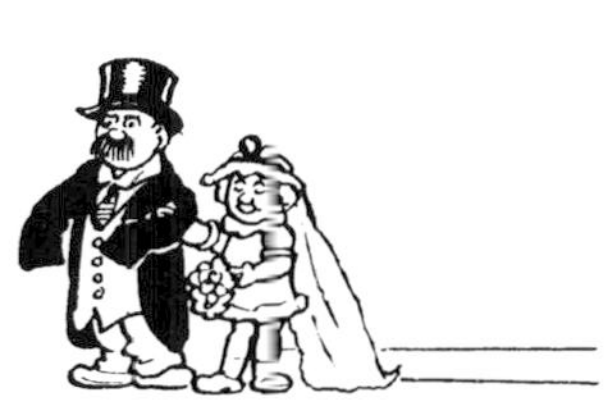

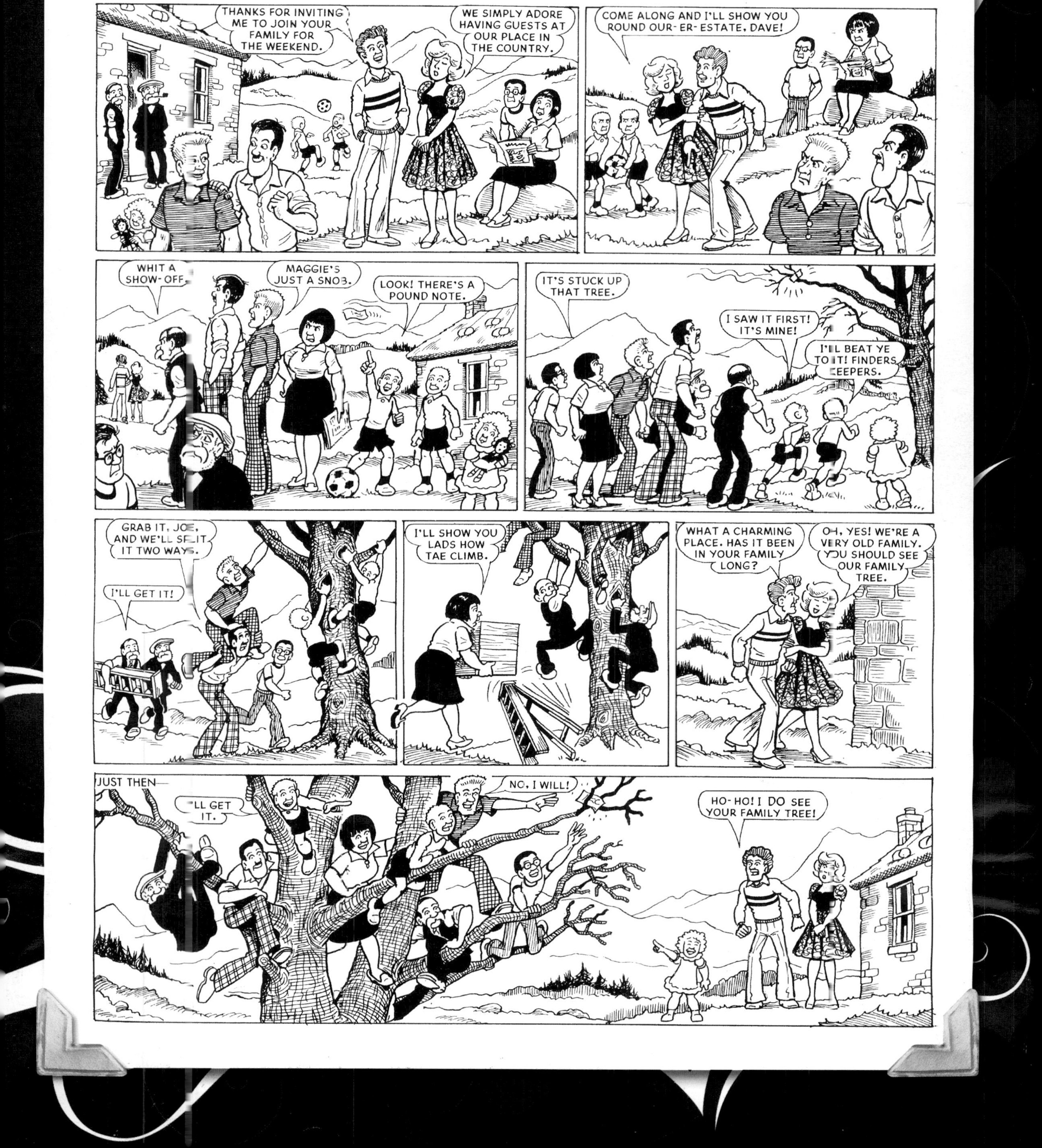

THANKS FOR INVITING ME TO JOIN YOUR FAMILY FOR THE WEEKEND.
WE SIMPLY ADORE HAVING GUESTS AT OUR PLACE IN THE COUNTRY.
COME ALONG AND I'LL SHOW YOU ROUND OUR-ER-ESTATE, DAVE!
WHIT A SHOW-OFF.
MAGGIE'S JUST A SNOB.
LOOK! THERE'S A POUND NOTE.
IT'S STUCK UP THAT TREE.
I SAW IT FIRST! IT'S MINE!
I'LL BEAT YE TO IT! FINDERS KEEPERS.
GRAB IT, JOE, AND WE'LL SPLIT IT TWO WAYS.
I'LL GET IT!
I'LL SHOW YOU LADS HOW TAE CLIMB.
WHAT A CHARMING PLACE. HAS IT BEEN IN YOUR FAMILY LONG?
OH, YES! WE'RE A VERY OLD FAMILY. YOU SHOULD SEE OUR FAMILY TREE.
JUST THEN—
I'LL GET IT.
NO, I WILL!
HO-HO! I DO SEE YOUR FAMILY TREE!

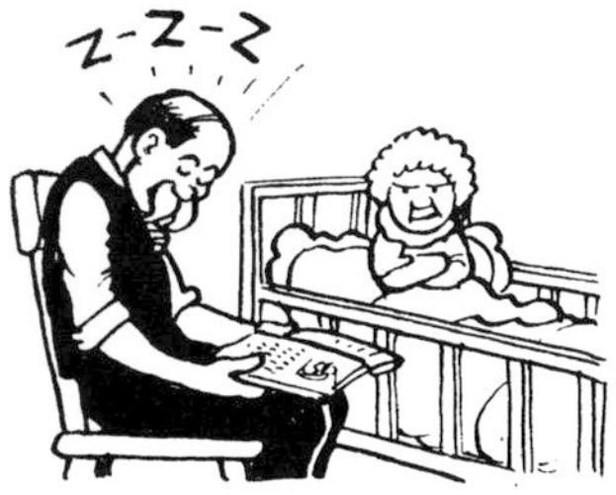
Z-Z-Z

Poor Paw's in a sorry plight—

It seems he can't tell left from right!

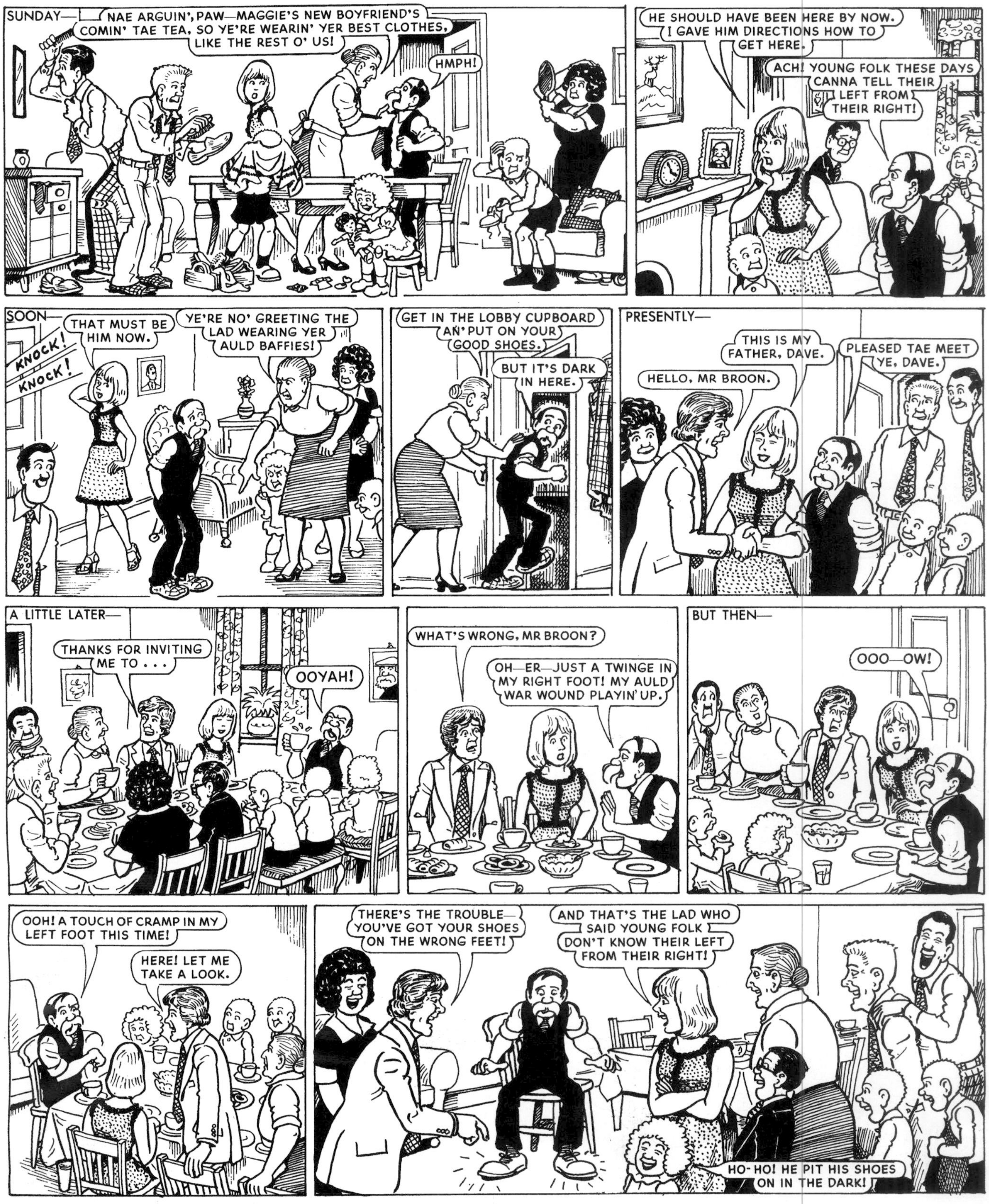
SUNDAY—
NAE ARGUIN', PAW—MAGGIE'S NEW BOYFRIEND'S COMIN' TAE TEA, SO YE'RE WEARIN' YER BEST CLOTHES, LIKE THE REST O' US!
HMPH!
HE SHOULD HAVE BEEN HERE BY NOW. I GAVE HIM DIRECTIONS HOW TO GET HERE.
ACH! YOUNG FOLK THESE DAYS CANNA TELL THEIR LEFT FROM THEIR RIGHT!
SOON—
KNOCK! KNOCK!
THAT MUST BE HIM NOW.
YE'RE NO' GREETING THE LAD WEARING YER AULD BAFFIES!
GET IN THE LOBBY CUPBOARD AN' PUT ON YOUR GOOD SHOES.
BUT IT'S DARK IN HERE.
PRESENTLY—
THIS IS MY FATHER, DAVE.
HELLO, MR BROON.
PLEASED TAE MEET YE, DAVE.
A LITTLE LATER—
THANKS FOR INVITING ME TO . . .
OOYAH!
WHAT'S WRONG, MR BROON?
OH—ER—JUST A TWINGE IN MY RIGHT FOOT! MY AULD WAR WOUND PLAYIN' UP.
BUT THEN—
OOO—OW!
OOH! A TOUCH OF CRAMP IN MY LEFT FOOT THIS TIME!
HERE! LET ME TAKE A LOOK.
THERE'S THE TROUBLE— YOU'VE GOT YOUR SHOES ON THE WRONG FEET!
AND THAT'S THE LAD WHO SAID YOUNG FOLK DON'T KNOW THEIR LEFT FROM THEIR RIGHT!
HO-HO! HE PIT HIS SHOES ON IN THE DARK!

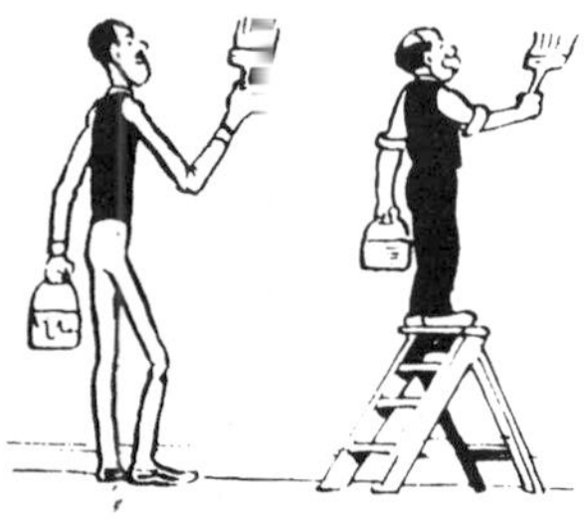

What a to-do—

When the clock strikes two!

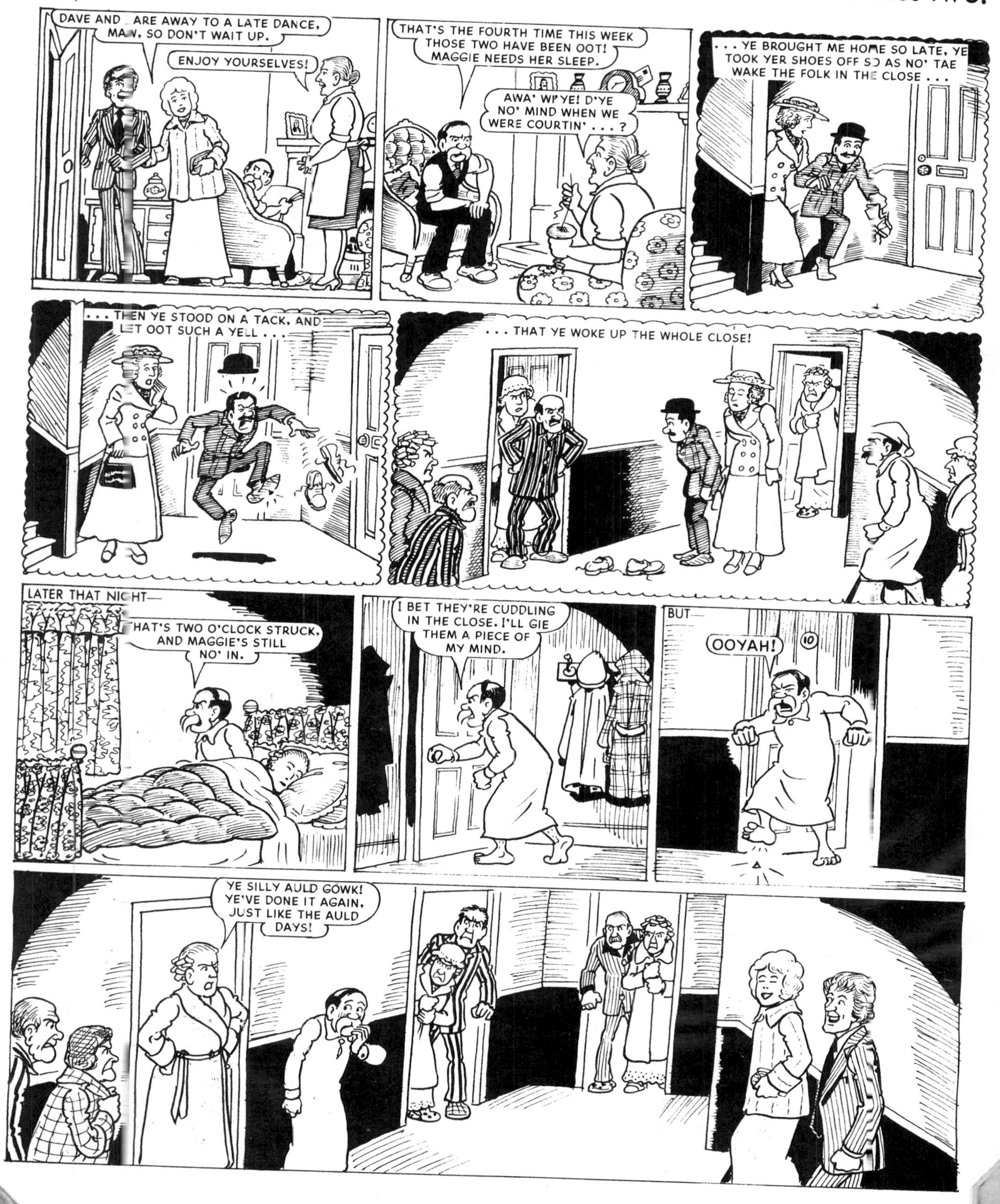
DAVE AND ARE AWAY TO A LATE DANCE, MAW, SO DON'T WAIT UP.
ENJOY YOURSELVES!
THAT'S THE FOURTH TIME THIS WEEK THOSE TWO HAVE BEEN OOT! MAGGIE NEEDS HER SLEEP.
AWA' WI' YE! D'YE NO' MIND WHEN WE WERE COURTIN' . . . ?
. . . YE BROUGHT ME HOME SO LATE, YE TOOK YER SHOES OFF SO AS NO' TAE WAKE THE FOLK IN THE CLOSE . . .
. . . THEN YE STOOD ON A TACK, AND LET OOT SUCH A YELL . . .
. . . THAT YE WOKE UP THE WHOLE CLOSE!
LATER THAT NIGHT—
THAT'S TWO O'CLOCK STRUCK, AND MAGGIE'S STILL NO' IN.
I BET THEY'RE CUDDLING IN THE CLOSE. I'LL GIE THEM A PIECE OF MY MIND.
BUT—
OOYAH!
10
YE SILLY AULD GOWK! YE'VE DONE IT AGAIN, JUST LIKE THE AULD DAYS!

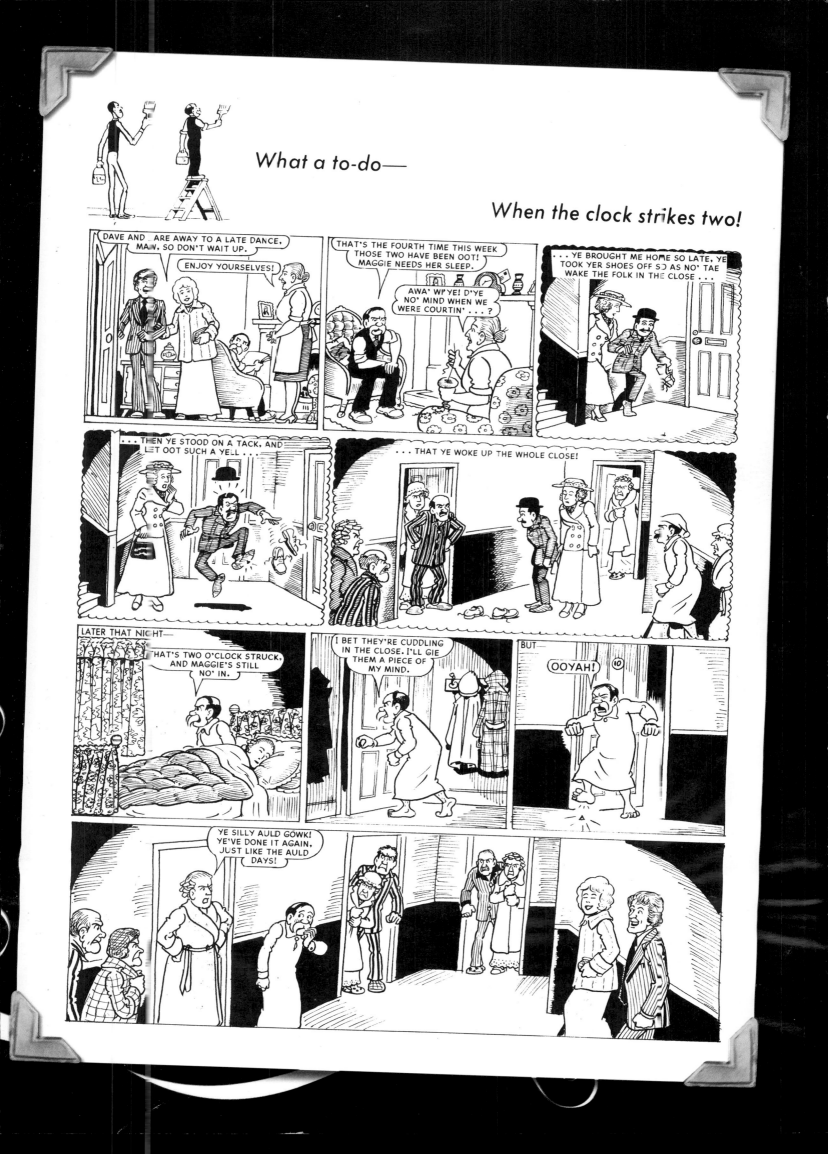

THIS country run—

Isn't much fun!

THAT'S MAGGIE'S LAD'S CAR. SMASHIN', EH?
AYE! AN' THAT'S THE THIRD TIME THIS WEEK HE'S VISITED THE HOOSE.
10
HELLO . . . PANT . . . THESE STAIRS . . . GASP . . . ARE TOO MUCH . . . PUFF . . . AFTER A DAY'S WORK!
I'M OOT O' BREATH AS WELL.
WE WERE ADMIRING YOUR CAR, DAVE. IT'S A BEAUTY.
THANKS, JOE.
LISTEN, LADS, MAGGIE'S WASHING HER HAIR TONIGHT, SO I COULD TAKE YOU OUT FOR A RUN.
WE CAN GO OUT BY POWRIE LOCH.
WE'VE GOT PLENTY TIME. LET'S GO FARTHER THAN THAT.
OKAY! GET YOUR SHORTS ON. MY KIT'S IN THE CAR.
EH?
HO-HO! DID YE NO' KEN—DAVE'S A P.E. TEACHER!
I'LL SOON HAVE YOU FIT FOR CLIMBING THE STAIRS. JOGGING'S JUST THE THING TO GET YOU IN SHAPE!
AND YOU . . . PUFF . . . SAID WE COULD GO FARTHER . . . PANT . . . THAN POWRIE LOCH!
POWRIE LOCH. 2 MILES

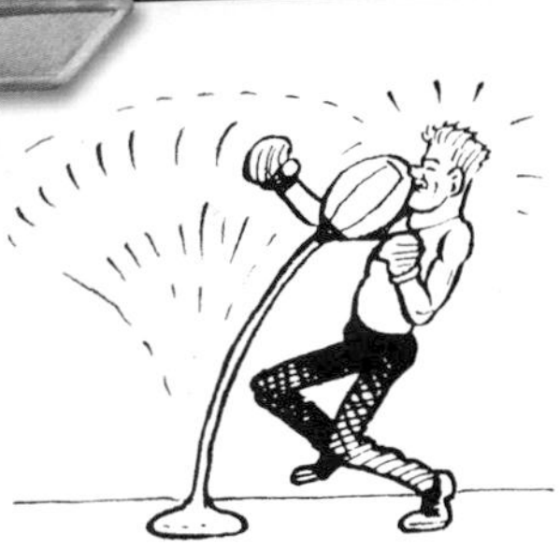

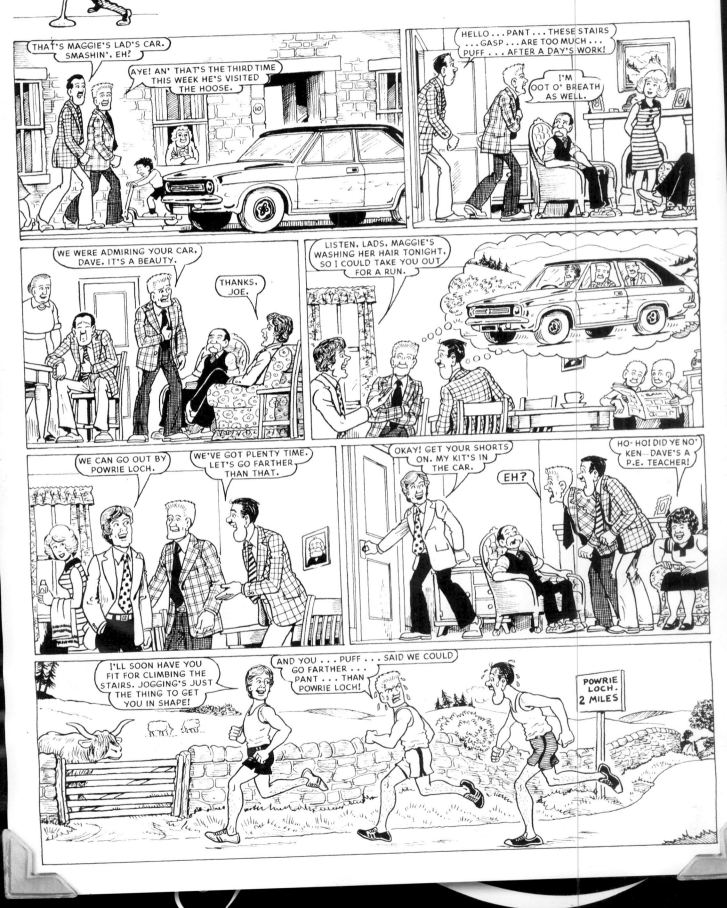

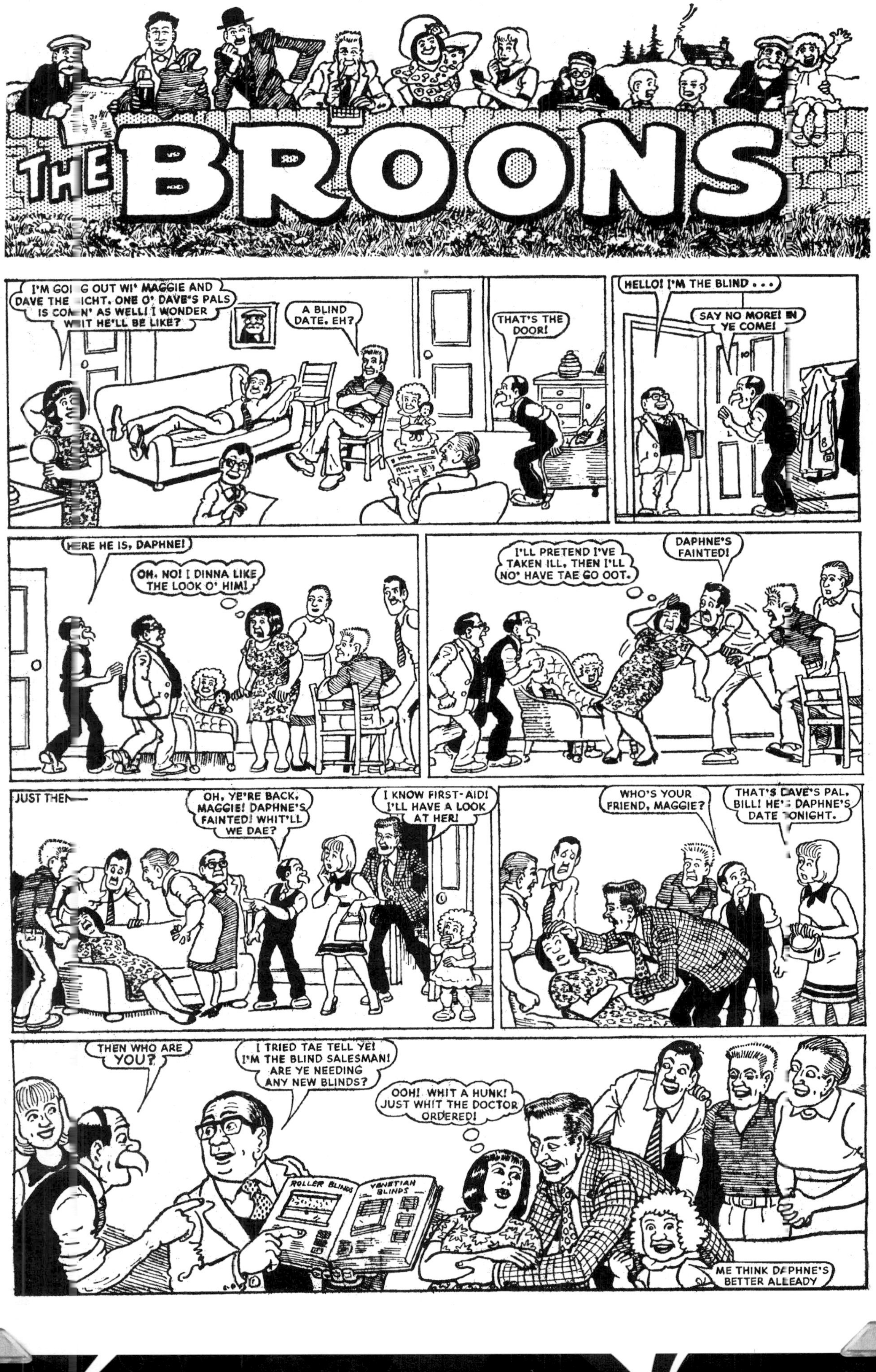
THE BROONS
I'M GOING OUT WI' MAGGIE AND DAVE THE NICHT. ONE O' DAVE'S PALS IS COMIN' AS WELL! I WONDER WHIT HE'LL BE LIKE?
A BLIND DATE, EH?
THAT'S THE DOOR!
HELLO! I'M THE BLIND . . .
SAY NO MORE! IN YE COME!
HERE HE IS, DAPHNE!
OH, NO! I DINNA LIKE THE LOOK O' HIM!
I'LL PRETEND I'VE TAKEN ILL, THEN I'LL NO' HAVE TAE GO OOT.
DAPHNE'S FAINTED!
JUST THEN—
OH, YE'RE BACK, MAGGIE! DAPHNE'S FAINTED! WHIT'LL WE DAE?
I KNOW FIRST-AID! I'LL HAVE A LOOK AT HER!
WHO'S YOUR FRIEND, MAGGIE?
THAT'S DAVE'S PAL, BILL! HE'S DAPHNE'S DATE TONIGHT.
THEN WHO ARE YOU?
I TRIED TAE TELL YE! I'M THE BLIND SALESMAN! ARE YE NEEDING ANY NEW BLINDS?
OOH! WHIT A HUNK! JUST WHIT THE DOCTOR ORDERED!
ROLLER BLINDS
VENETIAN BLINDS
ME THINK DAPHNE'S BETTER ALREADY

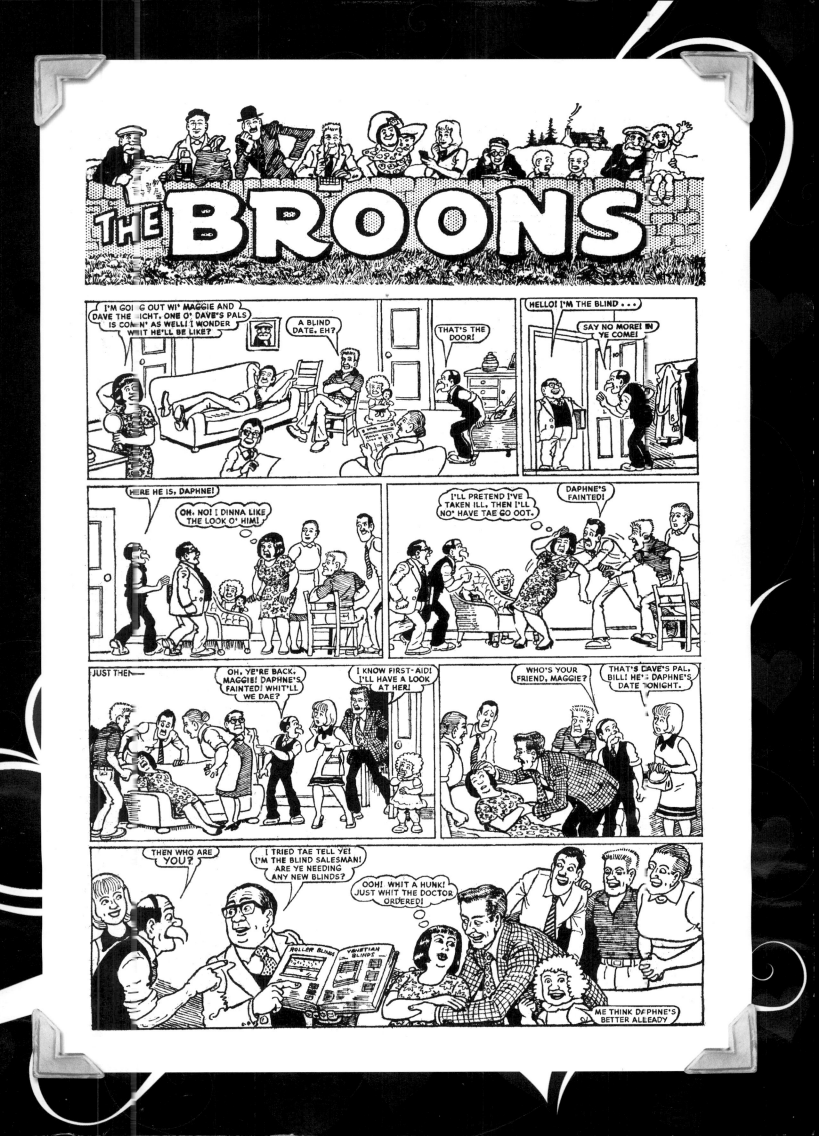

Maggie's bein' an awfy bore—

But, jings, she's got a shock in store!

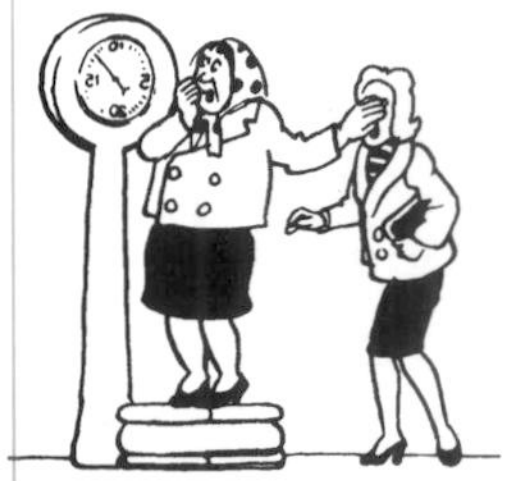

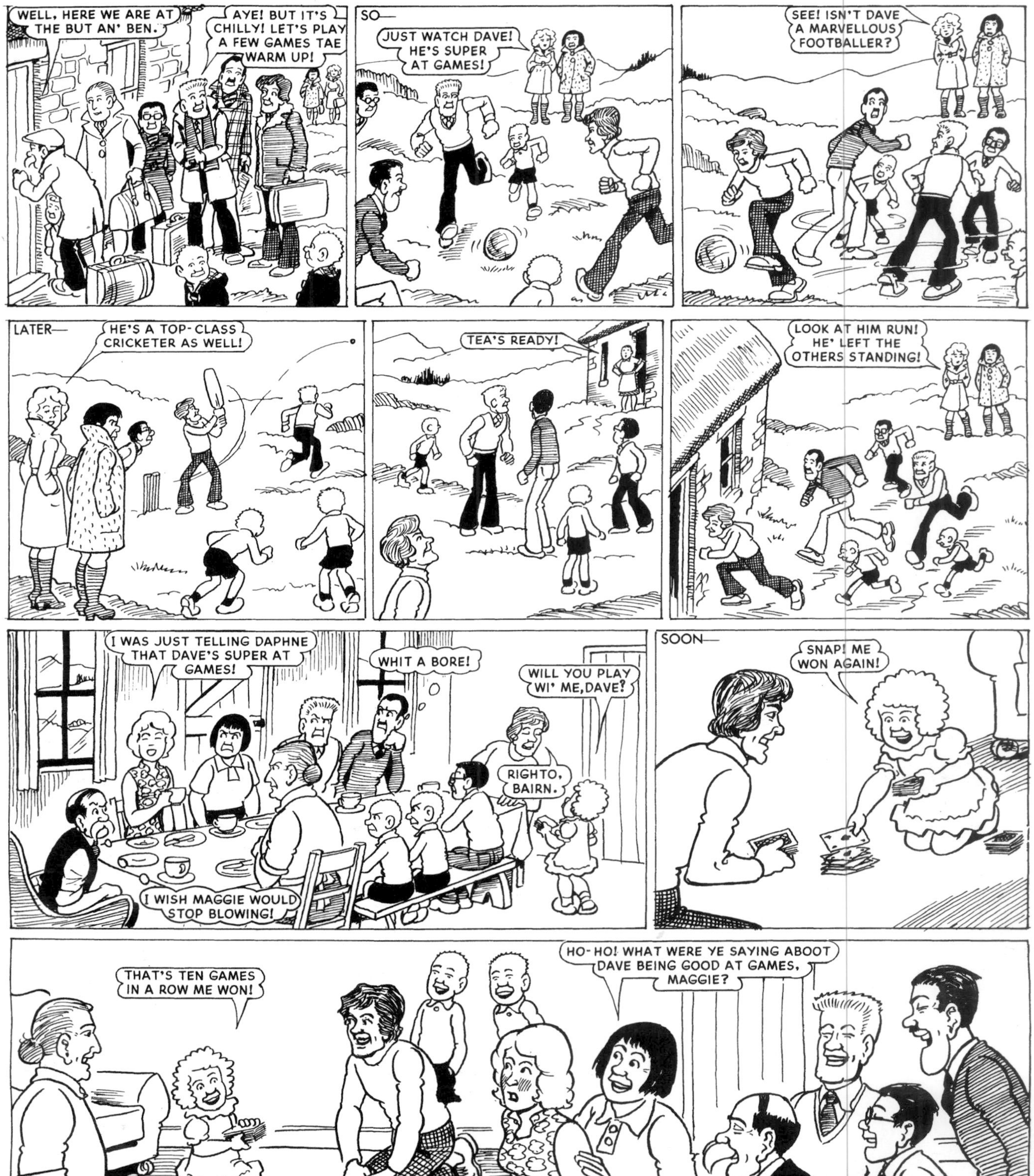

WELL, HERE WE ARE AT THE BUT AN' BEN.
AYE! BUT IT'S CHILLY! LET'S PLAY A FEW GAMES TAE WARM UP!
SO—
JUST WATCH DAVE! HE'S SUPER AT GAMES!
SEE! ISN'T DAVE A MARVELLOUS FOOTBALLER?
LATER—
HE'S A TOP-CLASS CRICKETER AS WELL!
TEA'S READY!
LOOK AT HIM RUN! HE' LEFT THE OTHERS STANDING!
I WAS JUST TELLING DAPHNE THAT DAVE'S SUPER AT GAMES!
WHIT A BORE!
WILL YOU PLAY WI' ME, DAVE?
RIGHTO, BAIRN.
I WISH MAGGIE WOULD STOP BLOWING!
SOON—
SNAP! ME WON AGAIN!
THAT'S TEN GAMES IN A ROW ME WON!
HO-HO! WHAT WERE YE SAYING ABOOT DAVE BEING GOOD AT GAMES, MAGGIE?

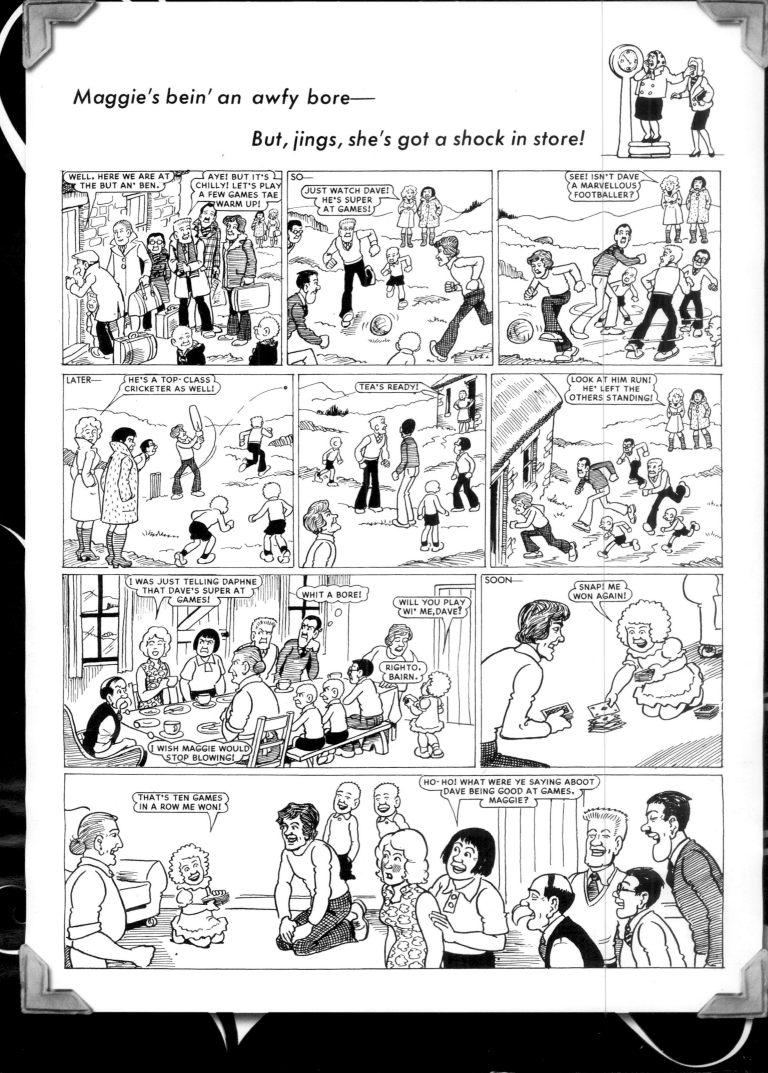

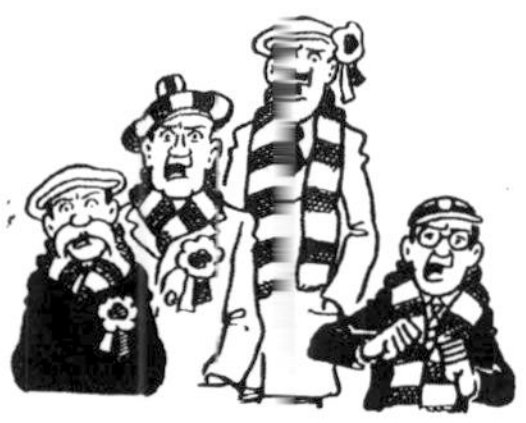

There's no " ifs " and " buts "—

These lads are going " nuts!"

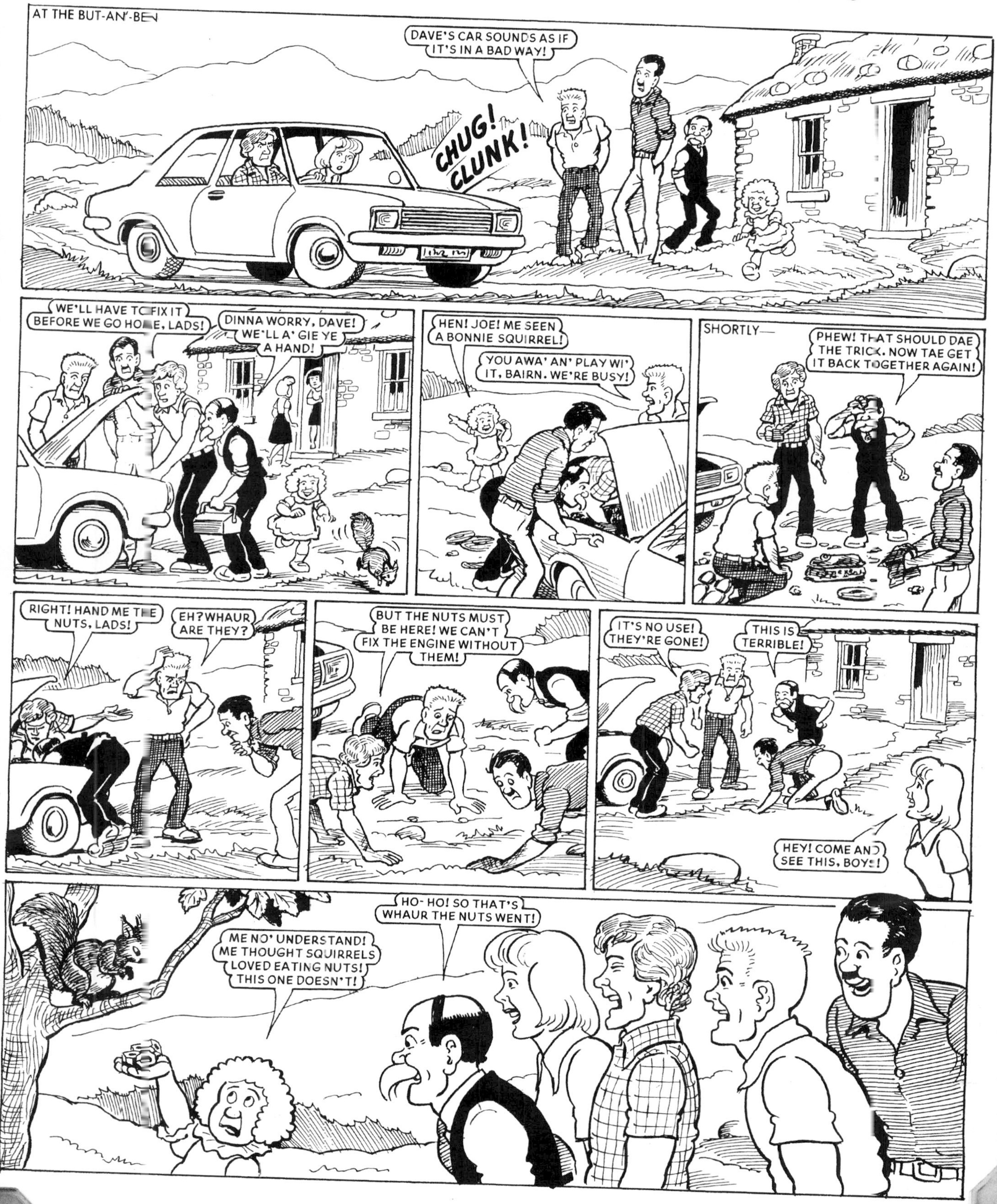

AT THE BUT-AN'-BEN
DAVE'S CAR SOUNDS AS IF IT'S IN A BAD WAY!
CHUG! CLUNK!
WE'LL HAVE TO FIX IT BEFORE WE GO HOME, LADS!
DINNA WORRY, DAVE! WE'LL A' GIE YE A HAND!
HEN! JOE! ME SEEN A BONNIE SQUIRREL!
YOU AWA' AN' PLAY WI' IT, BAIRN. WE'RE BUSY!
SHORTLY—
PHEW! THAT SHOULD DAE THE TRICK. NOW TAE GET IT BACK TOGETHER AGAIN!
RIGHT! HAND ME THE NUTS, LADS!
EH? WHAUR ARE THEY?
BUT THE NUTS MUST BE HERE! WE CAN'T FIX THE ENGINE WITHOUT THEM!
IT'S NO USE! THEY'RE GONE!
THIS IS TERRIBLE!
HEY! COME AND SEE THIS, BOYS!
HO-HO! SO THAT'S WHAUR THE NUTS WENT!
ME NO' UNDERSTAND! ME THOUGHT SQUIRRELS LOVED EATING NUTS! THIS ONE DOESN'T!

Be my Valentine!

00075 REG CINE ADMIT Matinee

Darling Maggie,

I couldnae sleep for thinking aboot you, well that an' the second helpin' o' dumplin' your Maw gied me when we got back last nicht, so I wrote you this poem.

Maggie Broon, oh Maggie Broon,
Maggie, Maggie, Maggie Broon,
You're the niftiest chick in the toon,
I really am ower the moon.

Canna wait tae see you again.

Dave xx

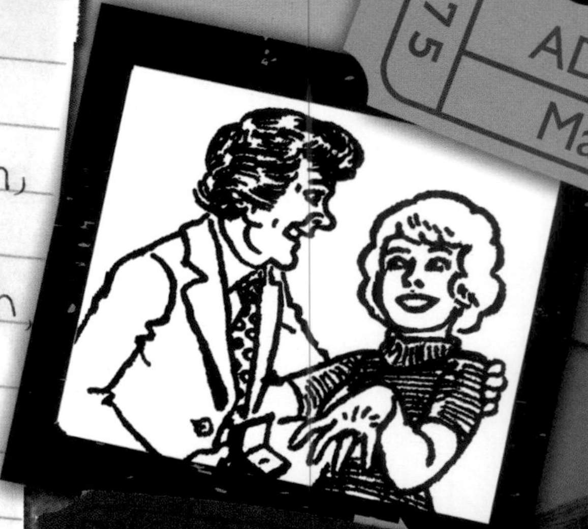

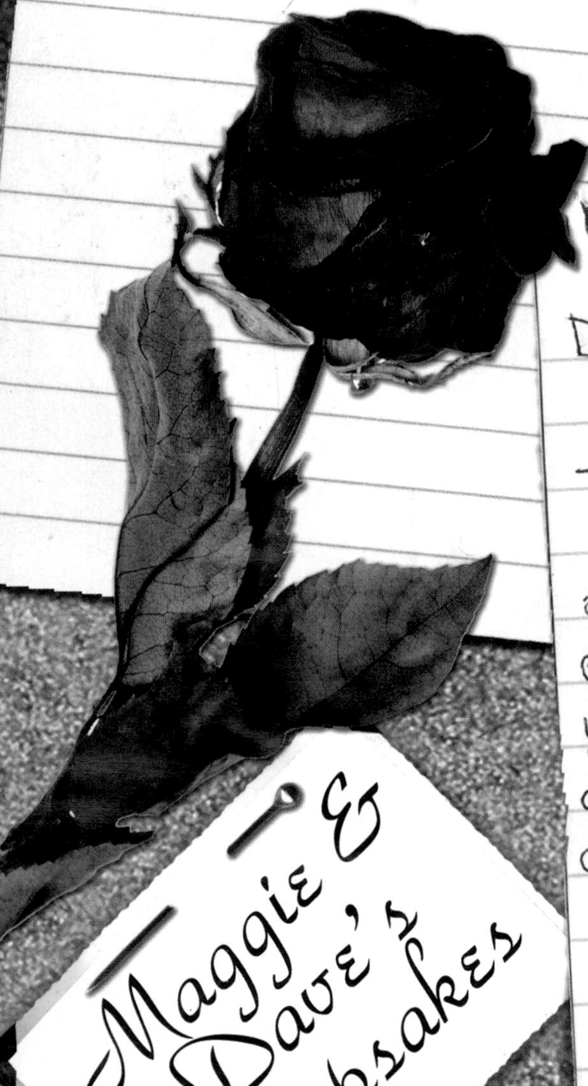

Dear Maggie,

I cannae believe the best lookin' lassie in Auchentoogle has agreed tae go oot wi' me. I couldnae tak' my eyes aff you in the street yesterday and walked right intae auld Bella Shaw. She ca'd me a mugger and walloped me wi' her handbag, but it was worth it – even though Bella must hae bricks in her bag. I'll pick you up at seven.

I wish it was seven. Dave.

Maggie & Dave's Keepsakes

Dearest darling Maggie,
Aye yer Paw gave me a bit o' the verbals for gettin' you hame so late last night but it was worth it. I'd pit my new velvet jacket ower a puddle for you, darling. I've kept the paper plate your stories came in but I canna find the plastic fork. I thought you looked better than Farrah Fawcett last night when you were angry. Never be angry-wangy with your Davilans. Xx

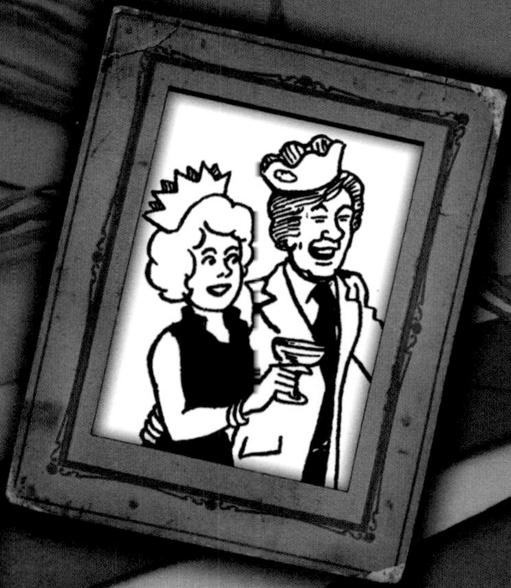

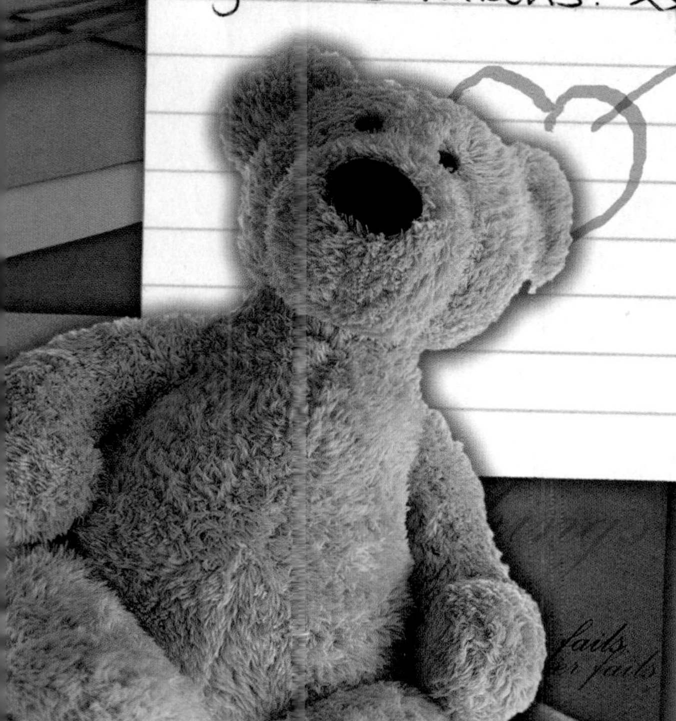

Darling Maggie,
I was so jealous when I saw you in Peem's car that I nearly ran after it and kicked his bumper, even though I was wearing the new platforms that cost me thirty bob in auld money. Peem wis smirkin' at me when I saw him in the chipper but Susie behind the counter didnae salt his chips. I think she fancies me but dinnae you be jealous. Dave.

XXX

My darling,
I love you more than Archie Gemmill or my Hillman Hunter. I want to marry you. Please be mine

Dave xxxxxx

Blackpool 1973

Jams galore—

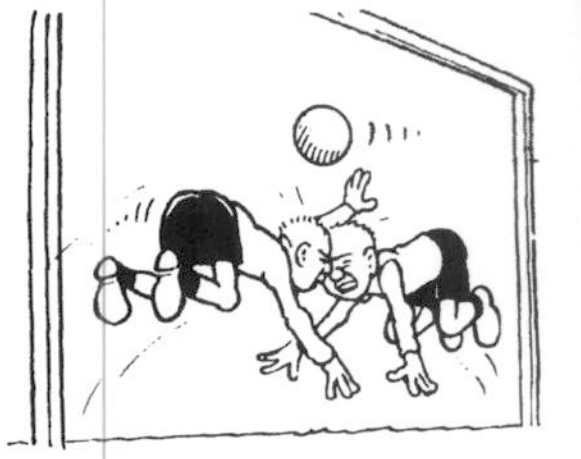

And then some more!

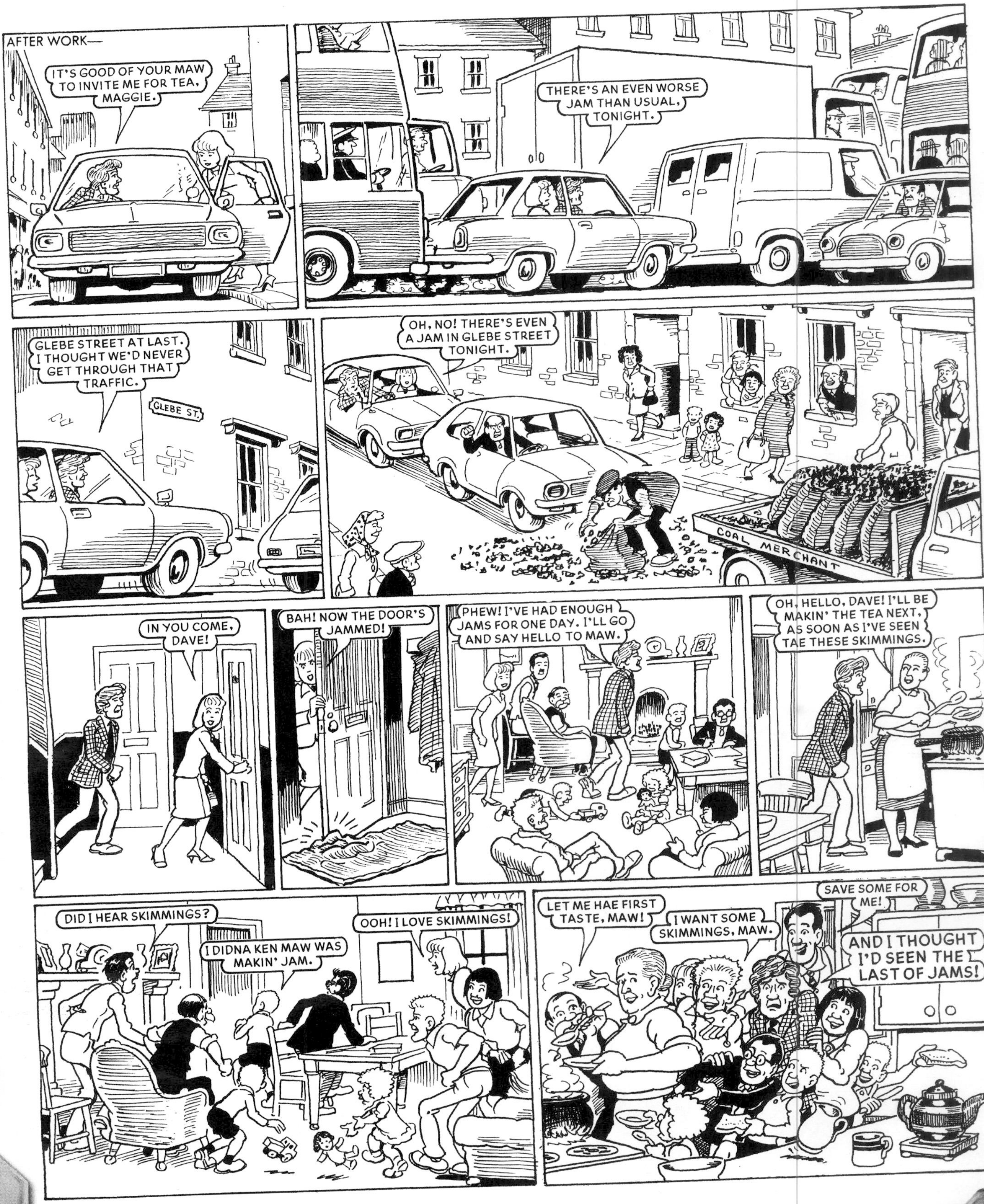

AFTER WORK—
IT'S GOOD OF YOUR MAW TO INVITE ME FOR TEA, MAGGIE.
THERE'S AN EVEN WORSE JAM THAN USUAL, TONIGHT.
GLEBE STREET AT LAST. I THOUGHT WE'D NEVER GET THROUGH THAT TRAFFIC.
GLEBE ST.
OH, NO! THERE'S EVEN A JAM IN GLEBE STREET TONIGHT.
COAL MERCHANT
IN YOU COME, DAVE!
BAH! NOW THE DOOR'S JAMMED!
PHEW! I'VE HAD ENOUGH JAMS FOR ONE DAY. I'LL GO AND SAY HELLO TO MAW.
OH, HELLO, DAVE! I'LL BE MAKIN' THE TEA NEXT, AS SOON AS I'VE SEEN TAE THESE SKIMMINGS.
DID I HEAR SKIMMINGS?
I DIDNA KEN MAW WAS MAKIN' JAM.
OOH! I LOVE SKIMMINGS!
LET ME HAE FIRST TASTE, MAW!
I WANT SOME SKIMMINGS, MAW.
SAVE SOME FOR ME!
AND I THOUGHT I'D SEEN THE LAST OF JAMS!

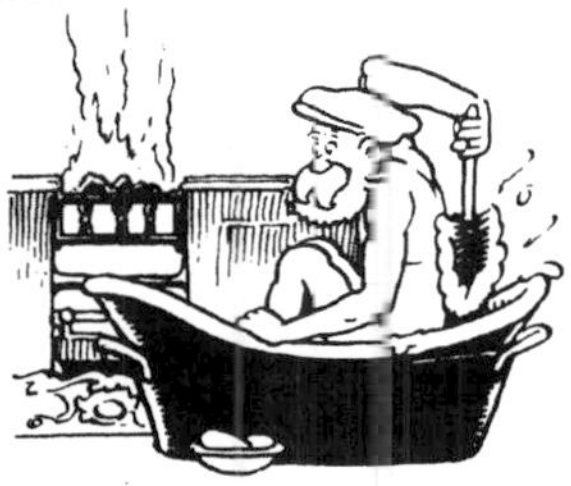

A punch on the nose, a broken arm—

Nae wonder Paw's filled with alarm!

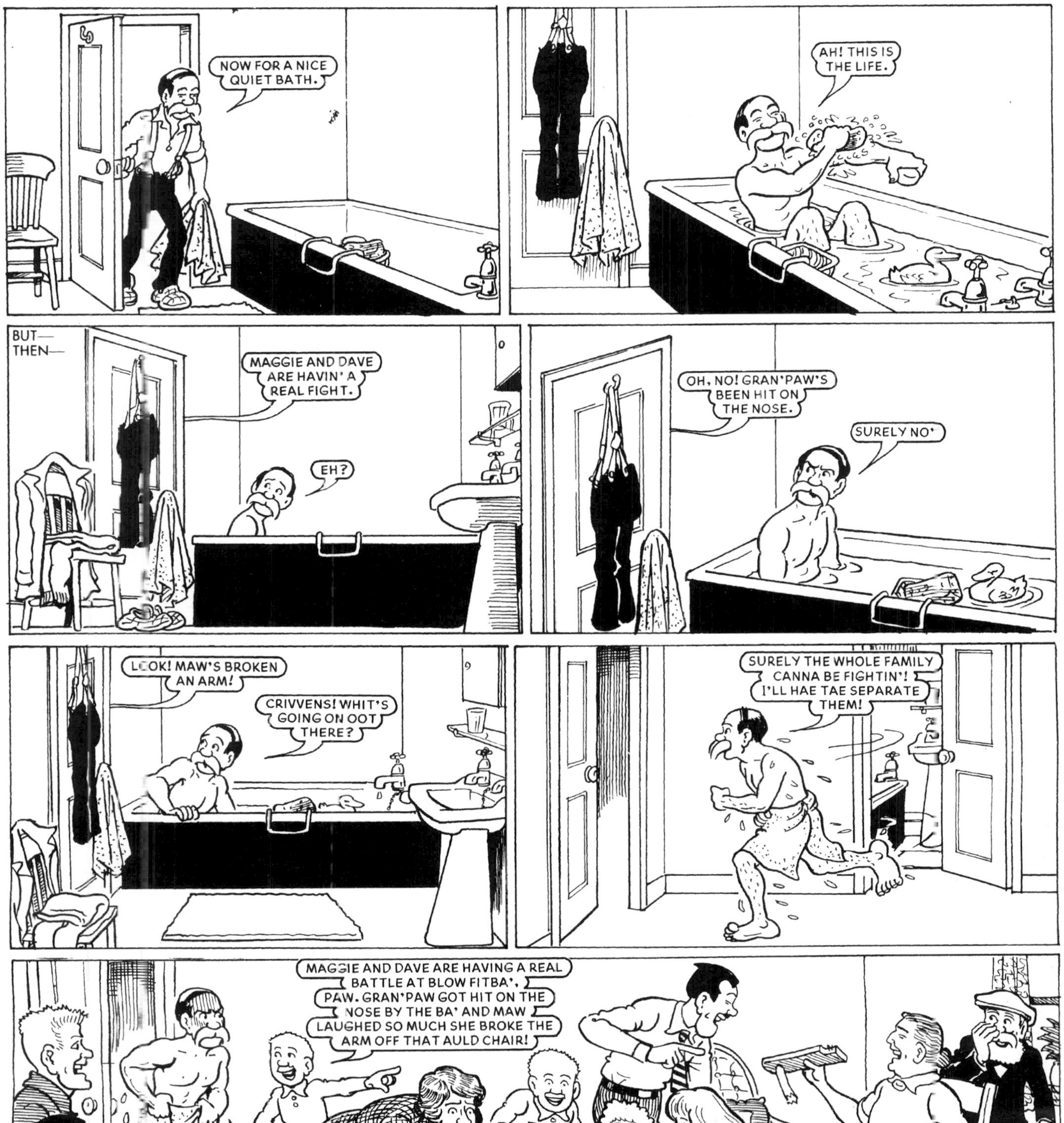
NOW FOR A NICE QUIET BATH.
AH! THIS IS THE LIFE.
BUT— THEN—
MAGGIE AND DAVE ARE HAVIN' A REAL FIGHT.
EH?
OH, NO! GRAN'PAW'S BEEN HIT ON THE NOSE.
SURELY NO'
LOOK! MAW'S BROKEN AN ARM!
CRIVVENS! WHIT'S GOING ON OOT THERE?
SURELY THE WHOLE FAMILY CANNA BE FIGHTIN'! I'LL HAE TAE SEPARATE THEM!
MAGGIE AND DAVE ARE HAVING A REAL BATTLE AT BLOW FITBA', PAW. GRAN'PAW GOT HIT ON THE NOSE BY THE BA' AND MAW LAUGHED SO MUCH SHE BROKE THE ARM OFF THAT AULD CHAIR!

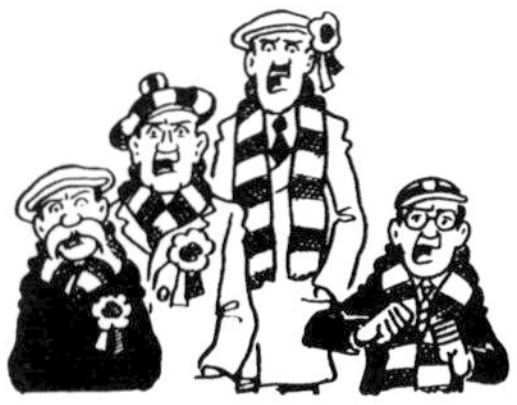

. . . but there's a catch—

At this fitba match!

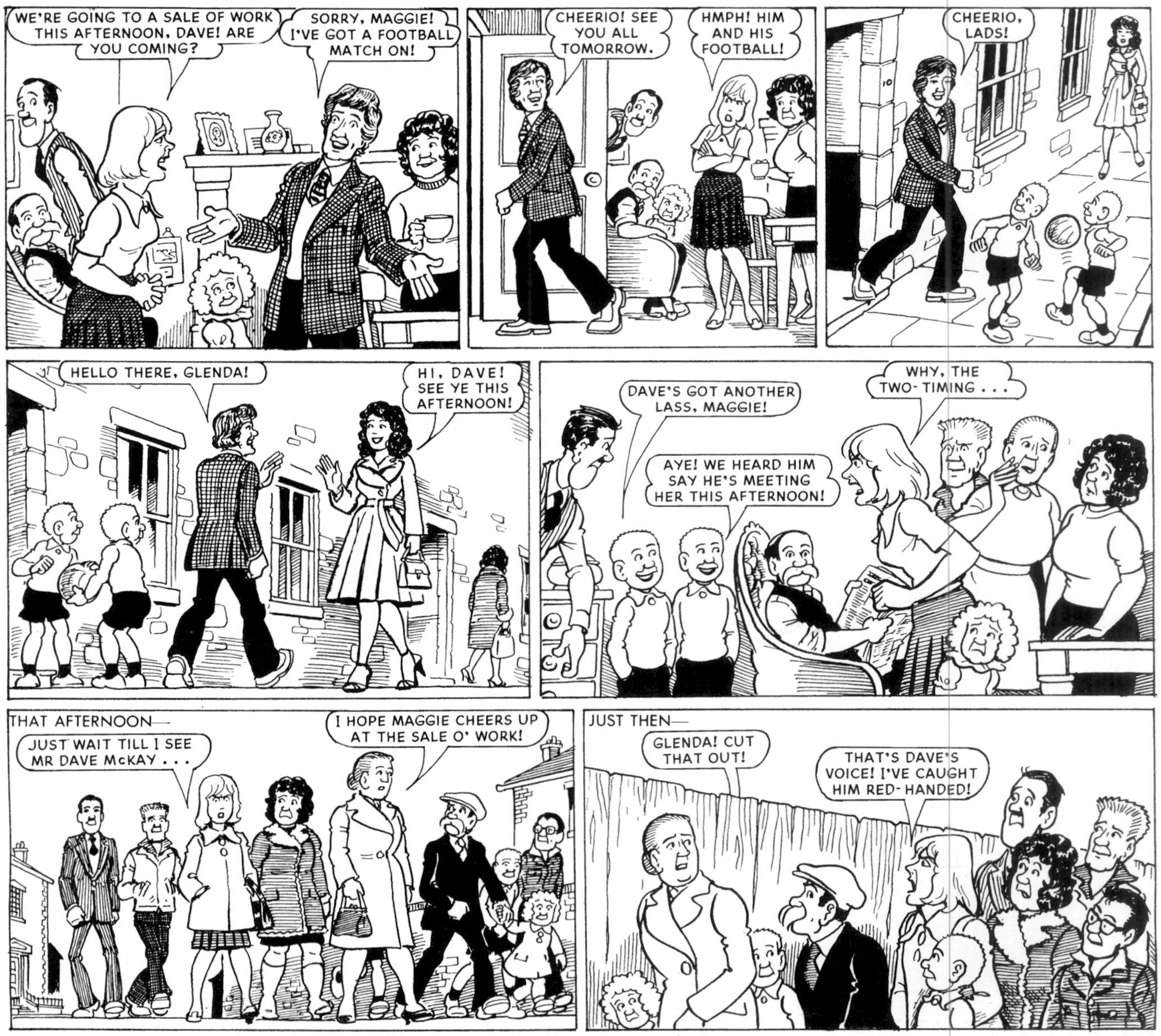

WE'RE GOING TO A SALE OF WORK THIS AFTERNOON, DAVE! ARE YOU COMING?
SORRY, MAGGIE! I'VE GOT A FOOTBALL MATCH ON!
CHEERIO! SEE YOU ALL TOMORROW.
HMPH! HIM AND HIS FOOTBALL!
CHEERIO, LADS!
HELLO THERE, GLENDA!
HI, DAVE! SEE YE THIS AFTERNOON!
DAVE'S GOT ANOTHER LASS, MAGGIE!
AYE! WE HEARD HIM SAY HE'S MEETING HER THIS AFTERNOON!
WHY, THE TWO-TIMING . . .
THAT AFTERNOON—
JUST WAIT TILL I SEE MR DAVE McKAY . . .
I HOPE MAGGIE CHEERS UP AT THE SALE O' WORK!
JUST THEN—
GLENDA! CUT THAT OUT!
THAT'S DAVE'S VOICE! I'VE CAUGHT HIM RED-HANDED!
I'VE WARNED YOU BEFORE ABOUT THOSE HIGH KICKS, GLENDA!
HO-HO! DAVE'S REFEREEING A LADIES' FITBA' MATCH!

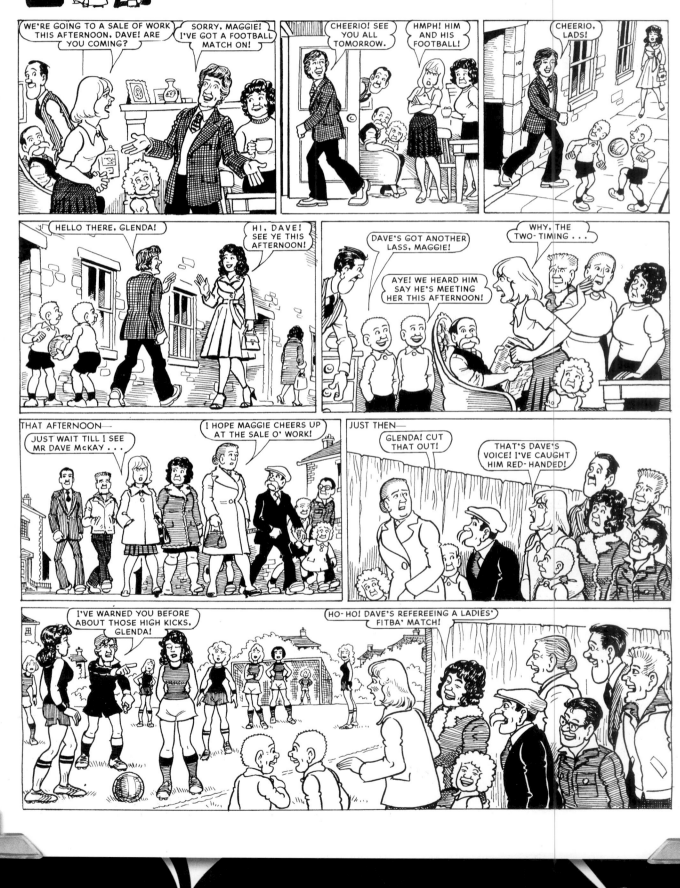

The lassies get a proper fright—

This "fortune teller's" always right!

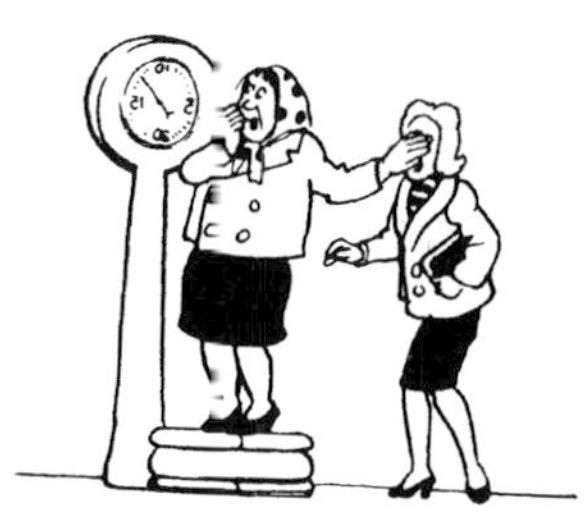

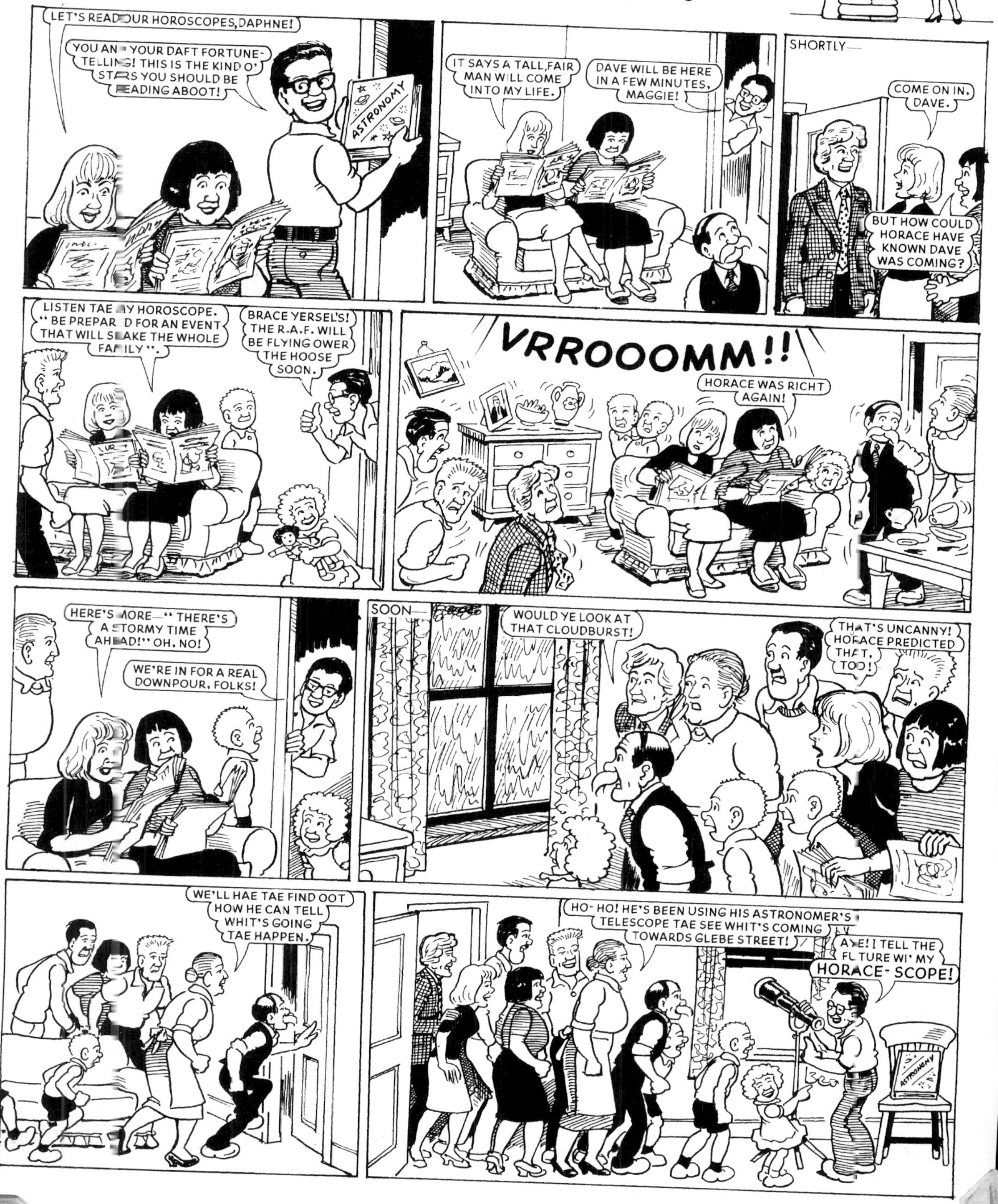

LET'S READ OUR HOROSCOPES, DAPHNE!
YOU AN' YOUR DAFT FORTUNE-TELLING! THIS IS THE KIND O' STARS YOU SHOULD BE READING ABOOT!
ASTRONOMY
IT SAYS A TALL, FAIR MAN WILL COME INTO MY LIFE.
DAVE WILL BE HERE IN A FEW MINUTES, MAGGIE!
SHORTLY—
COME ON IN, DAVE.
BUT HOW COULD HORACE HAVE KNOWN DAVE WAS COMING?
LISTEN TAE MY HOROSCOPE. "BE PREPARED FOR AN EVENT THAT WILL SHAKE THE WHOLE FAMILY".
BRACE YERSEL'S! THE R.A.F. WILL BE FLYING OWER THE HOOSE SOON.
VRROOOMM!!
HORACE WAS RICHT AGAIN!
HERE'S MORE—"THERE'S A STORMY TIME AHEAD!" OH, NO!
WE'RE IN FOR A REAL DOWNPOUR, FOLKS!
SOON—
WOULD YE LOOK AT THAT CLOUDBURST!
THAT'S UNCANNY! HORACE PREDICTED THAT, TOO!
WE'LL HAE TAE FIND OOT HOW HE CAN TELL WHIT'S GOING TAE HAPPEN.
HO-HO! HE'S BEEN USING HIS ASTRONOMER'S TELESCOPE TAE SEE WHIT'S COMING TOWARDS GLEBE STREET!
AYE! I TELL THE FUTURE WI' MY HORACE-SCOPE!
ASTRONOMY

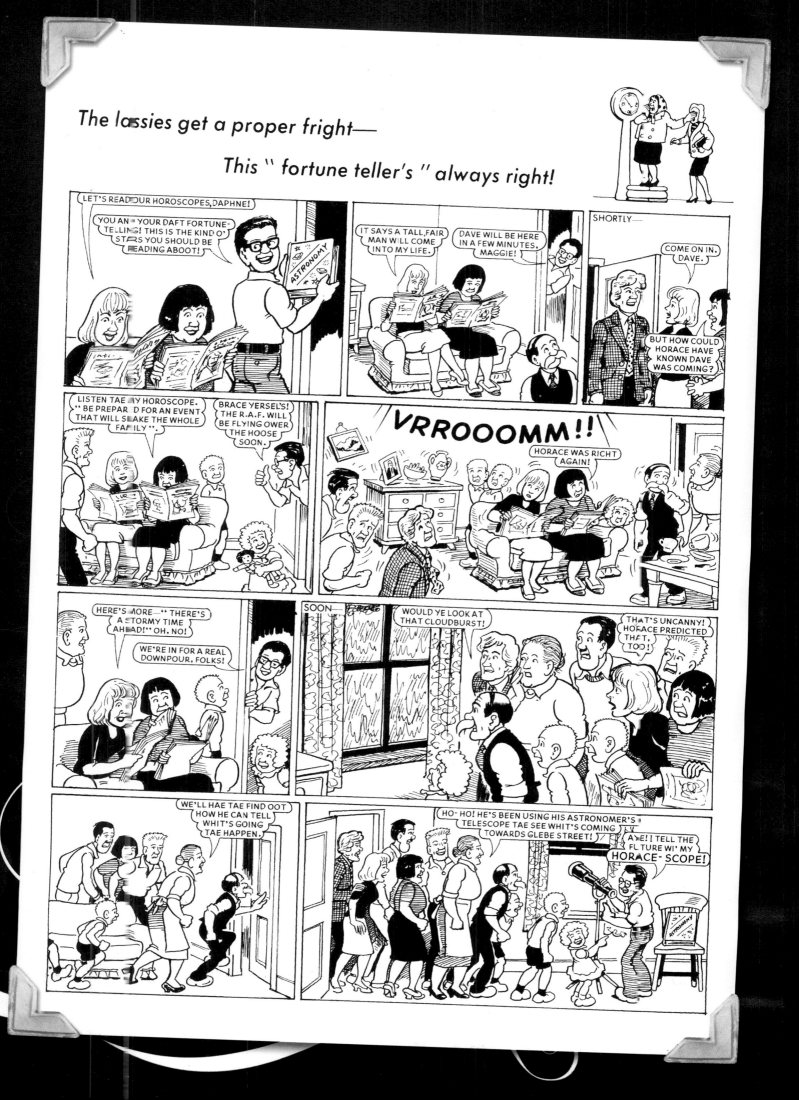

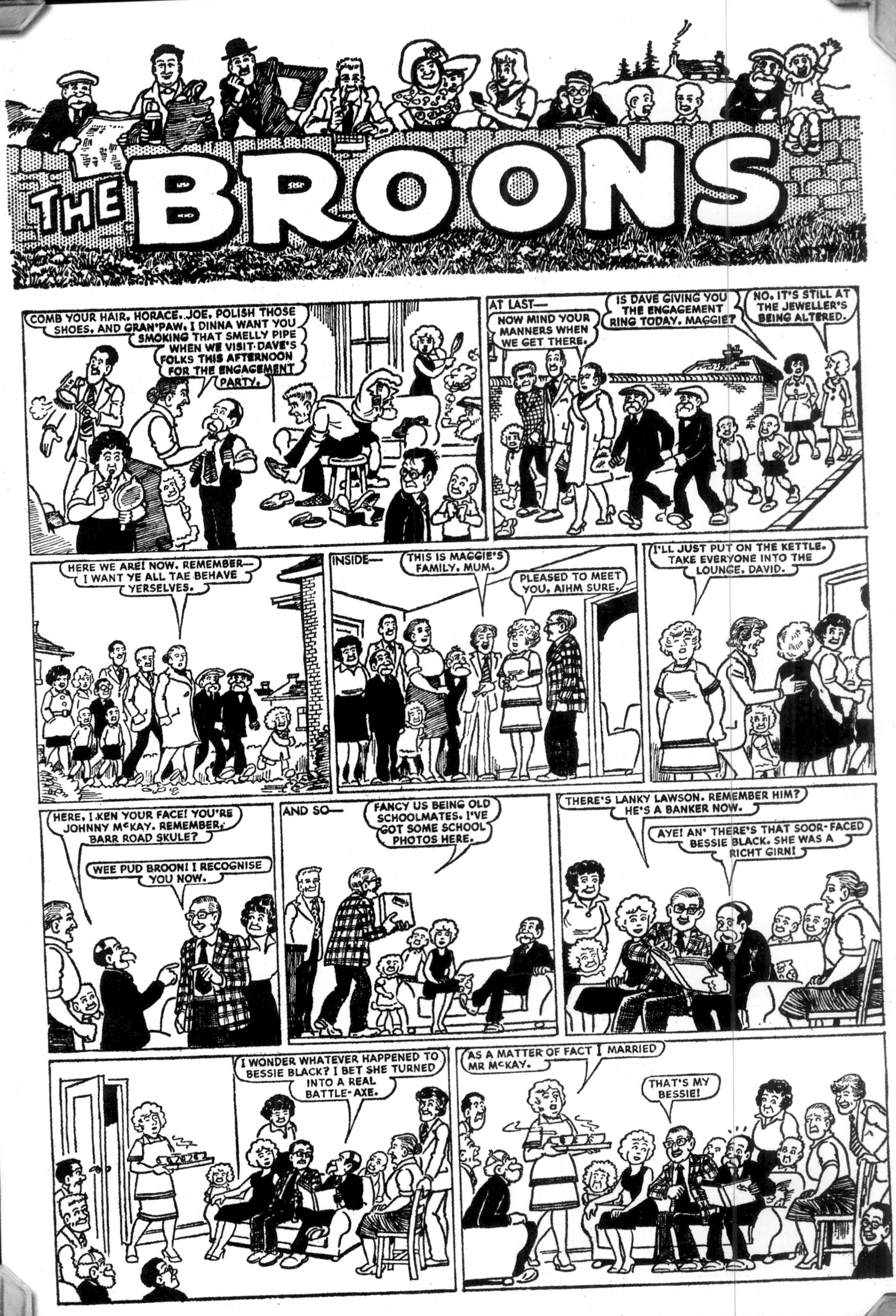
THE BROONS
COMB YOUR HAIR, HORACE. JOE, POLISH THOSE SHOES, AND GRAN'PAW, I DINNA WANT YOU SMOKING THAT SMELLY PIPE WHEN WE VISIT DAVE'S FOLKS THIS AFTERNOON FOR THE ENGAGEMENT PARTY.
AT LAST—
NOW MIND YOUR MANNERS WHEN WE GET THERE.
IS DAVE GIVING YOU THE ENGAGEMENT RING TODAY, MAGGIE?
NO, IT'S STILL AT THE JEWELLER'S BEING ALTERED.
HERE WE ARE! NOW, REMEMBER— I WANT YE ALL TAE BEHAVE YERSELVES.
INSIDE—
THIS IS MAGGIE'S FAMILY, MUM.
PLEASED TO MEET YOU, AIHM SURE.
I'LL JUST PUT ON THE KETTLE. TAKE EVERYONE INTO THE LOUNGE, DAVID.
HERE, I KEN YOUR FACE! YOU'RE JOHNNY McKAY, REMEMBER, BARR ROAD SKULE?
WEE PUD BROON! I RECOGNISE YOU NOW.
AND SO—
FANCY US BEING OLD SCHOOLMATES. I'VE GOT SOME SCHOOL PHOTOS HERE.
THERE'S LANKY LAWSON. REMEMBER HIM? HE'S A BANKER NOW.
AYE! AN' THERE'S THAT SOOR-FACED BESSIE BLACK. SHE WAS A RICHT GIRN!
I WONDER WHATEVER HAPPENED TO BESSIE BLACK? I BET SHE TURNED INTO A REAL BATTLE-AXE.
AS A MATTER OF FACT I MARRIED MR McKAY.
THAT'S MY BESSIE!

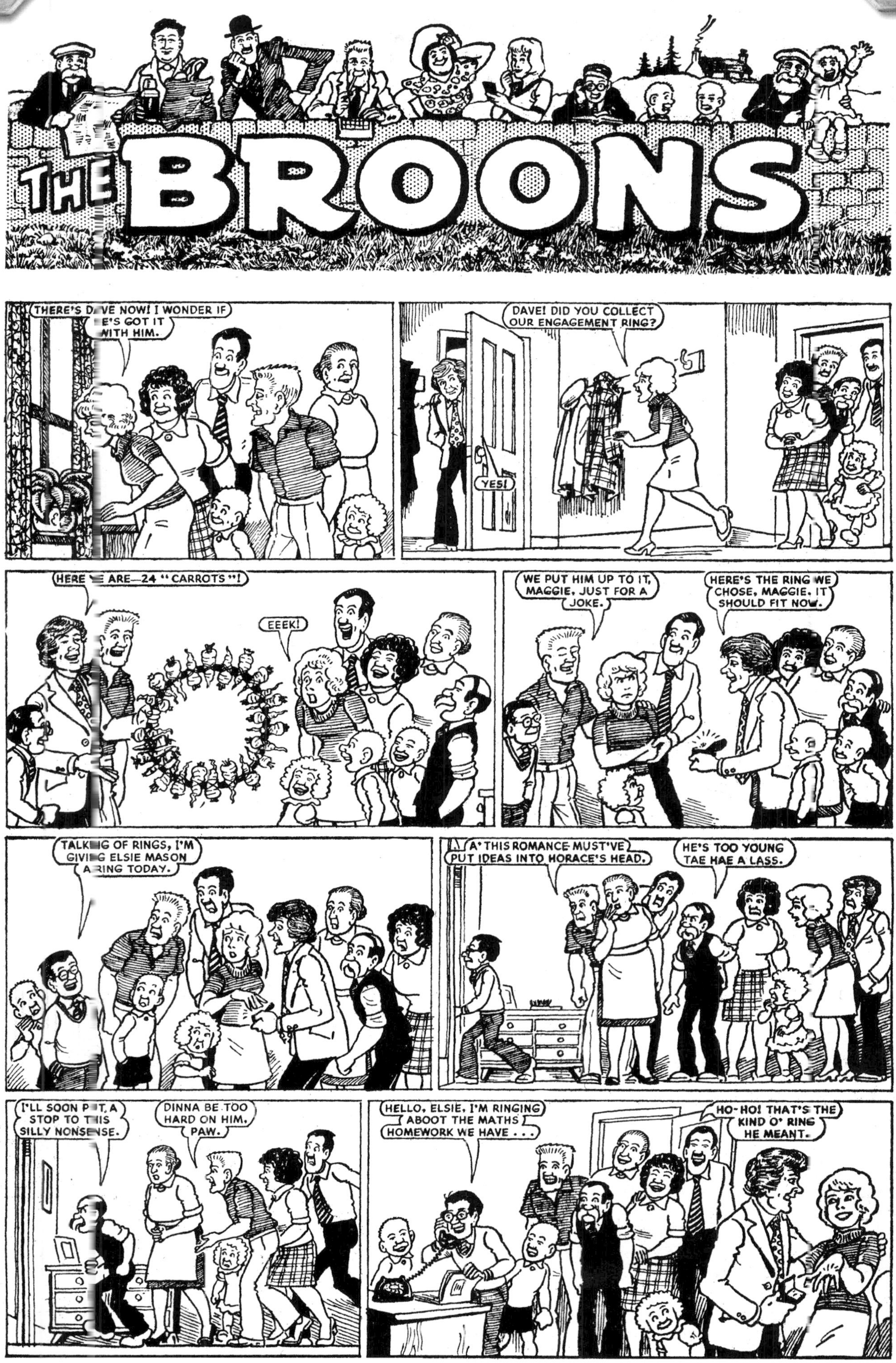
THE BROONS
THERE'S DAVE NOW! I WONDER IF HE'S GOT IT WITH HIM.
DAVE! DID YOU COLLECT OUR ENGAGEMENT RING?
YES!
HERE WE ARE—24 "CARROTS"!
EEEK!
WE PUT HIM UP TO IT, MAGGIE. JUST FOR A JOKE.
HERE'S THE RING WE CHOSE, MAGGIE. IT SHOULD FIT NOW.
TALKING OF RINGS, I'M GIVING ELSIE MASON A RING TODAY.
A' THIS ROMANCE MUST'VE PUT IDEAS INTO HORACE'S HEAD.
HE'S TOO YOUNG TAE HAE A LASS.
I'LL SOON PUT A STOP TO THIS SILLY NONSENSE.
DINNA BE TOO HARD ON HIM, PAW.
HELLO, ELSIE. I'M RINGING ABOOT THE MATHS HOMEWORK WE HAVE . . .
HO-HO! THAT'S THE KIND O' RING HE MEANT.

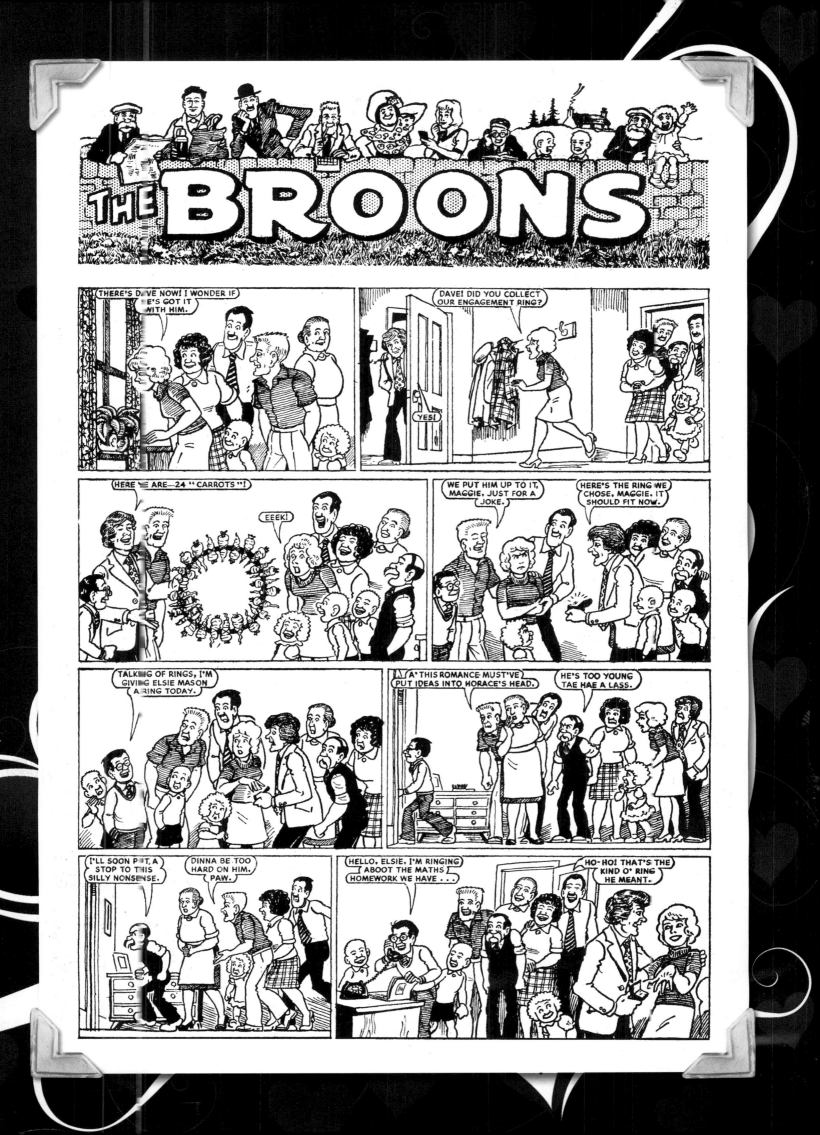

There's a " brush-off " in store—

For this bloke at the door!

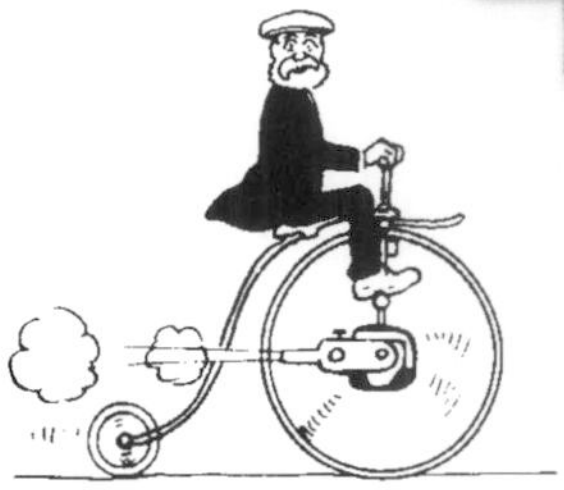

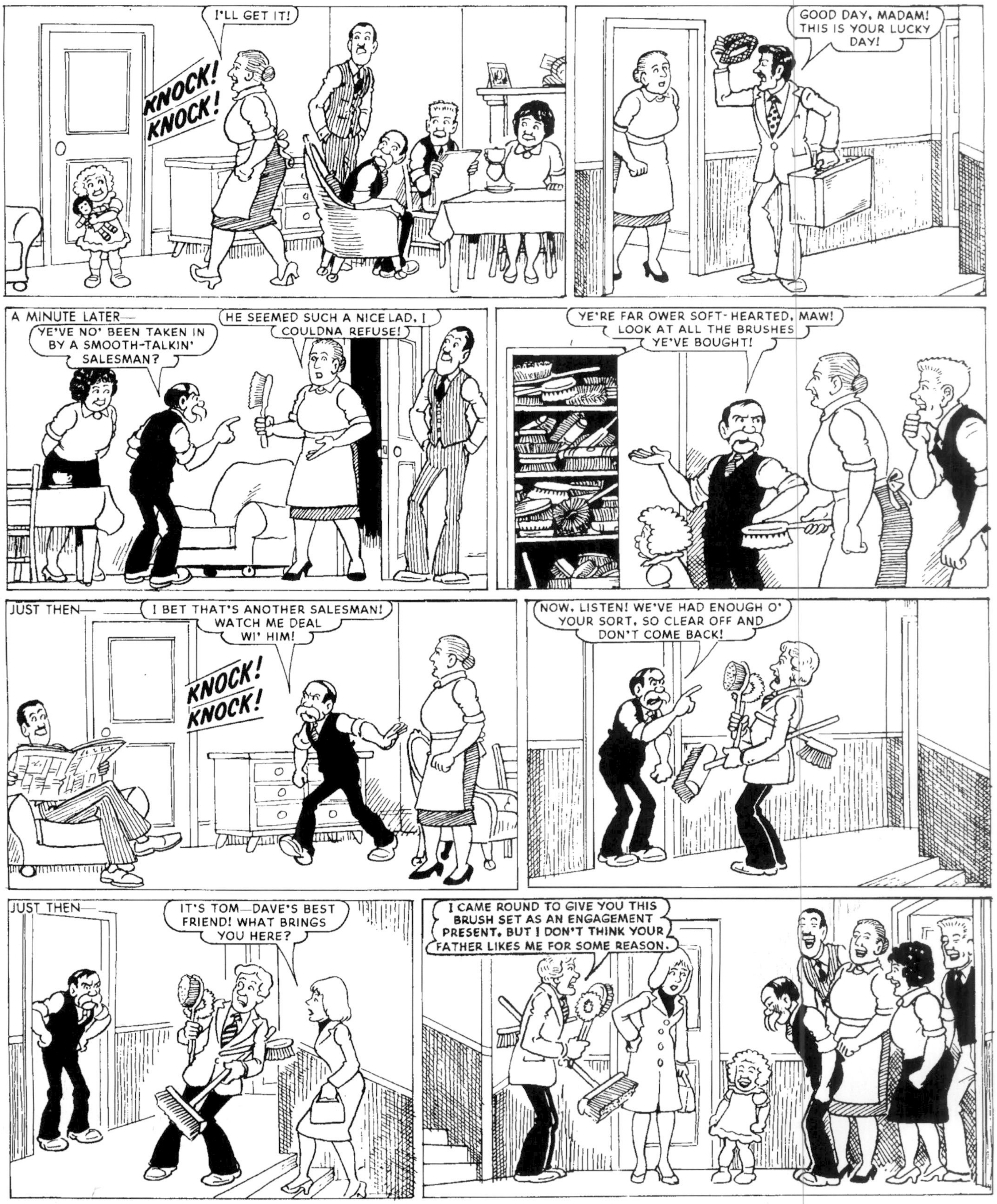
I'LL GET IT!
KNOCK! KNOCK!
GOOD DAY, MADAM! THIS IS YOUR LUCKY DAY!
A MINUTE LATER—
YE'VE NO' BEEN TAKEN IN BY A SMOOTH-TALKIN' SALESMAN?
HE SEEMED SUCH A NICE LAD, I COULDNA REFUSE!
YE'RE FAR OWER SOFT-HEARTED, MAW! LOOK AT ALL THE BRUSHES YE'VE BOUGHT!
JUST THEN—
I BET THAT'S ANOTHER SALESMAN! WATCH ME DEAL WI' HIM!
KNOCK! KNOCK!
NOW, LISTEN! WE'VE HAD ENOUGH O' YOUR SORT, SO CLEAR OFF AND DON'T COME BACK!
JUST THEN—
IT'S TOM—DAVE'S BEST FRIEND! WHAT BRINGS YOU HERE?
I CAME ROUND TO GIVE YOU THIS BRUSH SET AS AN ENGAGEMENT PRESENT, BUT I DON'T THINK YOUR FATHER LIKES ME FOR SOME REASON.

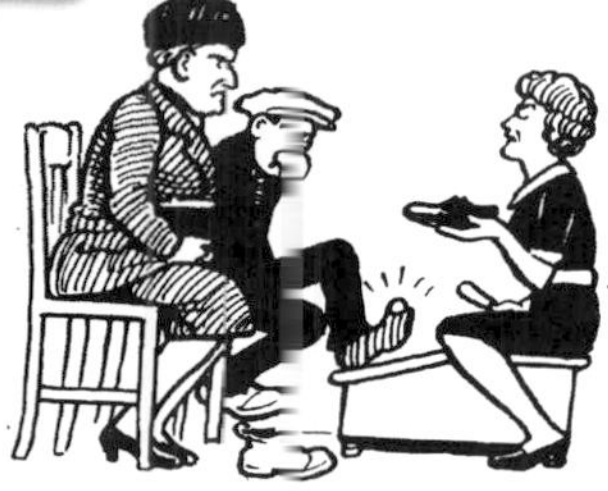

Help m'boab! Michty me!—

Here's a real CATastrophe!

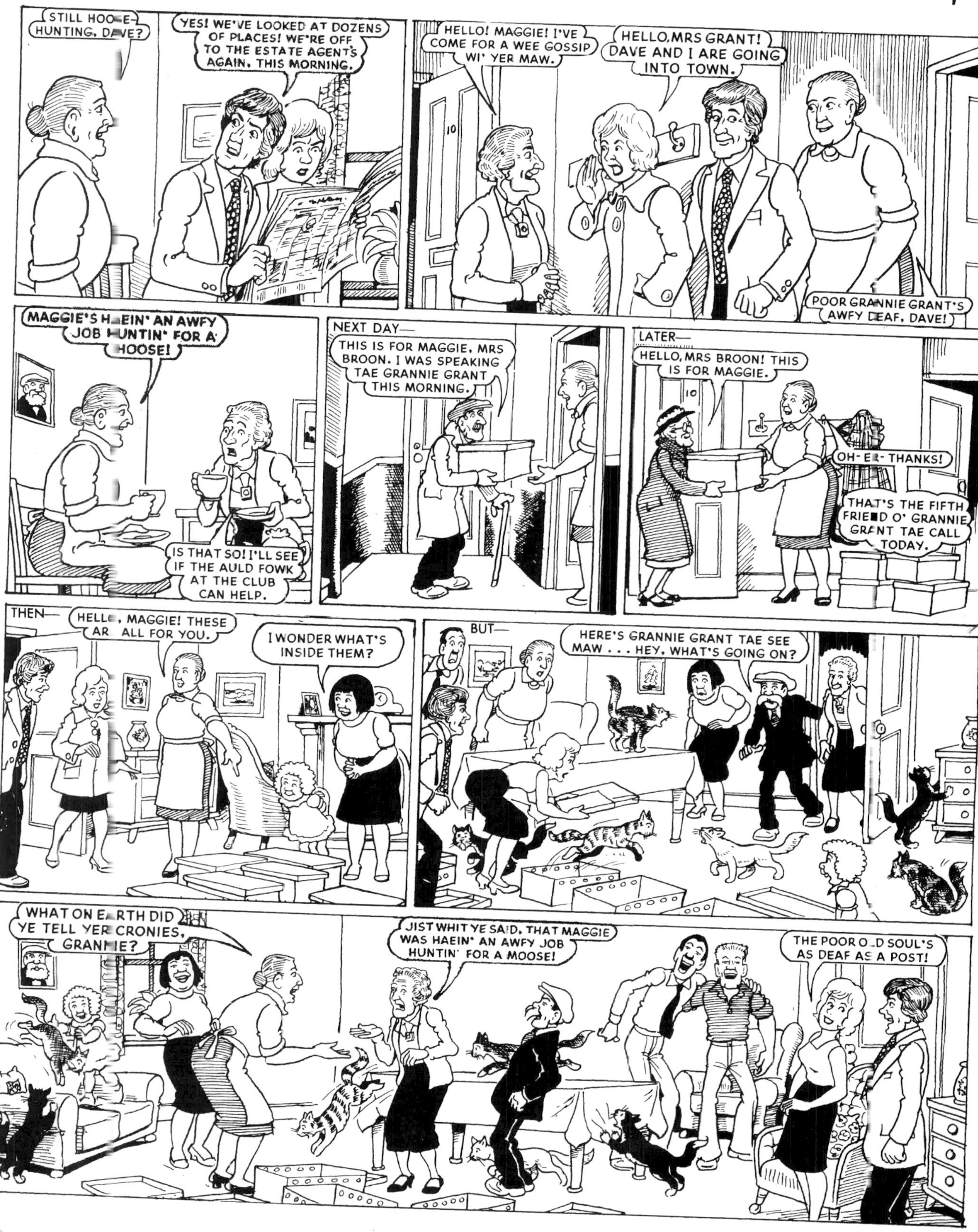

STILL HOOSE-HUNTING, DAVE?
YES! WE'VE LOOKED AT DOZENS OF PLACES! WE'RE OFF TO THE ESTATE AGENT'S AGAIN, THIS MORNING.
HELLO! MAGGIE! I'VE COME FOR A WEE GOSSIP WI' YER MAW.
HELLO, MRS GRANT! DAVE AND I ARE GOING INTO TOWN.
POOR GRANNIE GRANT'S AWFY DEAF, DAVE!
MAGGIE'S HAEIN' AN AWFY JOB HUNTIN' FOR A HOOSE!
IS THAT SO! I'LL SEE IF THE AULD FOWK AT THE CLUB CAN HELP.
NEXT DAY—
THIS IS FOR MAGGIE, MRS BROON. I WAS SPEAKING TAE GRANNIE GRANT THIS MORNING.
LATER—
HELLO, MRS BROON! THIS IS FOR MAGGIE.
OH-ER-THANKS!
THAT'S THE FIFTH FRIEND O' GRANNIE GRANT TAE CALL TODAY.
THEN—
HELLO, MAGGIE! THESE ARE ALL FOR YOU.
I WONDER WHAT'S INSIDE THEM?
BUT—
HERE'S GRANNIE GRANT TAE SEE MAW . . . HEY, WHAT'S GOING ON?
WHAT ON EARTH DID YE TELL YER CRONIES, GRANNIE?
JIST WHIT YE SAID. THAT MAGGIE WAS HAEIN' AN AWFY JOB HUNTIN' FOR A MOOSE!
THE POOR OLD SOUL'S AS DEAF AS A POST!

The Funny Side of Auld Romantics.

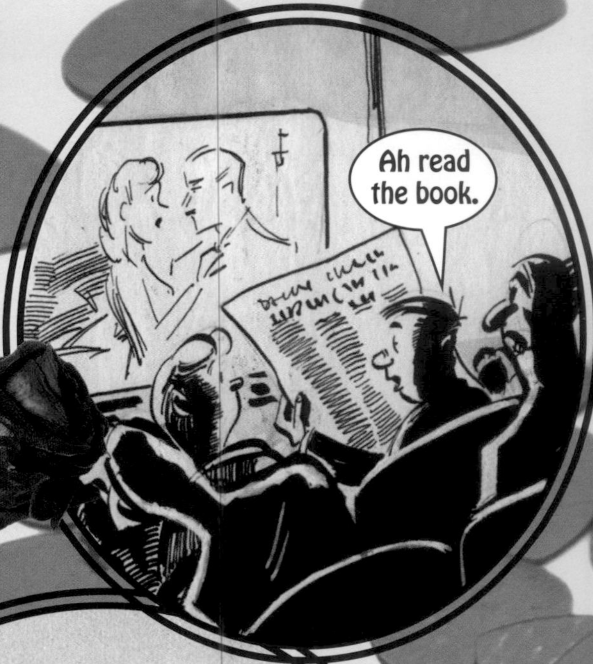

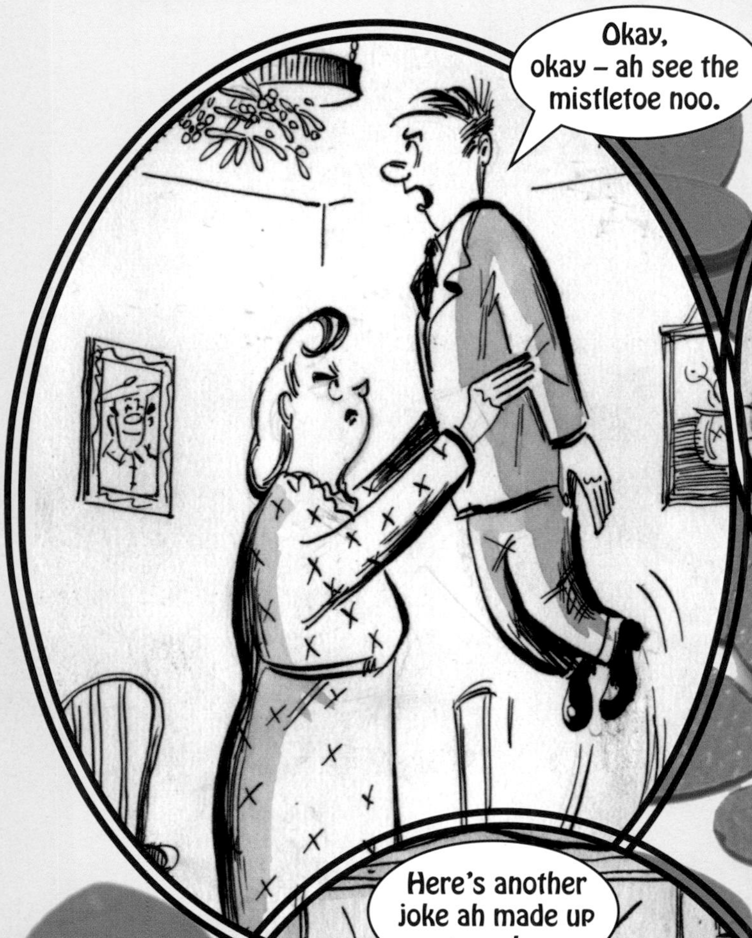

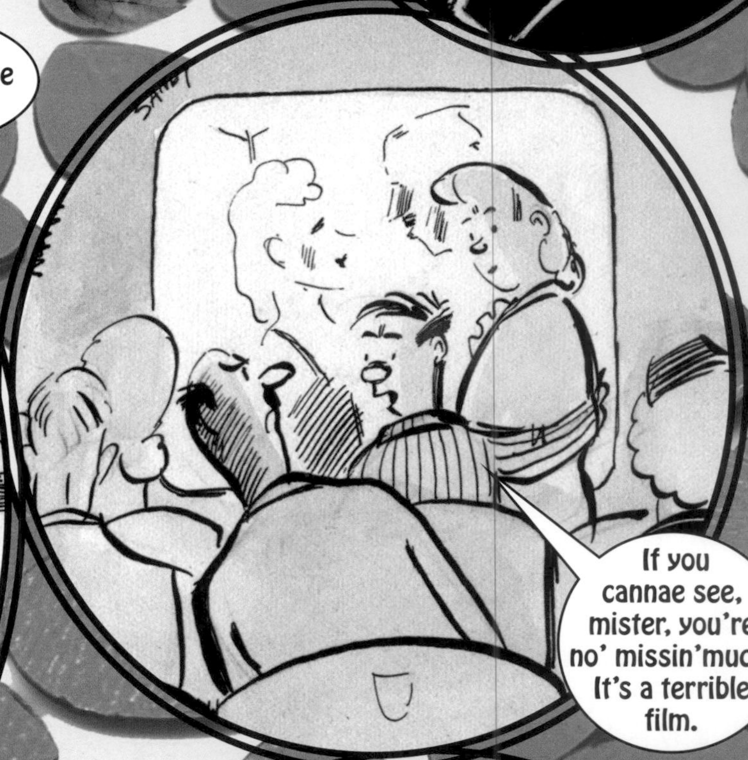

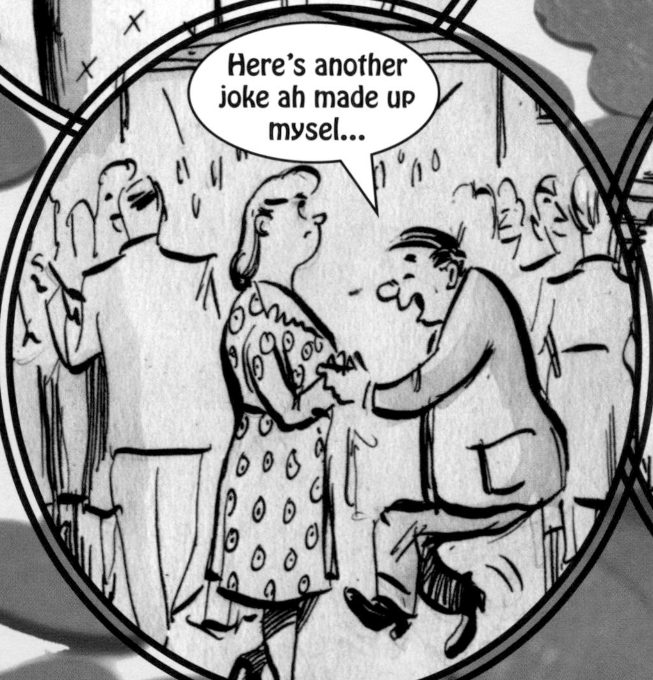

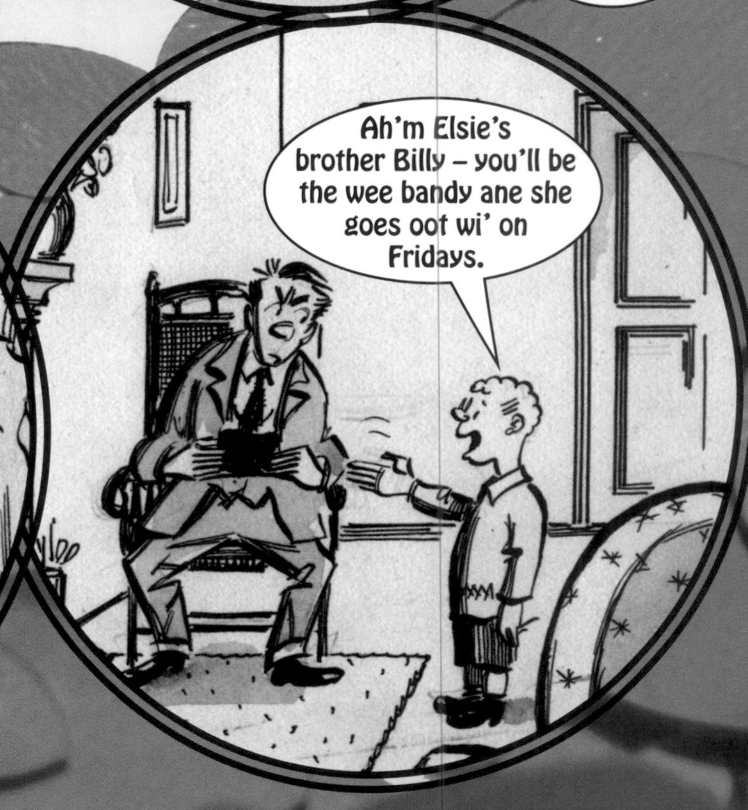

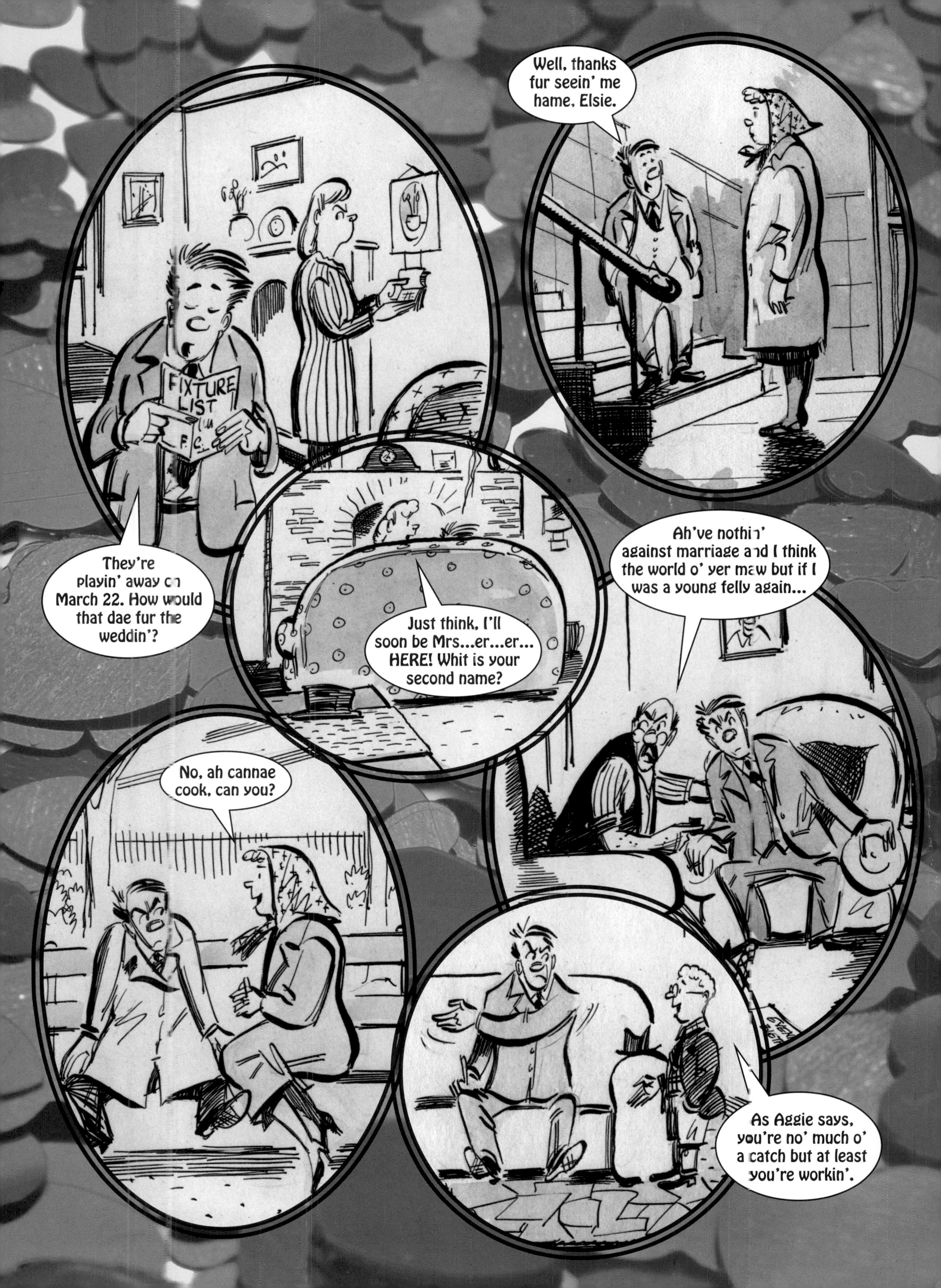
They're playin' away on March 22. How would that dae fur the weddin'?
Well, thanks fur seein' me hame, Elsie.
Just think, I'll soon be Mrs...er...er... HERE! Whit is your second name?
Ah've nothin' against marriage and I think the world o' yer maw but if I was a young felly again...
No, ah cannae cook, can you?
As Aggie says, you're no' much o' a catch but at least you're workin'.

This smart daughter—

Lands her Paw in " hot water "!

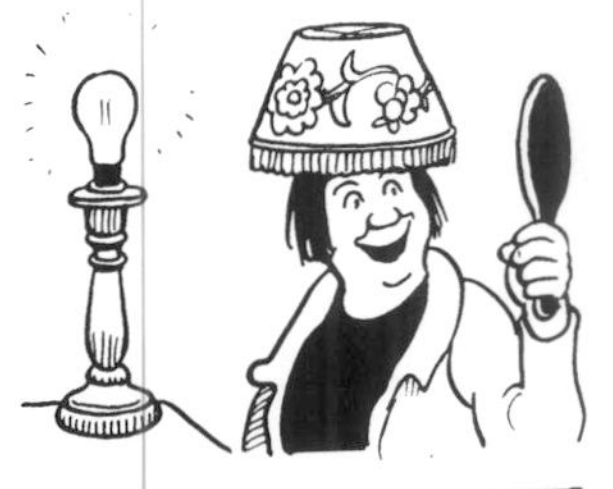

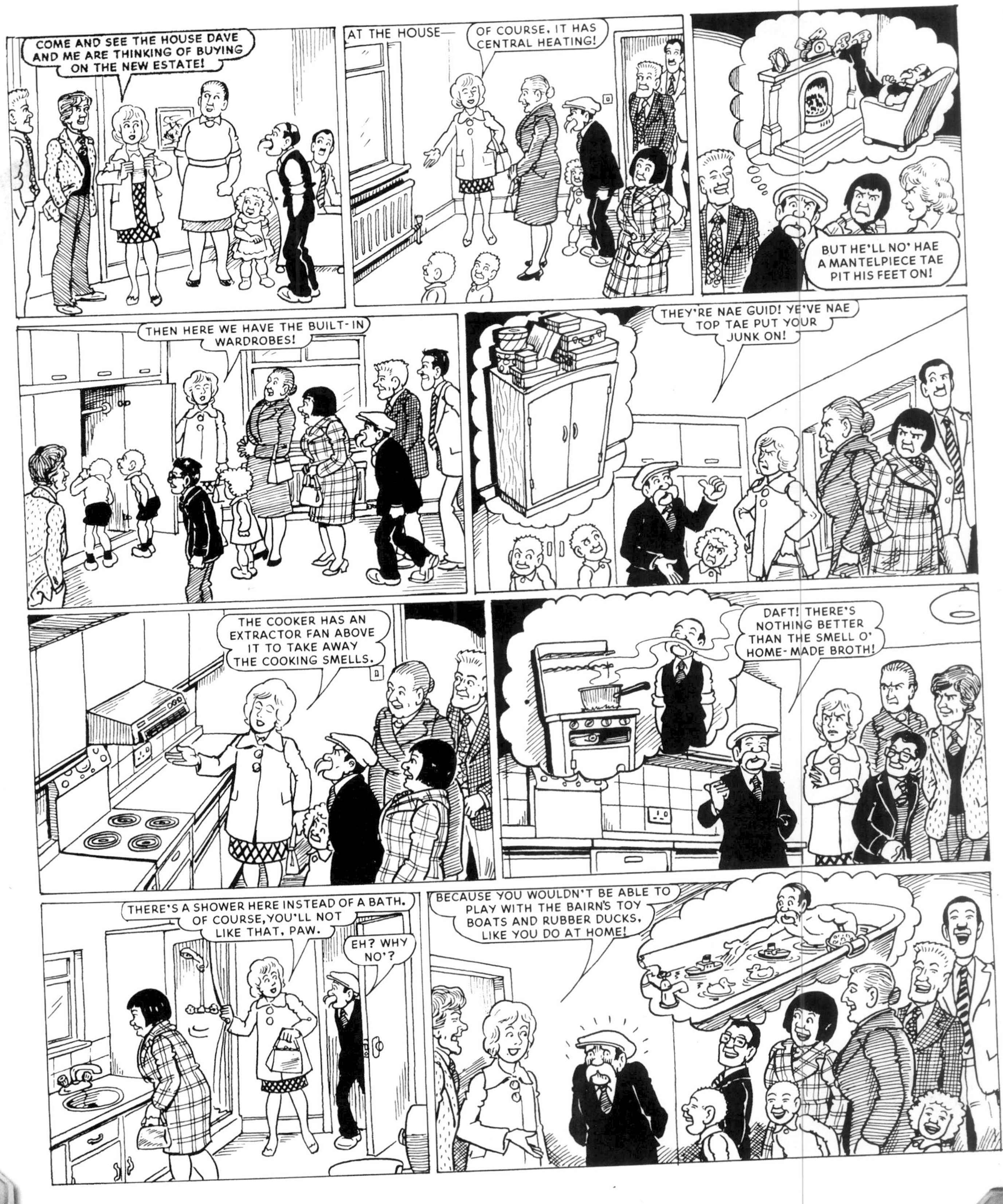

COME AND SEE THE HOUSE DAVE AND ME ARE THINKING OF BUYING ON THE NEW ESTATE!
AT THE HOUSE—
OF COURSE, IT HAS CENTRAL HEATING!
BUT HE'LL NO' HAE A MANTELPIECE TAE PIT HIS FEET ON!
THEN HERE WE HAVE THE BUILT-IN WARDROBES!
THEY'RE NAE GUID! YE'VE NAE TOP TAE PUT YOUR JUNK ON!
THE COOKER HAS AN EXTRACTOR FAN ABOVE IT TO TAKE AWAY THE COOKING SMELLS.
DAFT! THERE'S NOTHING BETTER THAN THE SMELL O' HOME-MADE BROTH!
THERE'S A SHOWER HERE INSTEAD OF A BATH. OF COURSE, YOU'LL NOT LIKE THAT, PAW.
EH? WHY NO'?
BECAUSE YOU WOULDN'T BE ABLE TO PLAY WITH THE BAIRN'S TOY BOATS AND RUBBER DUCKS, LIKE YOU DO AT HOME!

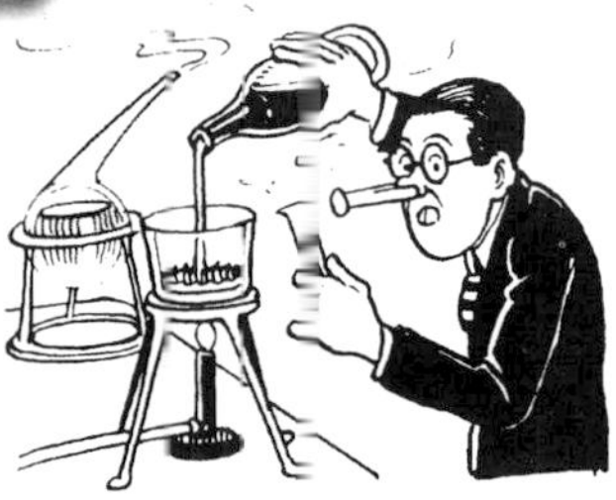

It's a real laughalot—

When they see what Paw's bought!

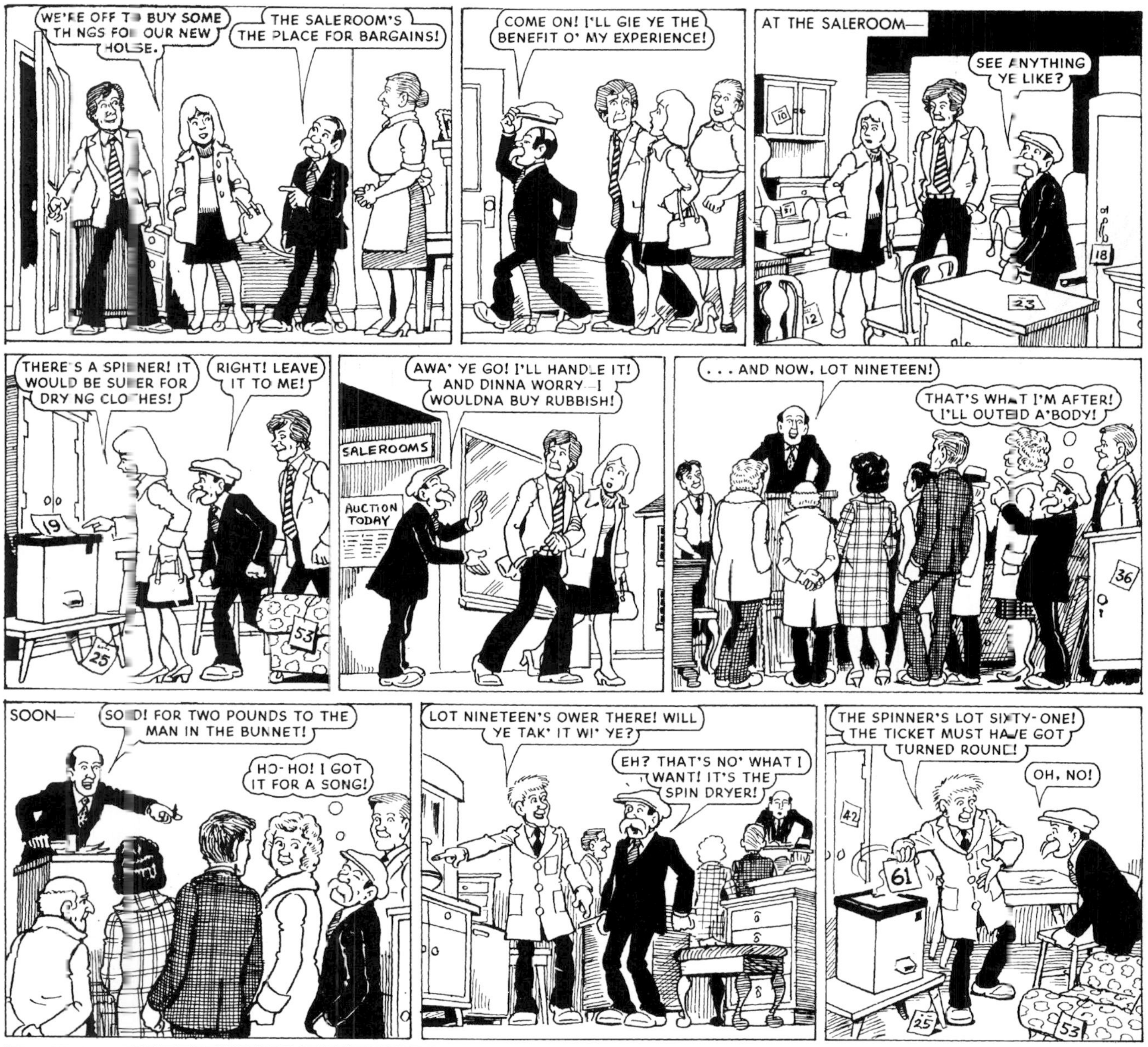

WE'RE OFF TO BUY SOME THINGS FOR OUR NEW HOUSE.
THE SALEROOM'S THE PLACE FOR BARGAINS!
COME ON! I'LL GIE YE THE BENEFIT O' MY EXPERIENCE!
AT THE SALEROOM—
SEE ANYTHING YE LIKE?
THERE'S A SPINNER! IT WOULD BE SUPER FOR DRYING CLOTHES!
RIGHT! LEAVE IT TO ME!
AWA' YE GO! I'LL HANDLE IT! AND DINNA WORRY—I WOULDNA BUY RUBBISH!
SALEROOMS
AUCTION TODAY
. . . AND NOW, LOT NINETEEN!
THAT'S WHAT I'M AFTER! I'LL OUTBID A'BODY!
SOON—
SOLD! FOR TWO POUNDS TO THE MAN IN THE BUNNET!
HO-HO! I GOT IT FOR A SONG!
LOT NINETEEN'S OWER THERE! WILL YE TAK' IT WI' YE?
EH? THAT'S NO' WHAT I WANT! IT'S THE SPIN DRYER!
THE SPINNER'S LOT SIXTY-ONE! THE TICKET MUST HAVE GOT TURNED ROUND!
OH, NO!
BACK HOME—
PAW'S STILL AT THE SALEROOM! HE'S GETTING US A GREAT THING FOR THE WASHING!
THEN—
HO-HO! THAT AULD MANGLE WILL CERTAINLY WRING YER CLAES, DAVE!
OH, NO! SO YOU WOULDN'T BUY RUBBISH, EH?

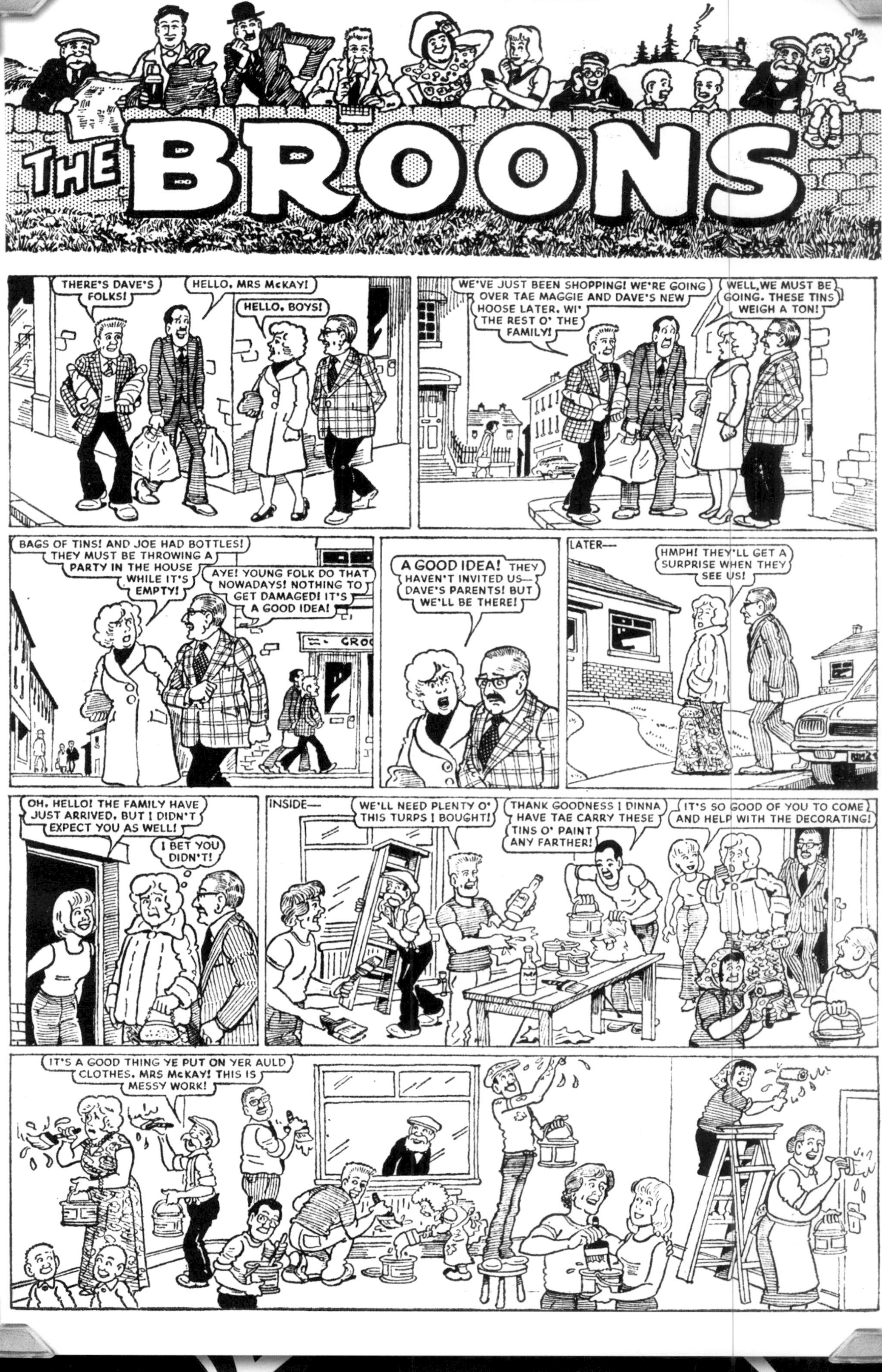
THE BROONS
THERE'S DAVE'S FOLKS!
HELLO, MRS McKAY!
HELLO, BOYS!
WE'VE JUST BEEN SHOPPING! WE'RE GOING OVER TAE MAGGIE AND DAVE'S NEW HOOSE LATER, WI' THE REST O' THE FAMILY!
WELL, WE MUST BE GOING. THESE TINS WEIGH A TON!
BAGS OF TINS! AND JOE HAD BOTTLES! THEY MUST BE THROWING A PARTY IN THE HOUSE WHILE IT'S EMPTY!
AYE! YOUNG FOLK DO THAT NOWADAYS! NOTHING TO GET DAMAGED! IT'S A GOOD IDEA!
A GOOD IDEA! THEY HAVEN'T INVITED US— DAVE'S PARENTS! BUT WE'LL BE THERE!
LATER—
HMPH! THEY'LL GET A SURPRISE WHEN THEY SEE US!
OH, HELLO! THE FAMILY HAVE JUST ARRIVED, BUT I DIDN'T EXPECT YOU AS WELL!
I BET YOU DIDN'T!
INSIDE—
WE'LL NEED PLENTY O' THIS TURPS I BOUGHT!
THANK GOODNESS I DINNA HAVE TAE CARRY THESE TINS O' PAINT ANY FARTHER!
IT'S SO GOOD OF YOU TO COME AND HELP WITH THE DECORATING!
IT'S A GOOD THING YE PUT ON YER AULD CLOTHES, MRS McKAY! THIS IS MESSY WORK!

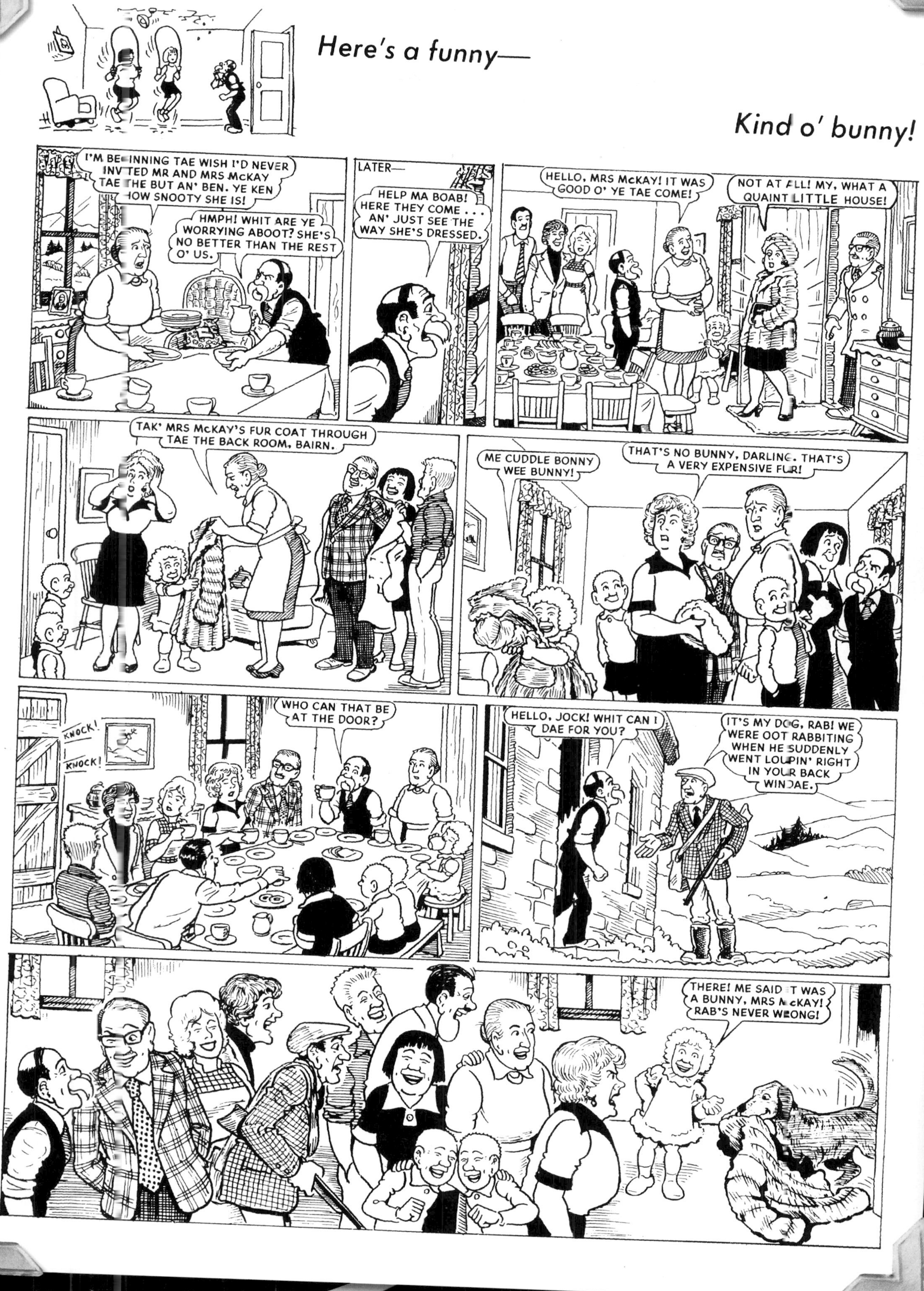
Here's a funny—
Kind o' bunny!
I'M BEGINNING TAE WISH I'D NEVER INVITED MR AND MRS McKAY TAE THE BUT AN' BEN. YE KEN HOW SNOOTY SHE IS!
HMPH! WHIT ARE YE WORRYING ABOOT? SHE'S NO BETTER THAN THE REST O' US.
LATER—
HELP MA BOAB! HERE THEY COME . . . AN' JUST SEE THE WAY SHE'S DRESSED.
HELLO, MRS McKAY! IT WAS GOOD O' YE TAE COME!
NOT AT ALL! MY, WHAT A QUAINT LITTLE HOUSE!
TAK' MRS McKAY'S FUR COAT THROUGH TAE THE BACK ROOM, BAIRN.
ME CUDDLE BONNY WEE BUNNY!
THAT'S NO BUNNY, DARLING. THAT'S A VERY EXPENSIVE FUR!
KNOCK! KNOCK!
WHO CAN THAT BE AT THE DOOR?
HELLO, JOCK! WHIT CAN I DAE FOR YOU?
IT'S MY DOG, RAB! WE WERE OOT RABBITING WHEN HE SUDDENLY WENT LOUPIN' RIGHT IN YOUR BACK WINDAE.
THERE! ME SAID IT WAS A BUNNY, MRS McKAY! RAB'S NEVER WRONG!

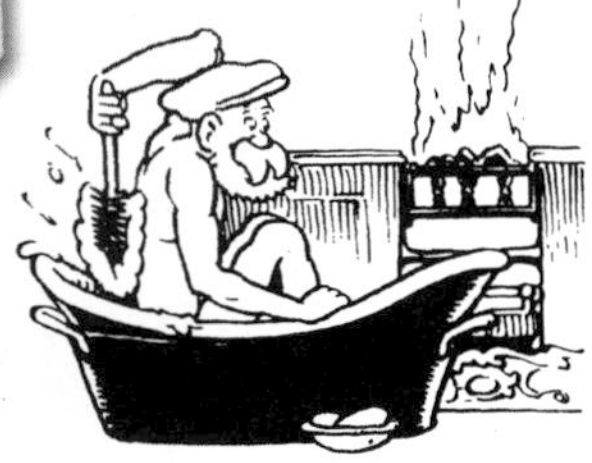

How to stay dry?—

Don't ask Mrs McKay!

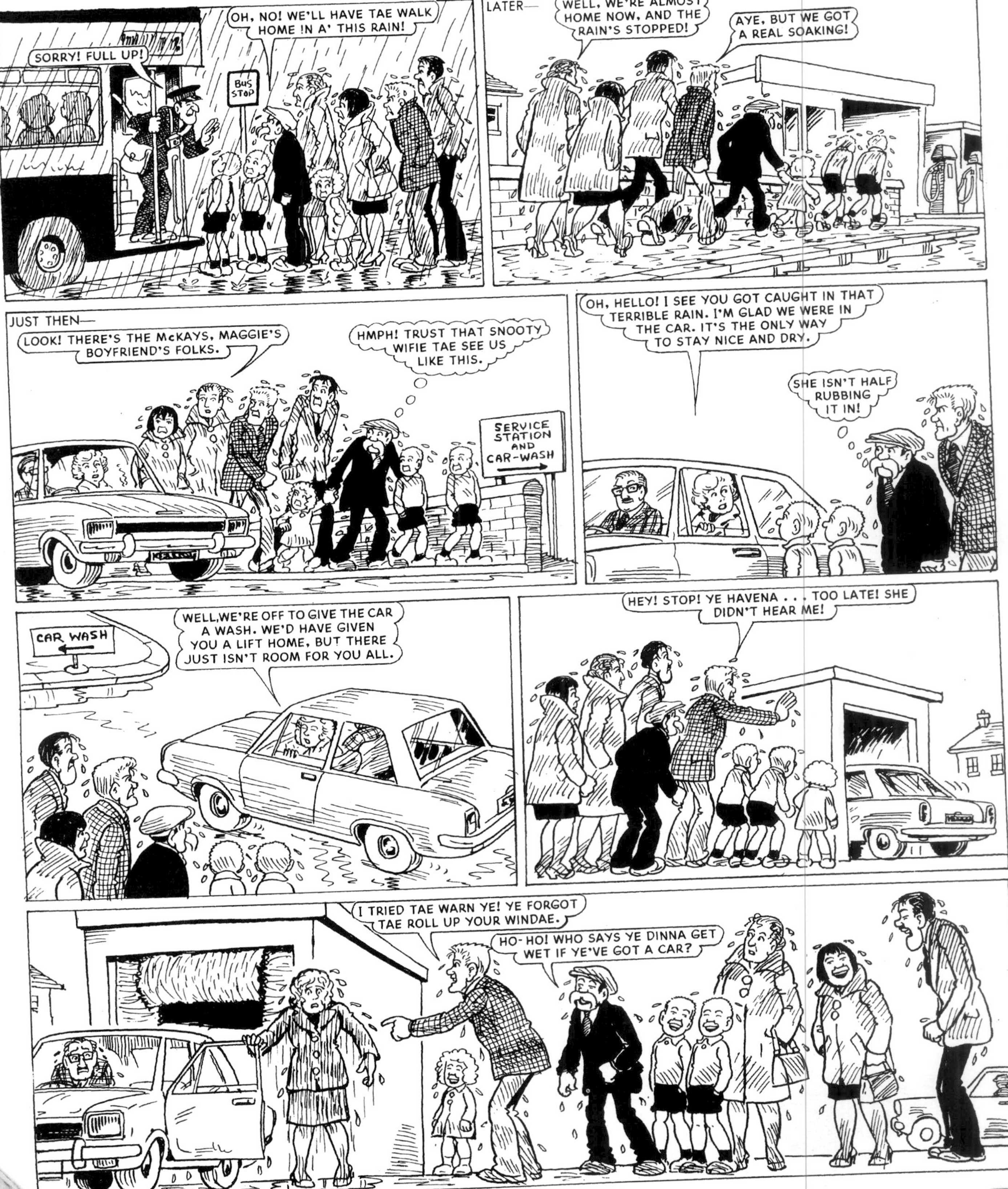

OH, NO! WE'LL HAVE TAE WALK HOME IN A' THIS RAIN!
SORRY! FULL UP!
BUS STOP
LATER—
WELL, WE'RE ALMOST HOME NOW, AND THE RAIN'S STOPPED!
AYE, BUT WE GOT A REAL SOAKING!
JUST THEN—
LOOK! THERE'S THE McKAYS, MAGGIE'S BOYFRIEND'S FOLKS.
HMPH! TRUST THAT SNOOTY WIFIE TAE SEE US LIKE THIS.
SERVICE STATION AND CAR-WASH
OH, HELLO! I SEE YOU GOT CAUGHT IN THAT TERRIBLE RAIN. I'M GLAD WE WERE IN THE CAR. IT'S THE ONLY WAY TO STAY NICE AND DRY.
SHE ISN'T HALF RUBBING IT IN!
CAR WASH
WELL, WE'RE OFF TO GIVE THE CAR A WASH. WE'D HAVE GIVEN YOU A LIFT HOME, BUT THERE JUST ISN'T ROOM FOR YOU ALL.
HEY! STOP! YE HAVENA . . . TOO LATE! SHE DIDN'T HEAR ME!
I TRIED TAE WARN YE! YE FORGOT TAE ROLL UP YOUR WINDAE.
HO-HO! WHO SAYS YE DINNA GET WET IF YE'VE GOT A CAR?

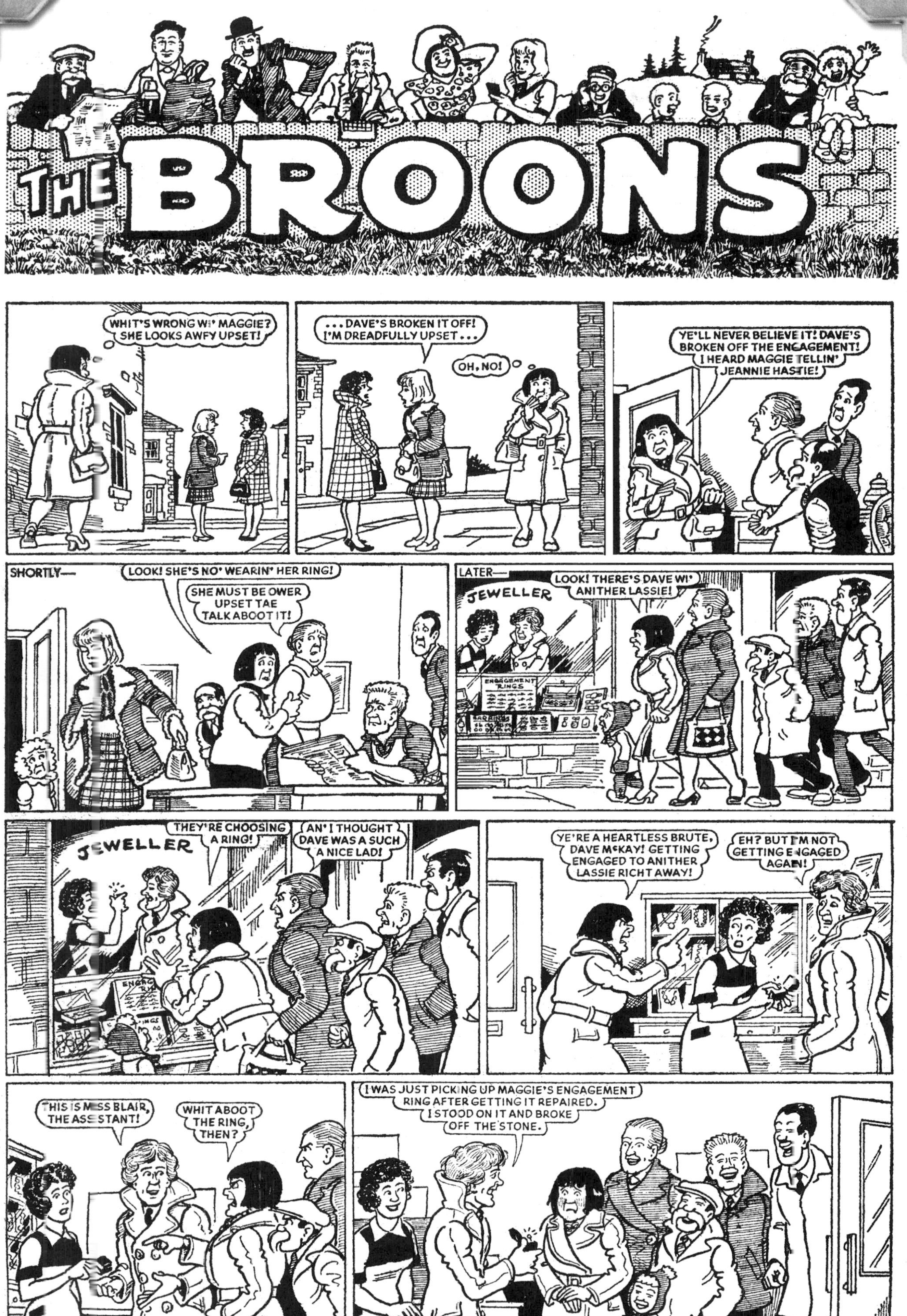
THE BROONS
WHIT'S WRONG WI' MAGGIE? SHE LOOKS AWFY UPSET!
...DAVE'S BROKEN IT OFF! I'M DREADFULLY UPSET...
OH, NO!
YE'LL NEVER BELIEVE IT! DAVE'S BROKEN OFF THE ENGAGEMENT! I HEARD MAGGIE TELLIN' JEANNIE HASTIE!
SHORTLY—
LOOK! SHE'S NO' WEARIN' HER RING!
SHE MUST BE OWER UPSET TAE TALK ABOOT IT!
LATER—
LOOK! THERE'S DAVE WI' ANITHER LASSIE!
JEWELLER
ENGAGEMENT RINGS
THEY'RE CHOOSING A RING!
AN' I THOUGHT DAVE WAS A SUCH A NICE LAD!
JEWELLER
YE'RE A HEARTLESS BRUTE, DAVE McKAY! GETTING ENGAGED TO ANITHER LASSIE RICHT AWAY!
EH? BUT I'M NOT GETTING ENGAGED AGAIN!
THIS IS MISS BLAIR, THE ASSISTANT!
WHIT ABOOT THE RING, THEN?
I WAS JUST PICKING UP MAGGIE'S ENGAGEMENT RING AFTER GETTING IT REPAIRED. I STOOD ON IT AND BROKE OFF THE STONE.

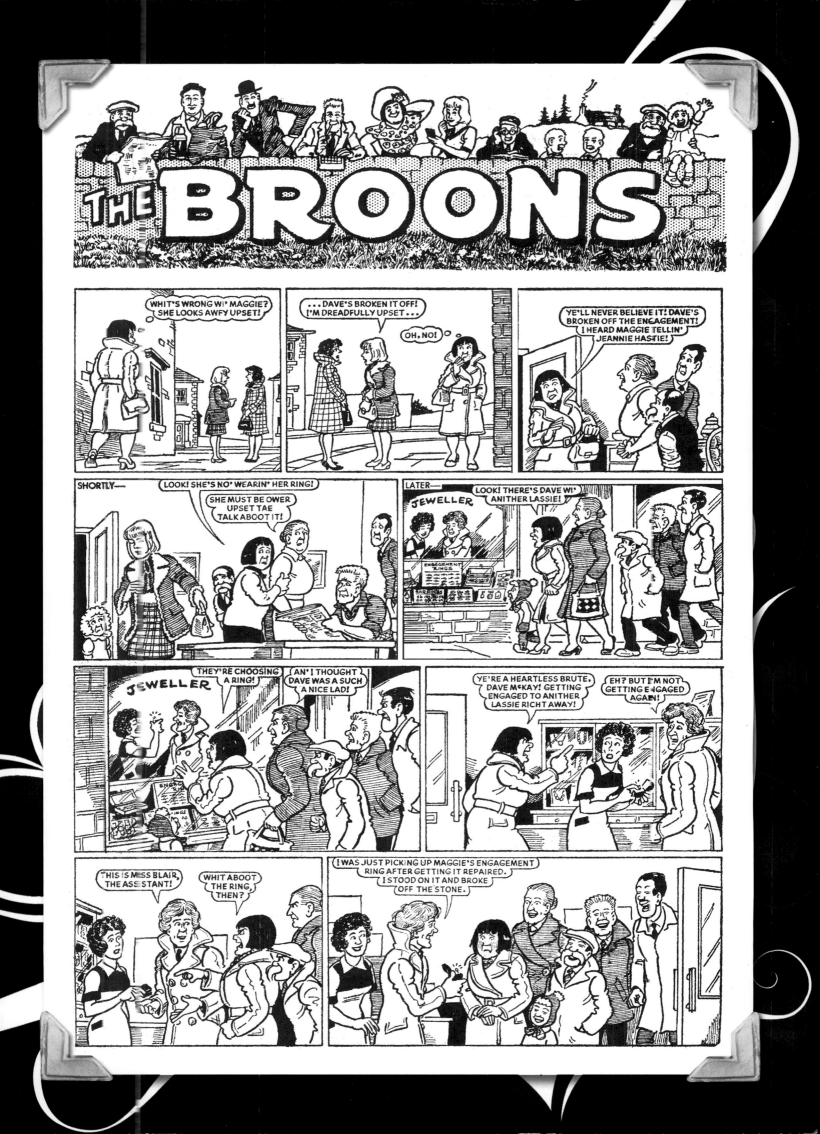

Their Christmas pud—

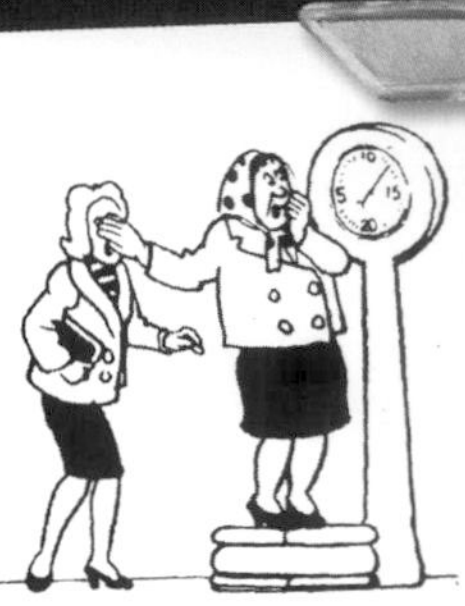

Is extra good!

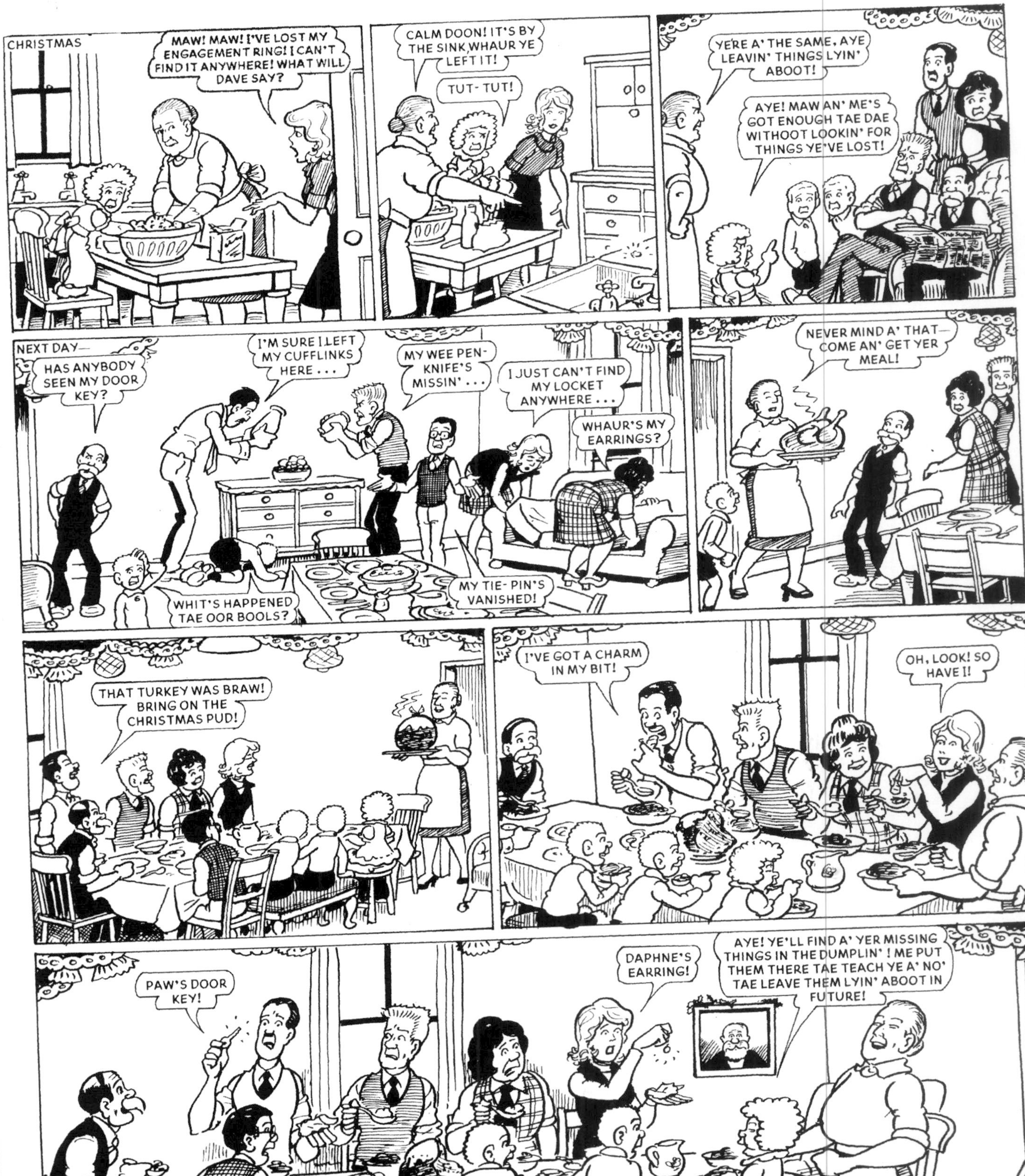

CHRISTMAS
MAW! MAW! I'VE LOST MY ENGAGEMENT RING! I CAN'T FIND IT ANYWHERE! WHAT WILL DAVE SAY?
CALM DOON! IT'S BY THE SINK, WHAUR YE LEFT IT!
TUT-TUT!
YE'RE A' THE SAME, AYE LEAVIN' THINGS LYIN' ABOOT!
AYE! MAW AN' ME'S GOT ENOUGH TAE DAE WITHOOT LOOKIN' FOR THINGS YE'VE LOST!
NEXT DAY—
HAS ANYBODY SEEN MY DOOR KEY?
I'M SURE I LEFT MY CUFFLINKS HERE . . .
MY WEE PEN-KNIFE'S MISSIN' . . .
I JUST CAN'T FIND MY LOCKET ANYWHERE . . .
WHAUR'S MY EARRINGS?
WHIT'S HAPPENED TAE OOR BOOLS?
MY TIE-PIN'S VANISHED!
NEVER MIND A' THAT— COME AN' GET YER MEAL!
THAT TURKEY WAS BRAW! BRING ON THE CHRISTMAS PUD!
I'VE GOT A CHARM IN MY BIT!
OH, LOOK! SO HAVE I!
PAW'S DOOR KEY!
DAPHNE'S EARRING!
AYE! YE'LL FIND A' YER MISSING THINGS IN THE DUMPLIN'! ME PUT THEM THERE TAE TEACH YE A' NO' TAE LEAVE THEM LYIN' ABOOT IN FUTURE!

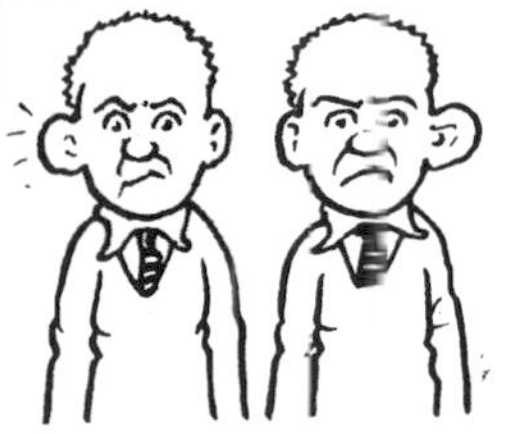

Michty me! What a shock!—

When guess-who calls at seven o'clock!

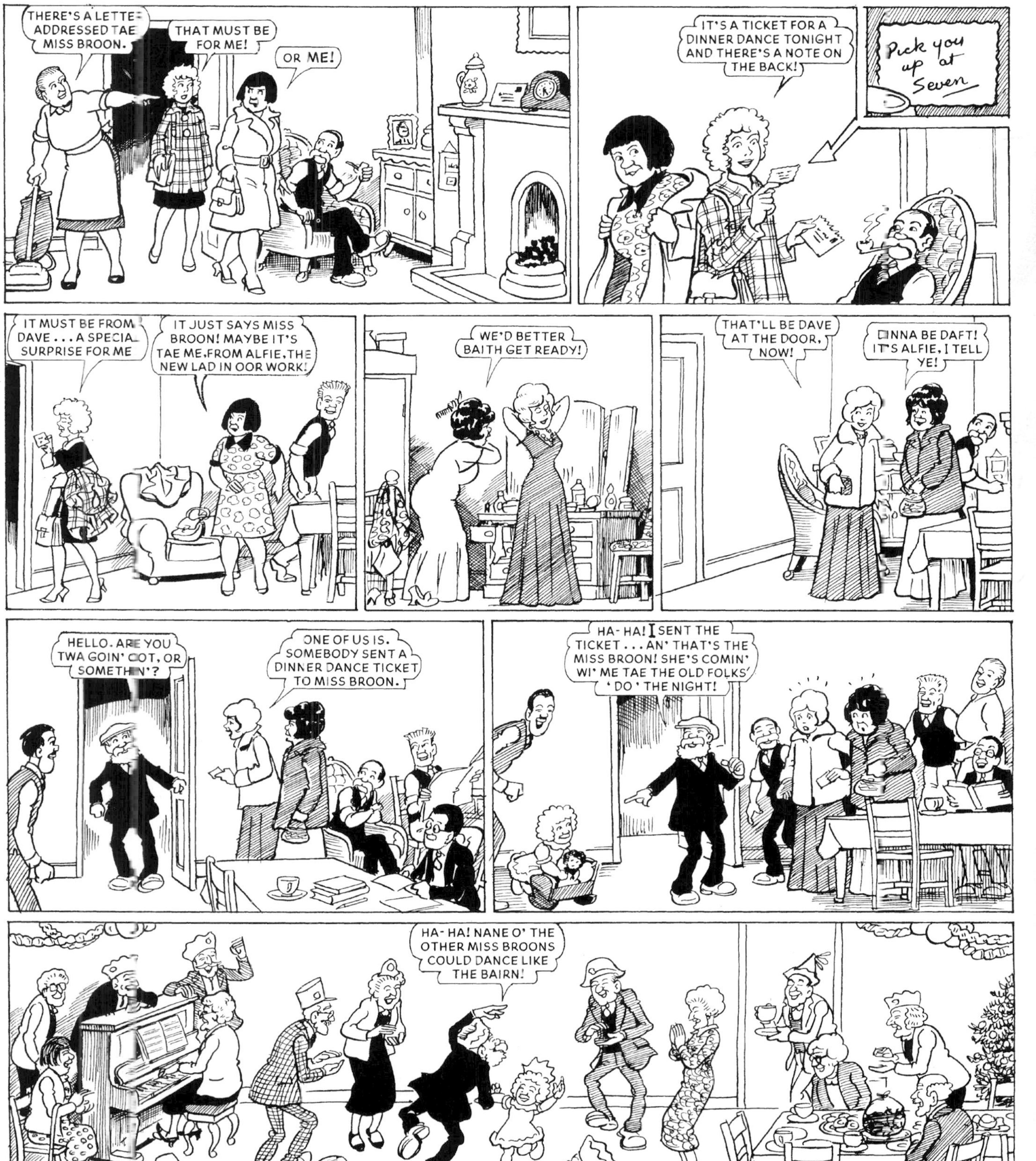

THERE'S A LETTER ADDRESSED TAE MISS BROON.
THAT MUST BE FOR ME!
OR ME!
IT'S A TICKET FOR A DINNER DANCE TONIGHT AND THERE'S A NOTE ON THE BACK!
Pick you up at Seven
IT MUST BE FROM DAVE . . . A SPECIAL SURPRISE FOR ME
IT JUST SAYS MISS BROON! MAYBE IT'S TAE ME, FROM ALFIE, THE NEW LAD IN OOR WORK!
WE'D BETTER BAITH GET READY!
THAT'LL BE DAVE AT THE DOOR, NOW!
DINNA BE DAFT! IT'S ALFIE, I TELL YE!
HELLO. ARE YOU TWA GOIN' OOT, OR SOMETHIN'?
ONE OF US IS. SOMEBODY SENT A DINNER DANCE TICKET TO MISS BROON.
HA-HA! I SENT THE TICKET . . . AN' THAT'S THE MISS BROON! SHE'S COMIN' WI' ME TAE THE OLD FOLKS' 'DO' THE NIGHT!
HA-HA! NANE O' THE OTHER MISS BROONS COULD DANCE LIKE THE BAIRN!

See the gloomy faces when—

It's Christmas Day at No. 10!

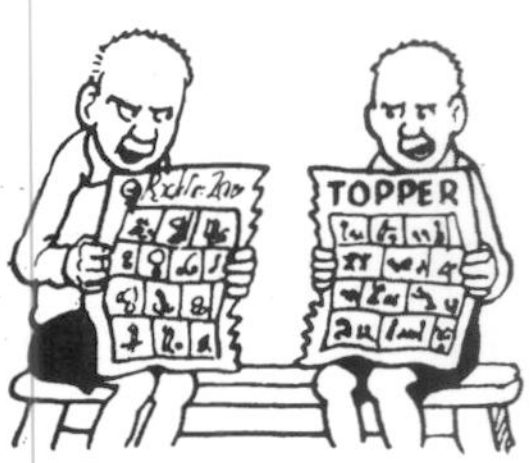
TOPPER

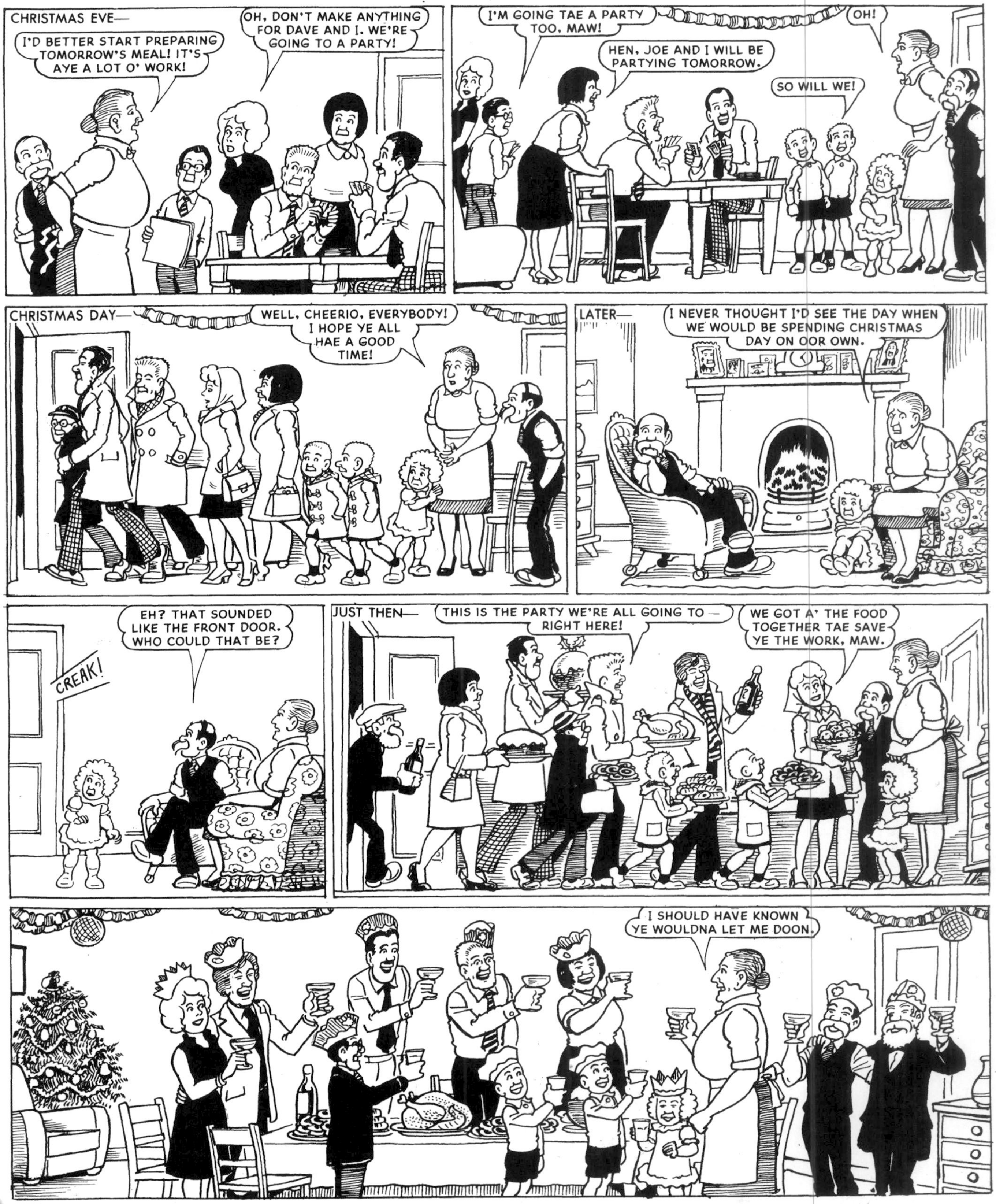
CHRISTMAS EVE—
I'D BETTER START PREPARING TOMORROW'S MEAL! IT'S AYE A LOT O' WORK!
OH, DON'T MAKE ANYTHING FOR DAVE AND I. WE'RE GOING TO A PARTY!
I'M GOING TAE A PARTY TOO, MAW!
HEN, JOE AND I WILL BE PARTYING TOMORROW.
SO WILL WE!
OH!
CHRISTMAS DAY—
WELL, CHEERIO, EVERYBODY! I HOPE YE ALL HAE A GOOD TIME!
LATER—
I NEVER THOUGHT I'D SEE THE DAY WHEN WE WOULD BE SPENDING CHRISTMAS DAY ON OOR OWN.
CREAK!
EH? THAT SOUNDED LIKE THE FRONT DOOR. WHO COULD THAT BE?
JUST THEN—
THIS IS THE PARTY WE'RE ALL GOING TO — RIGHT HERE!
WE GOT A' THE FOOD TOGETHER TAE SAVE YE THE WORK, MAW.
I SHOULD HAVE KNOWN YE WOULDNA LET ME DOON.

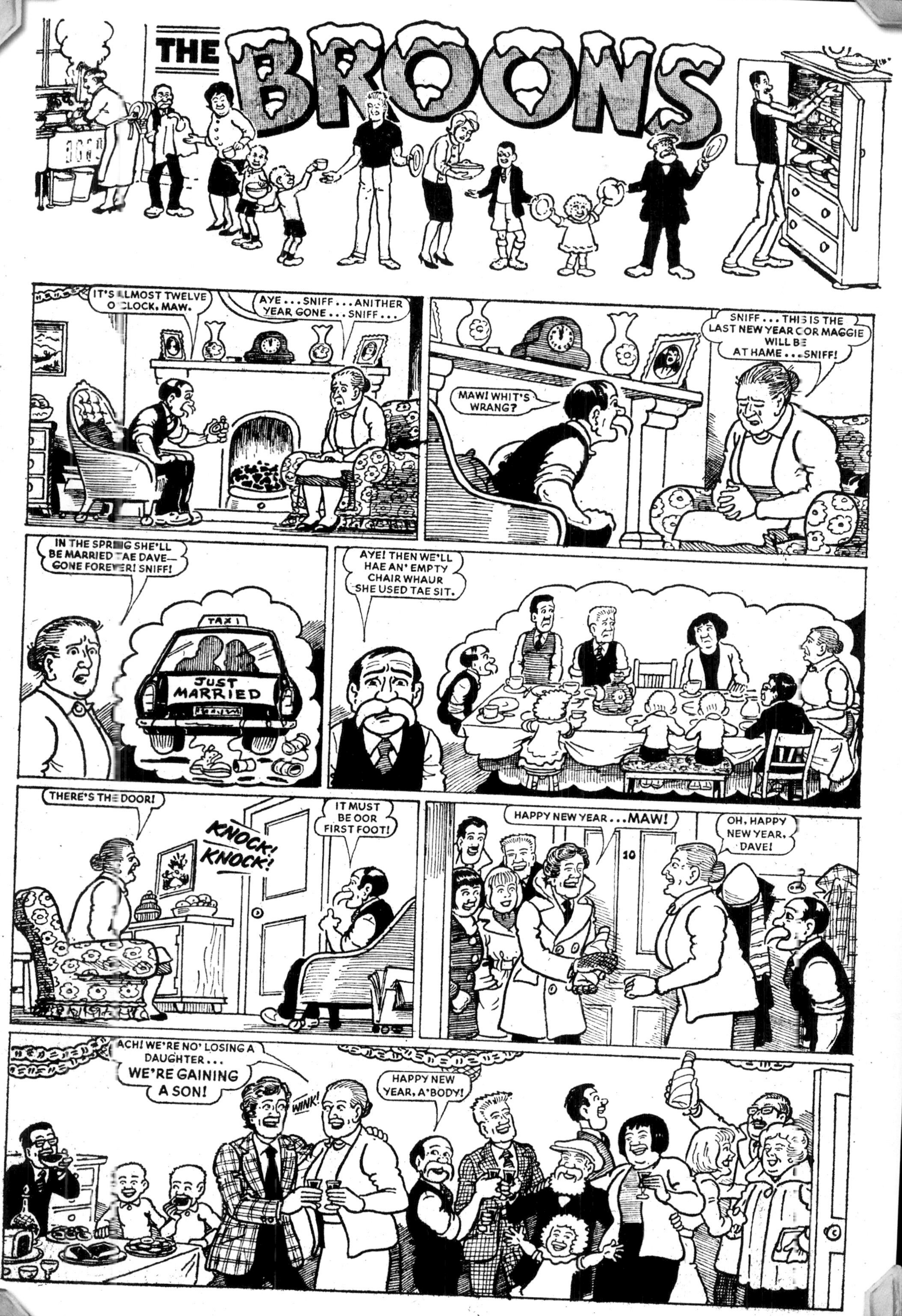
THE BROONS
IT'S ALMOST TWELVE O'CLOCK, MAW.
AYE . . . SNIFF . . . ANITHER YEAR GONE . . . SNIFF . . .
MAW! WHIT'S WRANG?
SNIFF . . . THIS IS THE LAST NEW YEAR OOR MAGGIE WILL BE AT HAME . . . SNIFF!
IN THE SPRING SHE'LL BE MARRIED TAE DAVE— GONE FOREVER! SNIFF!
TAXI
JUST MARRIED
AYE! THEN WE'LL HAE AN' EMPTY CHAIR WHAUR SHE USED TAE SIT.
THERE'S THE DOOR!
KNOCK! KNOCK!
IT MUST BE OOR FIRST FOOT!
HAPPY NEW YEAR . . . MAW!
OH, HAPPY NEW YEAR, DAVE!
ACH! WE'RE NO' LOSING A DAUGHTER . . .
WE'RE GAINING A SON!
WINK!
HAPPY NEW YEAR, A'BODY!

The Funny Side of Weddings

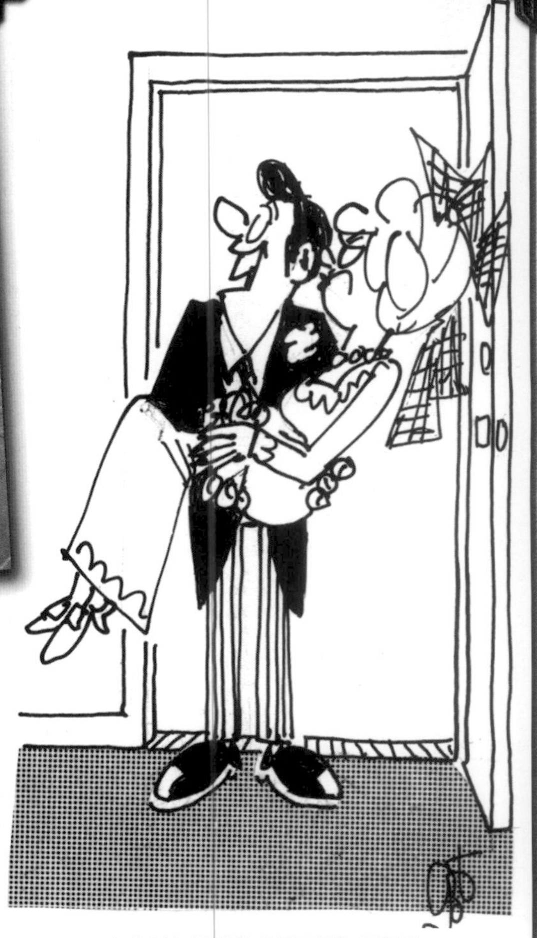

I CAN JUST SEE US NOW, PAYING OFF THE MORTGAGE – YOU DUMPY AND NAGGING, ME BALD AND BORED.

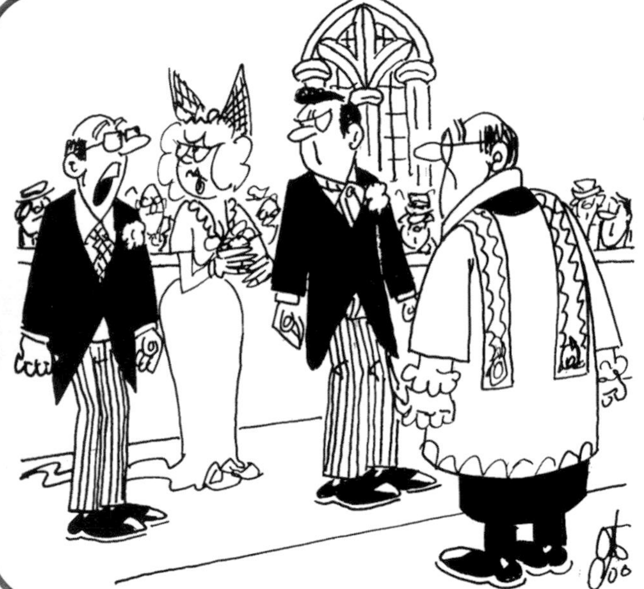

I GIVE THIS WOMAN – AND AFTER PAYING FOR THE WEDDING IT'S ABOUT ALL I HAVE LEFT TO GIVE.

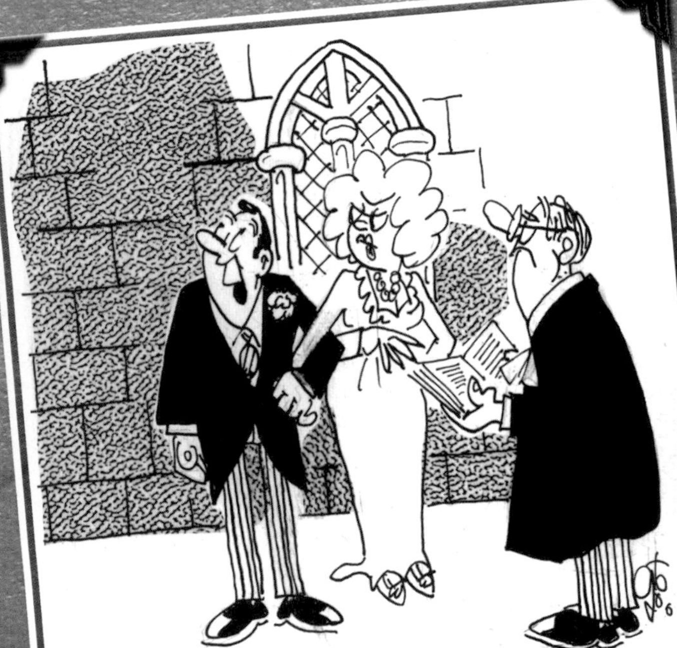

BACK HERE AGAIN. MUST SAY, THE OLD PLACE HASN'T CHANGED MUCH.

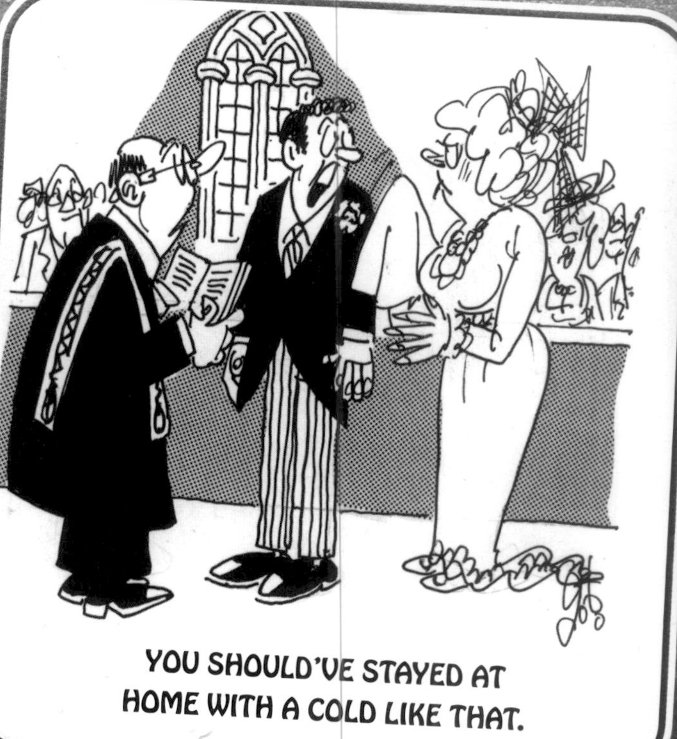

YOU SHOULD'VE STAYED AT HOME WITH A COLD LIKE THAT.

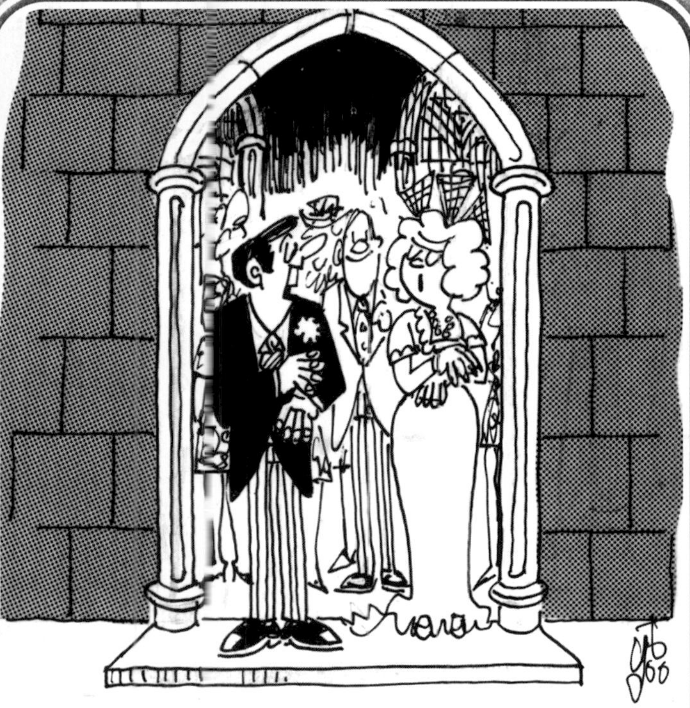

NOW CAN I STOP BEING NICE TO YOUR MOTHER?

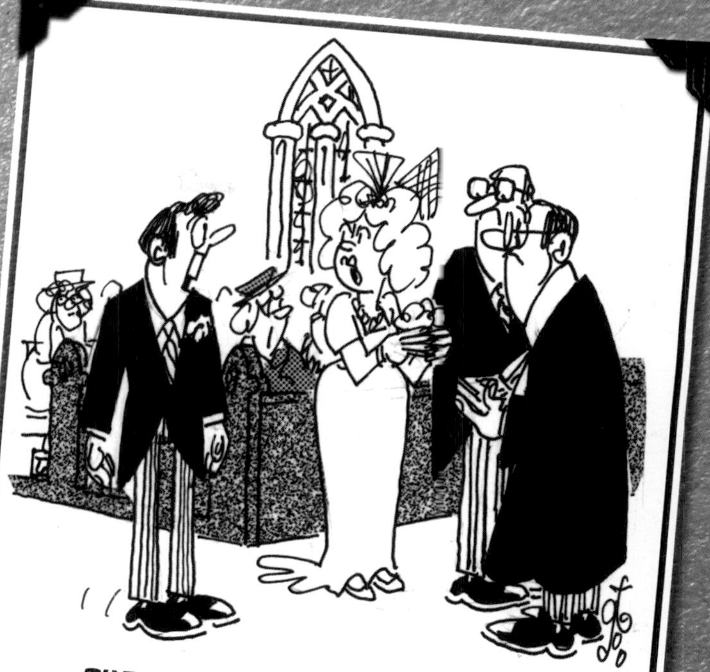

THE GROOM SAID IF HE WAS LATE WE WERE JUST TO START WITHOUT HIM.

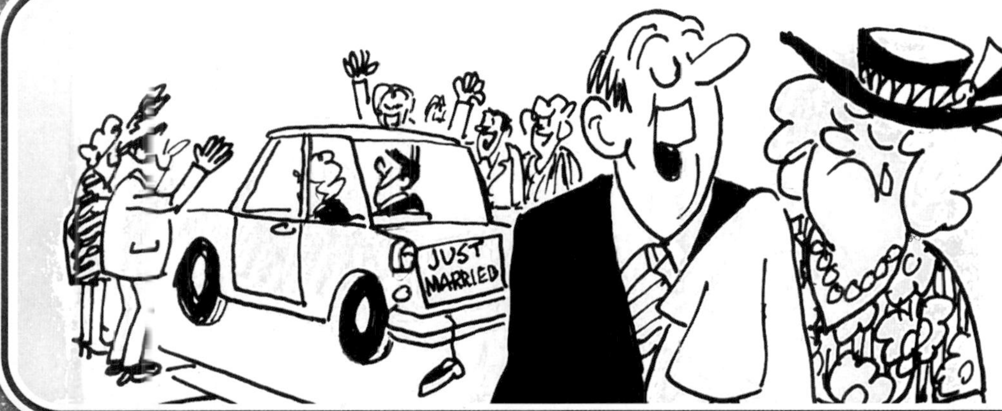
JUST MARRIED

WE'RE NOT LOSING A DAUGHTER, WE'RE GAINING A BATHROOM, KITCHEN AND REMOTE CONTROL.

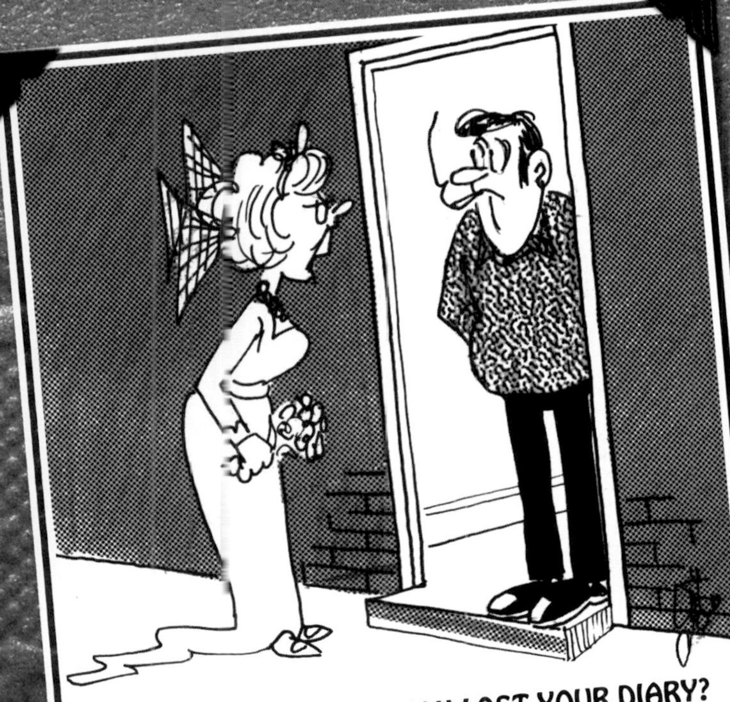

WHAT DO YOU MEAN, YOU LOST YOUR DIARY?

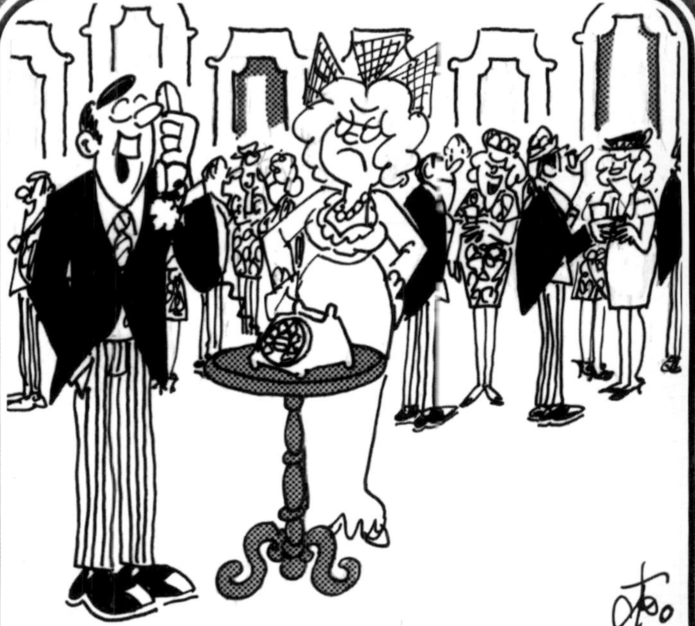

OH, I'M NOT DOING MUCH AT ALL. JUST THE SAME OLD STUFF.

This " antique " shopper—

Comes a cropper!

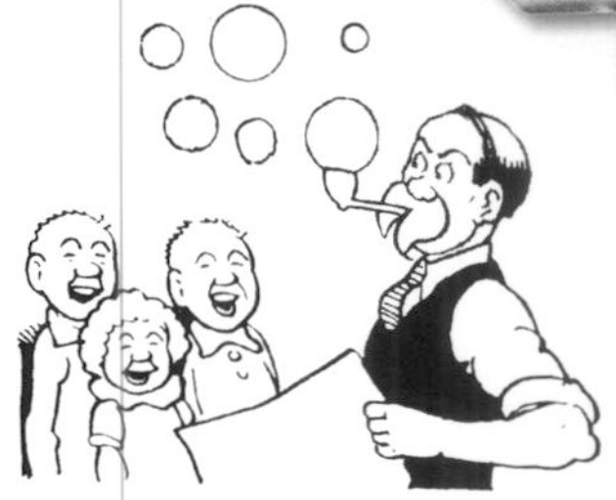

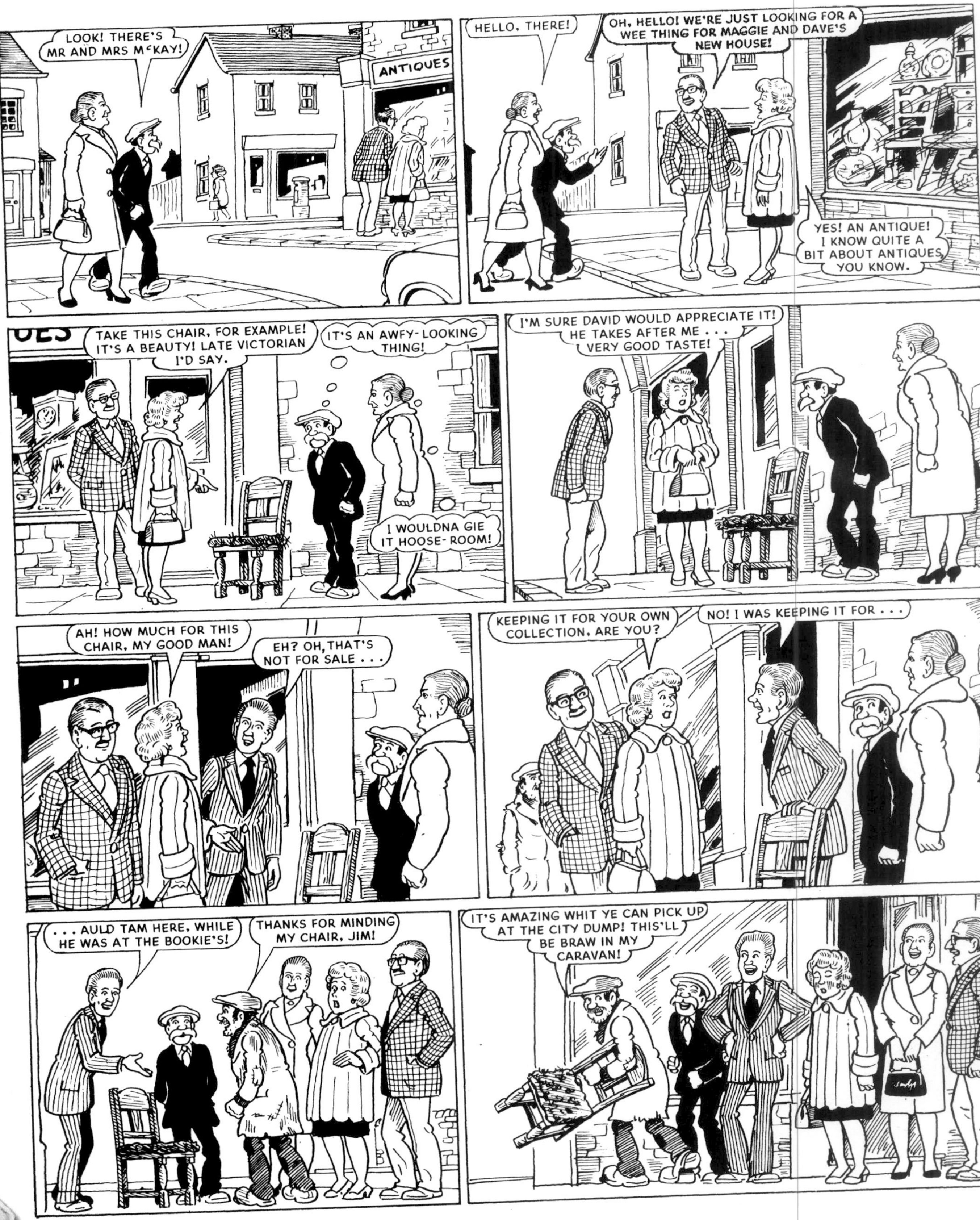
LOOK! THERE'S MR AND MRS McKAY!
ANTIQUES
HELLO, THERE!
OH, HELLO! WE'RE JUST LOOKING FOR A WEE THING FOR MAGGIE AND DAVE'S NEW HOUSE!
YES! AN ANTIQUE! I KNOW QUITE A BIT ABOUT ANTIQUES, YOU KNOW.
TAKE THIS CHAIR, FOR EXAMPLE! IT'S A BEAUTY! LATE VICTORIAN I'D SAY.
IT'S AN AWFY-LOOKING THING!
I WOULDNA GIE IT HOOSE-ROOM!
I'M SURE DAVID WOULD APPRECIATE IT! HE TAKES AFTER ME . . . VERY GOOD TASTE!
AH! HOW MUCH FOR THIS CHAIR, MY GOOD MAN!
EH? OH, THAT'S NOT FOR SALE . . .
KEEPING IT FOR YOUR OWN COLLECTION, ARE YOU?
NO! I WAS KEEPING IT FOR . . .
. . . AULD TAM HERE, WHILE HE WAS AT THE BOOKIE'S!
THANKS FOR MINDING MY CHAIR, JIM!
IT'S AMAZING WHIT YE CAN PICK UP AT THE CITY DUMP! THIS'LL BE BRAW IN MY CARAVAN!

An expert cook?—

Well, tak' a look!

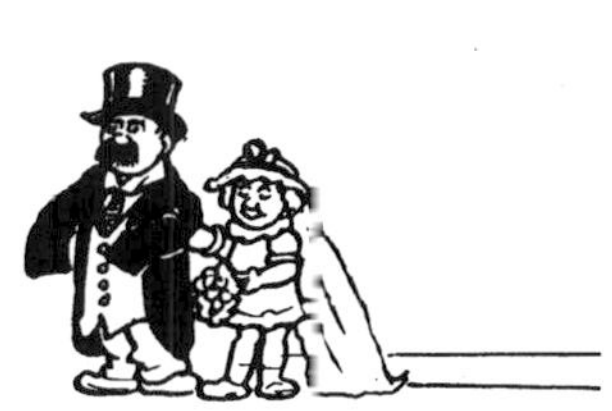

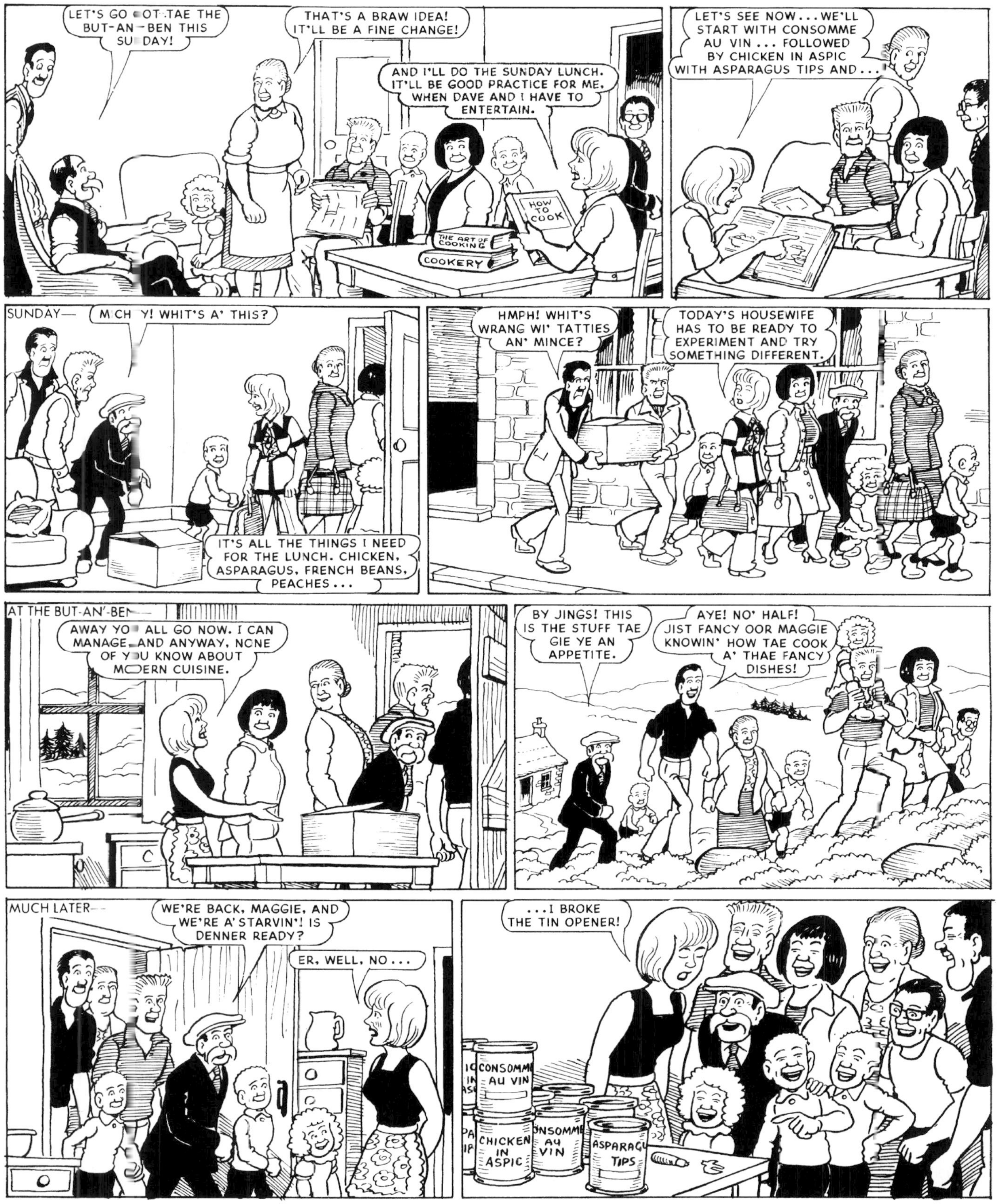
LET'S GO OOT TAE THE BUT-AN-BEN THIS SUNDAY!
THAT'S A BRAW IDEA! IT'LL BE A FINE CHANGE!
AND I'LL DO THE SUNDAY LUNCH. IT'LL BE GOOD PRACTICE FOR ME, WHEN DAVE AND I HAVE TO ENTERTAIN.
HOW TO COOK
THE ART OF COOKING
COOKERY
LET'S SEE NOW... WE'LL START WITH CONSOMME AU VIN ... FOLLOWED BY CHICKEN IN ASPIC WITH ASPARAGUS TIPS AND ...
SUNDAY—
MICHTY! WHIT'S A' THIS?
IT'S ALL THE THINGS I NEED FOR THE LUNCH. CHICKEN, ASPARAGUS, FRENCH BEANS, PEACHES ...
HMPH! WHIT'S WRANG WI' TATTIES AN' MINCE?
TODAY'S HOUSEWIFE HAS TO BE READY TO EXPERIMENT AND TRY SOMETHING DIFFERENT.
AT THE BUT-AN'-BEN—
AWAY YOU ALL GO NOW. I CAN MANAGE. AND ANYWAY, NONE OF YOU KNOW ABOUT MODERN CUISINE.
BY JINGS! THIS IS THE STUFF TAE GIE YE AN APPETITE.
AYE! NO' HALF! JIST FANCY OOR MAGGIE KNOWIN' HOW TAE COOK A' THAE FANCY DISHES!
MUCH LATER—
WE'RE BACK, MAGGIE, AND WE'RE A' STARVIN'! IS DENNER READY?
ER, WELL, NO ...
...I BROKE THE TIN OPENER!
CONSOMME AU VIN
CHICKEN IN ASPIC
ASPARAGUS TIPS

Is it the women or is it the men—

Who wear the breeks at No. 10?

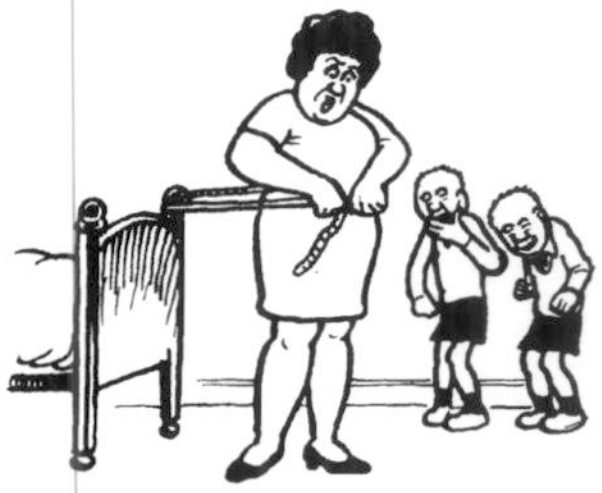

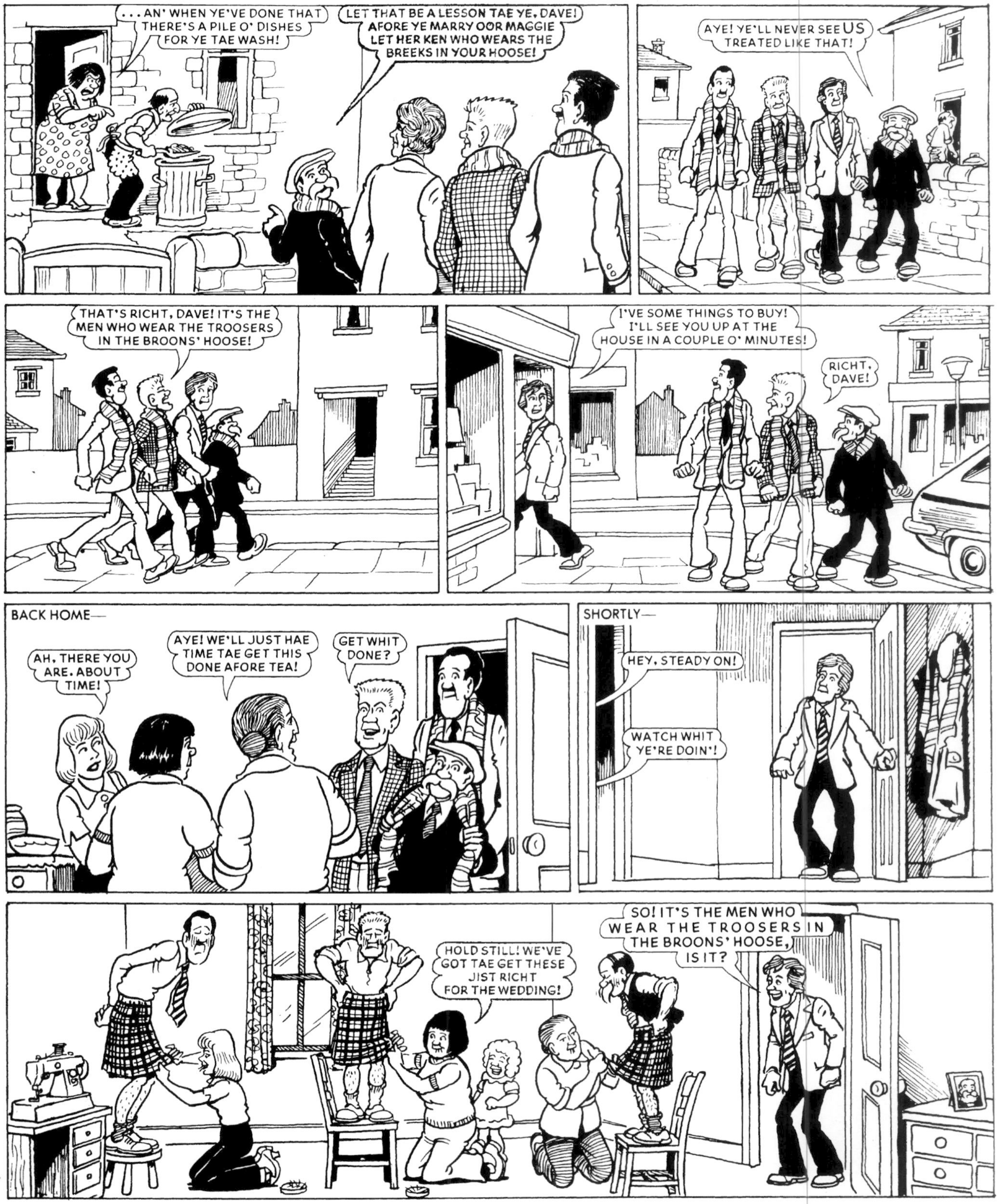
. . . AN' WHEN YE'VE DONE THAT THERE'S A PILE O' DISHES FOR YE TAE WASH!
LET THAT BE A LESSON TAE YE, DAVE! AFORE YE MARRY OOR MAGGIE LET HER KEN WHO WEARS THE BREEKS IN YOUR HOOSE!
AYE! YE'LL NEVER SEE US TREATED LIKE THAT!
THAT'S RICHT, DAVE! IT'S THE MEN WHO WEAR THE TROOSERS IN THE BROONS' HOOSE!
I'VE SOME THINGS TO BUY! I'LL SEE YOU UP AT THE HOUSE IN A COUPLE O' MINUTES!
RICHT, DAVE!
BACK HOME—
AH, THERE YOU ARE. ABOUT TIME!
AYE! WE'LL JUST HAE TIME TAE GET THIS DONE AFORE TEA!
GET WHIT DONE?
SHORTLY—
HEY, STEADY ON!
WATCH WHIT YE'RE DOIN'!
HOLD STILL! WE'VE GOT TAE GET THESE JIST RICHT FOR THE WEDDING!
SO! IT'S THE MEN WHO WEAR THE TROOSERS IN THE BROONS' HOOSE, IS IT?

Lots o' reek, lots o' puff—
Aye, that's really champion stuff!

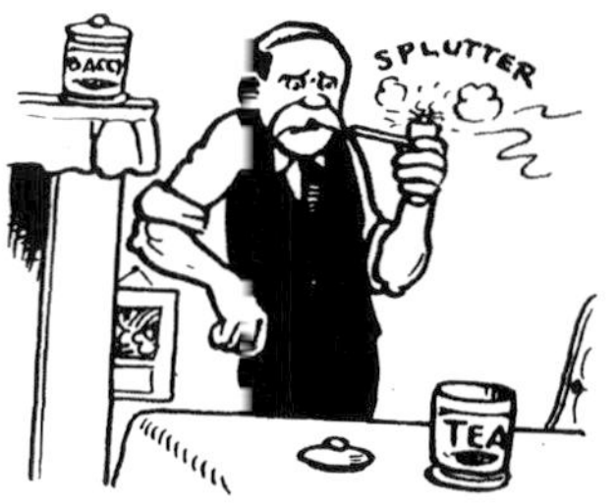

SPLUTTER
TEA

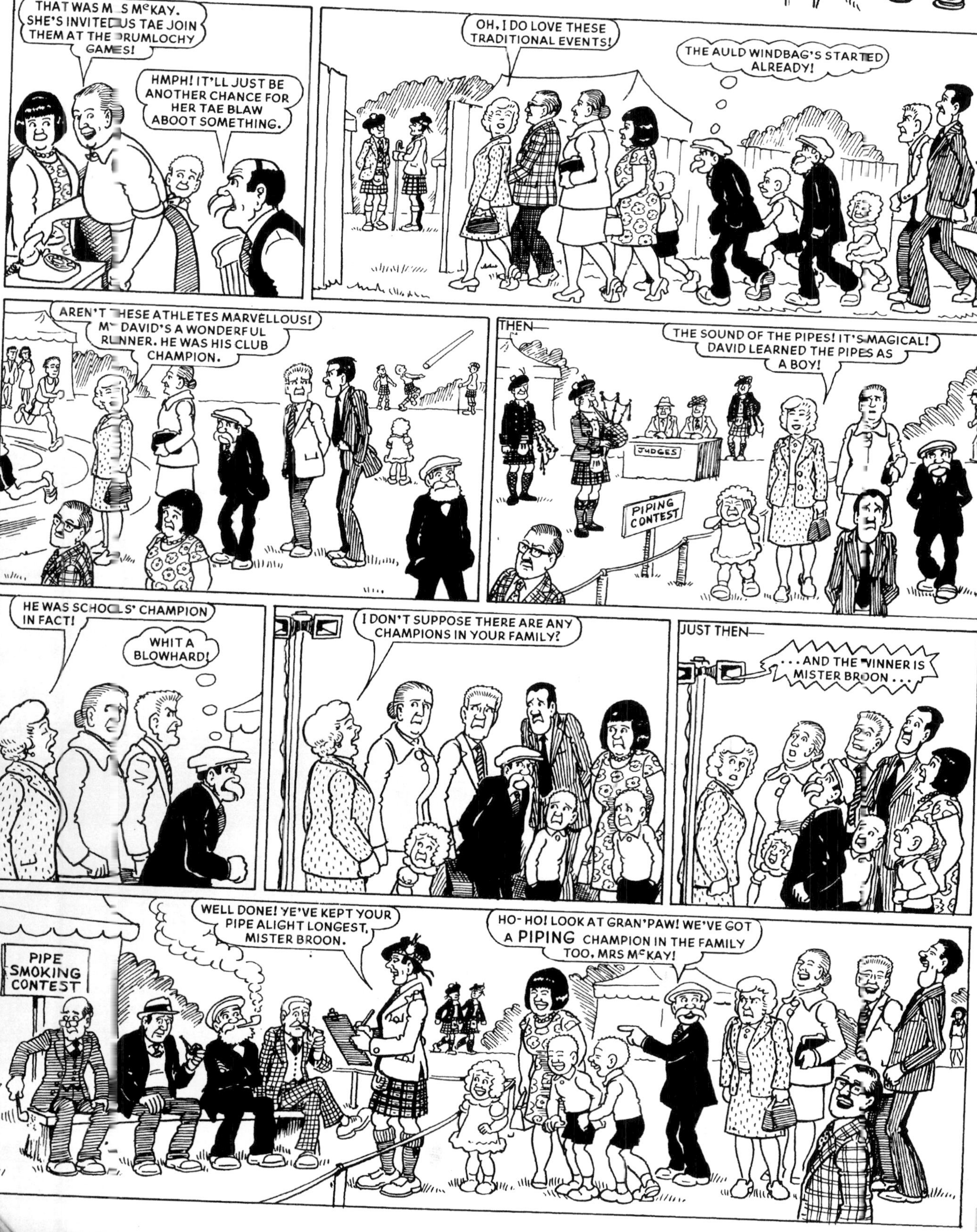

THAT WAS MRS McKAY. SHE'S INVITED US TAE JOIN THEM AT THE DRUMLOCHY GAMES!
HMPH! IT'LL JUST BE ANOTHER CHANCE FOR HER TAE BLAW ABOOT SOMETHING.
OH, I DO LOVE THESE TRADITIONAL EVENTS!
THE AULD WINDBAG'S STARTED ALREADY!
AREN'T THESE ATHLETES MARVELLOUS! MY DAVID'S A WONDERFUL RUNNER. HE WAS HIS CLUB CHAMPION.
THEN—
THE SOUND OF THE PIPES! IT'S MAGICAL! DAVID LEARNED THE PIPES AS A BOY!
JUDGES
PIPING CONTEST
HE WAS SCHOOLS' CHAMPION IN FACT!
WHIT A BLOWHARD!
I DON'T SUPPOSE THERE ARE ANY CHAMPIONS IN YOUR FAMILY?
JUST THEN—
. . . AND THE WINNER IS MISTER BROON . . .
PIPE SMOKING CONTEST
WELL DONE! YE'VE KEPT YOUR PIPE ALIGHT LONGEST, MISTER BROON.
HO-HO! LOOK AT GRAN'PAW! WE'VE GOT A PIPING CHAMPION IN THE FAMILY TOO, MRS McKAY!

Dave,

The floors ye sent me at work were brilliant. You should hae seen Ella McGlumfer! She was so jealous her face was as green as the leaves.

The poem was lovely, you could be writing songs for The Bay City Rollers.

Love Maggie. x

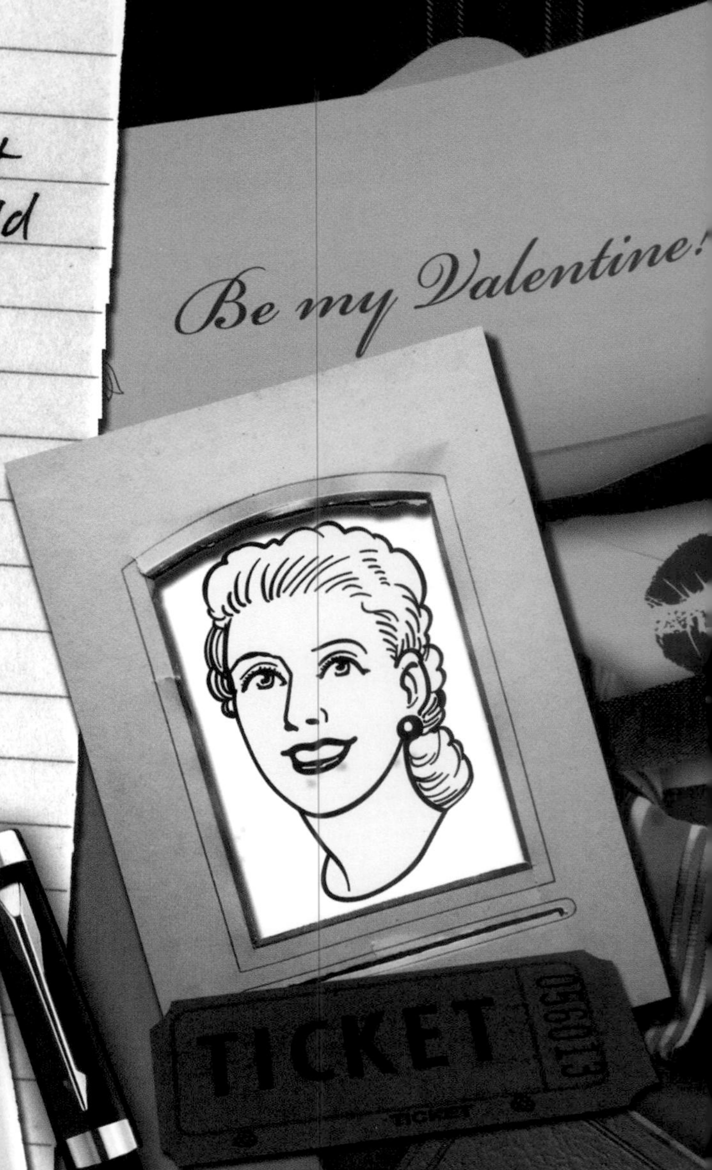
Be my Valentine!
TICKET
056013
TICKET

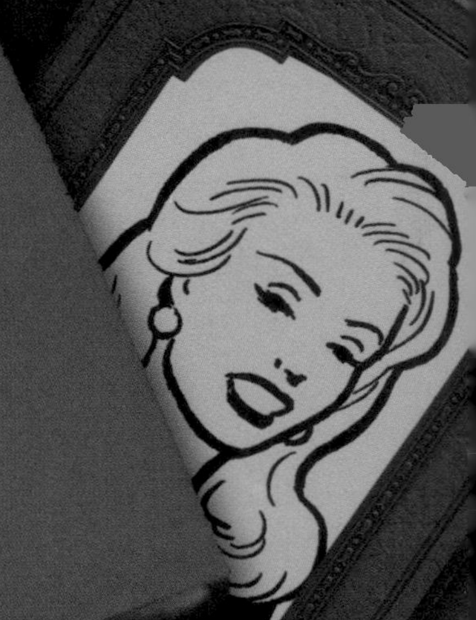

Dear David,

My phone number is Auchentogle 6125.

If I dinna answer the phone but another lassie does, it'll either be my Maw or my sister Daphne. If it's Maw be polite, if it's my sister Daphne, say nothing aboot comin' tae the hoose or she'll be awa' tightenin' her corsets and puttin' the full war pent on and you'll no' stand a chance.

Maggie x

P.S. You'll ken it's Daphne for she pits on a posh phone voice and tries tae sound like Angela Rippon.

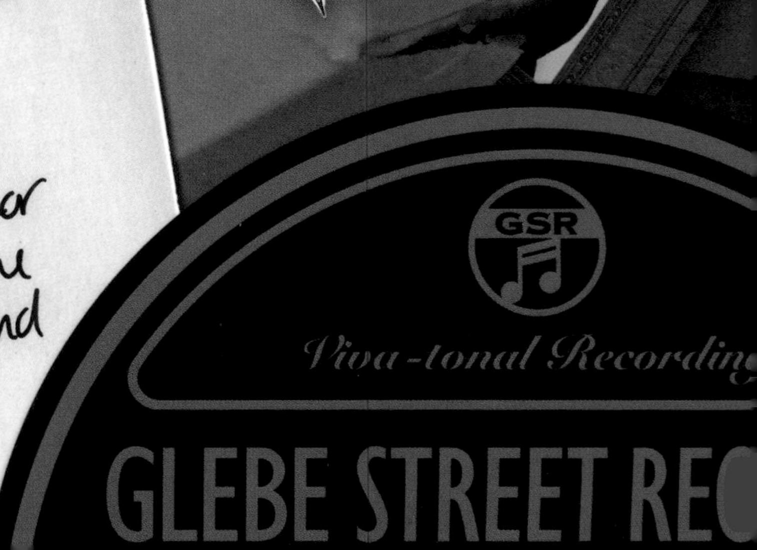
GSR
Viva-tonal Recording
GLEBE STREET REC

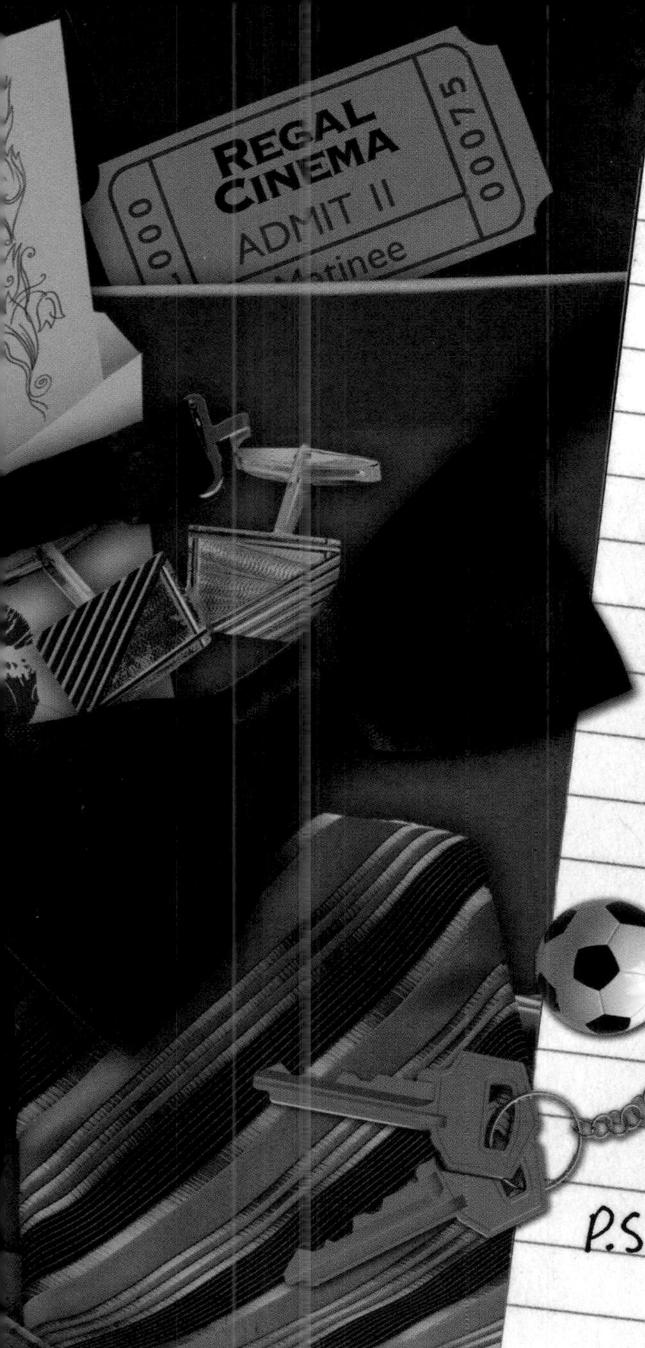
REGAL CINEMA
ADMIT II
Matinee
000075

Dearest Dave,

What a sweetie you are takin' the blame for me gettin' in so late frae the dancin'. And here we missed the last bus for I was bletherin' tae the lassies in the toilets. I was bletherin' aboot you, Dave. They a' think you look like John Travolta — and you did a bit last night until mah stories landed on yer heid. Sorry, I was aimin' for Ella.

Your Girl

Maggie xxx

P.S. Did Paw gie ye the "that never happened in mah day" efter I went in tae bed?

Davykins,

Please dinna believe what Peem Dodd says. I dinna fancy him one bit! I took a lift hame frae work wi' him because I didnae want my hair to go frizzy in the rain. I had my hair done for going oot wi' you sweetheart.

Love You,

Maggie xxx

Darling Dave,

Yes! Yes! Yes!

Yours for ever,

Maggie xxx

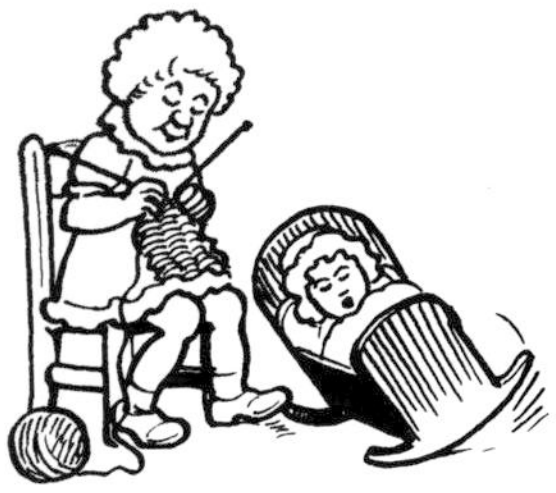

The family chuckle when they find—
Why the Bairn lags behind!

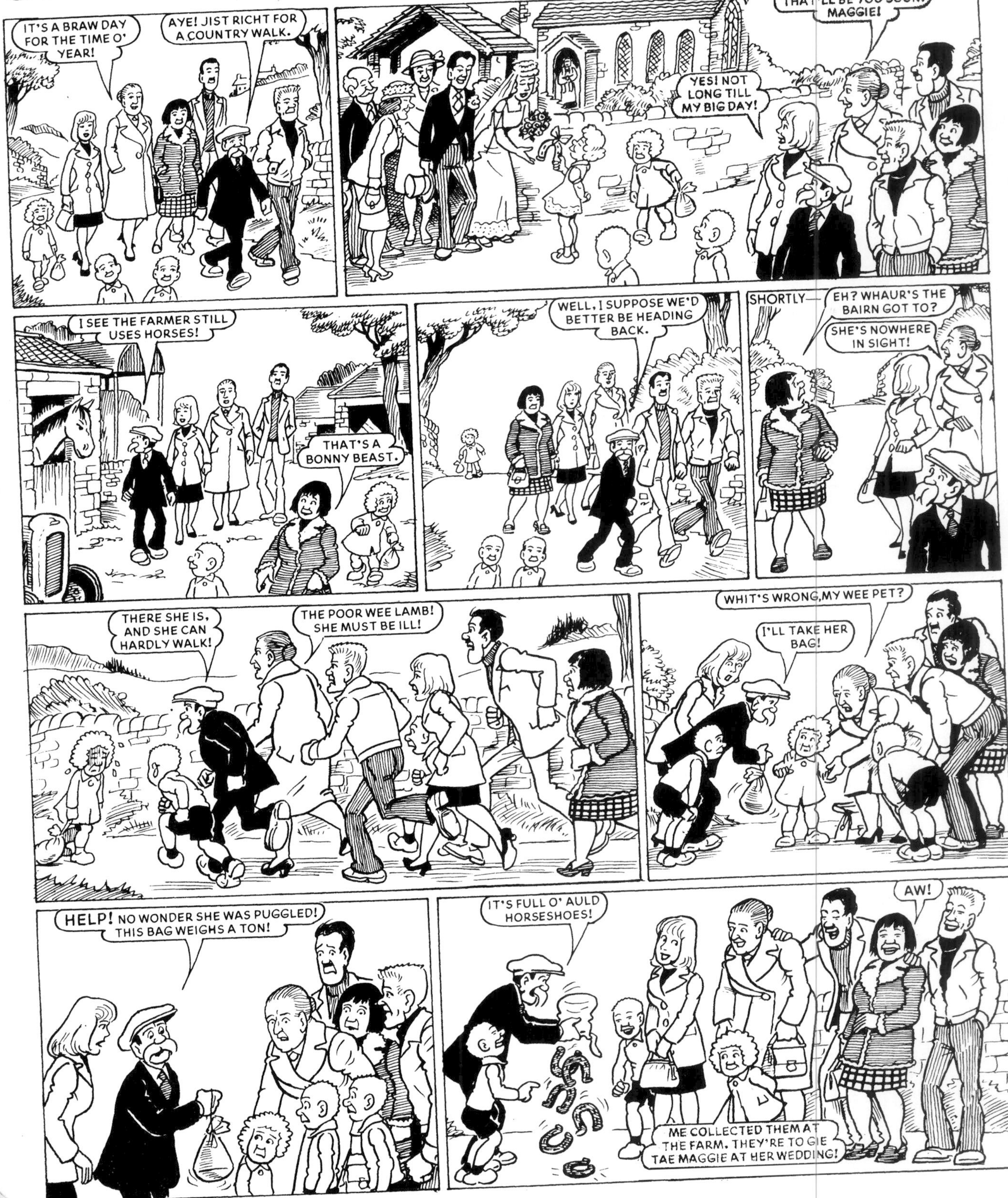
IT'S A BRAW DAY FOR THE TIME O' YEAR!
AYE! JIST RICHT FOR A COUNTRY WALK.
THAT'LL BE YOU SOON, MAGGIE!
YES! NOT LONG TILL MY BIG DAY!
I SEE THE FARMER STILL USES HORSES!
THAT'S A BONNY BEAST.
WELL, I SUPPOSE WE'D BETTER BE HEADING BACK.
SHORTLY—
EH? WHAUR'S THE BAIRN GOT TO?
SHE'S NOWHERE IN SIGHT!
THERE SHE IS, AND SHE CAN HARDLY WALK!
THE POOR WEE LAMB! SHE MUST BE ILL!
WHIT'S WRONG, MY WEE PET?
I'LL TAKE HER BAG!
HELP! NO WONDER SHE WAS PUGGLED! THIS BAG WEIGHS A TON!
IT'S FULL O' AULD HORSESHOES!
AW!
ME COLLECTED THEM AT THE FARM. THEY'RE TO GIE TAE MAGGIE AT HER WEDDING!

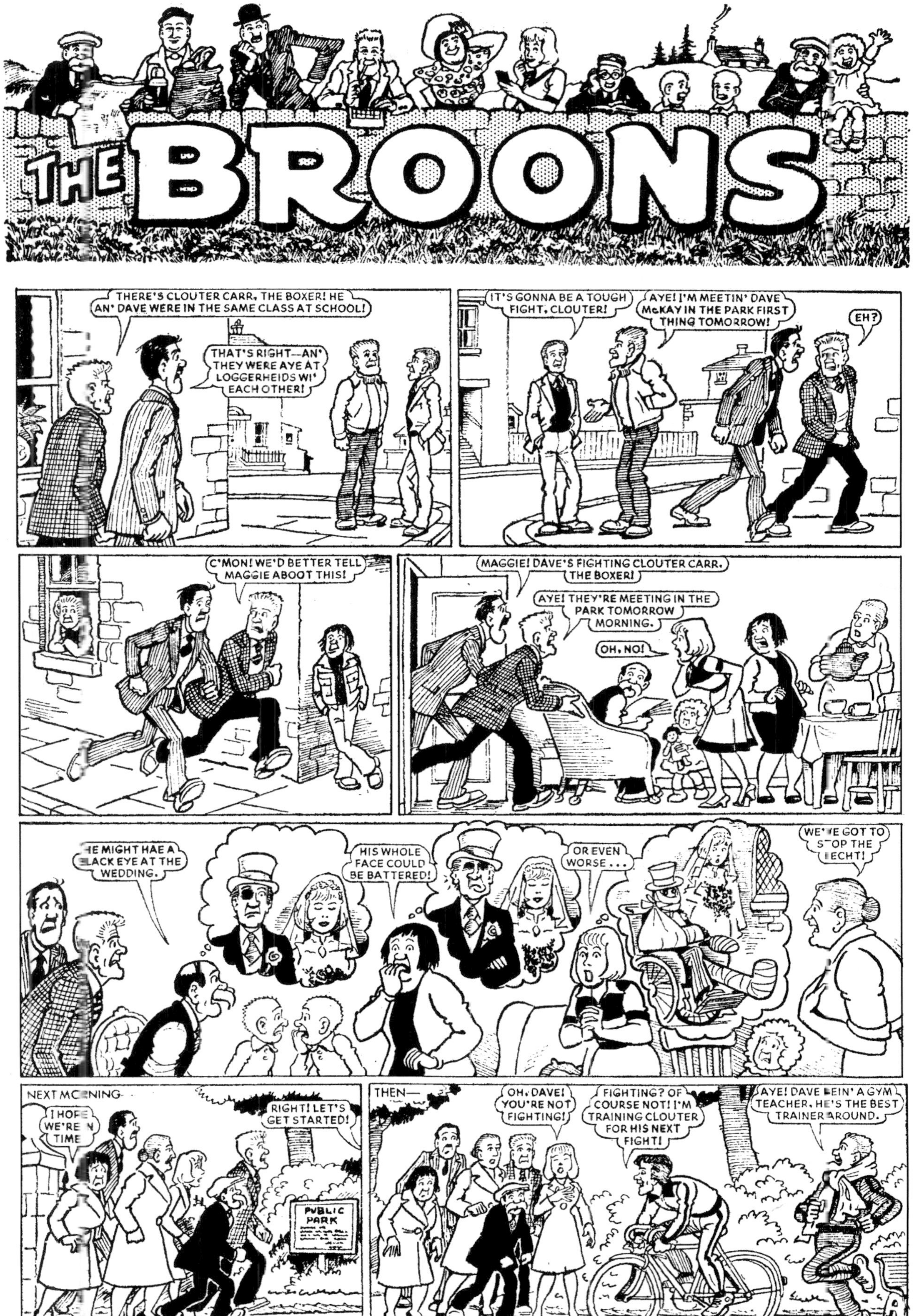
THE BROONS
THERE'S CLOUTER CARR, THE BOXER! HE AN' DAVE WERE IN THE SAME CLASS AT SCHOOL!
THAT'S RIGHT—AN' THEY WERE AYE AT LOGGERHEIDS WI' EACH OTHER!
IT'S GONNA BE A TOUGH FIGHT, CLOUTER!
AYE! I'M MEETIN' DAVE McKAY IN THE PARK FIRST THING TOMORROW!
EH?
C'MON! WE'D BETTER TELL MAGGIE ABOOT THIS!
MAGGIE! DAVE'S FIGHTING CLOUTER CARR, THE BOXER!
AYE! THEY'RE MEETING IN THE PARK TOMORROW MORNING.
OH, NO!
HE MIGHT HAE A BLACK EYE AT THE WEDDING.
HIS WHOLE FACE COULD BE BATTERED!
OR EVEN WORSE . . .
WE'VE GOT TO STOP THE FECHT!
NEXT MORNING—
I HOPE WE'RE IN TIME
RIGHT! LET'S GET STARTED!
PUBLIC PARK
THEN—
OH, DAVE! YOU'RE NOT FIGHTING!
FIGHTING? OF COURSE NOT! I'M TRAINING CLOUTER FOR HIS NEXT FIGHT!
AYE! DAVE BEIN' A GYM TEACHER, HE'S THE BEST TRAINER AROUND.

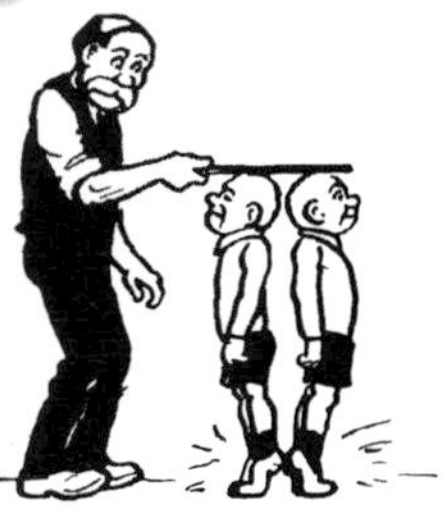

The list poor Paw makes—

Is full of mistakes!

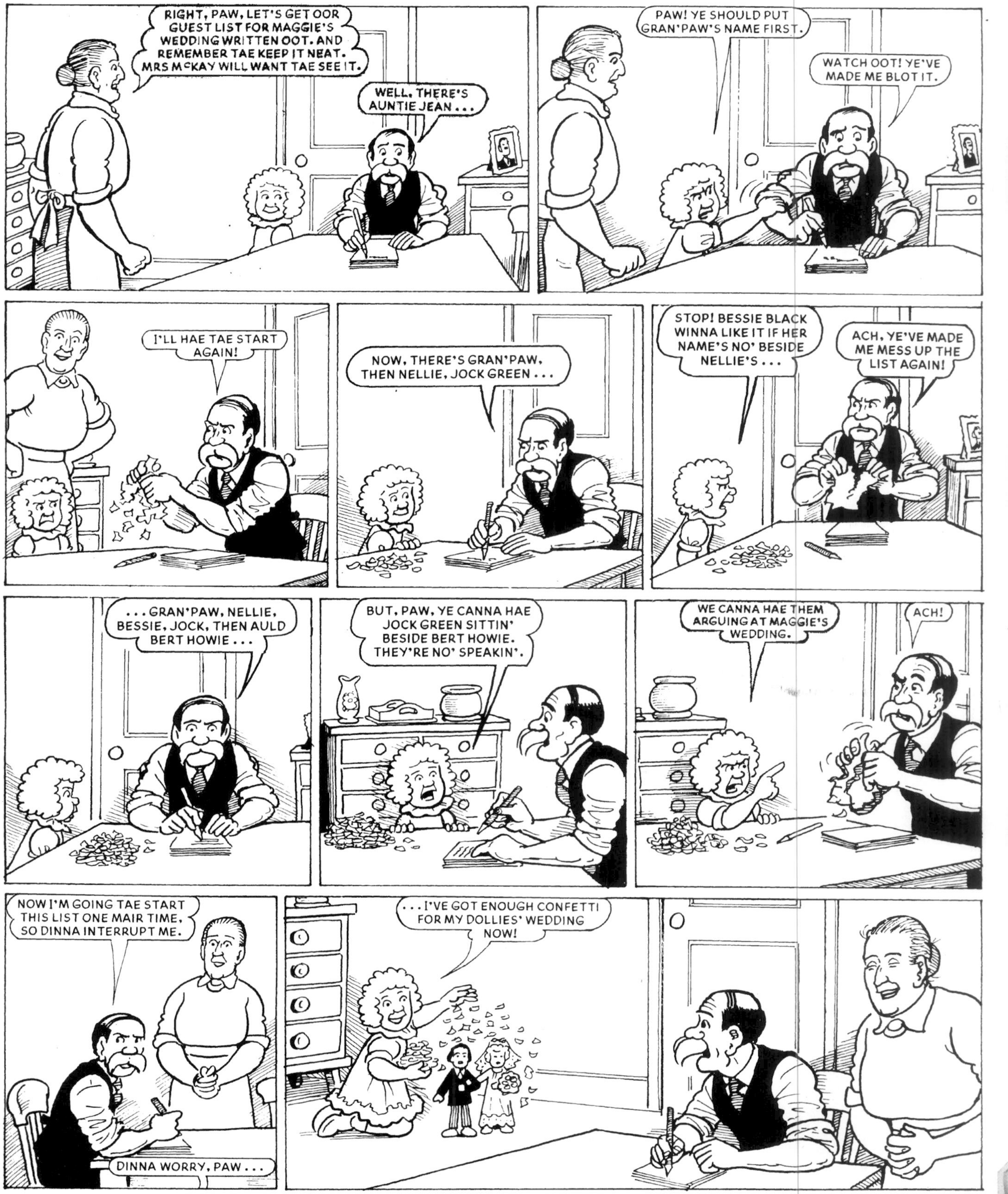

RIGHT, PAW, LET'S GET OOR GUEST LIST FOR MAGGIE'S WEDDING WRITTEN OOT. AND REMEMBER TAE KEEP IT NEAT. MRS McKAY WILL WANT TAE SEE IT.
WELL, THERE'S AUNTIE JEAN . . .
PAW! YE SHOULD PUT GRAN'PAW'S NAME FIRST.
WATCH OOT! YE'VE MADE ME BLOT IT.
I'LL HAE TAE START AGAIN!
NOW, THERE'S GRAN'PAW, THEN NELLIE, JOCK GREEN . . .
STOP! BESSIE BLACK WINNA LIKE IT IF HER NAME'S NO' BESIDE NELLIE'S . . .
ACH, YE'VE MADE ME MESS UP THE LIST AGAIN!
. . . GRAN'PAW, NELLIE, BESSIE, JOCK, THEN AULD BERT HOWIE . . .
BUT, PAW, YE CANNA HAE JOCK GREEN SITTIN' BESIDE BERT HOWIE. THEY'RE NO' SPEAKIN'.
WE CANNA HAE THEM ARGUING AT MAGGIE'S WEDDING.
ACH!
NOW I'M GOING TAE START THIS LIST ONE MAIR TIME, SO DINNA INTERRUPT ME.
DINNA WORRY, PAW . . .
. . . I'VE GOT ENOUGH CONFETTI FOR MY DOLLIES' WEDDING NOW!

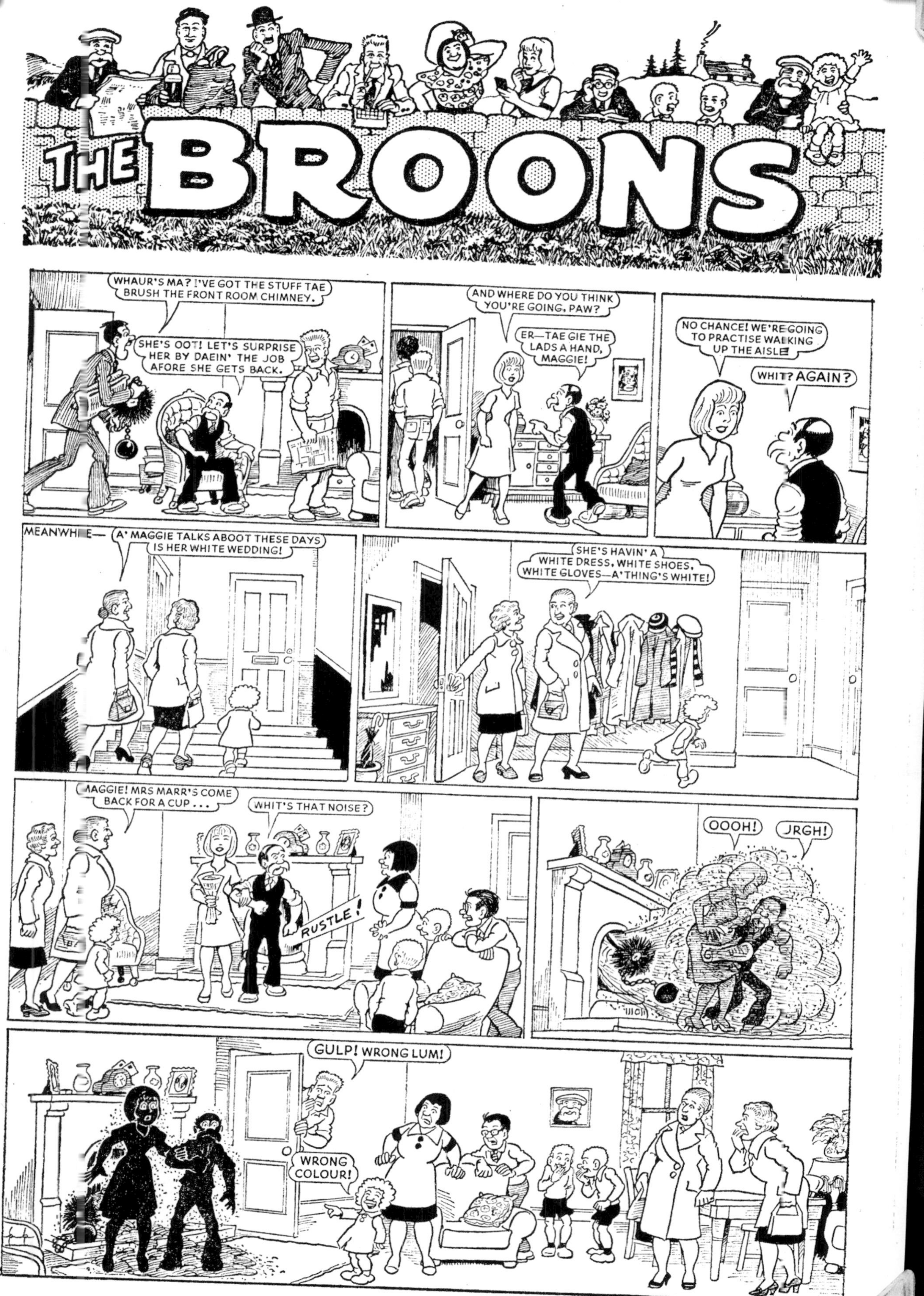
THE BROONS
WHAUR'S MA? I'VE GOT THE STUFF TAE BRUSH THE FRONT ROOM CHIMNEY.
SHE'S OOT! LET'S SURPRISE HER BY DAEIN' THE JOB AFORE SHE GETS BACK.
AND WHERE DO YOU THINK YOU'RE GOING, PAW?
ER—TAE GIE THE LADS A HAND, MAGGIE!
NO CHANCE! WE'RE GOING TO PRACTISE WALKING UP THE AISLE!
WHIT? AGAIN?
MEANWHILE—
A' MAGGIE TALKS ABOOT THESE DAYS IS HER WHITE WEDDING!
SHE'S HAVIN' A WHITE DRESS, WHITE SHOES, WHITE GLOVES—A' THING'S WHITE!
MAGGIE! MRS MARR'S COME BACK FOR A CUP . . .
WHIT'S THAT NOISE?
RUSTLE!
OOOH!
JRGH!
GULP! WRONG LUM!
WRONG COLOUR!

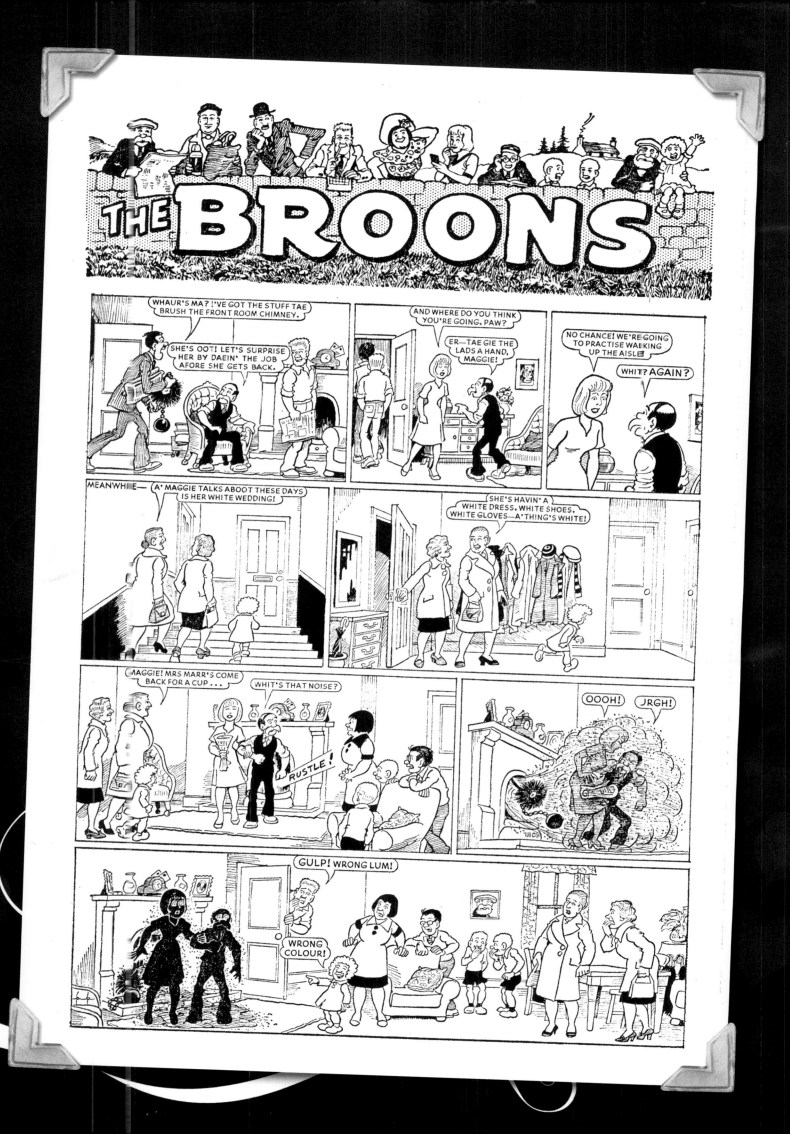

jings ... vens, help ma bo

Wedding Invitation

Mr and Mrs Broon invite Oor Wullie to the wedding of our daughter Maggie Broon to Dave McKay at Auchentogle Kirk.

And to the reception later at The Cooperative Hall.

Maw and Paw Broon

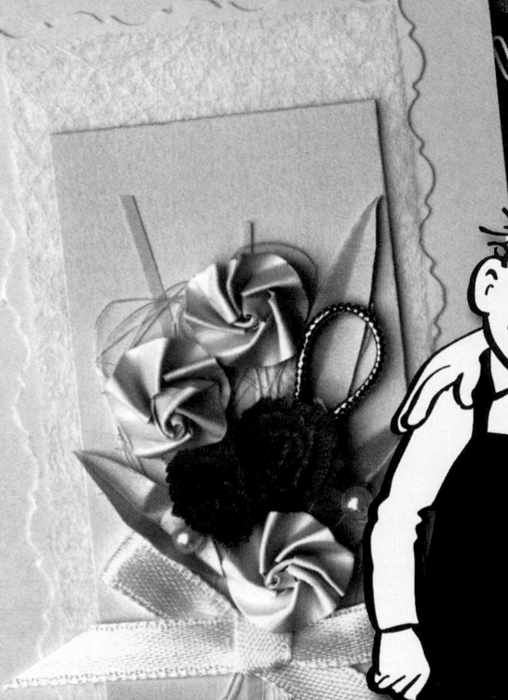

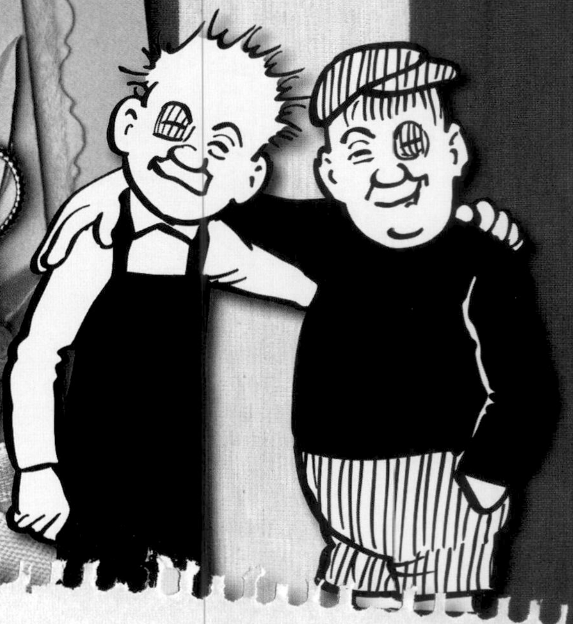

R.S.V.P.

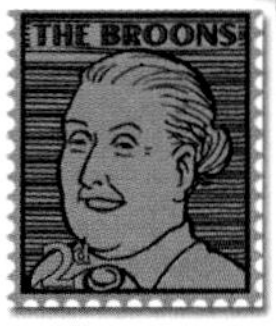
THE BROONS

The Broons,
10 Glebe Street

Dear Wullie,

Please come tae my wedding, I would really like a braw wee Scottish laddie like yersel' tae wish me luck. You hae been a braw freend tae me through a' the preparations, what wi' your runnin' errands and sending me that lucky horseshoe. It didnae matter tae me that Farmer Higgins came roond later tae ask for his horseshoe back – you're such a rascal! I dinna just want you tae bring one partner, though I'm told Primrose Patterson would be very keen tae come with you, bring a' your pals, Fat Bob, Soapy Soutar and Wee Eck. I'd love to see you a'.

Love, Maggie

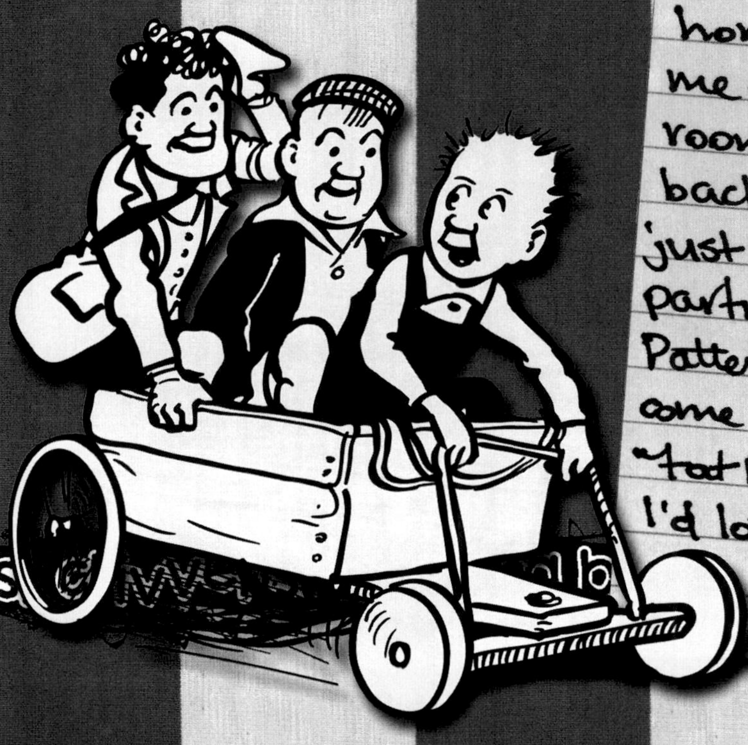

jings ... a bo

jings, crivvens, help ma boab! jings, crivvens, help ma
I USUALLY FIND WEDDIN'S BORIN' BUT THIS IS ANE I'LL ENJOY FINE. MAGGIE SAYS I DINNA HAE TAE DRESS UP POSH OR PRETEND TAE SING IN THE KIRK. AN BEST OF A', THE WEDDIN' BREAKFAST IS STOVIES.
jings, crivvens, help ma boab! jings, crivvens, help ma

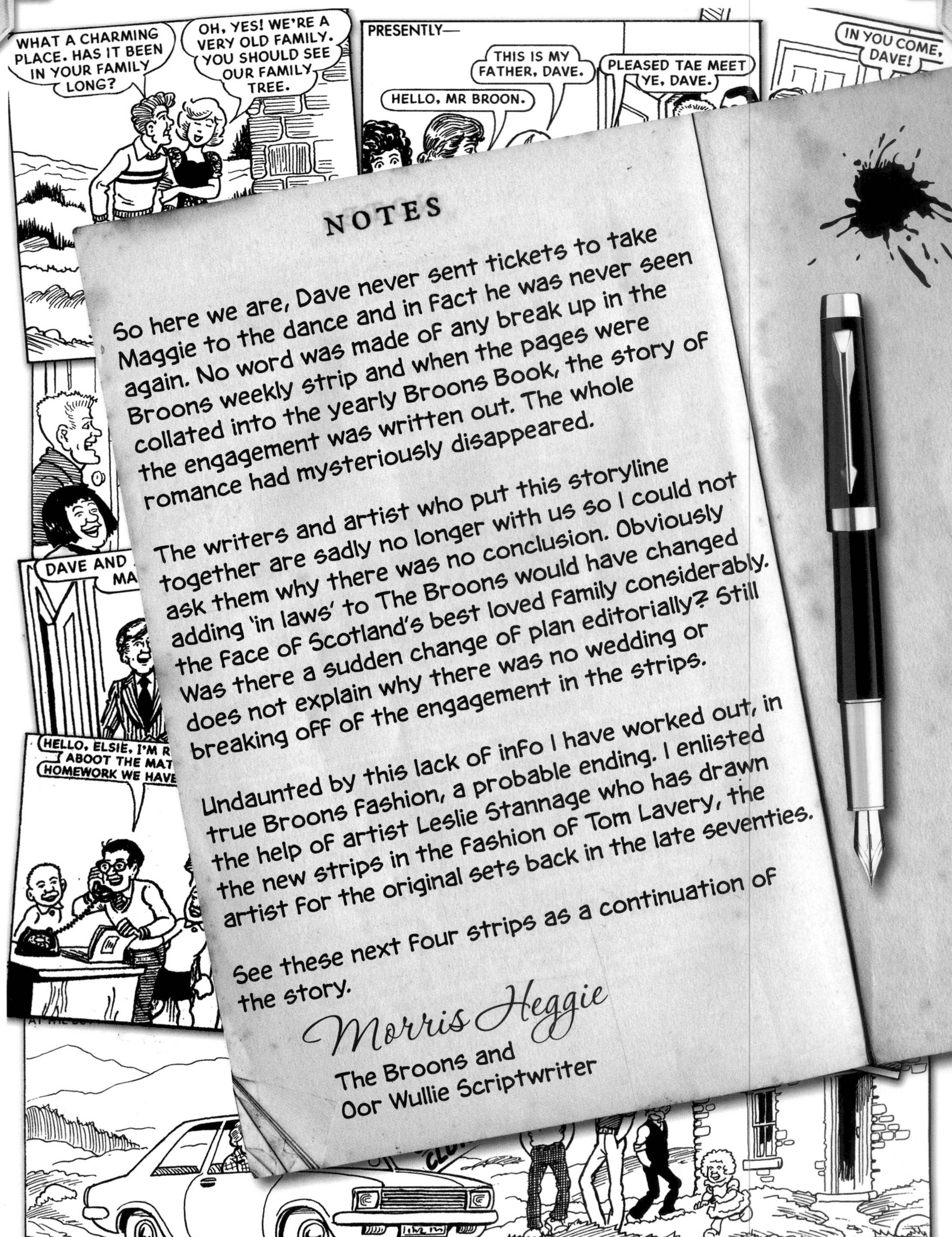
WHAT A CHARMING PLACE. HAS IT BEEN IN YOUR FAMILY LONG?
OH, YES! WE'RE A VERY OLD FAMILY. YOU SHOULD SEE OUR FAMILY TREE.
PRESENTLY—
THIS IS MY FATHER, DAVE.
PLEASED TAE MEET YE, DAVE.
HELLO, MR BROON.
IN YOU COME, DAVE!

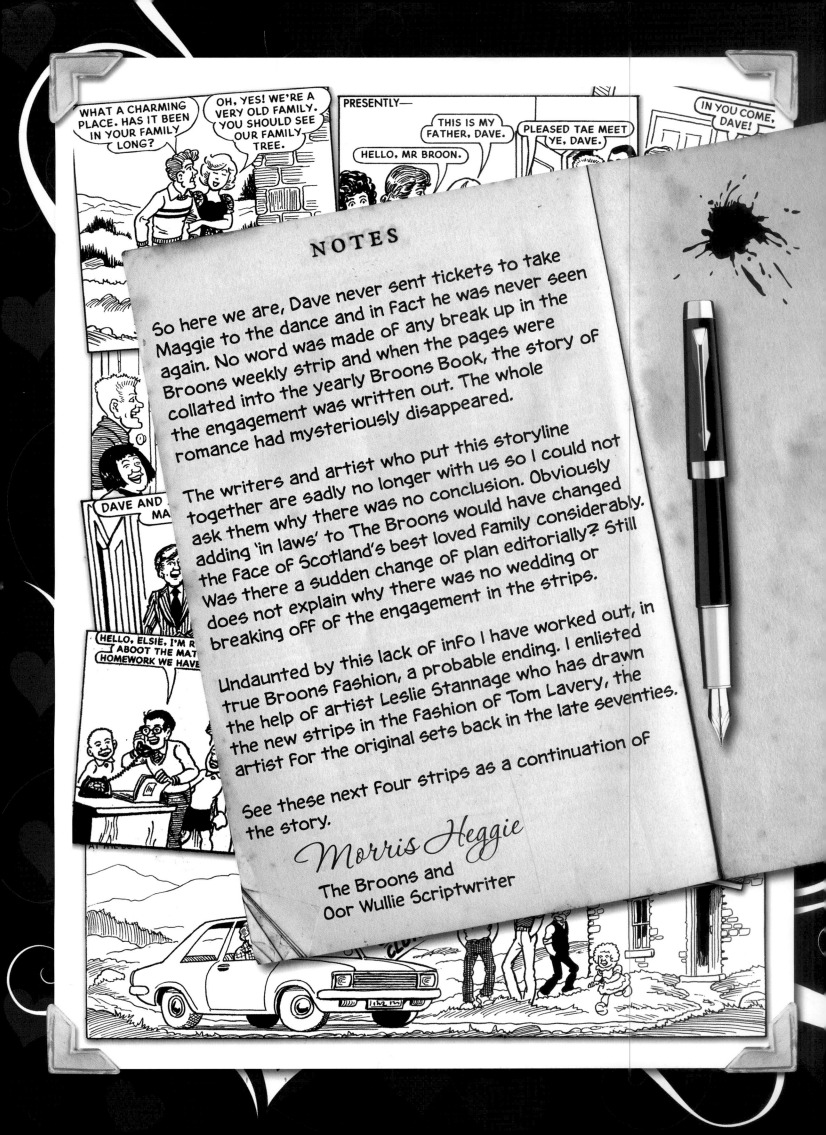

NOTES

So here we are, Dave never sent tickets to take Maggie to the dance and in fact he was never seen again. No word was made of any break up in the Broons weekly strip and when the pages were collated into the yearly Broons Book, the story of the engagement was written out. The whole romance had mysteriously disappeared.

The writers and artist who put this storyline together are sadly no longer with us so I could not ask them why there was no conclusion. Obviously adding 'in laws' to The Broons would have changed the face of Scotland's best loved family considerably. Was there a sudden change of plan editorially? Still does not explain why there was no wedding or breaking off of the engagement in the strips.

Undaunted by this lack of info I have worked out, in true Broons fashion, a probable ending. I enlisted the help of artist Leslie Stannage who has drawn the new strips in the fashion of Tom Lavery, the artist for the original sets back in the late seventies.

See these next four strips as a continuation of the story.

Morris Heggie

The Broons and
Oor Wullie Scriptwriter

Weddin' O' The Year

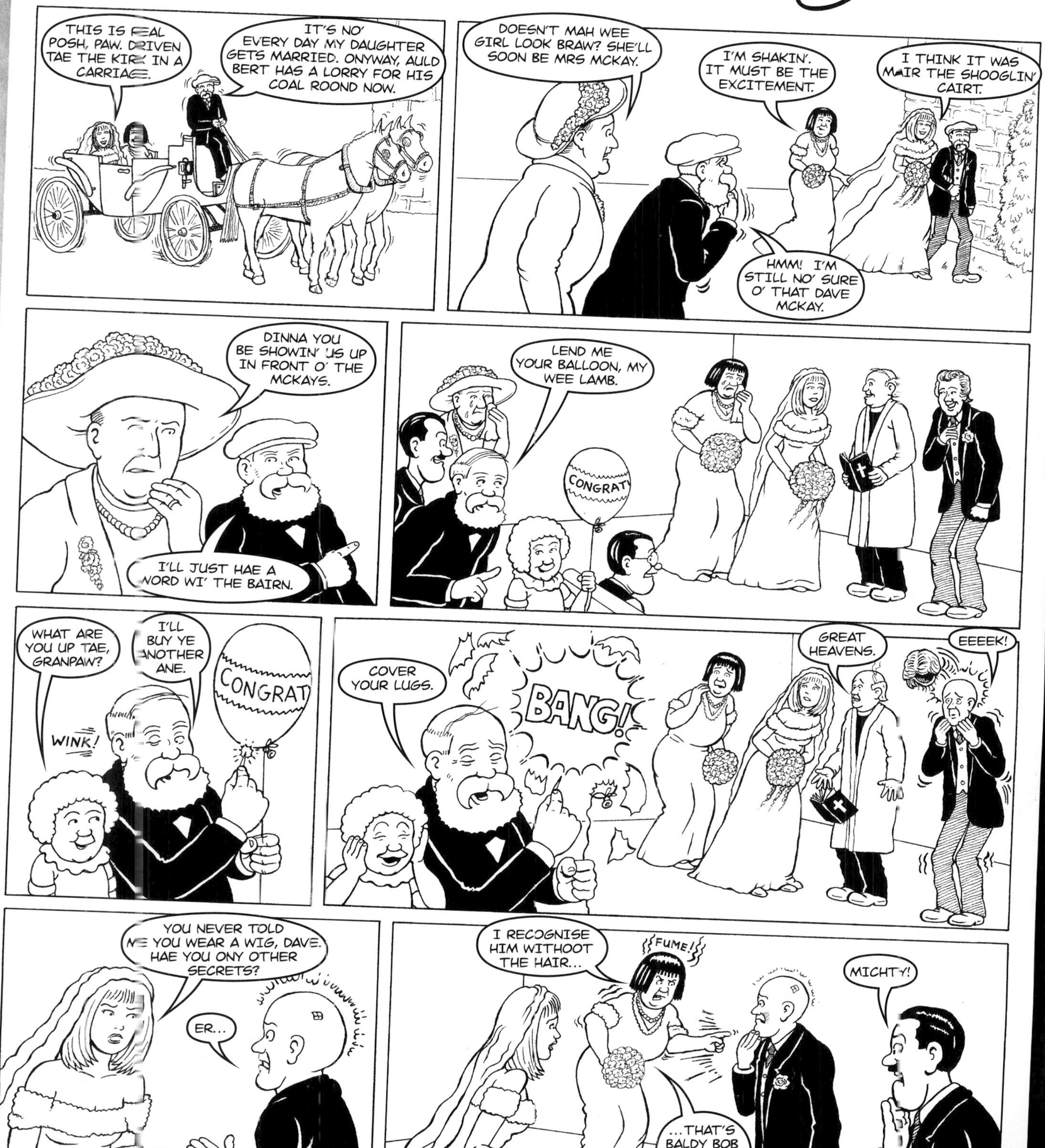

THIS IS REAL POSH, PAW. DRIVEN TAE THE KIRK IN A CARRIAGE.
IT'S NO' EVERY DAY MY DAUGHTER GETS MARRIED. ONYWAY, AULD BERT HAS A LORRY FOR HIS COAL ROOND NOW.
DOESN'T MAH WEE GIRL LOOK BRAW? SHE'LL SOON BE MRS MCKAY.
I'M SHAKIN'. IT MUST BE THE EXCITEMENT.
I THINK IT WAS MAIR THE SHOOGLIN' CAIRT.
HMM! I'M STILL NO' SURE O' THAT DAVE MCKAY.
DINNA YOU BE SHOWIN' US UP IN FRONT O' THE MCKAYS.
I'LL JUST HAE A WORD WI' THE BAIRN.
LEND ME YOUR BALLOON, MY WEE LAMB.
CONGRAT
WHAT ARE YOU UP TAE, GRANPAW?
WINK!
I'LL BUY YE ANOTHER ANE.
CONGRAT
COVER YOUR LUGS.
BANG!
GREAT HEAVENS.
EEEEK!
YOU NEVER TOLD ME YOU WEAR A WIG, DAVE. HAE YOU ONY OTHER SECRETS?
ER...
I RECOGNISE HIM WITHOOT THE HAIR...
FUME!
...THAT'S BALDY BOB FRAE MY SINGLES CLUB.
MICHTY!

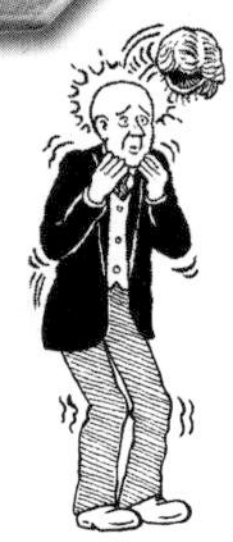

The bouquet whacks off poor Dave's head —

Could be he's not getting wed.

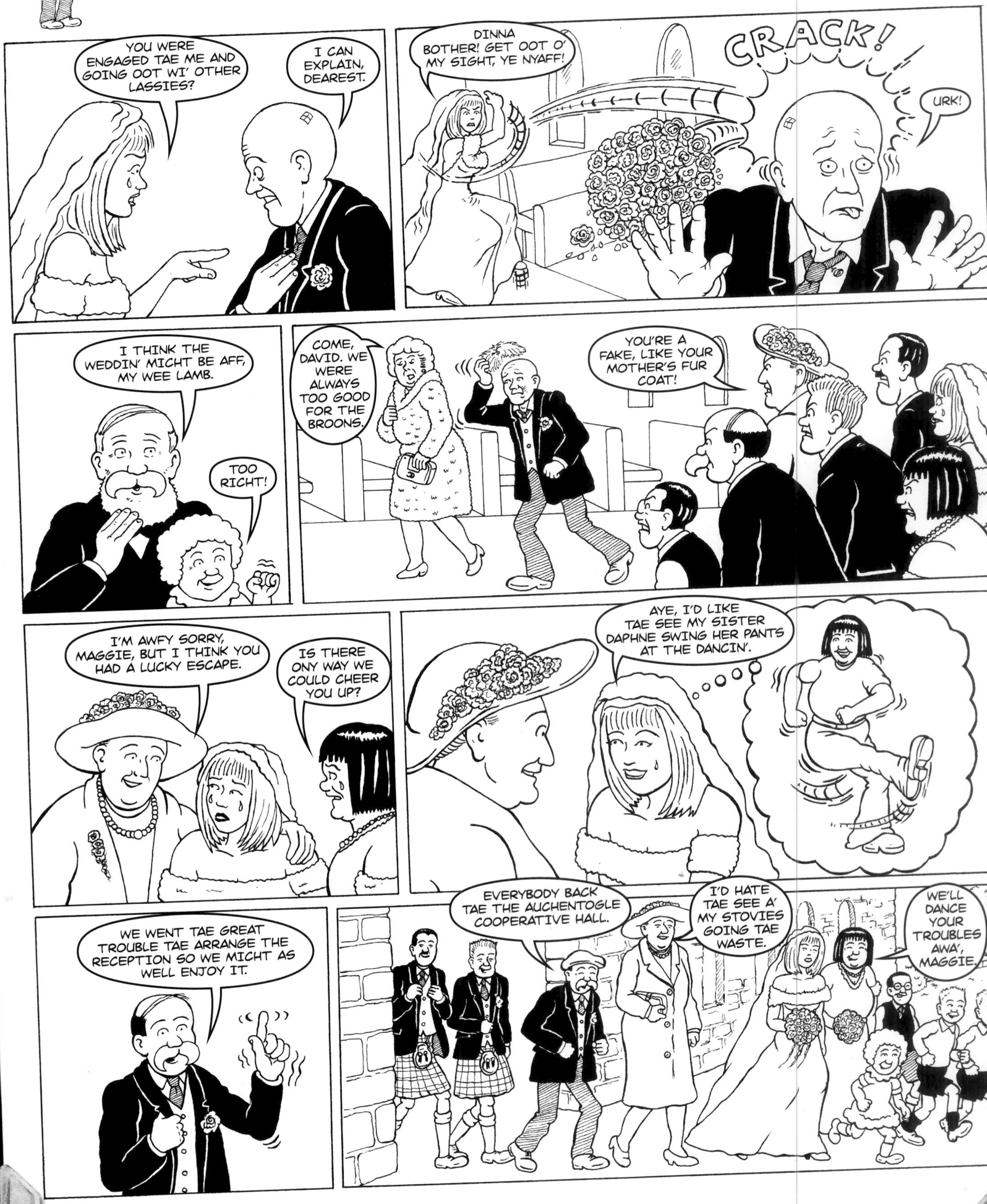

YOU WERE ENGAGED TAE ME AND GOING OOT WI' OTHER LASSIES?
I CAN EXPLAIN, DEAREST.
DINNA BOTHER! GET OOT O' MY SIGHT, YE NYAFF!
CRACK!
URK!
I THINK THE WEDDIN' MICHT BE AFF, MY WEE LAMB.
TOO RICHT!
COME, DAVID. WE WERE ALWAYS TOO GOOD FOR THE BROONS.
YOU'RE A FAKE, LIKE YOUR MOTHER'S FUR COAT!
I'M AWFY SORRY, MAGGIE, BUT I THINK YOU HAD A LUCKY ESCAPE.
IS THERE ONY WAY WE COULD CHEER YOU UP?
AYE, I'D LIKE TAE SEE MY SISTER DAPHNE SWING HER PANTS AT THE DANCIN'.
WE WENT TAE GREAT TROUBLE TAE ARRANGE THE RECEPTION SO WE MICHT AS WELL ENJOY IT.
EVERYBODY BACK TAE THE AUCHENTOGLE COOPERATIVE HALL.
I'D HATE TAE SEE A' MY STOVIES GOING TAE WASTE.
WE'LL DANCE YOUR TROUBLES AWA', MAGGIE.

The Cooperative Ha'

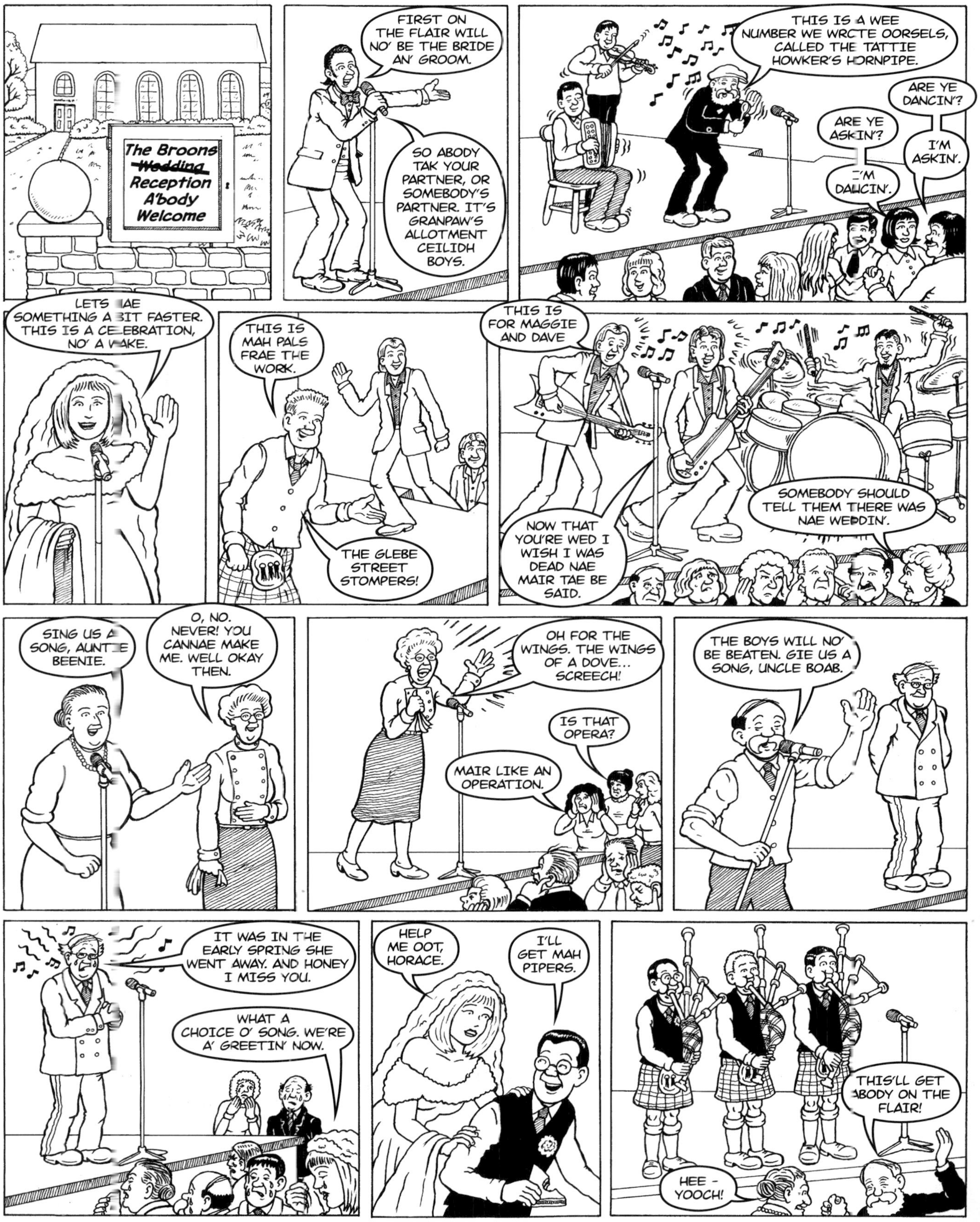

The Broons Wedding Reception A'body Welcome
FIRST ON THE FLAIR WILL NO' BE THE BRIDE AN' GROOM.
SO ABODY TAK YOUR PARTNER, OR SOMEBODY'S PARTNER. IT'S GRANPAW'S ALLOTMENT CEILIDH BOYS.
THIS IS A WEE NUMBER WE WROTE OORSELS, CALLED THE TATTIE HOWKER'S HORNPIPE.
ARE YE DANCIN'?
ARE YE ASKIN'?
I'M ASKIN'.
I'M DANCIN'.
LETS HAE SOMETHING A BIT FASTER. THIS IS A CELEBRATION, NO' A WAKE.
THIS IS MAH PALS FRAE THE WORK.
THE GLEBE STREET STOMPERS!
THIS IS FOR MAGGIE AND DAVE
NOW THAT YOU'RE WED I WISH I WAS DEAD NAE MAIR TAE BE SAID.
SOMEBODY SHOULD TELL THEM THERE WAS NAE WEDDIN'.
SING US A SONG, AUNTIE BEENIE.
O, NO. NEVER! YOU CANNAE MAKE ME. WELL OKAY THEN.
OH FOR THE WINGS. THE WINGS OF A DOVE... SCREECH!
IS THAT OPERA?
MAIR LIKE AN OPERATION.
THE BOYS WILL NO' BE BEATEN. GIE US A SONG, UNCLE BOAB.
IT WAS IN THE EARLY SPRING SHE WENT AWAY. AND HONEY I MISS YOU.
WHAT A CHOICE O' SONG. WE'RE A' GREETIN' NOW.
HELP ME OOT, HORACE.
I'LL GET MAH PIPERS.
THIS'LL GET ABODY ON THE FLAIR!
HEE - YOOCH!

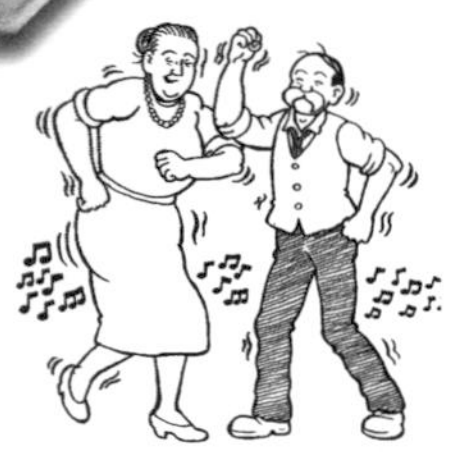

Pop, pipes, jigs and reels —

Make the Broons tak' tae their heels.

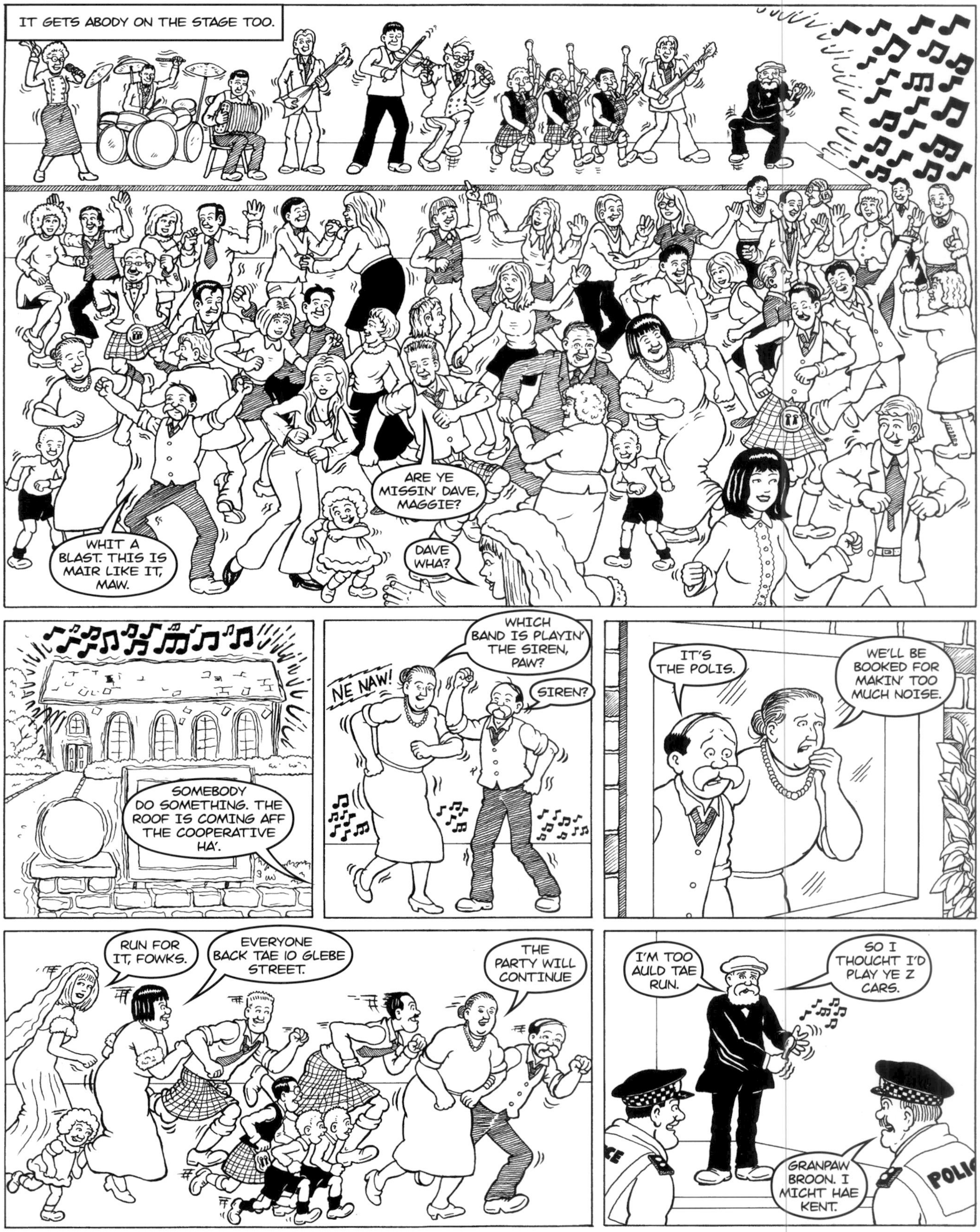

IT GETS ABODY ON THE STAGE TOO.
WHIT A BLAST. THIS IS MAIR LIKE IT, MAW.
ARE YE MISSIN' DAVE, MAGGIE?
DAVE WHA?
SOMEBODY DO SOMETHING. THE ROOF IS COMING AFF THE COOPERATIVE HA'.
NE NAW!
WHICH BAND IS PLAYIN' THE SIREN, PAW?
SIREN?
IT'S THE POLIS.
WE'LL BE BOOKED FOR MAKIN' TOO MUCH NOISE.
RUN FOR IT, FOWKS.
EVERYONE BACK TAE 10 GLEBE STREET.
THE PARTY WILL CONTINUE
I'M TOO AULD TAE RUN.
SO I THOUCHT I'D PLAY YE Z CARS.
GRANPAW BROON. I MICHT HAE KENT.

Wedding Invitation

And the gifts were returned

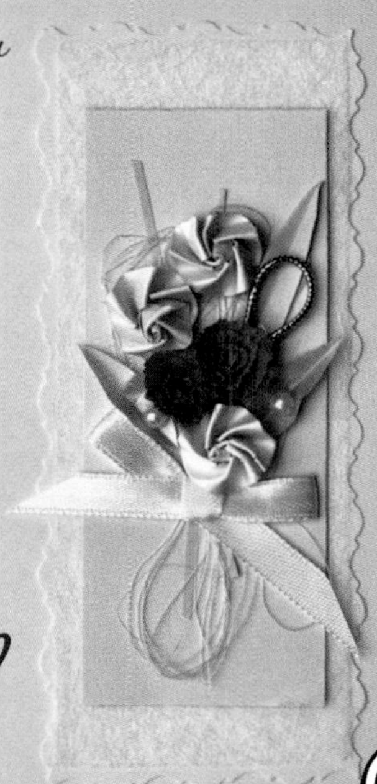

Dear Mr and Mrs McKay senior,

I am returning the casserole dish you gave to your grandson and myself for a wedding present. I see you got it from D and Q, maybe you could exchange it for a rat trap for when your grandson comes to visit.

Maggie Broon

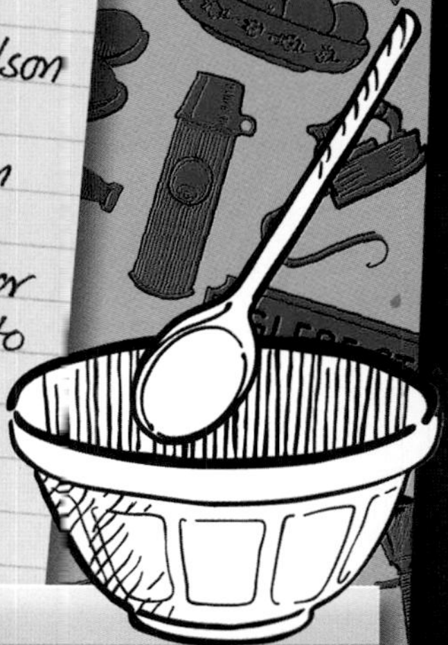

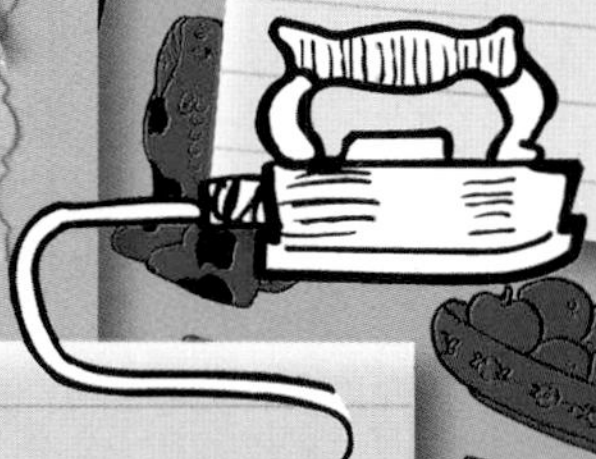

Dear Mrs McGinty,

I am returning your kind wedding present as my marriage didnae get aff the ground.

The lava lamp was a beautiful shade of purple—it reminded me of Dave's eye after Daphne had had a wee quiet word wi him.

Glad you enjoyed the reception. Your Hokey Cokey was amazing.

Yours

Maggie Broon

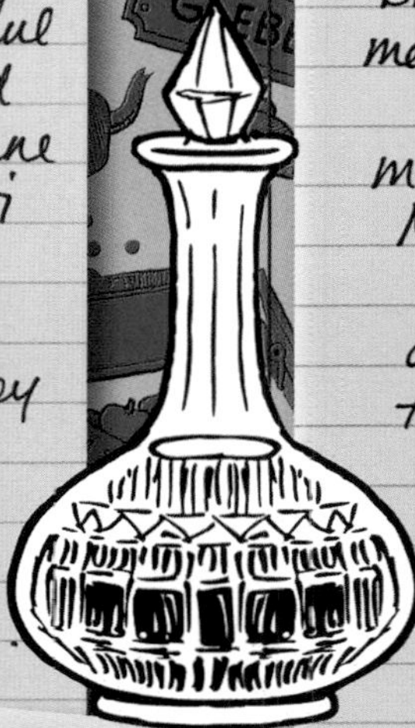

Dear Uncle Andrew and Auntie Moira,

I am returning your lovely wedding present. The rainbow tie dye curtains would have brightened up the house, not to mention the whole street.

I hope you can get your money back from Angus at Maharani's Luxury Rugs. If not kick Dave McKay's car as you go past on your way to work.

Your Loving niece,

Maggie

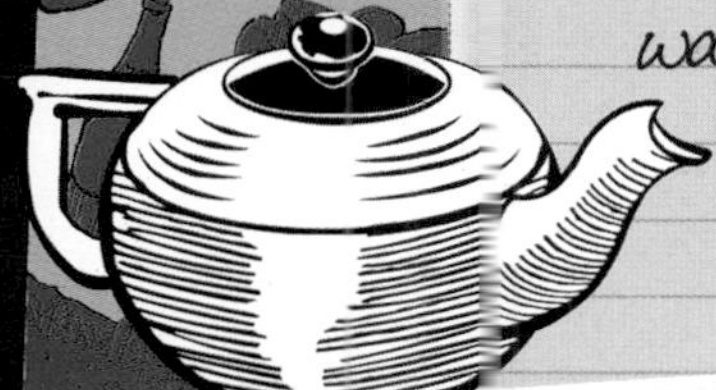

Dear Shirley

The marriage was a wash oot so I am returning your wedding present. The fondue set was a great idea.

Right now I'm no' fond o' a particular bald man. Did I see you daein the hustle wi' my brother Joe at the reception?

I aye thought you had yer eye on him.

Your Pal

Maggie

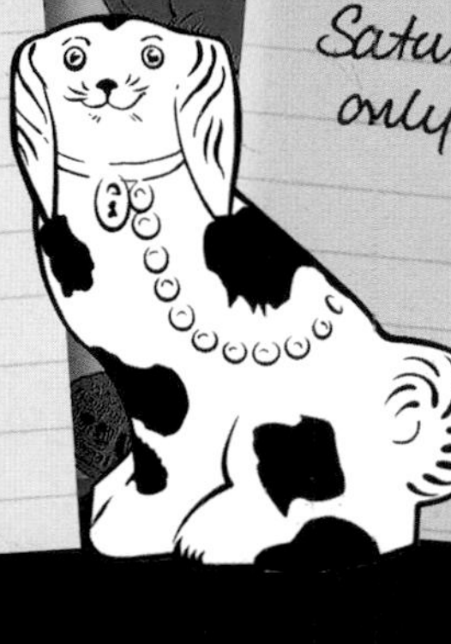

Dear Granpaw,

I am returning the lovely wedding present you sent me. The picture of the Chinese Girl is very nice but it has left a mark on your wall and I'm sure you'll miss it.

Thanks for what you did on Saturday and I'm glad the polis only kept you the one night.

Love you loads,

Maggie

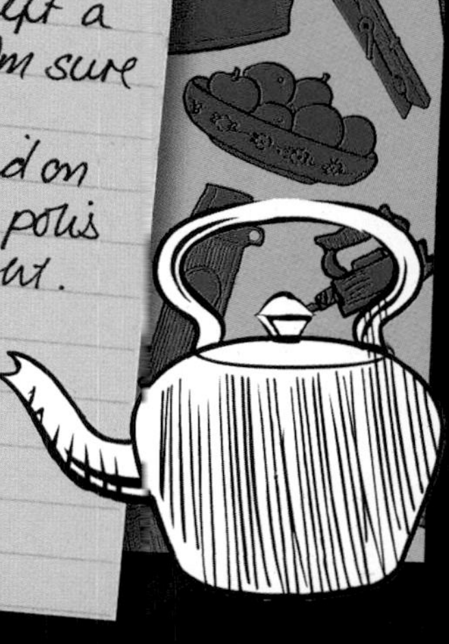

TOP VALUE FOR 7p

THE WEEKLY NEWS

No. 6358 APRIL 23, 1977 Price 7p

The Broons were not the only long running soap to have a wedding planned in 1977.

★ SIX GREAT PAGES OF MEMORABLE PICTURES AND STORIES FROM RIGHT BEHIND THE SCENES

CORONATION STREET WEDDING SOUVENIR

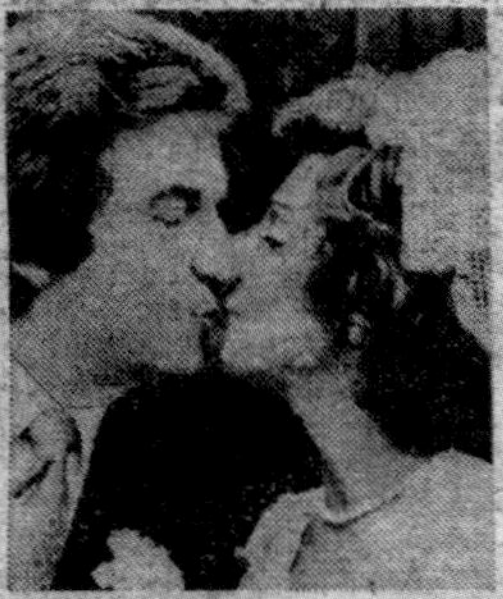

SEE PAGE 13 ONWARDS

DEIRDRE'S BABY STOPPED THE SHOW

ONLY MAKE-BELIEVE BUT REAL TEARS IN CHURCH

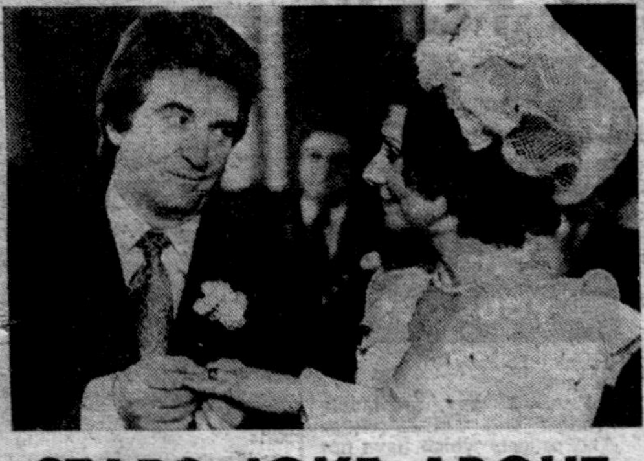

STARS JOKE ABOUT MEAL THAT NEVER WAS

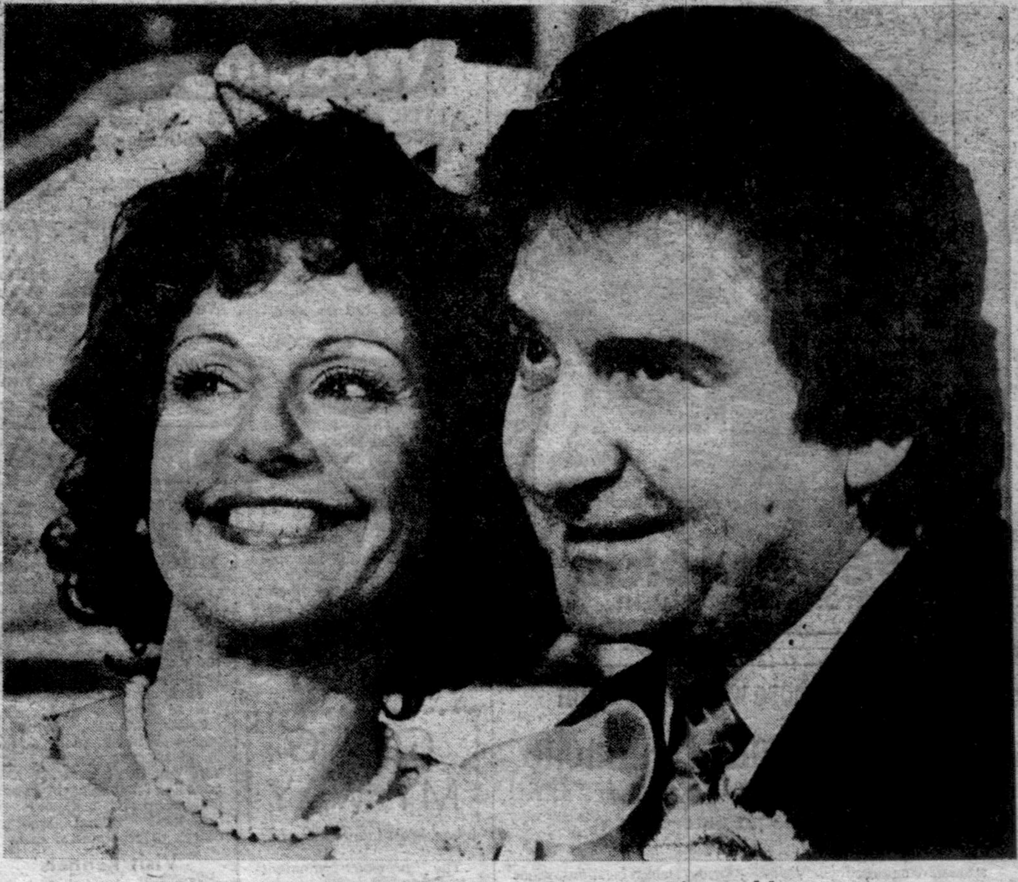

Barbara Mullaney and Peter Adamson as Rita and Len.

★ LAST-MINUTE PANIC TO RE-WRITE SCENE ★

TOP VALUE FOR 9p

THE WEEKLY NEWS

No. 6479 AUGUST 18, 1979 Price 9p

DREAM HOLIDAY ROMANCE

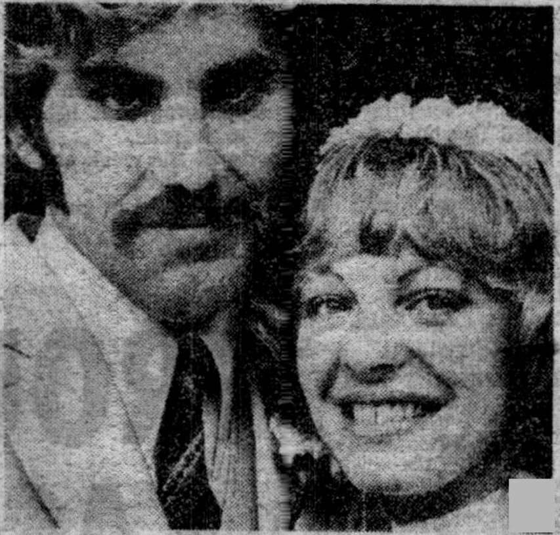

Marilyn and Richard.
FELL IN LOVE ON FIRST DAY.
Bride's own story on Page 16.

Daphne Broon would have been disappointed with this news.

COMPUTER PAIRINGS FOR DISCO DANCERS —Page 3

Arab offered £2 million for Blackpool's lights—Page 12

PRINCE CHARLES

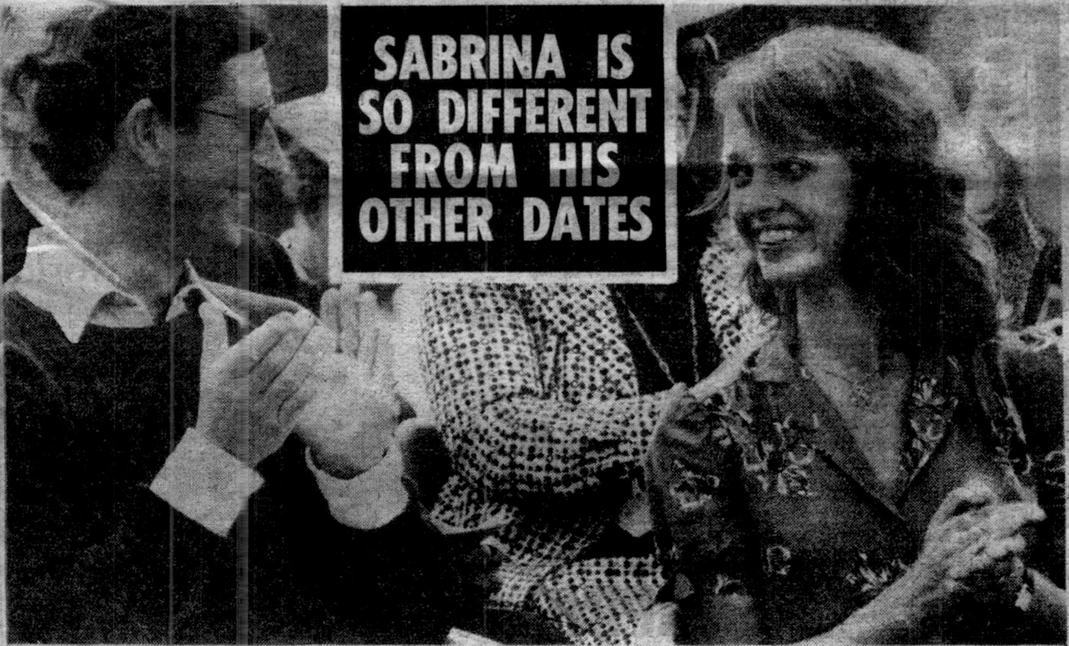

SABRINA IS SO DIFFERENT FROM HIS OTHER DATES

Prince Charles and Sabrina Guinness at Cowdray Park for the polo.

AND THE UNUSUAL GUINNESS HEIRESS

She has an adventurous spirit that took her to Hollywood to work as a nanny for a film star. Yet although her life has been a happy one, tragedy has touched the Guinness clan at times. Drugs, broken romances and fatal car crashes have all taken their toll.

FULL STORY ON PAGE 19

THE ROOTIN' TOOTIN' RIOTOUS LIFE OF HELLRAISER LEE MARVIN

HELD GIRL BY ONE LEG FROM HOTEL WINDOW

Laughs and surprises in the story of his outrageous exploits on Page 20.

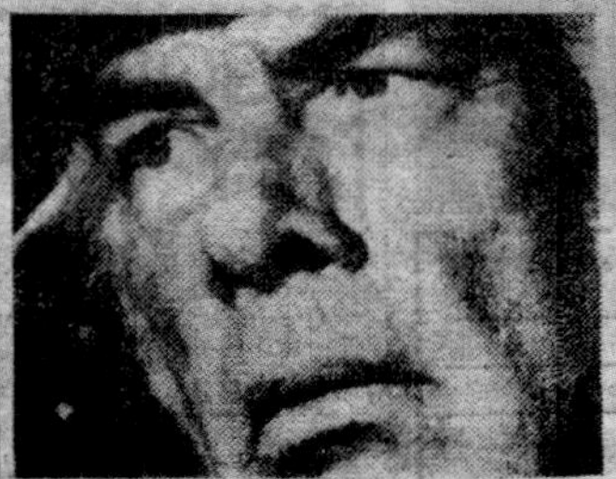

"BUT I'M MORE MELLOW NOW," HE SAID

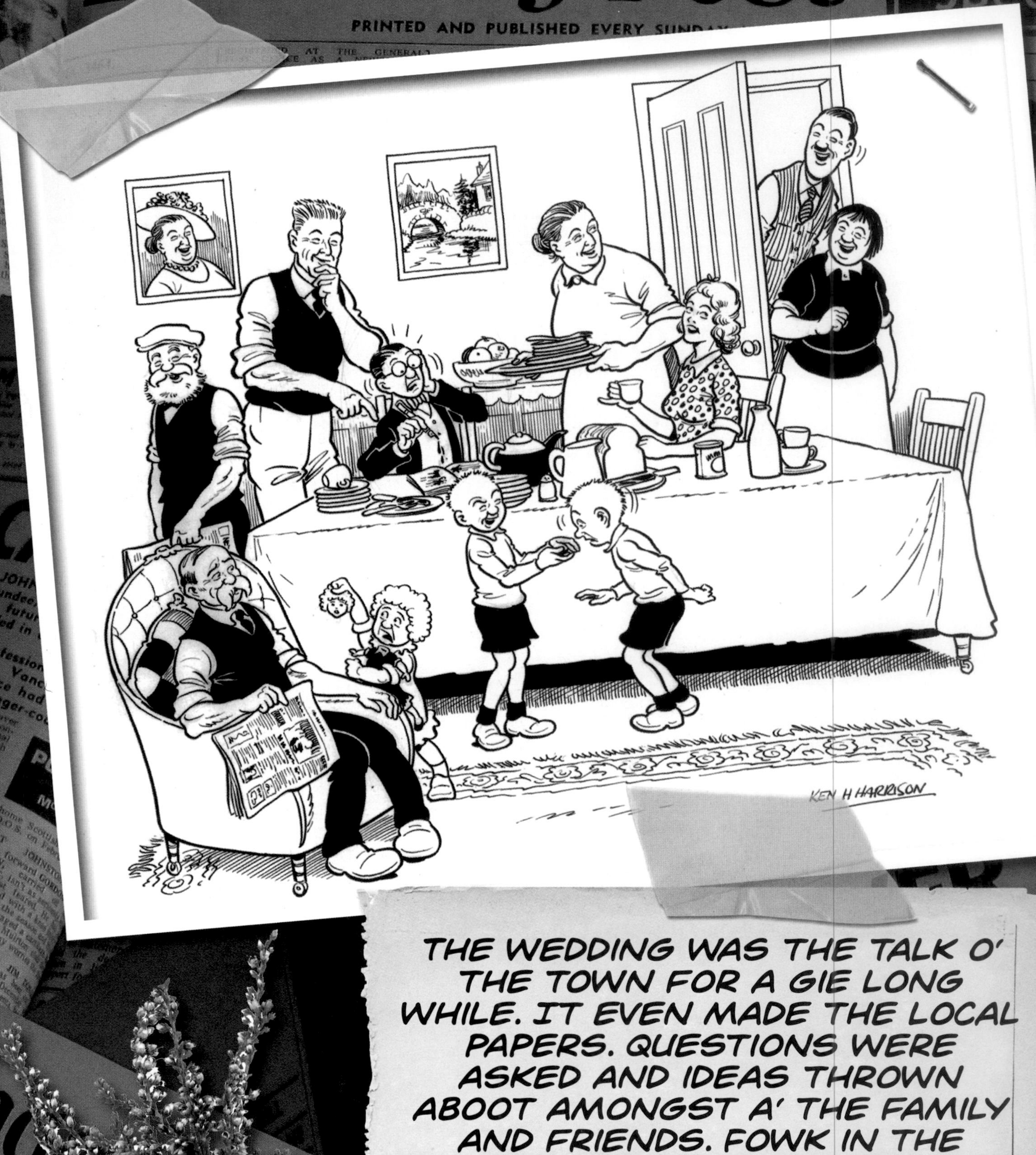
KEN H HARRISON

THE WEDDING WAS THE TALK O' THE TOWN FOR A GIE LONG WHILE. IT EVEN MADE THE LOCAL PAPERS. QUESTIONS WERE ASKED AND IDEAS THROWN ABOOT AMONGST A' THE FAMILY AND FRIENDS. FOWK IN THE STREET WID STOP AND GOSSIP ABOOT THE NEAR MISS THAT MAGGIE HAD. EVEN OWER IN AUCHENSHOOGLE PC MURDOCH WAS ASKED IF ANY ARRESTS WERE GOING TO BE MADE.

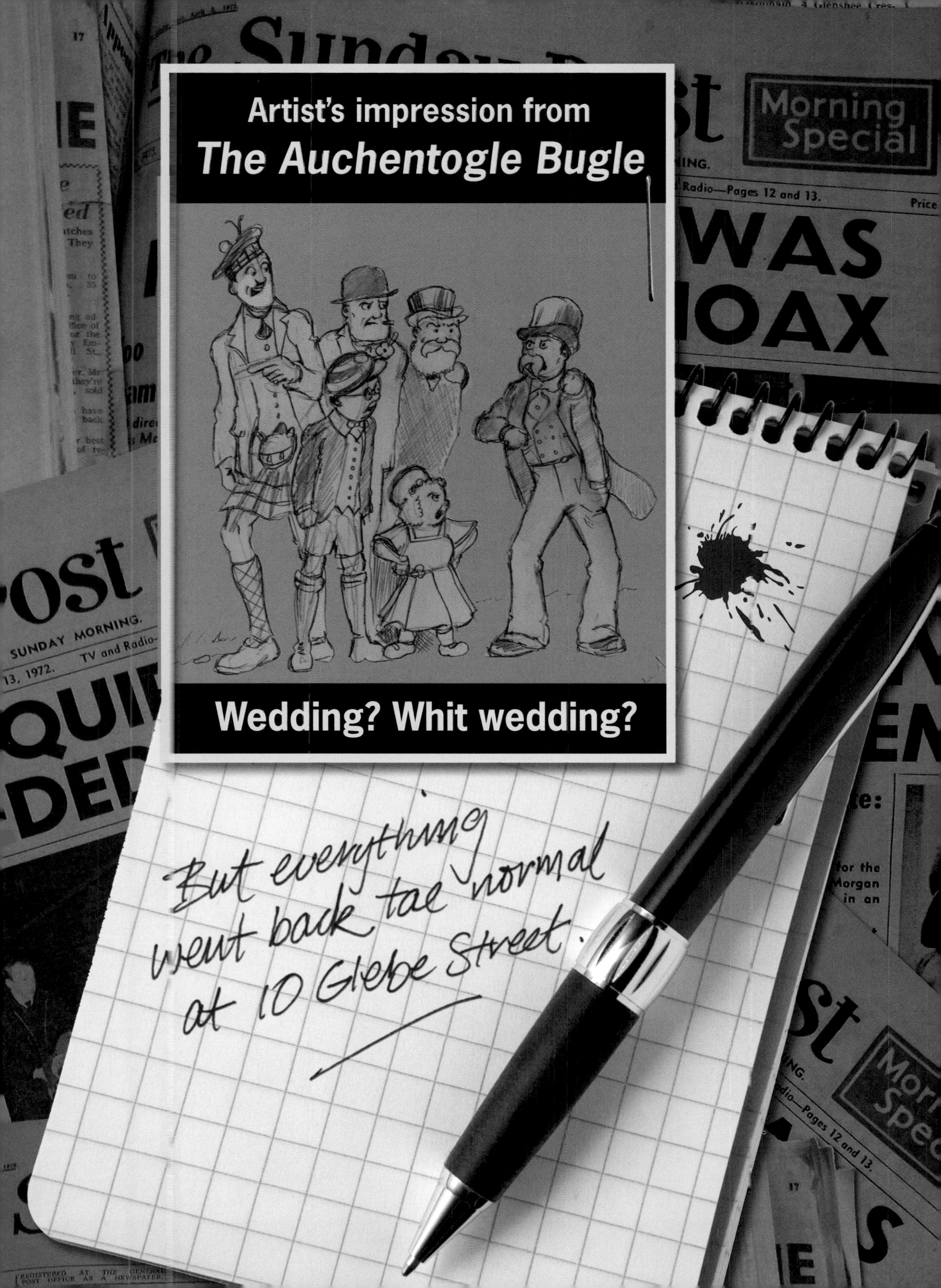
Artist's impression from
The Auchentogle Bugle
Wedding? Whit wedding?
But everything went back tae normal at 10 Glebe Street.
Morning Special
WAS HOAX
SUNDAY MORNING.

Help m'boab! It's no' half funny—

When Daphne turns into a bunny!

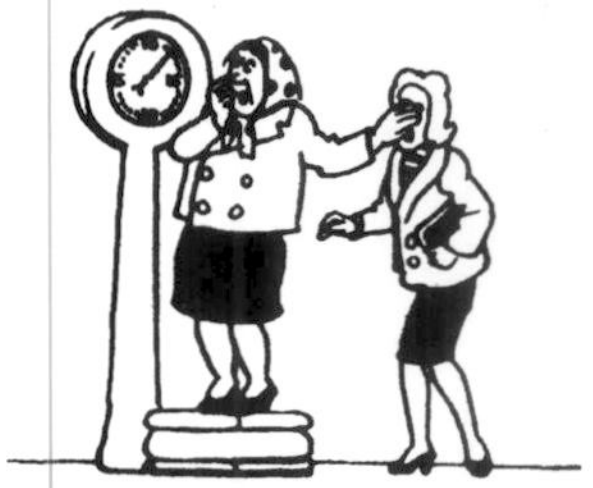

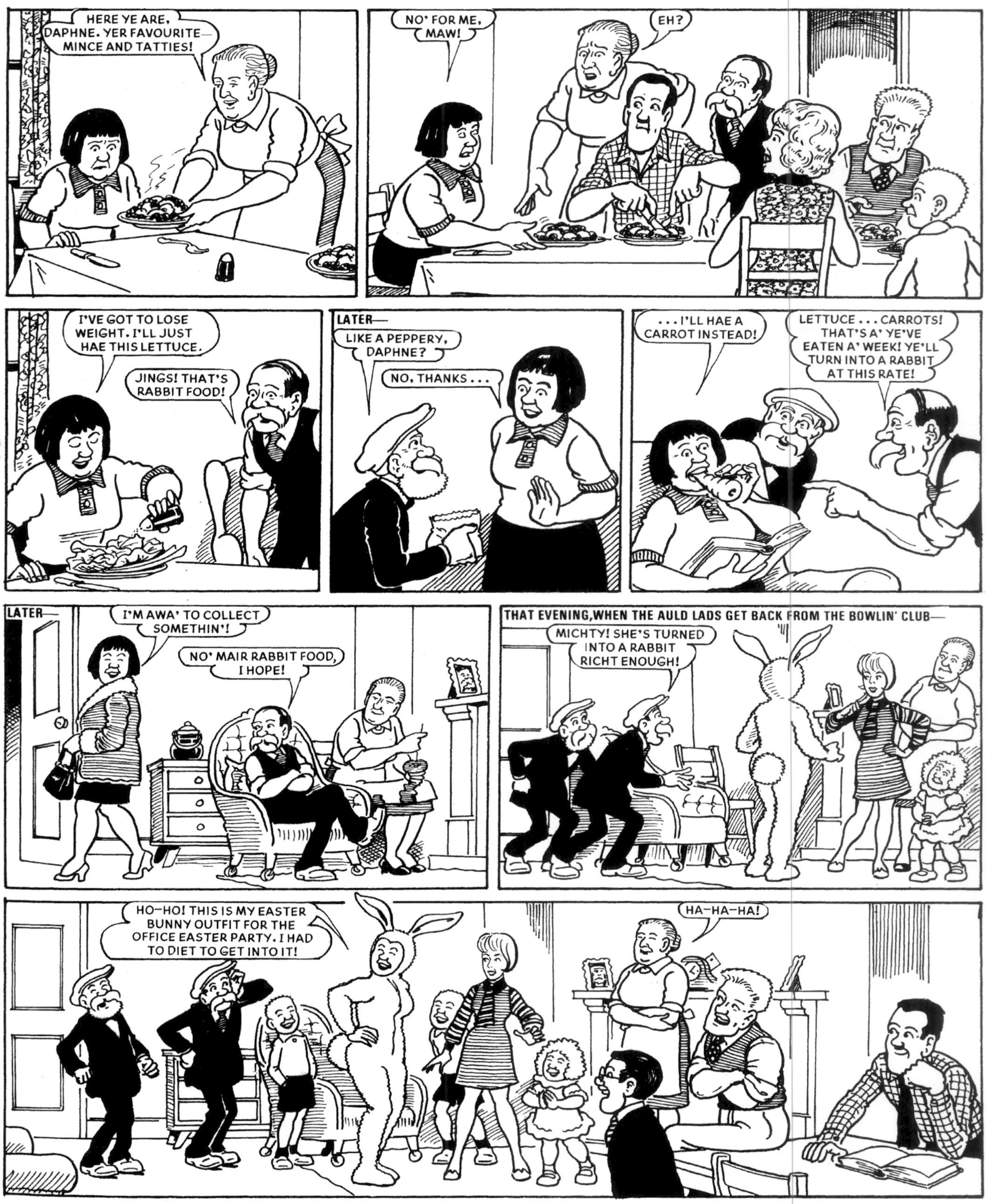

HERE YE ARE, DAPHNE. YER FAVOURITE— MINCE AND TATTIES!
NO' FOR ME, MAW!
EH?
I'VE GOT TO LOSE WEIGHT. I'LL JUST HAE THIS LETTUCE.
JINGS! THAT'S RABBIT FOOD!
LATER—
LIKE A PEPPERY, DAPHNE?
NO, THANKS . . .
. . . I'LL HAE A CARROT INSTEAD!
LETTUCE . . . CARROTS! THAT'S A' YE'VE EATEN A' WEEK! YE'LL TURN INTO A RABBIT AT THIS RATE!
LATER—
I'M AWA' TO COLLECT SOMETHIN'!
NO' MAIR RABBIT FOOD, I HOPE!
THAT EVENING, WHEN THE AULD LADS GET BACK FROM THE BOWLIN' CLUB—
MICHTY! SHE'S TURNED INTO A RABBIT RICHT ENOUGH!
HO-HO! THIS IS MY EASTER BUNNY OUTFIT FOR THE OFFICE EASTER PARTY. I HAD TO DIET TO GET INTO IT!
HA-HA-HA!

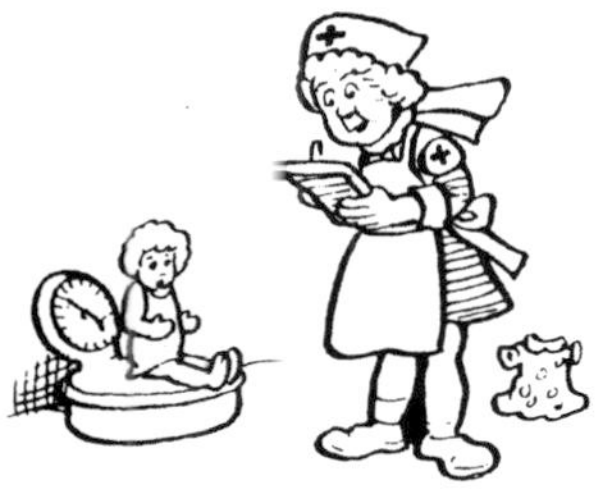

Is the Bairn famous—

Because o' where her name is?

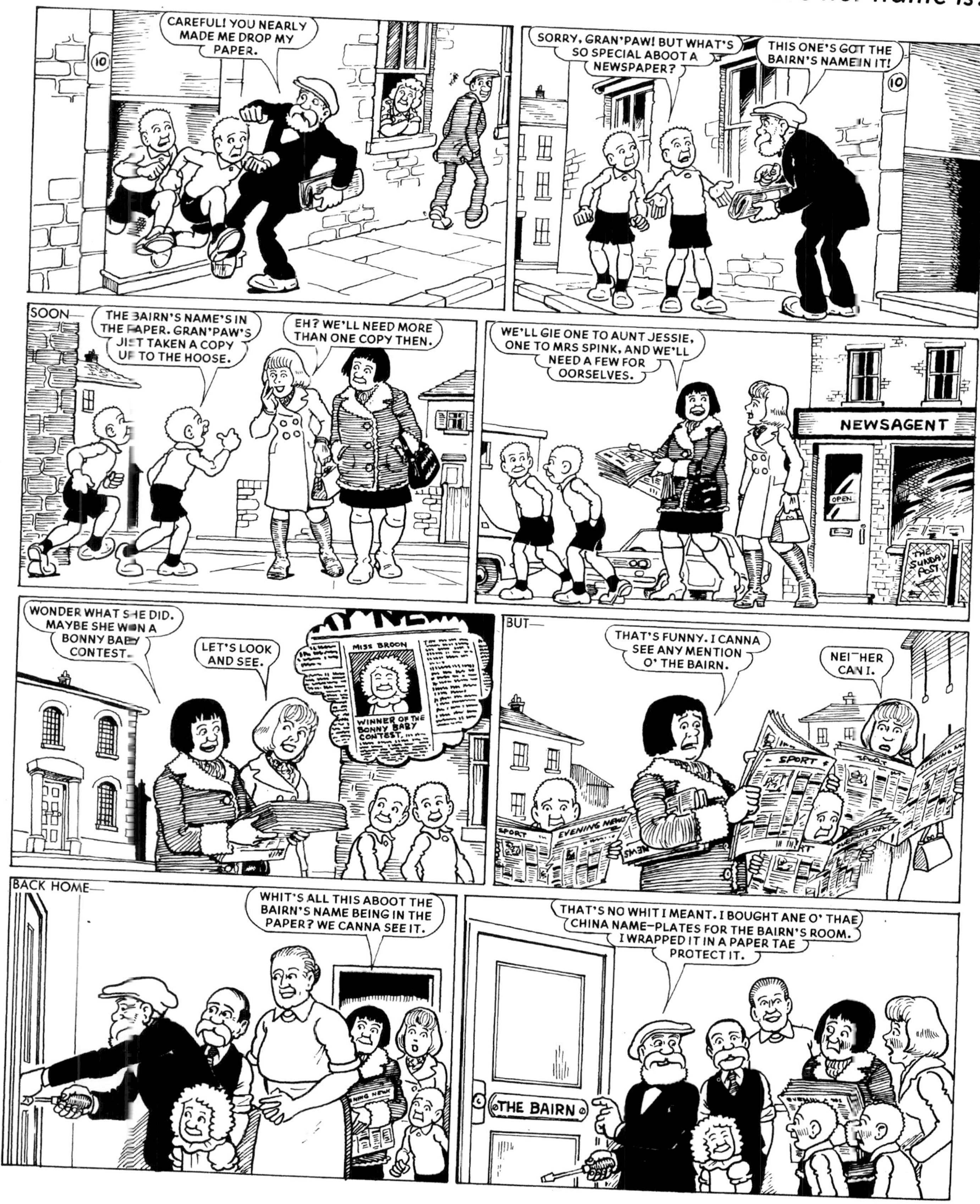

10
CAREFUL! YOU NEARLY MADE ME DROP MY PAPER.
SORRY, GRAN'PAW! BUT WHAT'S SO SPECIAL ABOOT A NEWSPAPER?
THIS ONE'S GOT THE BAIRN'S NAME IN IT!
10
SOON—
THE BAIRN'S NAME'S IN THE PAPER. GRAN'PAW'S JIST TAKEN A COPY UP TO THE HOOSE.
EH? WE'LL NEED MORE THAN ONE COPY THEN.
WE'LL GIE ONE TO AUNT JESSIE, ONE TO MRS SPINK, AND WE'LL NEED A FEW FOR OORSELVES.
NEWSAGENT
OPEN
THE SUNDAY POST
WONDER WHAT SHE DID. MAYBE SHE WON A BONNY BABY CONTEST.
LET'S LOOK AND SEE.
MISS BROON
WINNER OF THE BONNY BABY CONTEST.
BUT—
THAT'S FUNNY. I CANNA SEE ANY MENTION O' THE BAIRN.
NEITHER CAN I.
SPORT
EVENING NEWS
BACK HOME—
WHIT'S ALL THIS ABOOT THE BAIRN'S NAME BEING IN THE PAPER? WE CANNA SEE IT.
THAT'S NO WHIT I MEANT. I BOUGHT ANE O' THAE CHINA NAME-PLATES FOR THE BAIRN'S ROOM. I WRAPPED IT IN A PAPER TAE PROTECT IT.
THE BAIRN

PRINTED AND PUBLISHED EVERY SUNDAY MORNING.
SUNDAY, JANUARY 30, 1972. TV and Radio—Pages 12 and 13. Price 4p

A tall dark stranger? Whit a laugh!—

But it comes true for Hen, no' half!

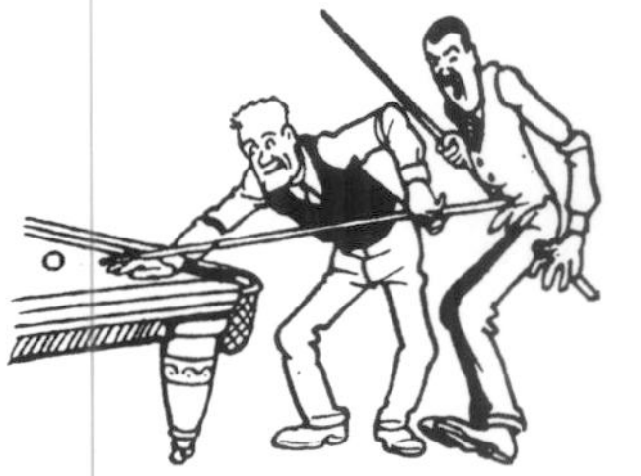

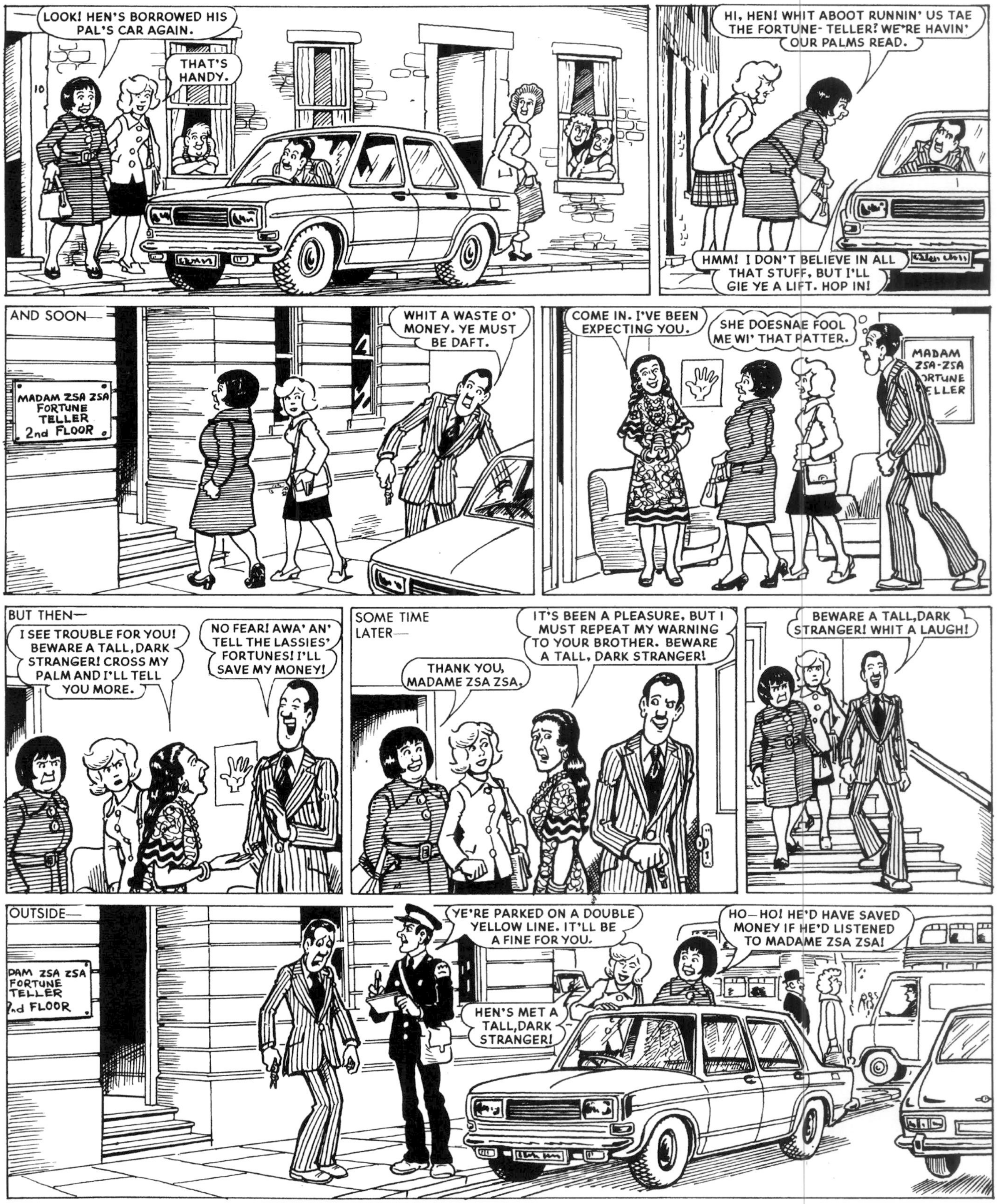

LOOK! HEN'S BORROWED HIS PAL'S CAR AGAIN.
THAT'S HANDY.
HI, HEN! WHIT ABOOT RUNNIN' US TAE THE FORTUNE-TELLER? WE'RE HAVIN' OUR PALMS READ.
HMM! I DON'T BELIEVE IN ALL THAT STUFF, BUT I'LL GIE YE A LIFT. HOP IN!
AND SOON—
MADAM ZSA ZSA FORTUNE TELLER 2nd FLOOR
WHIT A WASTE O' MONEY. YE MUST BE DAFT.
COME IN. I'VE BEEN EXPECTING YOU.
SHE DOESNAE FOOL ME WI' THAT PATTER.
BUT THEN—
I SEE TROUBLE FOR YOU! BEWARE A TALL, DARK STRANGER! CROSS MY PALM AND I'LL TELL YOU MORE.
NO FEAR! AWA' AN' TELL THE LASSIES' FORTUNES! I'LL SAVE MY MONEY!
SOME TIME LATER—
THANK YOU, MADAME ZSA ZSA.
IT'S BEEN A PLEASURE, BUT I MUST REPEAT MY WARNING TO YOUR BROTHER. BEWARE A TALL, DARK STRANGER!
BEWARE A TALL, DARK STRANGER! WHIT A LAUGH!
OUTSIDE—
YE'RE PARKED ON A DOUBLE YELLOW LINE. IT'LL BE A FINE FOR YOU.
HEN'S MET A TALL, DARK STRANGER!
HO—HO! HE'D HAVE SAVED MONEY IF HE'D LISTENED TO MADAME ZSA ZSA!

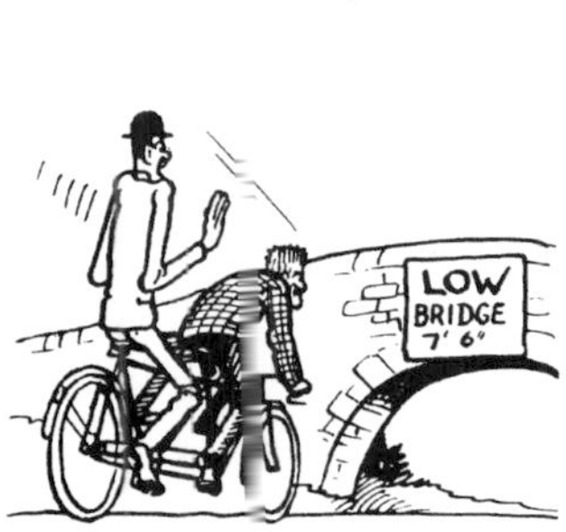
LOW BRIDGE 7' 6"

No " L " plates for Maw Broon now—

She's a driving star, and how!

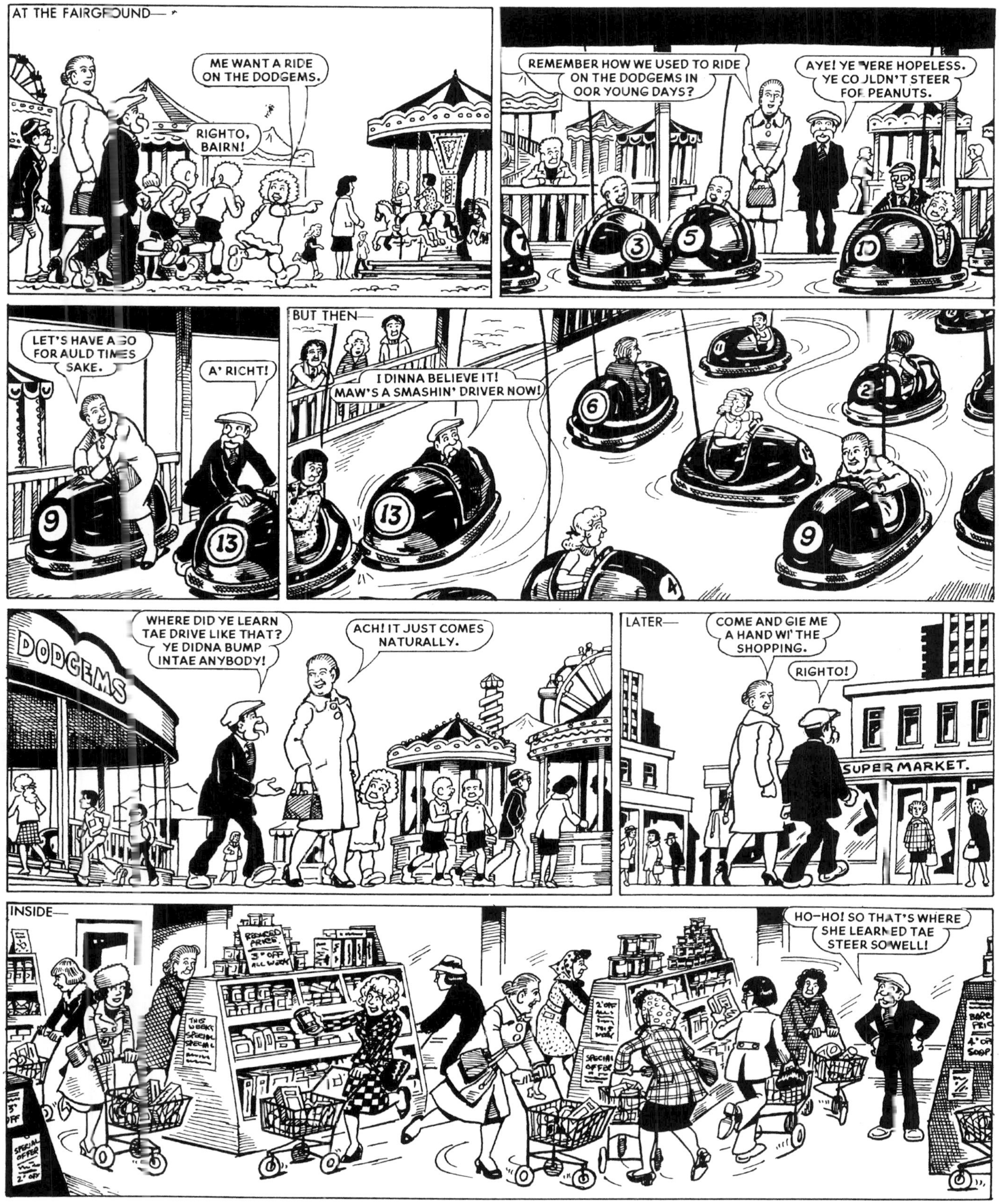
AT THE FAIRGROUND—
ME WANT A RIDE ON THE DODGEMS.
RIGHTO, BAIRN!
REMEMBER HOW WE USED TO RIDE ON THE DODGEMS IN OOR YOUNG DAYS?
AYE! YE WERE HOPELESS. YE COULDN'T STEER FOR PEANUTS.
LET'S HAVE A GO FOR AULD TIMES SAKE.
A' RICHT!
BUT THEN—
I DINNA BELIEVE IT! MAW'S A SMASHIN' DRIVER NOW!
DODGEMS
WHERE DID YE LEARN TAE DRIVE LIKE THAT? YE DIDNA BUMP INTAE ANYBODY!
ACH! IT JUST COMES NATURALLY.
LATER—
COME AND GIE ME A HAND WI' THE SHOPPING.
RIGHTO!
SUPER MARKET.
INSIDE—
HO-HO! SO THAT'S WHERE SHE LEARNED TAE STEER SO WELL!

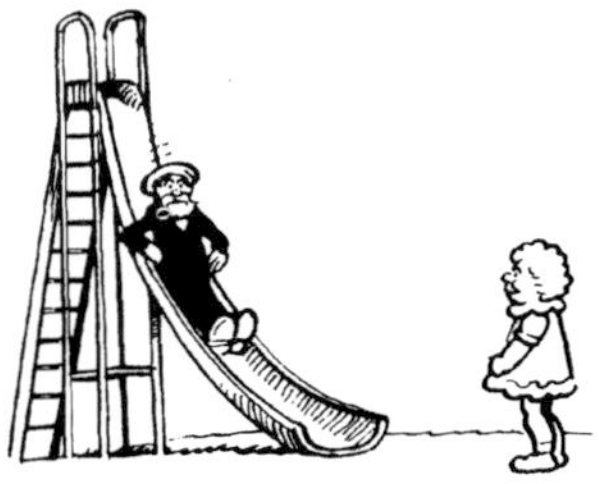

Gran'paw's got a date—

But wait . . !

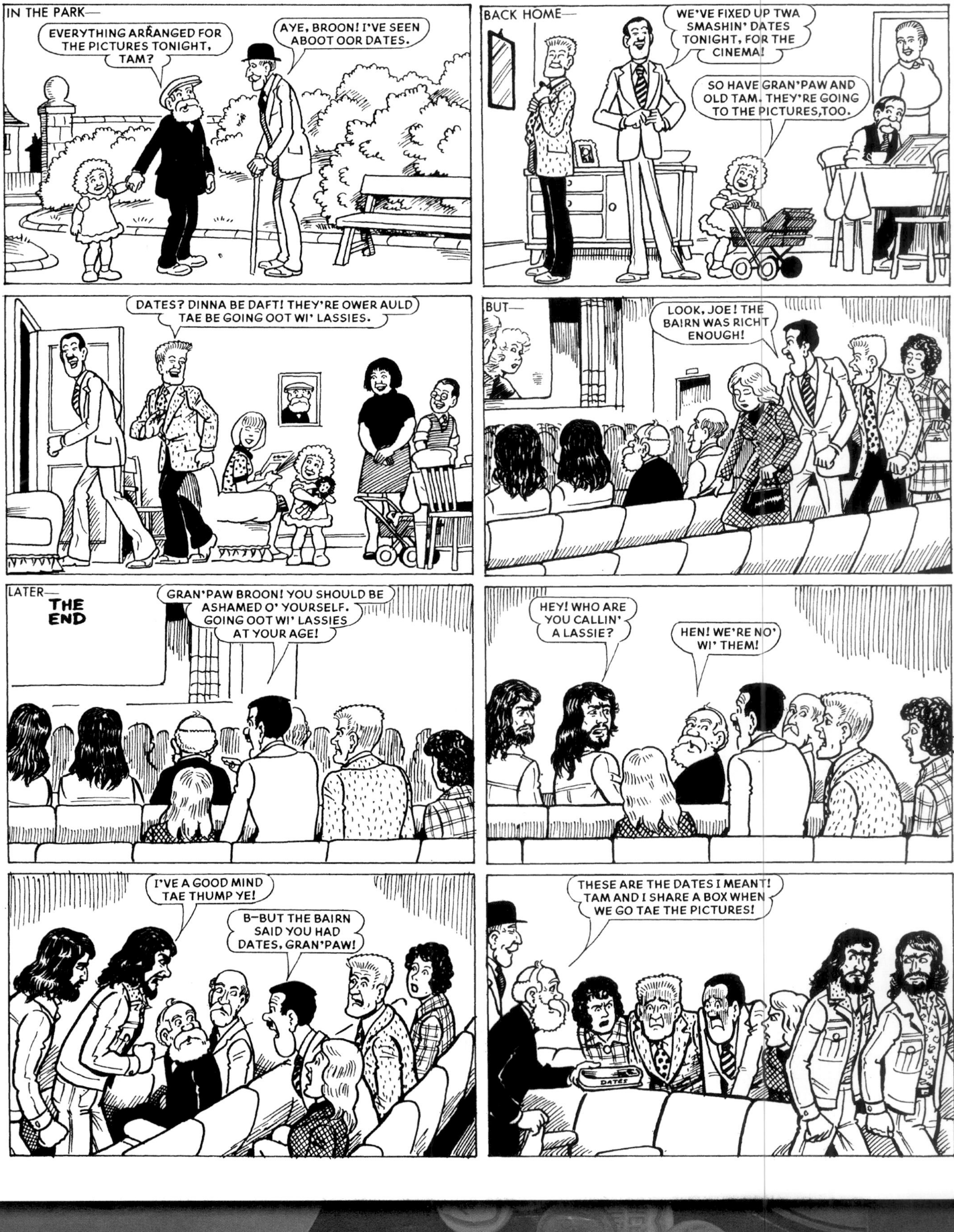

IN THE PARK—
EVERYTHING ARRANGED FOR THE PICTURES TONIGHT, TAM?
AYE, BROON! I'VE SEEN ABOOT OOR DATES.
BACK HOME—
WE'VE FIXED UP TWA SMASHIN' DATES TONIGHT, FOR THE CINEMA!
SO HAVE GRAN'PAW AND OLD TAM. THEY'RE GOING TO THE PICTURES, TOO.
DATES? DINNA BE DAFT! THEY'RE OWER AULD TAE BE GOING OOT WI' LASSIES.
BUT—
LOOK, JOE! THE BAIRN WAS RICHT ENOUGH!
LATER—
THE END
GRAN'PAW BROON! YOU SHOULD BE ASHAMED O' YOURSELF. GOING OOT WI' LASSIES AT YOUR AGE!
HEY! WHO ARE YOU CALLIN' A LASSIE?
HEN! WE'RE NO' WI' THEM!
I'VE A GOOD MIND TAE THUMP YE!
B–BUT THE BAIRN SAID YOU HAD DATES, GRAN'PAW!
THESE ARE THE DATES I MEANT! TAM AND I SHARE A BOX WHEN WE GO TAE THE PICTURES!
DATES

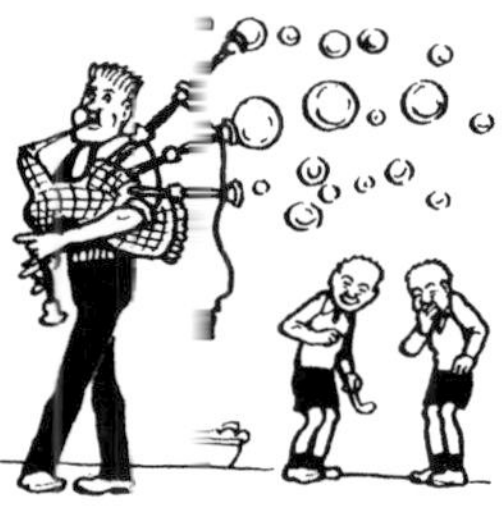

You can tell an awfy lot—

From the washing folk have got!

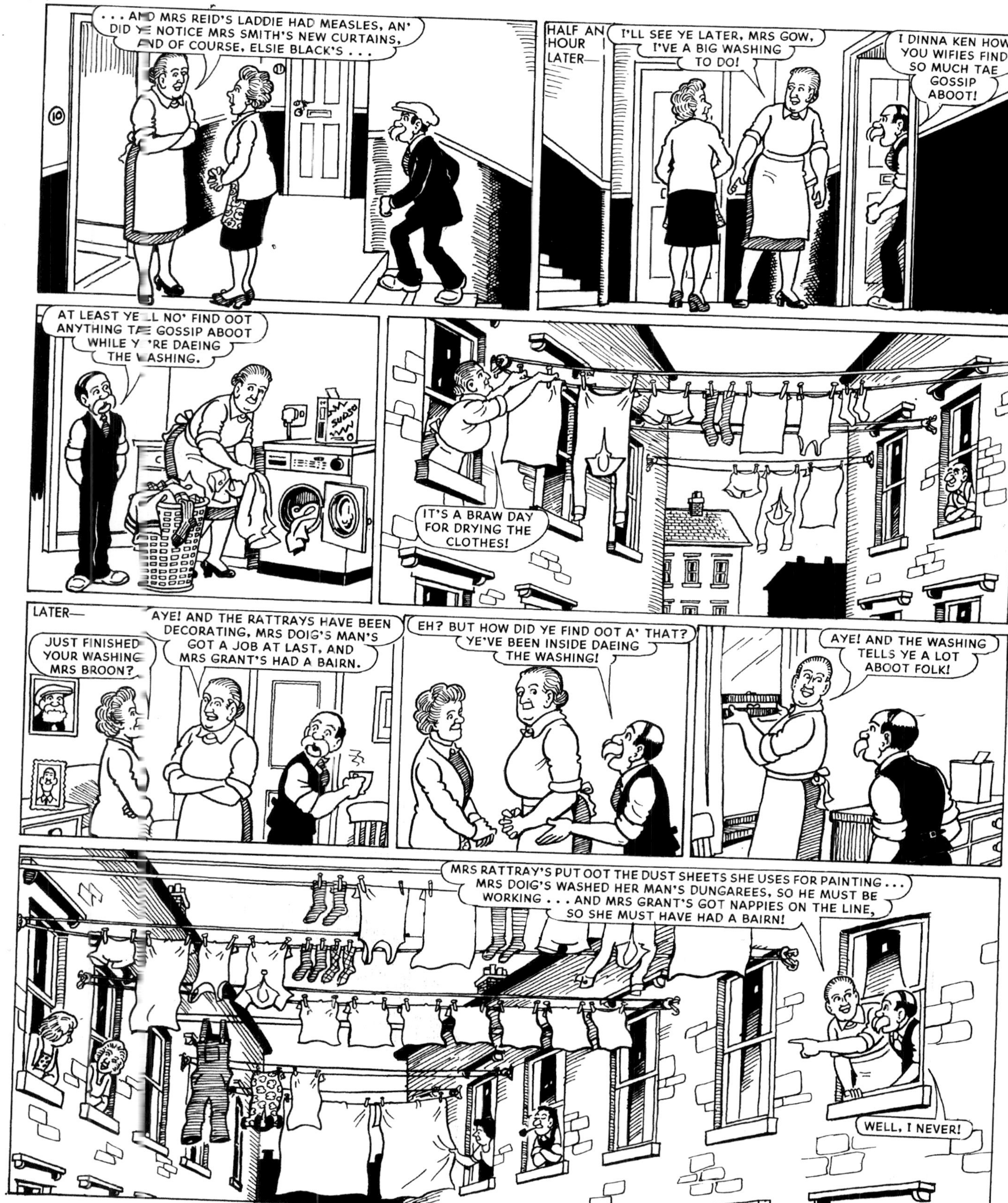

. . . AND MRS REID'S LADDIE HAD MEASLES, AN' DID YE NOTICE MRS SMITH'S NEW CURTAINS, AND OF COURSE, ELSIE BLACK'S . . .
10
11
HALF AN HOUR LATER—
I'LL SEE YE LATER, MRS GOW, I'VE A BIG WASHING TO DO!
I DINNA KEN HOW YOU WIFIES FIND SO MUCH TAE GOSSIP ABOOT!
AT LEAST YE'LL NO' FIND OOT ANYTHING TAE GOSSIP ABOOT WHILE YE'RE DAEING THE WASHING.
SUDSO
IT'S A BRAW DAY FOR DRYING THE CLOTHES!
LATER—
JUST FINISHED YOUR WASHING MRS BROON?
AYE! AND THE RATTRAYS HAVE BEEN DECORATING, MRS DOIG'S MAN'S GOT A JOB AT LAST, AND MRS GRANT'S HAD A BAIRN.
EH? BUT HOW DID YE FIND OOT A' THAT? YE'VE BEEN INSIDE DAEING THE WASHING!
AYE! AND THE WASHING TELLS YE A LOT ABOOT FOLK!
MRS RATTRAY'S PUT OOT THE DUST SHEETS SHE USES FOR PAINTING . . . MRS DOIG'S WASHED HER MAN'S DUNGAREES, SO HE MUST BE WORKING . . . AND MRS GRANT'S GOT NAPPIES ON THE LINE, SO SHE MUST HAVE HAD A BAIRN!
WELL, I NEVER!

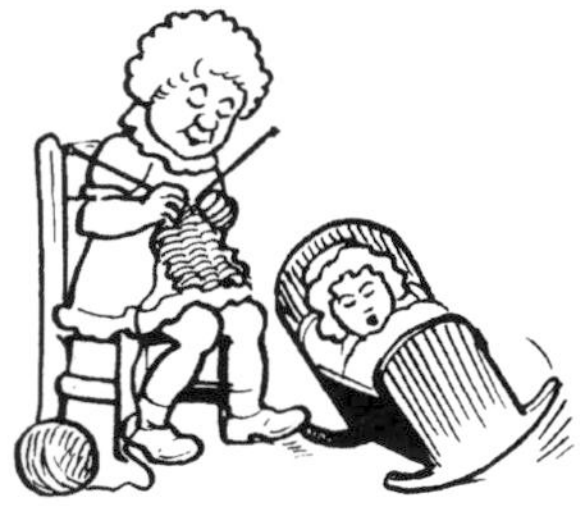

Gran'paw shouldn't eat—

This special kind of sweet!

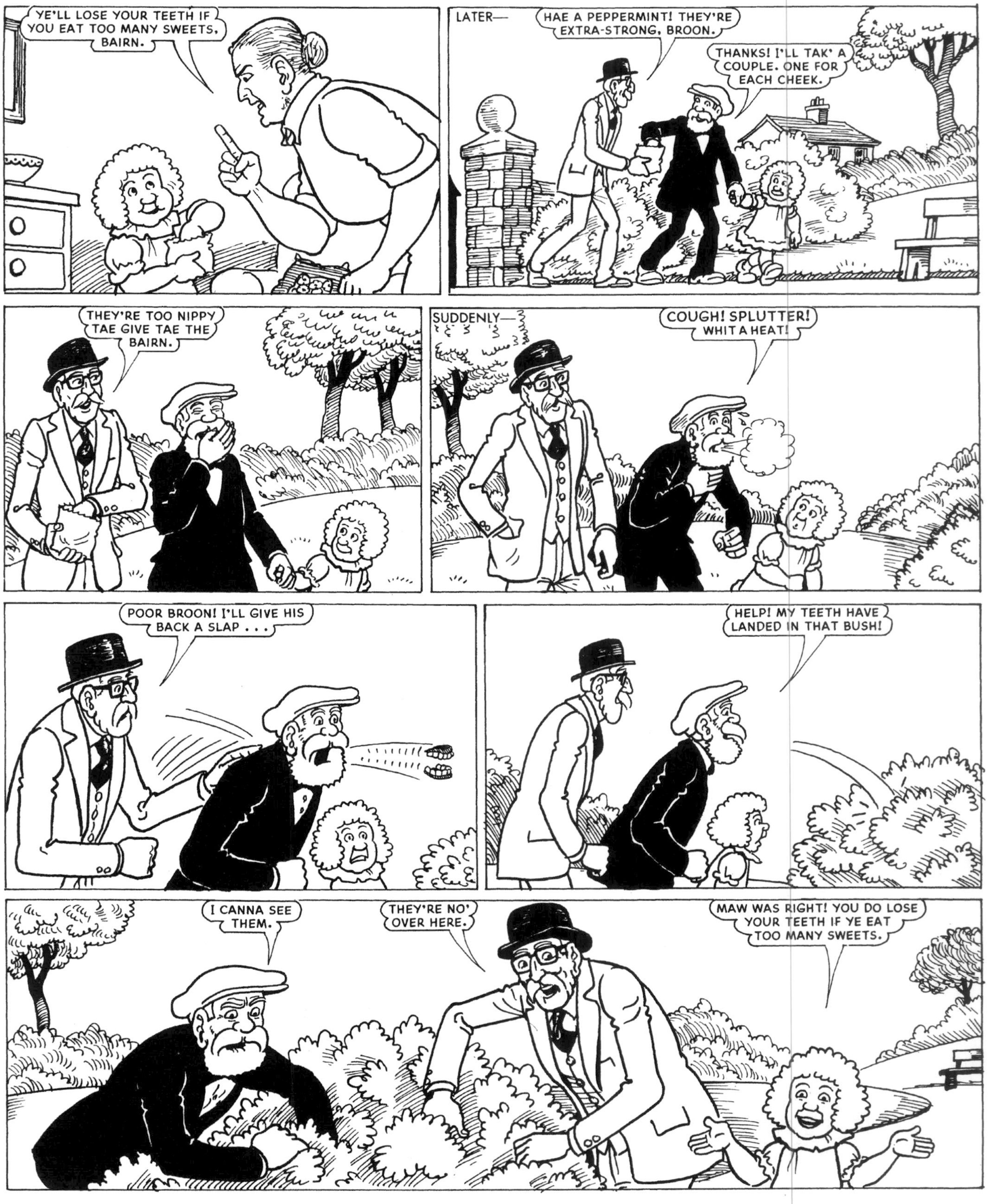
YE'LL LOSE YOUR TEETH IF YOU EAT TOO MANY SWEETS, BAIRN.
LATER—
HAE A PEPPERMINT! THEY'RE EXTRA-STRONG, BROON.
THANKS! I'LL TAK' A COUPLE. ONE FOR EACH CHEEK.
THEY'RE TOO NIPPY TAE GIVE TAE THE BAIRN.
SUDDENLY—
COUGH! SPLUTTER! WHIT A HEAT!
POOR BROON! I'LL GIVE HIS BACK A SLAP . . .
HELP! MY TEETH HAVE LANDED IN THAT BUSH!
I CANNA SEE THEM.
THEY'RE NO' OVER HERE.
MAW WAS RIGHT! YOU DO LOSE YOUR TEETH IF YE EAT TOO MANY SWEETS.

There are black looks for Paw Broon—

When this visitor sits doon!

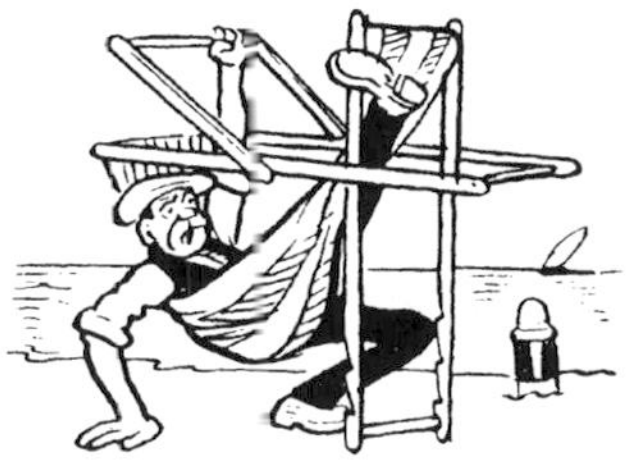

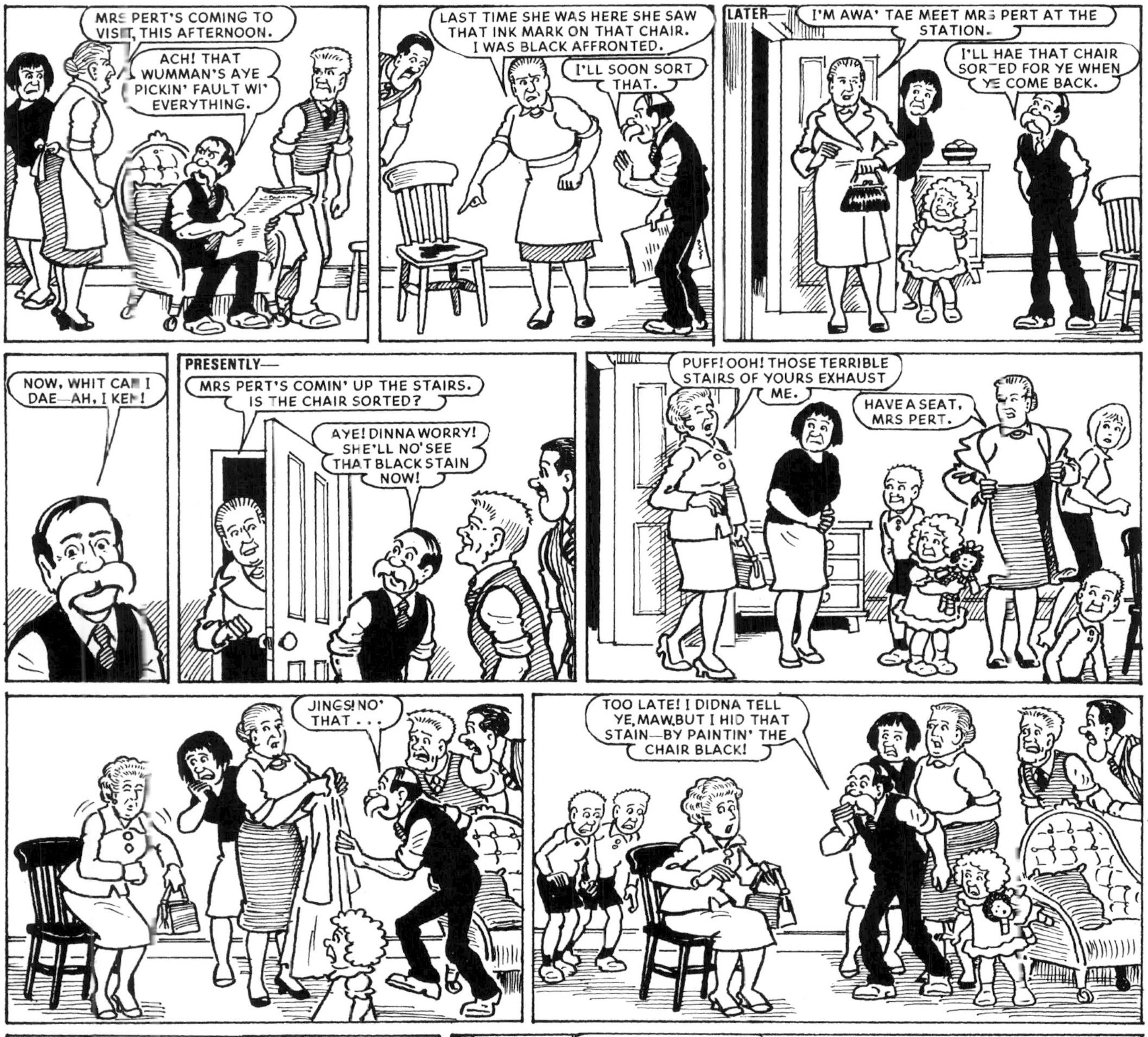
MRS PERT'S COMING TO VISIT, THIS AFTERNOON.
ACH! THAT WUMMAN'S AYE PICKIN' FAULT WI' EVERYTHING.
LAST TIME SHE WAS HERE SHE SAW THAT INK MARK ON THAT CHAIR. I WAS BLACK AFFRONTED.
I'LL SOON SORT THAT.
LATER—
I'M AWA' TAE MEET MRS PERT AT THE STATION.
I'LL HAE THAT CHAIR SORTED FOR YE WHEN YE COME BACK.
NOW, WHIT CAN I DAE—AH, I KEN!
PRESENTLY—
MRS PERT'S COMIN' UP THE STAIRS. IS THE CHAIR SORTED?
AYE! DINNA WORRY! SHE'LL NO' SEE THAT BLACK STAIN NOW!
PUFF! OOH! THOSE TERRIBLE STAIRS OF YOURS EXHAUST ME.
HAVE A SEAT, MRS PERT.
JINGS! NO' THAT . . .
TOO LATE! I DIDNA TELL YE, MAW, BUT I HID THAT STAIN—BY PAINTIN' THE CHAIR BLACK!
AND NOW YE'RE BLACK AFFRONTED AGAIN!
OH!
I'M LEAVING! MY NEW SUIT'S RUINED.
MRS PERT'S NO' BLACK AFFRONTED—SHE'S BLACK BEHINDED!

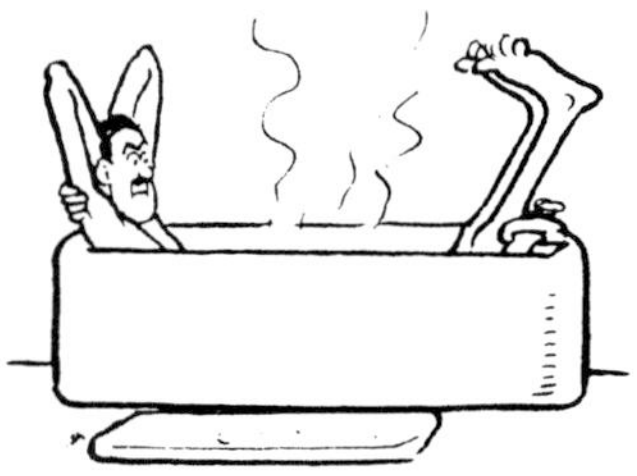

Too many trips to the barber's chair—

Leave poor Hen Broon in despair!

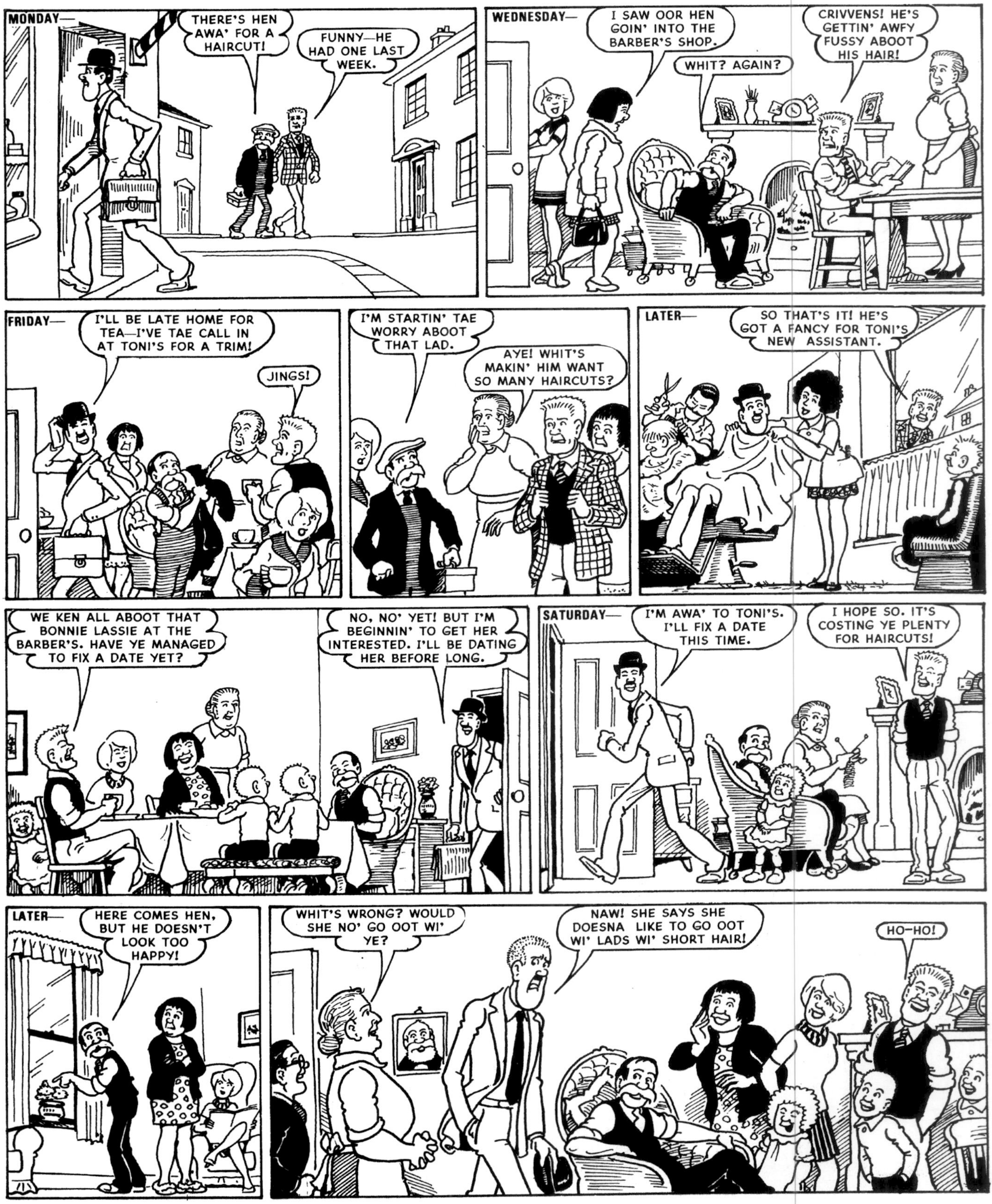
MONDAY—
THERE'S HEN AWA' FOR A HAIRCUT!
FUNNY—HE HAD ONE LAST WEEK.
WEDNESDAY—
I SAW OOR HEN GOIN' INTO THE BARBER'S SHOP.
WHIT? AGAIN?
CRIVVENS! HE'S GETTIN' AWFY FUSSY ABOOT HIS HAIR!
FRIDAY—
I'LL BE LATE HOME FOR TEA—I'VE TAE CALL IN AT TONI'S FOR A TRIM!
JINGS!
I'M STARTIN' TAE WORRY ABOOT THAT LAD.
AYE! WHIT'S MAKIN' HIM WANT SO MANY HAIRCUTS?
LATER—
SO THAT'S IT! HE'S GOT A FANCY FOR TONI'S NEW ASSISTANT.
WE KEN ALL ABOOT THAT BONNIE LASSIE AT THE BARBER'S. HAVE YE MANAGED TO FIX A DATE YET?
NO, NO' YET! BUT I'M BEGINNIN' TO GET HER INTERESTED. I'LL BE DATING HER BEFORE LONG.
SATURDAY—
I'M AWA' TO TONI'S. I'LL FIX A DATE THIS TIME.
I HOPE SO. IT'S COSTING YE PLENTY FOR HAIRCUTS!
LATER—
HERE COMES HEN, BUT HE DOESN'T LOOK TOO HAPPY!
WHIT'S WRONG? WOULD SHE NO' GO OOT WI' YE?
NAW! SHE SAYS SHE DOESNA LIKE TO GO OOT WI' LADS WI' SHORT HAIR!
HO-HO!

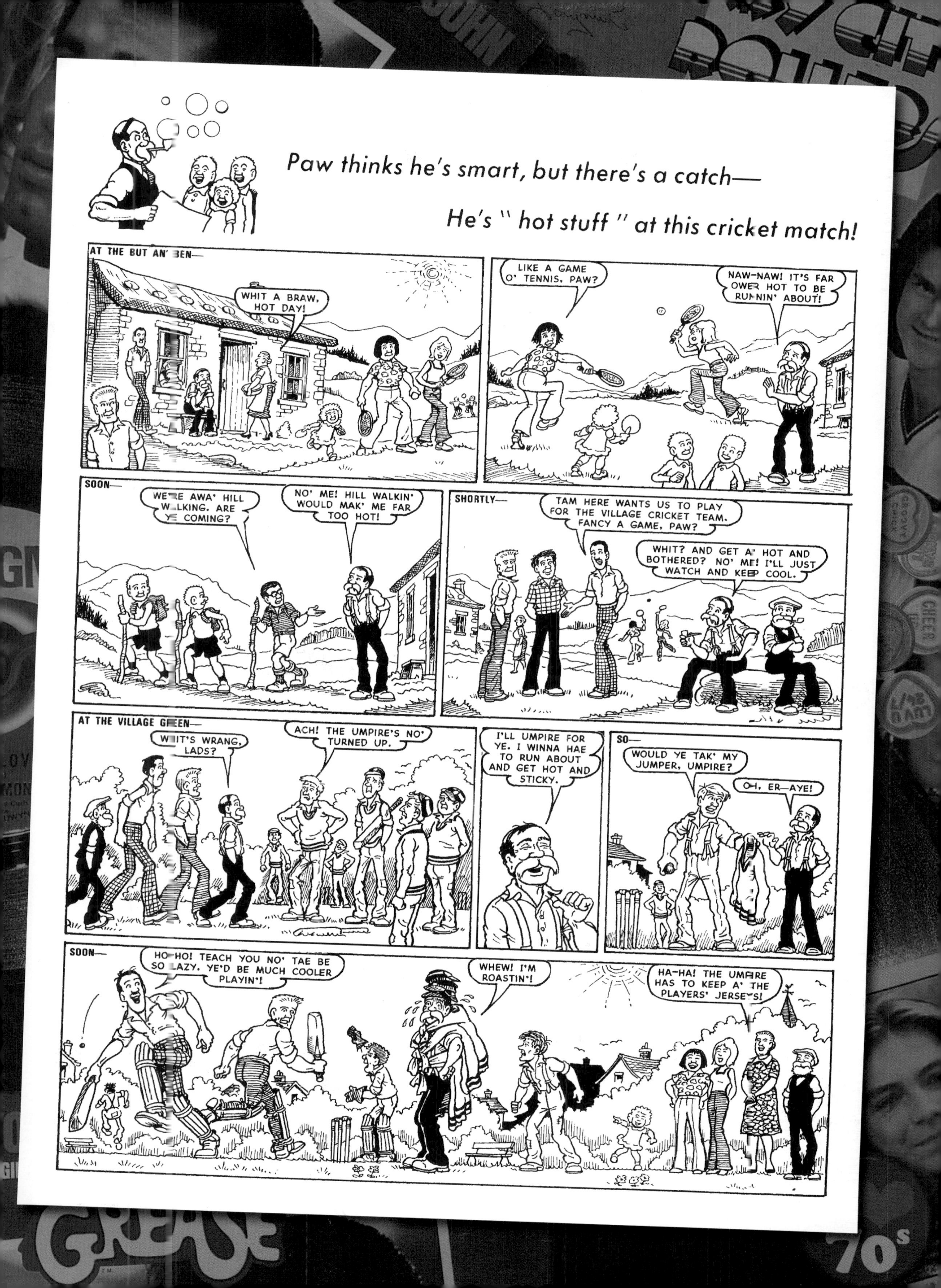
Paw thinks he's smart, but there's a catch—
He's " hot stuff " at this cricket match!
AT THE BUT AN' BEN—
WHIT A BRAW, HOT DAY!
LIKE A GAME O' TENNIS, PAW?
NAW-NAW! IT'S FAR OWER HOT TO BE RUNNIN' ABOUT!
SOON—
WE'RE AWA' HILL WALKING. ARE YE COMING?
NO' ME! HILL WALKIN' WOULD MAK' ME FAR TOO HOT!
SHORTLY—
TAM HERE WANTS US TO PLAY FOR THE VILLAGE CRICKET TEAM. FANCY A GAME, PAW?
WHIT? AND GET A' HOT AND BOTHERED? NO' ME! I'LL JUST WATCH AND KEEP COOL.
AT THE VILLAGE GREEN—
WHIT'S WRANG, LADS?
ACH! THE UMPIRE'S NO' TURNED UP.
I'LL UMPIRE FOR YE. I WINNA HAE TO RUN ABOUT AND GET HOT AND STICKY.
SO—
WOULD YE TAK' MY JUMPER, UMPIRE?
OH, ER—AYE!
SOON—
HO-HO! TEACH YOU NO' TAE BE SO LAZY. YE'D BE MUCH COOLER PLAYIN'!
WHEW! I'M ROASTIN'!
HA-HA! THE UMPIRE HAS TO KEEP A' THE PLAYERS' JERSEYS!
GREASE
70s

Paw thinks the rest are silly asses—

But see HIS kind o' fancy glasses!

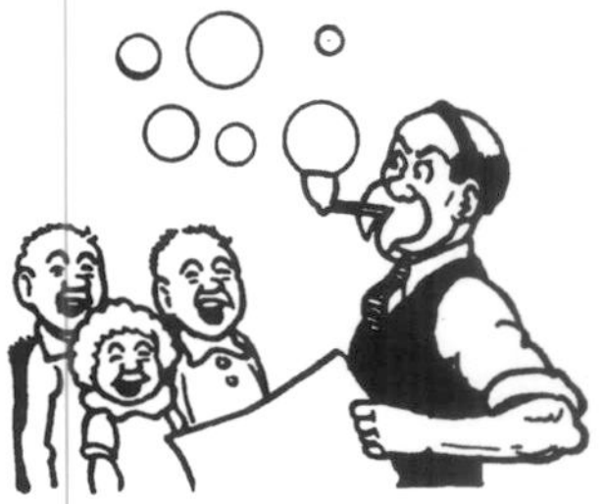

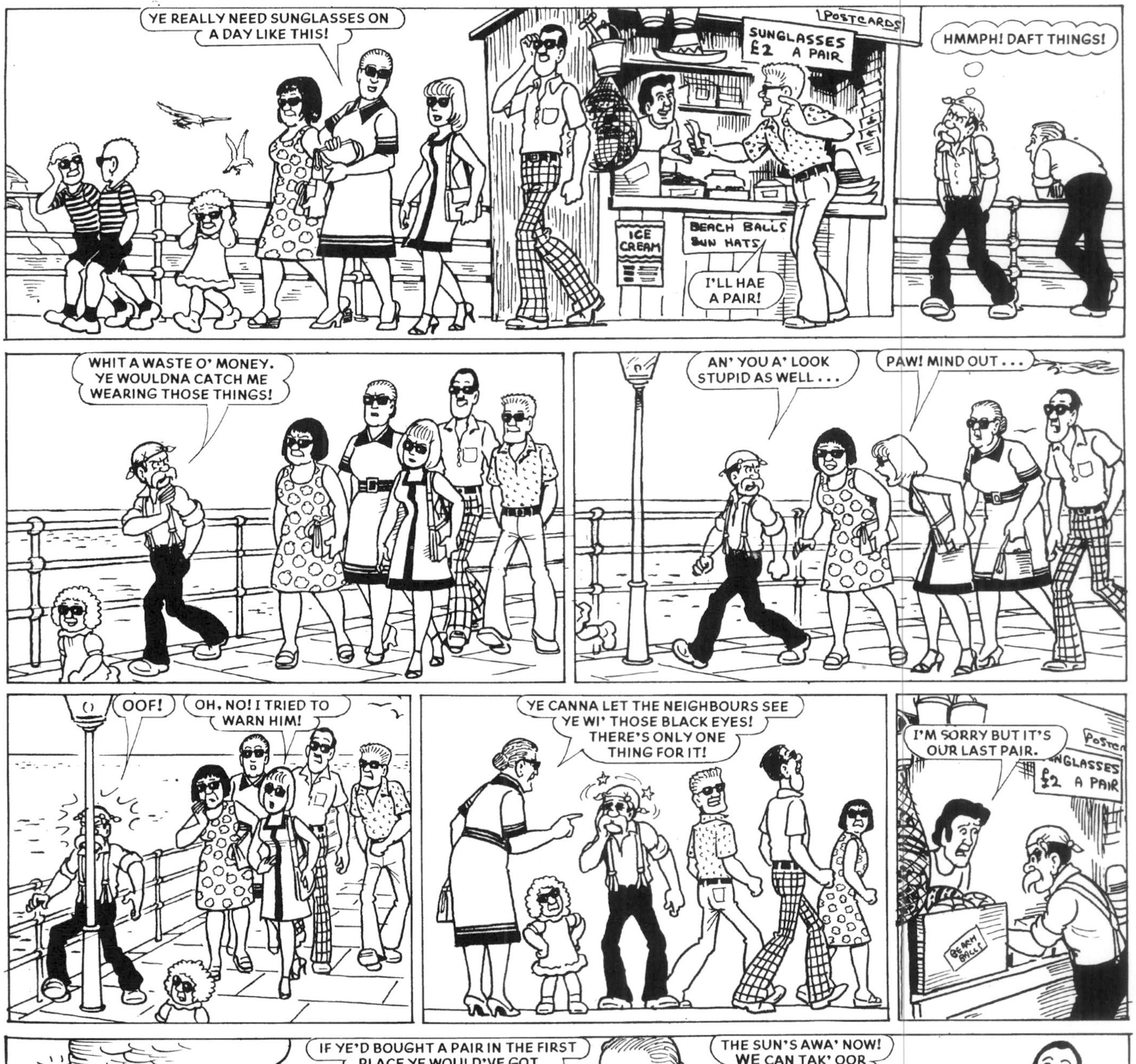
YE REALLY NEED SUNGLASSES ON A DAY LIKE THIS!
POSTCARDS
SUNGLASSES £2 A PAIR
ICE CREAM
BEACH BALLS SUN HATS
I'LL HAE A PAIR!
HMMPH! DAFT THINGS!
WHIT A WASTE O' MONEY. YE WOULDNA CATCH ME WEARING THOSE THINGS!
AN' YOU A' LOOK STUPID AS WELL . . .
PAW! MIND OUT . . .
OOF!
OH, NO! I TRIED TO WARN HIM!
YE CANNA LET THE NEIGHBOURS SEE YE WI' THOSE BLACK EYES! THERE'S ONLY ONE THING FOR IT!
I'M SORRY BUT IT'S OUR LAST PAIR.
IF YE'D BOUGHT A PAIR IN THE FIRST PLACE YE WOULD'VE GOT ORDINARY ONES.
THE SUN'S AWA' NOW! WE CAN TAK' OOR SPECS AFF!

It disnae go far— but it's a smashing car!

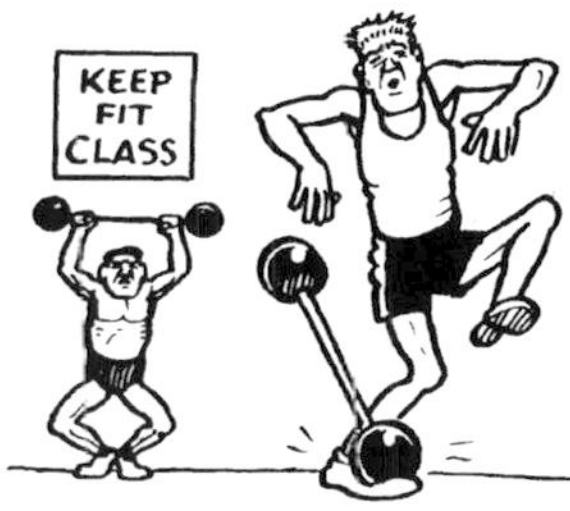
KEEP FIT CLASS

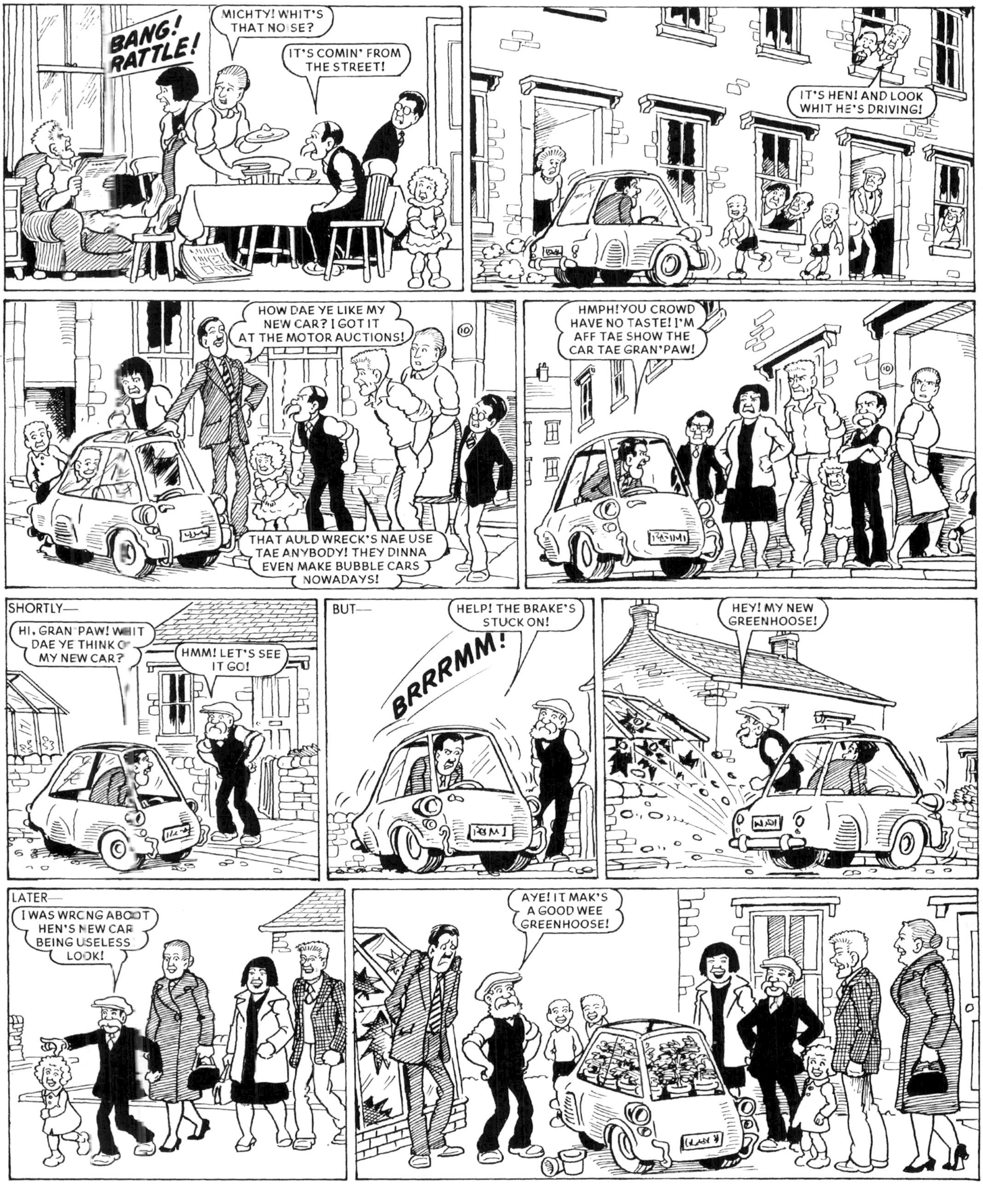
BANG! RATTLE!
MICHTY! WHIT'S THAT NOISE?
IT'S COMIN' FROM THE STREET!
IT'S HEN! AND LOOK WHIT HE'S DRIVING!
HOW DAE YE LIKE MY NEW CAR? I GOT IT AT THE MOTOR AUCTIONS!
THAT AULD WRECK'S NAE USE TAE ANYBODY! THEY DINNA EVEN MAKE BUBBLE CARS NOWADAYS!
HMPH! YOU CROWD HAVE NO TASTE! I'M AFF TAE SHOW THE CAR TAE GRAN'PAW!
SHORTLY—
HI, GRAN'PAW! WHIT DAE YE THINK O' MY NEW CAR?
HMM! LET'S SEE IT GO!
BUT—
HELP! THE BRAKE'S STUCK ON!
BRRRMM!
HEY! MY NEW GREENHOOSE!
LATER—
I WAS WRONG ABOOT HEN'S NEW CAR BEING USELESS. LOOK!
AYE! IT MAK'S A GOOD WEE GREENHOOSE!

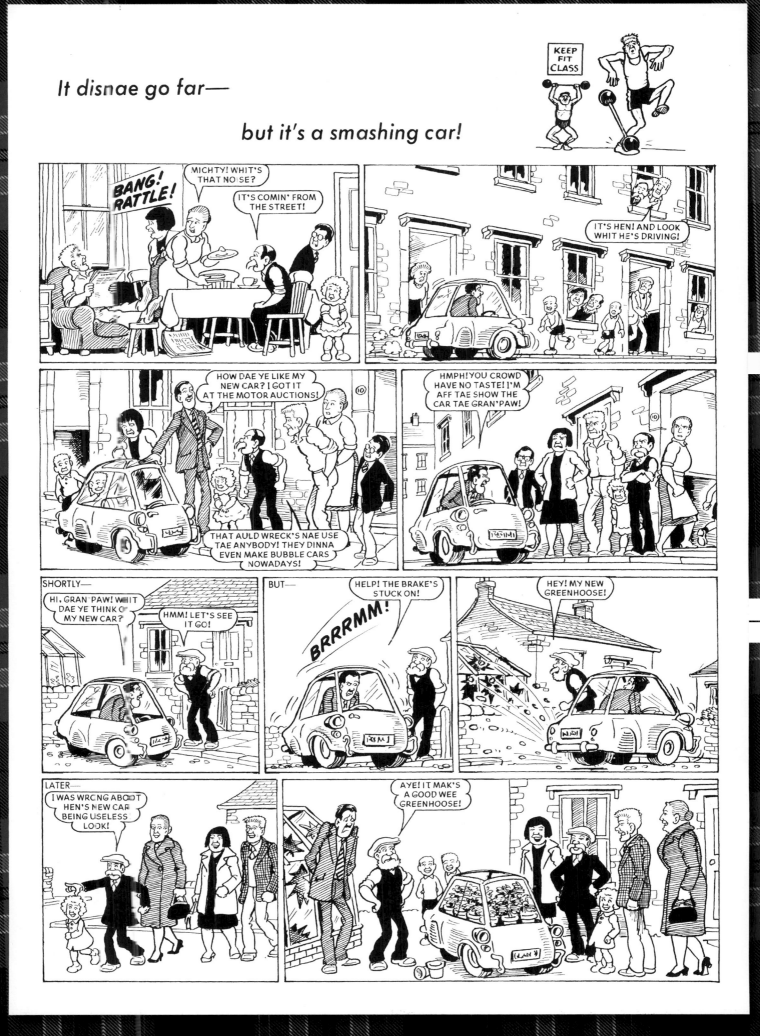

The Funny Side of Seventies Romance.

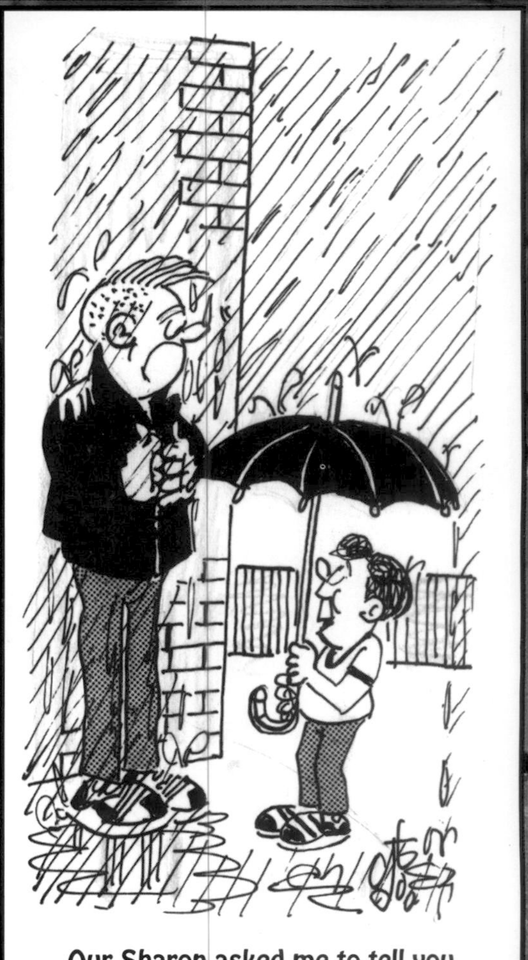

Our Sharon asked me to tell you she'll come when it stops raining.

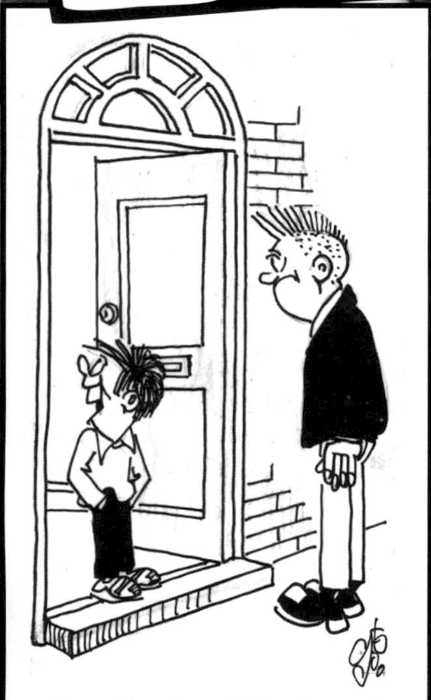

Hey, Sis! A walk in the park with a bag of chips is here.

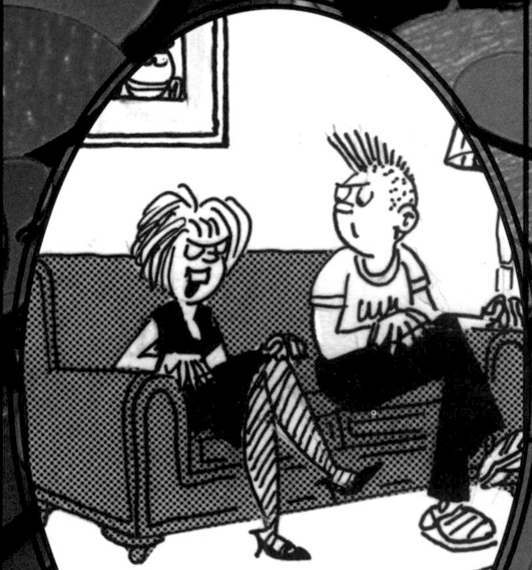

Of course there's no one else – not tonight anyway.

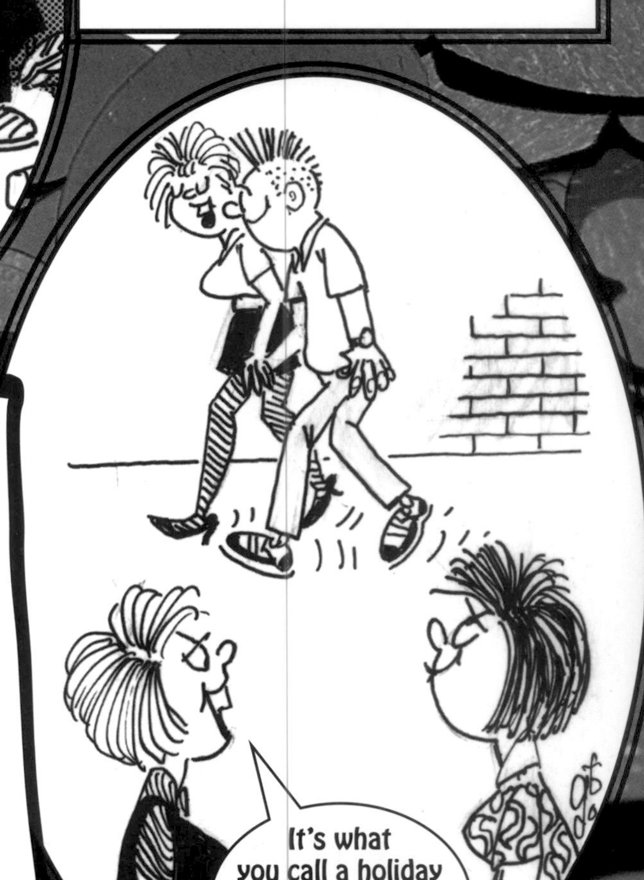
It's what you call a holiday romance. Her boyfriend is in Benidorm.

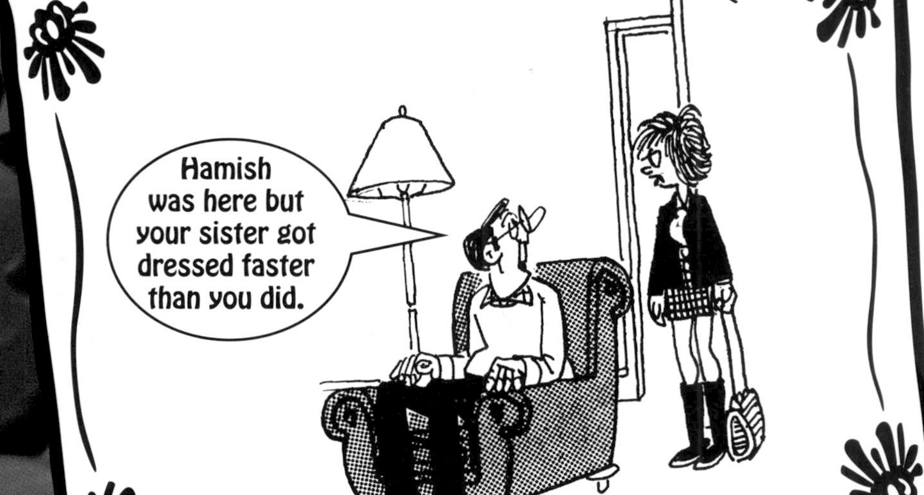
Hamish was here but your sister got dressed faster than you did.

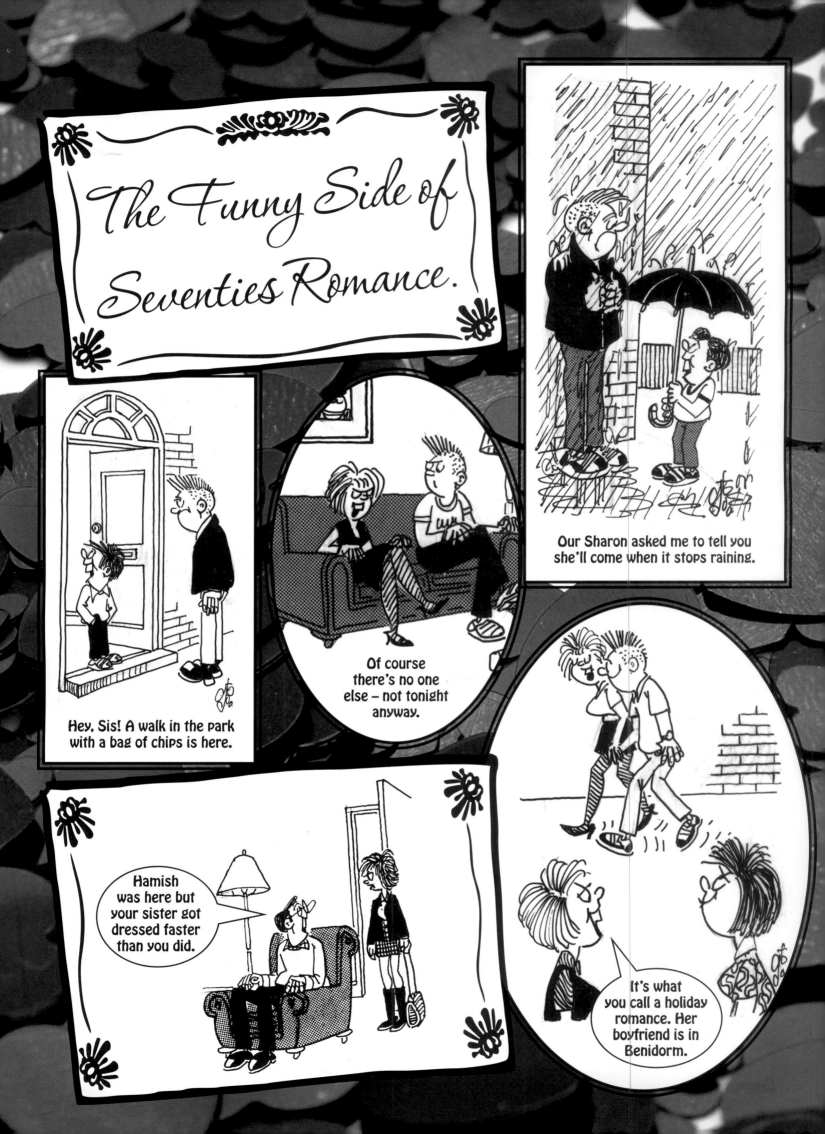

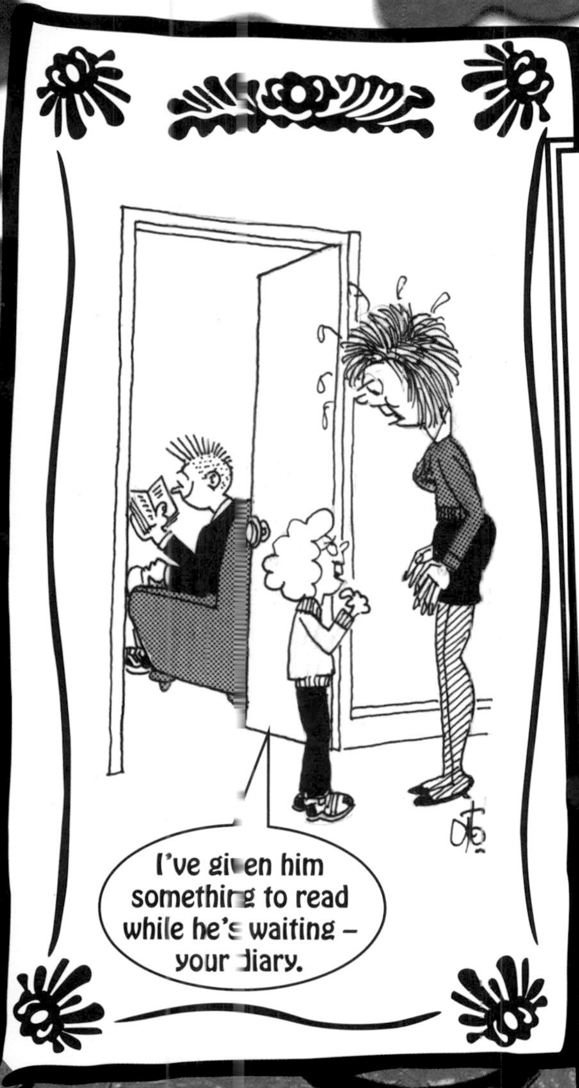
I've given him something to read while he's waiting – your diary.

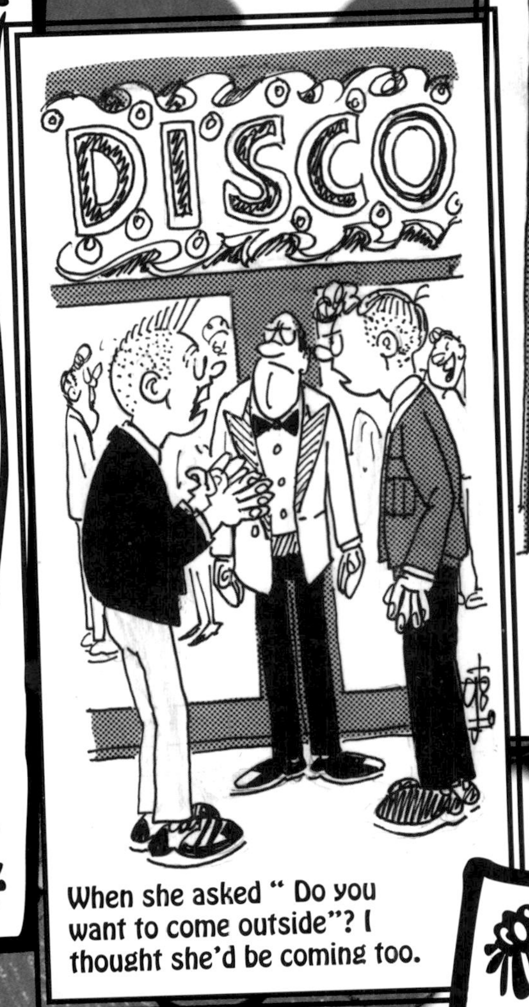
DISCO
When she asked " Do you want to come outside"? I thought she'd be coming too.

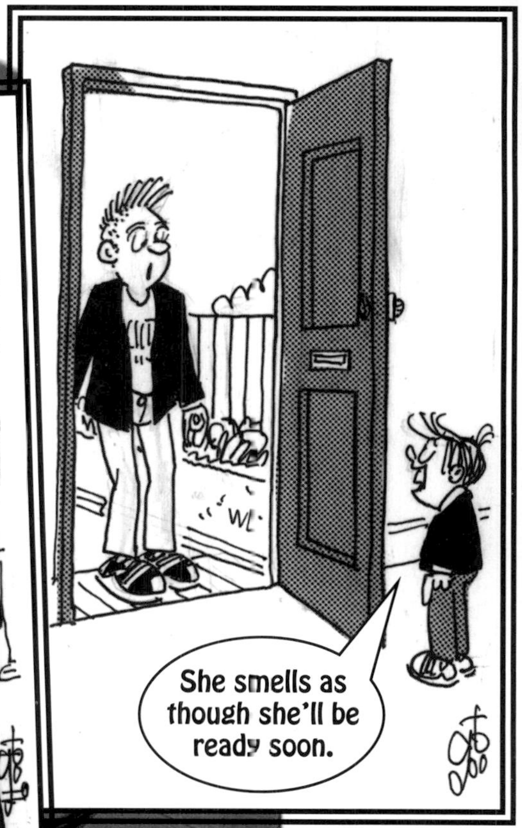
She smells as though she'll be ready soon.

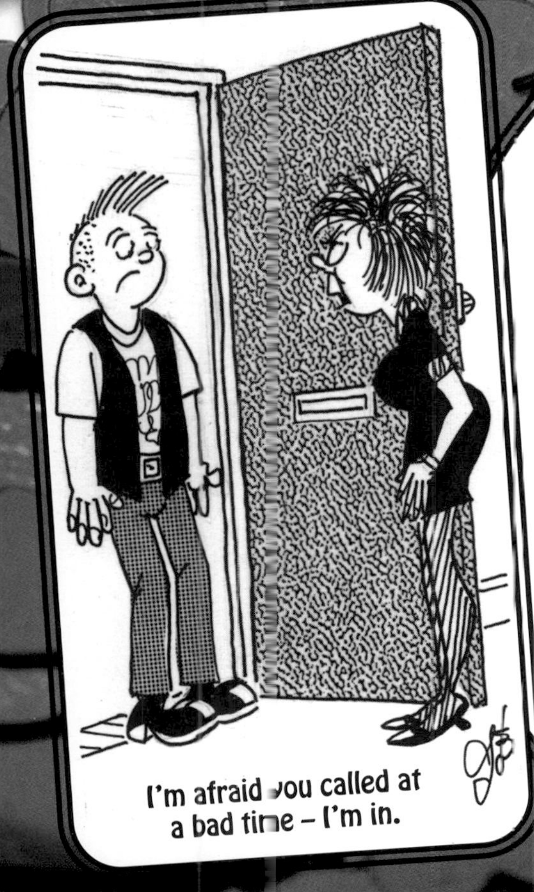
I'm afraid you called at a bad time – I'm in.

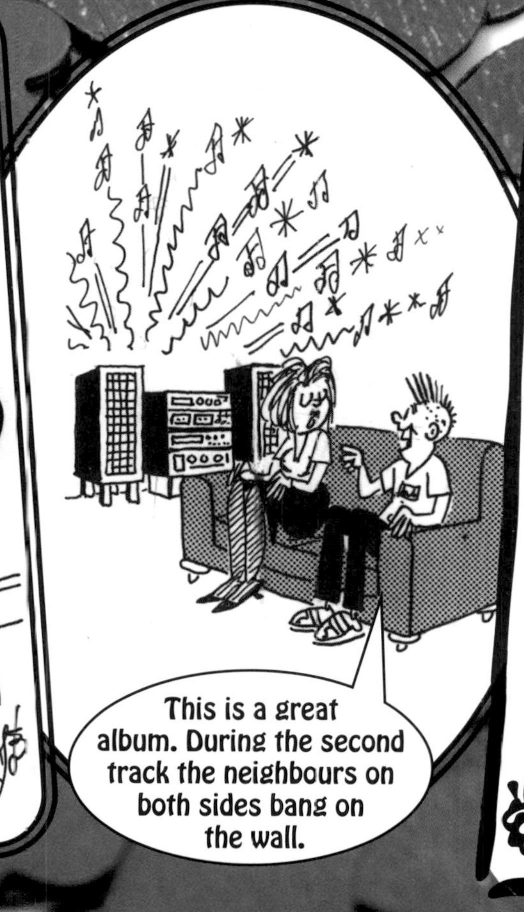
This is a great album. During the second track the neighbours on both sides bang on the wall.

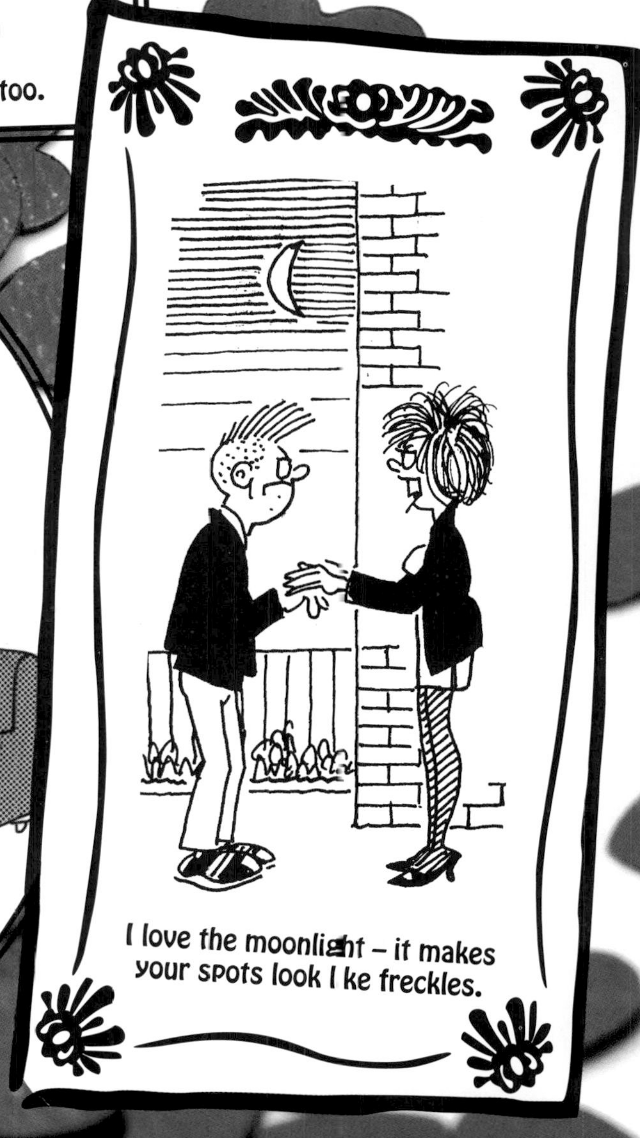
I love the moonlight – it makes your spots look like freckles.

There's a funny sight standin'—

On the Broons' landin'!

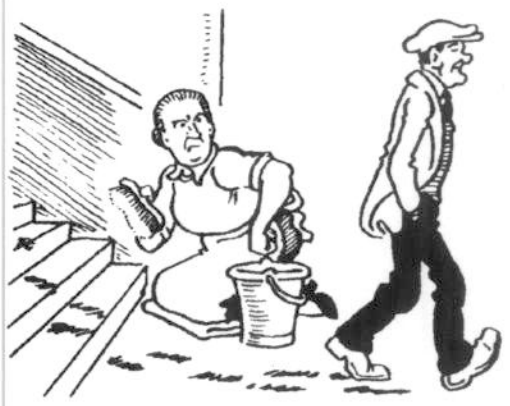

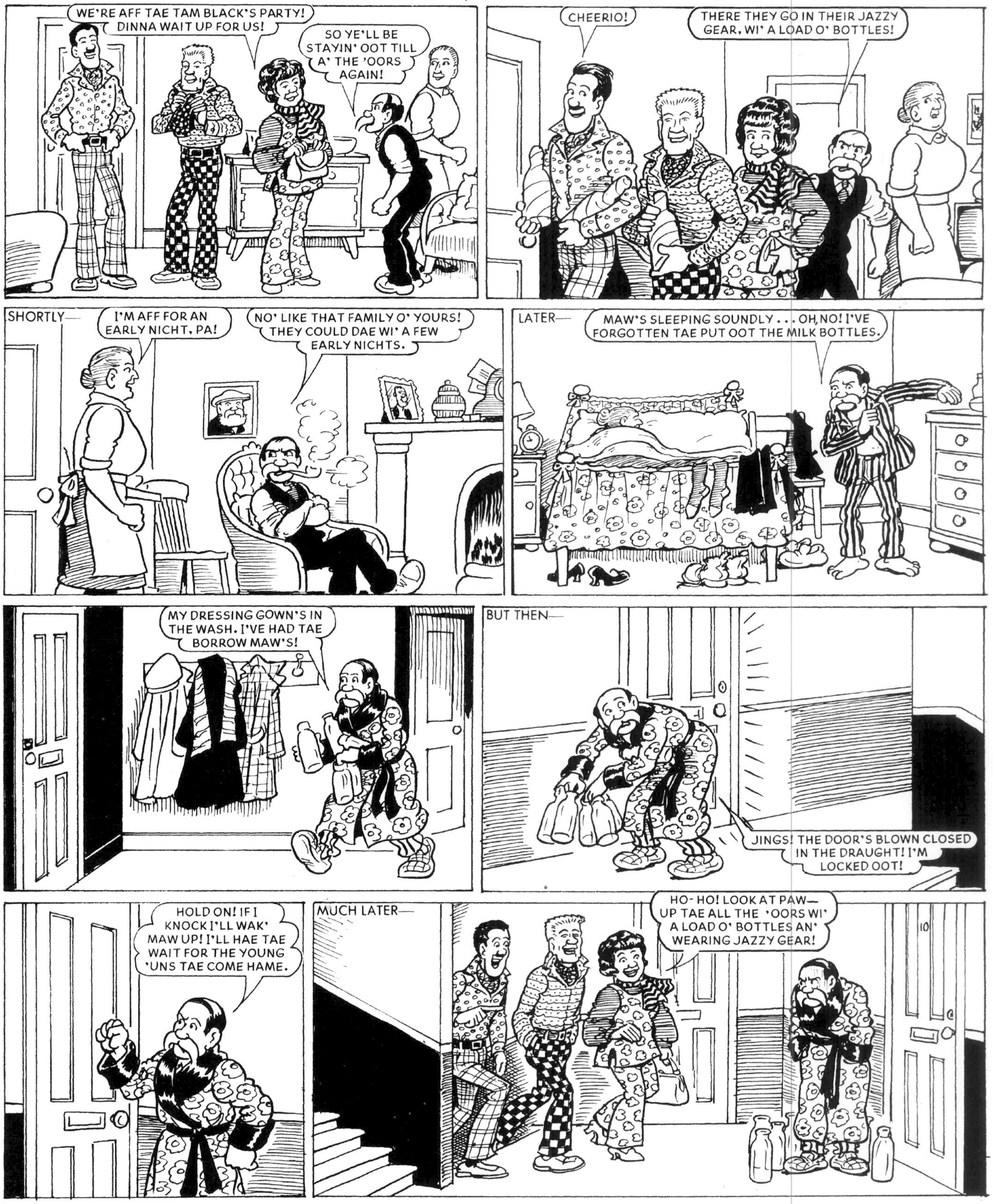

WE'RE AFF TAE TAM BLACK'S PARTY! DINNA WAIT UP FOR US!
SO YE'LL BE STAYIN' OOT TILL A' THE 'OORS AGAIN!
CHEERIO!
THERE THEY GO IN THEIR JAZZY GEAR, WI' A LOAD O' BOTTLES!
SHORTLY—
I'M AFF FOR AN EARLY NICHT, PA!
NO' LIKE THAT FAMILY O' YOURS! THEY COULD DAE WI' A FEW EARLY NICHTS.
LATER—
MAW'S SLEEPING SOUNDLY . . . OH, NO! I'VE FORGOTTEN TAE PUT OOT THE MILK BOTTLES.
MY DRESSING GOWN'S IN THE WASH. I'VE HAD TAE BORROW MAW'S!
BUT THEN—
JINGS! THE DOOR'S BLOWN CLOSED IN THE DRAUGHT! I'M LOCKED OOT!
HOLD ON! IF I KNOCK I'LL WAK' MAW UP! I'LL HAE TAE WAIT FOR THE YOUNG 'UNS TAE COME HAME.
MUCH LATER—
HO-HO! LOOK AT PAW—UP TAE ALL THE 'OORS WI' A LOAD O' BOTTLES AN' WEARING JAZZY GEAR!
10

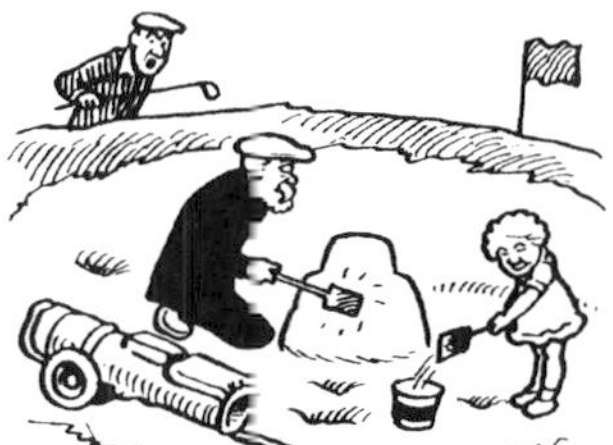

Prince Charming and his " Cinderellie "—

Her foot's just perfect for that wellie!

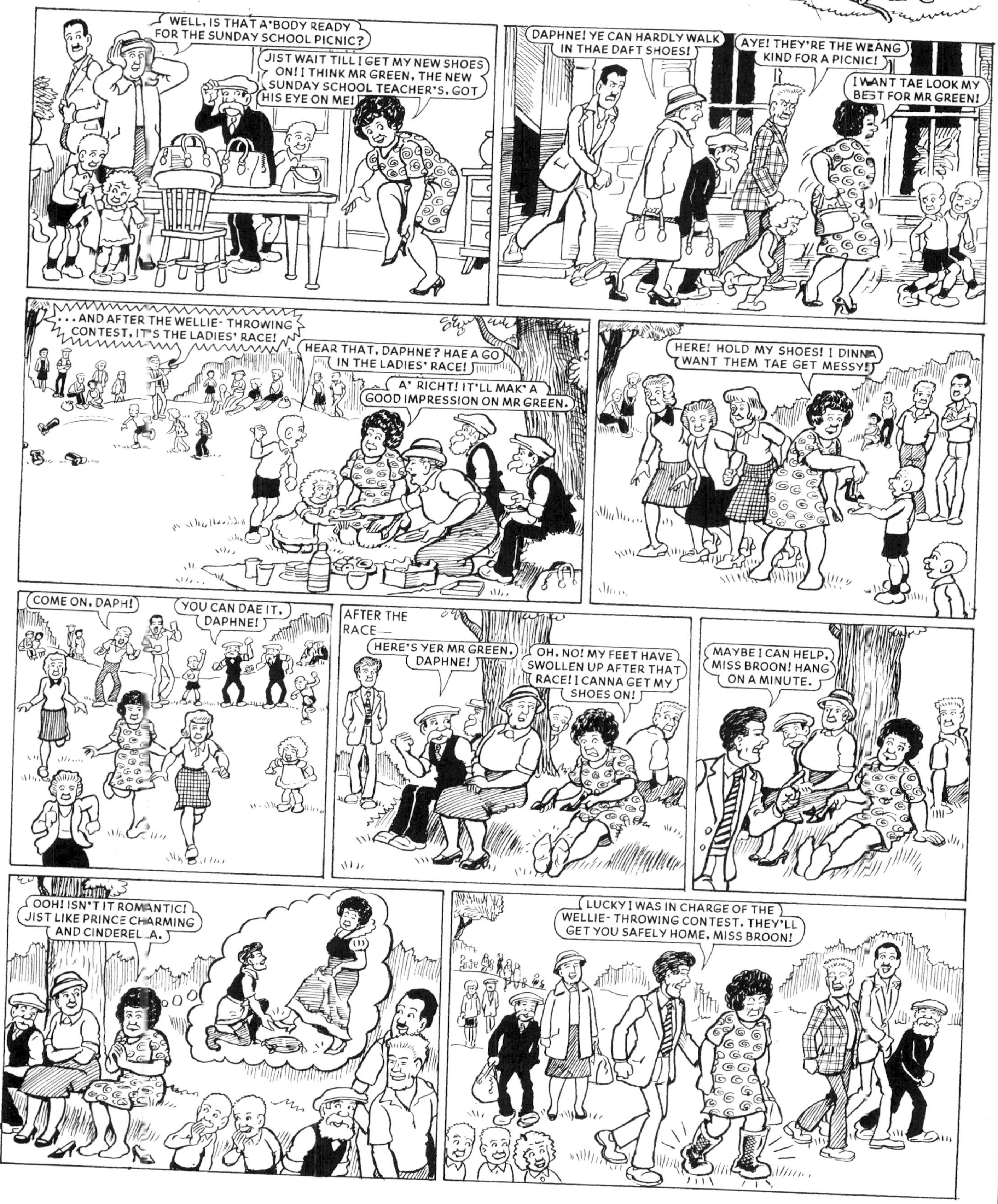
WELL, IS THAT A'BODY READY FOR THE SUNDAY SCHOOL PICNIC?
JIST WAIT TILL I GET MY NEW SHOES ON! I THINK MR GREEN, THE NEW SUNDAY SCHOOL TEACHER'S, GOT HIS EYE ON ME!
DAPHNE! YE CAN HARDLY WALK IN THAE DAFT SHOES!
AYE! THEY'RE THE WRANG KIND FOR A PICNIC!
I WANT TAE LOOK MY BEST FOR MR GREEN!
...AND AFTER THE WELLIE-THROWING CONTEST, IT'S THE LADIES' RACE!
HEAR THAT, DAPHNE? HAE A GO IN THE LADIES' RACE!
A' RICHT! IT'LL MAK' A GOOD IMPRESSION ON MR GREEN.
HERE! HOLD MY SHOES! I DINNA WANT THEM TAE GET MESSY!
COME ON, DAPH!
YOU CAN DAE IT, DAPHNE!
AFTER THE RACE—
HERE'S YER MR GREEN, DAPHNE!
OH, NO! MY FEET HAVE SWOLLEN UP AFTER THAT RACE! I CANNA GET MY SHOES ON!
MAYBE I CAN HELP, MISS BROON! HANG ON A MINUTE.
OOH! ISN'T IT ROMANTIC! JIST LIKE PRINCE CHARMING AND CINDERELLA.
LUCKY I WAS IN CHARGE OF THE WELLIE-THROWING CONTEST. THEY'LL GET YOU SAFELY HOME, MISS BROON!

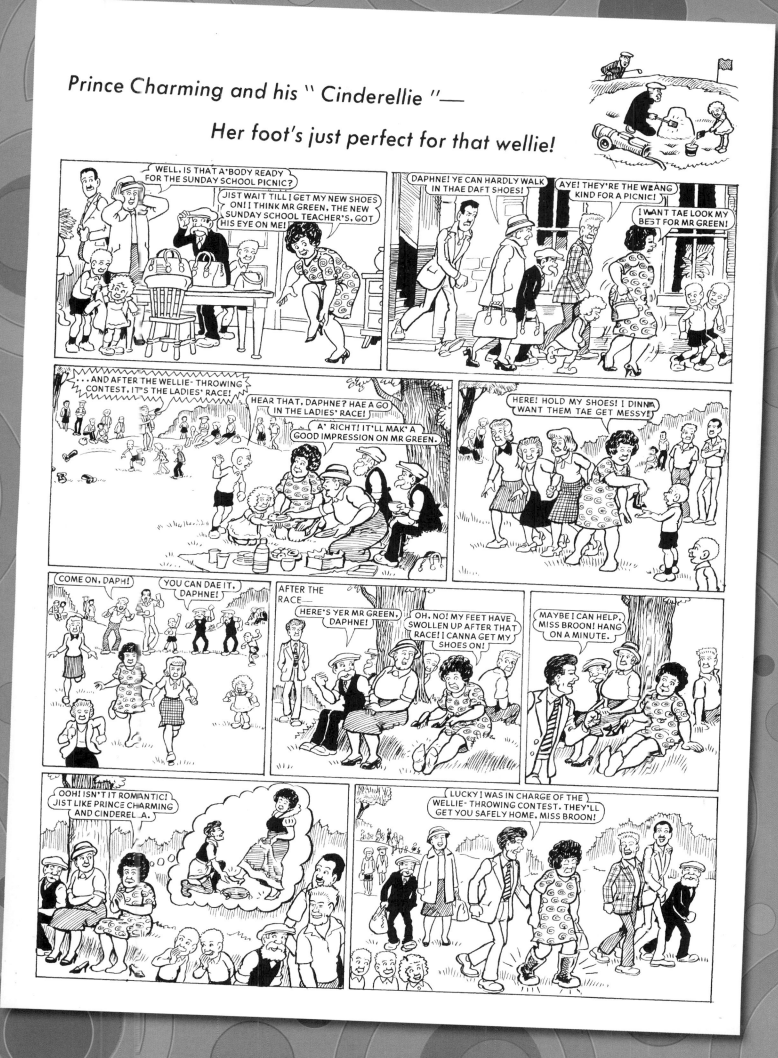

Fancy breeks and shirt wi' flowers—

Nae wonder Maw Broon gasps and glowers!

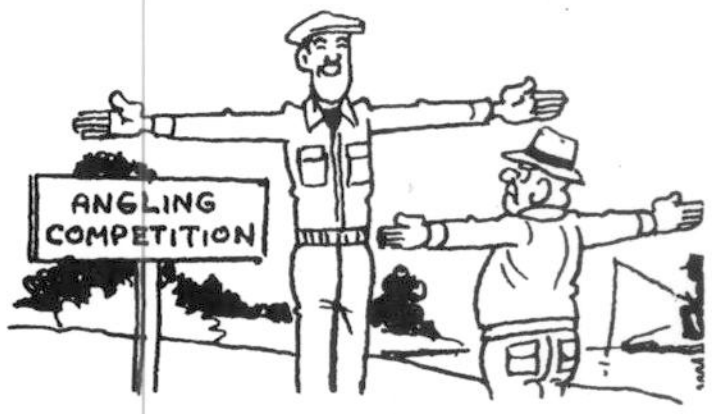
ANGLING COMPETITION

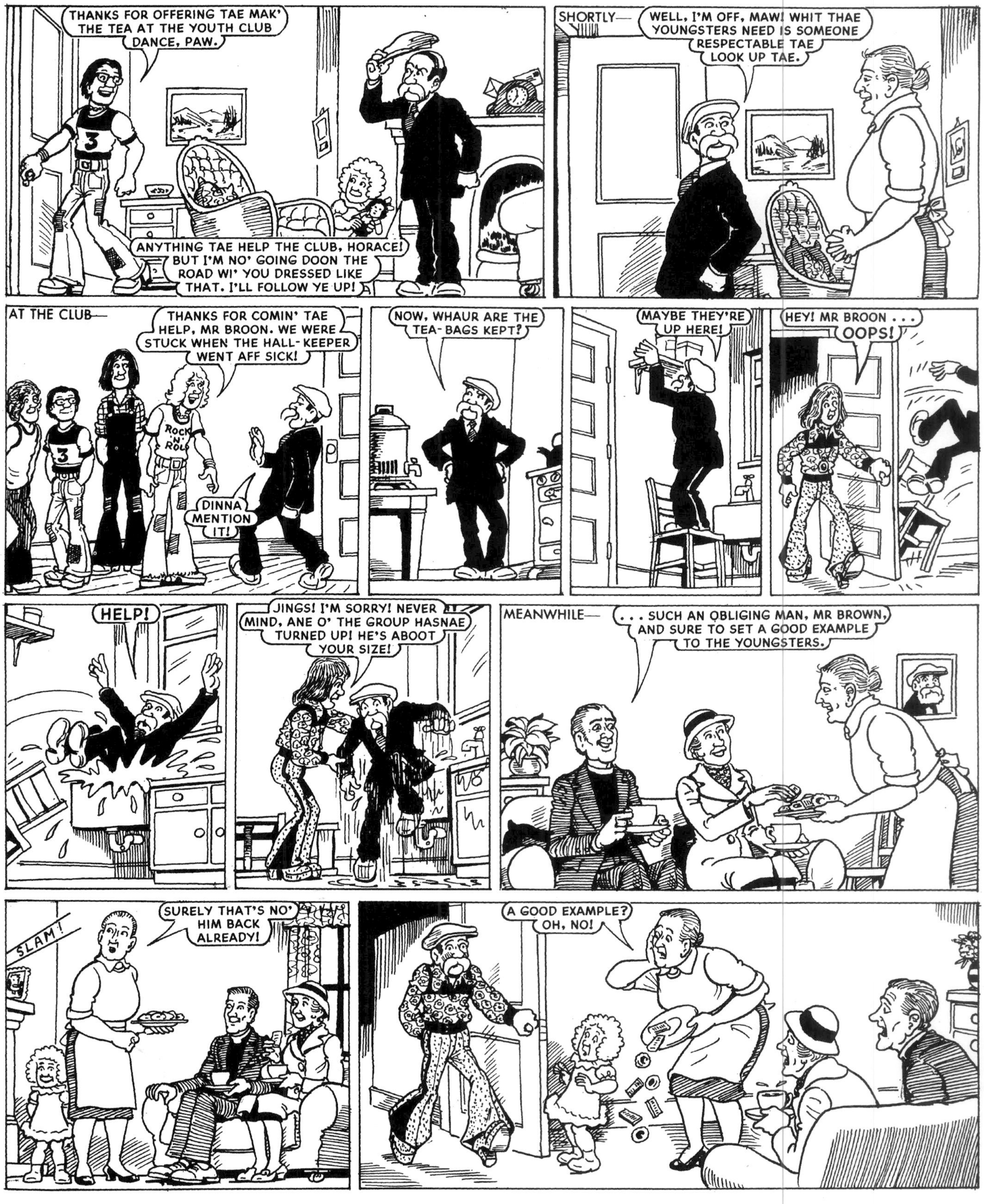
THANKS FOR OFFERING TAE MAK' THE TEA AT THE YOUTH CLUB DANCE, PAW.
ANYTHING TAE HELP THE CLUB, HORACE! BUT I'M NO' GOING DOON THE ROAD WI' YOU DRESSED LIKE THAT. I'LL FOLLOW YE UP!
SHORTLY—
WELL, I'M OFF, MAW! WHIT THAE YOUNGSTERS NEED IS SOMEONE RESPECTABLE TAE LOOK UP TAE.
AT THE CLUB—
THANKS FOR COMIN' TAE HELP, MR BROON. WE WERE STUCK WHEN THE HALL-KEEPER WENT AFF SICK!
DINNA MENTION IT!
ROCK 'N' ROLL
NOW, WHAUR ARE THE TEA-BAGS KEPT?
MAYBE THEY'RE UP HERE!
HEY! MR BROON . . .
OOPS!
HELP!
JINGS! I'M SORRY! NEVER MIND, ANE O' THE GROUP HASNAE TURNED UP! HE'S ABOOT YOUR SIZE!
MEANWHILE—
. . . SUCH AN OBLIGING MAN, MR BROWN, AND SURE TO SET A GOOD EXAMPLE TO THE YOUNGSTERS.
SLAM!
SURELY THAT'S NO' HIM BACK ALREADY!
A GOOD EXAMPLE? OH, NO!

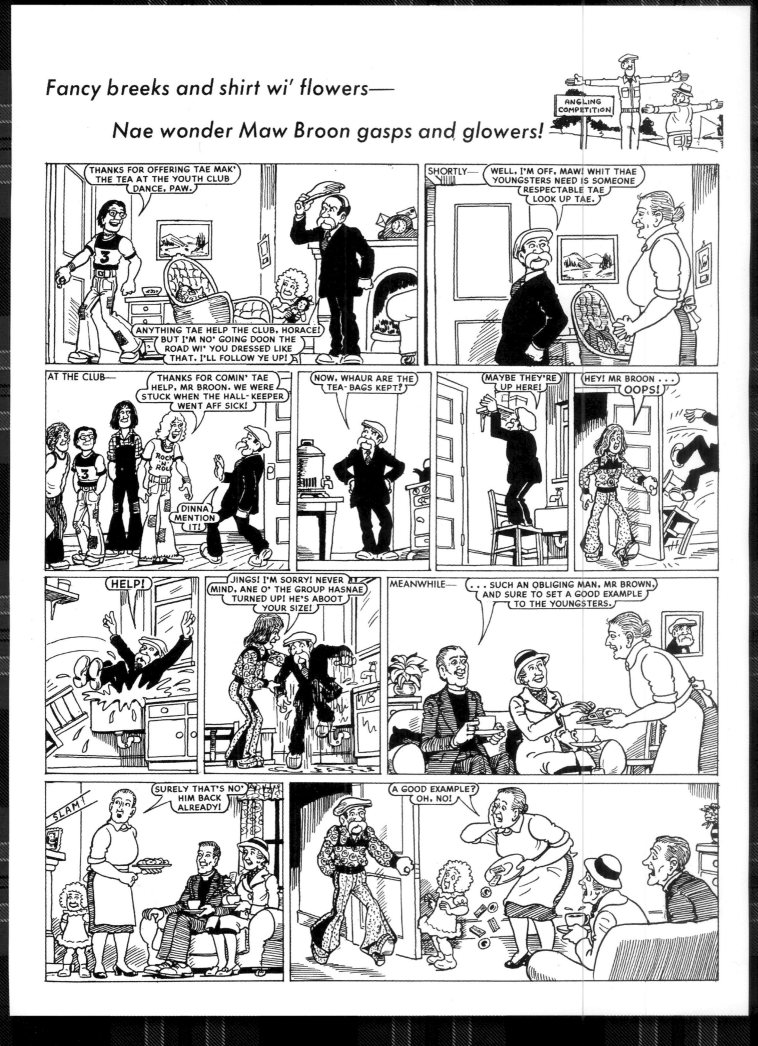

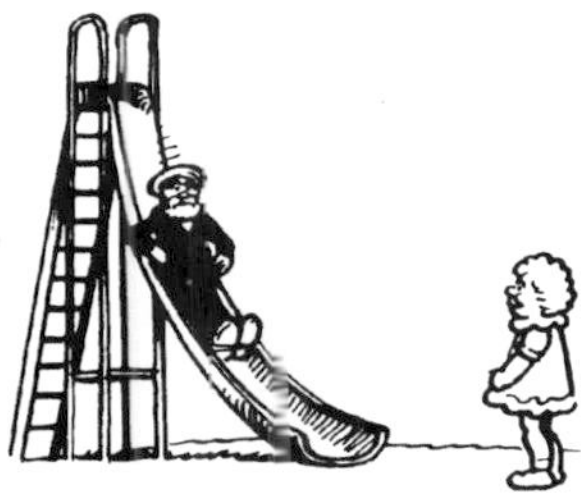

. . . but things were just as bad—

When this auld chap was a lad!

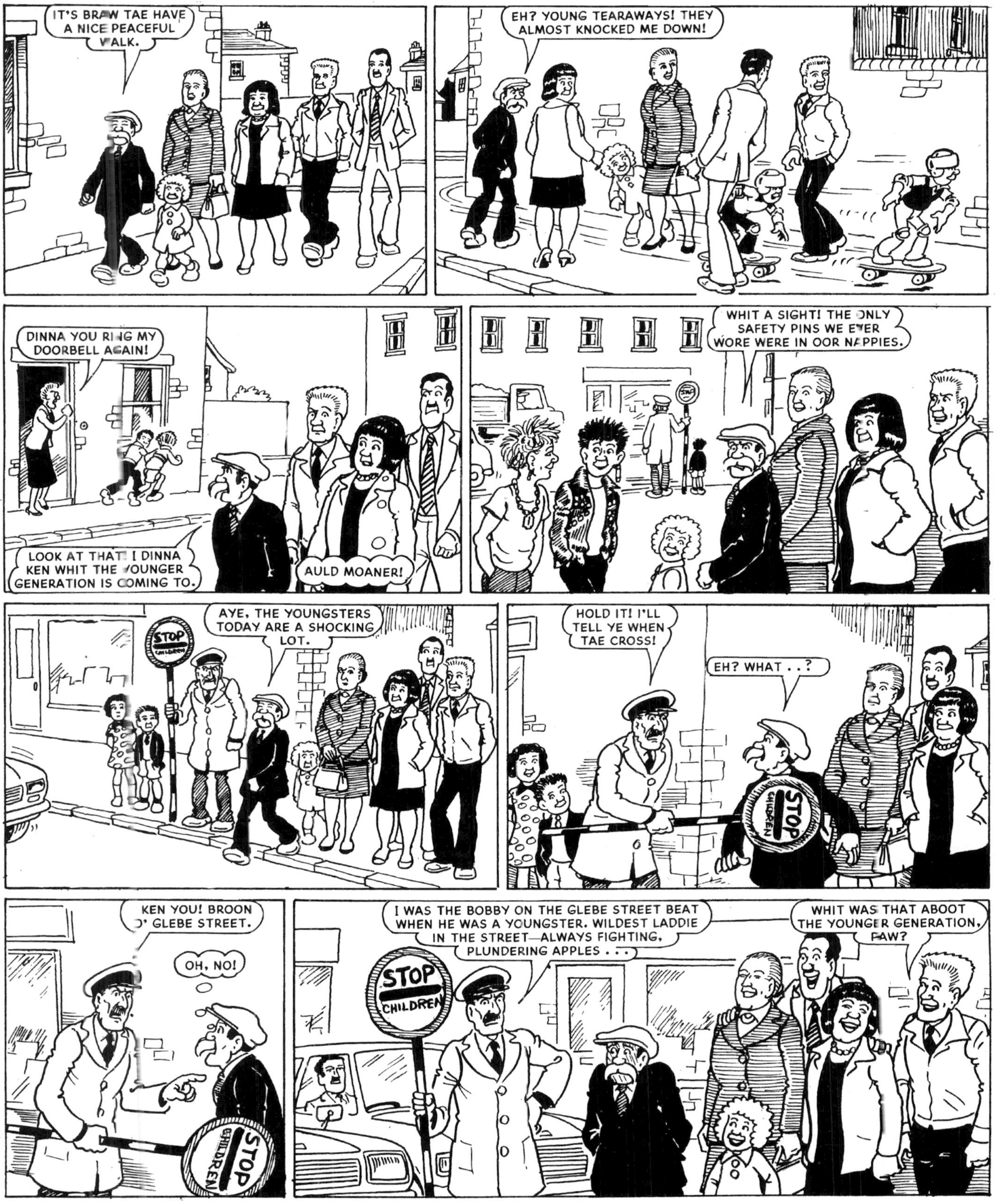

IT'S BRAW TAE HAVE A NICE PEACEFUL WALK.
EH? YOUNG TEARAWAYS! THEY ALMOST KNOCKED ME DOWN!
DINNA YOU RING MY DOORBELL AGAIN!
LOOK AT THAT! I DINNA KEN WHIT THE YOUNGER GENERATION IS COMING TO.
AULD MOANER!
WHIT A SIGHT! THE ONLY SAFETY PINS WE EVER WORE WERE IN OOR NAPPIES.
STOP CHILDREN
AYE, THE YOUNGSTERS TODAY ARE A SHOCKING LOT.
HOLD IT! I'LL TELL YE WHEN TAE CROSS!
EH? WHAT . . ?
STOP CHILDREN
KEN YOU! BROON O' GLEBE STREET.
OH, NO!
STOP CHILDREN
I WAS THE BOBBY ON THE GLEBE STREET BEAT WHEN HE WAS A YOUNGSTER. WILDEST LADDIE IN THE STREET—ALWAYS FIGHTING, PLUNDERING APPLES . . .
STOP CHILDREN
WHIT WAS THAT ABOOT THE YOUNGER GENERATION, PAW?

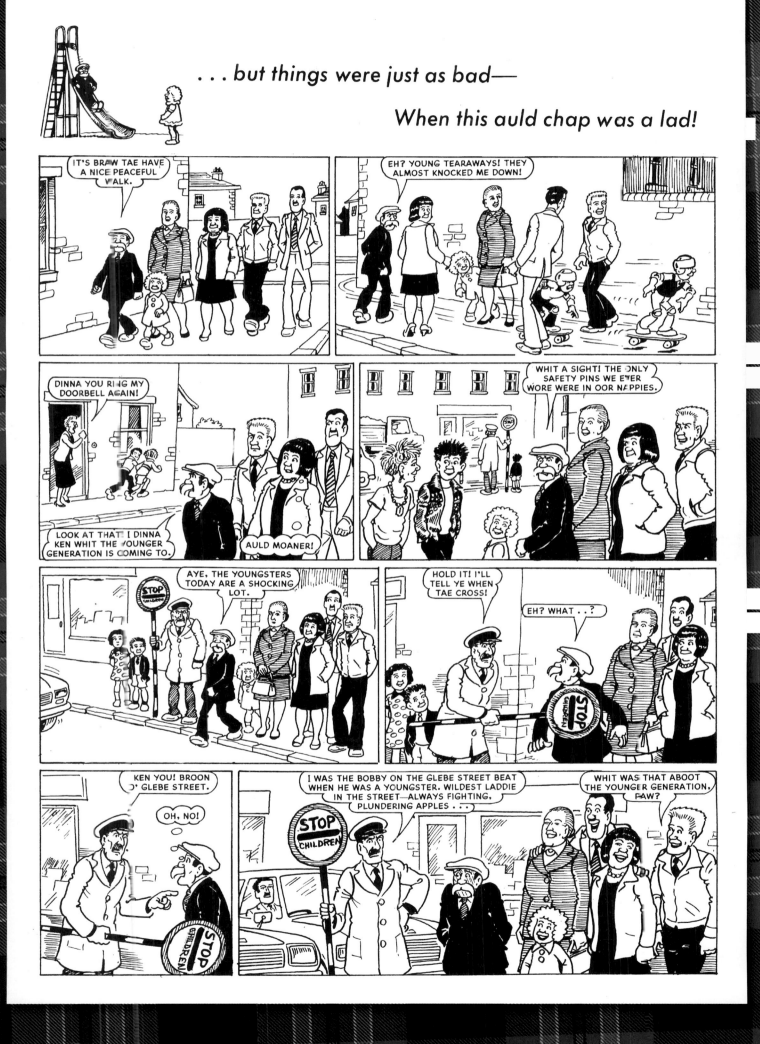

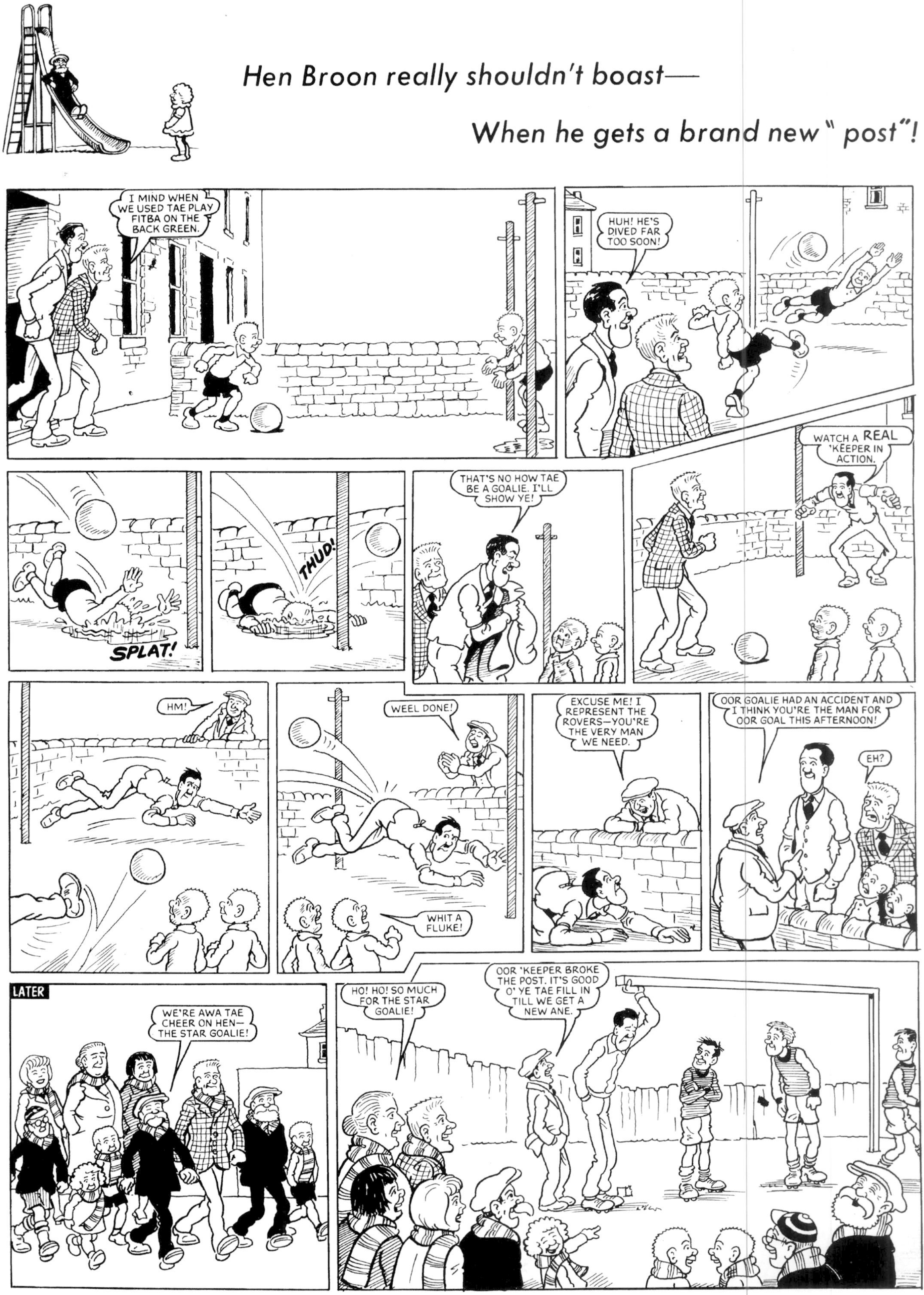
Hen Broon really shouldn't boast—
When he gets a brand new "post"!
I MIND WHEN WE USED TAE PLAY FITBA ON THE BACK GREEN.
HUH! HE'S DIVED FAR TOO SOON!
WATCH A REAL 'KEEPER IN ACTION.
SPLAT!
THUD!
THAT'S NO HOW TAE BE A GOALIE. I'LL SHOW YE!
HM!
WEEL DONE!
WHIT A FLUKE!
EXCUSE ME! I REPRESENT THE ROVERS—YOU'RE THE VERY MAN WE NEED.
OOR GOALIE HAD AN ACCIDENT AND I THINK YOU'RE THE MAN FOR OOR GOAL THIS AFTERNOON!
EH?
LATER
WE'RE AWA TAE CHEER ON HEN—THE STAR GOALIE!
HO! HO! SO MUCH FOR THE STAR GOALIE!
OOR 'KEEPER BROKE THE POST. IT'S GOOD O' YE TAE FILL IN TILL WE GET A NEW ANE.

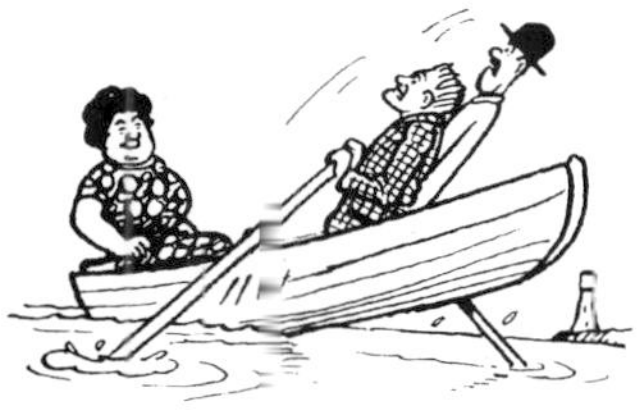

It's just no joke—

The day the brake broke!

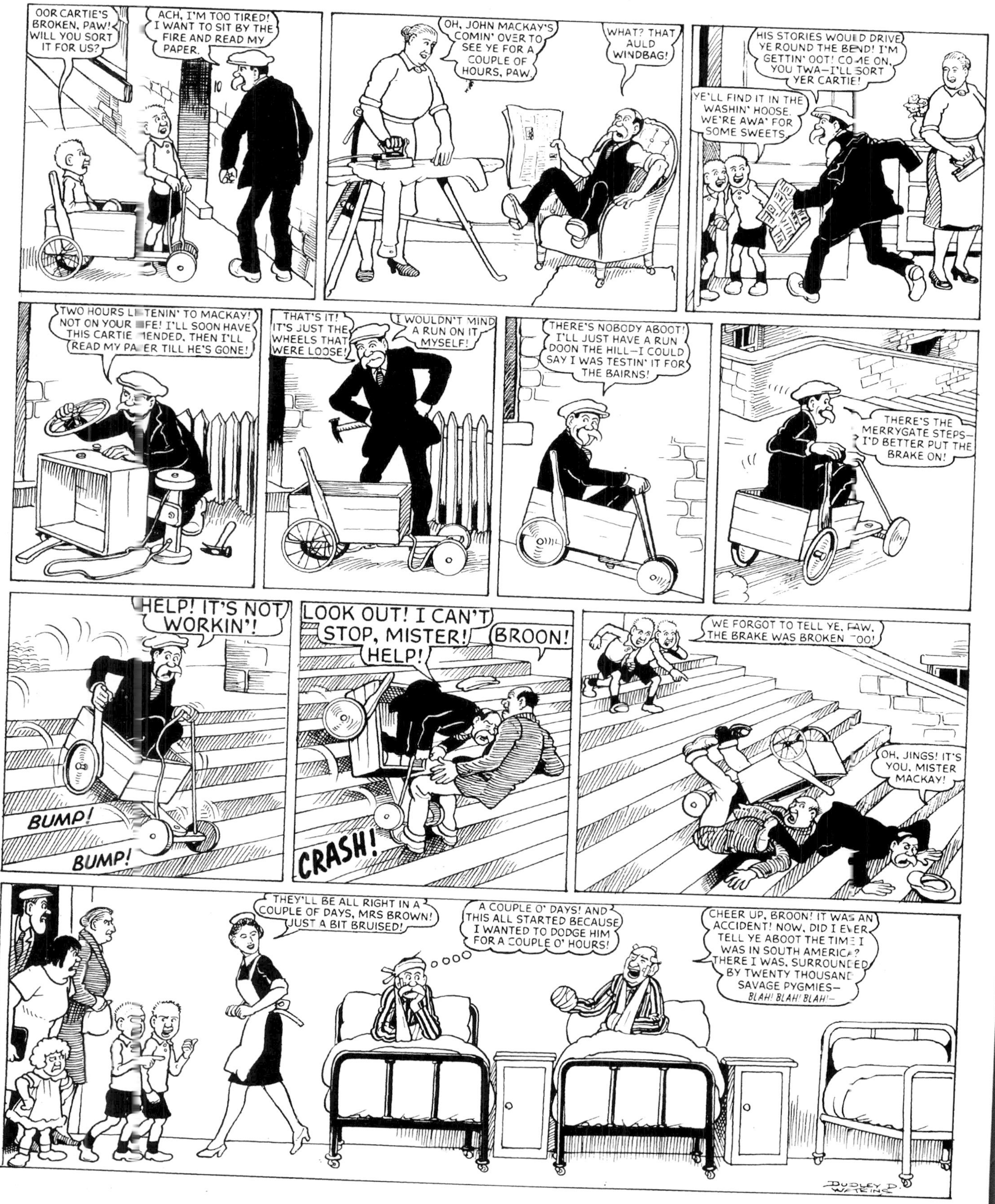

OOR CARTIE'S BROKEN, PAW! WILL YOU SORT IT FOR US?
ACH, I'M TOO TIRED! I WANT TO SIT BY THE FIRE AND READ MY PAPER.
10
OH, JOHN MACKAY'S COMIN' OVER TO SEE YE FOR A COUPLE OF HOURS, PAW.
WHAT? THAT AULD WINDBAG!
HIS STORIES WOULD DRIVE YE ROUND THE BEND! I'M GETTIN' OOT! COME ON, YOU TWA—I'LL SORT YER CARTIE!
YE'LL FIND IT IN THE WASHIN' HOOSE. WE'RE AWA' FOR SOME SWEETS.
TWO HOURS LISTENIN' TO MACKAY! NOT ON YOUR LIFE! I'LL SOON HAVE THIS CARTIE MENDED, THEN I'LL READ MY PAPER TILL HE'S GONE!
THAT'S IT! IT'S JUST THE WHEELS THAT WERE LOOSE!
I WOULDN'T MIND A RUN ON IT MYSELF!
THERE'S NOBODY ABOOT! I'LL JUST HAVE A RUN DOON THE HILL—I COULD SAY I WAS TESTIN' IT FOR THE BAIRNS!
THERE'S THE MERRYGATE STEPS—I'D BETTER PUT THE BRAKE ON!
HELP! IT'S NOT WORKIN'!
BUMP!
BUMP!
LOOK OUT! I CAN'T STOP, MISTER! HELP!
BROON!
CRASH!
WE FORGOT TO TELL YE, PAW. THE BRAKE WAS BROKEN TOO!
OH, JINGS! IT'S YOU, MISTER MACKAY!
THEY'LL BE ALL RIGHT IN A COUPLE OF DAYS, MRS BROWN! JUST A BIT BRUISED!
A COUPLE O' DAYS! AND THIS ALL STARTED BECAUSE I WANTED TO DODGE HIM FOR A COUPLE O' HOURS!
CHEER UP, BROON! IT WAS AN ACCIDENT! NOW, DID I EVER TELL YE ABOOT THE TIME I WAS IN SOUTH AMERICA? THERE I WAS, SURROUNDED BY TWENTY THOUSAND SAVAGE PYGMIES—
BLAH! BLAH! BLAH!—
DUDLEY D. WATKINS

The sad tale o' a pie—

And a big black eye!

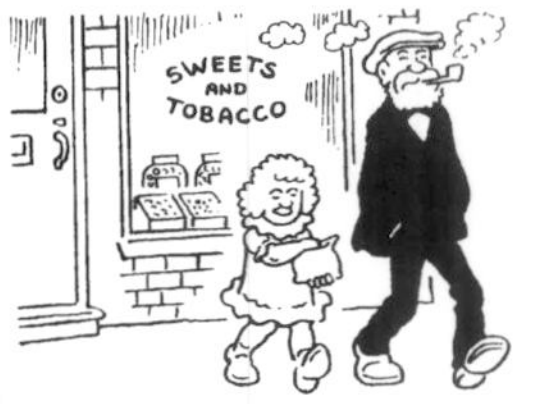
SWEETS AND TOBACCO

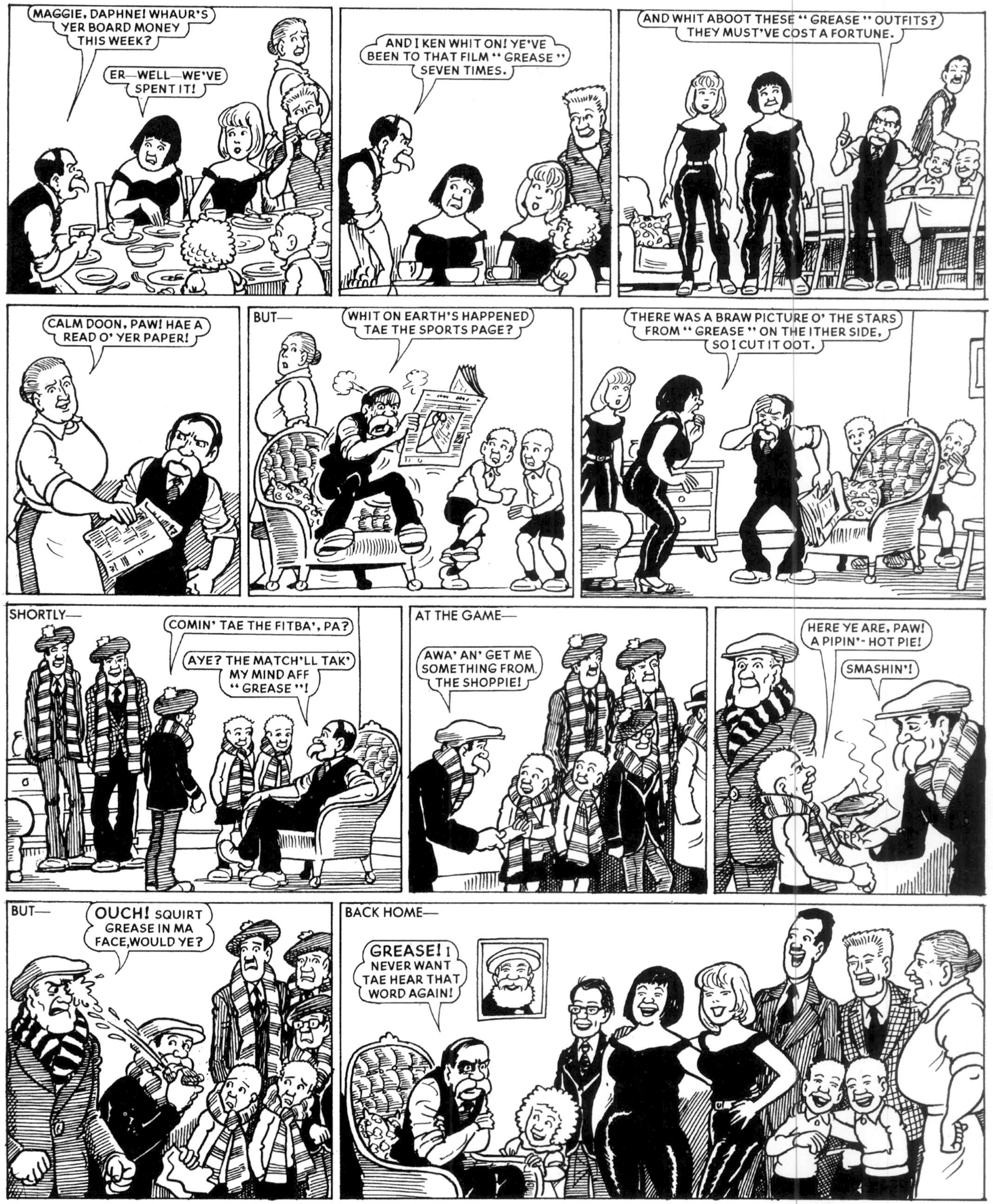
MAGGIE, DAPHNE! WHAUR'S YER BOARD MONEY THIS WEEK?
ER—WELL—WE'VE SPENT IT!
AND I KEN WHIT ON! YE'VE BEEN TO THAT FILM "GREASE" SEVEN TIMES.
AND WHIT ABOOT THESE "GREASE" OUTFITS? THEY MUST'VE COST A FORTUNE.
CALM DOON, PAW! HAE A READ O' YER PAPER!
BUT—
WHIT ON EARTH'S HAPPENED TAE THE SPORTS PAGE?
THERE WAS A BRAW PICTURE O' THE STARS FROM "GREASE" ON THE ITHER SIDE, SO I CUT IT OOT.
SHORTLY—
COMIN' TAE THE FITBA', PA?
AYE? THE MATCH'LL TAK' MY MIND AFF "GREASE"!
AT THE GAME—
AWA' AN' GET ME SOMETHING FROM THE SHOPPIE!
HERE YE ARE, PAW! A PIPIN'-HOT PIE!
SMASHIN'!
BUT—
OUCH! SQUIRT GREASE IN MA FACE, WOULD YE?
BACK HOME—
GREASE! I NEVER WANT TAE HEAR THAT WORD AGAIN!

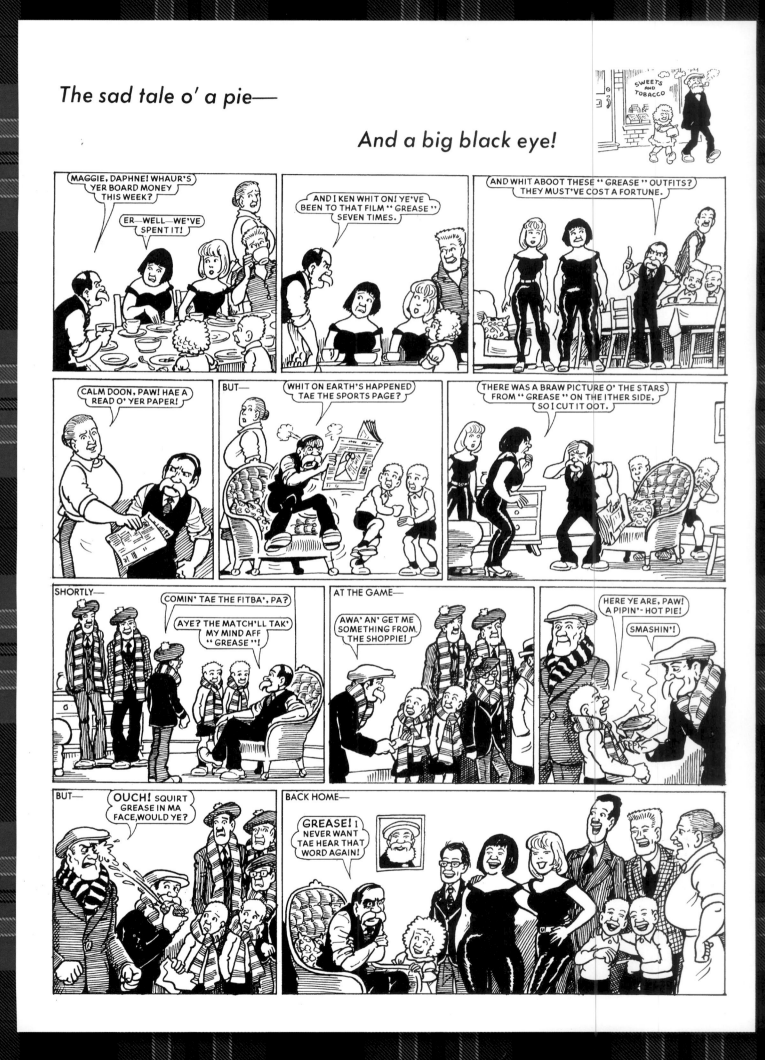

It's a very funny sight indeed—

When they go to work full speed!

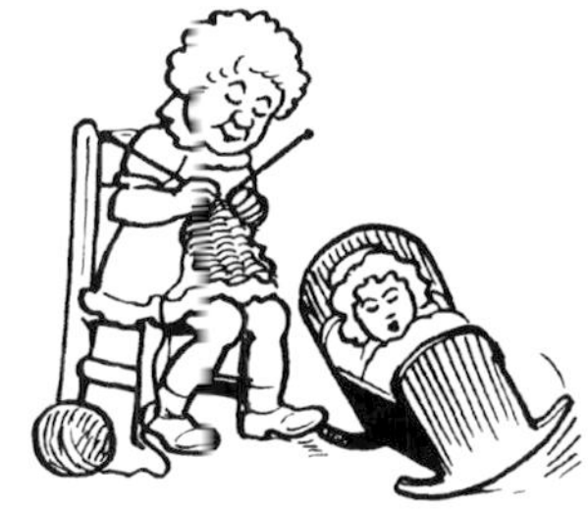

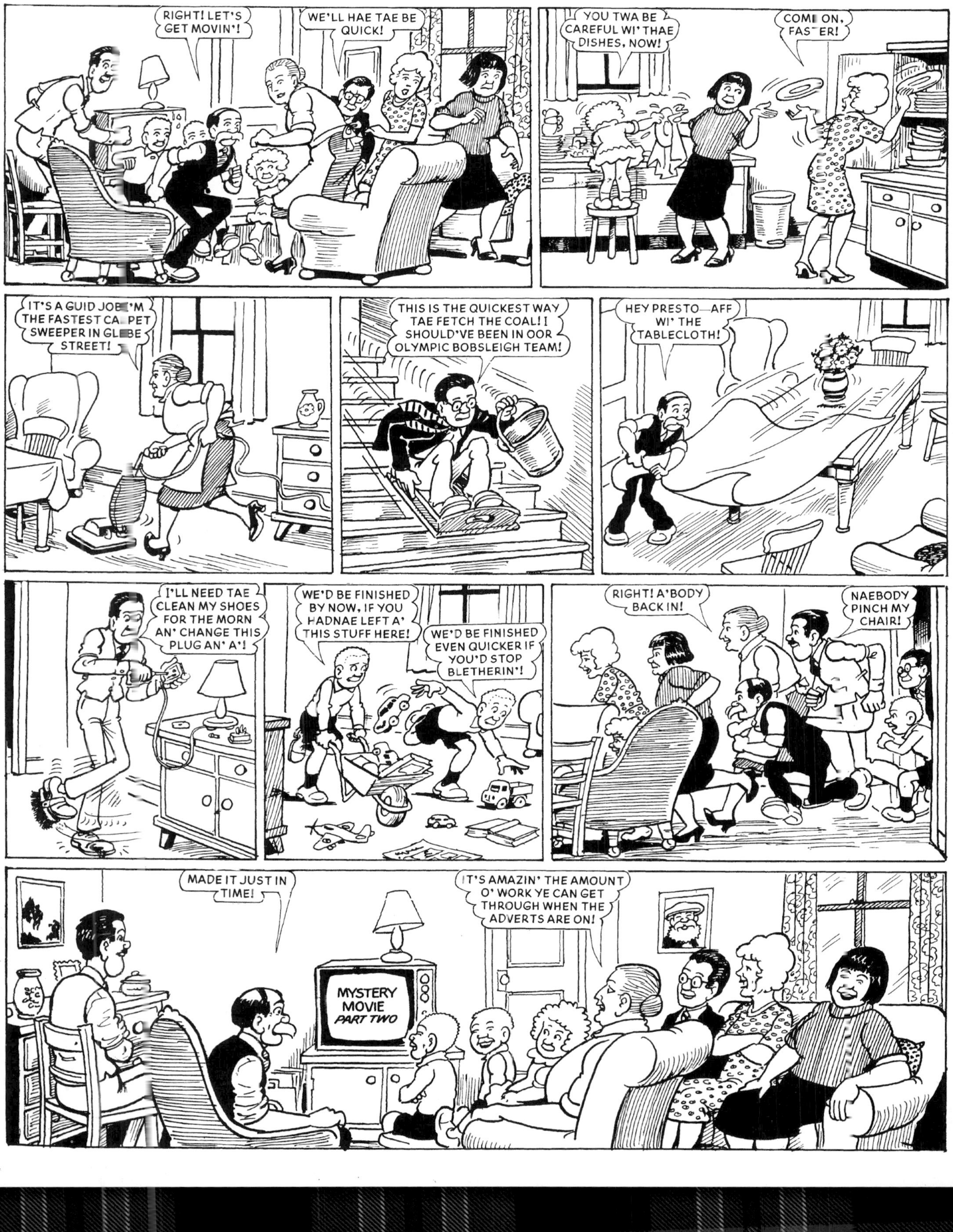
RIGHT! LET'S GET MOVIN'!
WE'LL HAE TAE BE QUICK!
YOU TWA BE CAREFUL WI' THAE DISHES, NOW!
COME ON, FASTER!
IT'S A GUID JOB I'M THE FASTEST CARPET SWEEPER IN GLEBE STREET!
THIS IS THE QUICKEST WAY TAE FETCH THE COAL! I SHOULD'VE BEEN IN OOR OLYMPIC BOBSLEIGH TEAM!
HEY PRESTO—AFF WI' THE TABLECLOTH!
I'LL NEED TAE CLEAN MY SHOES FOR THE MORN AN' CHANGE THIS PLUG AN' A'!
WE'D BE FINISHED BY NOW, IF YOU HADNAE LEFT A' THIS STUFF HERE!
WE'D BE FINISHED EVEN QUICKER IF YOU'D STOP BLETHERIN'!
RIGHT! A'BODY BACK IN!
NAEBODY PINCH MY CHAIR!
MADE IT JUST IN TIME!
IT'S AMAZIN' THE AMOUNT O' WORK YE CAN GET THROUGH WHEN THE ADVERTS ARE ON!
MYSTERY MOVIE PART TWO

There's many a " Hen "—

At No. 10!

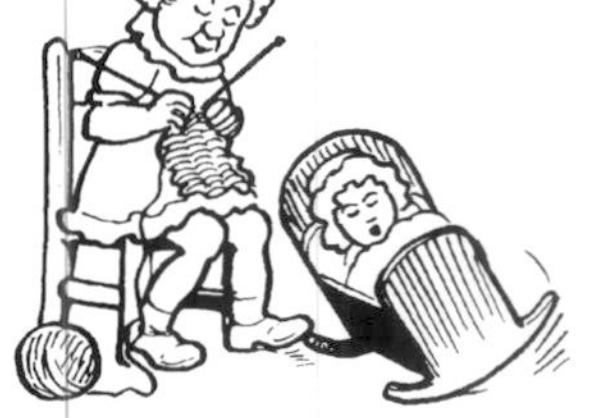

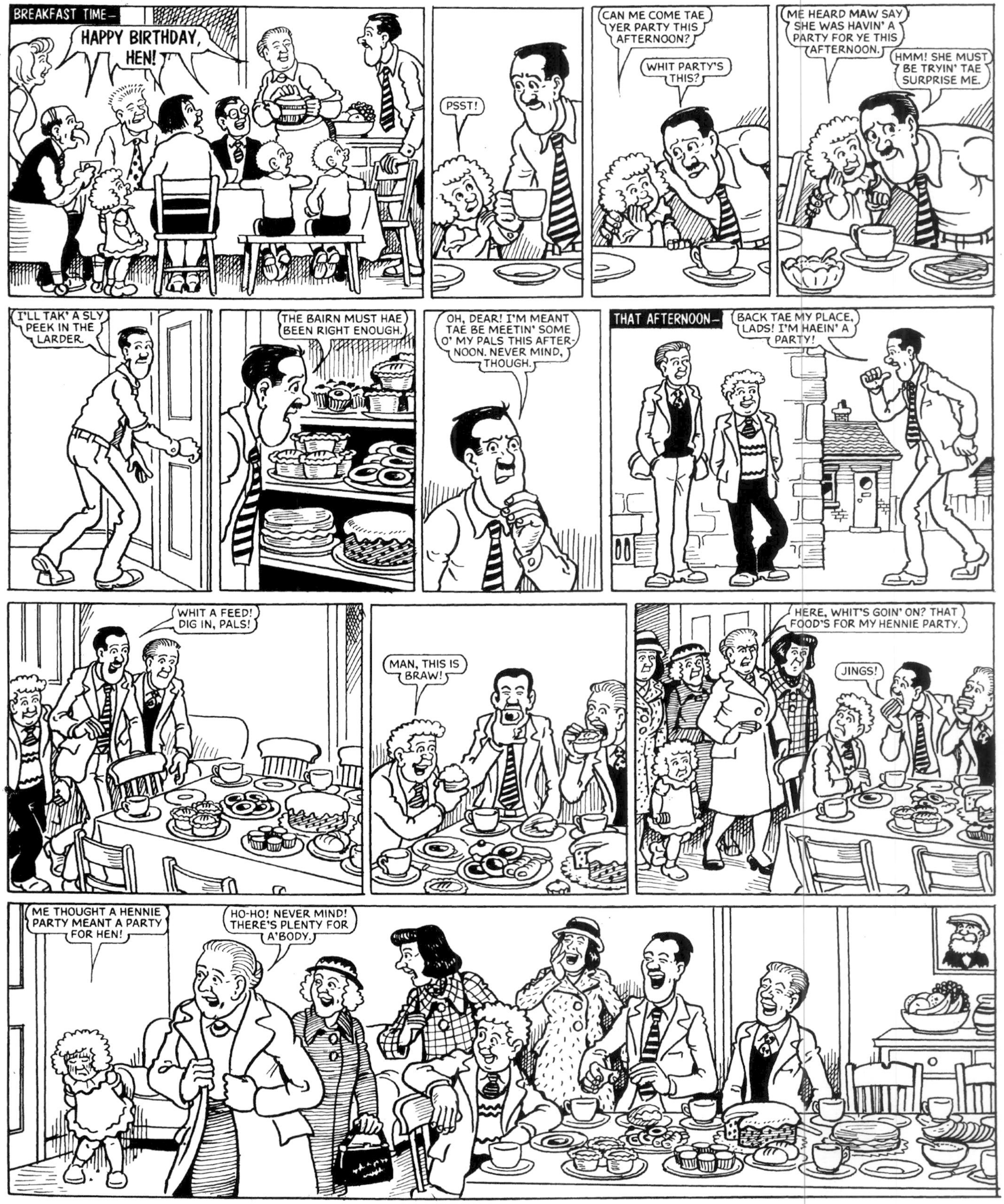

BREAKFAST TIME—
HAPPY BIRTHDAY, HEN!
PSST!
CAN ME COME TAE YER PARTY THIS AFTERNOON?
WHIT PARTY'S THIS?
ME HEARD MAW SAY SHE WAS HAVIN' A PARTY FOR YE THIS AFTERNOON.
HMM! SHE MUST BE TRYIN' TAE SURPRISE ME.
I'LL TAK' A SLY PEEK IN THE LARDER.
THE BAIRN MUST HAE BEEN RIGHT ENOUGH.
OH, DEAR! I'M MEANT TAE BE MEETIN' SOME O' MY PALS THIS AFTER-NOON. NEVER MIND, THOUGH.
THAT AFTERNOON—
BACK TAE MY PLACE, LADS! I'M HAEIN' A PARTY!
WHIT A FEED! DIG IN, PALS!
MAN, THIS IS BRAW!
HERE, WHIT'S GOIN' ON? THAT FOOD'S FOR MY HENNIE PARTY.
JINGS!
ME THOUGHT A HENNIE PARTY MEANT A PARTY FOR HEN!
HO-HO! NEVER MIND! THERE'S PLENTY FOR A'BODY.

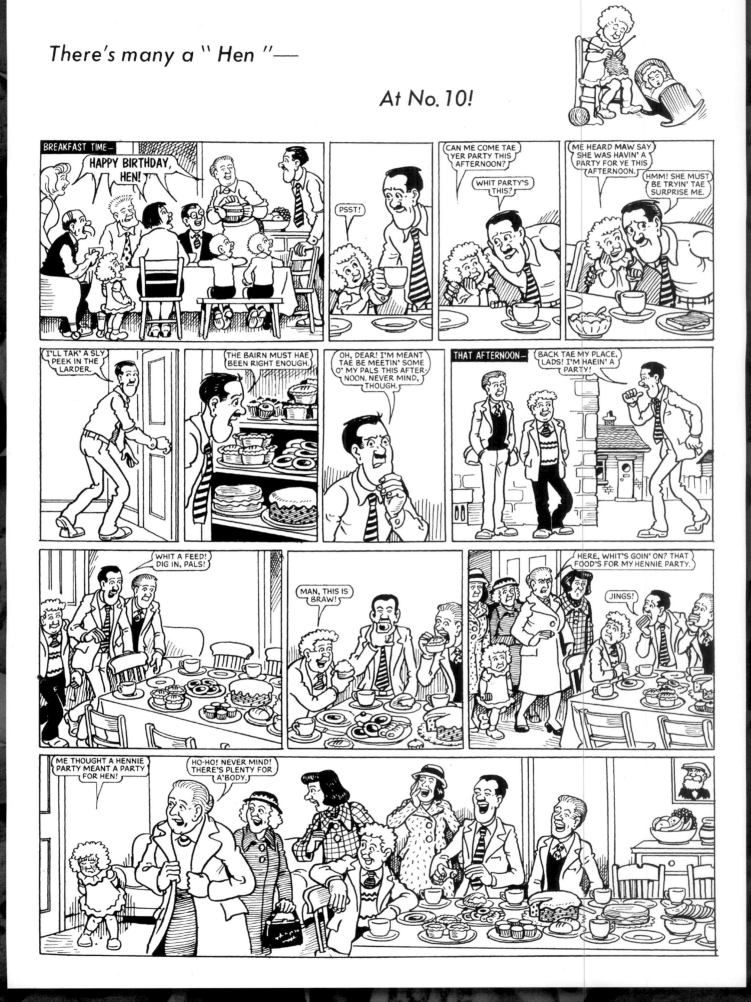

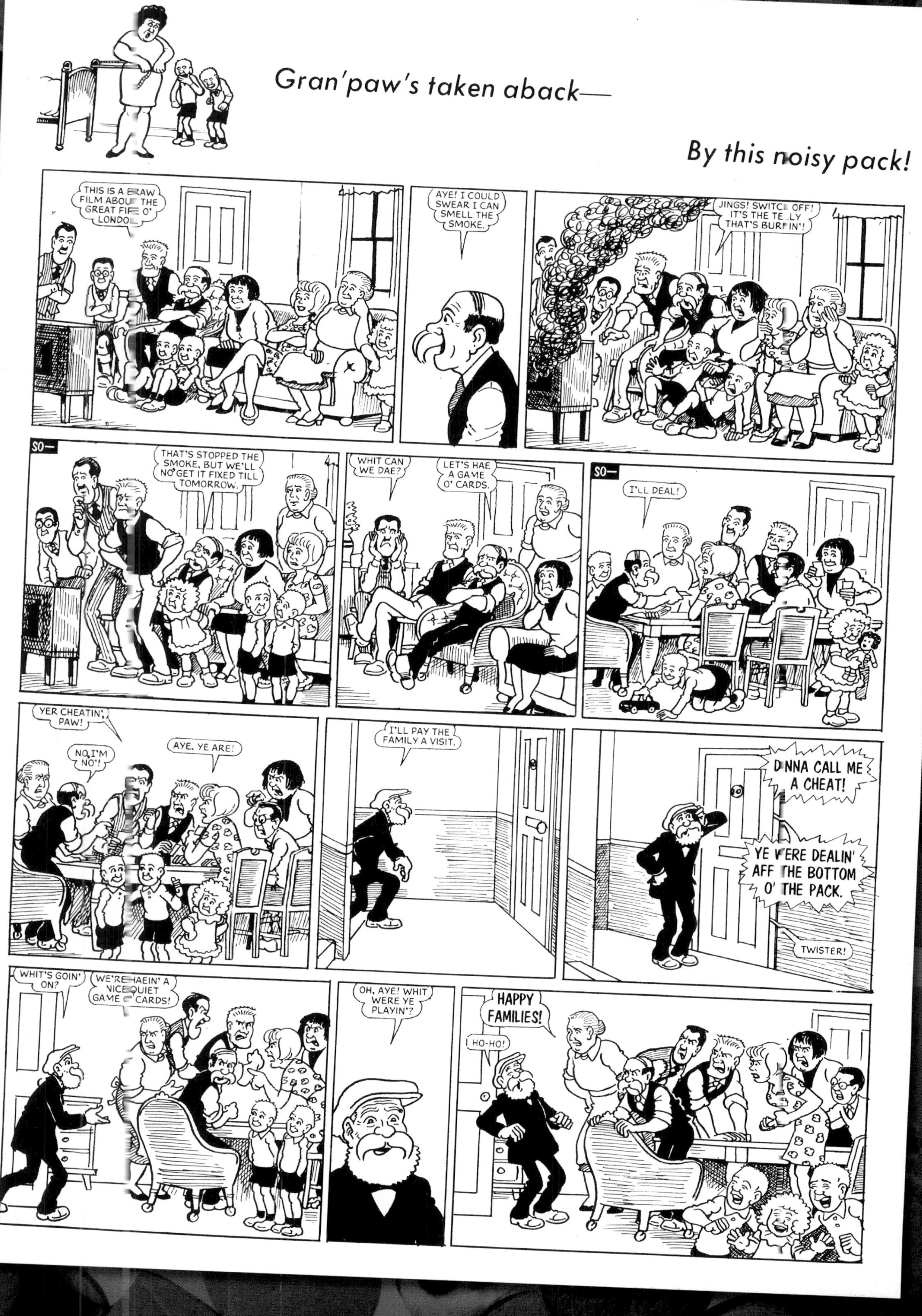
Gran'paw's taken aback—
By this noisy pack!
THIS IS A BRAW FILM ABOUT THE GREAT FIRE O' LONDON.
AYE! I COULD SWEAR I CAN SMELL THE SMOKE.
JINGS! SWITCH OFF! IT'S THE TELLY THAT'S BURNIN'!
SO—
THAT'S STOPPED THE SMOKE, BUT WE'LL NO' GET IT FIXED TILL TOMORROW.
WHIT CAN WE DAE?
LET'S HAE A GAME O' CARDS.
SO—
I'LL DEAL!
YER CHEATIN', PAW!
NO, I'M NO'!
AYE, YE ARE!
I'LL PAY THE FAMILY A VISIT.
DINNA CALL ME A CHEAT!
YE WERE DEALIN' AFF THE BOTTOM O' THE PACK.
TWISTER!
WHIT'S GOIN' ON?
WE'RE HAEIN' A NICE QUIET GAME O' CARDS!
OH, AYE! WHIT WERE YE PLAYIN'?
HAPPY FAMILIES!
HO-HO!

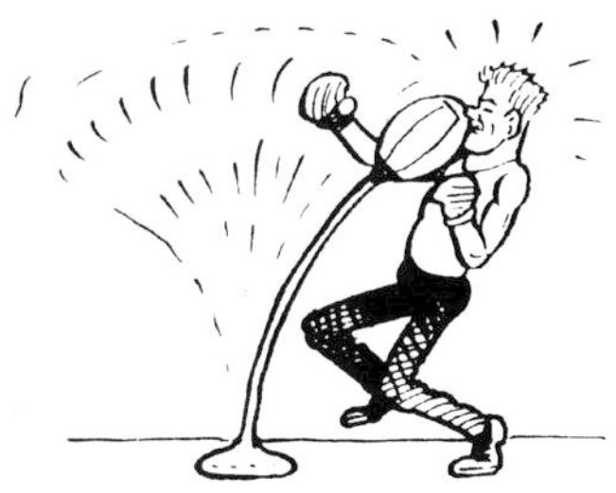

As a wrestler, Paw Broon's bad—

He's soon on the " deck", poor lad!

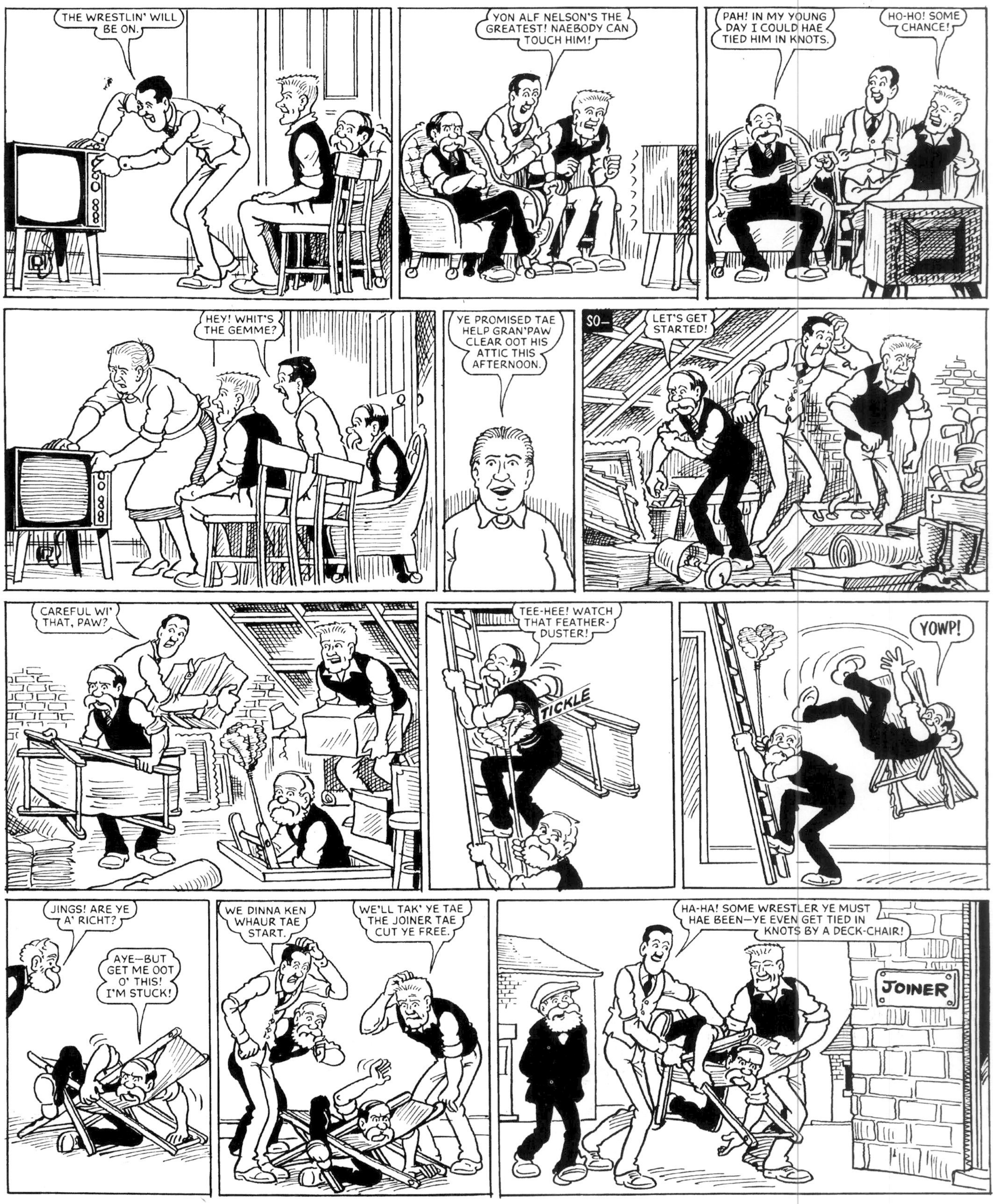
THE WRESTLIN' WILL BE ON.
YON ALF NELSON'S THE GREATEST! NAEBODY CAN TOUCH HIM!
PAH! IN MY YOUNG DAY I COULD HAE TIED HIM IN KNOTS.
HO-HO! SOME CHANCE!
HEY! WHIT'S THE GEMME?
YE PROMISED TAE HELP GRAN'PAW CLEAR OOT HIS ATTIC THIS AFTERNOON.
SO—
LET'S GET STARTED!
CAREFUL WI' THAT, PAW?
TEE-HEE! WATCH THAT FEATHER-DUSTER!
TICKLE
YOWP!
JINGS! ARE YE A' RICHT?
AYE—BUT GET ME OOT O' THIS! I'M STUCK!
WE DINNA KEN WHAUR TAE START.
WE'LL TAK' YE TAE THE JOINER TAE CUT YE FREE.
HA-HA! SOME WRESTLER YE MUST HAE BEEN—YE EVEN GET TIED IN KNOTS BY A DECK-CHAIR!
JOINER

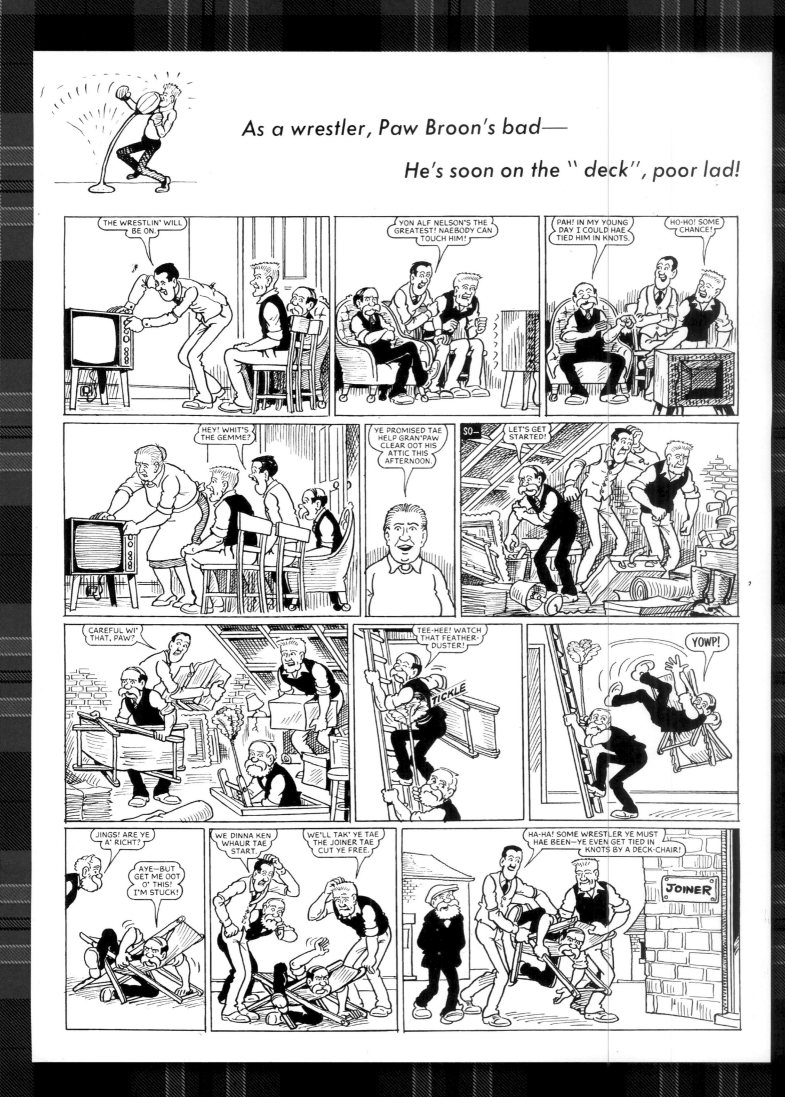

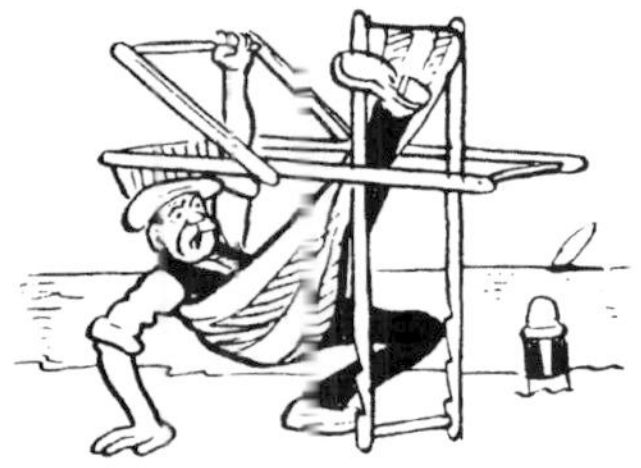

You'll get a hoot—

At Joe's "new" suit!

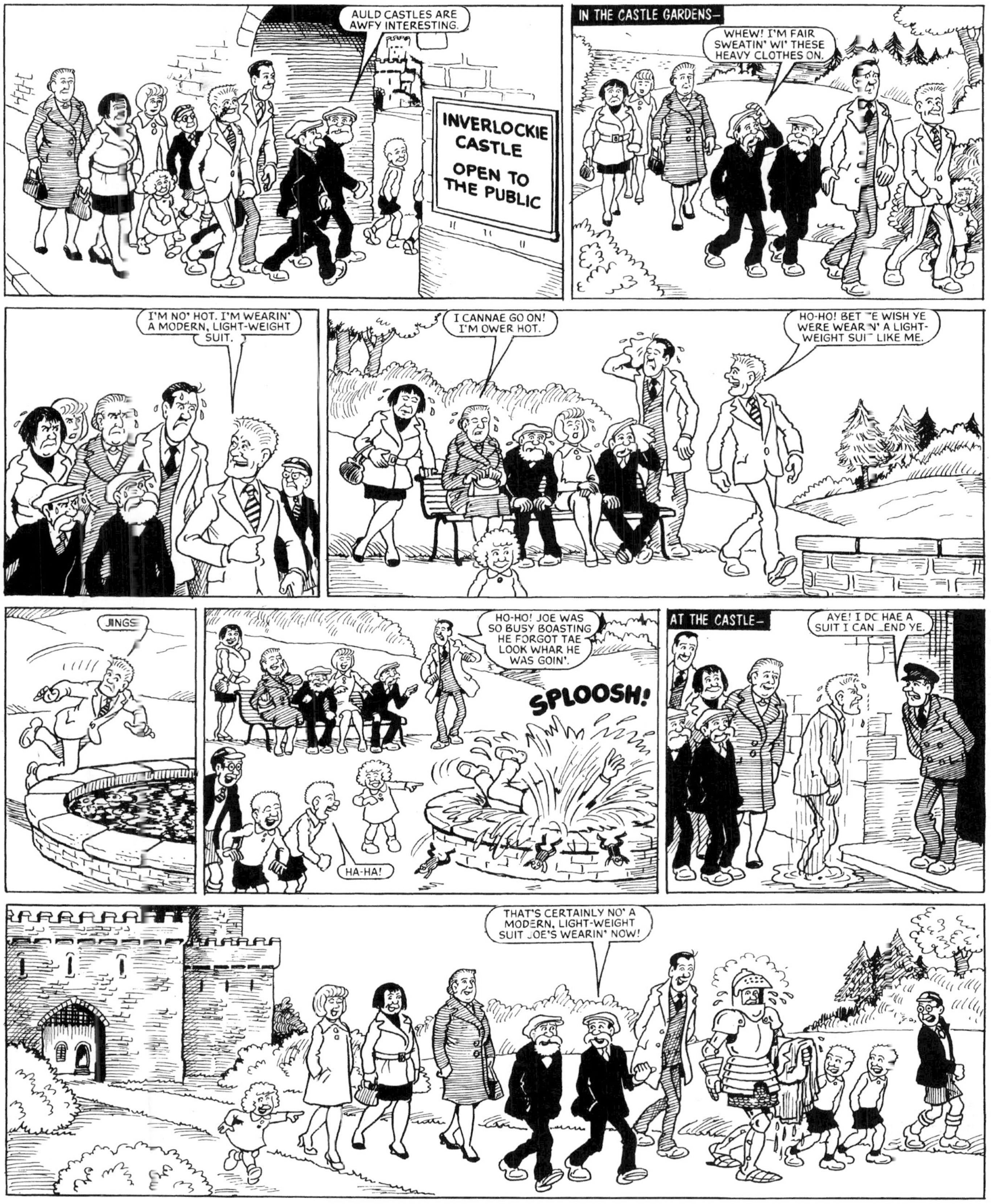

AULD CASTLES ARE AWFY INTERESTING.
INVERLOCKIE CASTLE OPEN TO THE PUBLIC
IN THE CASTLE GARDENS—
WHEW! I'M FAIR SWEATIN' WI' THESE HEAVY CLOTHES ON.
I'M NO' HOT. I'M WEARIN' A MODERN, LIGHT-WEIGHT SUIT.
I CANNAE GO ON! I'M OWER HOT.
HO-HO! BET YE WISH YE WERE WEARIN' A LIGHT-WEIGHT SUIT LIKE ME.
JINGS!
HO-HO! JOE WAS SO BUSY BOASTING HE FORGOT TAE LOOK WHAR HE WAS GOIN'.
SPLOOSH!
HA-HA!
AT THE CASTLE—
AYE! I DO HAE A SUIT I CAN LEND YE.
THAT'S CERTAINLY NO' A MODERN, LIGHT-WEIGHT SUIT JOE'S WEARIN' NOW!

Just for Maw's sake—

The Broons take a break!

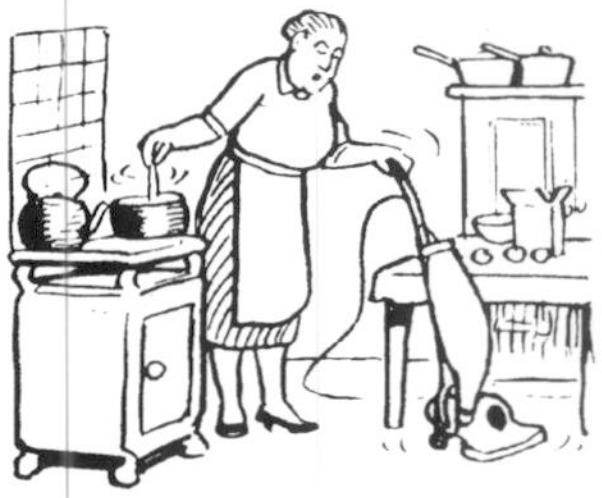

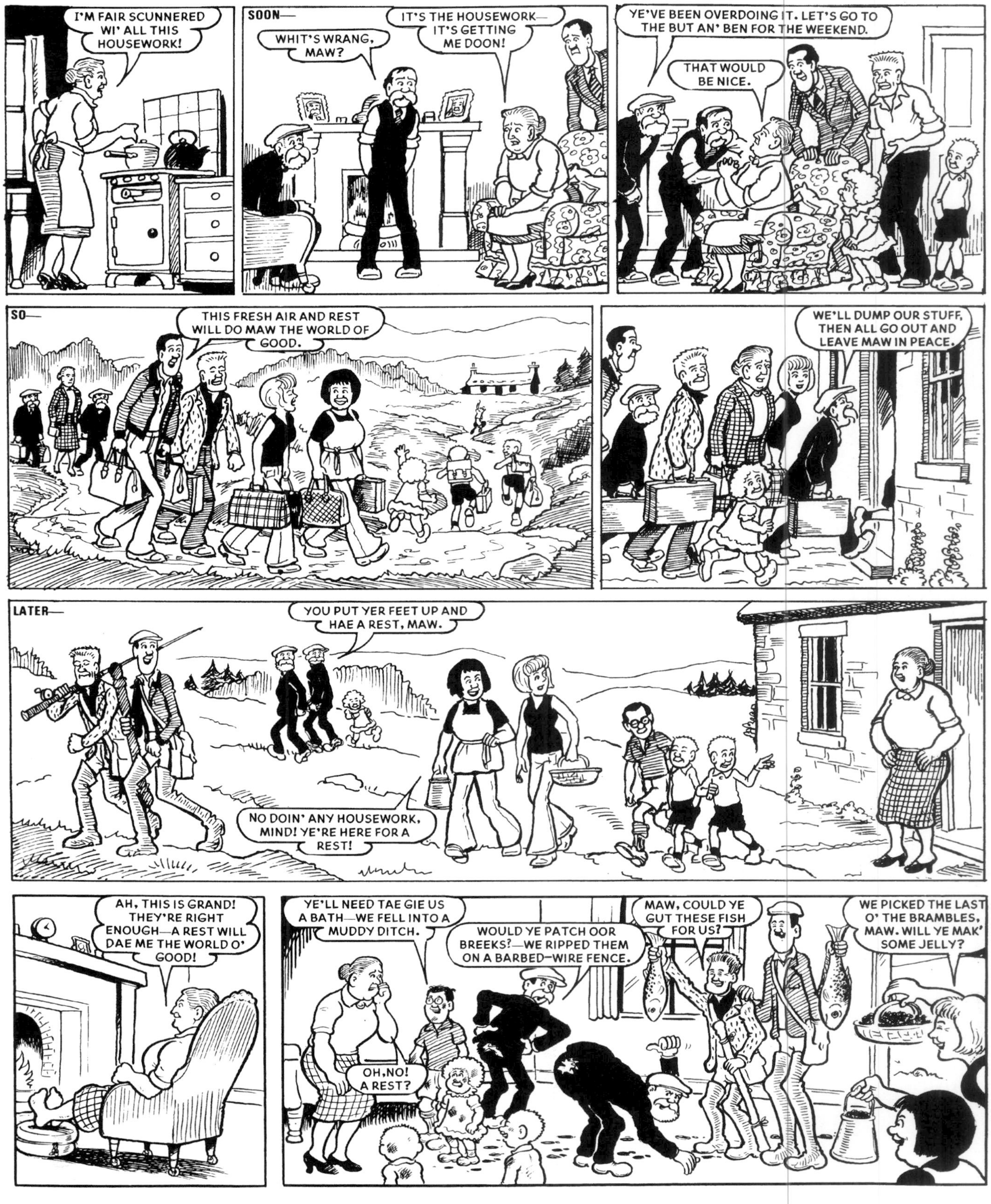
I'M FAIR SCUNNERED WI' ALL THIS HOUSEWORK!
SOON—
WHIT'S WRANG, MAW?
IT'S THE HOUSEWORK—IT'S GETTING ME DOON!
YE'VE BEEN OVERDOING IT. LET'S GO TO THE BUT AN' BEN FOR THE WEEKEND.
THAT WOULD BE NICE.
SO—
THIS FRESH AIR AND REST WILL DO MAW THE WORLD OF GOOD.
WE'LL DUMP OUR STUFF, THEN ALL GO OUT AND LEAVE MAW IN PEACE.
LATER—
YOU PUT YER FEET UP AND HAE A REST, MAW.
NO DOIN' ANY HOUSEWORK, MIND! YE'RE HERE FOR A REST!
AH, THIS IS GRAND! THEY'RE RIGHT ENOUGH—A REST WILL DAE ME THE WORLD O' GOOD!
YE'LL NEED TAE GIE US A BATH—WE FELL INTO A MUDDY DITCH.
WOULD YE PATCH OOR BREEKS?—WE RIPPED THEM ON A BARBED–WIRE FENCE.
MAW, COULD YE GUT THESE FISH FOR US?
WE PICKED THE LAST O' THE BRAMBLES, MAW. WILL YE MAK' SOME JELLY?
OH, NO! A REST?

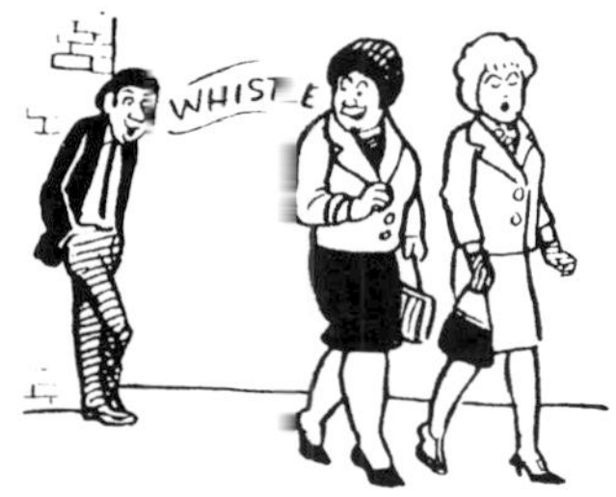

Gran'paw's up tae tricks, but then—

There's another " big bairn " at No. 10!

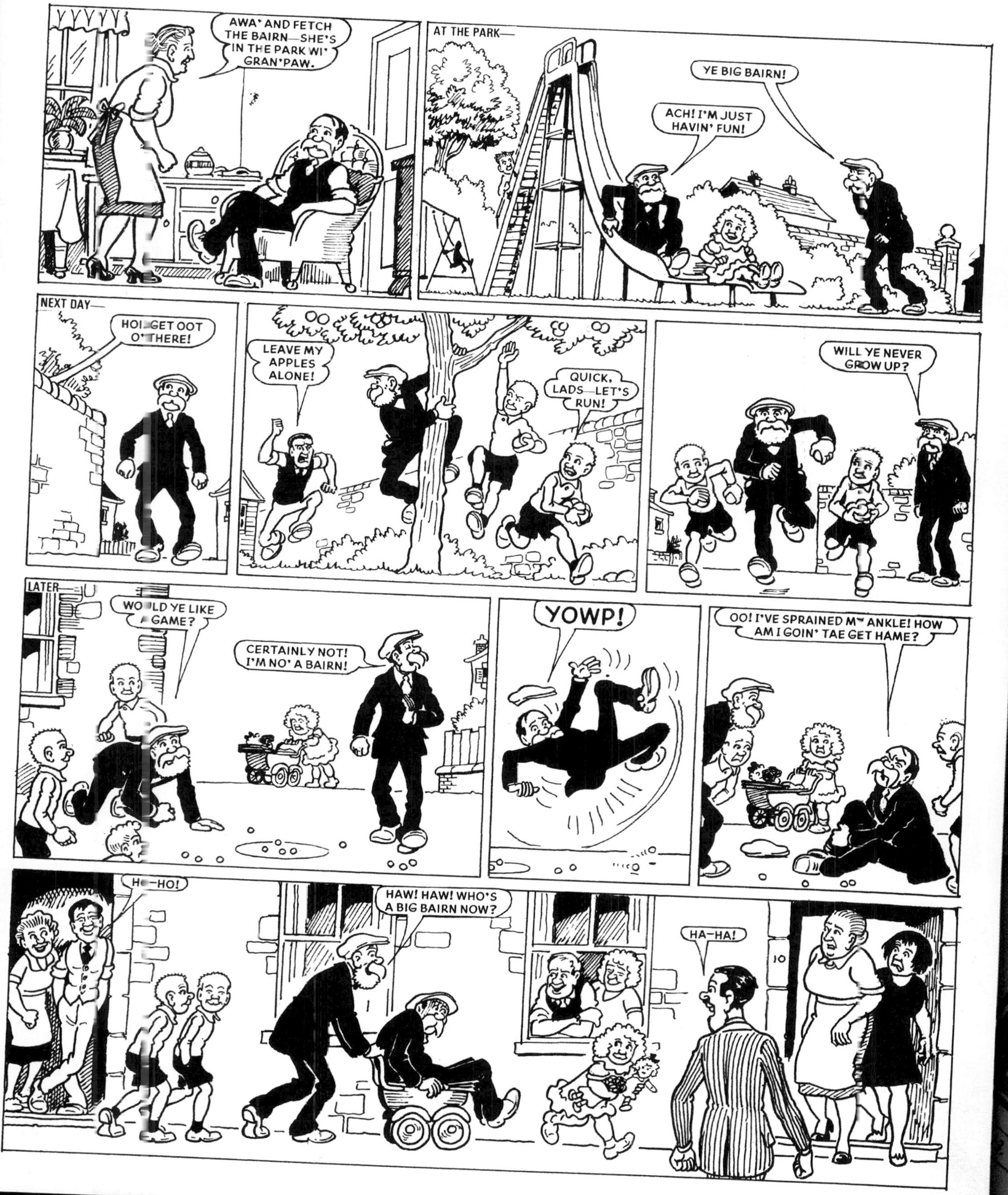
AWA' AND FETCH THE BAIRN—SHE'S IN THE PARK WI' GRAN'PAW.
AT THE PARK—
YE BIG BAIRN!
ACH! I'M JUST HAVIN' FUN!
NEXT DAY—
HOI! GET OOT O' THERE!
LEAVE MY APPLES ALONE!
QUICK, LADS—LET'S RUN!
WILL YE NEVER GROW UP?
LATER—
WOULD YE LIKE A GAME?
CERTAINLY NOT! I'M NO' A BAIRN!
YOWP!
OO! I'VE SPRAINED MY ANKLE! HOW AM I GOIN' TAE GET HAME?
HO-HO!
HAW! HAW! WHO'S A BIG BAIRN NOW?
HA-HA!
10

Wullie, Bob, Soapy and Primrose had an amazing array of comics to choose from in the 70s.

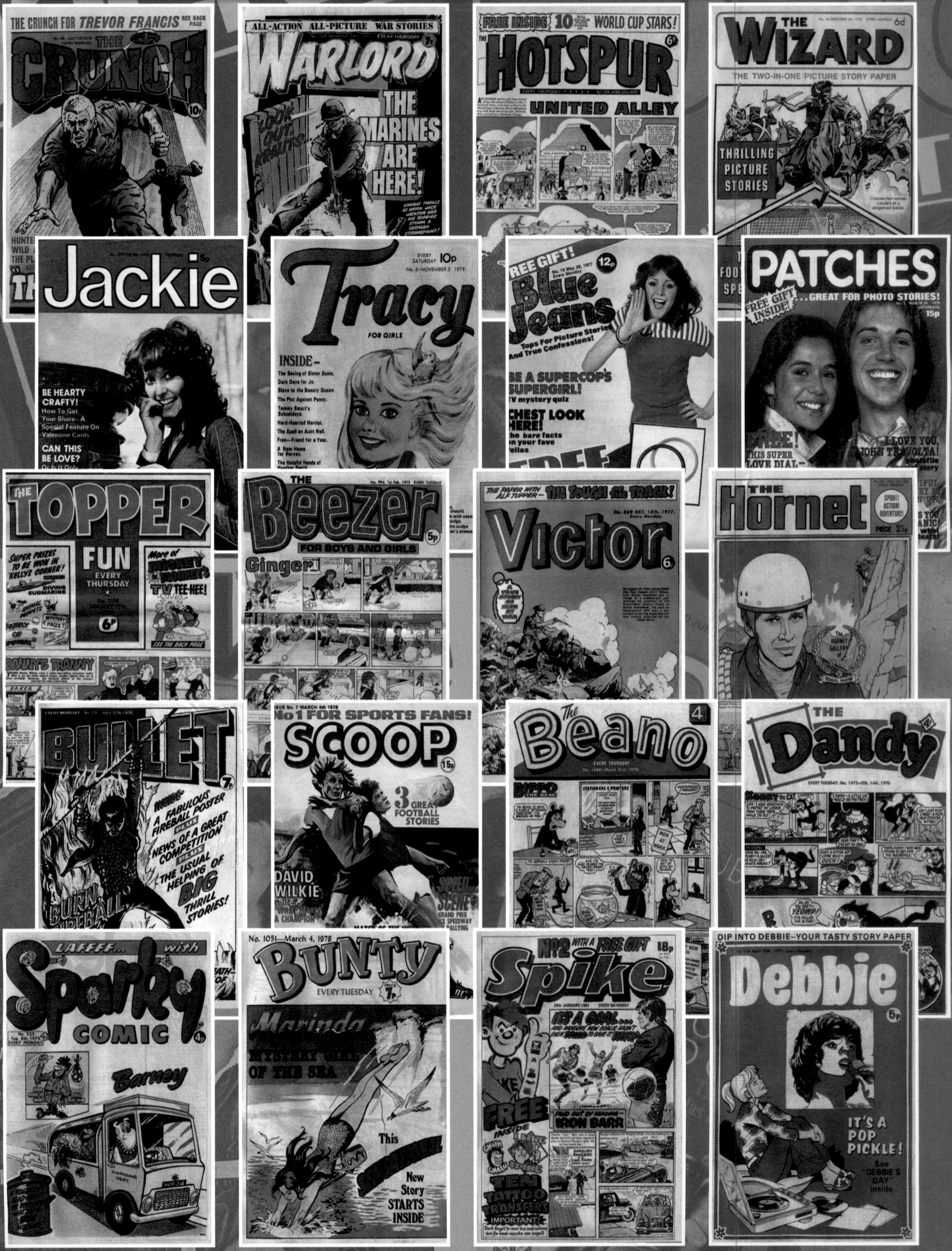
THE CRUNCH FOR TREVOR FRANCIS
THE CRUNCH
ALL-ACTION ALL-PICTURE WAR STORIES
WARLORD
THE MARINES ARE HERE!
FREE INSIDE 10 WORLD CUP STARS!
THE HOTSPUR
UNITED ALLEY
THE WIZARD
THE TWO-IN-ONE PICTURE STORY PAPER
THRILLING PICTURE STORIES
Jackie
BE HEARTY CRAFTY!
CAN THIS BE LOVE?
Tracy
FOR GIRLS
FREE GIFT!
Blue Jeans
BE A SUPERCOP'S SUPERGIRL!
CHEST LOOK HERE!
PATCHES
...GREAT FOR PHOTO STORIES!
I LOVE YOU, JOHN TRAVOLTA!
THE TOPPER
FUN EVERY THURSDAY
TV TEE-HEE!
THE Beezer
FOR BOYS AND GIRLS
Ginger
THE PAPER WITH ALF TUPPER - THE TOUGH OF THE TRACK!
Victor
THE Hornet
BULLET
SCOOP
No1 FOR SPORTS FANS!
3 GREAT FOOTBALL STORIES
DAVID WILKIE
The Beano
The Dandy
LAFFFF... with Sparky COMIC
Barney
No. 1051—March 4, 1978
BUNTY
EVERY TUESDAY
Marinda
MYSTERY GIRL OF THE SEA
New Story STARTS INSIDE
No2 WITH A FREE GIFT
Spike
IRON BARR
DIP INTO DEBBIE—YOUR TASTY STORY PAPER
Debbie
IT'S A POP PICKLE!

OOR WULLIE®

Oor Wullie and his pals enjoyed lively times in the 70s

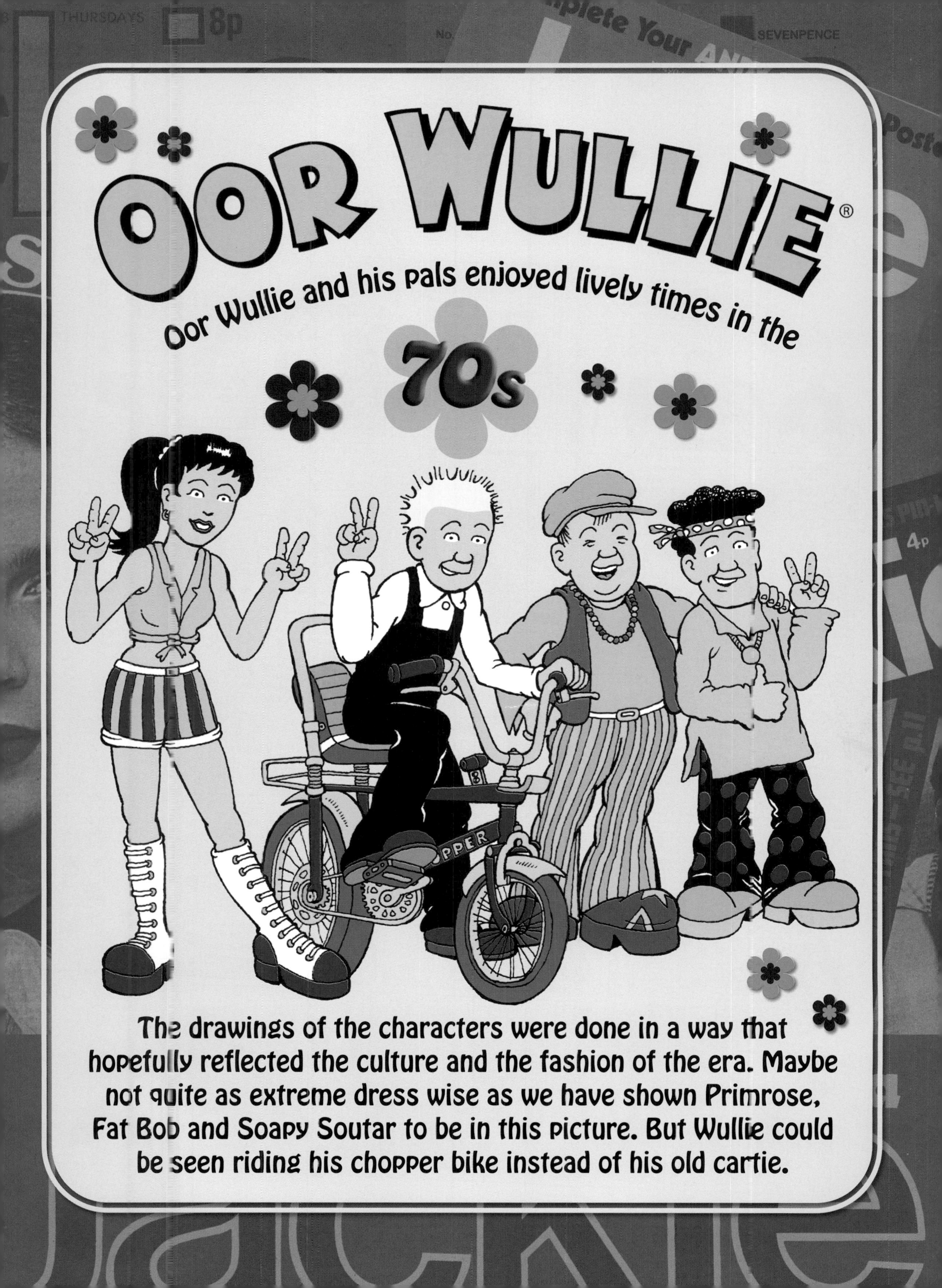

PPER

The drawings of the characters were done in a way that hopefully reflected the culture and the fashion of the era. Maybe not quite as extreme dress wise as we have shown Primrose, Fat Bob and Soapy Soutar to be in this picture. But Wullie could be seen riding his chopper bike instead of his old cartie.

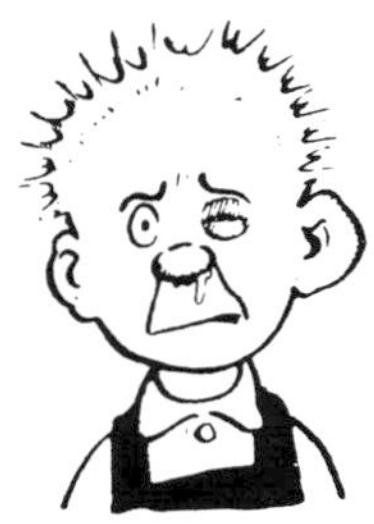

Poor Oor Wullie comes off worst—

When the lads' new ba' is burst!

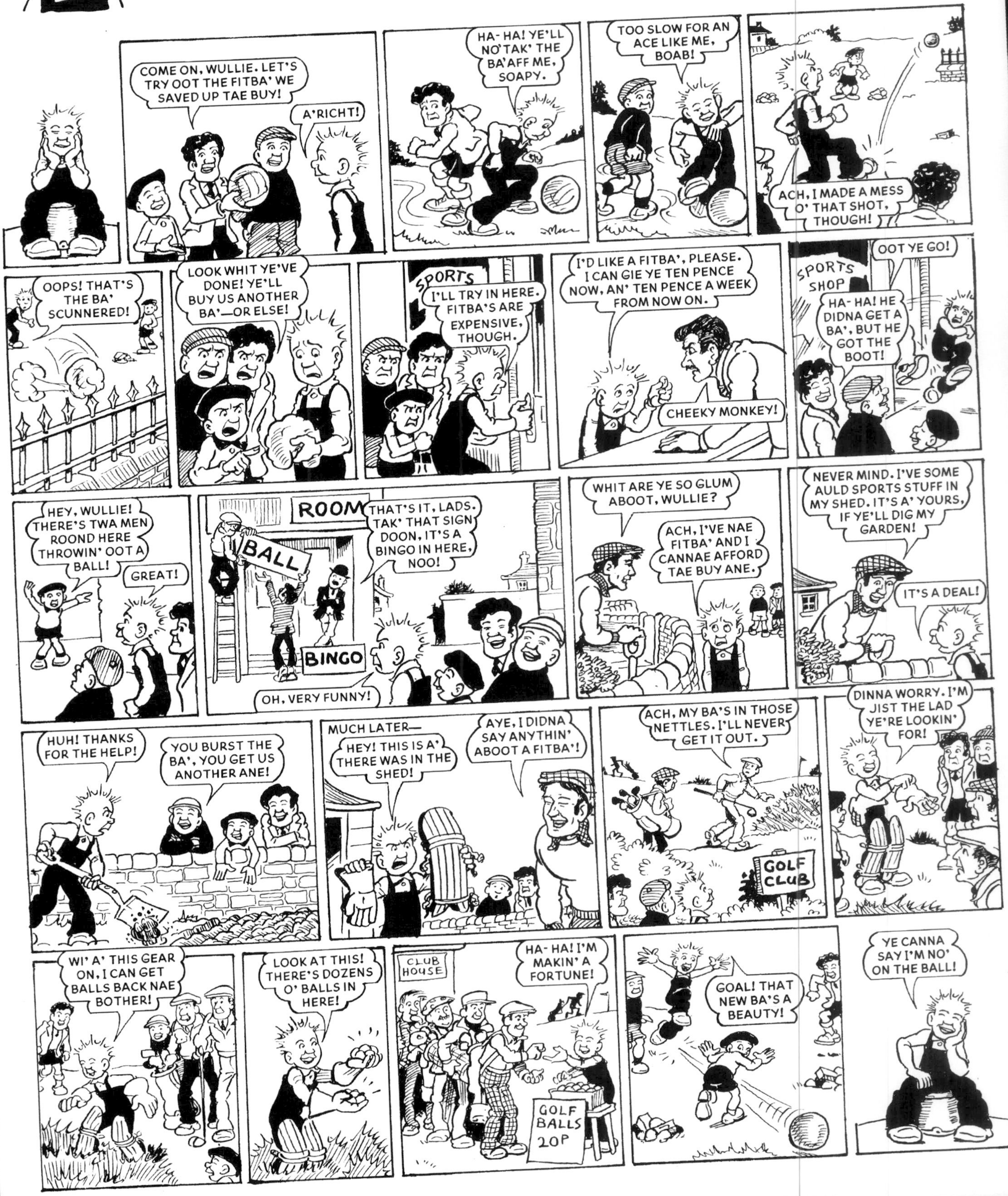

COME ON, WULLIE. LET'S TRY OOT THE FITBA' WE SAVED UP TAE BUY!
A'RICHT!
HA-HA! YE'LL NO'TAK' THE BA' AFF ME, SOAPY.
TOO SLOW FOR AN ACE LIKE ME, BOAB!
ACH, I MADE A MESS O' THAT SHOT, THOUGH!
OOPS! THAT'S THE BA' SCUNNERED!
LOOK WHIT YE'VE DONE! YE'LL BUY US ANOTHER BA'—OR ELSE!
SPORTS
I'LL TRY IN HERE. FITBA'S ARE EXPENSIVE, THOUGH.
I'D LIKE A FITBA', PLEASE. I CAN GIE YE TEN PENCE NOW, AN' TEN PENCE A WEEK FROM NOW ON.
CHEEKY MONKEY!
SPORTS SHOP
OOT YE GO!
HA-HA! HE DIDNA GET A BA', BUT HE GOT THE BOOT!
HEY, WULLIE! THERE'S TWA MEN ROOND HERE THROWIN' OOT A BALL!
GREAT!
ROOM
BALL
THAT'S IT, LADS. TAK' THAT SIGN DOON, IT'S A BINGO IN HERE, NOO!
BINGO
OH, VERY FUNNY!
WHIT ARE YE SO GLUM ABOOT, WULLIE?
ACH, I'VE NAE FITBA' AND I CANNAE AFFORD TAE BUY ANE.
NEVER MIND. I'VE SOME AULD SPORTS STUFF IN MY SHED. IT'S A' YOURS, IF YE'LL DIG MY GARDEN!
IT'S A DEAL!
HUH! THANKS FOR THE HELP!
YOU BURST THE BA', YOU GET US ANOTHER ANE!
MUCH LATER—
HEY! THIS IS A' THERE WAS IN THE SHED!
AYE, I DIDNA SAY ANYTHIN' ABOOT A FITBA'!
ACH, MY BA'S IN THOSE NETTLES. I'LL NEVER GET IT OUT.
GOLF CLUB
DINNA WORRY. I'M JIST THE LAD YE'RE LOOKIN' FOR!
WI' A' THIS GEAR ON, I CAN GET BALLS BACK NAE BOTHER!
LOOK AT THIS! THERE'S DOZENS O' BALLS IN HERE!
CLUB HOUSE
HA-HA! I'M MAKIN' A FORTUNE!
GOLF BALLS 20P
GOAL! THAT NEW BA'S A BEAUTY!
YE CANNA SAY I'M NO' ON THE BALL!

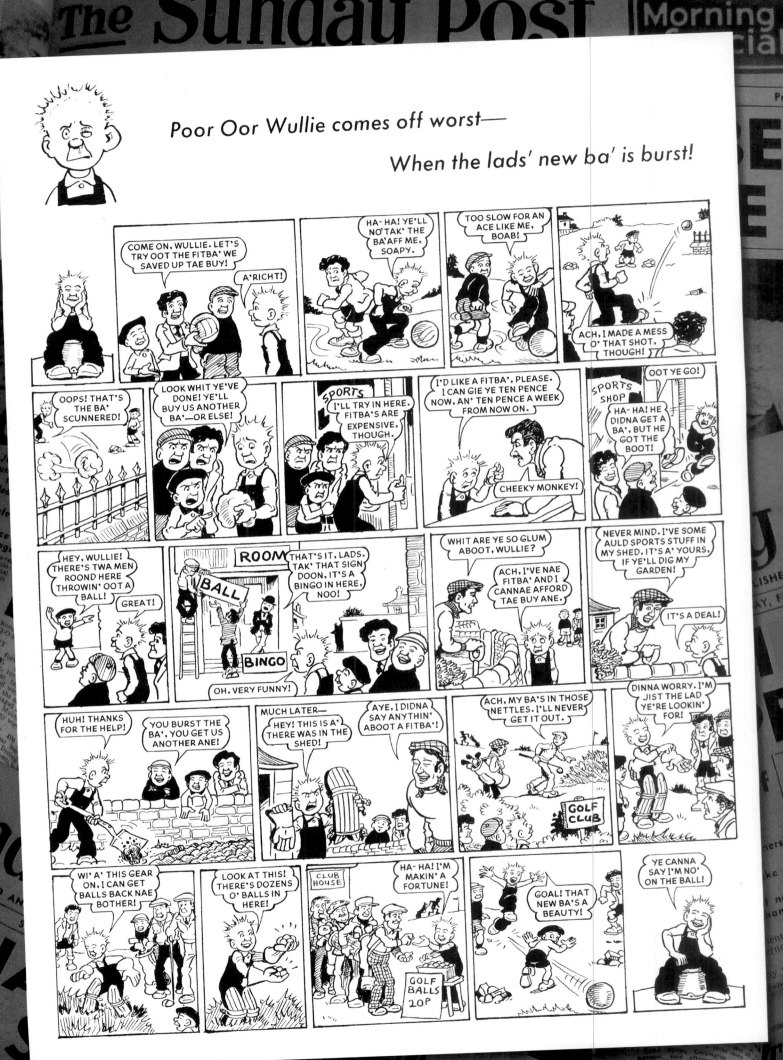

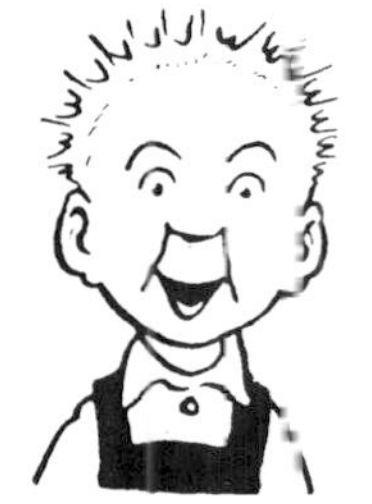

Wull's oot tae see the fitba', free—

Up high on stilts, or in a tree!

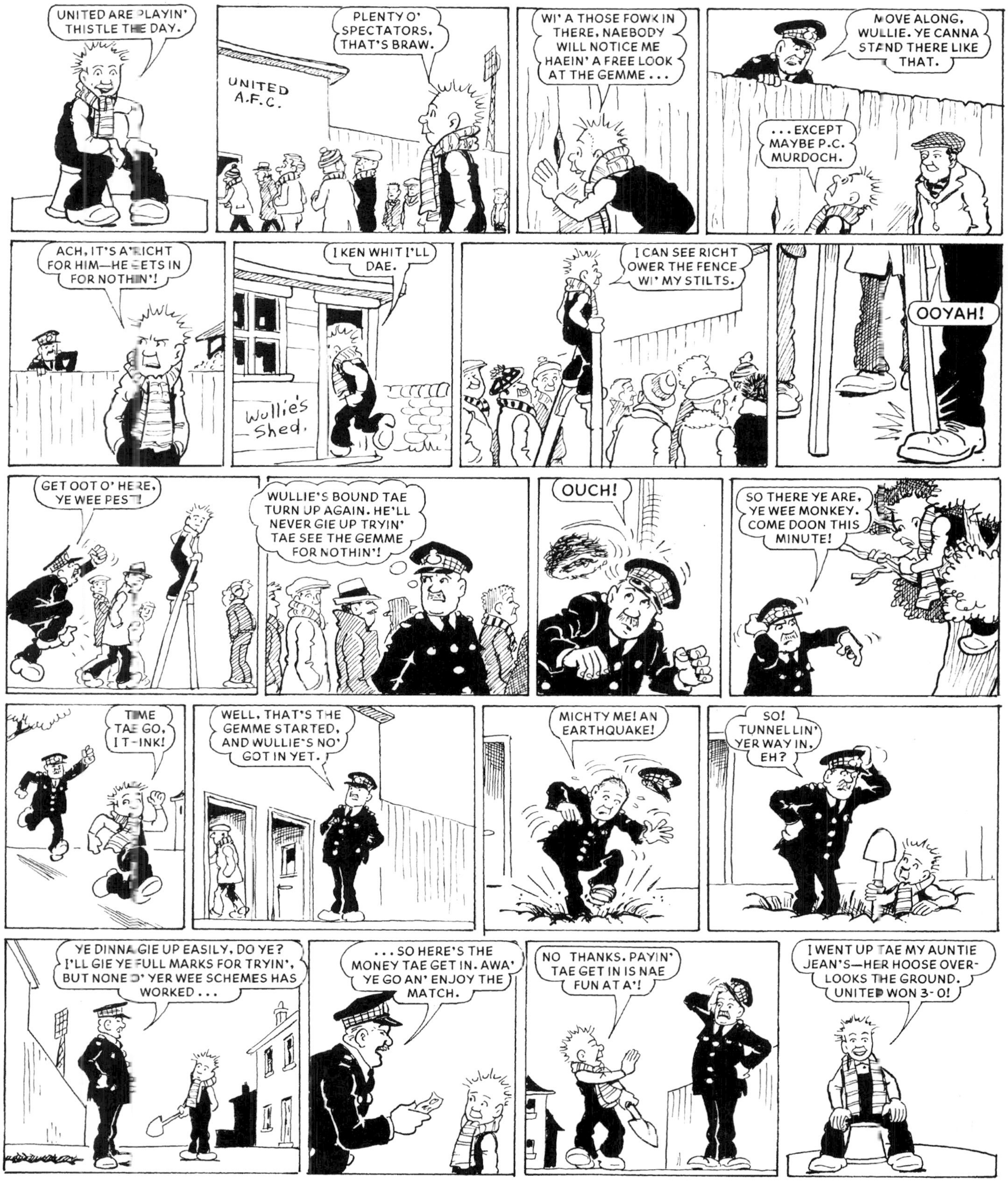

UNITED ARE PLAYIN' THISTLE THE DAY.
PLENTY O' SPECTATORS, THAT'S BRAW.
UNITED A.F.C.
WI' A THOSE FOWK IN THERE, NAEBODY WILL NOTICE ME HAEIN' A FREE LOOK AT THE GEMME . . .
MOVE ALONG, WULLIE. YE CANNA STAND THERE LIKE THAT.
. . . EXCEPT MAYBE P.C. MURDOCH.
ACH, IT'S A'RICHT FOR HIM—HE GETS IN FOR NOTHIN'!
I KEN WHIT I'LL DAE.
Wullie's Shed.
I CAN SEE RICHT OWER THE FENCE WI' MY STILTS.
OOYAH!
GET OOT O' HERE, YE WEE PEST!
WULLIE'S BOUND TAE TURN UP AGAIN. HE'LL NEVER GIE UP TRYIN' TAE SEE THE GEMME FOR NOTHIN'!
OUCH!
SO THERE YE ARE, YE WEE MONKEY. COME DOON THIS MINUTE!
TIME TAE GO, I T-INK!
WELL, THAT'S THE GEMME STARTED, AND WULLIE'S NO' GOT IN YET.
MICHTY ME! AN EARTHQUAKE!
SO! TUNNELLIN' YER WAY IN, EH?
YE DINNA GIE UP EASILY, DO YE? I'LL GIE YE FULL MARKS FOR TRYIN', BUT NONE O' YER WEE SCHEMES HAS WORKED . . .
. . . SO HERE'S THE MONEY TAE GET IN. AWA' YE GO AN' ENJOY THE MATCH.
NO THANKS. PAYIN' TAE GET IN IS NAE FUN AT A'!
I WENT UP TAE MY AUNTIE JEAN'S—HER HOOSE OVERLOOKS THE GROUND. UNITED WON 3-0!

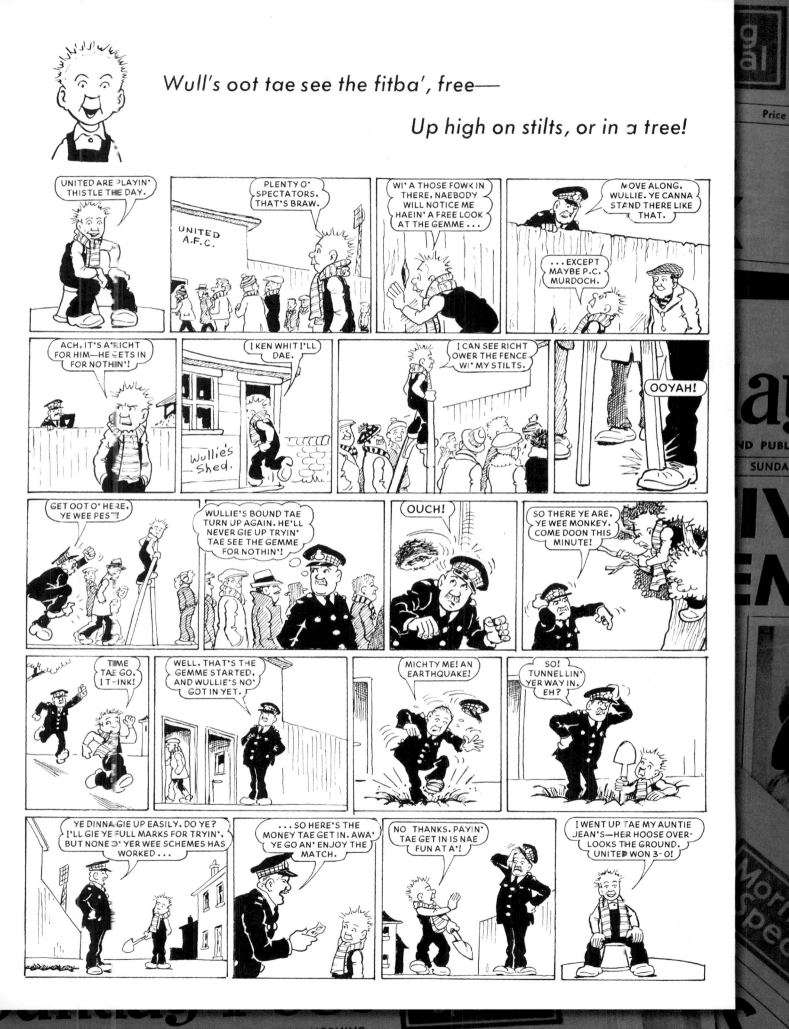

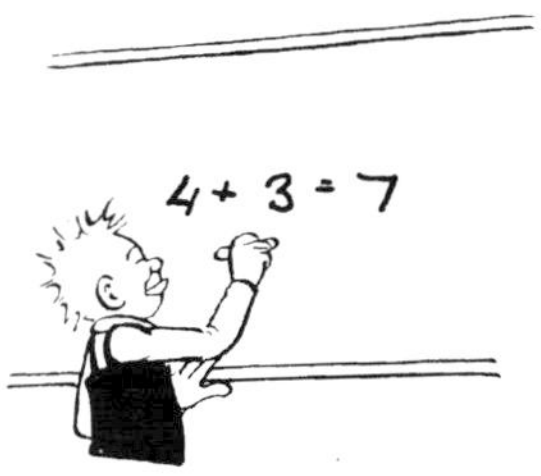
4 + 3 = 7

Wull wants to get his hair trimmed, but—

He'd rather see the PRICES cut!

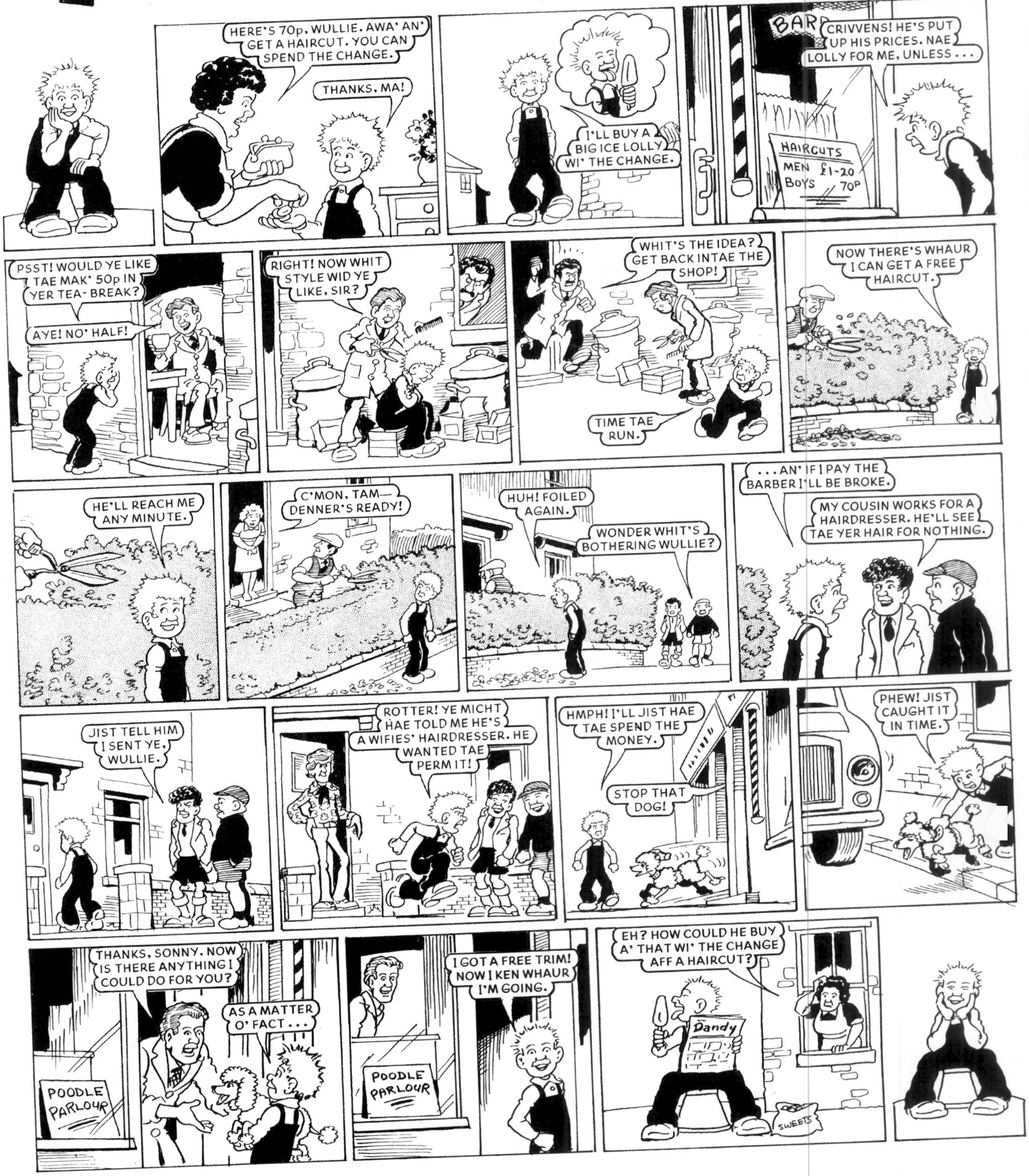
HERE'S 70p, WULLIE. AWA' AN' GET A HAIRCUT. YOU CAN SPEND THE CHANGE.
THANKS, MA!
I'LL BUY A BIG ICE LOLLY WI' THE CHANGE.
CRIVVENS! HE'S PUT UP HIS PRICES. NAE LOLLY FOR ME, UNLESS . . .
HAIRCUTS
MEN £1-20
BOYS 70P
PSST! WOULD YE LIKE TAE MAK' 50p IN YER TEA-BREAK?
AYE! NO' HALF!
RIGHT! NOW WHIT STYLE WID YE LIKE, SIR?
WHIT'S THE IDEA? GET BACK INTAE THE SHOP!
TIME TAE RUN.
NOW THERE'S WHAUR I CAN GET A FREE HAIRCUT.
HE'LL REACH ME ANY MINUTE.
C'MON, TAM— DENNER'S READY!
HUH! FOILED AGAIN.
WONDER WHIT'S BOTHERING WULLIE?
. . . AN' IF I PAY THE BARBER I'LL BE BROKE.
MY COUSIN WORKS FOR A HAIRDRESSER. HE'LL SEE TAE YER HAIR FOR NOTHING.
JIST TELL HIM I SENT YE, WULLIE.
ROTTER! YE MICHT HAE TOLD ME HE'S A WIFIES' HAIRDRESSER. HE WANTED TAE PERM IT!
HMPH! I'LL JIST HAE TAE SPEND THE MONEY.
STOP THAT DOG!
PHEW! JIST CAUGHT IT IN TIME.
THANKS, SONNY. NOW IS THERE ANYTHING I COULD DO FOR YOU?
AS A MATTER O' FACT . . .
POODLE PARLOUR
I GOT A FREE TRIM! NOW I KEN WHAUR I'M GOING.
POODLE PARLOUR
EH? HOW COULD HE BUY A' THAT WI' THE CHANGE AFF A HAIRCUT?
Dandy
SWEETS

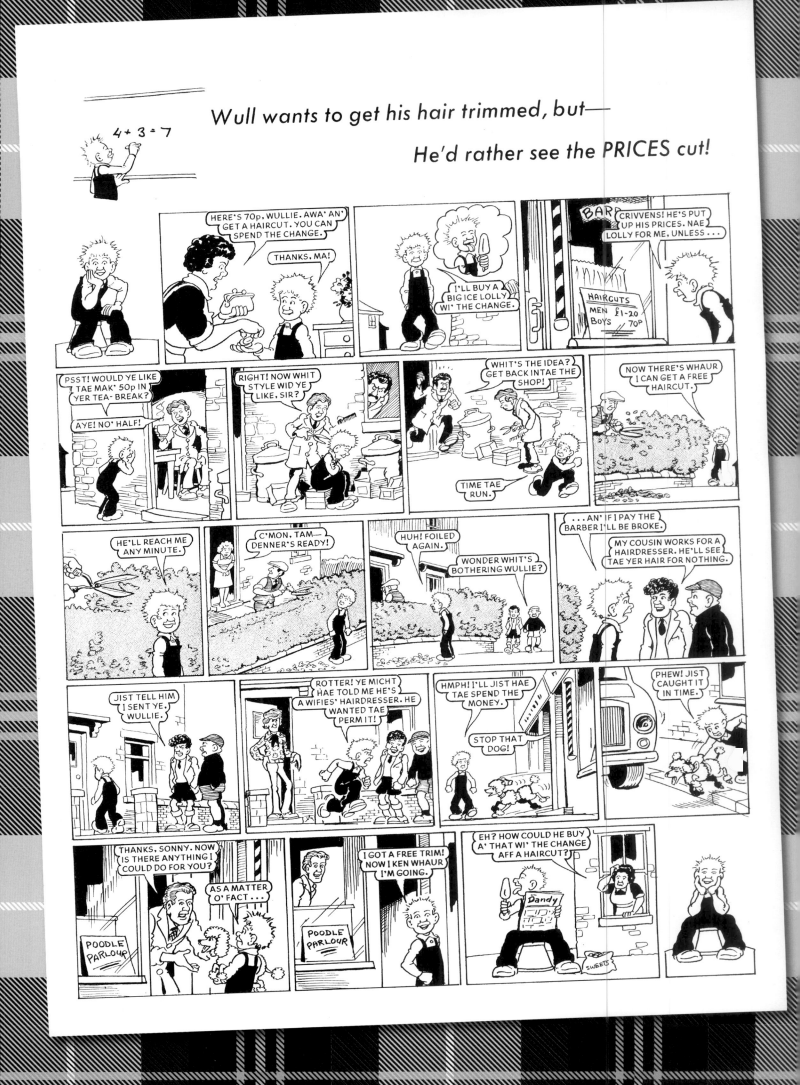

Heap big fun with Wullie now—

He's a real smart chief, and " how!"

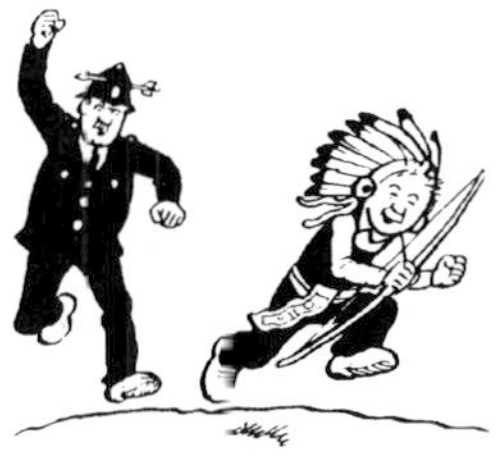

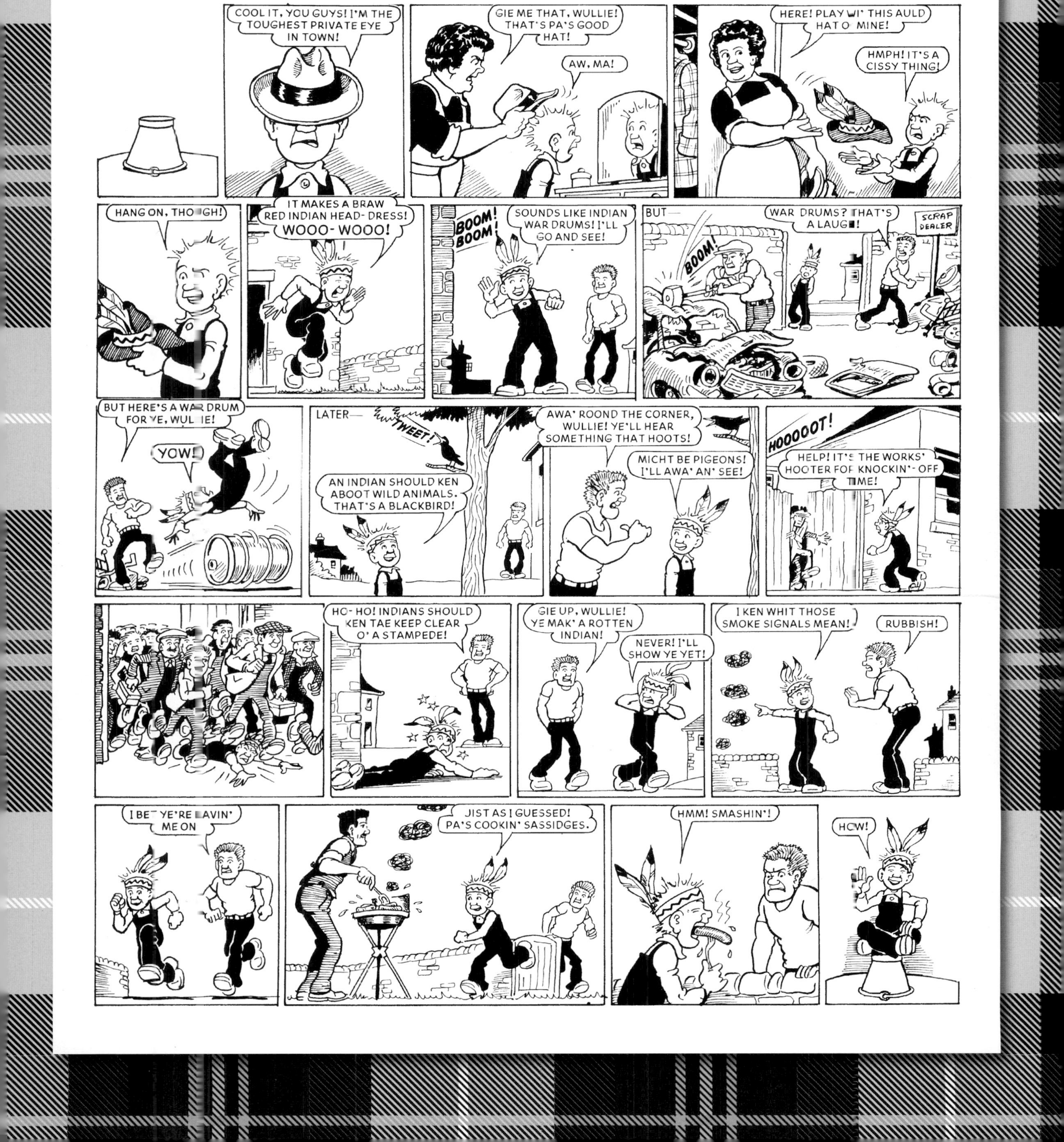

COOL IT, YOU GUYS! I'M THE TOUGHEST PRIVATE EYE IN TOWN!
GIE ME THAT, WULLIE! THAT'S PA'S GOOD HAT!
AW, MA!
HERE! PLAY WI' THIS AULD HAT O' MINE!
HMPH! IT'S A CISSY THING!
HANG ON, THOUGH!
IT MAKES A BRAW RED INDIAN HEAD-DRESS! WOOO-WOOO!
BOOM! BOOM!
SOUNDS LIKE INDIAN WAR DRUMS! I'LL GO AND SEE!
BUT—
WAR DRUMS? THAT'S A LAUGH!
SCRAP DEALER
BOOM!
BUT HERE'S A WAR DRUM FOR YE, WULLIE!
YOW!
LATER—
TWEET!
AN INDIAN SHOULD KEN ABOOT WILD ANIMALS. THAT'S A BLACKBIRD!
AWA' ROOND THE CORNER, WULLIE! YE'LL HEAR SOMETHING THAT HOOTS!
MICHT BE PIGEONS! I'LL AWA' AN' SEE!
HOOOOOT!
HELP! IT'S THE WORKS' HOOTER FOR KNOCKIN'-OFF TIME!
HO-HO! INDIANS SHOULD KEN TAE KEEP CLEAR O' A STAMPEDE!
GIE UP, WULLIE! YE MAK' A ROTTEN INDIAN!
NEVER! I'LL SHOW YE YET!
I KEN WHIT THOSE SMOKE SIGNALS MEAN!
RUBBISH!
I BET YE'RE HAVIN' ME ON
JIST AS I GUESSED! PA'S COOKIN' SASSIDGES.
HMM! SMASHIN'!
HOW!

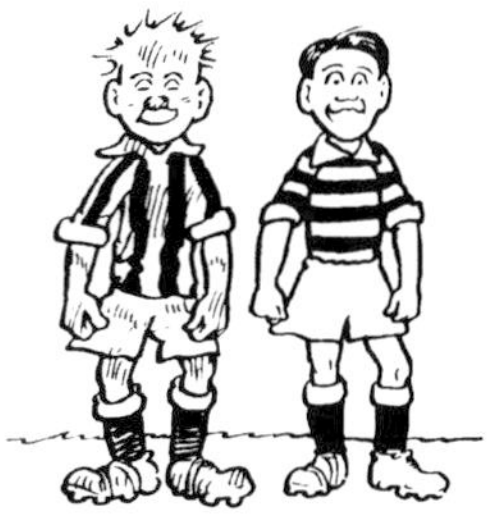

Here's the smartest—

Comic artist!

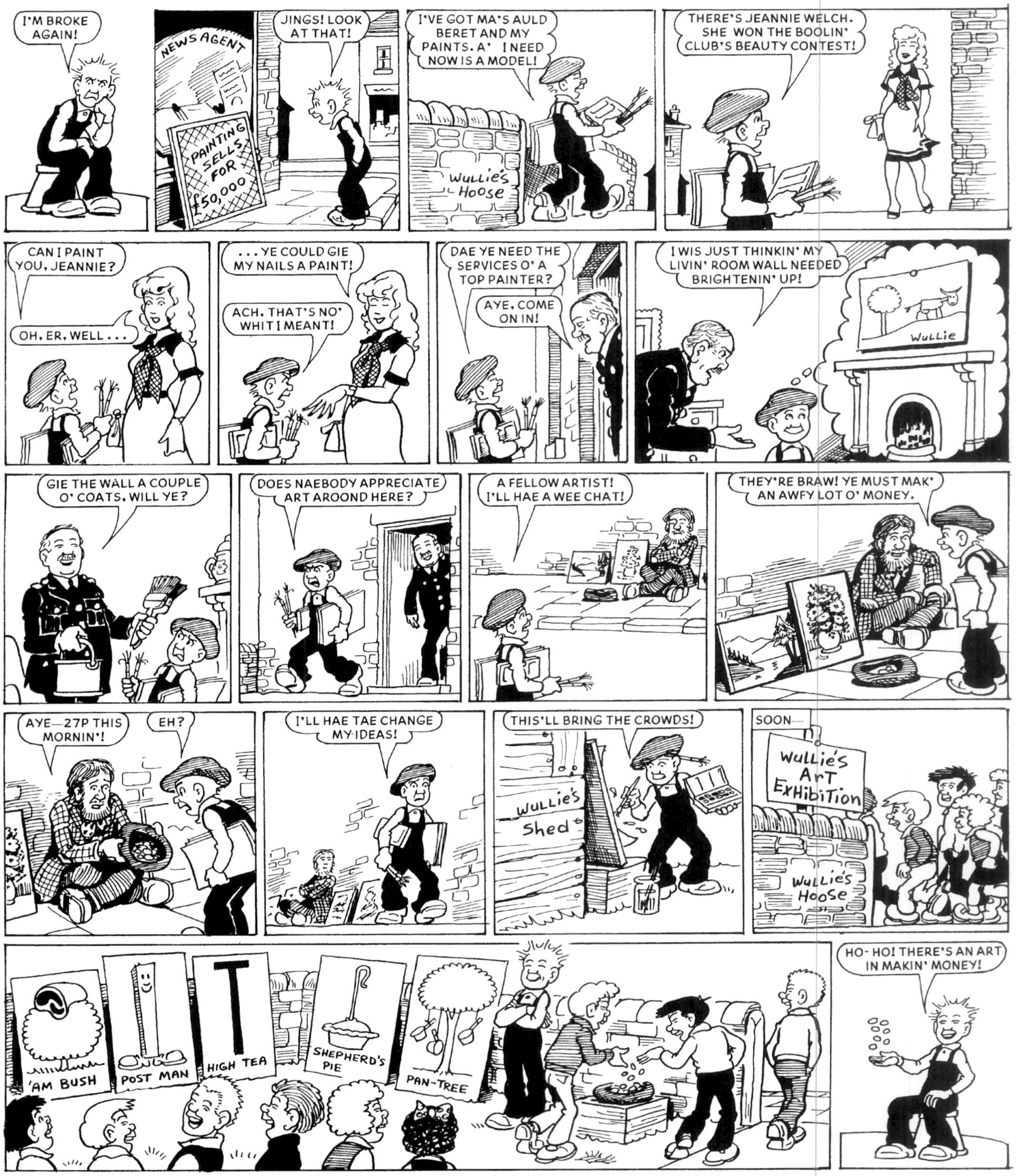

I'M BROKE AGAIN!
NEWS AGENT
PAINTING SELLS FOR £50,000
JINGS! LOOK AT THAT!
I'VE GOT MA'S AULD BERET AND MY PAINTS. A' I NEED NOW IS A MODEL!
WULLIE'S HOOSE
THERE'S JEANNIE WELCH. SHE WON THE BOOLIN' CLUB'S BEAUTY CONTEST!
CAN I PAINT YOU, JEANNIE?
OH, ER, WELL . . .
. . . YE COULD GIE MY NAILS A PAINT!
ACH, THAT'S NO' WHIT I MEANT!
DAE YE NEED THE SERVICES O' A TOP PAINTER?
AYE, COME ON IN!
I WIS JUST THINKIN' MY LIVIN' ROOM WALL NEEDED BRIGHTENIN' UP!
WULLIE
GIE THE WALL A COUPLE O' COATS, WILL YE?
DOES NAEBODY APPRECIATE ART AROOND HERE?
A FELLOW ARTIST! I'LL HAE A WEE CHAT!
THEY'RE BRAW! YE MUST MAK' AN AWFY LOT O' MONEY.
AYE—27P THIS MORNIN'!
EH?
I'LL HAE TAE CHANGE MY IDEAS!
THIS'LL BRING THE CROWDS!
WULLIE'S SHED
SOON—
WULLIE'S ART EXHIBITION
WULLIE'S HOOSE
'AM BUSH
POST MAN
HIGH TEA
SHEPHERD'S PIE
PAN-TREE
HO-HO! THERE'S AN ART IN MAKIN' MONEY!

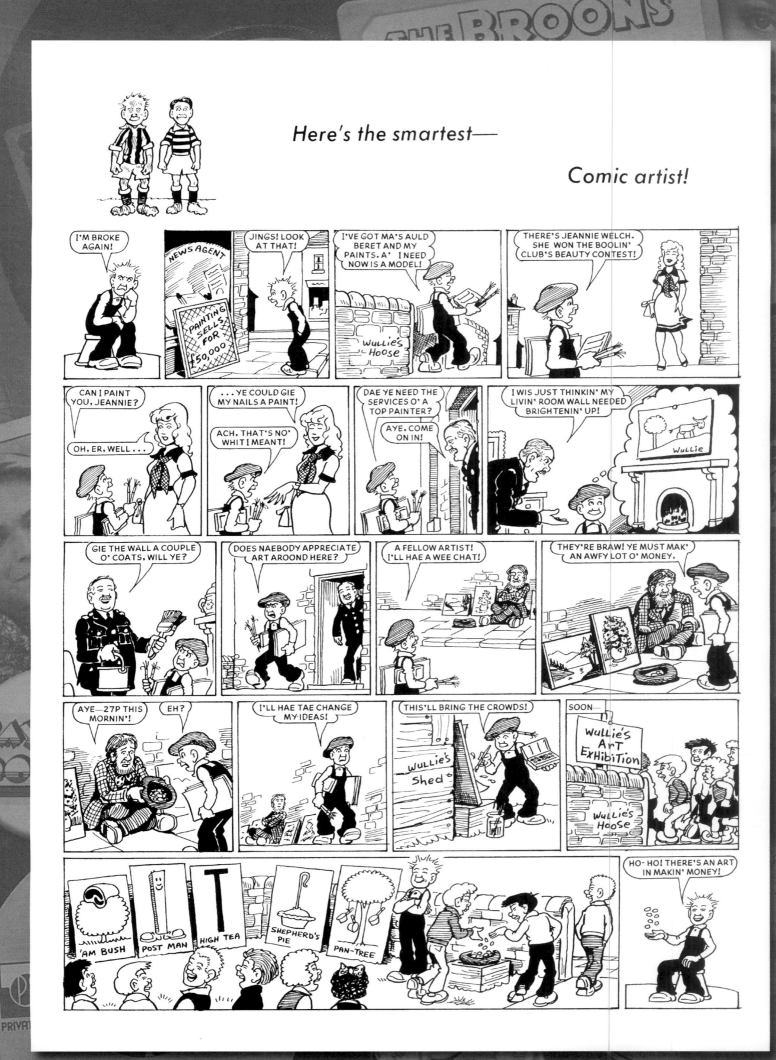

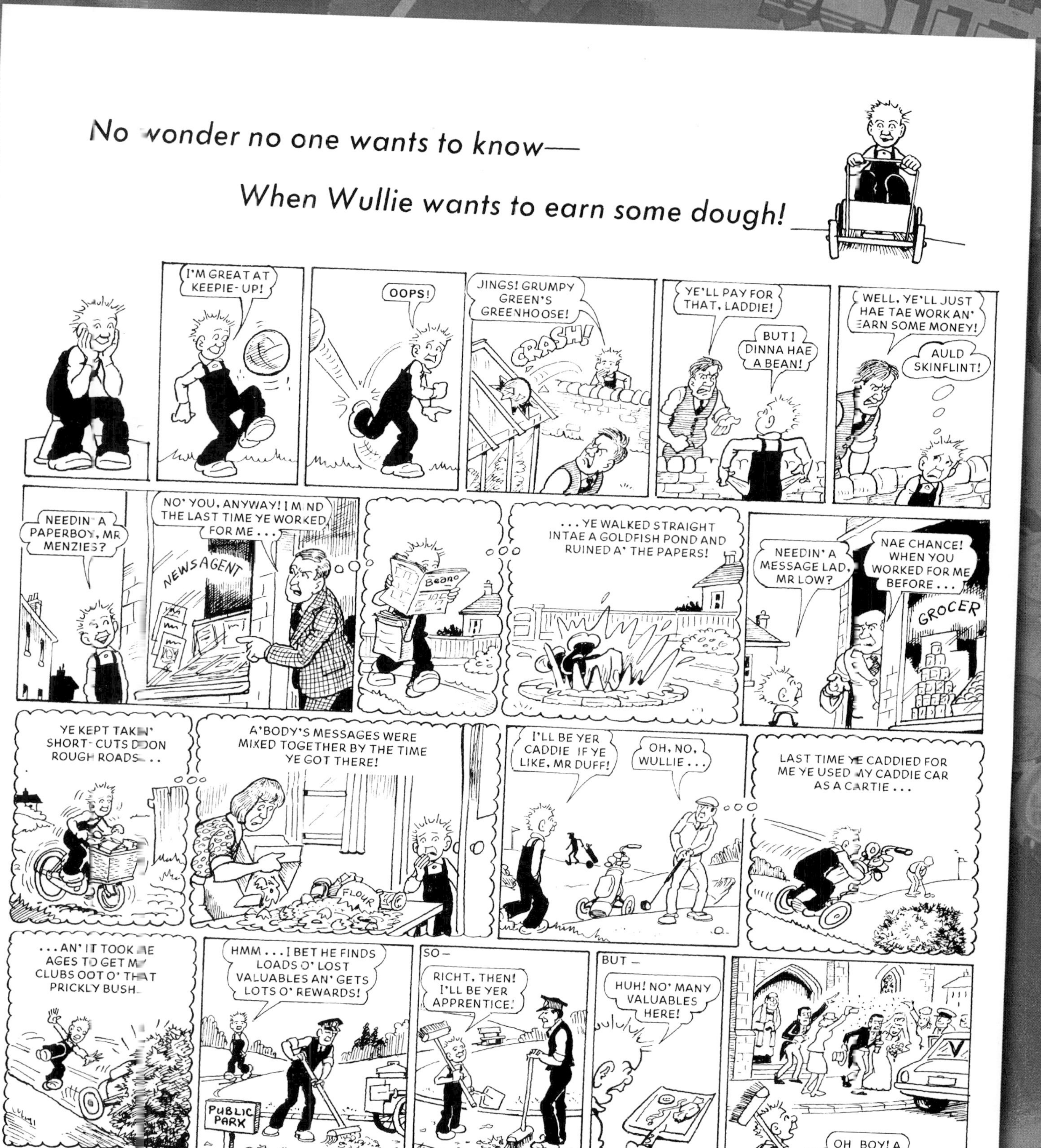
No wonder no one wants to know—
When Wullie wants to earn some dough!
I'M GREAT AT KEEPIE-UP!
OOPS!
JINGS! GRUMPY GREEN'S GREENHOOSE!
CRASH!
YE'LL PAY FOR THAT, LADDIE!
BUT I DINNA HAE A BEAN!
WELL, YE'LL JUST HAE TAE WORK AN' EARN SOME MONEY!
AULD SKINFLINT!
NEEDIN' A PAPERBOY, MR MENZIES?
NO' YOU, ANYWAY! I MIND THE LAST TIME YE WORKED FOR ME . . .
NEWSAGENT
Beano
. . . YE WALKED STRAIGHT INTAE A GOLDFISH POND AND RUINED A' THE PAPERS!
NEEDIN' A MESSAGE LAD, MR LOW?
NAE CHANCE! WHEN YOU WORKED FOR ME BEFORE . . .
GROCER
YE KEPT TAKIN' SHORT-CUTS DOON ROUGH ROADS . . .
A'BODY'S MESSAGES WERE MIXED TOGETHER BY THE TIME YE GOT THERE!
FLOUR
I'LL BE YER CADDIE IF YE LIKE, MR DUFF!
OH, NO, WULLIE . . .
LAST TIME YE CADDIED FOR ME YE USED MY CADDIE CAR AS A CARTIE . . .
. . . AN' IT TOOK ME AGES TO GET MY CLUBS OOT O' THAT PRICKLY BUSH.
HMM . . . I BET HE FINDS LOADS O' LOST VALUABLES AN' GETS LOTS O' REWARDS!
PUBLIC PARK
SO—
RICHT, THEN! I'LL BE YER APPRENTICE!
BUT—
HUH! NO' MANY VALUABLES HERE!
OH BOY! A WEDDIN'!
NOW I CAN REALLY CLEAN UP!
I'M MAKIN' A FORTUNE!
THERE SHOULD BE ENOUGH TO PAY FOR YOUR GLASS THERE, MR GREEN!

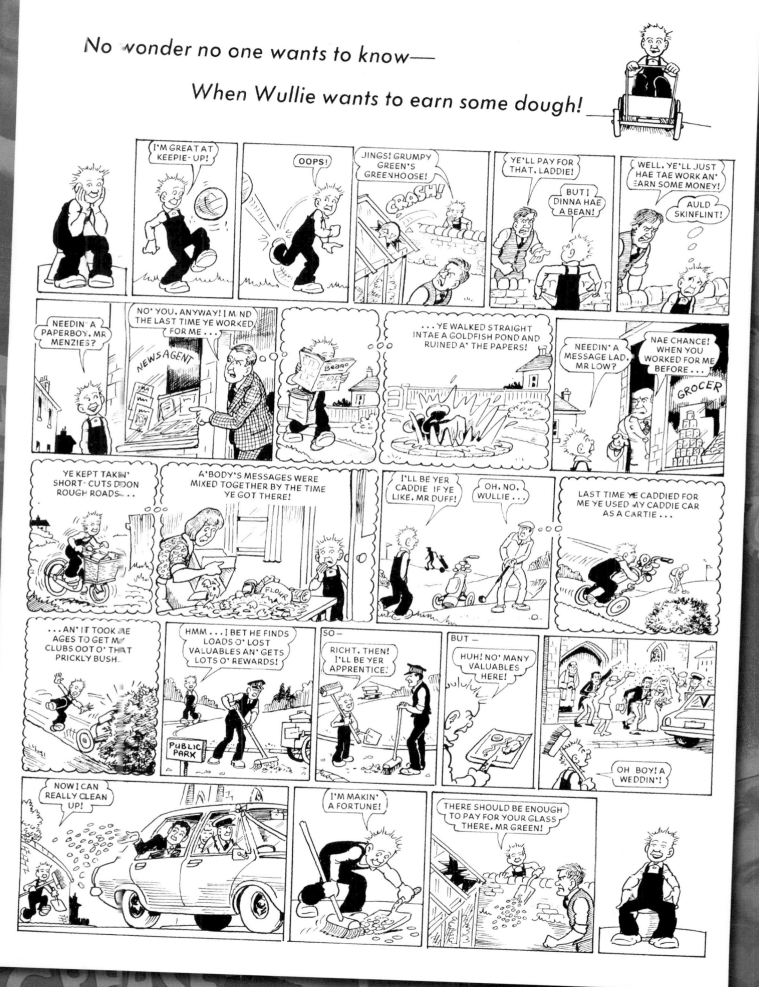

When Wullie tries his latest trick—

He finds Pa has a BONE to pick!

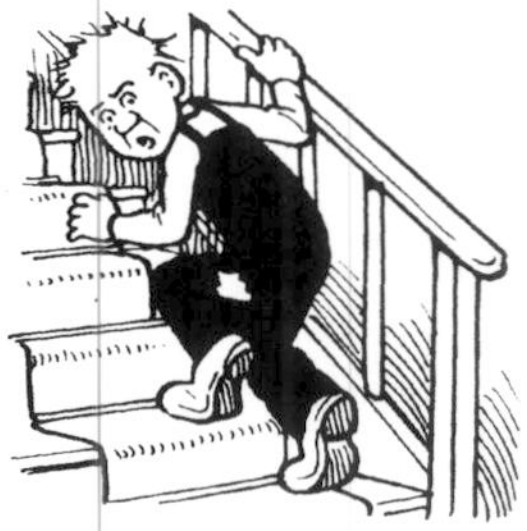

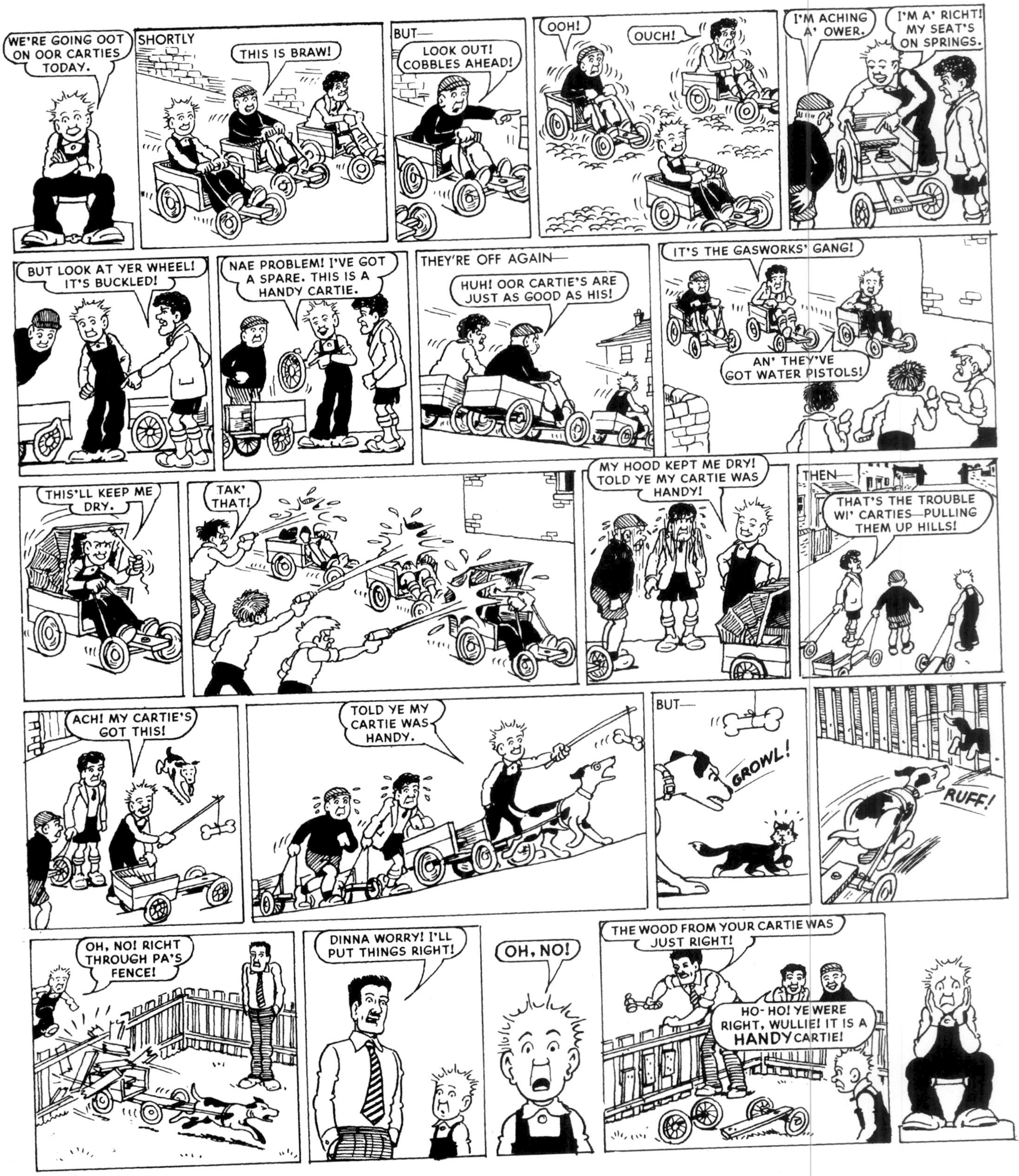

WE'RE GOING OOT ON OOR CARTIES TODAY.
SHORTLY
THIS IS BRAW!
BUT—
LOOK OUT! COBBLES AHEAD!
OOH!
OUCH!
I'M ACHING A' OWER.
I'M A' RICHT! MY SEAT'S ON SPRINGS.
BUT LOOK AT YER WHEEL! IT'S BUCKLED!
NAE PROBLEM! I'VE GOT A SPARE. THIS IS A HANDY CARTIE.
THEY'RE OFF AGAIN—
HUH! OOR CARTIE'S ARE JUST AS GOOD AS HIS!
IT'S THE GASWORKS' GANG!
AN' THEY'VE GOT WATER PISTOLS!
THIS'LL KEEP ME DRY.
TAK' THAT!
MY HOOD KEPT ME DRY! TOLD YE MY CARTIE WAS HANDY!
THEN—
THAT'S THE TROUBLE WI' CARTIES—PULLING THEM UP HILLS!
ACH! MY CARTIE'S GOT THIS!
TOLD YE MY CARTIE WAS HANDY.
BUT—
GROWL!
RUFF!
OH, NO! RICHT THROUGH PA'S FENCE!
DINNA WORRY! I'LL PUT THINGS RIGHT!
OH, NO!
THE WOOD FROM YOUR CARTIE WAS JUST RIGHT!
HO-HO! YE WERE RIGHT, WULLIE! IT IS A HANDY CARTIE!

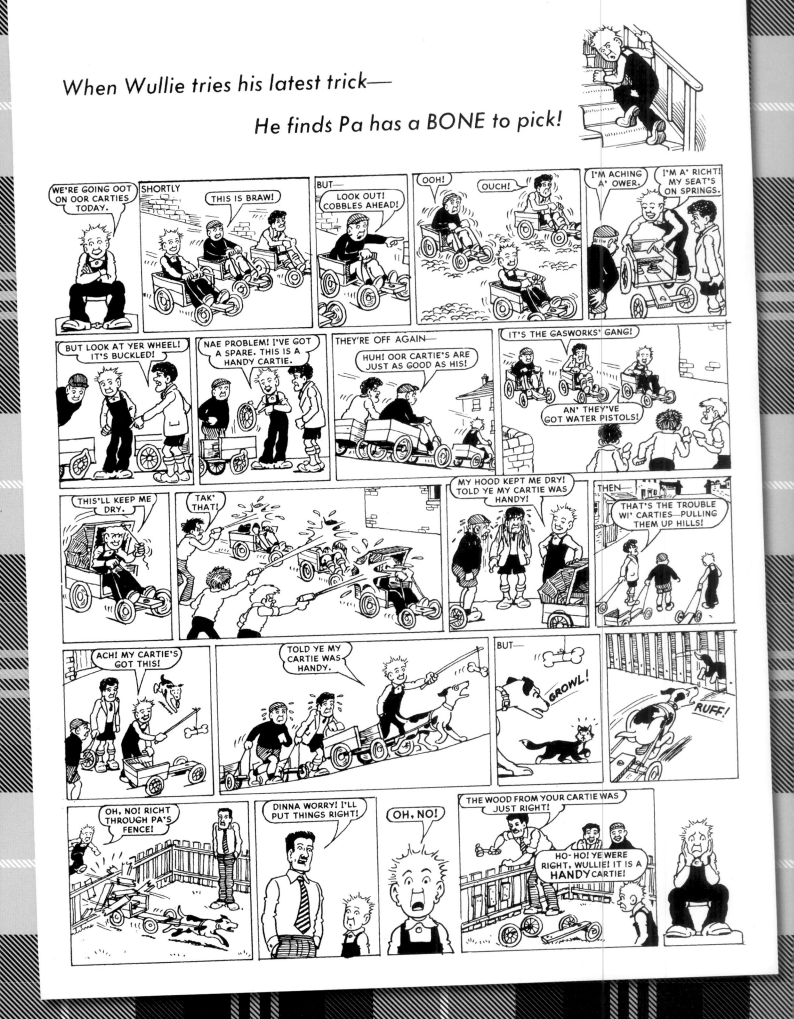

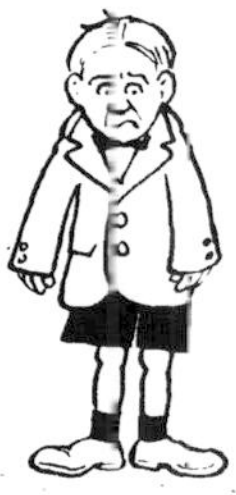

Lots o' shocks—

Wi' curly locks!

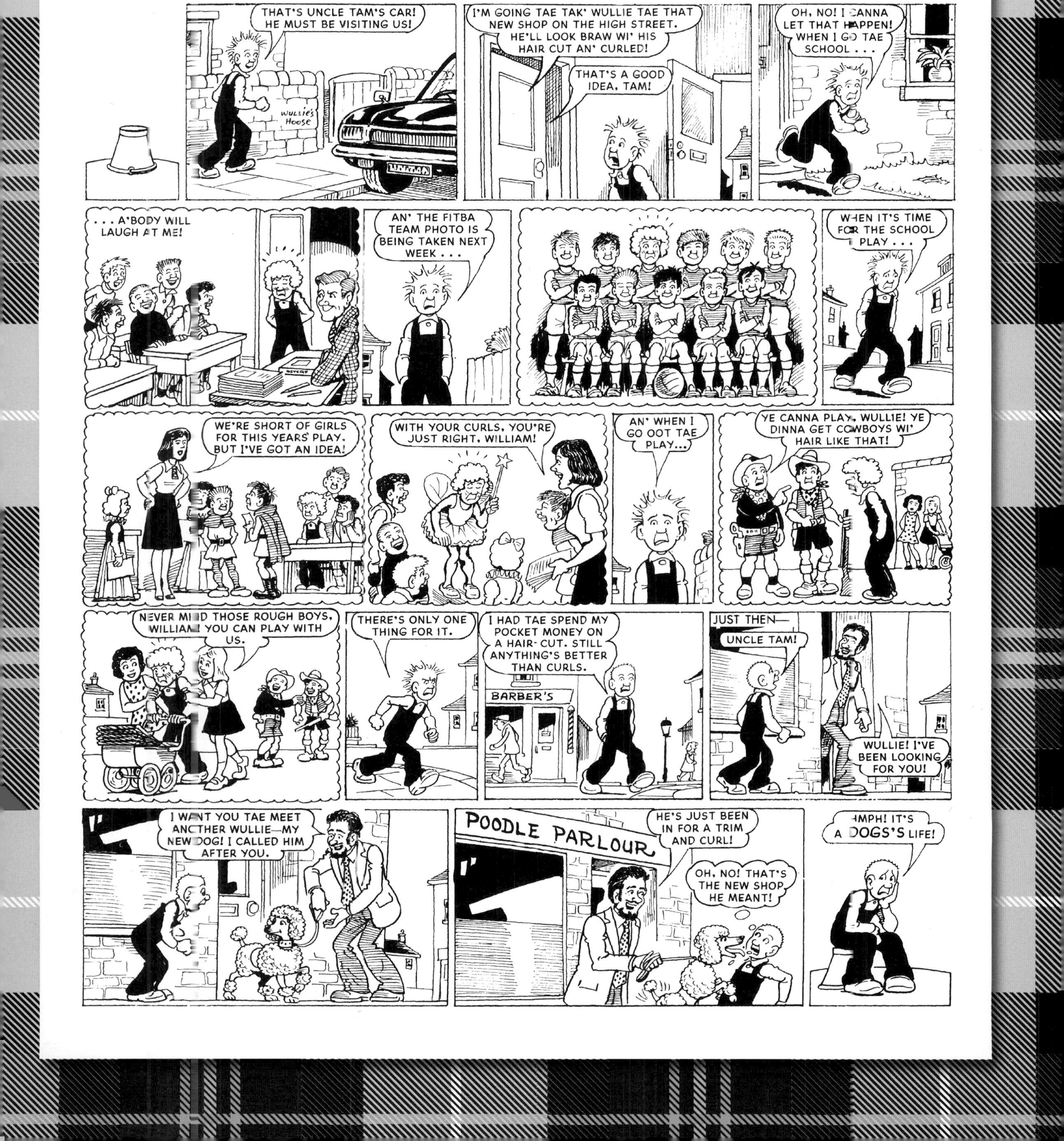

THAT'S UNCLE TAM'S CAR! HE MUST BE VISITING US!
WULLIE'S HOOSE
I'M GOING TAE TAK' WULLIE TAE THAT NEW SHOP ON THE HIGH STREET. HE'LL LOOK BRAW WI' HIS HAIR CUT AN' CURLED!
THAT'S A GOOD IDEA, TAM!
OH, NO! I CANNA LET THAT HAPPEN! WHEN I GO TAE SCHOOL . . .
. . . A'BODY WILL LAUGH AT ME!
AN' THE FITBA TEAM PHOTO IS BEING TAKEN NEXT WEEK . . .
WHEN IT'S TIME FOR THE SCHOOL PLAY . . .
WE'RE SHORT OF GIRLS FOR THIS YEARS PLAY. BUT I'VE GOT AN IDEA!
WITH YOUR CURLS, YOU'RE JUST RIGHT, WILLIAM!
AN' WHEN I GO OOT TAE PLAY...
YE CANNA PLAY, WULLIE! YE DINNA GET COWBOYS WI' HAIR LIKE THAT!
NEVER MIND THOSE ROUGH BOYS, WILLIAM! YOU CAN PLAY WITH US.
THERE'S ONLY ONE THING FOR IT.
I HAD TAE SPEND MY POCKET MONEY ON A HAIR-CUT. STILL ANYTHING'S BETTER THAN CURLS.
BARBER'S
JUST THEN—
UNCLE TAM!
WULLIE! I'VE BEEN LOOKING FOR YOU!
I WANT YOU TAE MEET ANOTHER WULLIE—MY NEW DOG! I CALLED HIM AFTER YOU.
POODLE PARLOUR
HE'S JUST BEEN IN FOR A TRIM AND CURL!
OH, NO! THAT'S THE NEW SHOP HE MEANT!
HMPH! IT'S A DOGS'S LIFE!

Wull fools his Pa, and teacher, too—

But things look bad for you-know-who!

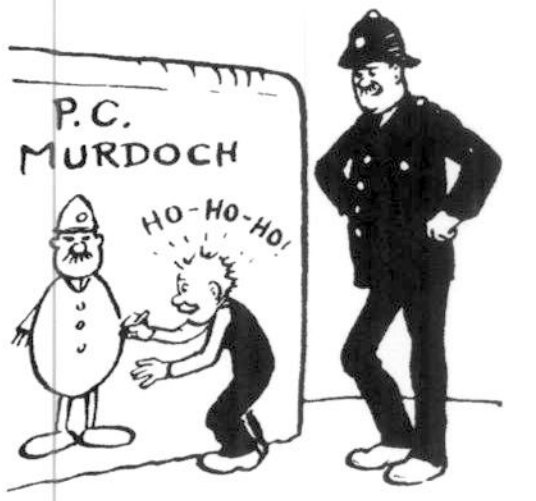

P.C. MURDOCH
HO-HO-HO!

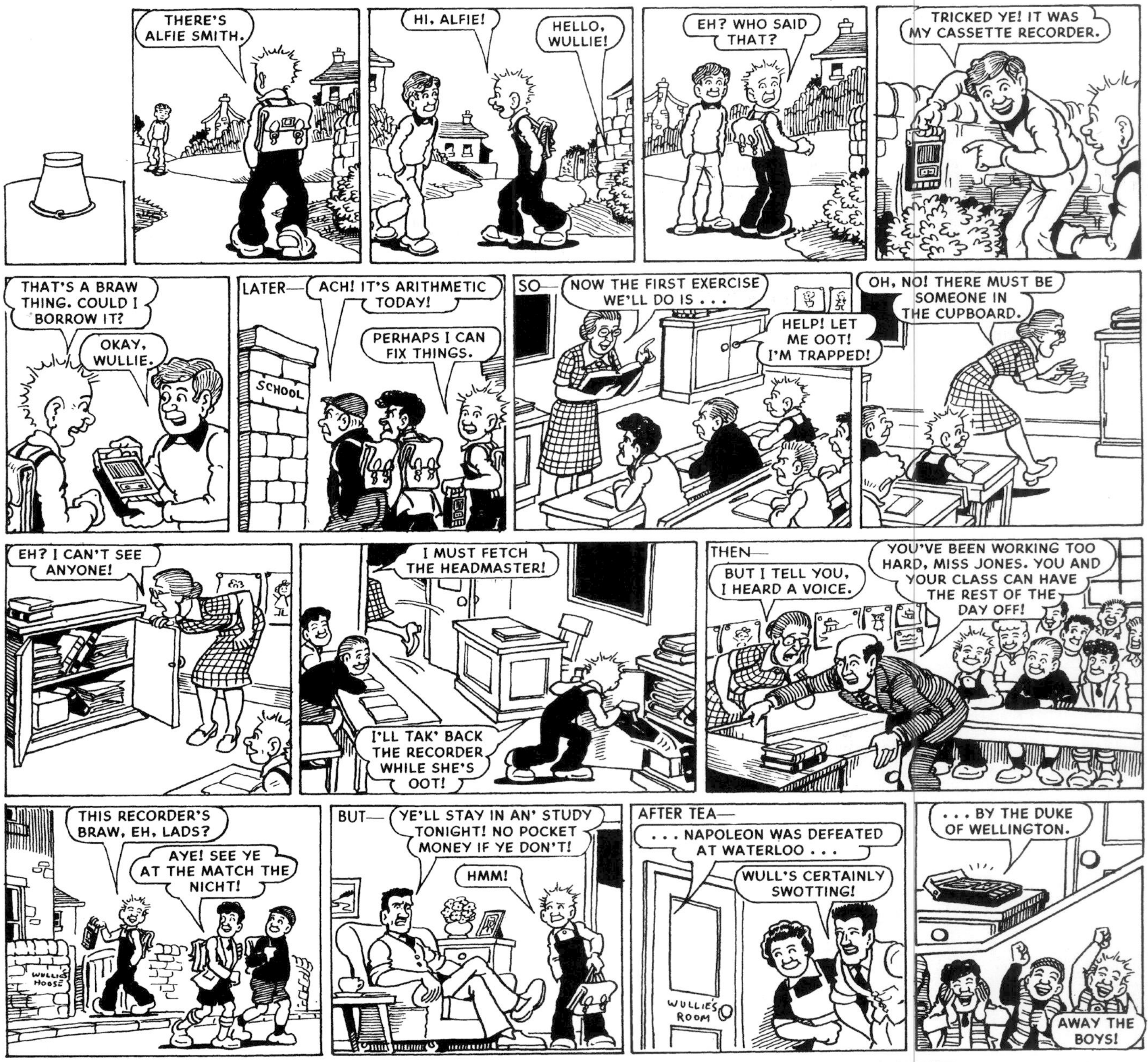

THERE'S ALFIE SMITH.
HI, ALFIE!
HELLO, WULLIE!
EH? WHO SAID THAT?
TRICKED YE! IT WAS MY CASSETTE RECORDER.
THAT'S A BRAW THING. COULD I BORROW IT?
OKAY, WULLIE.
LATER—
ACH! IT'S ARITHMETIC TODAY!
PERHAPS I CAN FIX THINGS.
SCHOOL
SO—
NOW THE FIRST EXERCISE WE'LL DO IS . . .
HELP! LET ME OOT! I'M TRAPPED!
OH, NO! THERE MUST BE SOMEONE IN THE CUPBOARD.
EH? I CAN'T SEE ANYONE!
I MUST FETCH THE HEADMASTER!
I'LL TAK' BACK THE RECORDER WHILE SHE'S OOT!
THEN—
BUT I TELL YOU, I HEARD A VOICE.
YOU'VE BEEN WORKING TOO HARD, MISS JONES. YOU AND YOUR CLASS CAN HAVE THE REST OF THE DAY OFF!
THIS RECORDER'S BRAW, EH, LADS?
AYE! SEE YE AT THE MATCH THE NICHT!
WULLIE'S HOOSE
BUT—
YE'LL STAY IN AN' STUDY TONIGHT! NO POCKET MONEY IF YE DON'T!
HMM!
AFTER TEA—
. . . NAPOLEON WAS DEFEATED AT WATERLOO . . .
WULL'S CERTAINLY SWOTTING!
WULLIE'S ROOM
. . . BY THE DUKE OF WELLINGTON.
AWAY THE BOYS!
NEXT DAY—
HERE'S YER POCKET MONEY, WULLIE!
THANKS, PAW!
HERE YE ARE, ALFIE. THAT'S A GREAT RECORDER YE'VE GOT.
LET'S RECORD SOMETHING NOW, WULLIE!
BUT—
HEY! IT'S NOT WORKING! YOU'VE USED UP THE BATTERIES!
CLICK!
PAY UP! I'LL HAVE TO BUY NEW BATTERIES!
THERE GOES MY POCKET MONEY!
WHIT DID I SAY ABOOT TAPE RECORDERS?

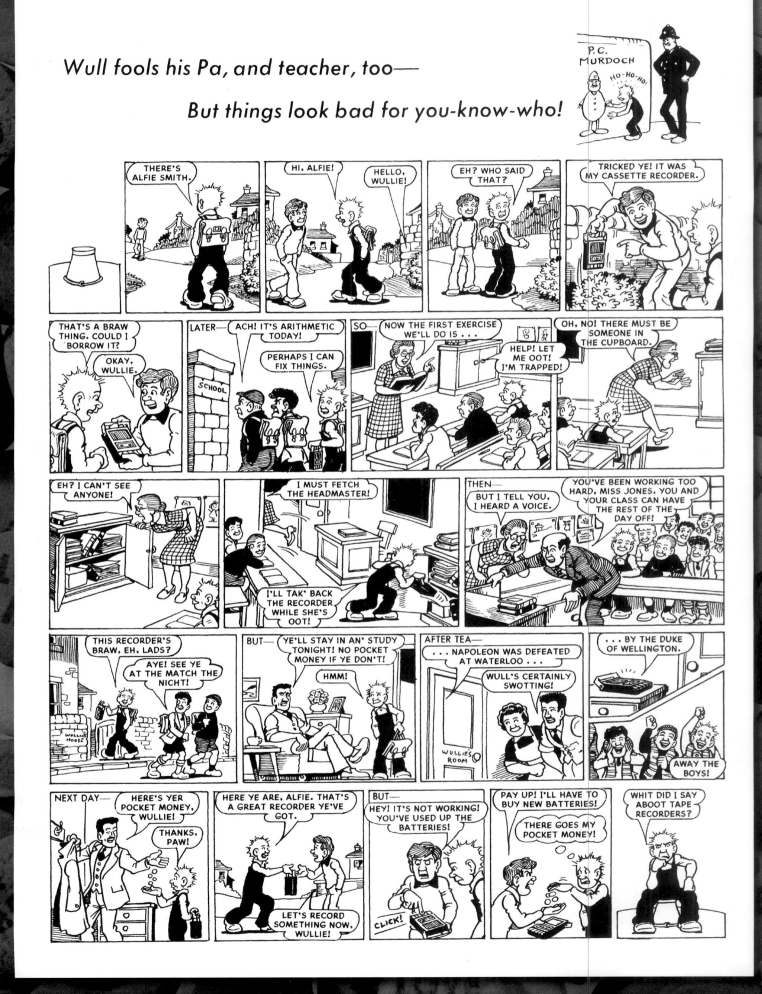

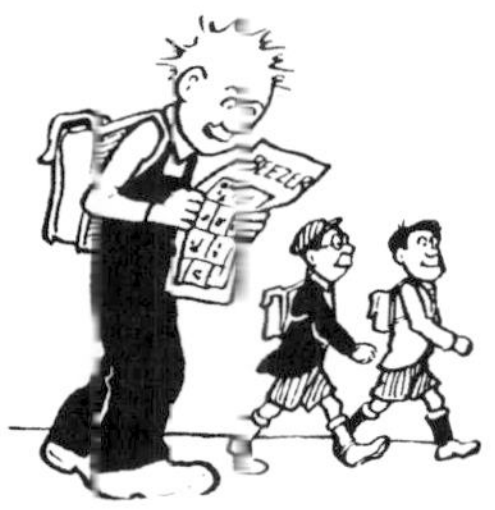

Is Wullie ill, or going saft?—

His chums think so—but he's no daft!

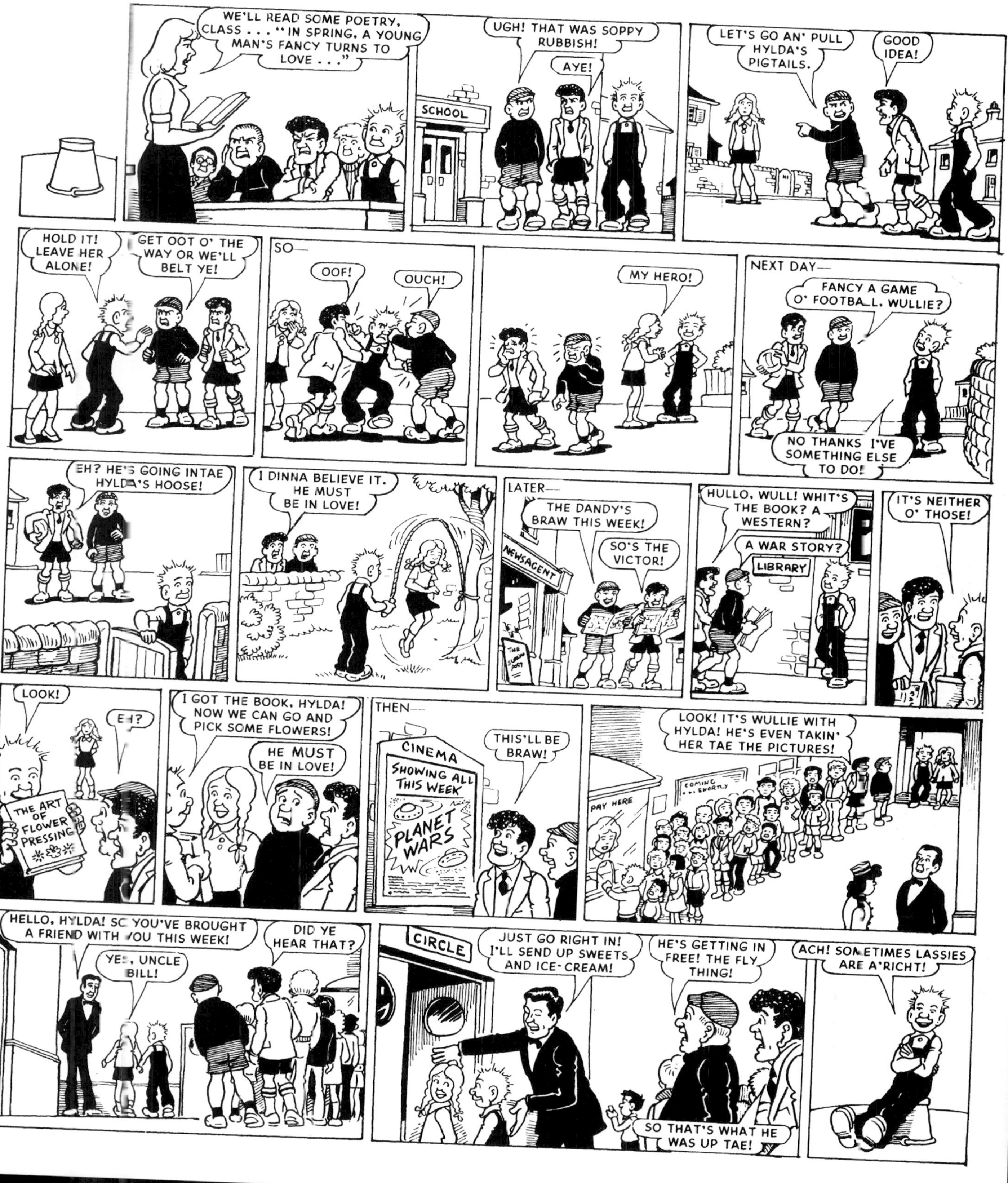
WE'LL READ SOME POETRY, CLASS . . . "IN SPRING, A YOUNG MAN'S FANCY TURNS TO LOVE . . ."
UGH! THAT WAS SOPPY RUBBISH!
AYE!
SCHOOL
LET'S GO AN' PULL HYLDA'S PIGTAILS.
GOOD IDEA!
HOLD IT! LEAVE HER ALONE!
GET OOT O' THE WAY OR WE'LL BELT YE!
SO—
OOF!
OUCH!
MY HERO!
NEXT DAY—
FANCY A GAME O' FOOTBALL, WULLIE?
NO THANKS I'VE SOMETHING ELSE TO DO!
EH? HE'S GOING INTAE HYLDA'S HOOSE!
I DINNA BELIEVE IT. HE MUST BE IN LOVE!
LATER—
THE DANDY'S BRAW THIS WEEK!
SO'S THE VICTOR!
NEWSAGENT
HULLO, WULL! WHIT'S THE BOOK? A WESTERN?
A WAR STORY?
LIBRARY
IT'S NEITHER O' THOSE!
LOOK!
EH?
THE ART OF FLOWER PRESSING
I GOT THE BOOK, HYLDA! NOW WE CAN GO AND PICK SOME FLOWERS!
HE MUST BE IN LOVE!
THEN—
CINEMA
SHOWING ALL THIS WEEK
PLANET WARS
THIS'LL BE BRAW!
LOOK! IT'S WULLIE WITH HYLDA! HE'S EVEN TAKIN' HER TAE THE PICTURES!
PAY HERE
HELLO, HYLDA! SO YOU'VE BROUGHT A FRIEND WITH YOU THIS WEEK!
YES, UNCLE BILL!
DID YE HEAR THAT?
CIRCLE
JUST GO RIGHT IN! I'LL SEND UP SWEETS AND ICE-CREAM!
HE'S GETTING IN FREE! THE FLY THING!
SO THAT'S WHAT HE WAS UP TAE!
ACH! SOMETIMES LASSIES ARE A'RICHT!

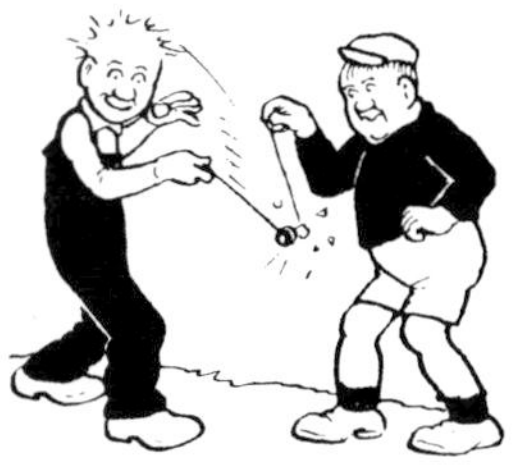

It's the brawest thing they've ever seen— When Wullie takes on Grouchie Greene!

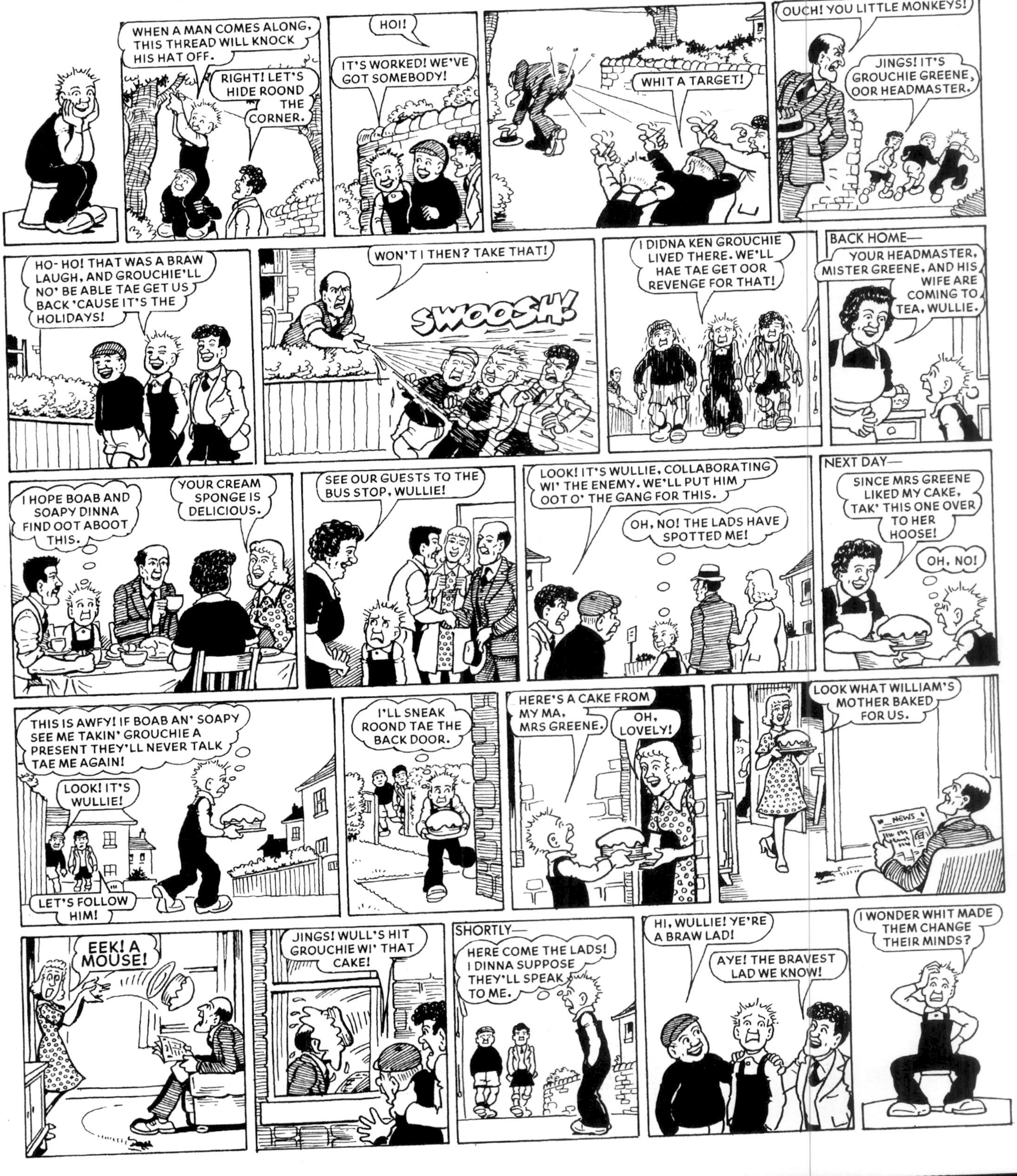
WHEN A MAN COMES ALONG, THIS THREAD WILL KNOCK HIS HAT OFF.
RIGHT! LET'S HIDE ROOND THE CORNER.
HOI!
IT'S WORKED! WE'VE GOT SOMEBODY!
WHIT A TARGET!
OUCH! YOU LITTLE MONKEYS!
JINGS! IT'S GROUCHIE GREENE, OOR HEADMASTER.
HO-HO! THAT WAS A BRAW LAUGH, AND GROUCHIE'LL NO' BE ABLE TAE GET US BACK 'CAUSE IT'S THE HOLIDAYS!
WON'T I THEN? TAKE THAT!
SWOOSH!
I DIDNA KEN GROUCHIE LIVED THERE. WE'LL HAE TAE GET OOR REVENGE FOR THAT!
BACK HOME—
YOUR HEADMASTER, MISTER GREENE, AND HIS WIFE ARE COMING TO TEA, WULLIE.
I HOPE BOAB AND SOAPY DINNA FIND OOT ABOOT THIS.
YOUR CREAM SPONGE IS DELICIOUS.
SEE OUR GUESTS TO THE BUS STOP, WULLIE!
LOOK! IT'S WULLIE, COLLABORATING WI' THE ENEMY. WE'LL PUT HIM OOT O' THE GANG FOR THIS.
OH, NO! THE LADS HAVE SPOTTED ME!
NEXT DAY—
SINCE MRS GREENE LIKED MY CAKE, TAK' THIS ONE OVER TO HER HOOSE!
OH, NO!
THIS IS AWFY! IF BOAB AN' SOAPY SEE ME TAKIN' GROUCHIE A PRESENT THEY'LL NEVER TALK TAE ME AGAIN!
LOOK! IT'S WULLIE!
LET'S FOLLOW HIM!
I'LL SNEAK ROOND TAE THE BACK DOOR.
HERE'S A CAKE FROM MY MA, MRS GREENE.
OH, LOVELY!
LOOK WHAT WILLIAM'S MOTHER BAKED FOR US.
NEWS
EEK! A MOUSE!
JINGS! WULL'S HIT GROUCHIE WI' THAT CAKE!
SHORTLY—
HERE COME THE LADS! I DINNA SUPPOSE THEY'LL SPEAK TO ME.
HI, WULLIE! YE'RE A BRAW LAD!
AYE! THE BRAVEST LAD WE KNOW!
I WONDER WHIT MADE THEM CHANGE THEIR MINDS?

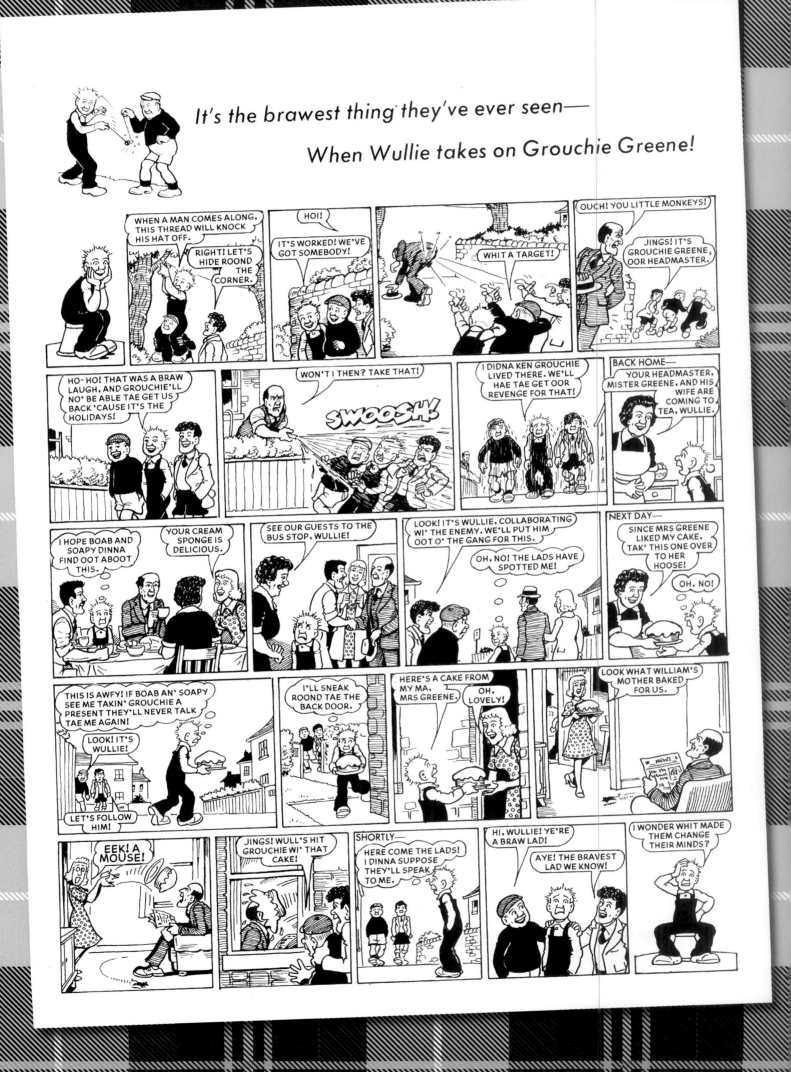

You'll never guess what—

He should have bought!

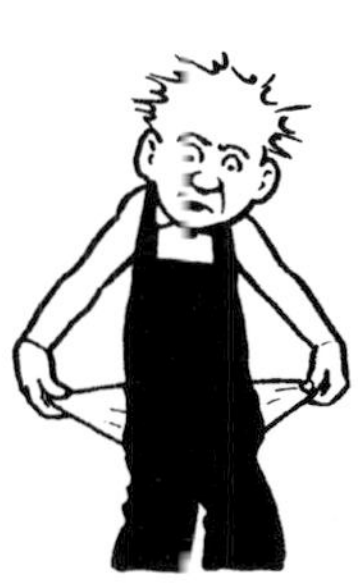

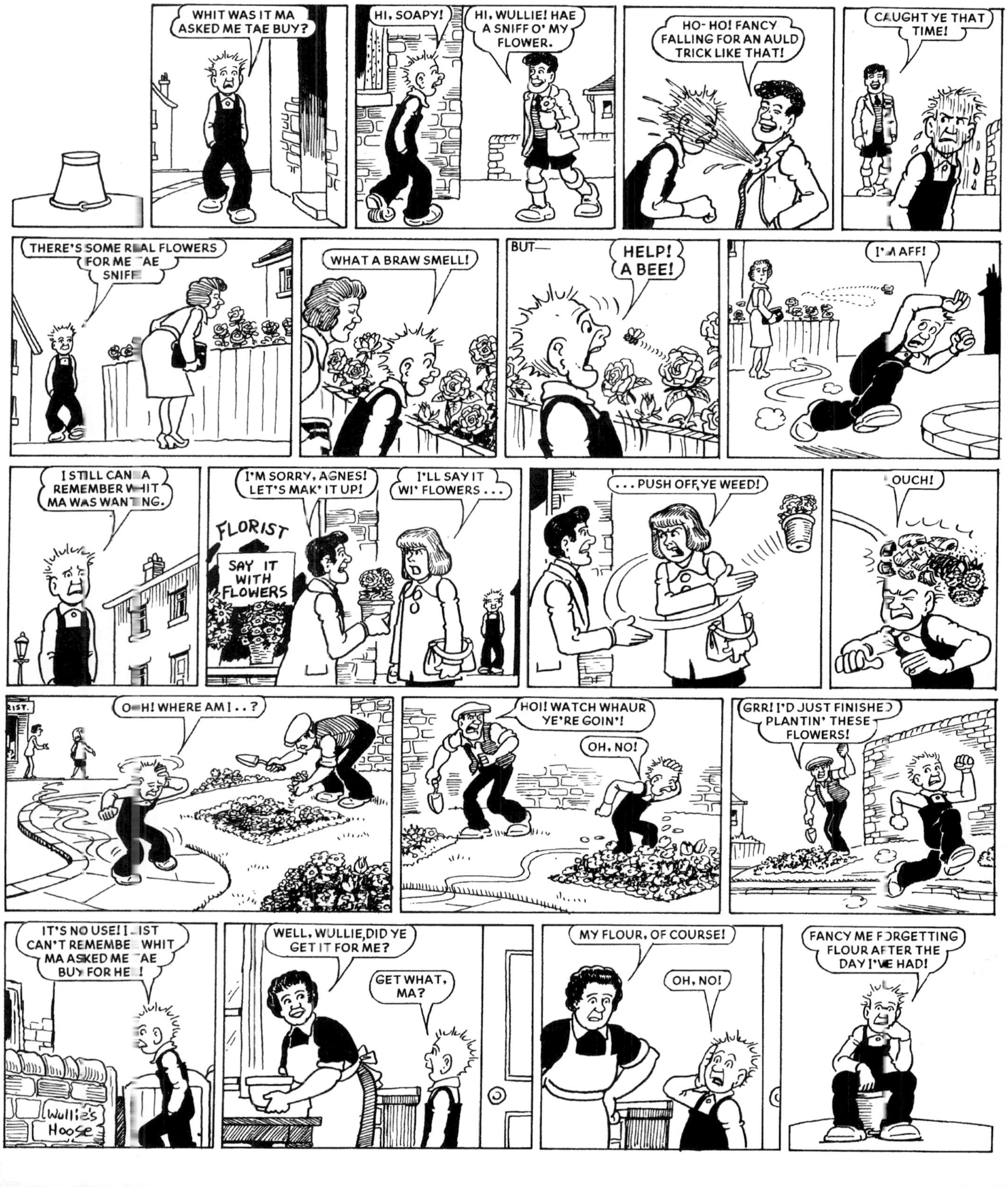

WHIT WAS IT MA ASKED ME TAE BUY?
HI, SOAPY!
HI, WULLIE! HAE A SNIFF O' MY FLOWER.
HO-HO! FANCY FALLING FOR AN AULD TRICK LIKE THAT!
CAUGHT YE THAT TIME!
THERE'S SOME REAL FLOWERS FOR ME TAE SNIFF.
WHAT A BRAW SMELL!
BUT—
HELP! A BEE!
I'M AFF!
I STILL CAN'A REMEMBER WHIT MA WAS WANTING.
I'M SORRY, AGNES! LET'S MAK' IT UP!
I'LL SAY IT WI' FLOWERS . . .
FLORIST
SAY IT WITH FLOWERS
. . . PUSH OFF, YE WEED!
OUCH!
OOH! WHERE AM I . . ?
HOI! WATCH WHAUR YE'RE GOIN'!
OH, NO!
GRR! I'D JUST FINISHED PLANTIN' THESE FLOWERS!
IT'S NO USE! I JIST CAN'T REMEMBER WHIT MA ASKED ME TAE BUY FOR HER!
Wullie's Hoose
WELL, WULLIE, DID YE GET IT FOR ME?
GET WHAT, MA?
MY FLOUR, OF COURSE!
OH, NO!
FANCY ME FORGETTING FLOUR AFTER THE DAY I'VE HAD!

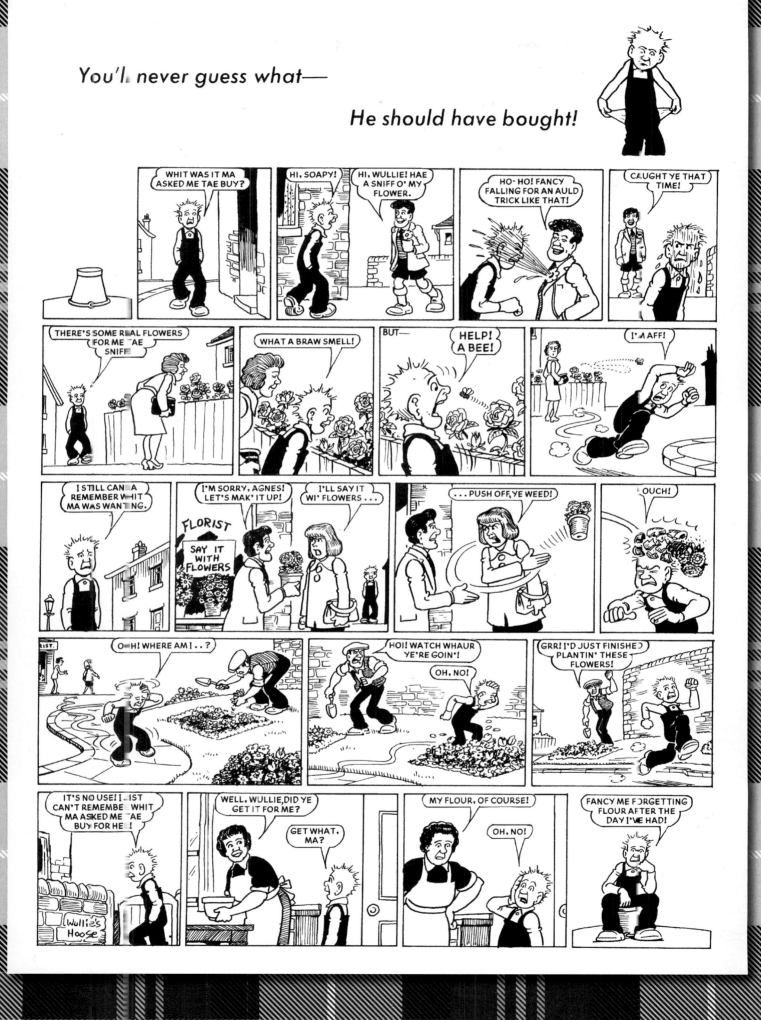

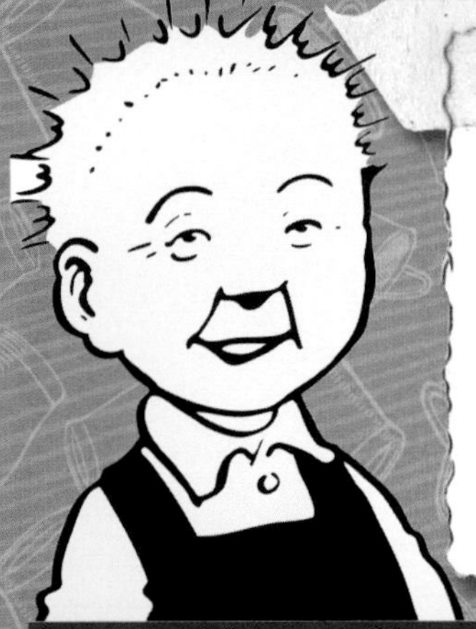

In the seventies The Sunday Post newspaper was breaking records circulation-wise and the popularity of The Broons and Oor Wullie was immense. The colourful Oor Wullie books of this decade sold out every Christmas. A great many were sent to Scots living abroad and must have been a hilarious reminder of life in 'the auld country'. Most people will recognise some of these covers, in fact many people carefully kept and stored their old Oor Wullie books.

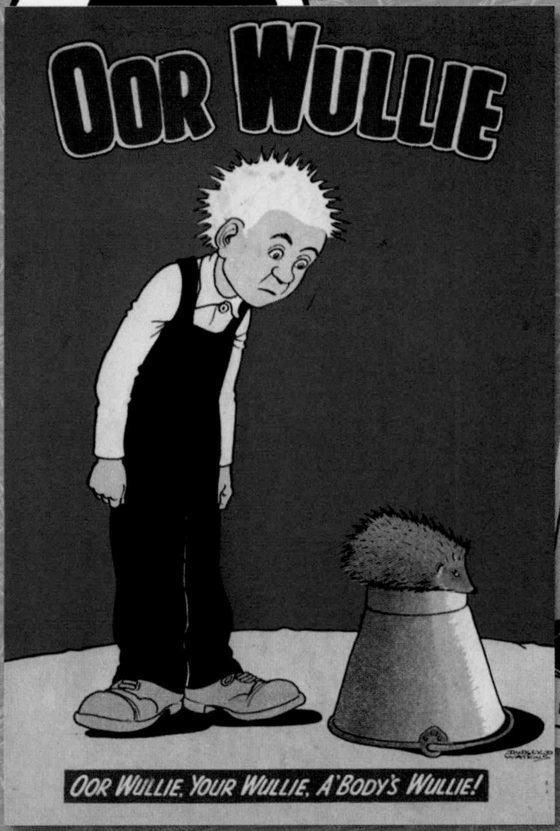
OOR WULLIE
OOR WULLIE, YOUR WULLIE, A'BODY'S WULLIE!

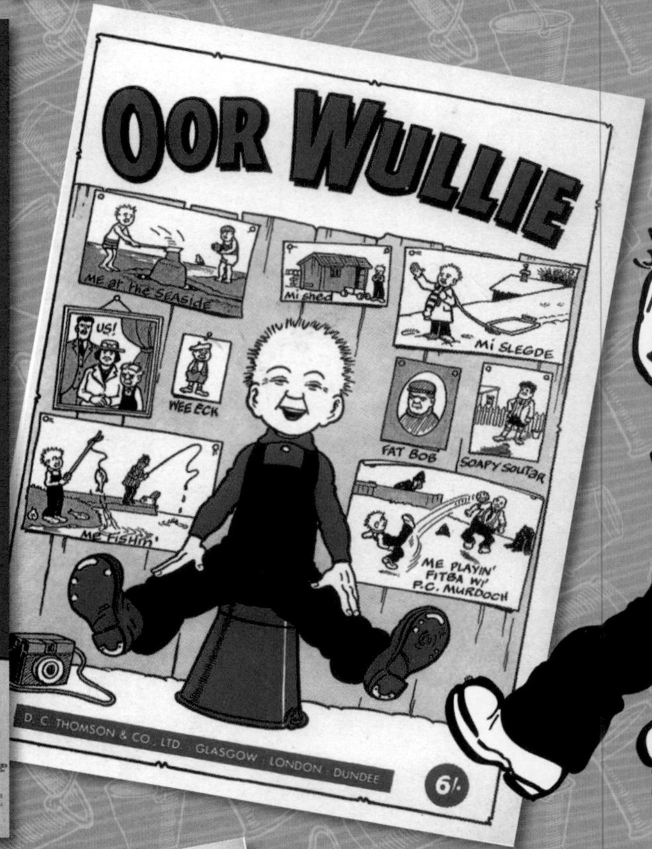
OOR WULLIE
ME at the SEASIDE
Mi shed
Mi SLEGDE
US!
WEE ECK
FAT BOB
SOAPY SOUTAR
ME FISHIN'
ME PLAYIN' FITBA WI' P.C. MURDOCH
D. C. THOMSON & CO., LTD. GLASGOW · LONDON · DUNDEE
6/-

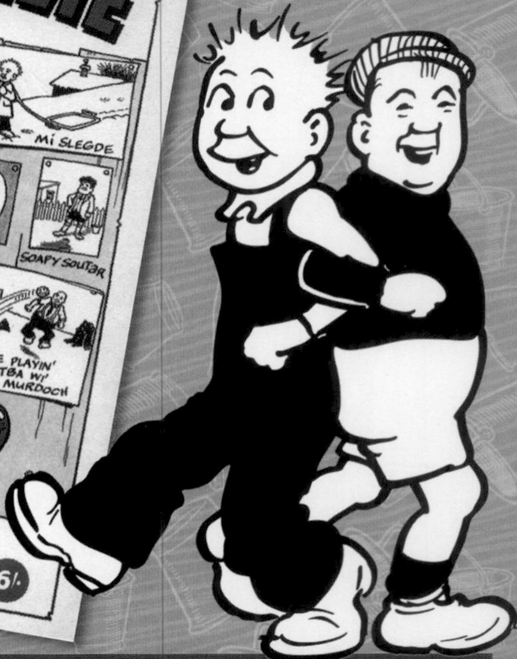

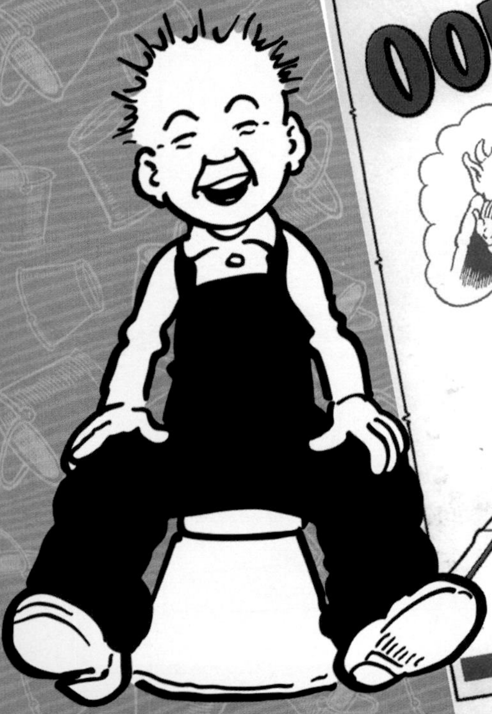

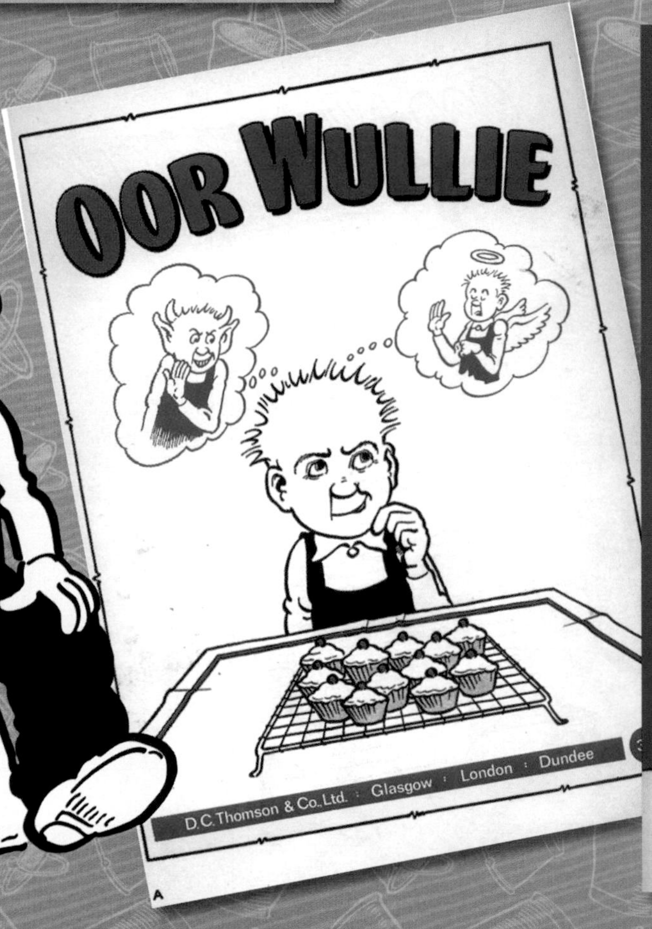
OOR WULLIE
D.C.Thomson & Co.,Ltd. Glasgow London Dundee

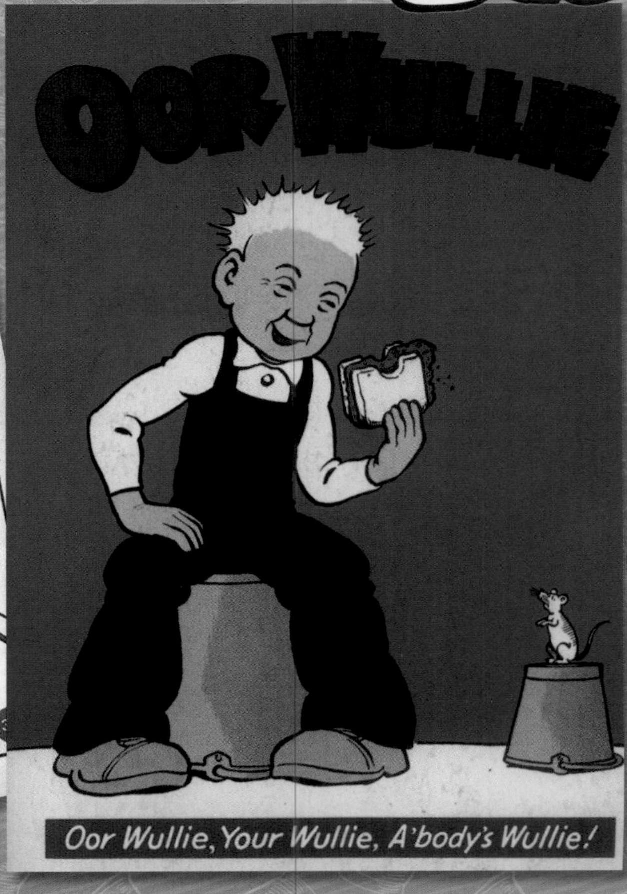
OOR WULLIE
Oor Wullie, Your Wullie, A'body's Wullie!

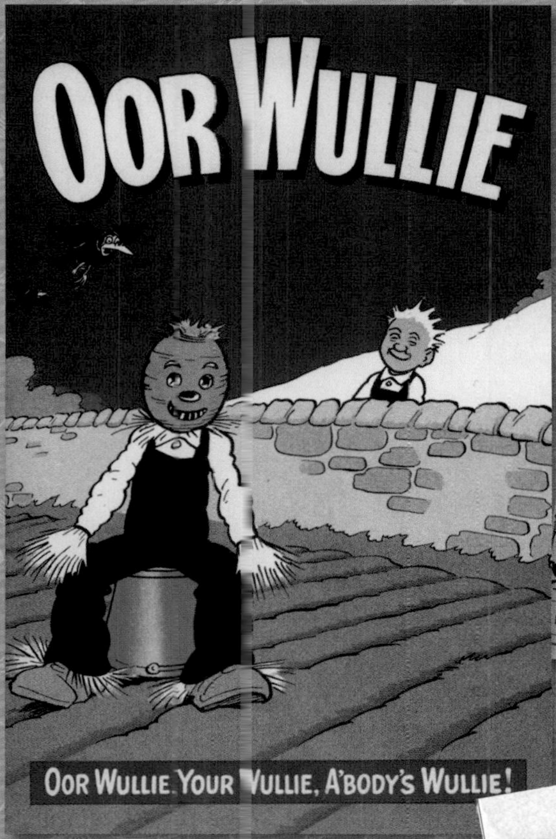
OOR WULLIE
OOR WULLIE. YOUR WULLIE, A'BODY'S WULLIE!

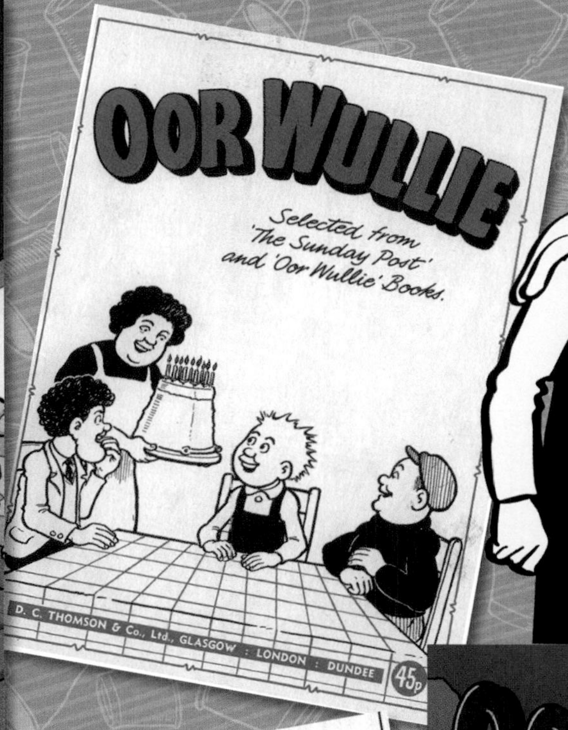
OOR WULLIE
Selected from 'The Sunday Post' and 'Oor Wullie' Books.
D. C. THOMSON & Co., Ltd., GLASGOW : LONDON : DUNDEE
45p

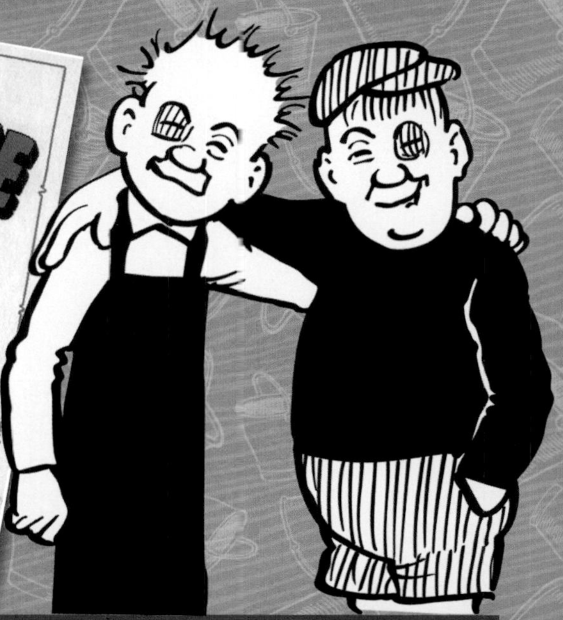

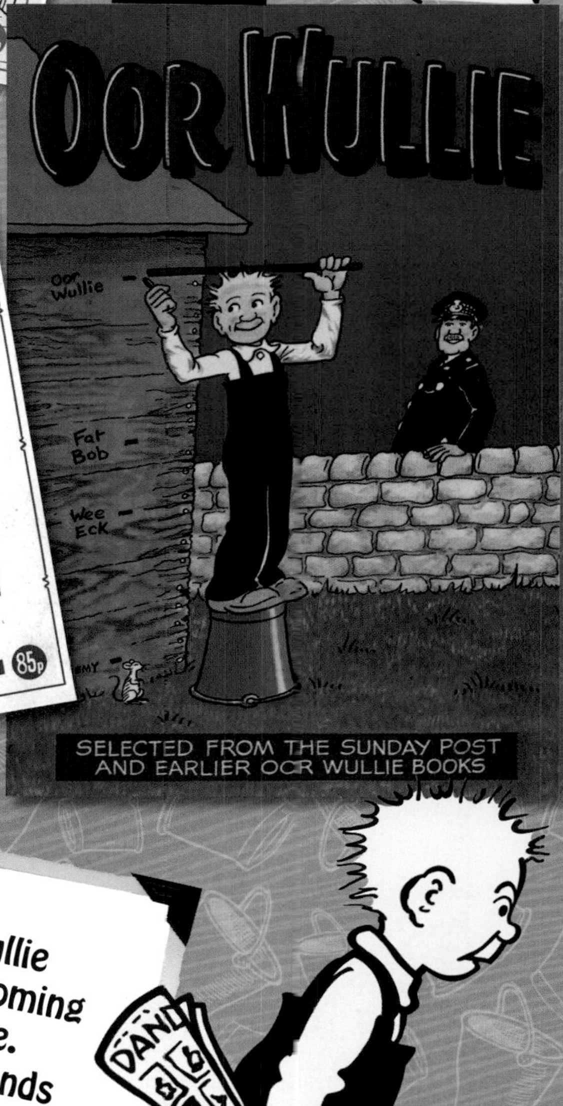
OOR WULLIE
Oor Wullie
Fat Bob
Wee Eck
SELECTED FROM THE SUNDAY POST AND EARLIER OOR WULLIE BOOKS

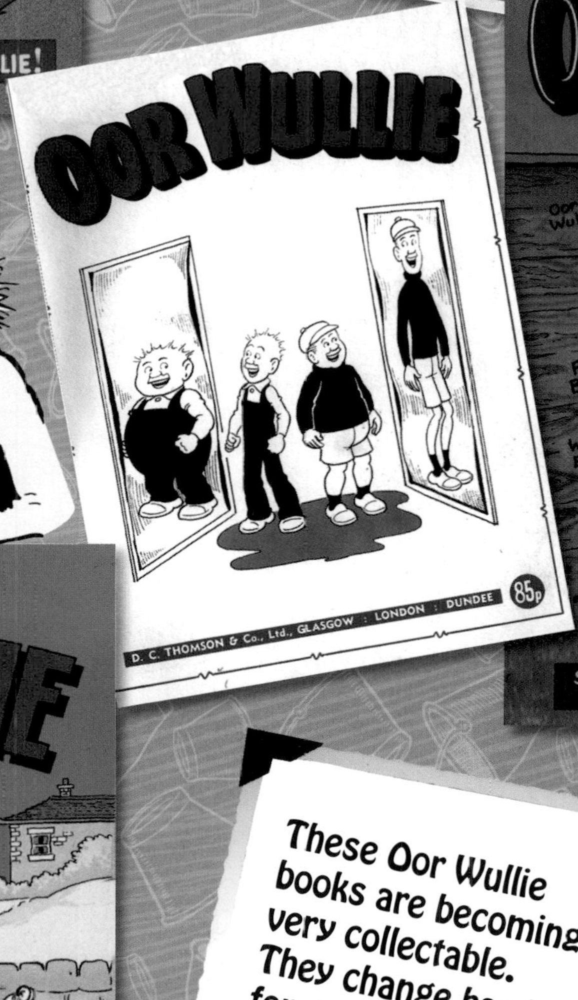
OOR WULLIE
D. C. THOMSON & Co., Ltd., GLASGOW : LONDON : DUNDEE
85p

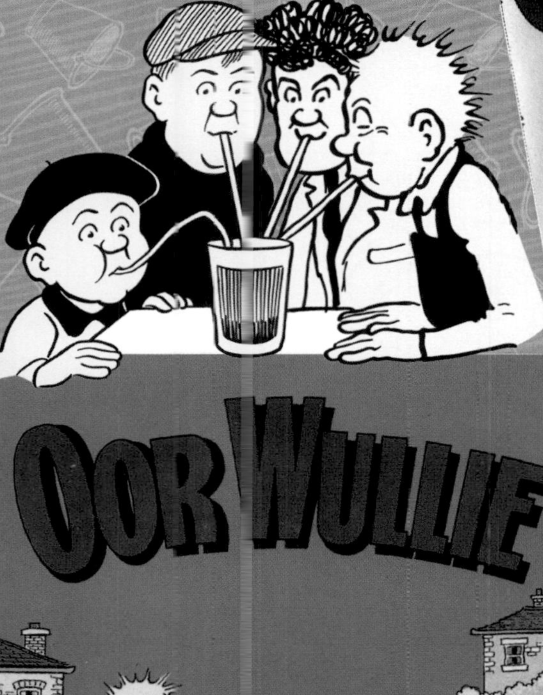

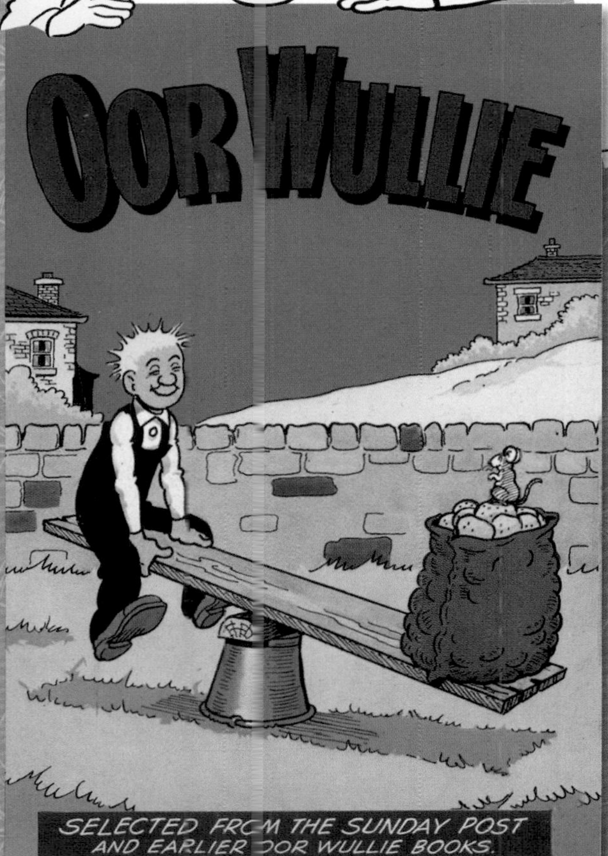
OOR WULLIE
SELECTED FROM THE SUNDAY POST AND EARLIER OOR WULLIE BOOKS.

These Oor Wullie books are becoming very collectable. They change hands for good prices if in top condition. Trouble is, most people read and re-read their Oor Wullie books over and over again so very few are in mint condition.

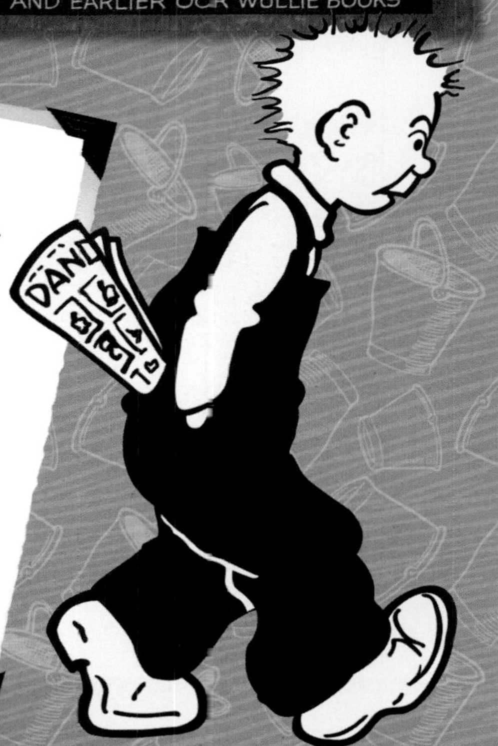

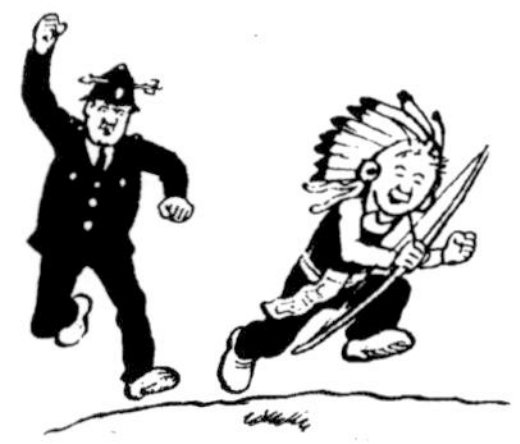

Pa's money's safe, or so it seems—

But one BAD shot upsets Pa's schemes!

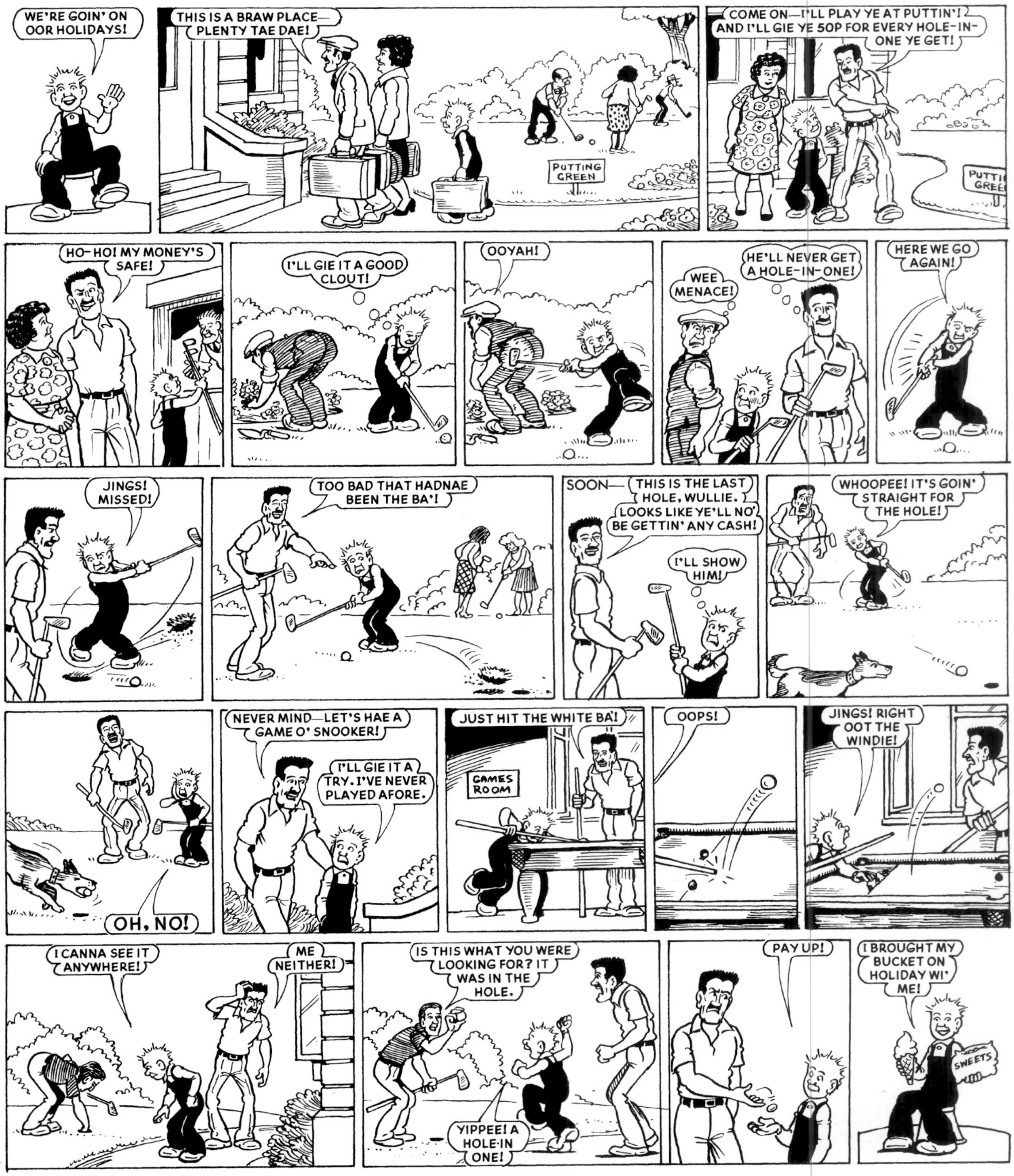
WE'RE GOIN' ON OOR HOLIDAYS!
THIS IS A BRAW PLACE—PLENTY TAE DAE!
PUTTING GREEN
COME ON—I'LL PLAY YE AT PUTTIN'! AND I'LL GIE YE 50P FOR EVERY HOLE-IN-ONE YE GET!
HO-HO! MY MONEY'S SAFE!
I'LL GIE IT A GOOD CLOUT!
OOYAH!
WEE MENACE!
HE'LL NEVER GET A HOLE-IN-ONE!
HERE WE GO AGAIN!
JINGS! MISSED!
TOO BAD THAT HADNAE BEEN THE BA'!
SOON—
THIS IS THE LAST HOLE, WULLIE. LOOKS LIKE YE'LL NO' BE GETTIN' ANY CASH!
I'LL SHOW HIM!
WHOOPEE! IT'S GOIN' STRAIGHT FOR THE HOLE!
OH, NO!
NEVER MIND—LET'S HAE A GAME O' SNOOKER!
I'LL GIE IT A TRY. I'VE NEVER PLAYED AFORE.
JUST HIT THE WHITE BA'!
GAMES ROOM
OOPS!
JINGS! RIGHT OOT THE WINDIE!
I CANNA SEE IT ANYWHERE!
ME NEITHER!
IS THIS WHAT YOU WERE LOOKING FOR? IT WAS IN THE HOLE.
YIPPEE! A HOLE-IN ONE!
PAY UP!
I BROUGHT MY BUCKET ON HOLIDAY WI' ME!
SWEETS

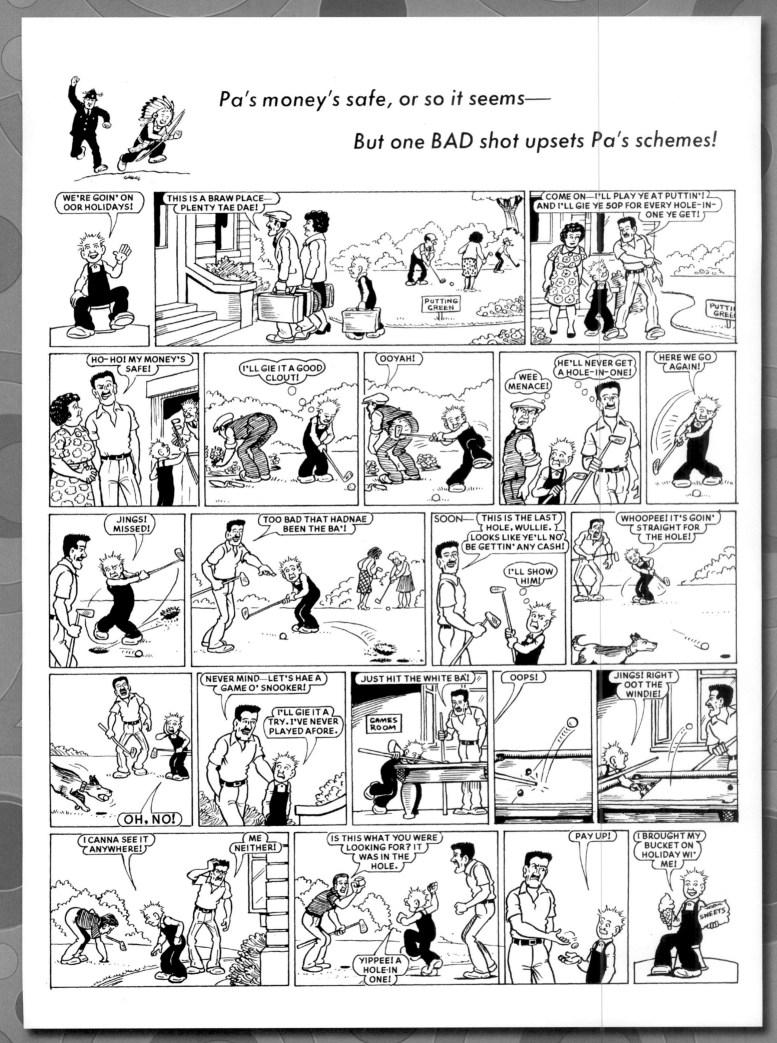

He's the best wee pet—

Wull could ever get!

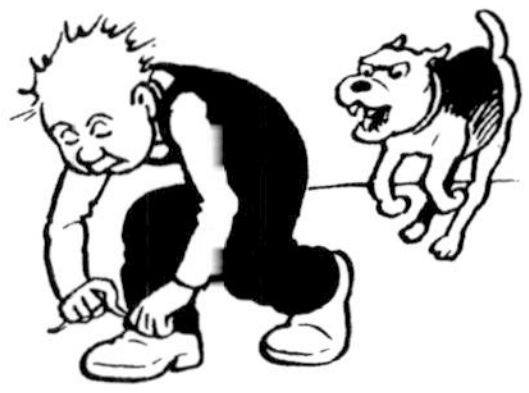

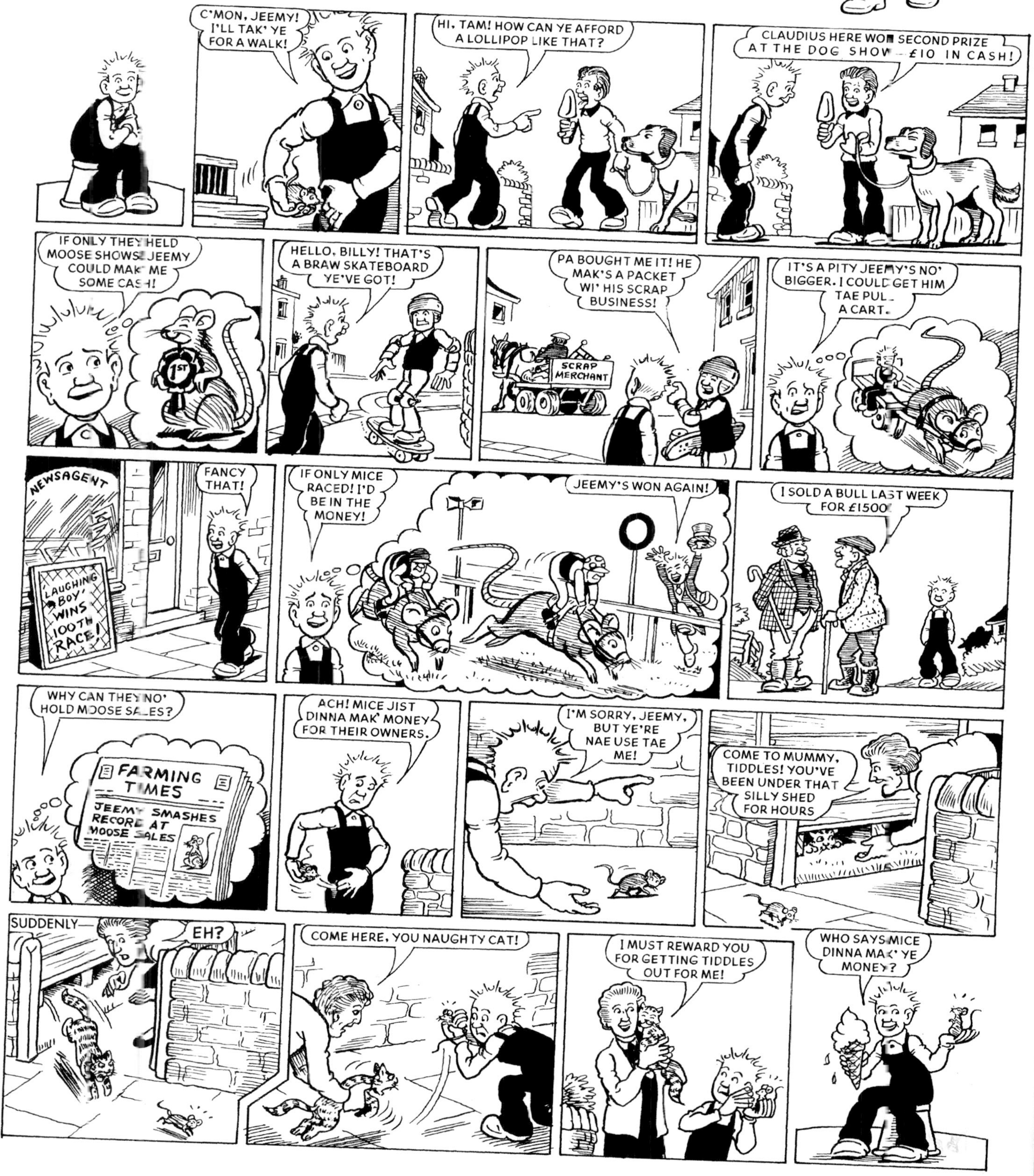
C'MON, JEEMY! I'LL TAK' YE FOR A WALK!
HI, TAM! HOW CAN YE AFFORD A LOLLIPOP LIKE THAT?
CLAUDIUS HERE WON SECOND PRIZE AT THE DOG SHOW—£10 IN CASH!
IF ONLY THEY HELD MOOSE SHOWS, JEEMY COULD MAK' ME SOME CASH!
1ST
HELLO, BILLY! THAT'S A BRAW SKATEBOARD YE'VE GOT!
PA BOUGHT ME IT! HE MAK'S A PACKET WI' HIS SCRAP BUSINESS!
SCRAP MERCHANT
IT'S A PITY JEEMY'S NO' BIGGER. I COULD GET HIM TAE PULL A CART.
NEWSAGENT
LAUGHING BOY WINS 100TH RACE!
FANCY THAT!
IF ONLY MICE RACED! I'D BE IN THE MONEY!
JEEMY'S WON AGAIN!
I SOLD A BULL LAST WEEK FOR £1500!
WHY CAN THEY NO' HOLD MOOSE SALES?
FARMING TIMES
JEEMY SMASHES RECORD AT MOOSE SALES
ACH! MICE JIST DINNA MAK' MONEY FOR THEIR OWNERS.
I'M SORRY, JEEMY, BUT YE'RE NAE USE TAE ME!
COME TO MUMMY, TIDDLES! YOU'VE BEEN UNDER THAT SILLY SHED FOR HOURS
SUDDENLY—
EH?
COME HERE, YOU NAUGHTY CAT!
I MUST REWARD YOU FOR GETTING TIDDLES OUT FOR ME!
WHO SAYS MICE DINNA MAK' YE MONEY?

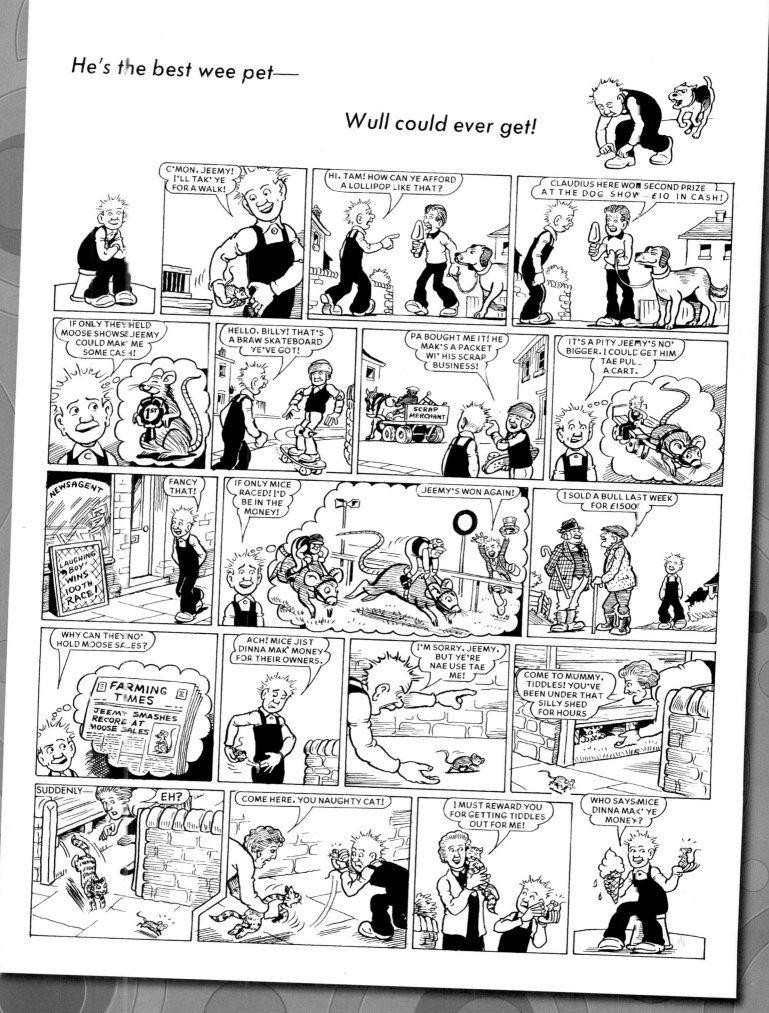

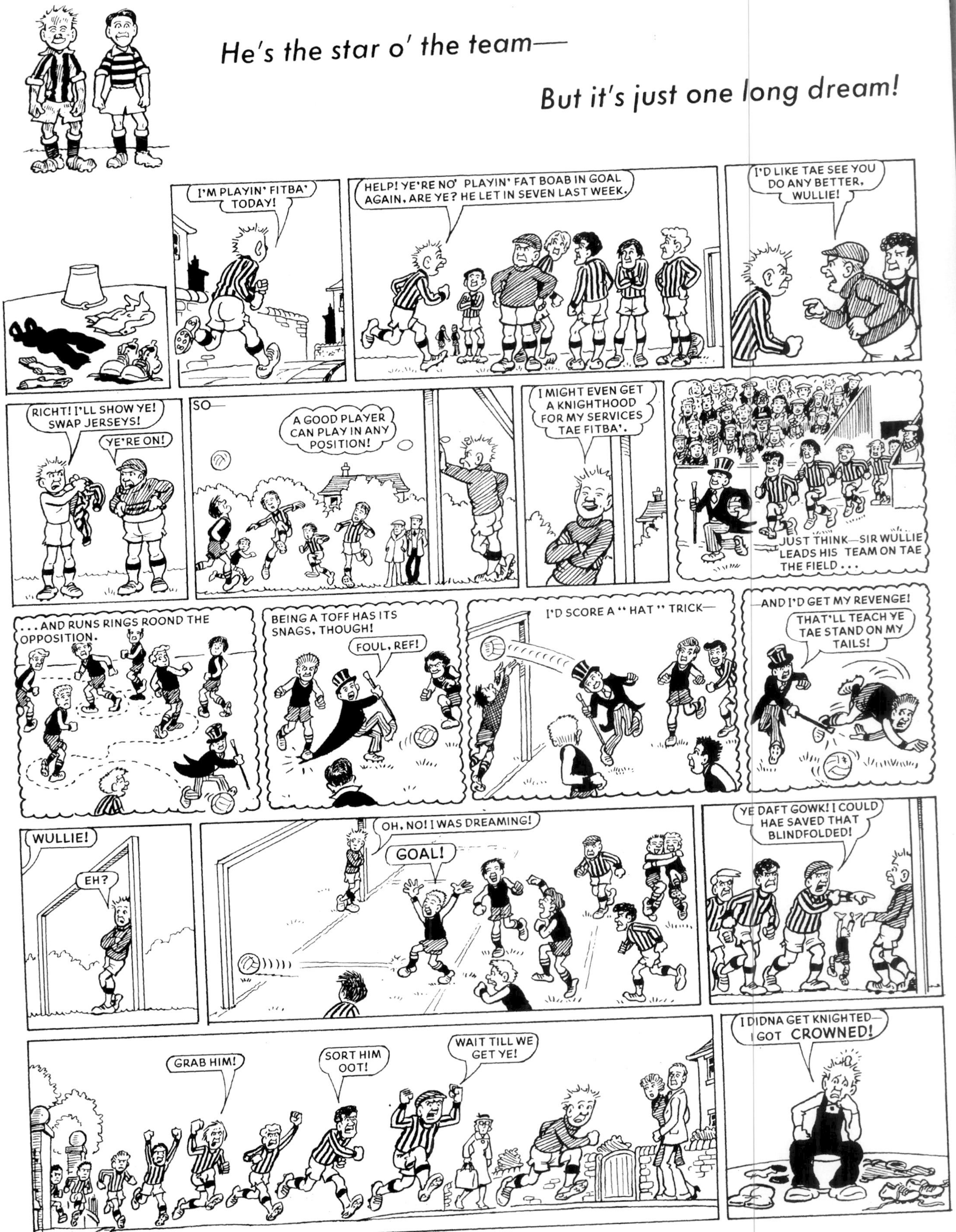

He's the star o' the team—
But it's just one long dream!
I'M PLAYIN' FITBA' TODAY!
HELP! YE'RE NO' PLAYIN' FAT BOAB IN GOAL AGAIN, ARE YE? HE LET IN SEVEN LAST WEEK.
I'D LIKE TAE SEE YOU DO ANY BETTER, WULLIE!
RICHT! I'LL SHOW YE! SWAP JERSEYS!
YE'RE ON!
SO—
A GOOD PLAYER CAN PLAY IN ANY POSITION!
I MIGHT EVEN GET A KNIGHTHOOD FOR MY SERVICES TAE FITBA'.
JUST THINK—SIR WULLIE LEADS HIS TEAM ON TAE THE FIELD . . .
. . . AND RUNS RINGS ROOND THE OPPOSITION.
BEING A TOFF HAS ITS SNAGS, THOUGH!
FOUL, REF!
I'D SCORE A " HAT " TRICK—
—AND I'D GET MY REVENGE!
THAT'LL TEACH YE TAE STAND ON MY TAILS!
WULLIE!
EH?
OH, NO! I WAS DREAMING!
GOAL!
YE DAFT GOWK! I COULD HAE SAVED THAT BLINDFOLDED!
GRAB HIM!
SORT HIM OOT!
WAIT TILL WE GET YE!
I DIDNA GET KNIGHTED—I GOT CROWNED!

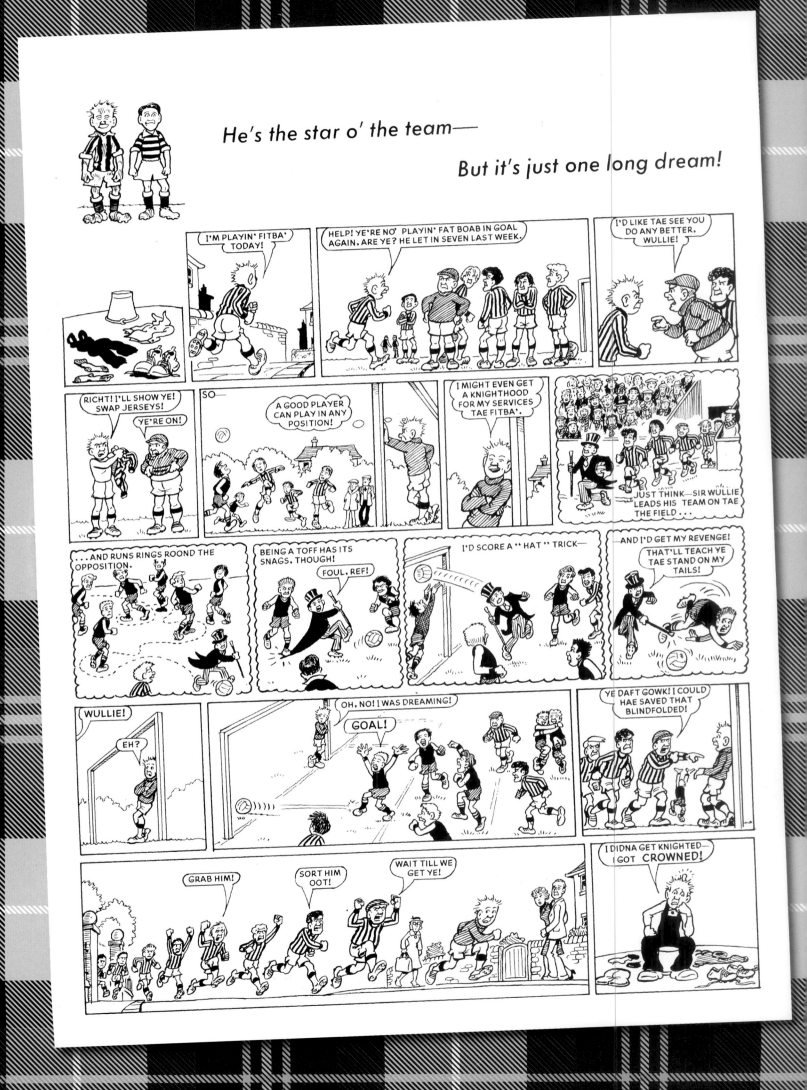

Look at what Oor Wullie's found—

His new pal's a muckle hound!

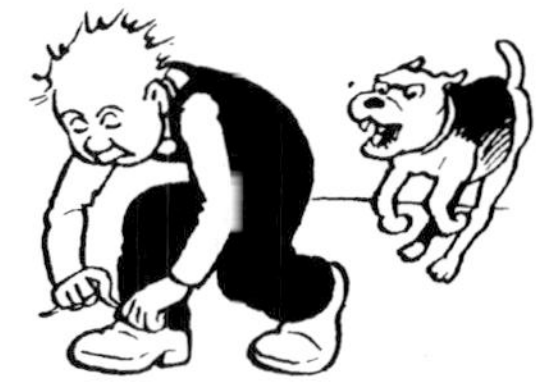

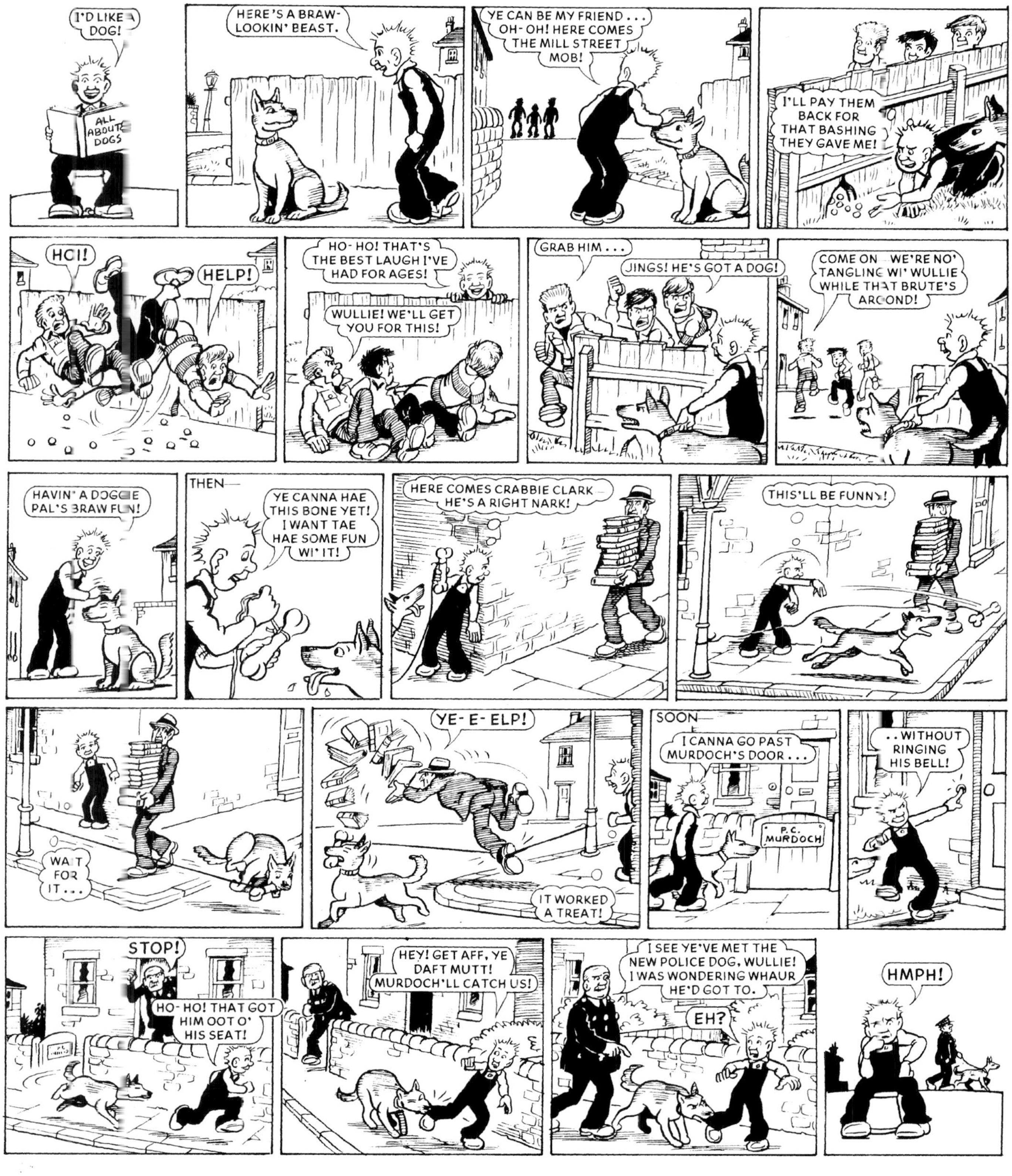
I'D LIKE A DOG!
ALL ABOUT DOGS
HERE'S A BRAW-LOOKIN' BEAST.
YE CAN BE MY FRIEND . . . OH-OH! HERE COMES THE MILL STREET MOB!
I'LL PAY THEM BACK FOR THAT BASHING THEY GAVE ME!
HOI!
HELP!
HO-HO! THAT'S THE BEST LAUGH I'VE HAD FOR AGES!
WULLIE! WE'LL GET YOU FOR THIS!
GRAB HIM . . .
JINGS! HE'S GOT A DOG!
COME ON—WE'RE NO' TANGLING WI' WULLIE WHILE THAT BRUTE'S AROOND!
HAVIN' A DOGGIE PAL'S BRAW FUN!
THEN—
YE CANNA HAE THIS BONE YET! I WANT TAE HAE SOME FUN WI' IT!
HERE COMES CRABBIE CLARK—HE'S A RIGHT NARK!
THIS'LL BE FUNNY!
WAIT FOR IT . . .
YE-E-ELP!
IT WORKED A TREAT!
SOON—
I CANNA GO PAST MURDOCH'S DOOR . . .
P.C. MURDOCH
. . WITHOUT RINGING HIS BELL!
STOP!
HO-HO! THAT GOT HIM OOT O' HIS SEAT!
HEY! GET AFF, YE DAFT MUTT! MURDOCH'LL CATCH US!
I SEE YE'VE MET THE NEW POLICE DOG, WULLIE! I WAS WONDERING WHAUR HE'D GOT TO.
EH?
HMPH!

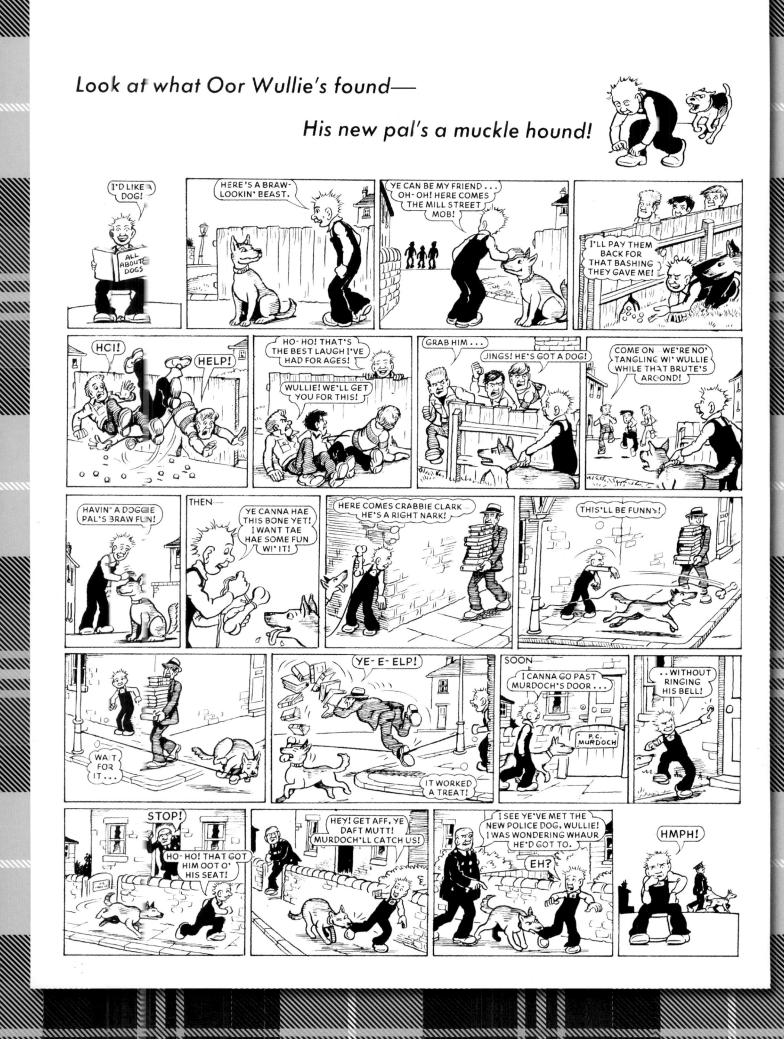

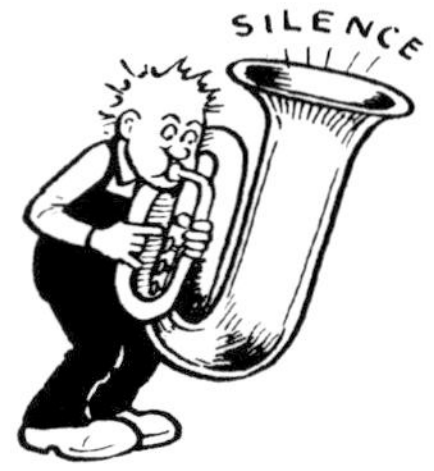
SILENCE

As half-past twelve at last draws near—

There's one sound Wullie waits to hear!

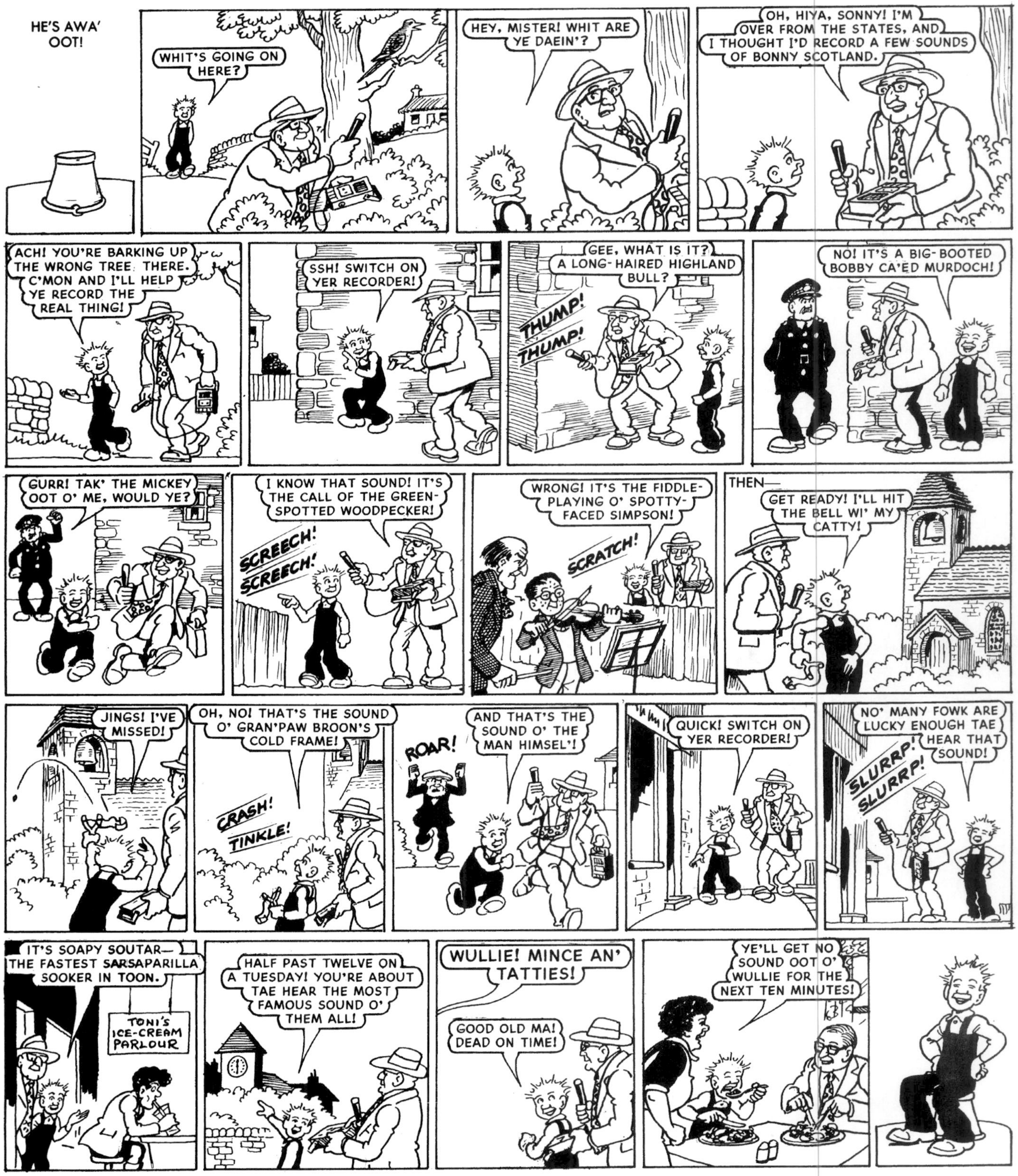
HE'S AWA' OOT!
WHIT'S GOING ON HERE?
HEY, MISTER! WHIT ARE YE DAEIN'?
OH, HIYA, SONNY! I'M OVER FROM THE STATES, AND I THOUGHT I'D RECORD A FEW SOUNDS OF BONNY SCOTLAND.
ACH! YOU'RE BARKING UP THE WRONG TREE, THERE. C'MON AND I'LL HELP YE RECORD THE REAL THING!
SSH! SWITCH ON YER RECORDER!
GEE, WHAT IS IT? A LONG-HAIRED HIGHLAND BULL?
THUMP! THUMP!
NO! IT'S A BIG-BOOTED BOBBY CA'ED MURDOCH!
GURR! TAK' THE MICKEY OOT O' ME, WOULD YE?
I KNOW THAT SOUND! IT'S THE CALL OF THE GREEN-SPOTTED WOODPECKER!
SCREECH! SCREECH!
WRONG! IT'S THE FIDDLE-PLAYING O' SPOTTY-FACED SIMPSON!
SCRATCH!
THEN—
GET READY! I'LL HIT THE BELL WI' MY CATTY!
JINGS! I'VE MISSED!
OH, NO! THAT'S THE SOUND O' GRAN'PAW BROON'S COLD FRAME!
CRASH! TINKLE!
AND THAT'S THE SOUND O' THE MAN HIMSEL'!
ROAR!
QUICK! SWITCH ON YER RECORDER!
NO' MANY FOWK ARE LUCKY ENOUGH TAE HEAR THAT SOUND!
SLURRP! SLURRP!
IT'S SOAPY SOUTAR— THE FASTEST SARSAPARILLA SOOKER IN TOON.
TONI'S ICE-CREAM PARLOUR
HALF PAST TWELVE ON A TUESDAY! YOU'RE ABOUT TAE HEAR THE MOST FAMOUS SOUND O' THEM ALL!
WULLIE! MINCE AN' TATTIES!
GOOD OLD MA! DEAD ON TIME!
YE'LL GET NO SOUND OOT O' WULLIE FOR THE NEXT TEN MINUTES!

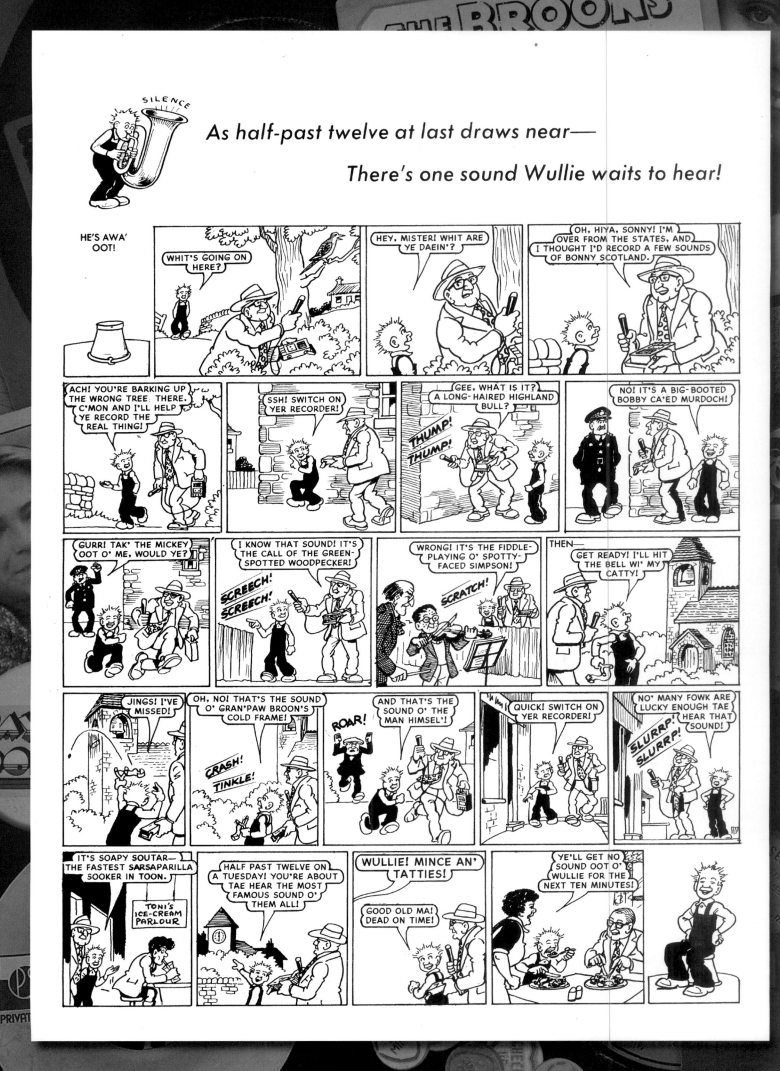

Michty me! There's something wrong—

Wullie's arms are four-feet long!

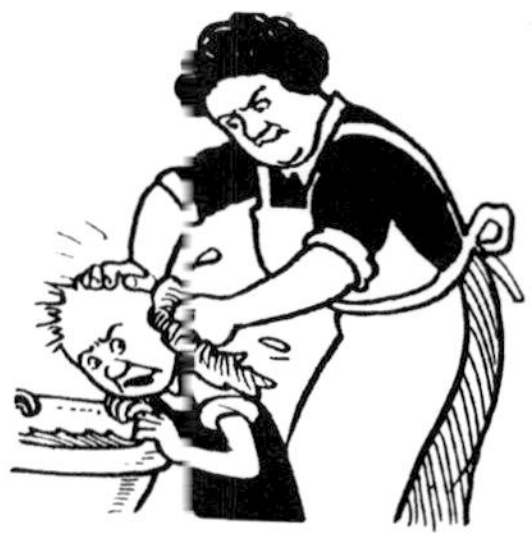

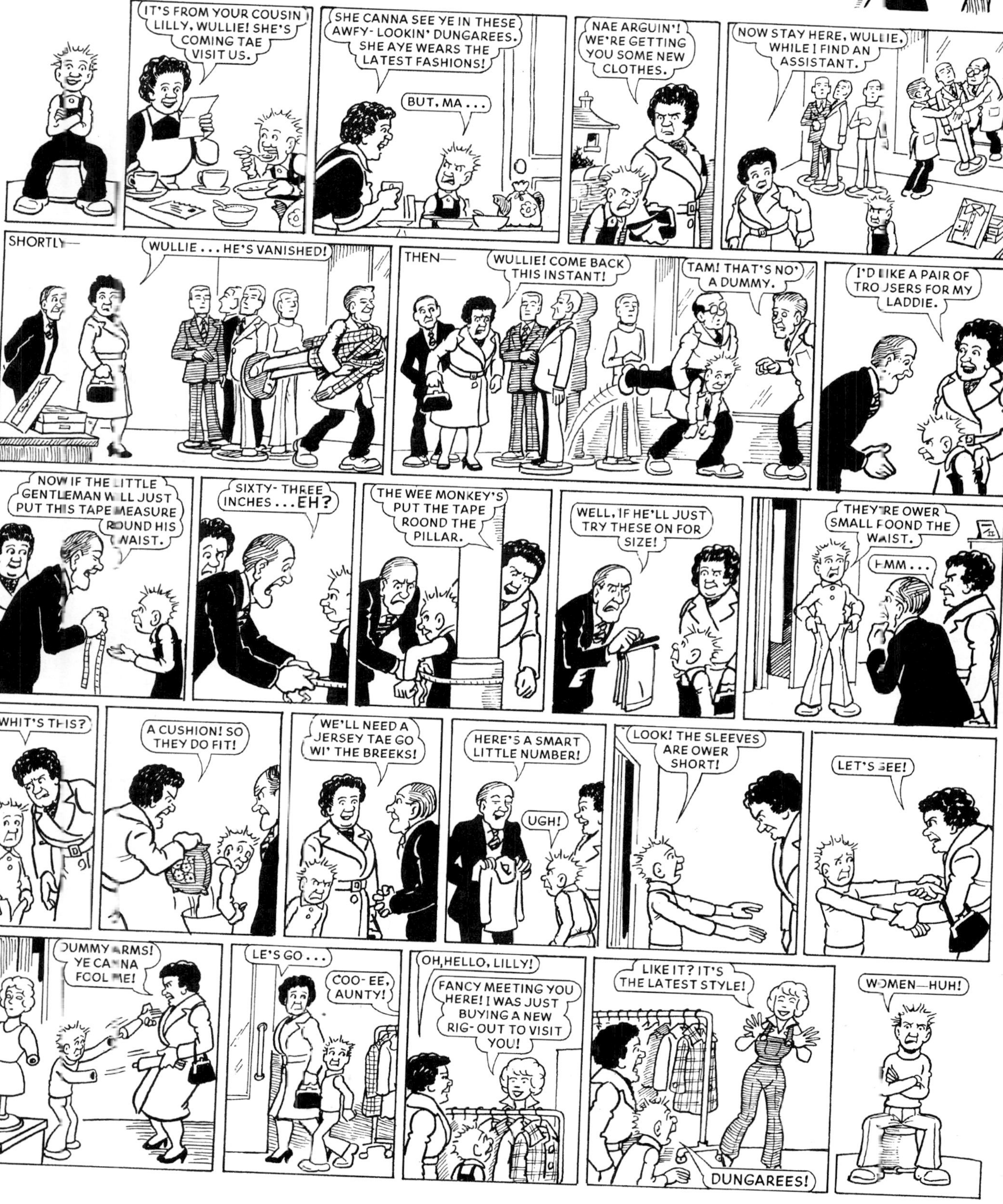

IT'S FROM YOUR COUSIN LILLY, WULLIE! SHE'S COMING TAE VISIT US.
SHE CANNA SEE YE IN THESE AWFY- LOOKIN' DUNGAREES. SHE AYE WEARS THE LATEST FASHIONS!
BUT, MA . . .
NAE ARGUIN'! WE'RE GETTING YOU SOME NEW CLOTHES.
NOW STAY HERE, WULLIE, WHILE I FIND AN ASSISTANT.
SHORTLY—
WULLIE . . . HE'S VANISHED!
THEN—
WULLIE! COME BACK THIS INSTANT!
TAM! THAT'S NO' A DUMMY.
I'D LIKE A PAIR OF TROUSERS FOR MY LADDIE.
NOW IF THE LITTLE GENTLEMAN WILL JUST PUT THIS TAPE MEASURE ROUND HIS WAIST.
SIXTY- THREE INCHES . . . EH?
THE WEE MONKEY'S PUT THE TAPE ROOND THE PILLAR.
WELL, IF HE'LL JUST TRY THESE ON FOR SIZE!
THEY'RE OWER SMALL ROOND THE WAIST.
HMM . . .
WHIT'S THIS?
A CUSHION! SO THEY DO FIT!
WE'LL NEED A JERSEY TAE GO WI' THE BREEKS!
HERE'S A SMART LITTLE NUMBER!
UGH!
LOOK! THE SLEEVES ARE OWER SHORT!
LET'S SEE!
DUMMY ARMS! YE CANNA FOOL ME!
LE'S GO . . .
COO- EE, AUNTY!
OH, HELLO, LILLY!
FANCY MEETING YOU HERE! I WAS JUST BUYING A NEW RIG- OUT TO VISIT YOU!
LIKE IT? IT'S THE LATEST STYLE!
DUNGAREES!
WOMEN—HUH!

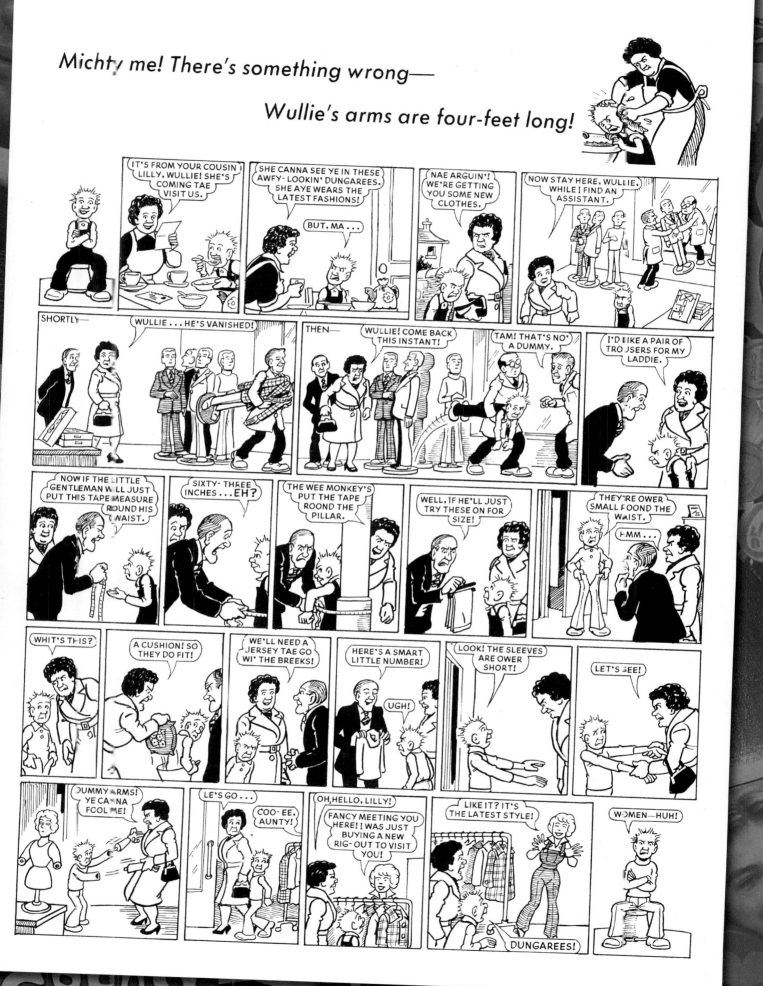

Three lads go for a cartie run—

And they soon have TREEmendous fun!

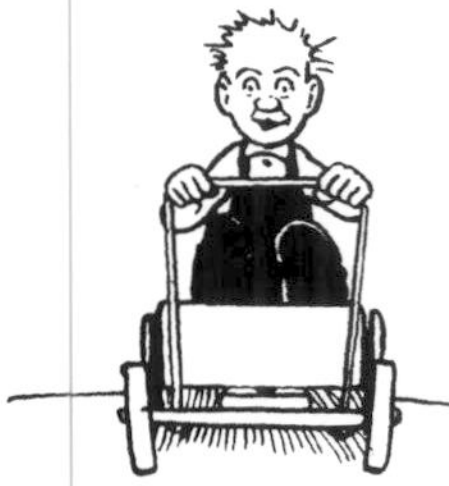

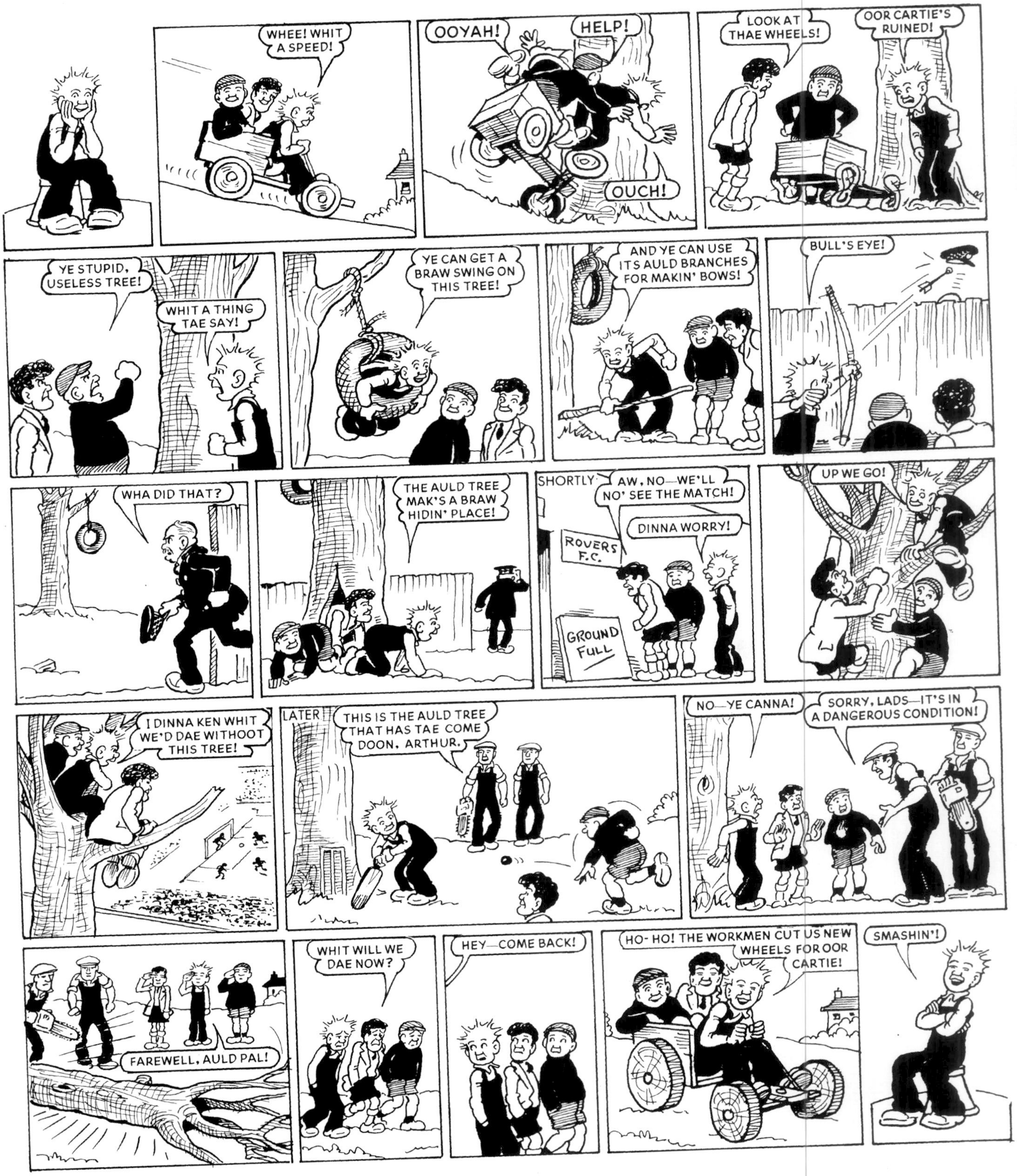

WHEE! WHIT A SPEED!
OOYAH!
HELP!
OUCH!
LOOK AT THAE WHEELS!
OOR CARTIE'S RUINED!
YE STUPID, USELESS TREE!
WHIT A THING TAE SAY!
YE CAN GET A BRAW SWING ON THIS TREE!
AND YE CAN USE ITS AULD BRANCHES FOR MAKIN' BOWS!
BULL'S EYE!
WHA DID THAT?
THE AULD TREE MAK'S A BRAW HIDIN' PLACE!
SHORTLY
AW, NO—WE'LL NO' SEE THE MATCH!
ROVERS F.C.
DINNA WORRY!
GROUND FULL
UP WE GO!
I DINNA KEN WHIT WE'D DAE WITHOOT THIS TREE!
LATER
THIS IS THE AULD TREE THAT HAS TAE COME DOON, ARTHUR.
NO—YE CANNA!
SORRY, LADS—IT'S IN A DANGEROUS CONDITION!
FAREWELL, AULD PAL!
WHIT WILL WE DAE NOW?
HEY—COME BACK!
HO-HO! THE WORKMEN CUT US NEW WHEELS FOR OOR CARTIE!
SMASHIN'!

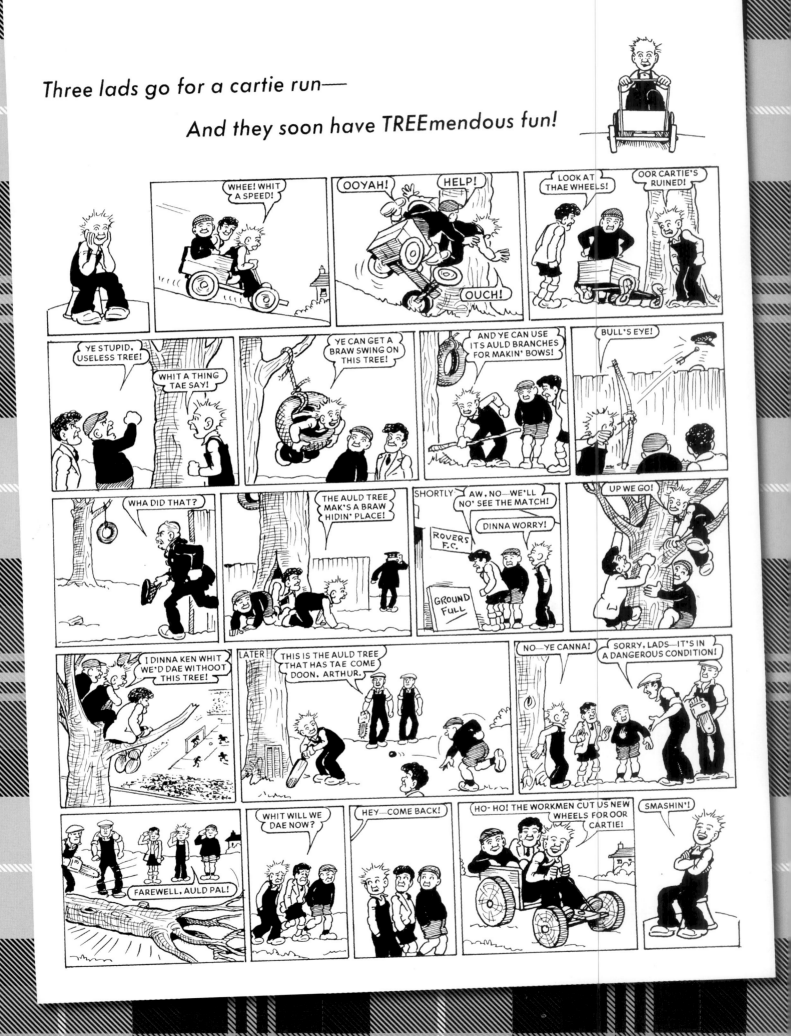

Though Wull's in trouble as a rule—

Today he's teacher's pet at school!

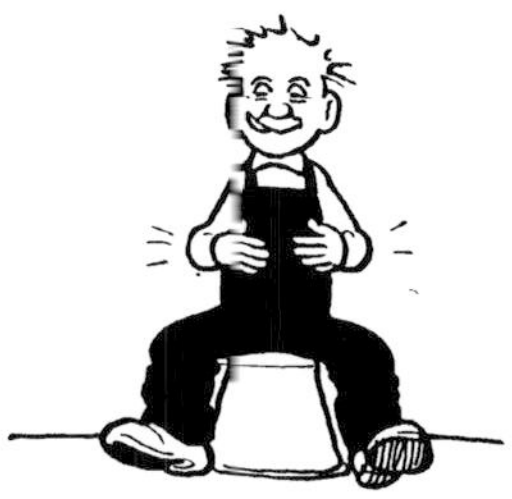

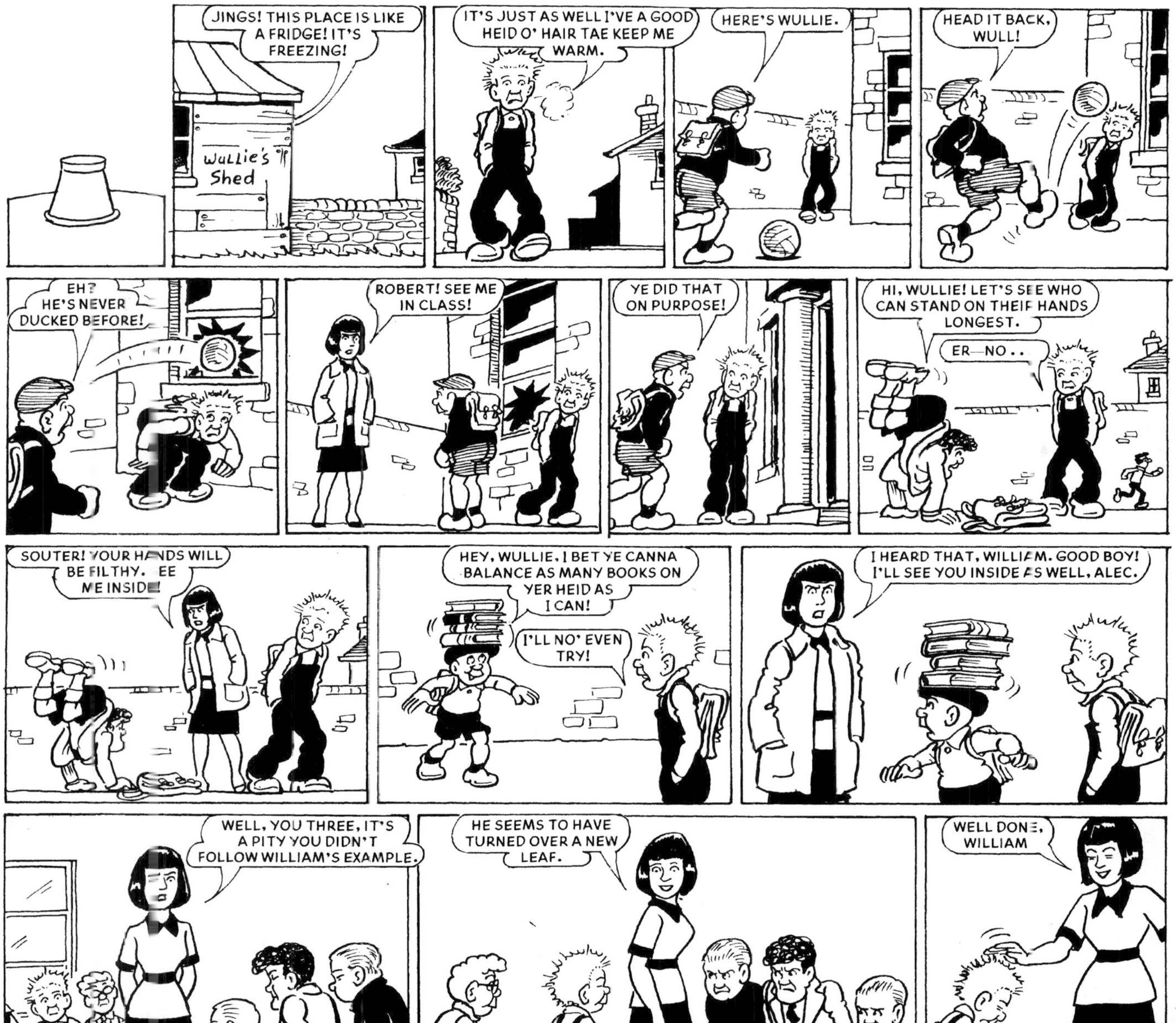

Faces Of The 70s

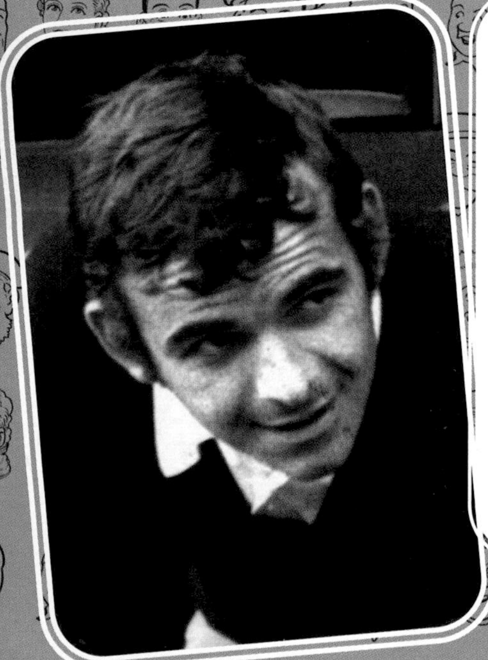

1970

Four years after England's glorious triumph in the World Cup, came their defence, or probably more precisely, the lack of it. This World Cup saw probably the best international team ever seen...Brazil.

England's BIG sporting achievement of 1970 was that of Tony Jacklin who followed up his Open win in 1969 with victory in The US Open. The first Englishman to triumph since Cyril Walker in 1924.

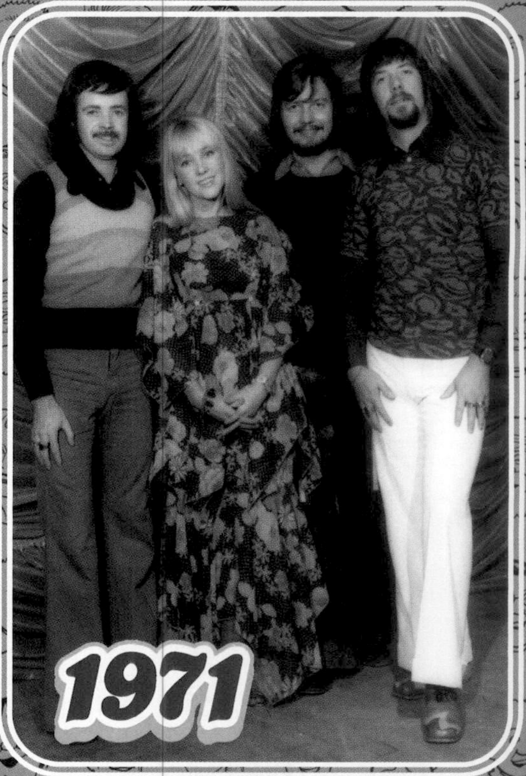

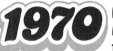

1971

Chirpy Chirpy Cheep Cheep was one of the big hits of 1971. Sung by Middle of the Road, fronted by Sally Carr, the song became one of those get up and dance classics.

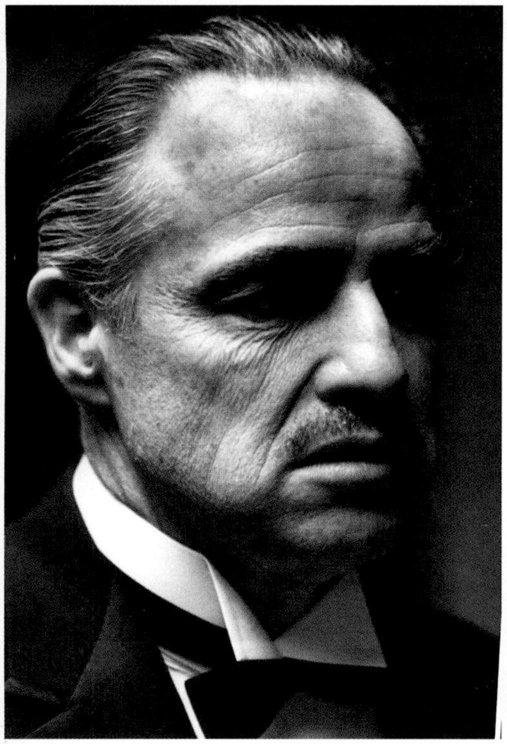

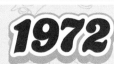

1972

Probably THE face of the 1970s, Marlon Brando as Don Corleone in the classic, Godfather.

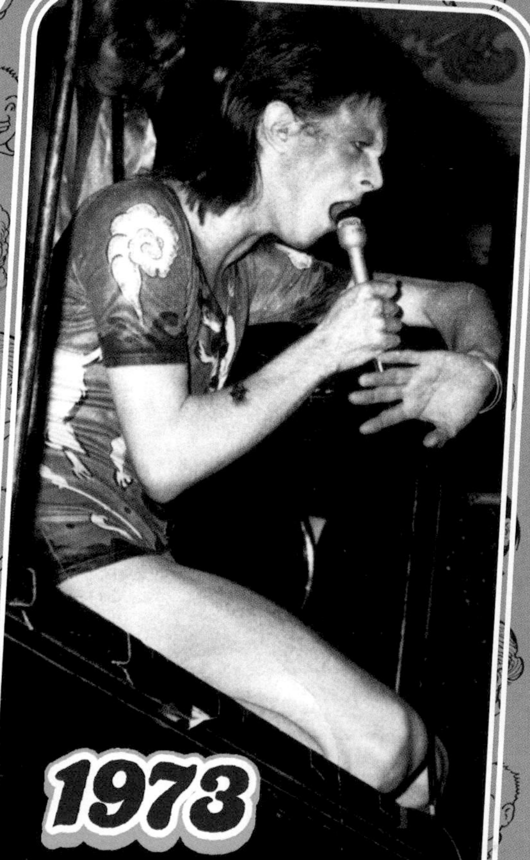

1973

David Bowie in Ziggy Stardust mode was one of the music sensations of the 1970s.

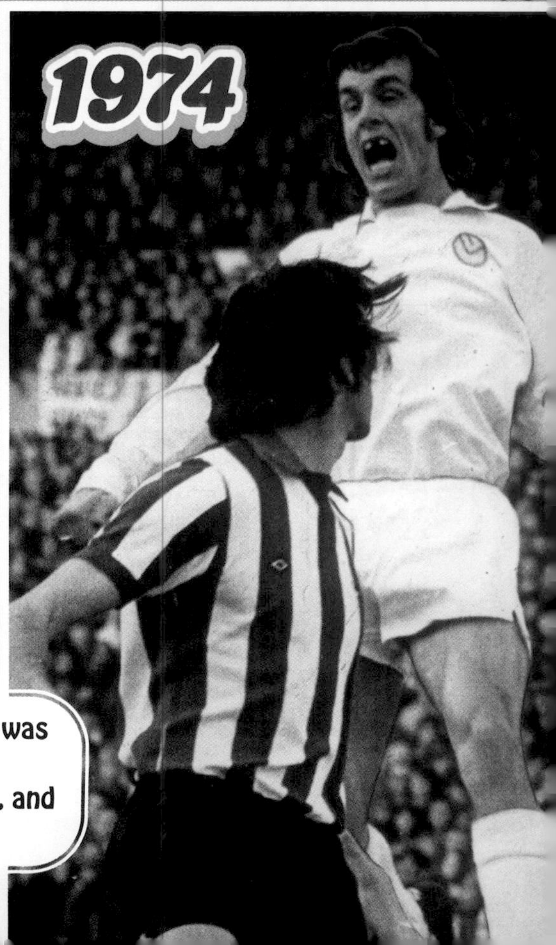

1974

The face of Scottish football circa 1974 was Joe Jordan. His heroics in World Cup qualifying are legend. Scotland qualified, and ...er...England didn't.

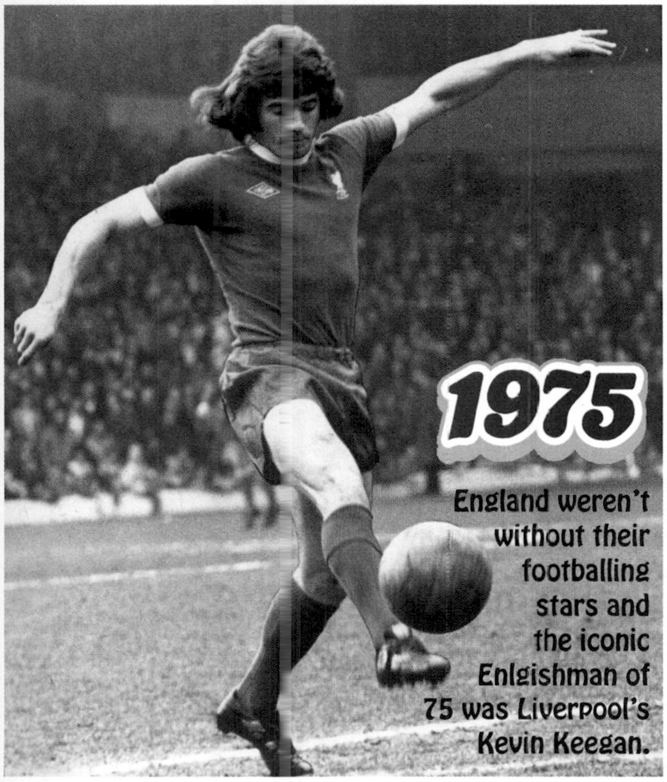

1975

England weren't without their footballing stars and the iconic Enlgishman of 75 was Liverpool's Kevin Keegan.

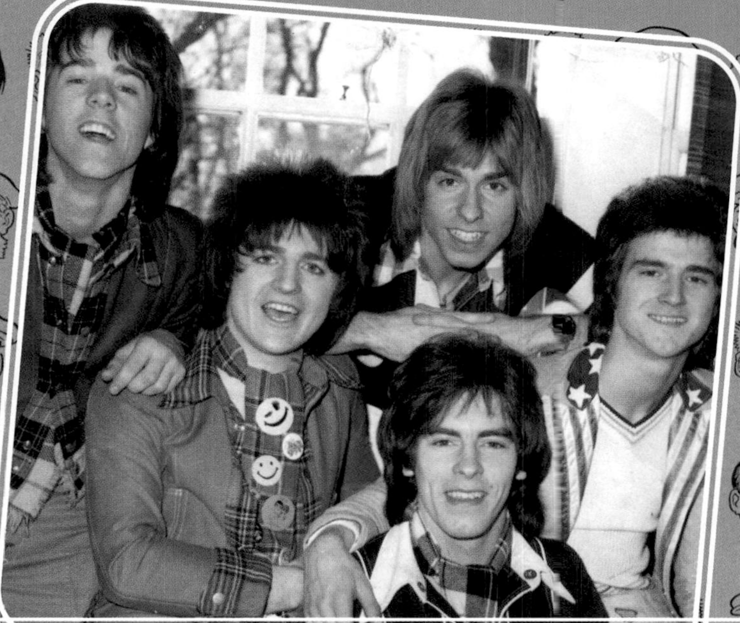

1976

The Bay City Rollers, already a British sensational hit it big on the other side of the Atlantic with a string of top ten albums and singles.

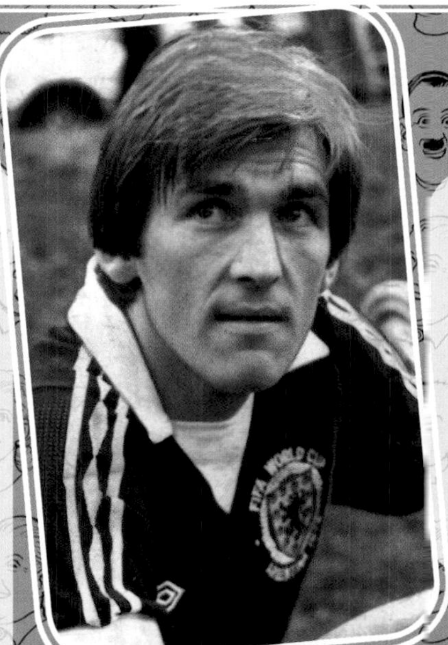

1977

Kenny Dalglish is one of a handful of Scottish players revered both sides of the border. He left Celtic for Liverpool in August and repeated his home success by becoming a Liverpool legend.

1978

Grease hit the screens in 78 with John Travolta and Olivia Neutron Bomb the stars. Who can forget the flower of Australian womanhood in this massive box office smash.

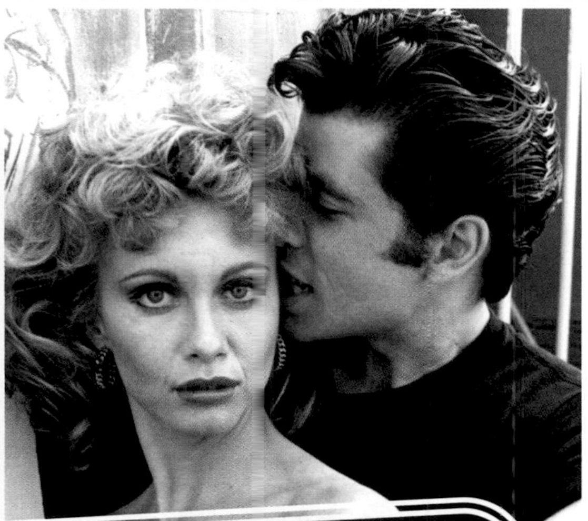

The other major event of 1978 was the World Cup in Argentina. Scotland were there and England weren't. Scotland did nothing except cuff one of the finalists. If it hadn't been for two of the world's great soccer powers in their group, Iran and Peru, it would have been Scotland and Argentina in the final. And we would have won with style. We, or Wee Archie, won the goal of the tournament with that goal!!! Pictured is Denis Law presenting Archie Gemmill with a silver shield in recognition of the best goal ever scored in any World Cup before or after. Now, if only Denis had taken his boots to Argentina just think what Scotland could have done.

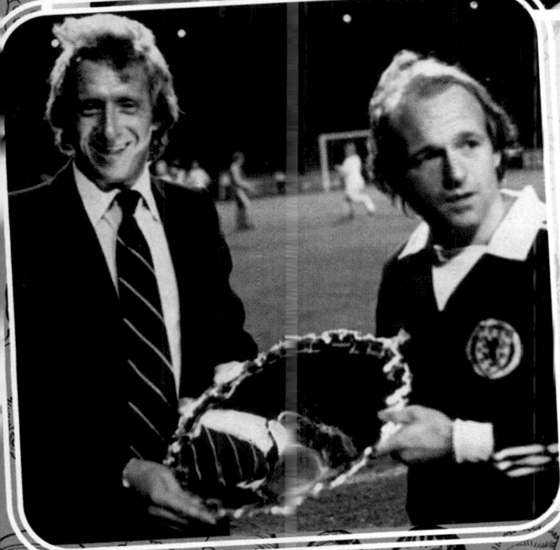

1979

With punk firmly established, many bands hung onto the coat tails of this genre and the Boomtown Rats were one of the outstanding post punk, new wave bands. I don't like Mondays, was the second of their two number one hits.

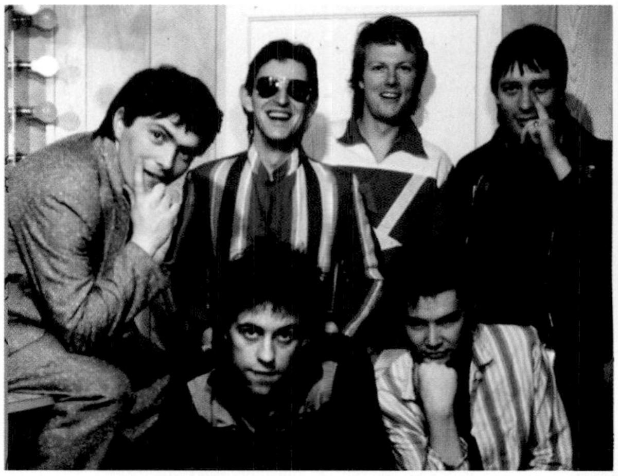

A two-wheeled hut—

Sounds smashing, but . . .

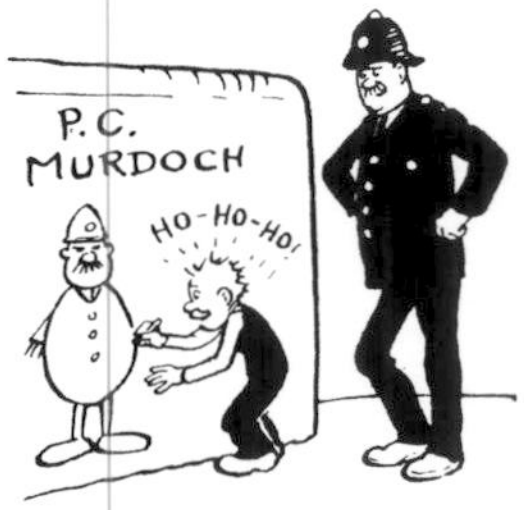
P.C. MURDOCH
HO-HO-HO!

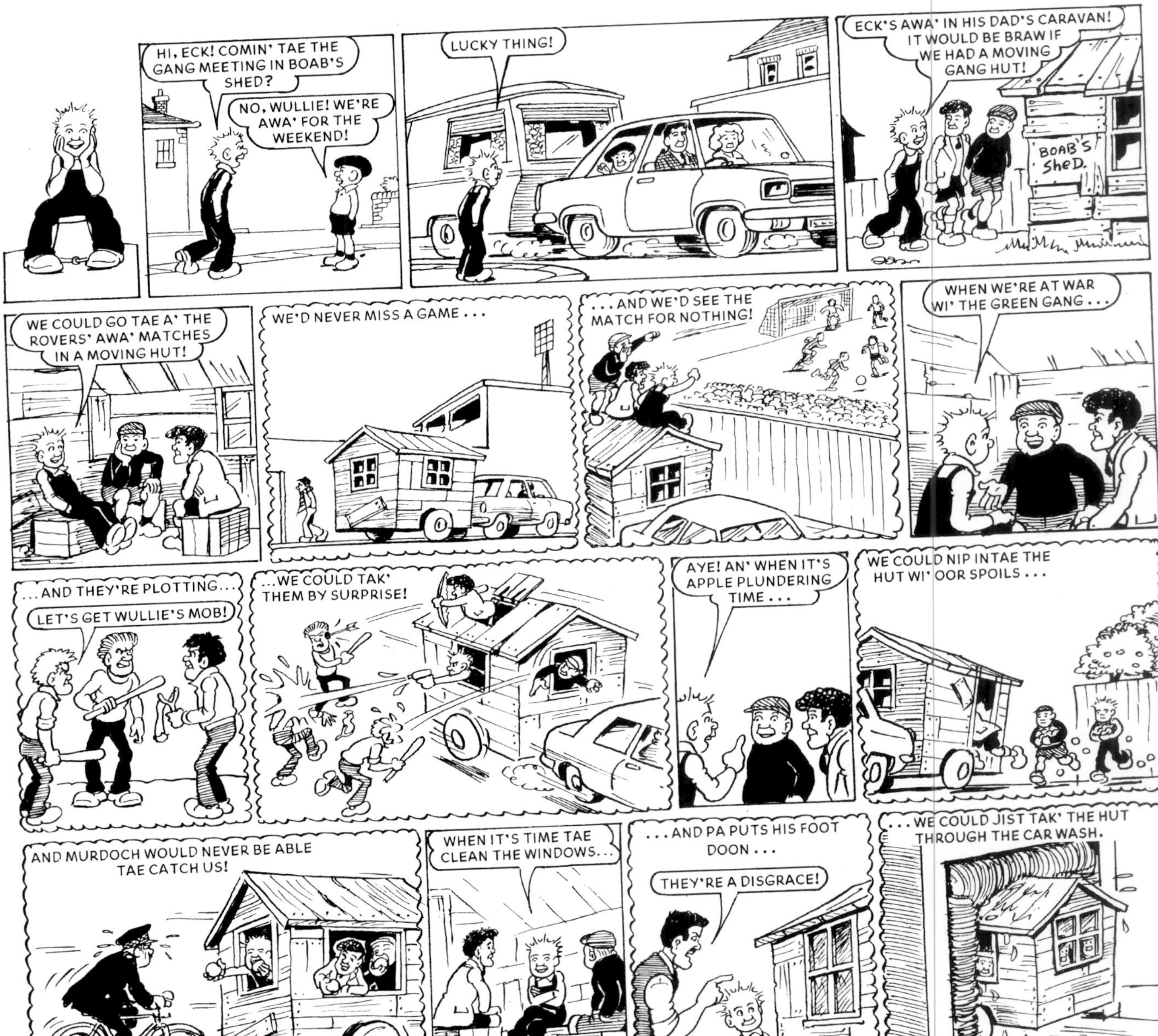
HI, ECK! COMIN' TAE THE GANG MEETING IN BOAB'S SHED?
NO, WULLIE! WE'RE AWA' FOR THE WEEKEND!
LUCKY THING!
ECK'S AWA' IN HIS DAD'S CARAVAN! IT WOULD BE BRAW IF WE HAD A MOVING GANG HUT!
BOAB'S SheD.
WE COULD GO TAE A' THE ROVERS' AWA' MATCHES IN A MOVING HUT!
WE'D NEVER MISS A GAME . . .
. . . AND WE'D SEE THE MATCH FOR NOTHING!
WHEN WE'RE AT WAR WI' THE GREEN GANG . . .
. . . AND THEY'RE PLOTTING . . .
LET'S GET WULLIE'S MOB!
. . . WE COULD TAK' THEM BY SURPRISE!
AYE! AN' WHEN IT'S APPLE PLUNDERING TIME . . .
WE COULD NIP INTAE THE HUT WI' OOR SPOILS . . .
AND MURDOCH WOULD NEVER BE ABLE TAE CATCH US!
WHEN IT'S TIME TAE CLEAN THE WINDOWS . . .
. . . AND PA PUTS HIS FOOT DOON . . .
THEY'RE A DISGRACE!
. . . WE COULD JIST TAK' THE HUT THROUGH THE CAR WASH.
YE'RE RIGHT, WULLIE! A MOVING HUT WOULD BE BRAW!
HELP! THE WALL'S COLLAPSIN'!
OOH! WE GOT A MOVING HUT— BUT NO' THE KIND WE WANTED!

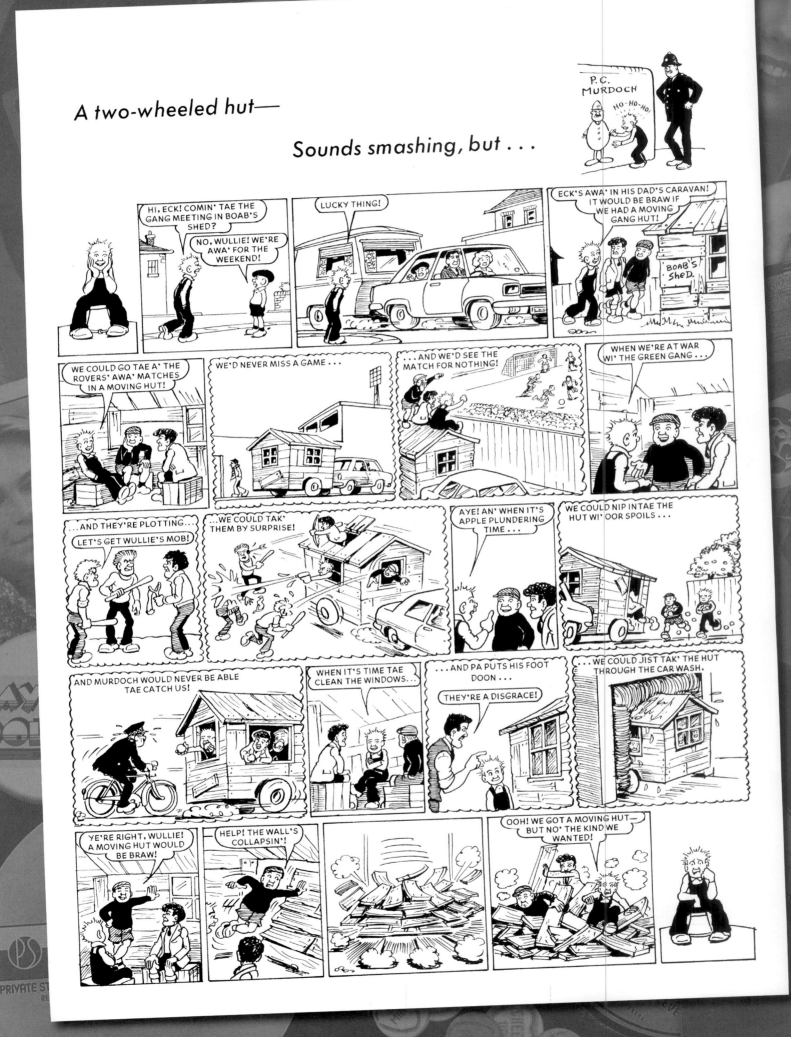

When the snow lies deep and thick—

Oor lad gets up to every trick!

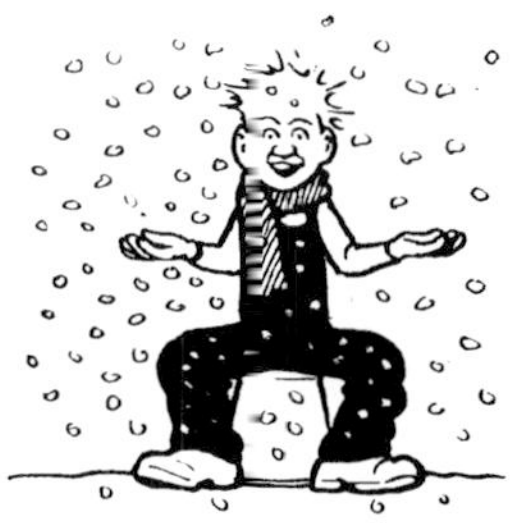

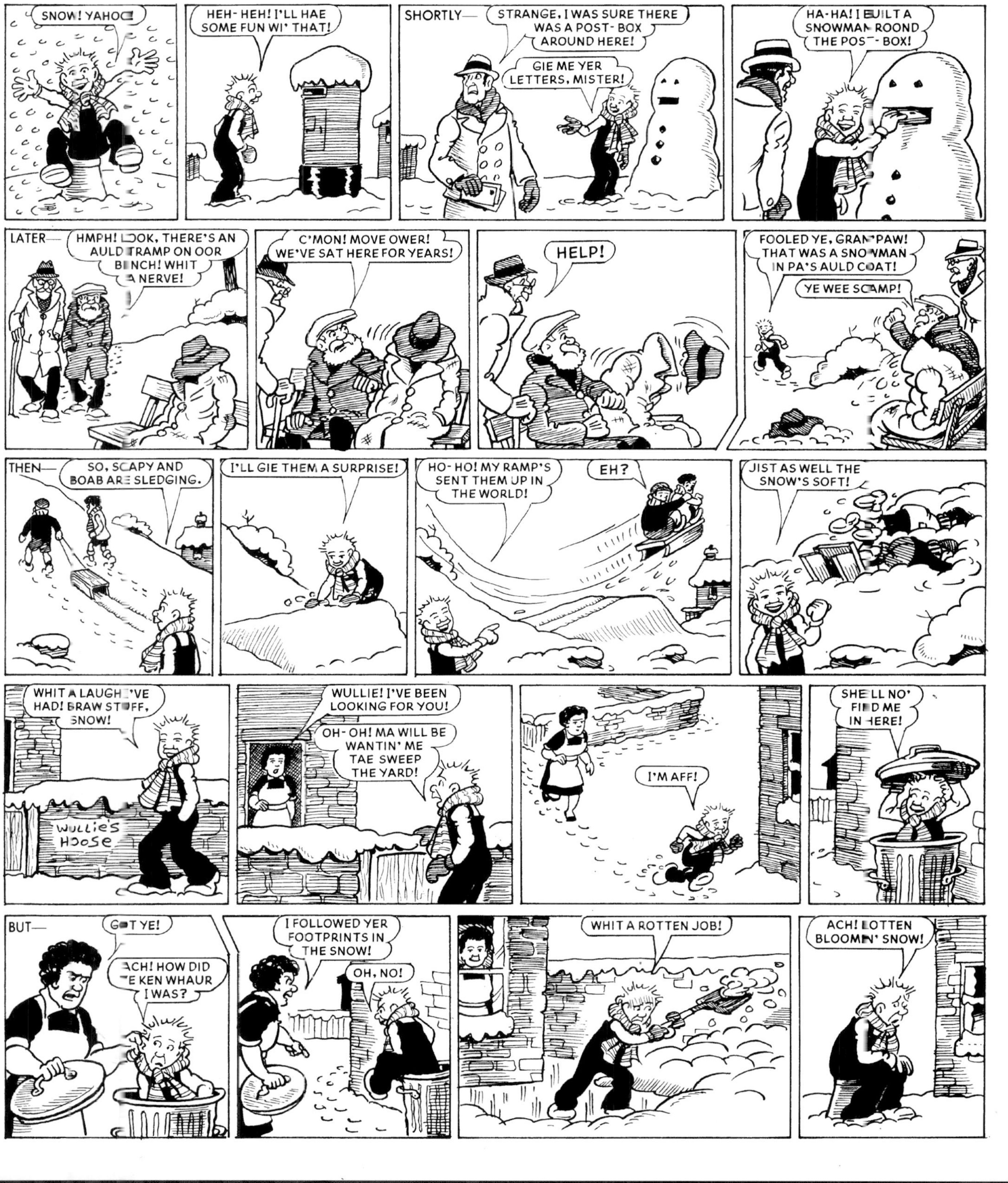
SNOW! YAHOO!
HEH-HEH! I'LL HAE SOME FUN WI' THAT!
SHORTLY—
STRANGE, I WAS SURE THERE WAS A POST-BOX AROUND HERE!
GIE ME YER LETTERS, MISTER!
HA-HA! I BUILT A SNOWMAN ROOND THE POST-BOX!
LATER—
HMPH! LOOK, THERE'S AN AULD TRAMP ON OOR BINCH! WHIT A NERVE!
C'MON! MOVE OWER! WE'VE SAT HERE FOR YEARS!
HELP!
FOOLED YE, GRAN'PAW! THAT WAS A SNOWMAN IN PA'S AULD COAT!
YE WEE SCAMP!
THEN—
SO, SCAPY AND BOAB ARE SLEDGING.
I'LL GIE THEM A SURPRISE!
HO-HO! MY RAMP'S SENT THEM UP IN THE WORLD!
EH?
JIST AS WELL THE SNOW'S SOFT!
WHIT A LAUGH I'VE HAD! BRAW STUFF, SNOW!
WULLIE'S HOOSE
WULLIE! I'VE BEEN LOOKING FOR YOU!
OH-OH! MA WILL BE WANTIN' ME TAE SWEEP THE YARD!
I'M AFF!
SHE'LL NO' FIND ME IN HERE!
BUT—
GOT YE!
ACH! HOW DID YE KEN WHAUR I WAS?
I FOLLOWED YER FOOTPRINTS IN THE SNOW!
OH, NO!
WHIT A ROTTEN JOB!
ACH! ROTTEN BLOOMIN' SNOW!

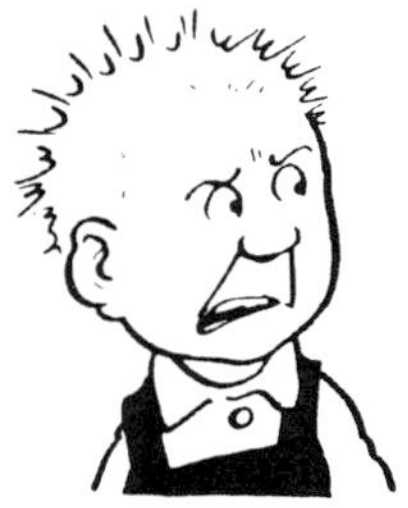

There's trouble for you-know-who—

On a bicycle built for two!

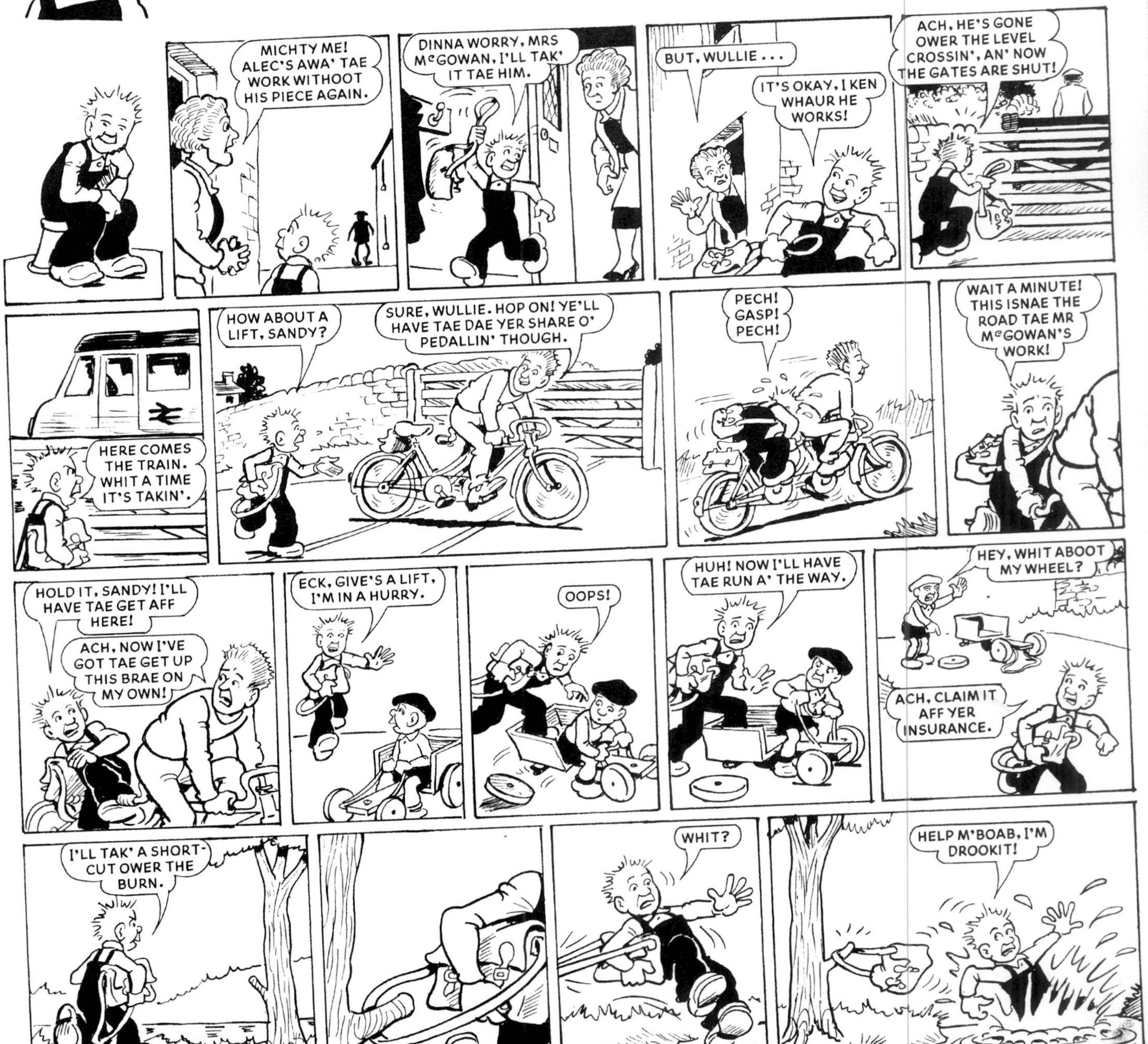

MICHTY ME! ALEC'S AWA' TAE WORK WITHOOT HIS PIECE AGAIN.
DINNA WORRY, MRS McGOWAN, I'LL TAK' IT TAE HIM.
BUT, WULLIE . . .
IT'S OKAY, I KEN WHAUR HE WORKS!
ACH, HE'S GONE OWER THE LEVEL CROSSIN', AN' NOW THE GATES ARE SHUT!
HERE COMES THE TRAIN. WHIT A TIME IT'S TAKIN'.
HOW ABOUT A LIFT, SANDY?
SURE, WULLIE. HOP ON! YE'LL HAVE TAE DAE YER SHARE O' PEDALLIN' THOUGH.
PECH! GASP! PECH!
WAIT A MINUTE! THIS ISNAE THE ROAD TAE MR McGOWAN'S WORK!
HOLD IT, SANDY! I'LL HAVE TAE GET AFF HERE!
ACH, NOW I'VE GOT TAE GET UP THIS BRAE ON MY OWN!
ECK, GIVE'S A LIFT, I'M IN A HURRY.
OOPS!
HUH! NOW I'LL HAVE TAE RUN A' THE WAY.
HEY, WHIT ABOOT MY WHEEL?
ACH, CLAIM IT AFF YER INSURANCE.
I'LL TAK' A SHORT-CUT OWER THE BURN.
WHIT?
HELP M'BOAB, I'M DROOKIT!
EVENTUALLY—
CAUGHT YE AT LAST! I'VE GOT YER PIECE HERE, MR McGOWAN.
NO, I'VE GOT IT HERE, WULLIE.
WORKS ENTRANCE
YOU'VE GOT IT? THEN WHIT'S IN HERE?
CLOTHES PEGS?
AYE, I TRIED TO TELL YE, WULLIE. YE TOOK THE WRANG BAG!
WHIT A SCUNNER! STILL, THE CLOTHES PEGS CAME IN HANDY!

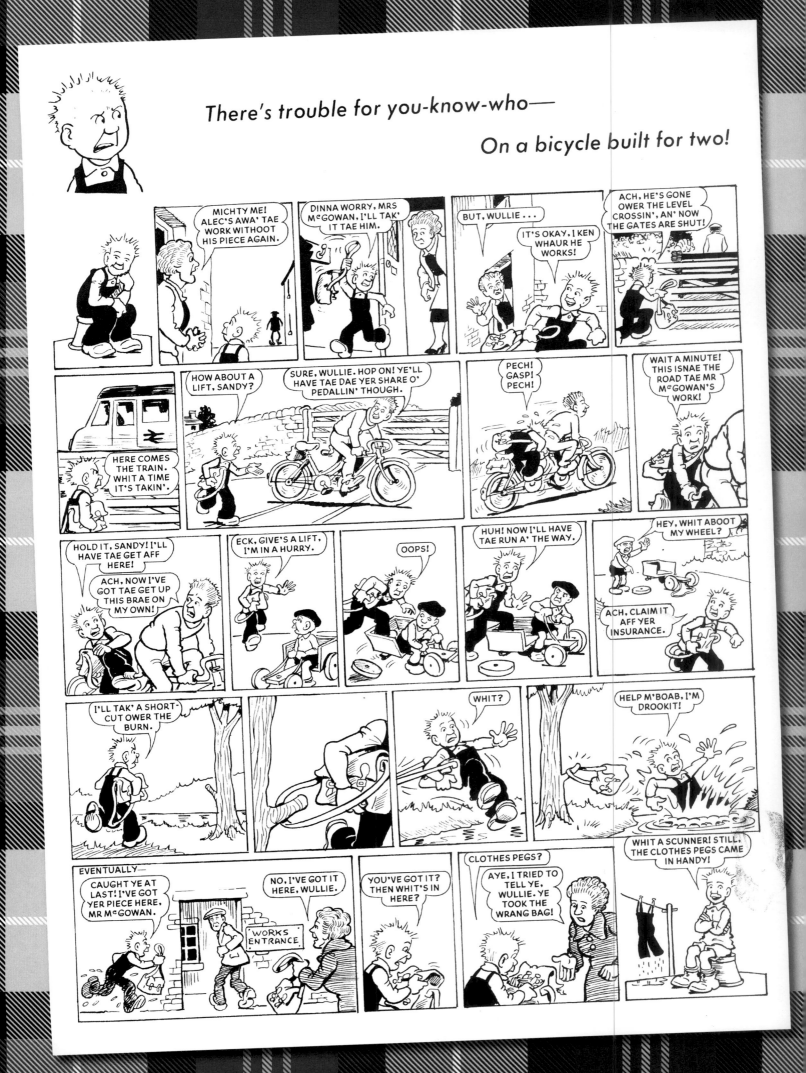

Wull does his best to guard that box—

But in the end, it gives him shocks.

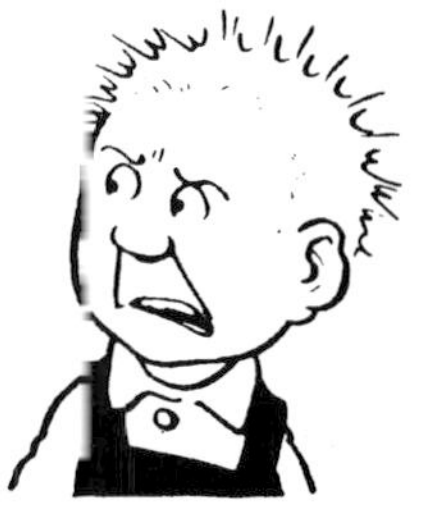

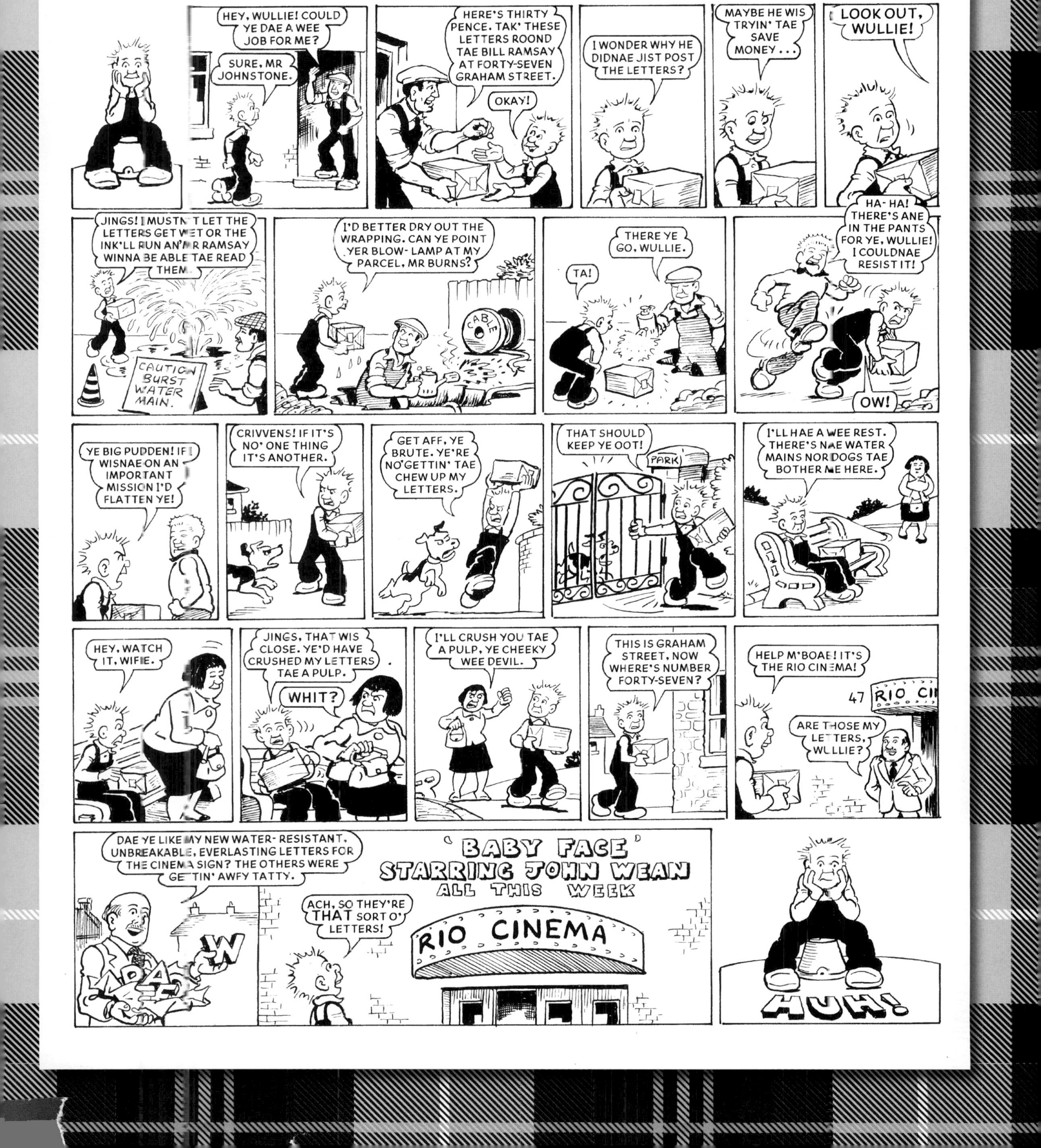

HEY, WULLIE! COULD YE DAE A WEE JOB FOR ME?
SURE, MR JOHNSTONE.
HERE'S THIRTY PENCE. TAK' THESE LETTERS ROOND TAE BILL RAMSAY AT FORTY-SEVEN GRAHAM STREET.
OKAY!
I WONDER WHY HE DIDNAE JIST POST THE LETTERS?
MAYBE HE WIS TRYIN' TAE SAVE MONEY . . .
LOOK OUT, WULLIE!
JINGS! I MUSTN'T LET THE LETTERS GET WET OR THE INK'LL RUN AN' MR RAMSAY WINNA BE ABLE TAE READ THEM.
CAUTION BURST WATER MAIN.
I'D BETTER DRY OUT THE WRAPPING. CAN YE POINT YER BLOW-LAMP AT MY PARCEL, MR BURNS?
CABLE
THERE YE GO, WULLIE.
TA!
HA-HA! THERE'S ANE IN THE PANTS FOR YE, WULLIE! I COULDNAE RESIST IT!
OW!
YE BIG PUDDEN! IF I WISNAE ON AN IMPORTANT MISSION I'D FLATTEN YE!
CRIVVENS! IF IT'S NO' ONE THING IT'S ANOTHER.
GET AFF, YE BRUTE. YE'RE NO' GETTIN' TAE CHEW UP MY LETTERS.
THAT SHOULD KEEP YE OOT!
PARK
I'LL HAE A WEE REST. THERE'S NAE WATER MAINS NOR DOGS TAE BOTHER ME HERE.
HEY, WATCH IT, WIFIE.
JINGS, THAT WIS CLOSE. YE'D HAVE CRUSHED MY LETTERS TAE A PULP.
WHIT?
I'LL CRUSH YOU TAE A PULP, YE CHEEKY WEE DEVIL.
THIS IS GRAHAM STREET, NOW WHERE'S NUMBER FORTY-SEVEN?
HELP M'BOAB! IT'S THE RIO CINEMA!
47
ARE THOSE MY LETTERS, WULLIE?
DAE YE LIKE MY NEW WATER-RESISTANT, UNBREAKABLE, EVERLASTING LETTERS FOR THE CINEMA SIGN? THE OTHERS WERE GETTIN' AWFY TATTY.
'BABY FACE' STARRING JOHN WEAN ALL THIS WEEK
ACH, SO THEY'RE THAT SORT O' LETTERS!
RIO CINEMA
HUH!

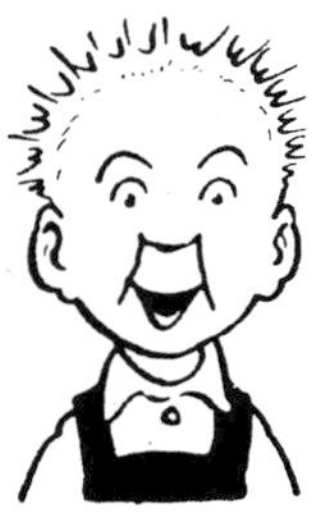

Lassies, teachers and P.C.'s—

They're all wearing dungarees!

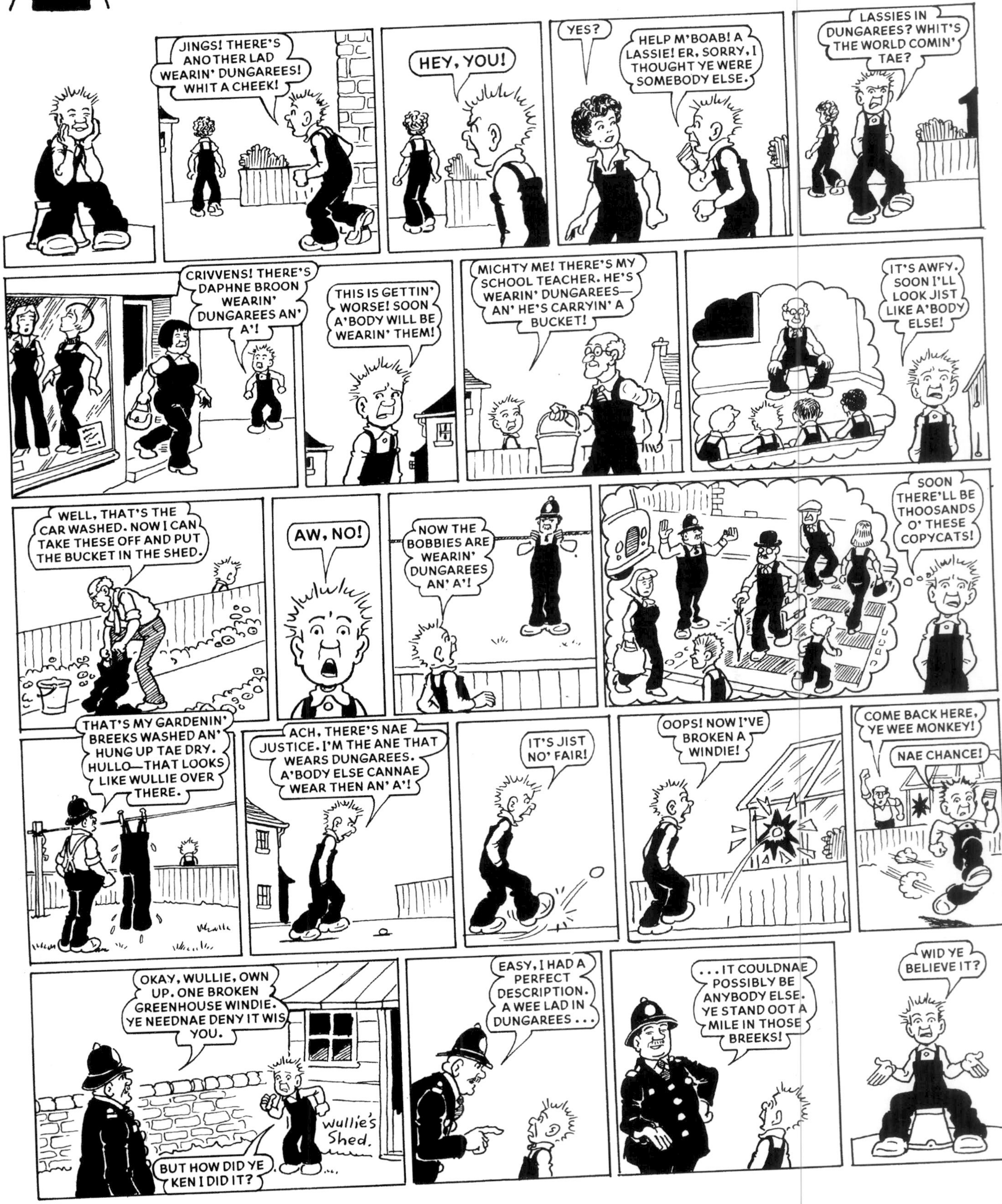

JINGS! THERE'S ANOTHER LAD WEARIN' DUNGAREES! WHIT A CHEEK!
HEY, YOU!
YES?
HELP M'BOAB! A LASSIE! ER, SORRY, I THOUGHT YE WERE SOMEBODY ELSE.
LASSIES IN DUNGAREES? WHIT'S THE WORLD COMIN' TAE?
CRIVVENS! THERE'S DAPHNE BROON WEARIN' DUNGAREES AN' A'!
THIS IS GETTIN' WORSE! SOON A'BODY WILL BE WEARIN' THEM!
MICHTY ME! THERE'S MY SCHOOL TEACHER. HE'S WEARIN' DUNGAREES— AN' HE'S CARRYIN' A BUCKET!
IT'S AWFY. SOON I'LL LOOK JIST LIKE A'BODY ELSE!
WELL, THAT'S THE CAR WASHED. NOW I CAN TAKE THESE OFF AND PUT THE BUCKET IN THE SHED.
AW, NO!
NOW THE BOBBIES ARE WEARIN' DUNGAREES AN' A'!
SOON THERE'LL BE THOOSANDS O' THESE COPYCATS!
THAT'S MY GARDENIN' BREEKS WASHED AN' HUNG UP TAE DRY. HULLO—THAT LOOKS LIKE WULLIE OVER THERE.
ACH, THERE'S NAE JUSTICE. I'M THE ANE THAT WEARS DUNGAREES. A'BODY ELSE CANNAE WEAR THEN AN' A'!
IT'S JIST NO' FAIR!
OOPS! NOW I'VE BROKEN A WINDIE!
COME BACK HERE, YE WEE MONKEY!
NAE CHANCE!
OKAY, WULLIE, OWN UP. ONE BROKEN GREENHOUSE WINDIE. YE NEEDNAE DENY IT WIS YOU.
BUT HOW DID YE KEN I DID IT?
wullie's Shed.
EASY, I HAD A PERFECT DESCRIPTION. A WEE LAD IN DUNGAREES . . .
. . . IT COULDNAE POSSIBLY BE ANYBODY ELSE. YE STAND OOT A MILE IN THOSE BREEKS!
WID YE BELIEVE IT?

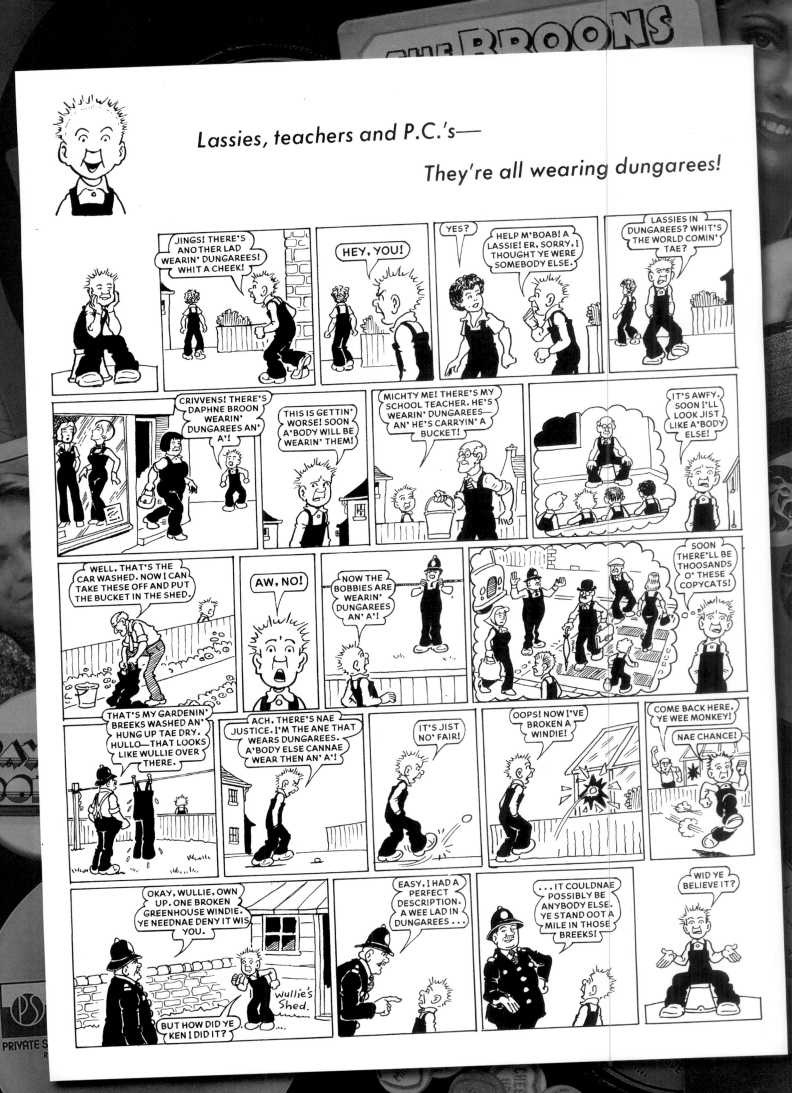

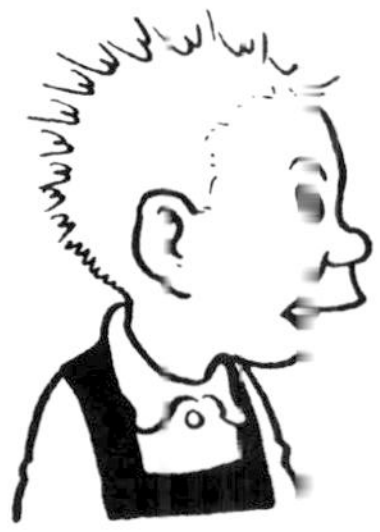

Oor Wullie's got a super plan—

To build himself a " cartie-van "!

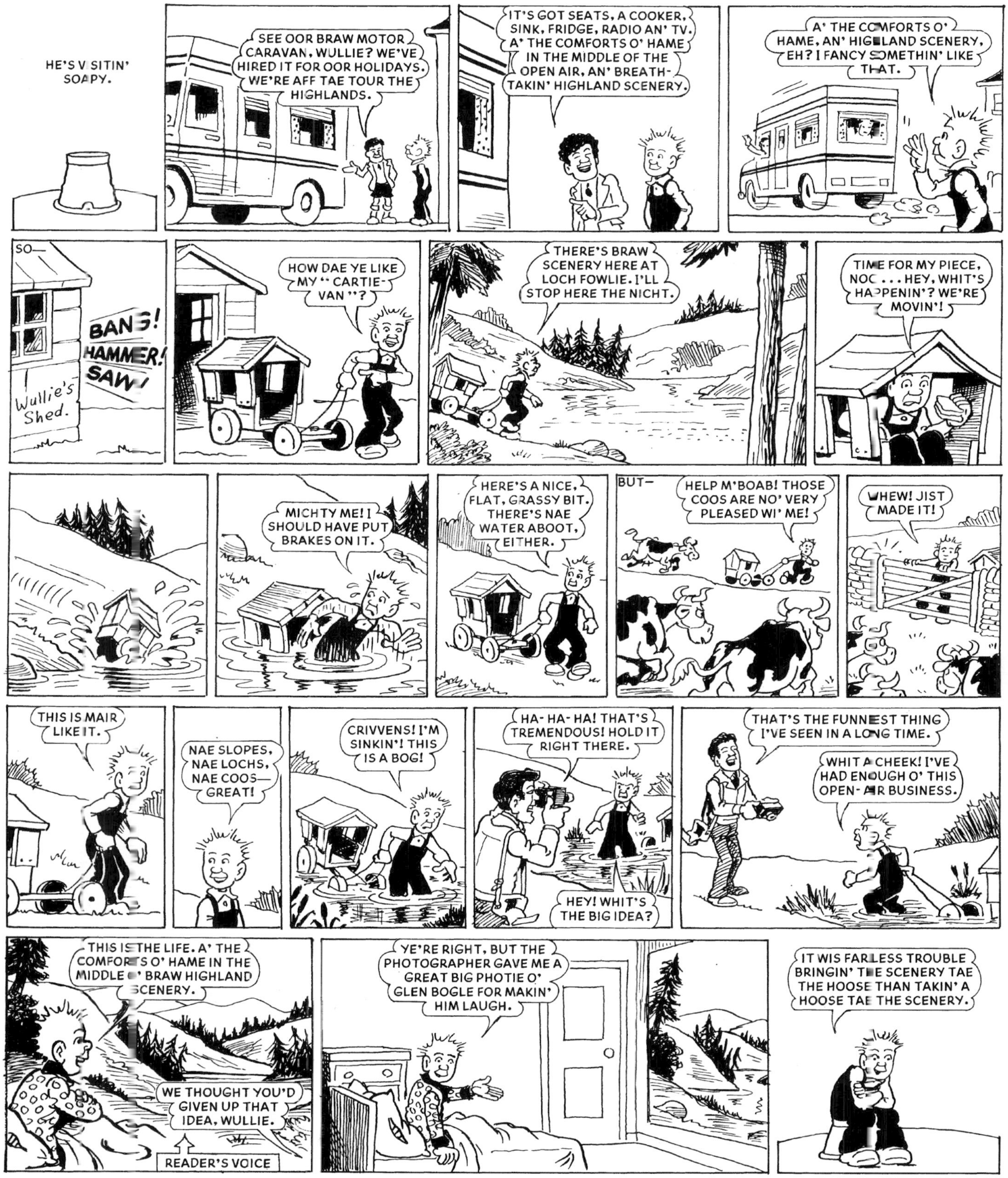

HE'S VISITIN' SOAPY.
SEE OOR BRAW MOTOR CARAVAN, WULLIE? WE'VE HIRED IT FOR OOR HOLIDAYS. WE'RE AFF TAE TOUR THE HIGHLANDS.
IT'S GOT SEATS, A COOKER, SINK, FRIDGE, RADIO AN' TV. A' THE COMFORTS O' HAME IN THE MIDDLE OF THE OPEN AIR, AN' BREATH-TAKIN' HIGHLAND SCENERY.
A' THE COMFORTS O' HAME, AN' HIGHLAND SCENERY, EH? I FANCY SOMETHIN' LIKE THAT.
SO—
BANG! HAMMER! SAW!
Wullie's Shed.
HOW DAE YE LIKE MY " CARTIE-VAN "?
THERE'S BRAW SCENERY HERE AT LOCH FOWLIE. I'LL STOP HERE THE NICHT.
TIME FOR MY PIECE, NOO . . . HEY, WHIT'S HAPPENIN'? WE'RE MOVIN'!
MICHTY ME! I SHOULD HAVE PUT BRAKES ON IT.
HERE'S A NICE, FLAT, GRASSY BIT. THERE'S NAE WATER ABOOT, EITHER.
BUT—
HELP M'BOAB! THOSE COOS ARE NO' VERY PLEASED WI' ME!
WHEW! JIST MADE IT!
THIS IS MAIR LIKE IT.
NAE SLOPES, NAE LOCHS, NAE COOS— GREAT!
CRIVVENS! I'M SINKIN'! THIS IS A BOG!
HA-HA-HA! THAT'S TREMENDOUS! HOLD IT RIGHT THERE.
HEY! WHIT'S THE BIG IDEA?
THAT'S THE FUNNIEST THING I'VE SEEN IN A LONG TIME.
WHIT A CHEEK! I'VE HAD ENOUGH O' THIS OPEN-AIR BUSINESS.
THIS IS THE LIFE. A' THE COMFORTS O' HAME IN THE MIDDLE O' BRAW HIGHLAND SCENERY.
WE THOUGHT YOU'D GIVEN UP THAT IDEA, WULLIE.
READER'S VOICE
YE'RE RIGHT, BUT THE PHOTOGRAPHER GAVE ME A GREAT BIG PHOTIE O' GLEN BOGLE FOR MAKIN' HIM LAUGH.
IT WIS FAR LESS TROUBLE BRINGIN' THE SCENERY TAE THE HOOSE THAN TAKIN' A HOOSE TAE THE SCENERY.

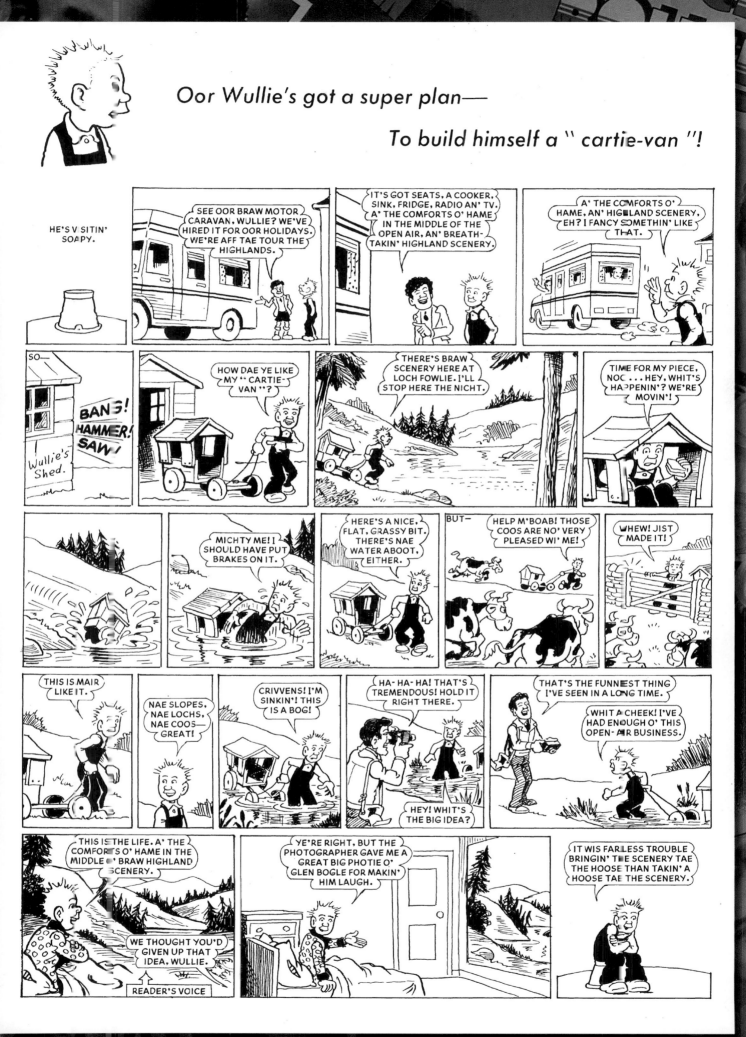

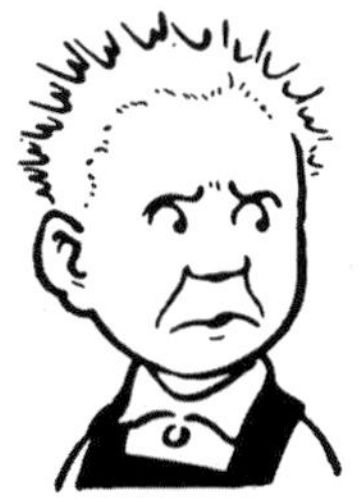

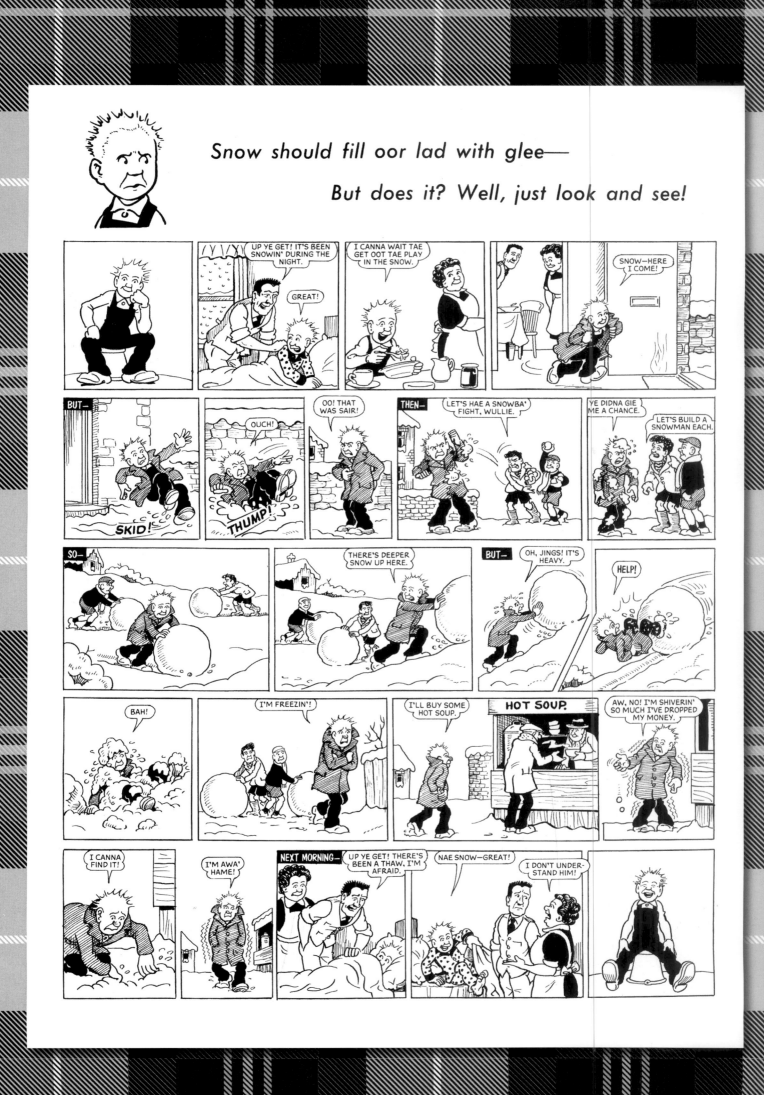

Snow should fill oor lad with glee—

But does it? Well, just look and see!

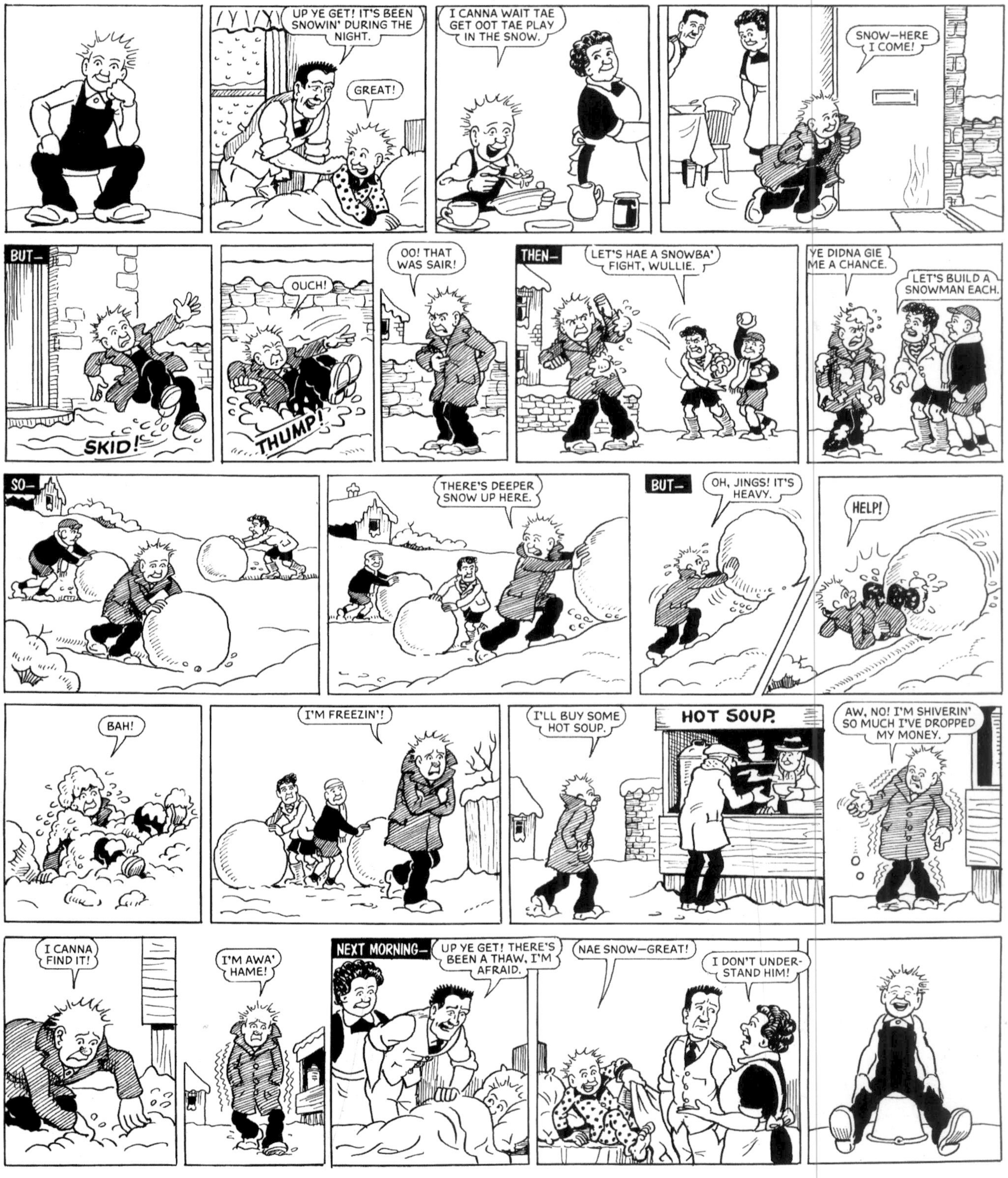
UP YE GET! IT'S BEEN SNOWIN' DURING THE NIGHT.
GREAT!
I CANNA WAIT TAE GET OOT TAE PLAY IN THE SNOW.
SNOW—HERE I COME!
BUT—
SKID!
OUCH!
THUMP!
OO! THAT WAS SAIR!
THEN—
LET'S HAE A SNOWBA' FIGHT, WULLIE.
YE DIDNA GIE ME A CHANCE.
LET'S BUILD A SNOWMAN EACH.
SO—
THERE'S DEEPER SNOW UP HERE.
BUT—
OH, JINGS! IT'S HEAVY.
HELP!
BAH!
I'M FREEZIN'!
I'LL BUY SOME HOT SOUP.
HOT SOUP
AW, NO! I'M SHIVERIN' SO MUCH I'VE DROPPED MY MONEY.
I CANNA FIND IT!
I'M AWA' HAME!
NEXT MORNING—
UP YE GET! THERE'S BEEN A THAW, I'M AFRAID.
NAE SNOW—GREAT!
I DON'T UNDER-STAND HIM!

There are three glum chums—

When the parkie comes!

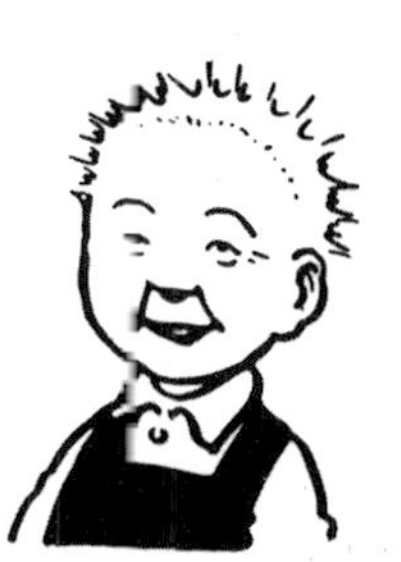

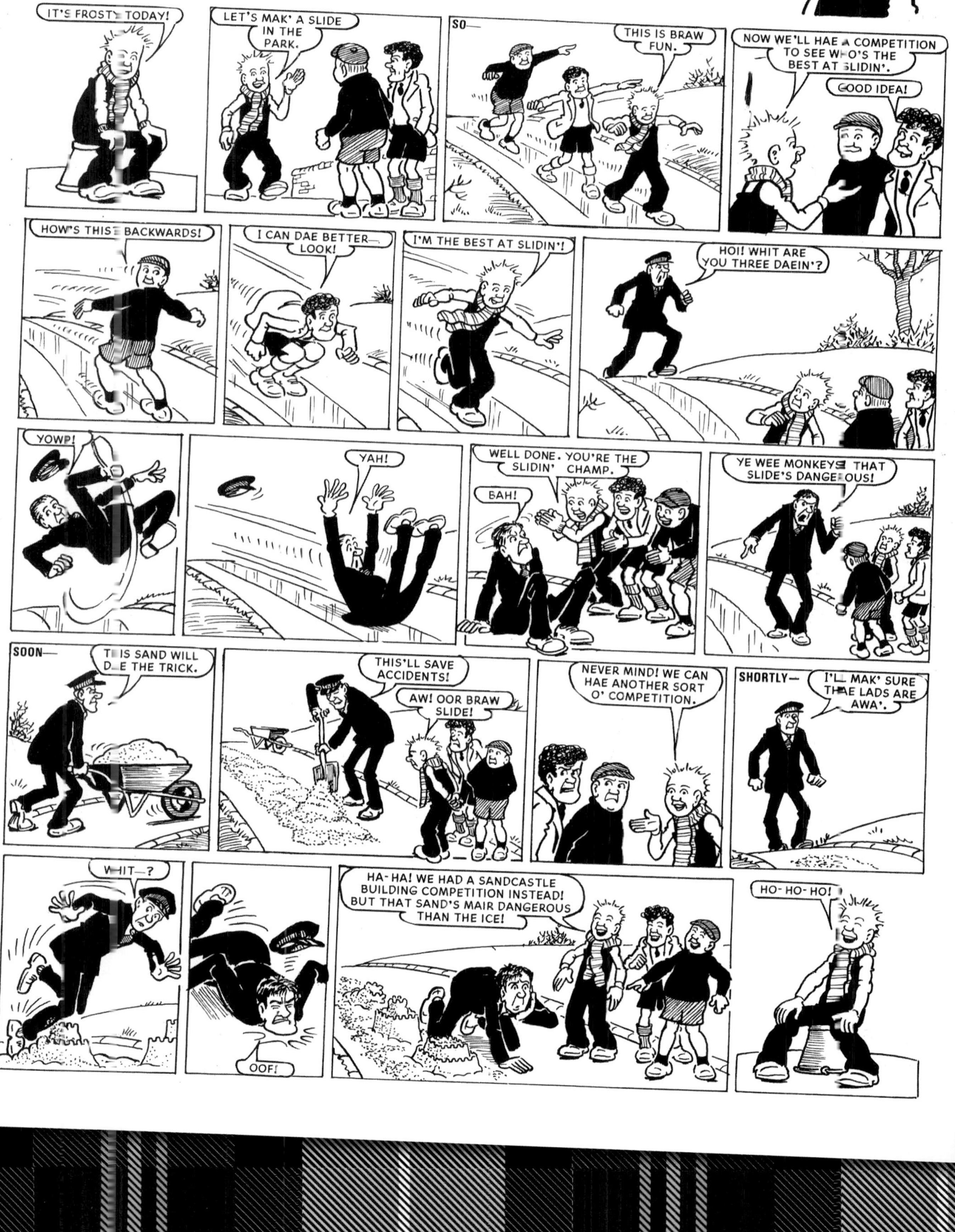
IT'S FROSTY TODAY!
LET'S MAK' A SLIDE IN THE PARK.
SO—
THIS IS BRAW FUN.
NOW WE'LL HAE A COMPETITION TO SEE WHO'S THE BEST AT SLIDIN'.
GOOD IDEA!
HOW'S THIS? BACKWARDS!
I CAN DAE BETTER— LOOK!
I'M THE BEST AT SLIDIN'!
HOI! WHIT ARE YOU THREE DAEIN'?
YOWP!
YAH!
WELL DONE. YOU'RE THE SLIDIN' CHAMP.
BAH!
YE WEE MONKEYS! THAT SLIDE'S DANGEROUS!
SOON—
THIS SAND WILL DAE THE TRICK.
THIS'LL SAVE ACCIDENTS!
AW! OOR BRAW SLIDE!
NEVER MIND! WE CAN HAE ANOTHER SORT O' COMPETITION.
SHORTLY—
I'LL MAK' SURE THAE LADS ARE AWA'.
WHIT—?
OOF!
HA-HA! WE HAD A SANDCASTLE BUILDING COMPETITION INSTEAD! BUT THAT SAND'S MAIR DANGEROUS THAN THE ICE!
HO-HO-HO!

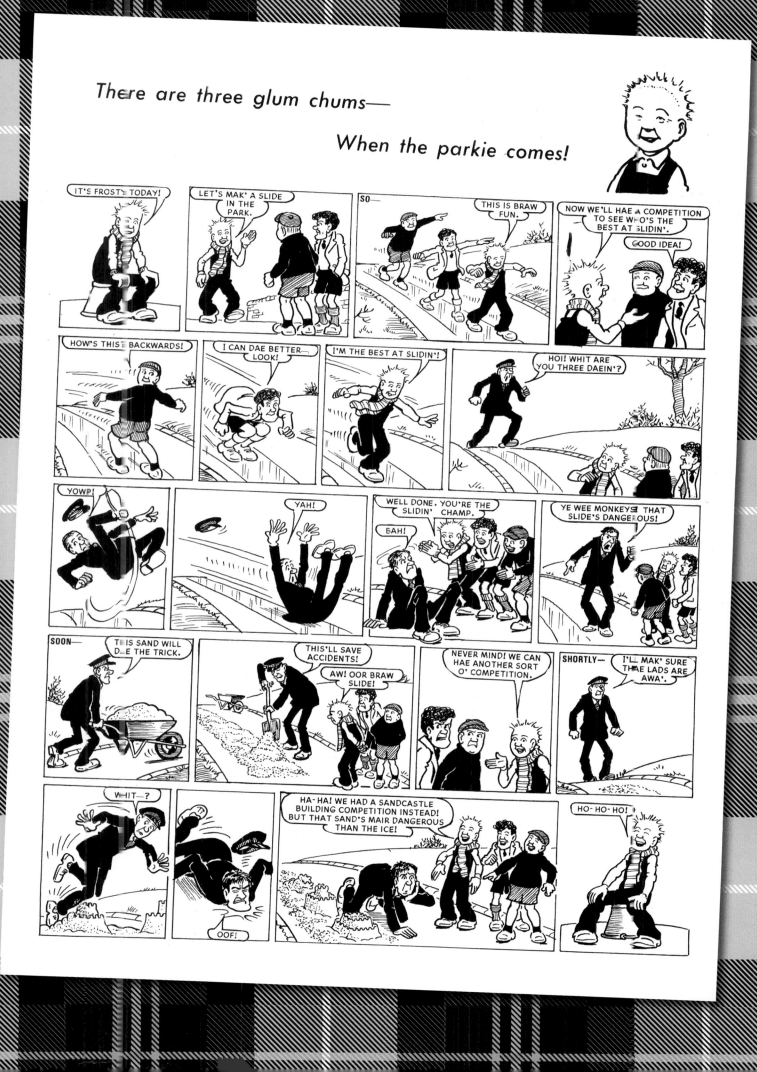

Wull's dancing lessons come up trumps—

When he learns ballet jumps!

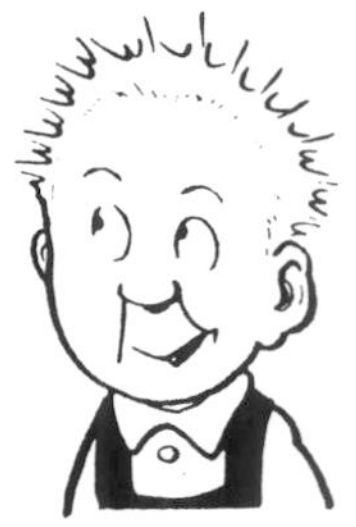

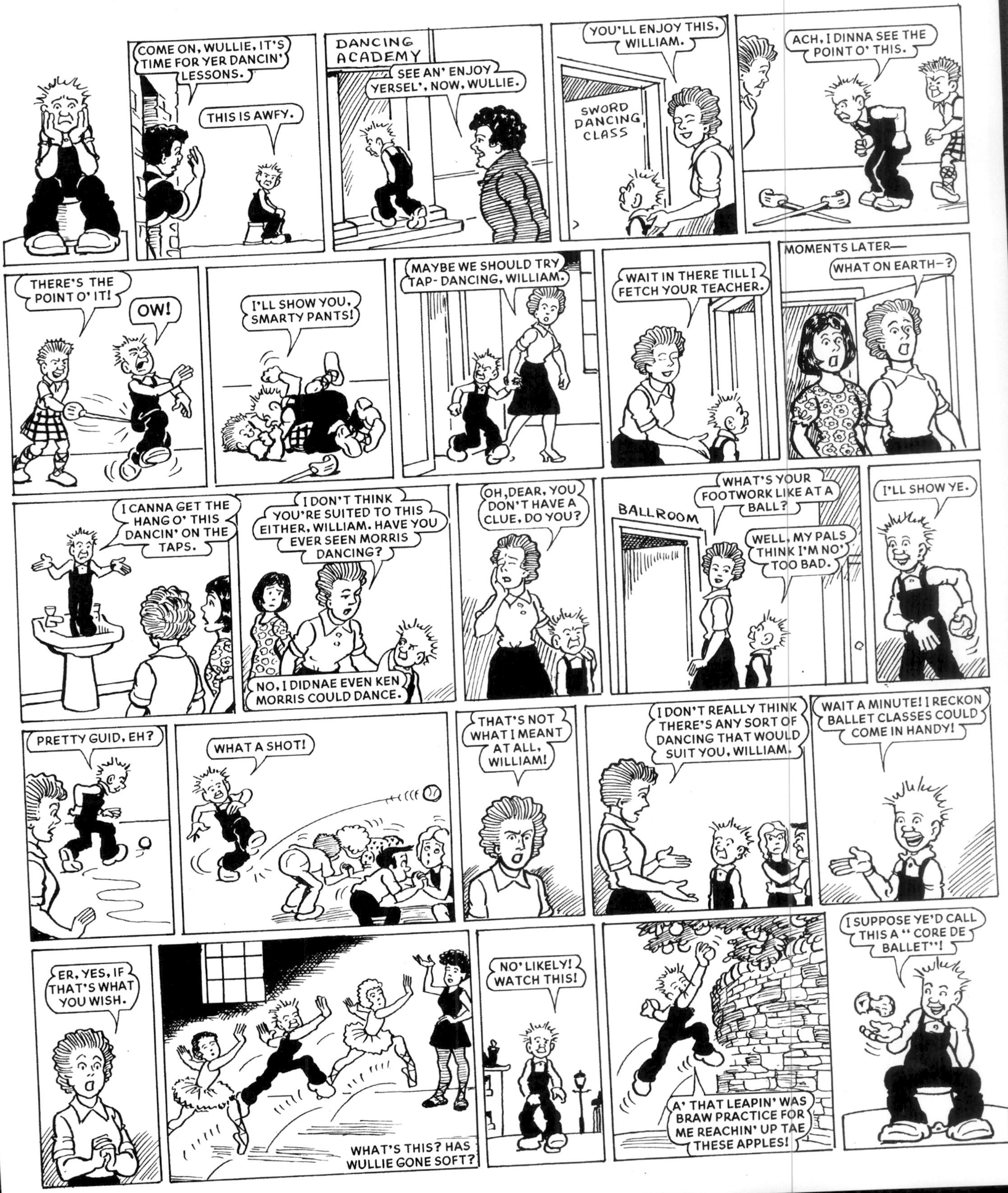
COME ON, WULLIE, IT'S TIME FOR YER DANCIN' LESSONS.
THIS IS AWFY.
DANCING ACADEMY
SEE AN' ENJOY YERSEL', NOW, WULLIE.
YOU'LL ENJOY THIS, WILLIAM.
SWORD DANCING CLASS
ACH, I DINNA SEE THE POINT O' THIS.
THERE'S THE POINT O' IT!
OW!
I'LL SHOW YOU, SMARTY PANTS!
MAYBE WE SHOULD TRY TAP-DANCING, WILLIAM.
WAIT IN THERE TILL I FETCH YOUR TEACHER.
MOMENTS LATER—
WHAT ON EARTH—?
I CANNA GET THE HANG O' THIS DANCIN' ON THE TAPS.
I DON'T THINK YOU'RE SUITED TO THIS EITHER, WILLIAM. HAVE YOU EVER SEEN MORRIS DANCING?
NO, I DIDNAE EVEN KEN MORRIS COULD DANCE.
OH, DEAR, YOU DON'T HAVE A CLUE, DO YOU?
BALLROOM
WHAT'S YOUR FOOTWORK LIKE AT A BALL?
WELL, MY PALS THINK I'M NO' TOO BAD.
I'LL SHOW YE.
PRETTY GUID, EH?
WHAT A SHOT!
THAT'S NOT WHAT I MEANT AT ALL, WILLIAM!
I DON'T REALLY THINK THERE'S ANY SORT OF DANCING THAT WOULD SUIT YOU, WILLIAM.
WAIT A MINUTE! I RECKON BALLET CLASSES COULD COME IN HANDY!
ER, YES, IF THAT'S WHAT YOU WISH.
WHAT'S THIS? HAS WULLIE GONE SOFT?
NO' LIKELY! WATCH THIS!
A' THAT LEAPIN' WAS BRAW PRACTICE FOR ME REACHIN' UP TAE THESE APPLES!
I SUPPOSE YE'D CALL THIS A "CORE DE BALLET"!

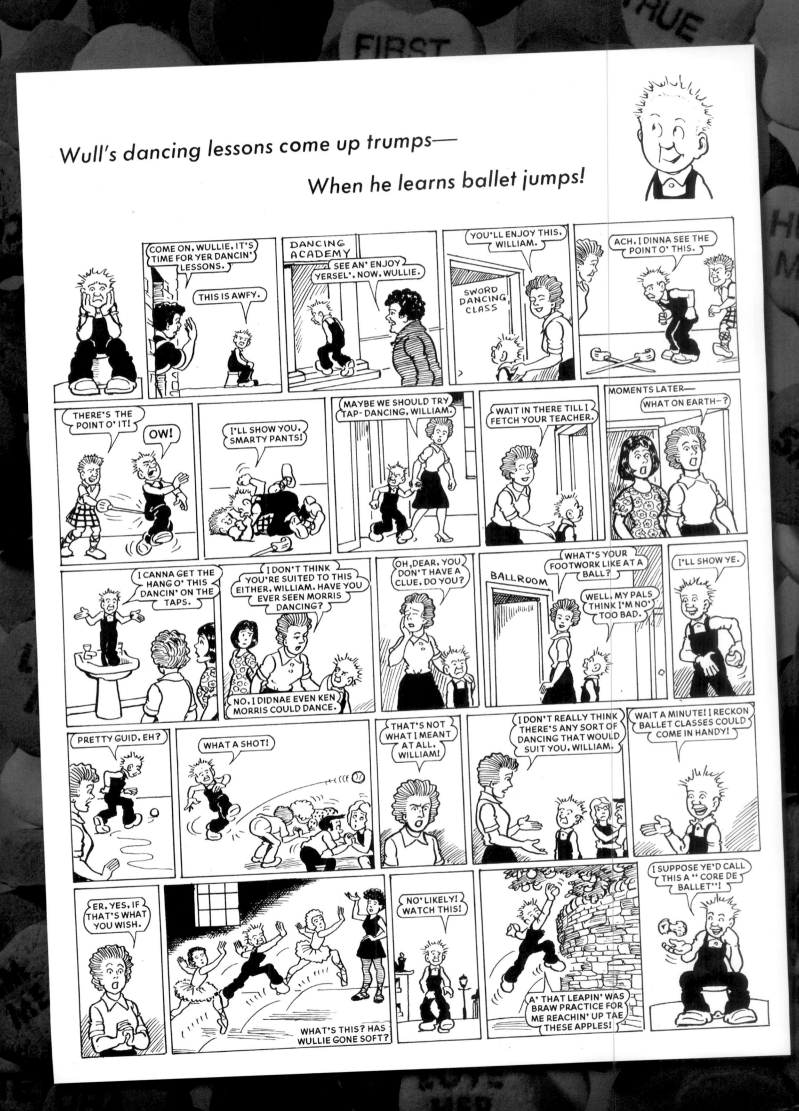

Wullie does a lot o' frettin'—

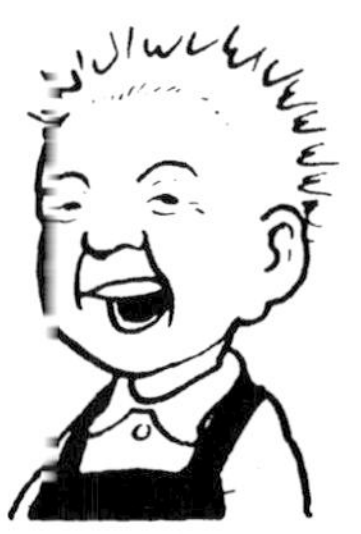

Until he sees what Murdoch's gettin!

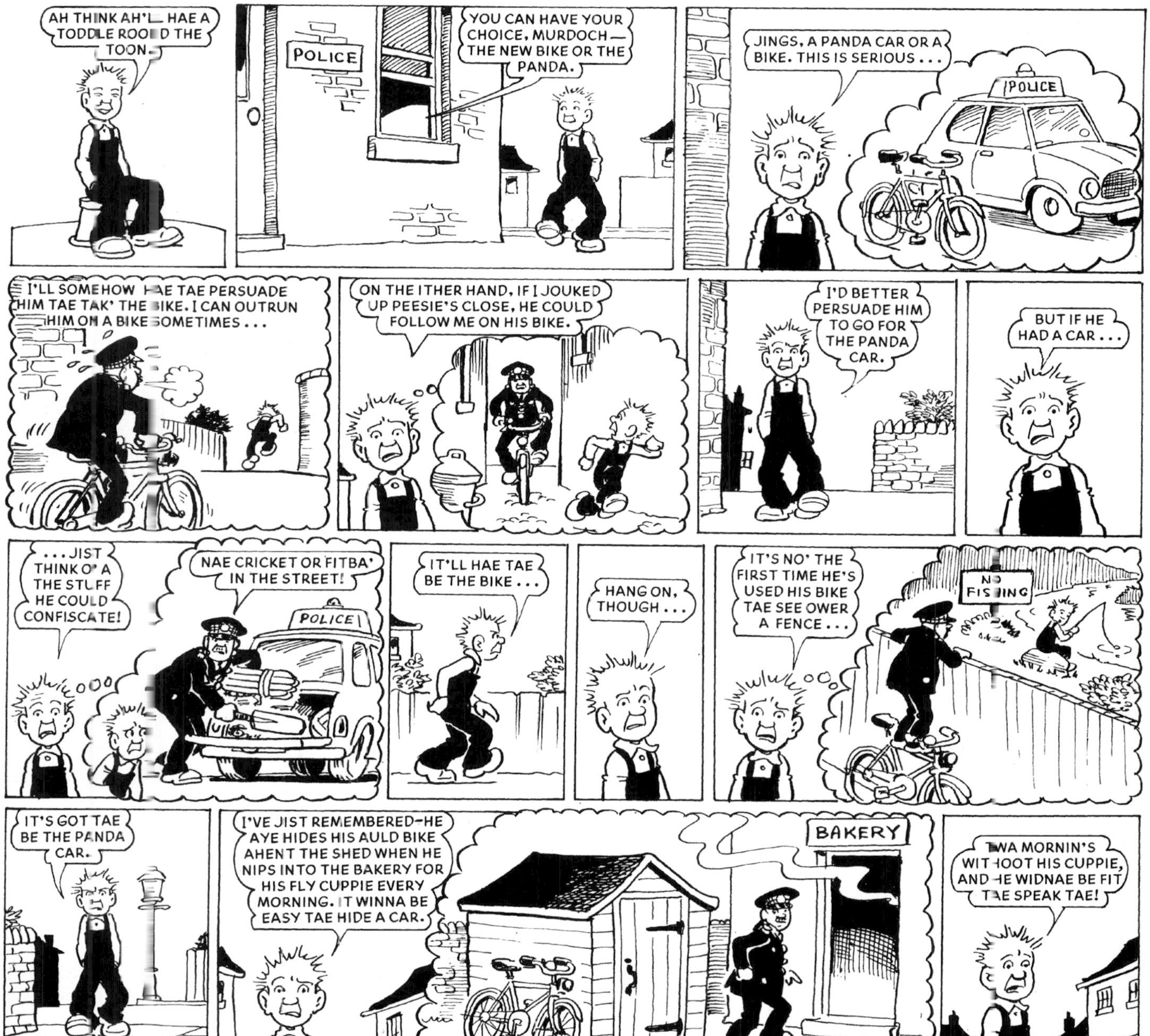

AH THINK AH'LL HAE A TODDLE ROOND THE TOON.
POLICE
YOU CAN HAVE YOUR CHOICE, MURDOCH — THE NEW BIKE OR THE PANDA.
JINGS, A PANDA CAR OR A BIKE. THIS IS SERIOUS . . .
POLICE
I'LL SOMEHOW HAE TAE PERSUADE HIM TAE TAK' THE BIKE. I CAN OUTRUN HIM ON A BIKE SOMETIMES . . .
ON THE ITHER HAND, IF I JOUKED UP PEESIE'S CLOSE, HE COULD FOLLOW ME ON HIS BIKE.
I'D BETTER PERSUADE HIM TO GO FOR THE PANDA CAR.
BUT IF HE HAD A CAR . . .
. . . JIST THINK O' A THE STUFF HE COULD CONFISCATE!
NAE CRICKET OR FITBA' IN THE STREET!
POLICE
IT'LL HAE TAE BE THE BIKE . . .
HANG ON, THOUGH . . .
IT'S NO' THE FIRST TIME HE'S USED HIS BIKE TAE SEE OWER A FENCE . . .
NO FISHING
IT'S GOT TAE BE THE PANDA CAR.
I'VE JIST REMEMBERED—HE AYE HIDES HIS AULD BIKE AHENT THE SHED WHEN HE NIPS INTO THE BAKERY FOR HIS FLY CUPPIE EVERY MORNING. IT WINNA BE EASY TAE HIDE A CAR.
BAKERY
TWA MORNIN'S WITHOOT HIS CUPPIE, AND HE WIDNAE BE FIT TAE SPEAK TAE!
SO IT'LL JIST HAE TAE BE THE NEW BIKE.
OOYAH!
HELLO, WULLIE, WHIT DAE YE THINK O' THE PANDA I WON FOR MY NEPHEW IN THE POLICE DRAW? I GOT THE CHOICE O' THIS OR A WEE BIKE.
ACH, A' THAT WORRYIN' FOR NOTHIN'!

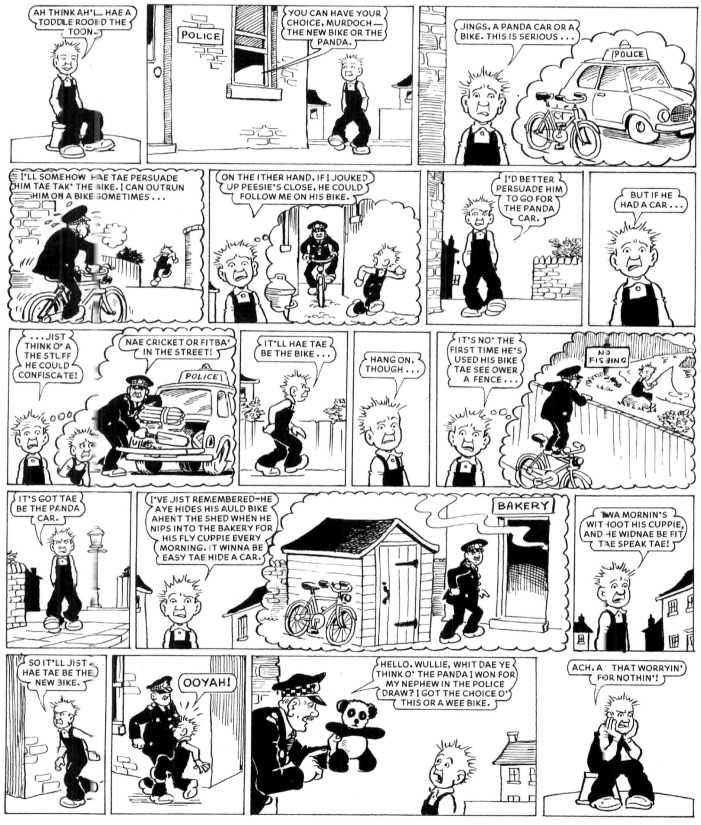

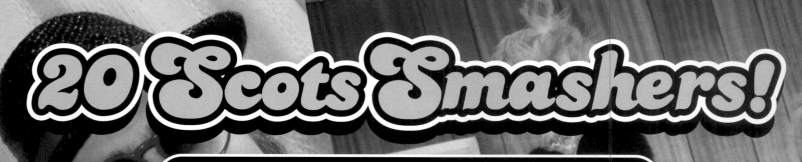

20 Scots Smashers!

Remember and reminisce.....

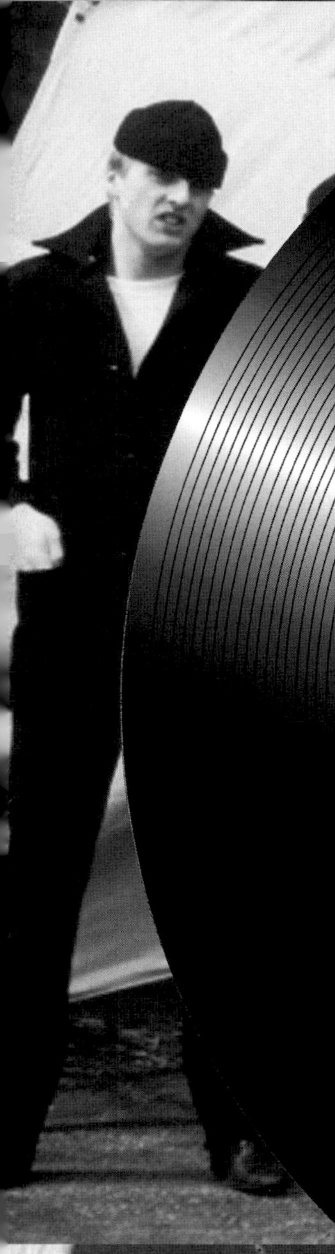

1. Name the Bay City Rollers.
2. Who was lead singer with The Sweet?
3. Which Bee Gee did Lulu marry?
4. Which military band had a number one hit with "Amazing Grace"?
5. Who performed in the folk scene with Billy Connolly as The Humblebums?
6. Name Middle of the Road's greatest hit.
8. What was the occasion for the "Ally's Tartan Army" song?
9. Which female vocalist's favourite months could be "January, February"?
10. Who had a massive hit with "Darlin'"?

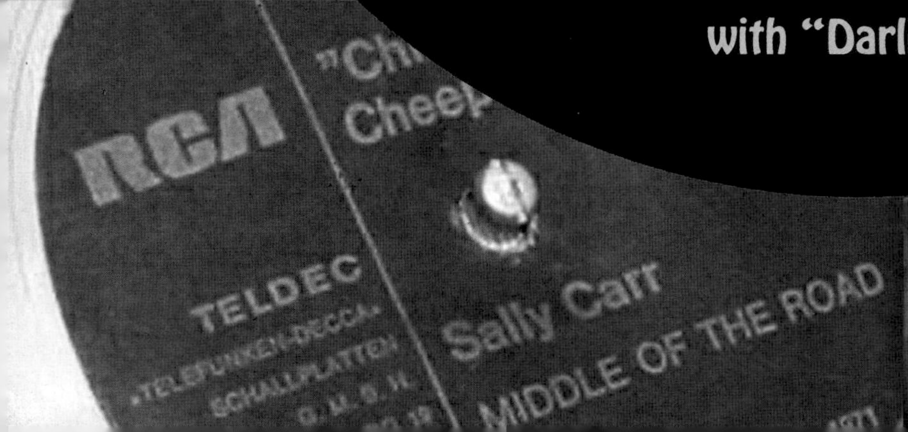
RCA
"Chi
Cheep
TELDEC
TELEFUNKEN-DECCA
SCHALLPLATTEN
Sally Carr
MIDDLE OF THE ROAD

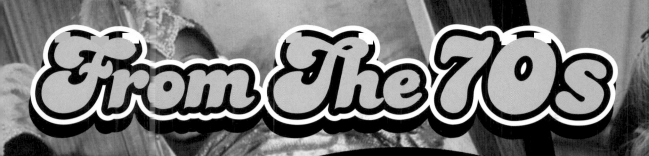

From The 70s

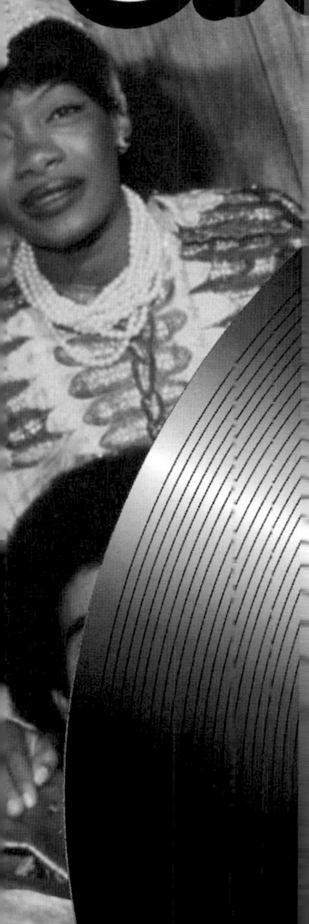
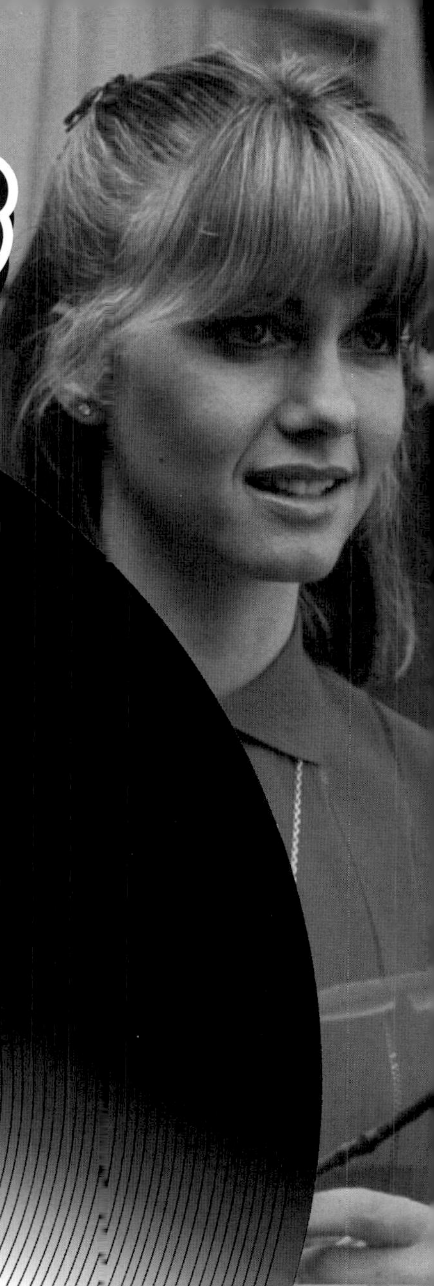

11. Name Simple Minds' lead singer.

12. Gregory's Girl sang with Altered Images. Who is she?

13. Which female singer was with The Tourists?

14. Apart from Tom Jones, Delilah was a huge hit for who?

15. Which duo made up McGuiness Flint?

16. Who sang about a Broken down Angel?

17. Which band did David Paton and Billy Lyall form?

18. Which Scottish town does Annie Lennox hail from?

19. What name is Derek Dick better known by?

20. Who sings the theme tune to "Taggart"?

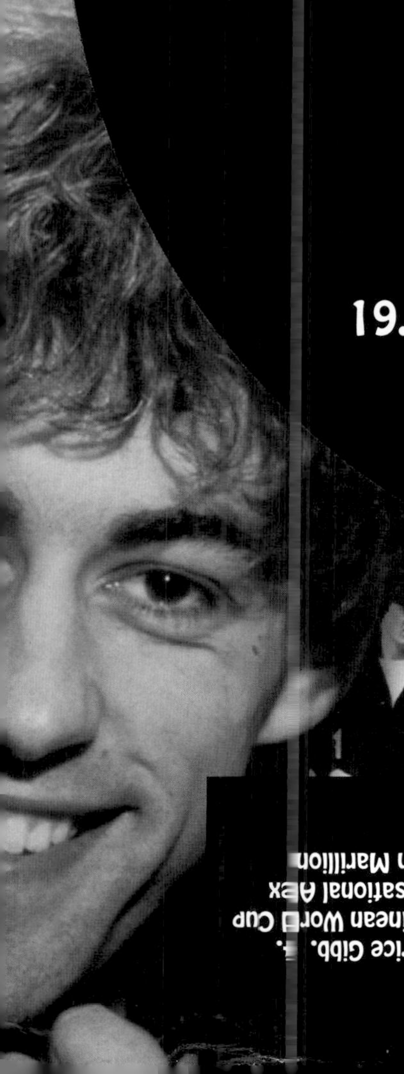
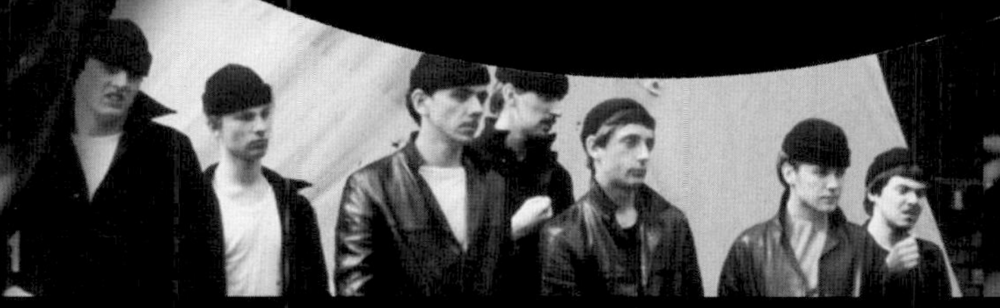
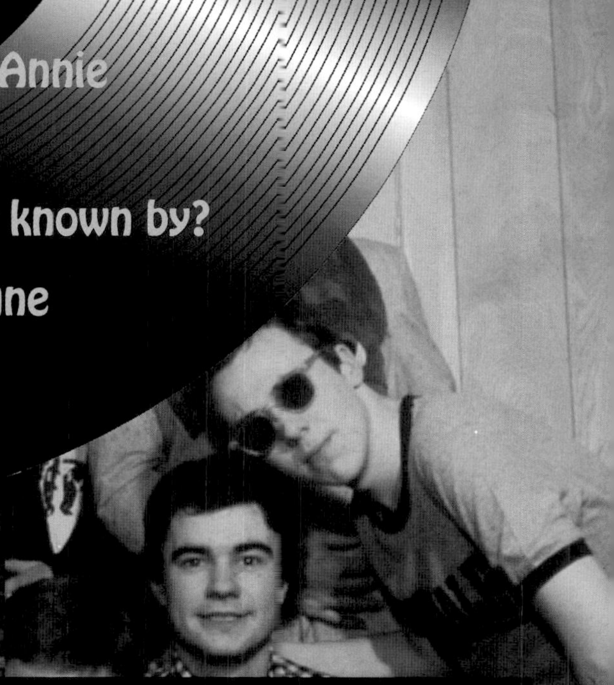

Answers:

1. Les McKeown, Alan Longmuir, Derek Longmuir, Eric Faulkner, Stuart Wood. 2. Brian Connolly. 3. Maurice Gibb. 4. Royal Scots Dragoon Guards. 5. Gerry Rafferty. 6. Chirpy, Chirpy, Cheep, Cheep. 7. Skids. 8. The Argentinean World Cup 1978. 9. Barbara Dickson. 10. Frankie Miller. 11. Jim Kerr. 12. Claire Grogan. 13. Annie Lennox. 14. Sensational Alex Harvey Band. 15. Benny Gallagher and Graham Lyle. 16. Nazareth. 17. Pilot. 18. Aberdeen. 19. Fish from Marillion 20. Maggie Bell.

Teeth here, teeth there, teeth everywhere—

Nae wonder Wull's filled wi' despair!

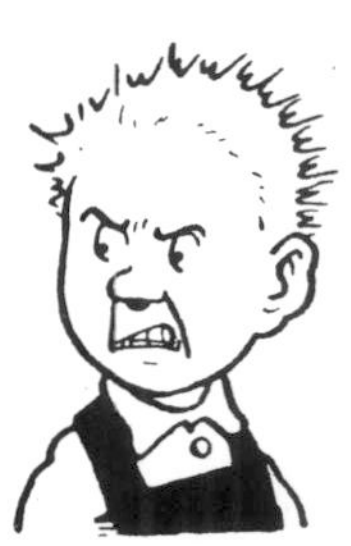

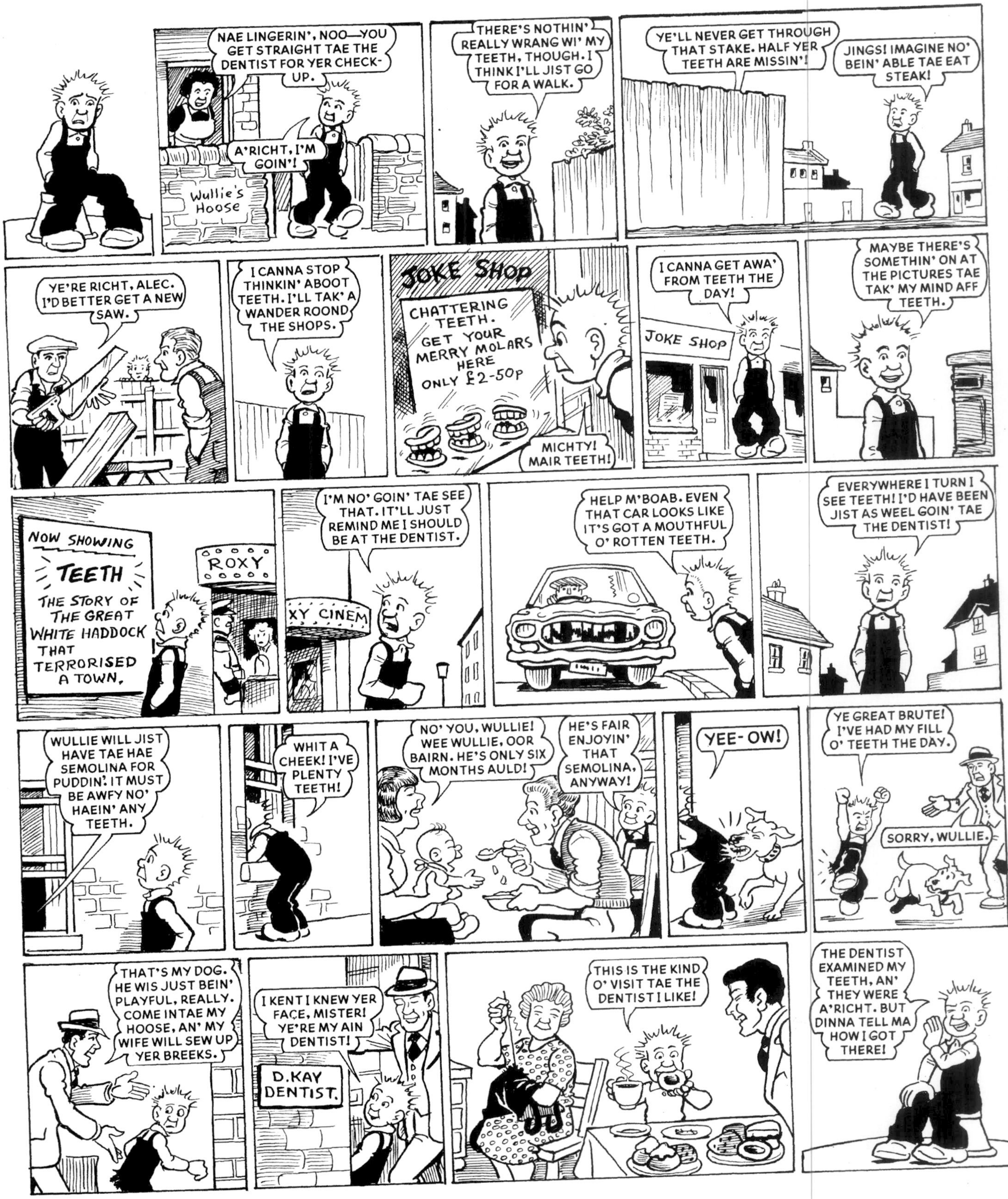
NAE LINGERIN', NOO—YOU GET STRAIGHT TAE THE DENTIST FOR YER CHECK-UP.
A'RICHT, I'M GOIN'!
Wullie's Hoose
THERE'S NOTHIN' REALLY WRANG WI' MY TEETH, THOUGH. I THINK I'LL JIST GO FOR A WALK.
YE'LL NEVER GET THROUGH THAT STAKE. HALF YER TEETH ARE MISSIN'!
JINGS! IMAGINE NO' BEIN' ABLE TAE EAT STEAK!
YE'RE RICHT, ALEC. I'D BETTER GET A NEW SAW.
I CANNA STOP THINKIN' ABOOT TEETH. I'LL TAK' A WANDER ROOND THE SHOPS.
JOKE SHOP
CHATTERING TEETH. GET YOUR MERRY MOLARS HERE ONLY £2-50P
MICHTY! MAIR TEETH!
I CANNA GET AWA' FROM TEETH THE DAY!
JOKE SHOP
MAYBE THERE'S SOMETHIN' ON AT THE PICTURES TAE TAK' MY MIND AFF TEETH.
NOW SHOWING TEETH THE STORY OF THE GREAT WHITE HADDOCK THAT TERRORISED A TOWN.
ROXY
I'M NO' GOIN' TAE SEE THAT. IT'LL JUST REMIND ME I SHOULD BE AT THE DENTIST.
XY CINEM
HELP M'BOAB. EVEN THAT CAR LOOKS LIKE IT'S GOT A MOUTHFUL O' ROTTEN TEETH.
EVERYWHERE I TURN I SEE TEETH! I'D HAVE BEEN JIST AS WEEL GOIN' TAE THE DENTIST!
WULLIE WILL JIST HAVE TAE HAE SEMOLINA FOR PUDDIN'. IT MUST BE AWFY NO' HAEIN' ANY TEETH.
WHIT A CHEEK! I'VE PLENTY TEETH!
NO' YOU, WULLIE! WEE WULLIE, OOR BAIRN. HE'S ONLY SIX MONTHS AULD!
HE'S FAIR ENJOYIN' THAT SEMOLINA, ANYWAY!
YEE-OW!
YE GREAT BRUTE! I'VE HAD MY FILL O' TEETH THE DAY.
SORRY, WULLIE.
THAT'S MY DOG. HE WIS JUST BEIN' PLAYFUL, REALLY. COME INTAE MY HOOSE, AN' MY WIFE WILL SEW UP YER BREEKS.
I KENT I KNEW YER FACE, MISTER! YE'RE MY AIN DENTIST!
D.KAY DENTIST.
THIS IS THE KIND O' VISIT TAE THE DENTIST I LIKE!
THE DENTIST EXAMINED MY TEETH, AN' THEY WERE A'RICHT. BUT DINNA TELL MA HOW I GOT THERE!

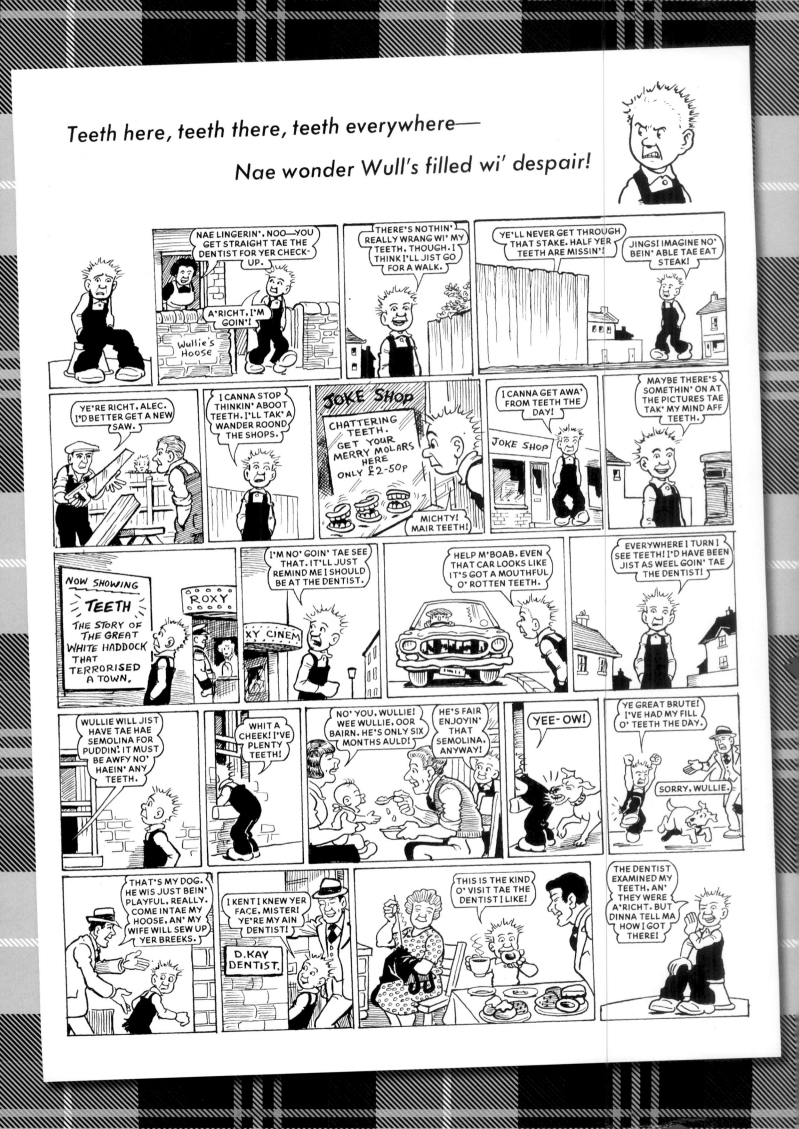

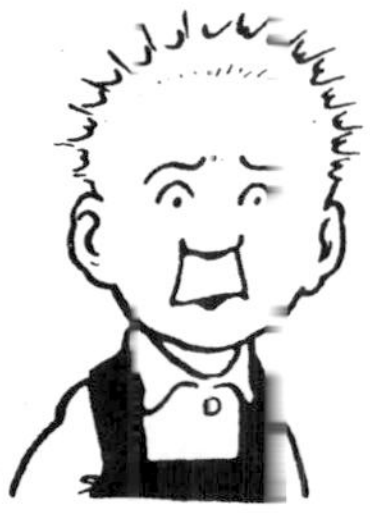

Archie Ologist? Who's he?—

Just tak' a look below and see!

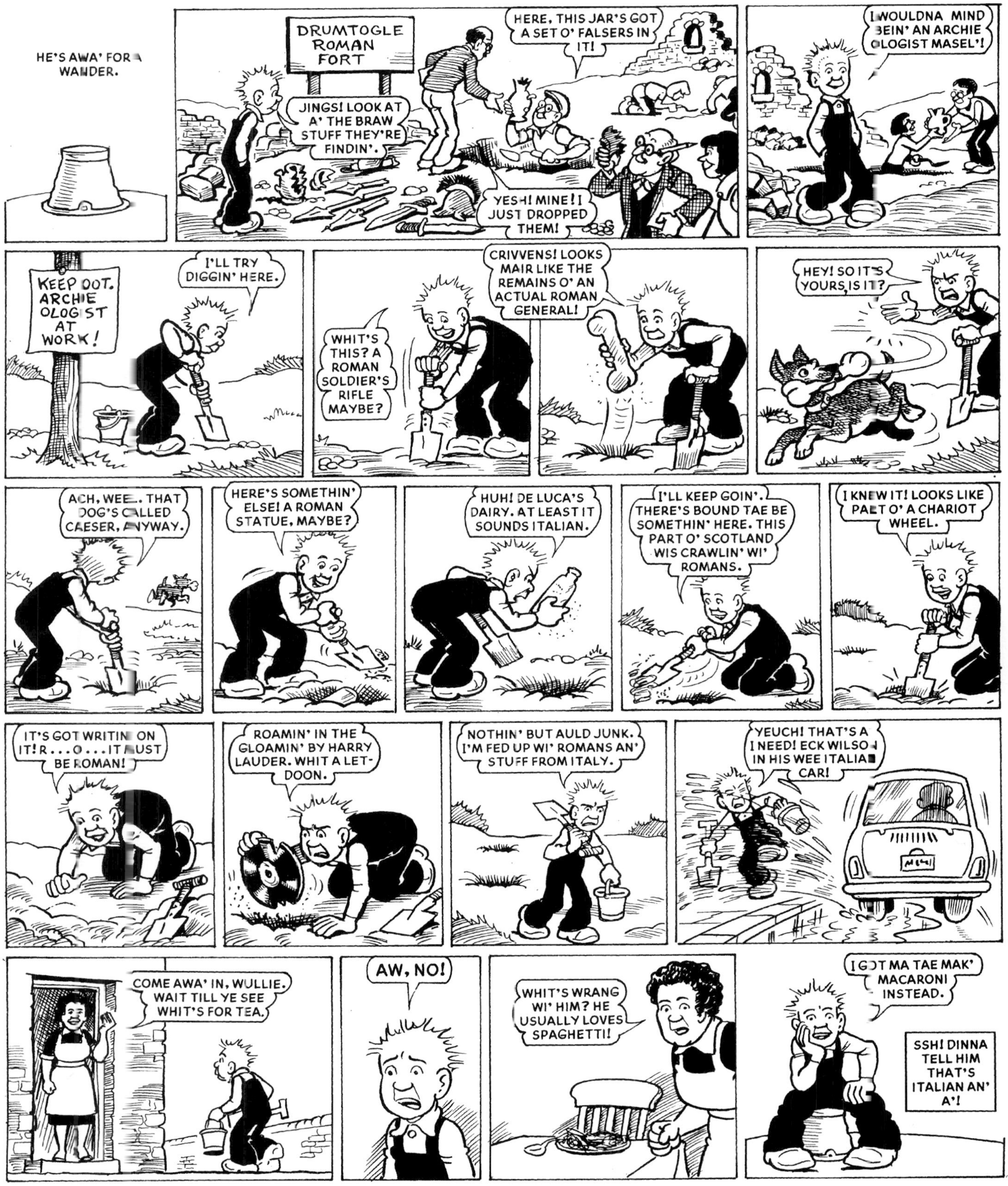

HE'S AWA' FOR A WANDER.
DRUMTOGLE ROMAN FORT
HERE, THIS JAR'S GOT A SET O' FALSERS IN IT!
JINGS! LOOK AT A' THE BRAW STUFF THEY'RE FINDIN'.
YESH! MINE! I JUST DROPPED THEM!
I WOULDNA MIND BEIN' AN ARCHIE OLOGIST MASEL'!
KEEP OOT. ARCHIE OLOGIST AT WORK!
I'LL TRY DIGGIN' HERE.
WHIT'S THIS? A ROMAN SOLDIER'S RIFLE MAYBE?
CRIVVENS! LOOKS MAIR LIKE THE REMAINS O' AN ACTUAL ROMAN GENERAL!
HEY! SO IT'S YOURS, IS IT?
ACH, WEEL. THAT DOG'S CALLED CAESER, ANYWAY.
HERE'S SOMETHIN' ELSE! A ROMAN STATUE, MAYBE?
HUH! DE LUCA'S DAIRY. AT LEAST IT SOUNDS ITALIAN.
I'LL KEEP GOIN'. THERE'S BOUND TAE BE SOMETHIN' HERE. THIS PART O' SCOTLAND WIS CRAWLIN' WI' ROMANS.
I KNEW IT! LOOKS LIKE PART O' A CHARIOT WHEEL.
IT'S GOT WRITIN' ON IT! R . . . O . . . IT MUST BE ROMAN!
ROAMIN' IN THE GLOAMIN' BY HARRY LAUDER. WHIT A LET-DOON.
NOTHIN' BUT AULD JUNK. I'M FED UP WI' ROMANS AN' STUFF FROM ITALY.
YEUCH! THAT'S A' I NEED! ECK WILSON IN HIS WEE ITALIAN CAR!
COME AWA' IN, WULLIE. WAIT TILL YE SEE WHIT'S FOR TEA.
AW, NO!
WHIT'S WRANG WI' HIM? HE USUALLY LOVES SPAGHETTI!
I GOT MA TAE MAK' MACARONI INSTEAD.
SSH! DINNA TELL HIM THAT'S ITALIAN AN' A'!

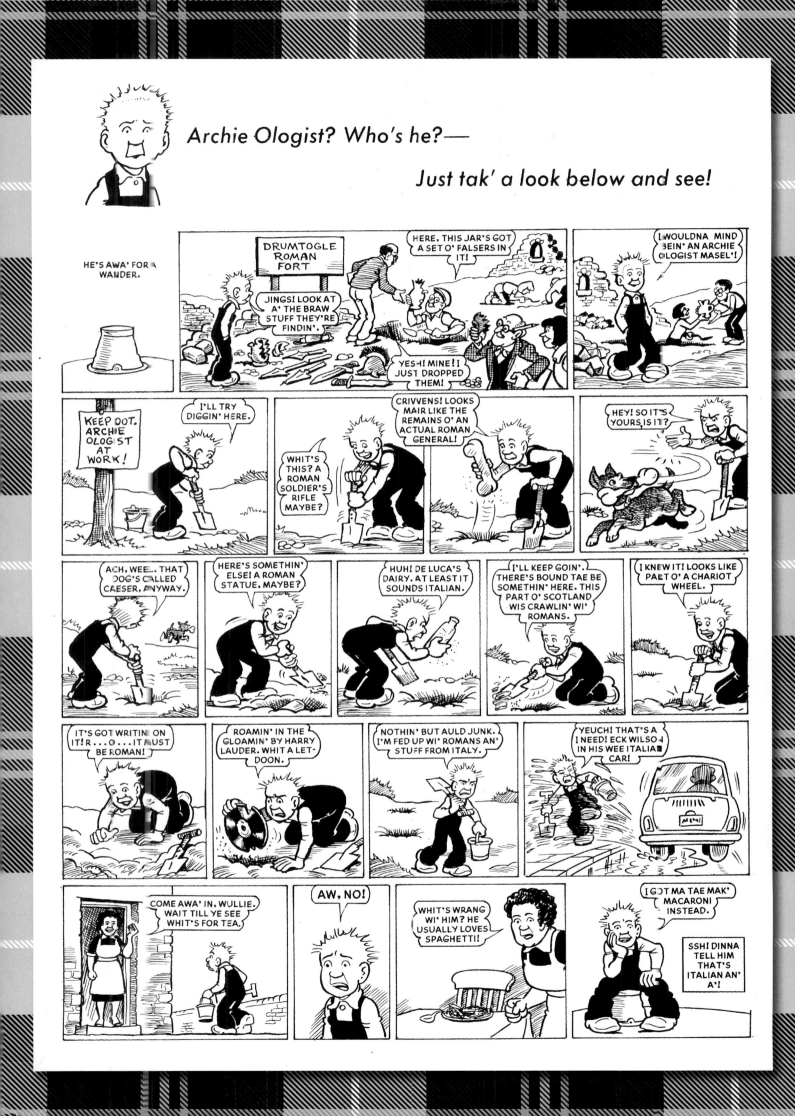

It's a proper laughalot—

When Wullie wants tae sail his yacht!

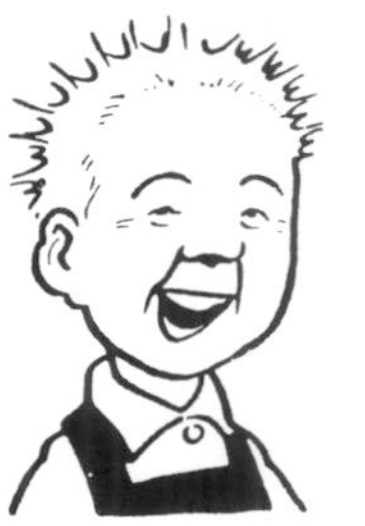

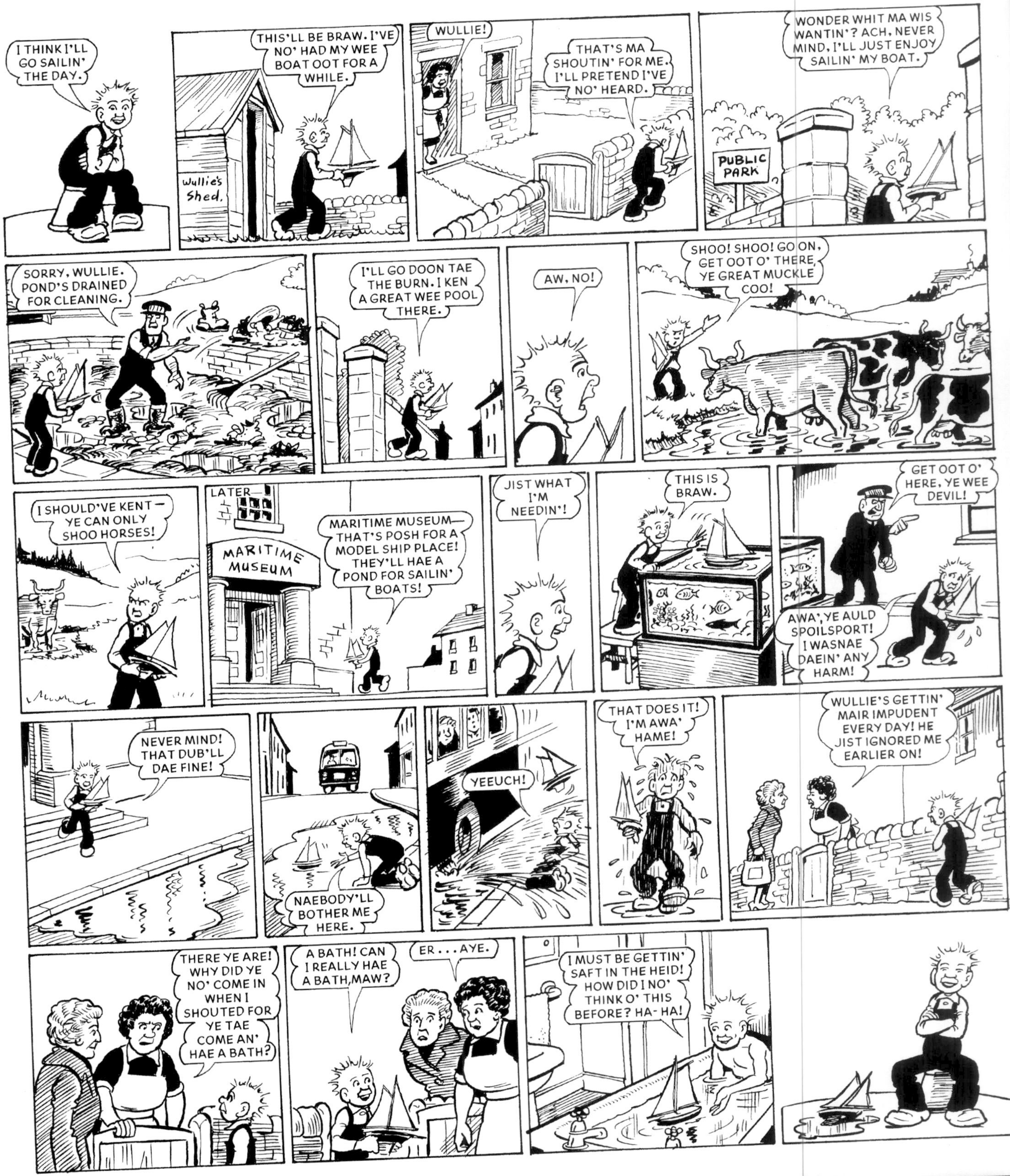

I THINK I'LL GO SAILIN' THE DAY.
THIS'LL BE BRAW. I'VE NO' HAD MY WEE BOAT OOT FOR A WHILE.
Wullie's Shed.
WULLIE!
THAT'S MA SHOUTIN' FOR ME. I'LL PRETEND I'VE NO' HEARD.
WONDER WHIT MA WIS WANTIN'? ACH, NEVER MIND, I'LL JUST ENJOY SAILIN' MY BOAT.
PUBLIC PARK
SORRY, WULLIE. POND'S DRAINED FOR CLEANING.
I'LL GO DOON TAE THE BURN. I KEN A GREAT WEE POOL THERE.
AW, NO!
SHOO! SHOO! GO ON, GET OOT O' THERE, YE GREAT MUCKLE COO!
I SHOULD'VE KENT — YE CAN ONLY SHOO HORSES!
LATER
MARITIME MUSEUM
MARITIME MUSEUM— THAT'S POSH FOR A MODEL SHIP PLACE! THEY'LL HAE A POND FOR SAILIN' BOATS!
JIST WHAT I'M NEEDIN'!
THIS IS BRAW.
GET OOT O' HERE, YE WEE DEVIL!
AWA', YE AULD SPOILSPORT! I WASNAE DAEIN' ANY HARM!
NEVER MIND! THAT DUB'LL DAE FINE!
NAEBODY'LL BOTHER ME HERE.
YEEUCH!
THAT DOES IT! I'M AWA' HAME!
WULLIE'S GETTIN' MAIR IMPUDENT EVERY DAY! HE JIST IGNORED ME EARLIER ON!
THERE YE ARE! WHY DID YE NO' COME IN WHEN I SHOUTED FOR YE TAE COME AN' HAE A BATH?
A BATH! CAN I REALLY HAE A BATH, MAW?
ER . . . AYE.
I MUST BE GETTIN' SAFT IN THE HEID! HOW DID I NO' THINK O' THIS BEFORE? HA-HA!

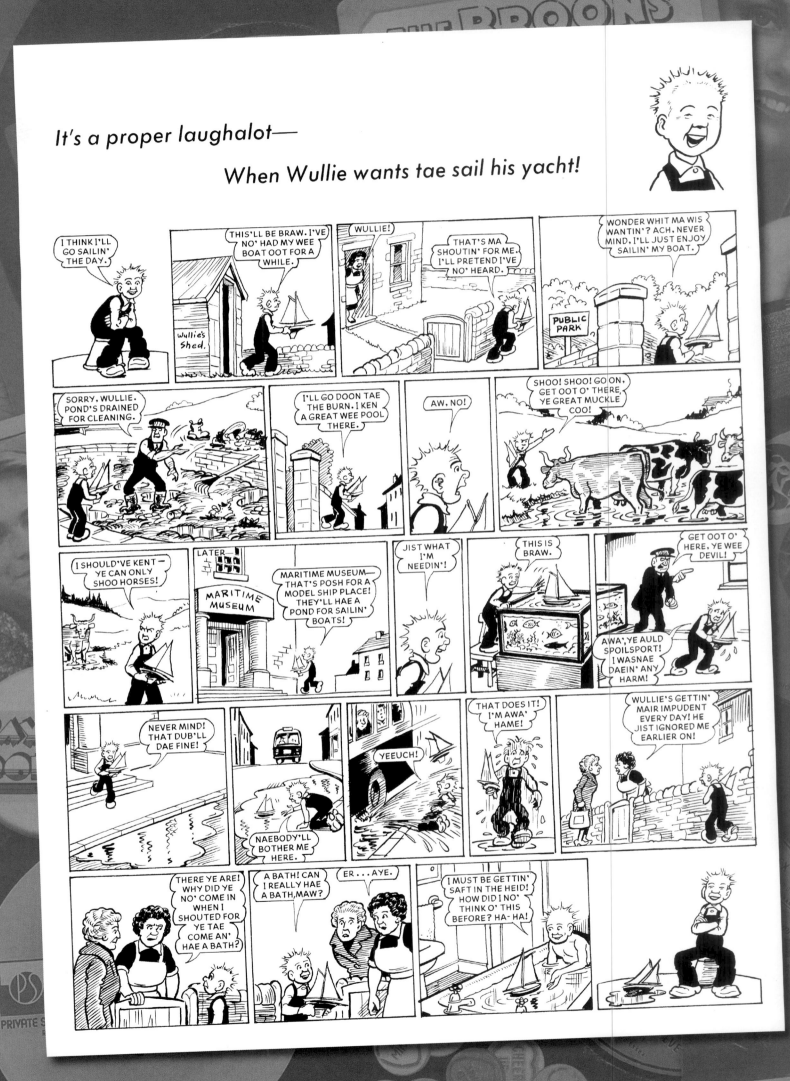

A sanctuary for birds? That's grand!—

But things don't go quite as Wull planned.

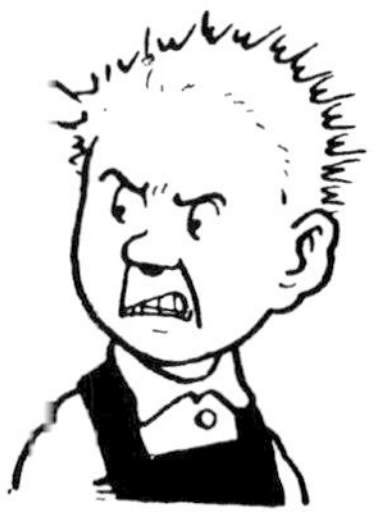

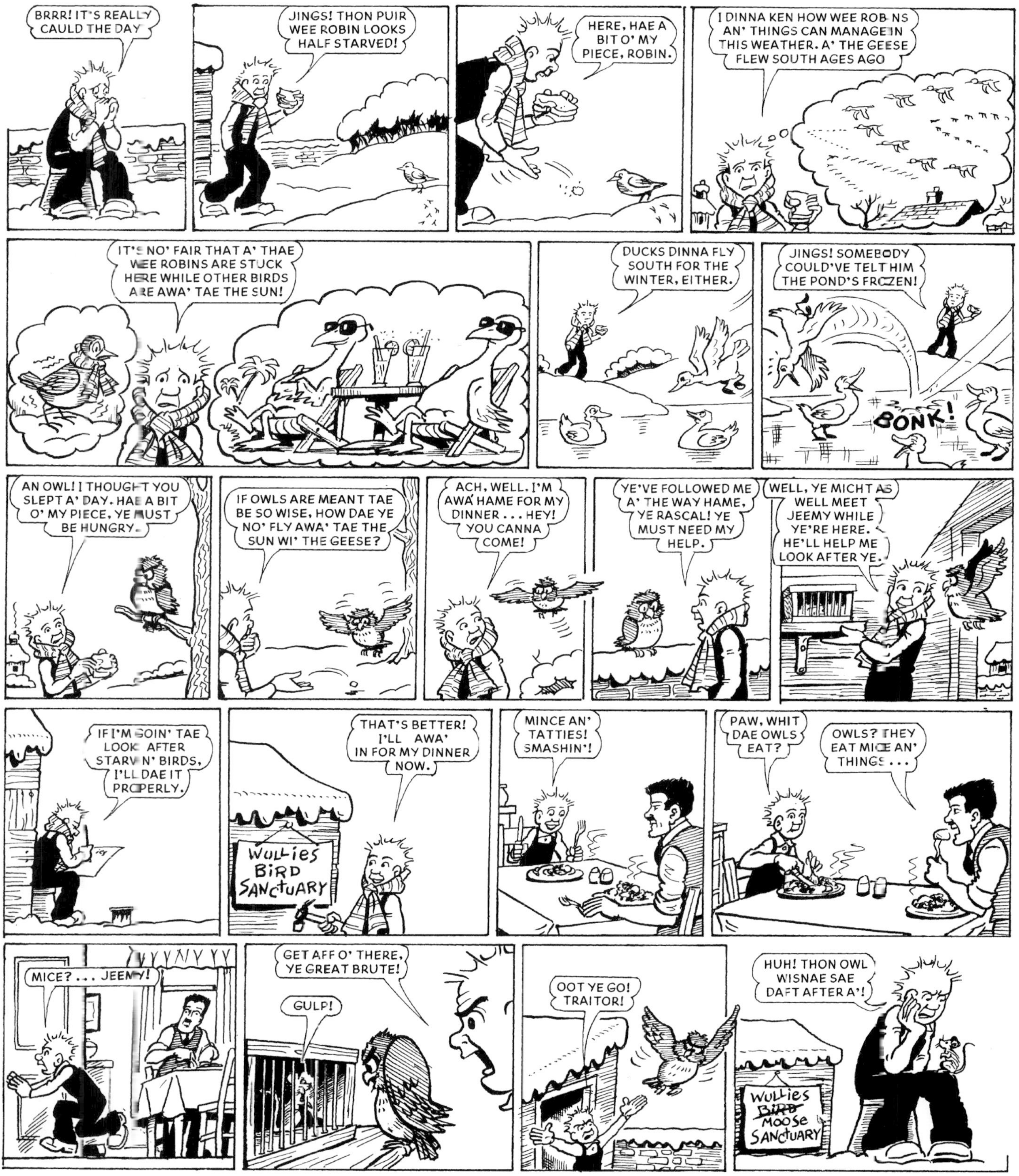

BRRR! IT'S REALLY CAULD THE DAY
JINGS! THON PUIR WEE ROBIN LOOKS HALF STARVED!
HERE, HAE A BIT O' MY PIECE, ROBIN.
I DINNA KEN HOW WEE ROBINS AN' THINGS CAN MANAGE IN THIS WEATHER. A' THE GEESE FLEW SOUTH AGES AGO
IT'S NO' FAIR THAT A' THAE WEE ROBINS ARE STUCK HERE WHILE OTHER BIRDS ARE AWA' TAE THE SUN!
DUCKS DINNA FLY SOUTH FOR THE WINTER, EITHER.
JINGS! SOMEBODY COULD'VE TELT HIM THE POND'S FROZEN!
BONK!
AN OWL! I THOUGHT YOU SLEPT A' DAY. HAE A BIT O' MY PIECE, YE MUST BE HUNGRY.
IF OWLS ARE MEANT TAE BE SO WISE, HOW DAE YE NO' FLY AWA' TAE THE SUN WI' THE GEESE?
ACH, WELL, I'M AWA' HAME FOR MY DINNER . . . HEY! YOU CANNA COME!
YE'VE FOLLOWED ME A' THE WAY HAME, YE RASCAL! YE MUST NEED MY HELP.
WELL, YE MICHT AS WELL MEET JEEMY WHILE YE'RE HERE. HE'LL HELP ME LOOK AFTER YE.
IF I'M GOIN' TAE LOOK AFTER STARVIN' BIRDS, I'LL DAE IT PROPERLY.
THAT'S BETTER! I'LL AWA' IN FOR MY DINNER NOW.
WULLIES BIRD SANCTUARY
MINCE AN' TATTIES! SMASHIN'!
PAW, WHIT DAE OWLS EAT?
OWLS? THEY EAT MICE AN' THINGS . . .
MICE? . . . JEEMY!
GET AFF O' THERE, YE GREAT BRUTE!
GULP!
OOT YE GO! TRAITOR!
HUH! THON OWL WISNAE SAE DAFT AFTER A'!
WULLIES BIRD MOOSE SANCTUARY

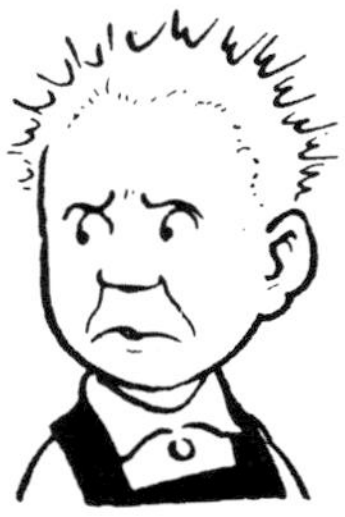

Help m' boab! What's happenin' here?—

When Wull's around, folk disappear!

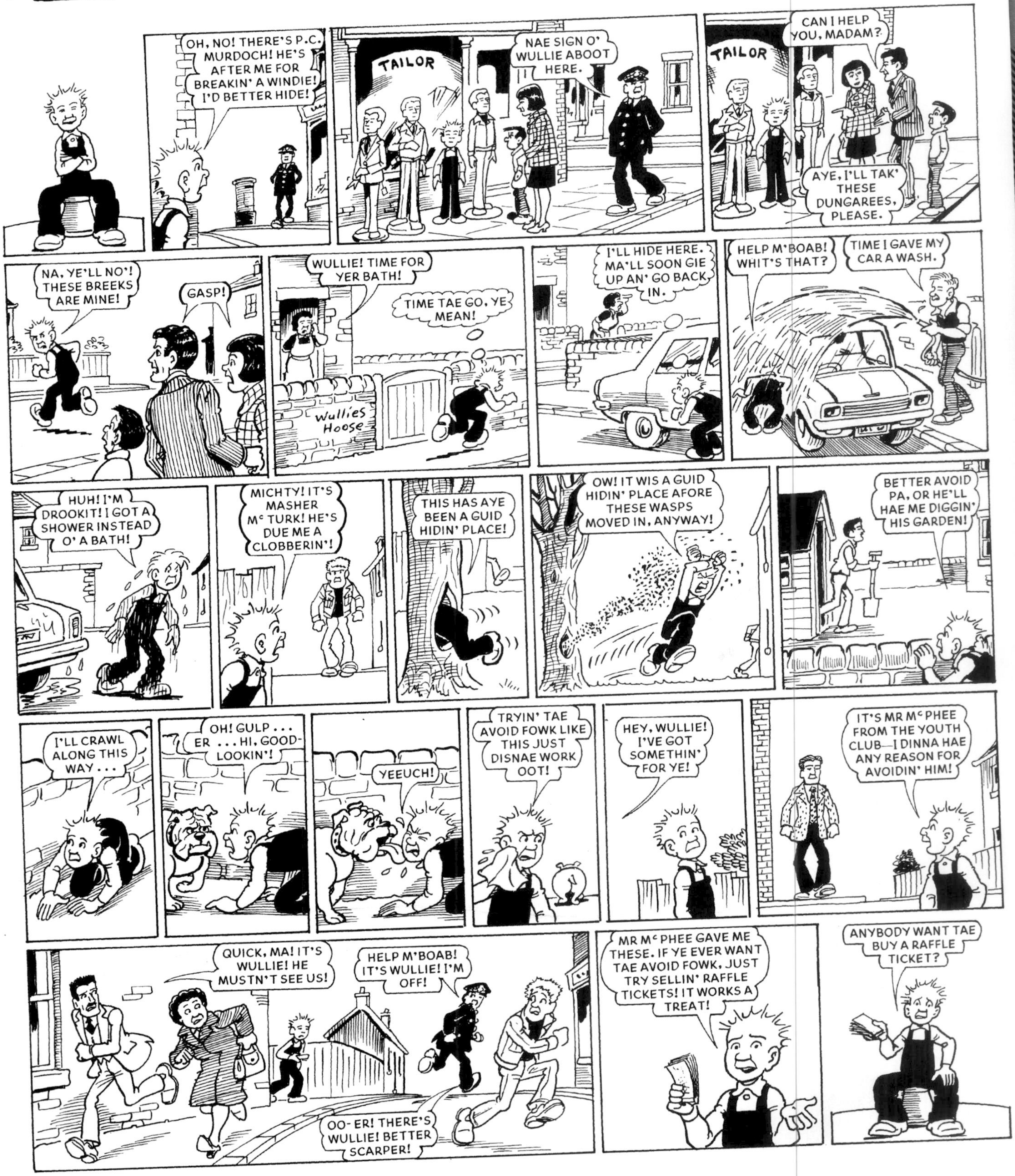

OH, NO! THERE'S P.C. MURDOCH! HE'S AFTER ME FOR BREAKIN' A WINDIE! I'D BETTER HIDE!
TAILOR
NAE SIGN O' WULLIE ABOOT HERE.
TAILOR
CAN I HELP YOU, MADAM?
AYE, I'LL TAK' THESE DUNGAREES, PLEASE.
NA, YE'LL NO'! THESE BREEKS ARE MINE!
GASP!
WULLIE! TIME FOR YER BATH!
TIME TAE GO, YE MEAN!
Wullies Hoose
I'LL HIDE HERE. MA'LL SOON GIE UP AN' GO BACK IN.
HELP M'BOAB! WHIT'S THAT?
TIME I GAVE MY CAR A WASH.
HUH! I'M DROOKIT! I GOT A SHOWER INSTEAD O' A BATH!
MICHTY! IT'S MASHER McTURK! HE'S DUE ME A CLOBBERIN'!
THIS HAS AYE BEEN A GUID HIDIN' PLACE!
OW! IT WIS A GUID HIDIN' PLACE AFORE THESE WASPS MOVED IN, ANYWAY!
BETTER AVOID PA, OR HE'LL HAE ME DIGGIN' HIS GARDEN!
I'LL CRAWL ALONG THIS WAY...
OH! GULP... ER ...HI, GOOD-LOOKIN'!
YEEUCH!
TRYIN' TAE AVOID FOWK LIKE THIS JUST DISNAE WORK OOT!
HEY, WULLIE! I'VE GOT SOMETHIN' FOR YE!
IT'S MR McPHEE FROM THE YOUTH CLUB—I DINNA HAE ANY REASON FOR AVOIDIN' HIM!
QUICK, MA! IT'S WULLIE! HE MUSTN'T SEE US!
HELP M'BOAB! IT'S WULLIE! I'M OFF!
OO-ER! THERE'S WULLIE! BETTER SCARPER!
MR McPHEE GAVE ME THESE. IF YE EVER WANT TAE AVOID FOWK, JUST TRY SELLIN' RAFFLE TICKETS! IT WORKS A TREAT!
ANYBODY WANT TAE BUY A RAFFLE TICKET?

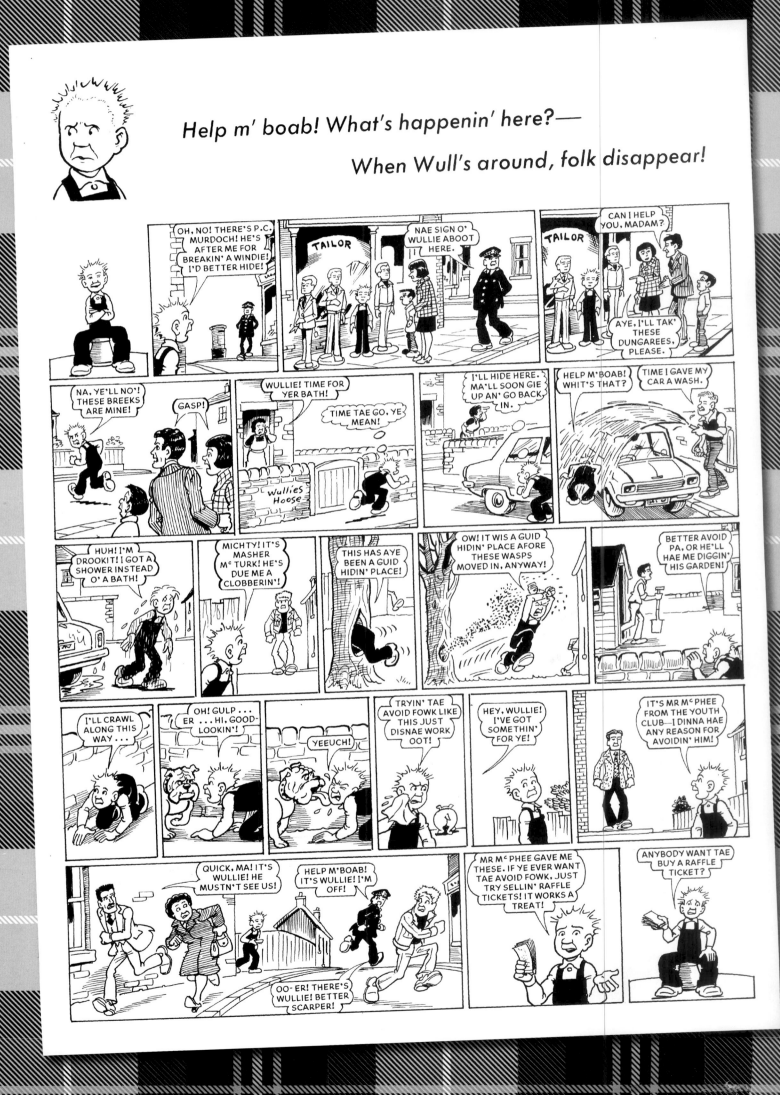

The folk line up for Wull's coach trip—

And sure enough, he gets a tip!

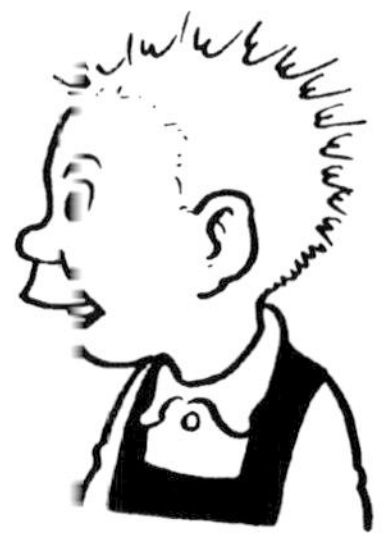

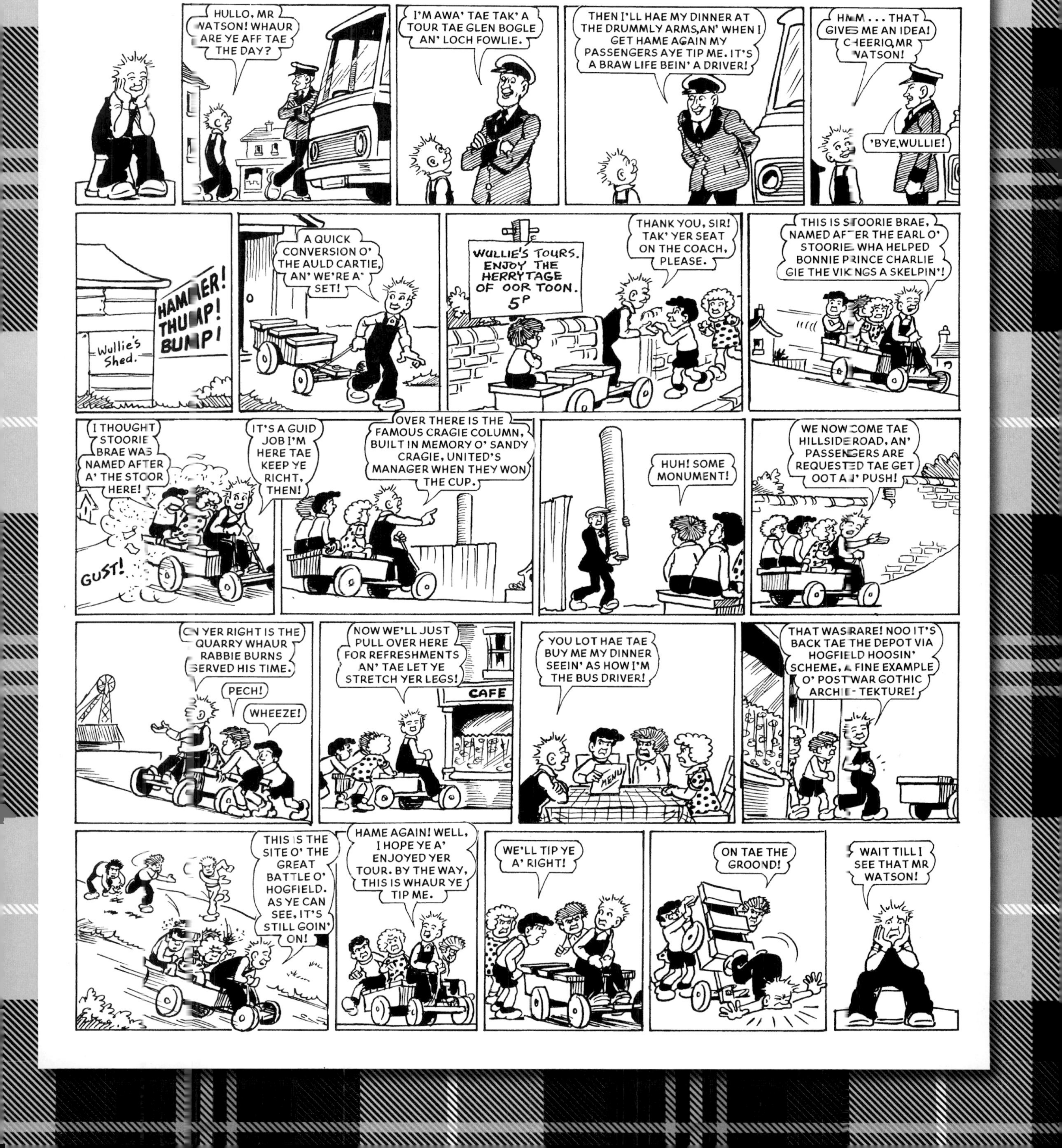
HULLO, MR WATSON! WHAUR ARE YE AFF TAE THE DAY?
I'M AWA' TAE TAK' A TOUR TAE GLEN BOGLE AN' LOCH FOWLIE.
THEN I'LL HAE MY DINNER AT THE DRUMMLY ARMS, AN' WHEN I GET HAME AGAIN MY PASSENGERS AYE TIP ME. IT'S A BRAW LIFE BEIN' A DRIVER!
HMM . . . THAT GIVES ME AN IDEA! CHEERIO, MR WATSON!
'BYE, WULLIE!
Wullie's Shed.
HAMMER! THUMP! BUMP!
A QUICK CONVERSION O' THE AULD CARTIE, AN' WE'RE A' SET!
WULLIE'S TOURS. ENJOY THE HERRYTAGE OF OOR TOON. 5P
THANK YOU, SIR! TAK' YER SEAT ON THE COACH, PLEASE.
THIS IS STOORIE BRAE, NAMED AFTER THE EARL O' STOORIE, WHA HELPED BONNIE PRINCE CHARLIE GIE THE VIKINGS A SKELPIN'!
I THOUGHT STOORIE BRAE WAS NAMED AFTER A' THE STOOR HERE!
IT'S A GUID JOB I'M HERE TAE KEEP YE RICHT, THEN!
GUST!
OVER THERE IS THE FAMOUS CRAGIE COLUMN, BUILT IN MEMORY O' SANDY CRAGIE, UNITED'S MANAGER WHEN THEY WON THE CUP.
HUH! SOME MONUMENT!
WE NOW COME TAE HILLSIDE ROAD, AN' PASSENGERS ARE REQUESTED TAE GET OOT AN' PUSH!
ON YER RIGHT IS THE QUARRY WHAUR RABBIE BURNS SERVED HIS TIME.
PECH!
WHEEZE!
NOW WE'LL JUST PULL OVER HERE FOR REFRESHMENTS AN' TAE LET YE STRETCH YER LEGS!
CAFE
YOU LOT HAE TAE BUY ME MY DINNER SEEIN' AS HOW I'M THE BUS DRIVER!
MENU
THAT WAS RARE! NOO IT'S BACK TAE THE DEPOT VIA HOGFIELD HOOSIN' SCHEME, A FINE EXAMPLE O' POSTWAR GOTHIC ARCHIE-TEKTURE!
THIS IS THE SITE O' THE GREAT BATTLE O' HOGFIELD. AS YE CAN SEE, IT'S STILL GOIN' ON!
HAME AGAIN! WELL, I HOPE YE A' ENJOYED YER TOUR. BY THE WAY, THIS IS WHAUR YE TIP ME.
WE'LL TIP YE A' RIGHT!
ON TAE THE GROOND!
WAIT TILL I SEE THAT MR WATSON!

All Oor Wullie wants to know—

Is what made Hen Broon grow and grow!

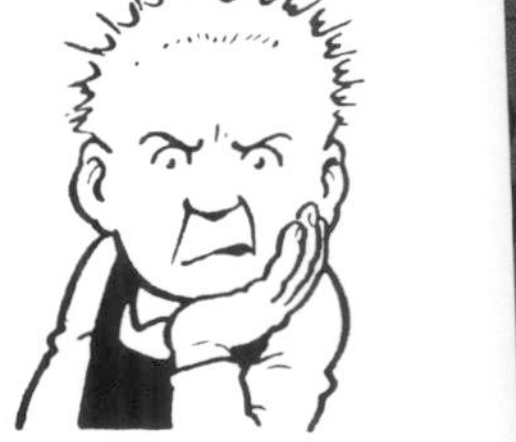

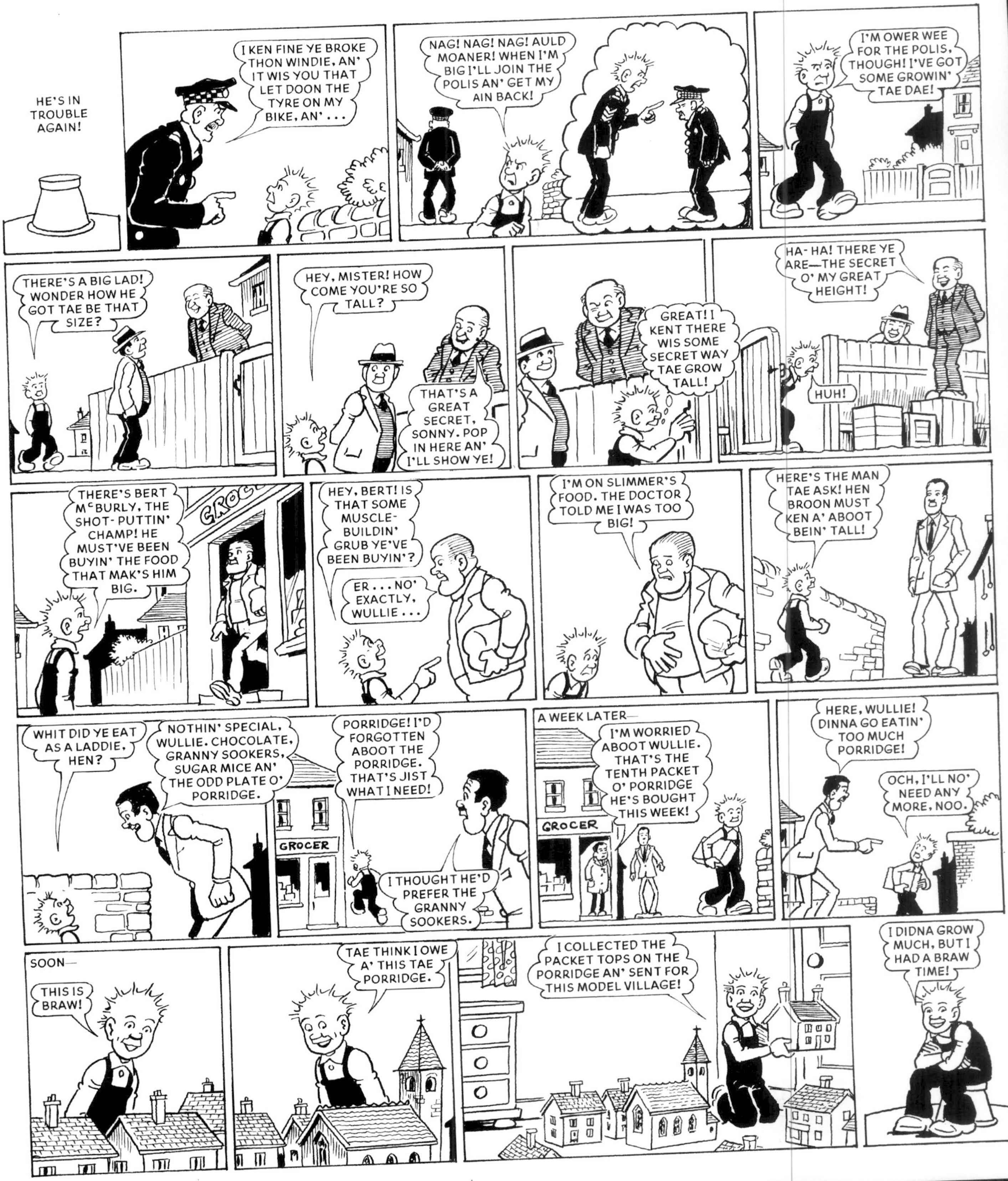

HE'S IN TROUBLE AGAIN!
I KEN FINE YE BROKE THON WINDIE, AN' IT WIS YOU THAT LET DOON THE TYRE ON MY BIKE, AN' . . .
NAG! NAG! NAG! AULD MOANER! WHEN I'M BIG I'LL JOIN THE POLIS AN' GET MY AIN BACK!
I'M OWER WEE FOR THE POLIS, THOUGH! I'VE GOT SOME GROWIN' TAE DAE!
THERE'S A BIG LAD! WONDER HOW HE GOT TAE BE THAT SIZE?
HEY, MISTER! HOW COME YOU'RE SO TALL?
THAT'S A GREAT SECRET, SONNY. POP IN HERE AN' I'LL SHOW YE!
GREAT! I KENT THERE WIS SOME SECRET WAY TAE GROW TALL!
HA-HA! THERE YE ARE—THE SECRET O' MY GREAT HEIGHT!
HUH!
THERE'S BERT McBURLY, THE SHOT-PUTTIN' CHAMP! HE MUST'VE BEEN BUYIN' THE FOOD THAT MAK'S HIM BIG.
GROC
HEY, BERT! IS THAT SOME MUSCLE-BUILDIN' GRUB YE'VE BEEN BUYIN'?
ER . . . NO' EXACTLY, WULLIE . . .
I'M ON SLIMMER'S FOOD. THE DOCTOR TOLD ME I WAS TOO BIG!
HERE'S THE MAN TAE ASK! HEN BROON MUST KEN A' ABOOT BEIN' TALL!
WHIT DID YE EAT AS A LADDIE, HEN?
NOTHIN' SPECIAL, WULLIE. CHOCOLATE, GRANNY SOOKERS, SUGAR MICE AN' THE ODD PLATE O' PORRIDGE.
PORRIDGE! I'D FORGOTTEN ABOOT THE PORRIDGE. THAT'S JIST WHAT I NEED!
GROCER
I THOUGHT HE'D PREFER THE GRANNY SOOKERS.
A WEEK LATER—
I'M WORRIED ABOOT WULLIE. THAT'S THE TENTH PACKET O' PORRIDGE HE'S BOUGHT THIS WEEK!
GROCER
HERE, WULLIE! DINNA GO EATIN' TOO MUCH PORRIDGE!
OCH, I'LL NO' NEED ANY MORE, NOO.
SOON—
THIS IS BRAW!
TAE THINK I OWE A' THIS TAE PORRIDGE.
I COLLECTED THE PACKET TOPS ON THE PORRIDGE AN' SENT FOR THIS MODEL VILLAGE!
I DIDNA GROW MUCH, BUT I HAD A BRAW TIME!

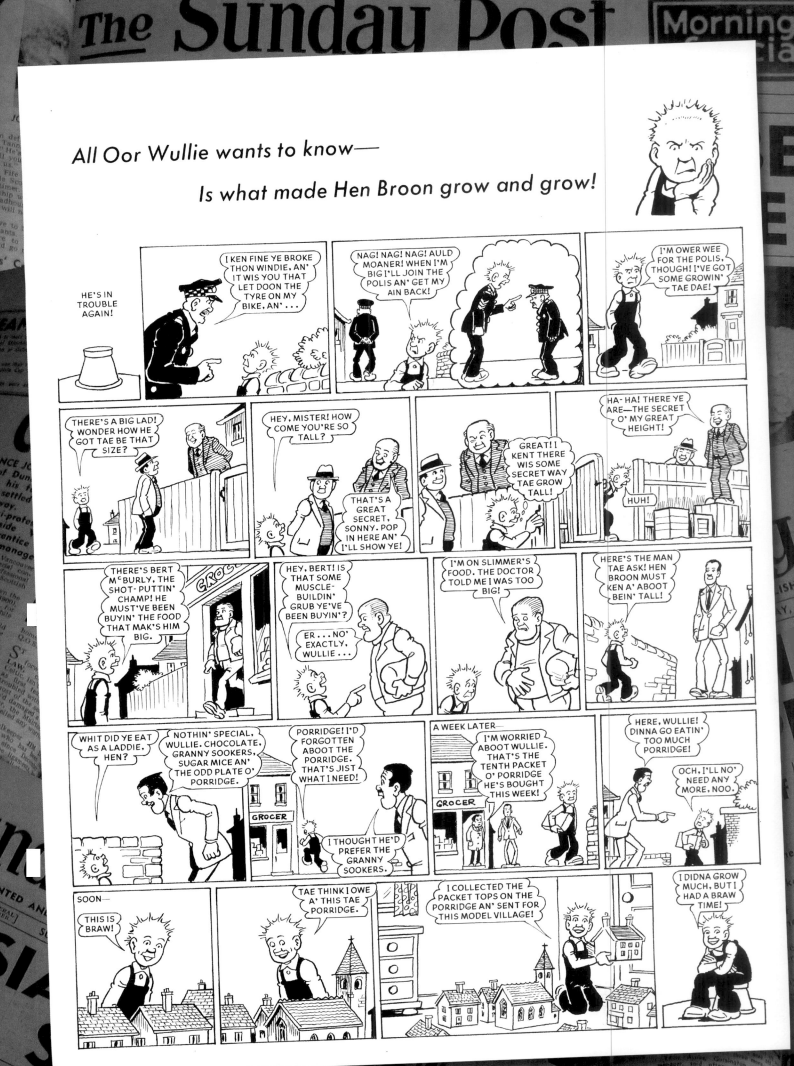

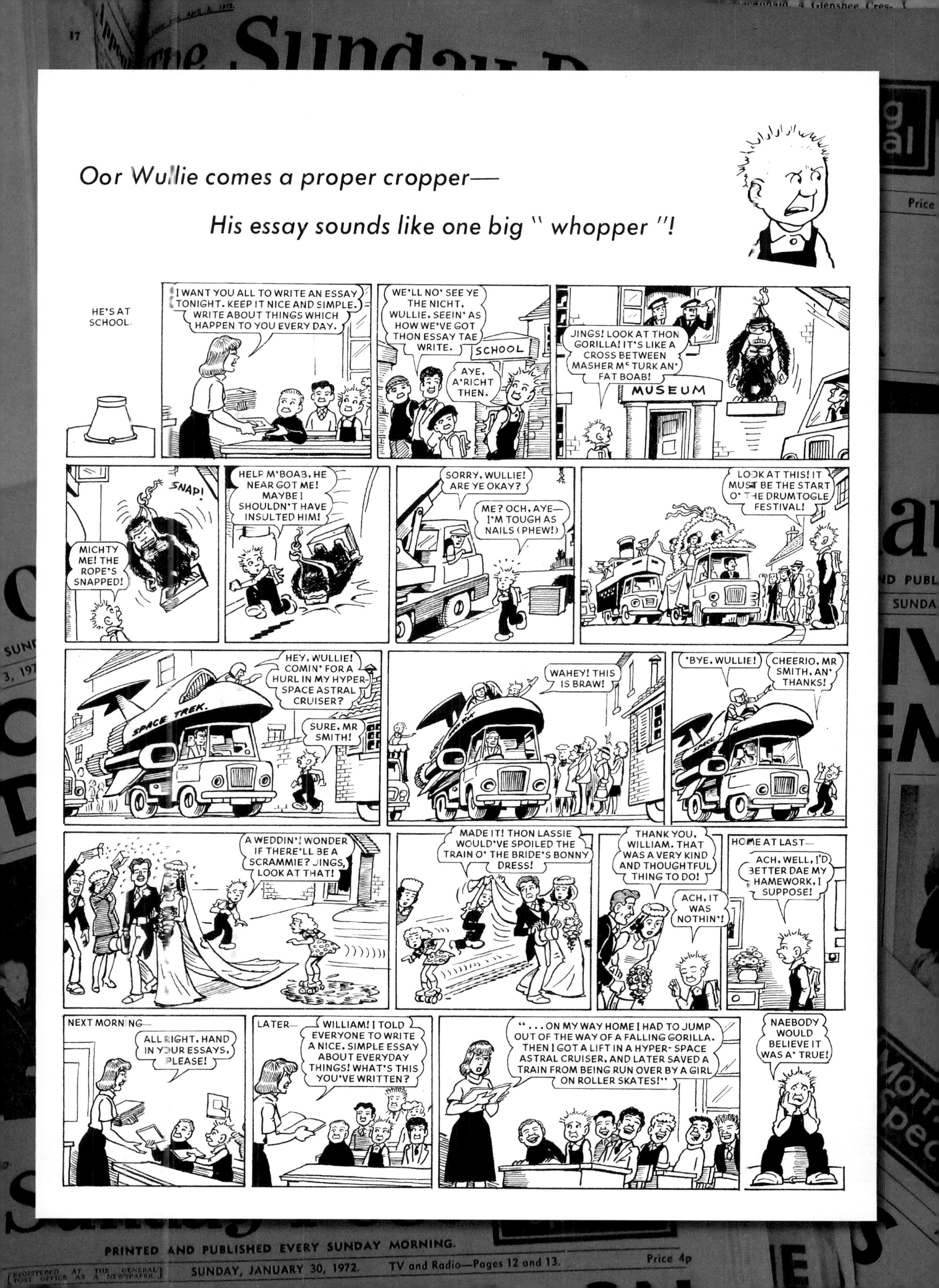
Oor Wullie comes a proper cropper—
His essay sounds like one big " whopper "!
HE'S AT SCHOOL.
I WANT YOU ALL TO WRITE AN ESSAY TONIGHT. KEEP IT NICE AND SIMPLE. WRITE ABOUT THINGS WHICH HAPPEN TO YOU EVERY DAY.
WE'LL NO' SEE YE THE NICHT, WULLIE, SEEIN' AS HOW WE'VE GOT THON ESSAY TAE WRITE.
SCHOOL
AYE, A'RICHT THEN.
JINGS! LOOK AT THON GORILLA! IT'S LIKE A CROSS BETWEEN MASHER M^c TURK AN' FAT BOAB!
MUSEUM
SNAP!
MICHTY ME! THE ROPE'S SNAPPED!
HELP M'BOAB, HE NEAR GOT ME! MAYBE I SHOULDN'T HAVE INSULTED HIM!
SORRY, WULLIE! ARE YE OKAY?
ME? OCH, AYE— I'M TOUGH AS NAILS (PHEW!)
LOOK AT THIS! IT MUST BE THE START O' THE DRUMTOGLE FESTIVAL!
HEY, WULLIE! COMIN' FOR A HURL IN MY HYPER-SPACE ASTRAL CRUISER?
SPACE TREK.
SURE, MR SMITH!
WAHEY! THIS IS BRAW!
'BYE, WULLIE!
CHEERIO, MR SMITH, AN' THANKS!
A WEDDIN'! WONDER IF THERE'LL BE A SCRAMMIE? JINGS, LOOK AT THAT!
MADE IT! THON LASSIE WOULD'VE SPOILED THE TRAIN O' THE BRIDE'S BONNY DRESS!
THANK YOU, WILLIAM. THAT WAS A VERY KIND AND THOUGHTFUL THING TO DO!
ACH, IT WAS NOTHIN'!
HOME AT LAST—
ACH, WELL, I'D BETTER DAE MY HAMEWORK, I SUPPOSE!
NEXT MORNING—
ALL RIGHT, HAND IN YOUR ESSAYS, PLEASE!
LATER—
WILLIAM! I TOLD EVERYONE TO WRITE A NICE, SIMPLE ESSAY ABOUT EVERYDAY THINGS! WHAT'S THIS YOU'VE WRITTEN?
". . . ON MY WAY HOME I HAD TO JUMP OUT OF THE WAY OF A FALLING GORILLA. THEN I GOT A LIFT IN A HYPER- SPACE ASTRAL CRUISER, AND LATER SAVED A TRAIN FROM BEING RUN OVER BY A GIRL ON ROLLER SKATES!"
NAEBODY WOULD BELIEVE IT WAS A' TRUE!
PRINTED AND PUBLISHED EVERY SUNDAY MORNING.
SUNDAY, JANUARY 30, 1972.
TV and Radio—Pages 12 and 13.
Price 4p

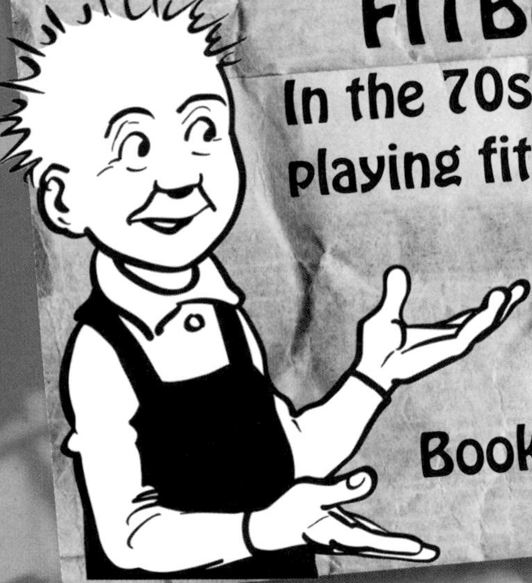

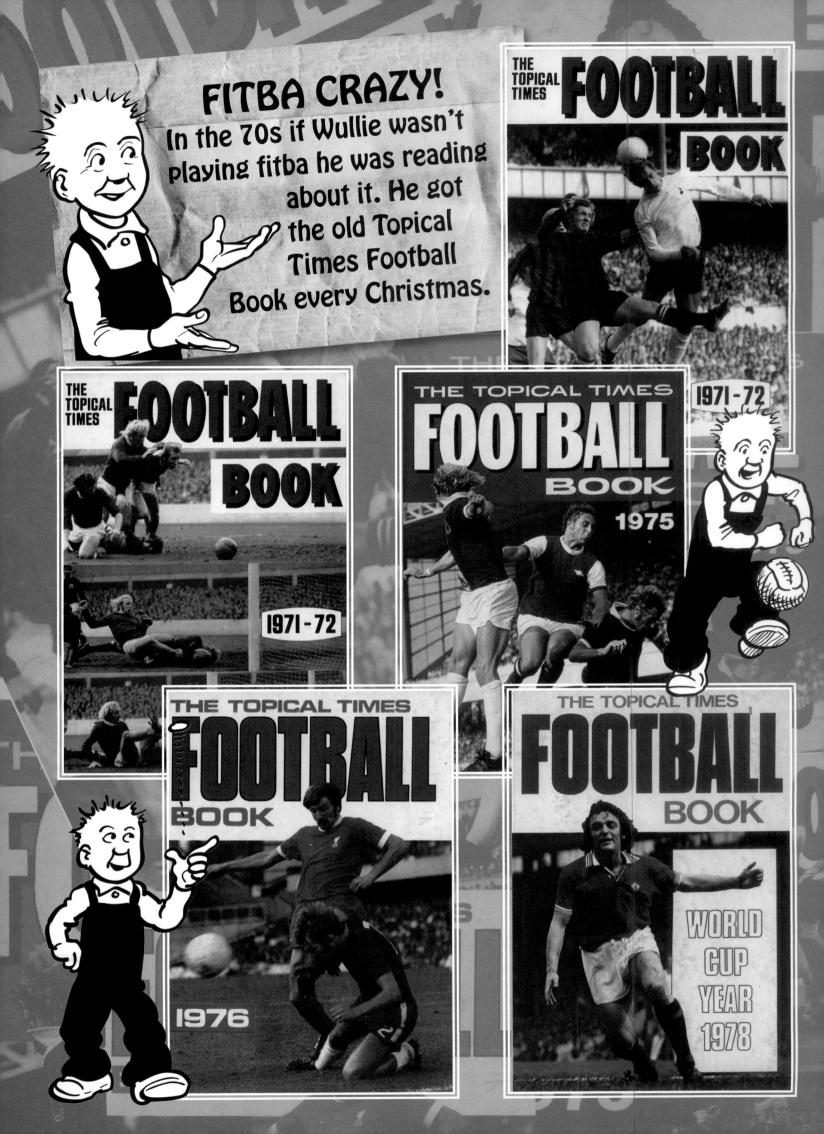

FITBA CRAZY!

In the 70s if Wullie wasn't playing fitba he was reading about it. He got the old Topical Times Football Book every Christmas.

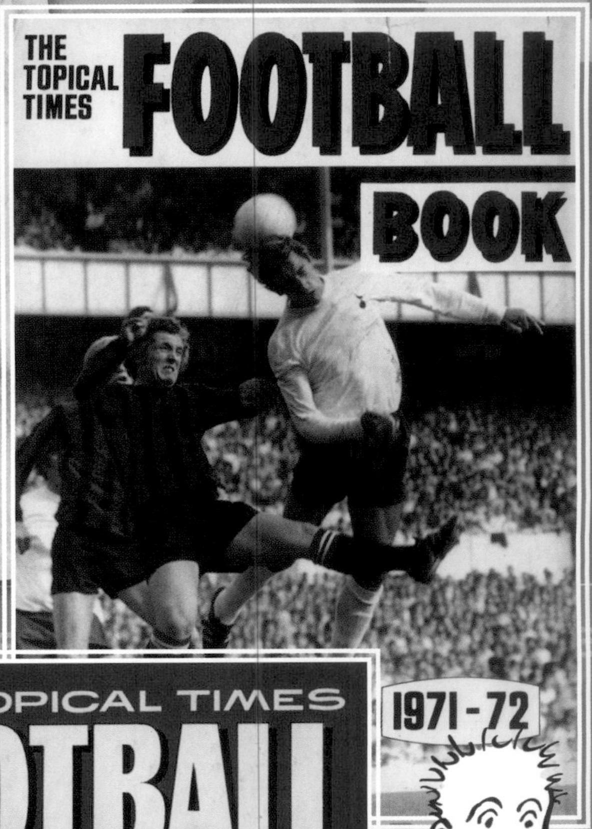
THE TOPICAL TIMES
FOOTBALL
BOOK
1971-72

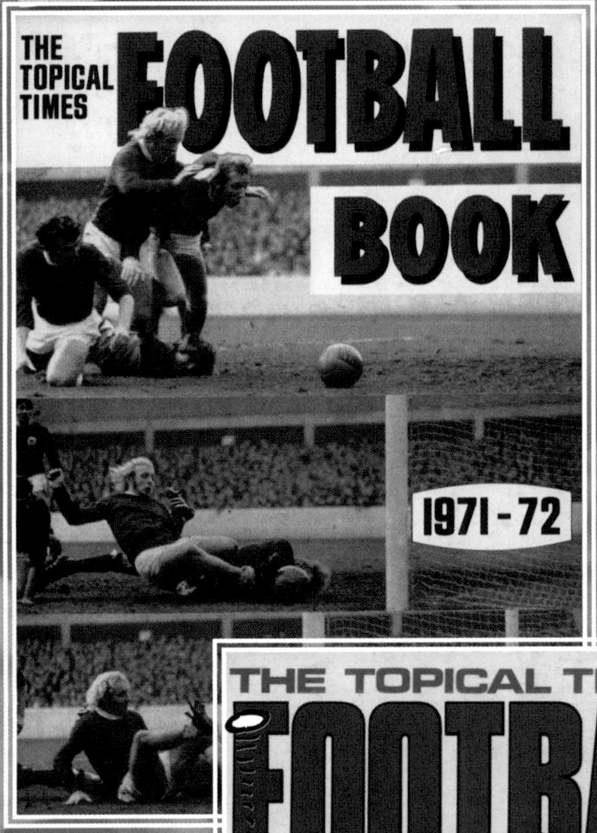
THE TOPICAL TIMES
FOOTBALL
BOOK
1971-72

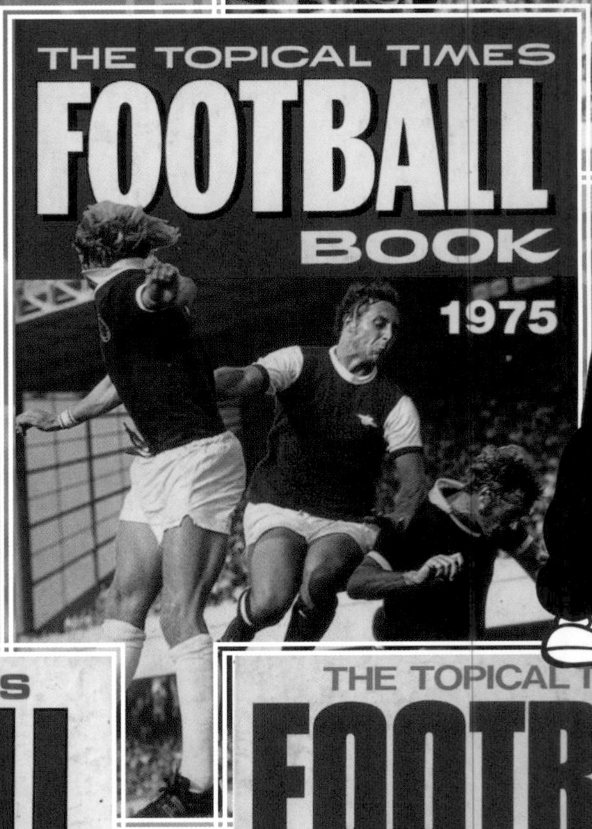
THE TOPICAL TIMES
FOOTBALL
BOOK
1975

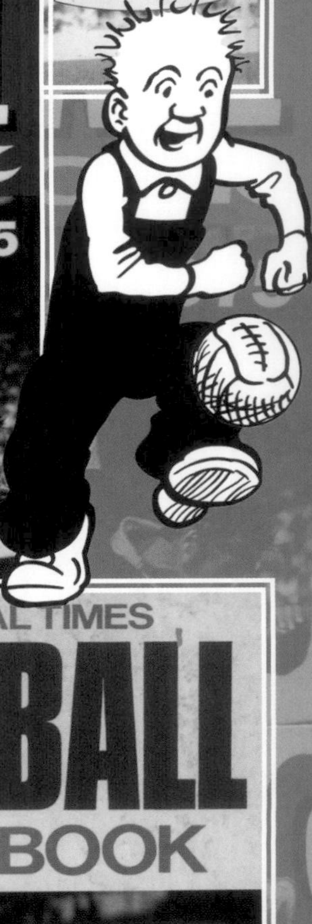

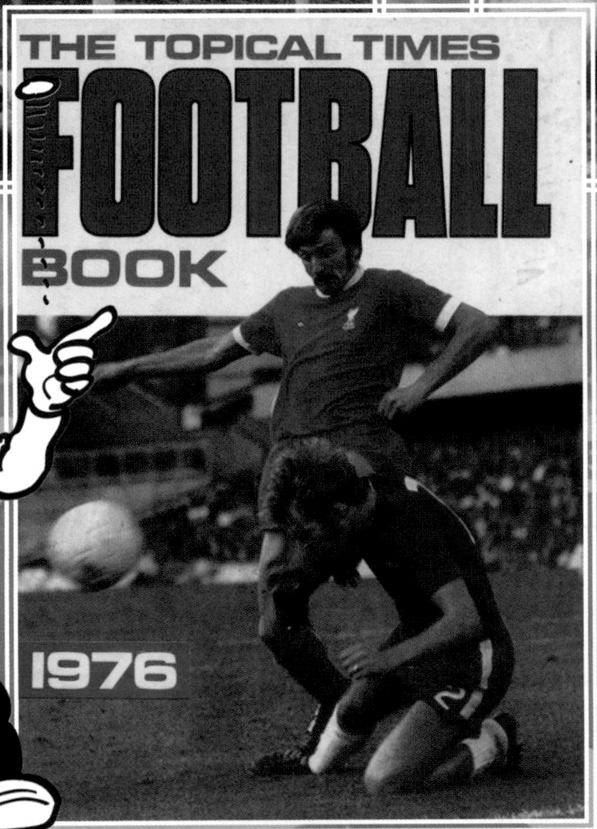
THE TOPICAL TIMES
FOOTBALL
BOOK
1976

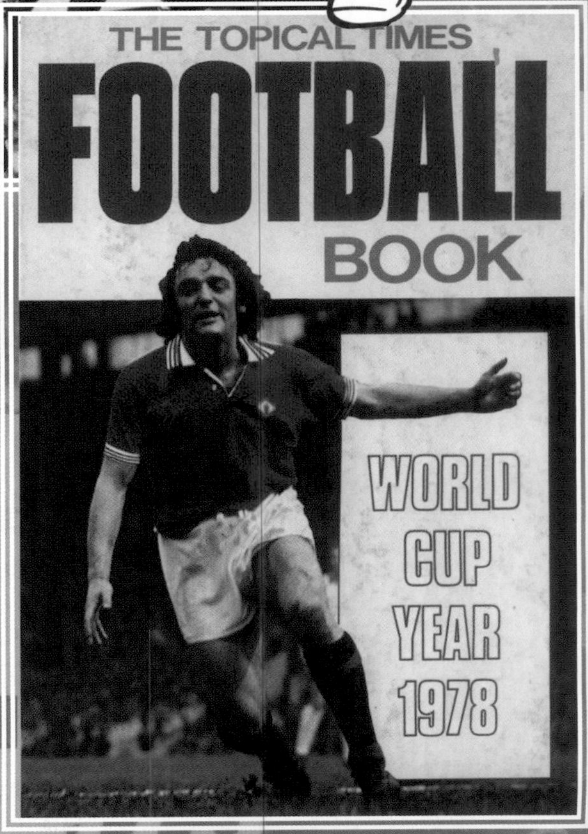
THE TOPICAL TIMES
FOOTBALL
BOOK
WORLD CUP YEAR 1978

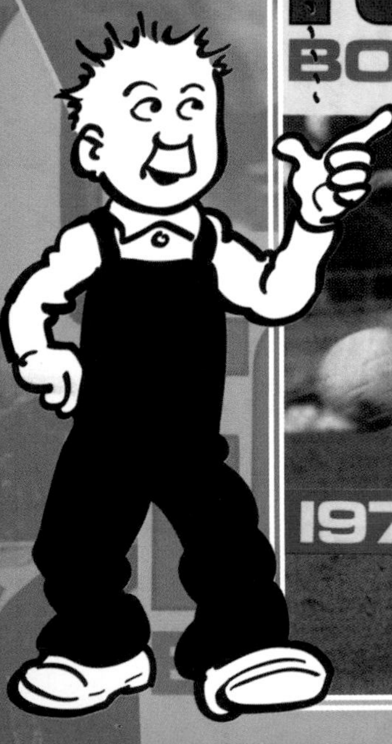

Scots wha hae... BRAWN!

Strain your brain and tug your memory back to 1960 – 85 to take this sporting challenge.

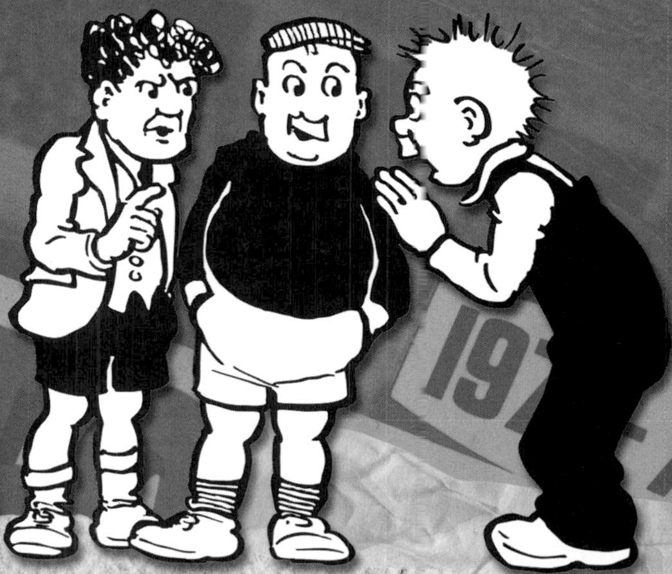

1. How many times has Kenny Dalglish been capped?
2. Which Formula One World Champion also won a British Skeet Shooting Championship?
3. Can you name three Scots who were British Lightweight Title holders?
4. Which Olympic medallist's athletics career started at Hawkhill Harriers Club?
5. Who won the gold for the 200 metre breaststroke in the Montreal Olympics in 1976?
6. Which athlete's time was so unusually fast in 1977 that the course was remeasured?
7. Who was the first jockey to the Queen?
8. Who was the manager of the Scottish team that qualified for the World Cup Final in 1982?
9. Name three other famous Scots born football managers.
10. Who won seven consecutive Grand Prix races?

Answers:

1. One hundred and two, 2. Jackie Stewart, 3. Jim Watt, Ken Buchanan, Dick McTaggart, 4. Liz McColgan, 5. David Wilkie, 6. Ian Stewart in the Michelin 10 mile road race in Staffordshire in the record time of 45 minutes 13 seconds, 7. Willie Carson, 8. Jock Stein, 9. Sir Matt Busby, Bill Shankly, Sir Alex Ferguson, 10. Jim Clark.

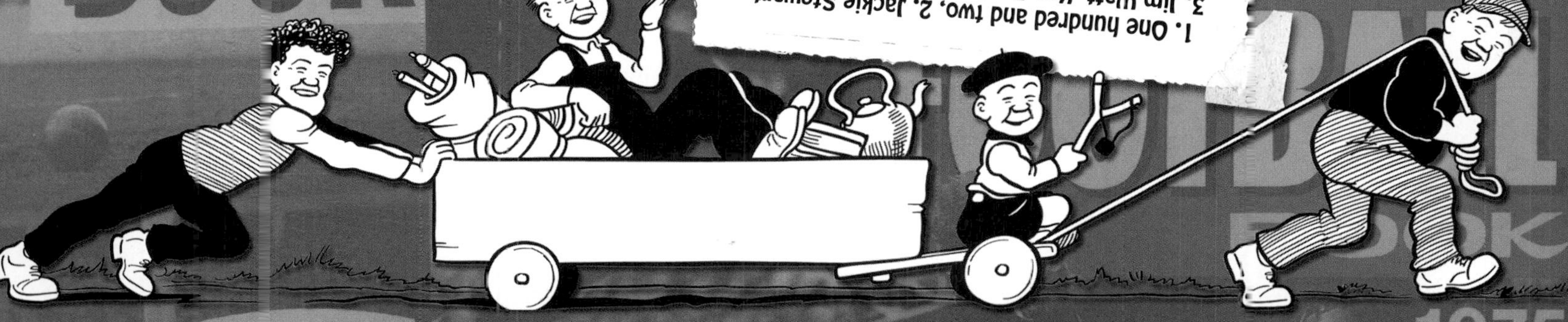

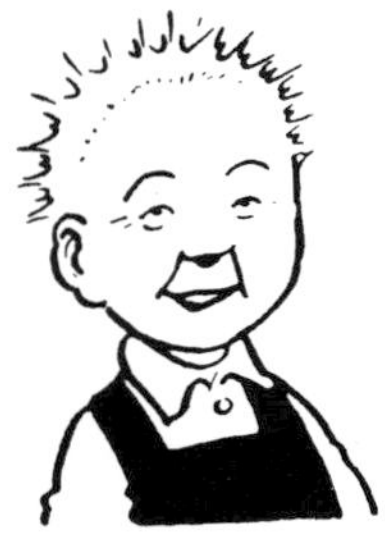

Some smart replies—

Then a big surprise!

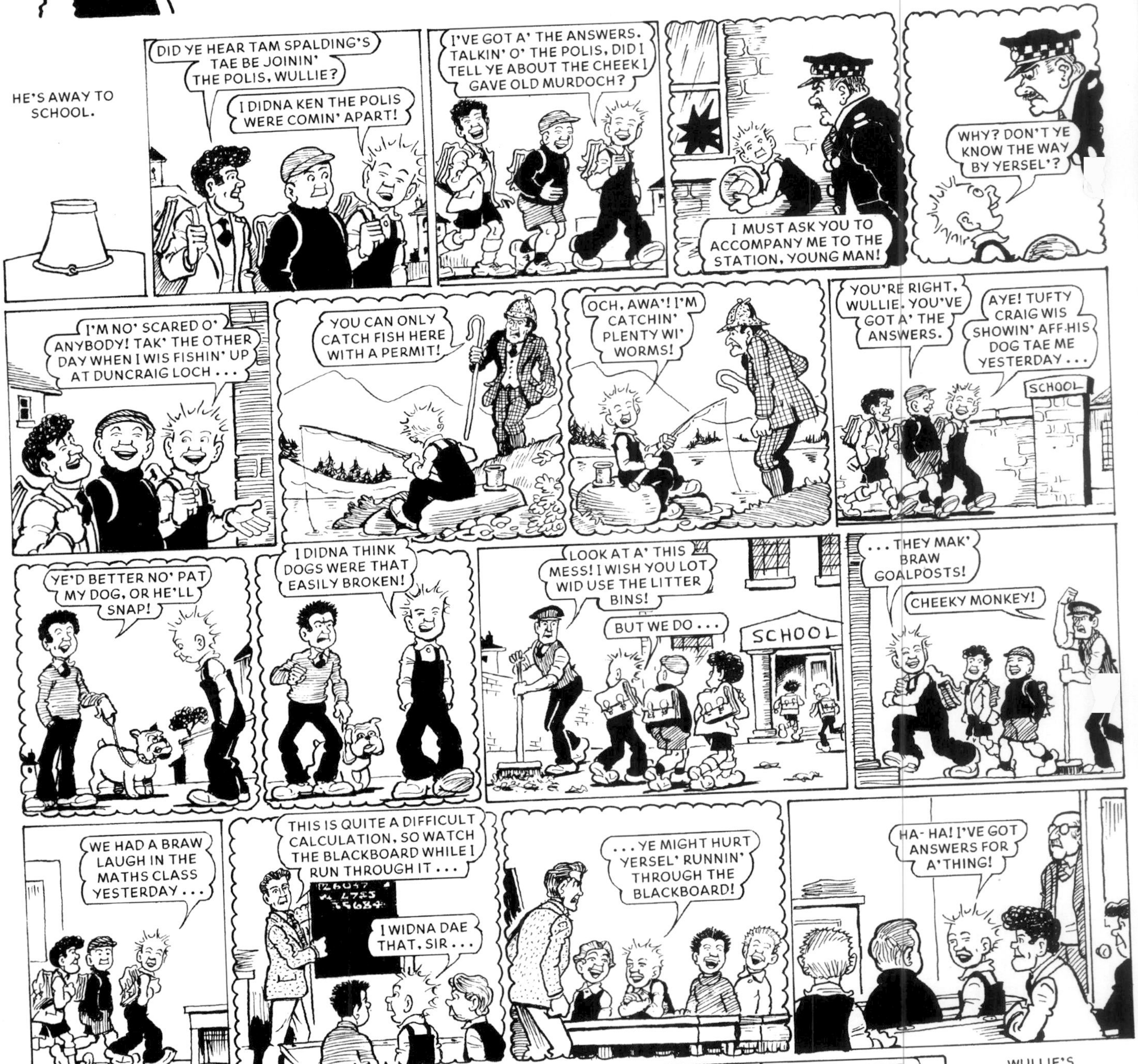
HE'S AWAY TO SCHOOL.
DID YE HEAR TAM SPALDING'S TAE BE JOININ' THE POLIS, WULLIE?
I DIDNA KEN THE POLIS WERE COMIN' APART!
I'VE GOT A' THE ANSWERS. TALKIN' O' THE POLIS, DID I TELL YE ABOUT THE CHEEK I GAVE OLD MURDOCH?
I MUST ASK YOU TO ACCOMPANY ME TO THE STATION, YOUNG MAN!
WHY? DON'T YE KNOW THE WAY BY YERSEL'?
I'M NO' SCARED O' ANYBODY! TAK' THE OTHER DAY WHEN I WIS FISHIN' UP AT DUNCRAIG LOCH . . .
YOU CAN ONLY CATCH FISH HERE WITH A PERMIT!
OCH, AWA'! I'M CATCHIN' PLENTY WI' WORMS!
YOU'RE RIGHT, WULLIE. YOU'VE GOT A' THE ANSWERS.
AYE! TUFTY CRAIG WIS SHOWIN' AFF HIS DOG TAE ME YESTERDAY . . .
SCHOOL
YE'D BETTER NO' PAT MY DOG, OR HE'LL SNAP!
I DIDNA THINK DOGS WERE THAT EASILY BROKEN!
LOOK AT A' THIS MESS! I WISH YOU LOT WID USE THE LITTER BINS!
BUT WE DO . . .
SCHOOL
. . . THEY MAK' BRAW GOALPOSTS!
CHEEKY MONKEY!
WE HAD A BRAW LAUGH IN THE MATHS CLASS YESTERDAY . . .
THIS IS QUITE A DIFFICULT CALCULATION, SO WATCH THE BLACKBOARD WHILE I RUN THROUGH IT . . .
I WIDNA DAE THAT, SIR . . .
. . . YE MIGHT HURT YERSEL' RUNNIN' THROUGH THE BLACKBOARD!
HA-HA! I'VE GOT ANSWERS FOR A' THING!
RIGHT, CLASS! TAKE OUT THE ANSWERS TO LAST NIGHT'S HOMEWORK EXERCISE!
JINGS! I'VE FORGOTTEN MINE!
TAKE 100 HUNDRED LINES, WILLIAM! THAT SHOULD TEACH YOU TO REMEMBER YOUR HOMEWORK!
HEE-HEE! PITY YE DIDNA HAE A' THE ANSWERS THERE, EH, WULLIE?
WULLIE'S SPEECHLESS—FOR ONCE!

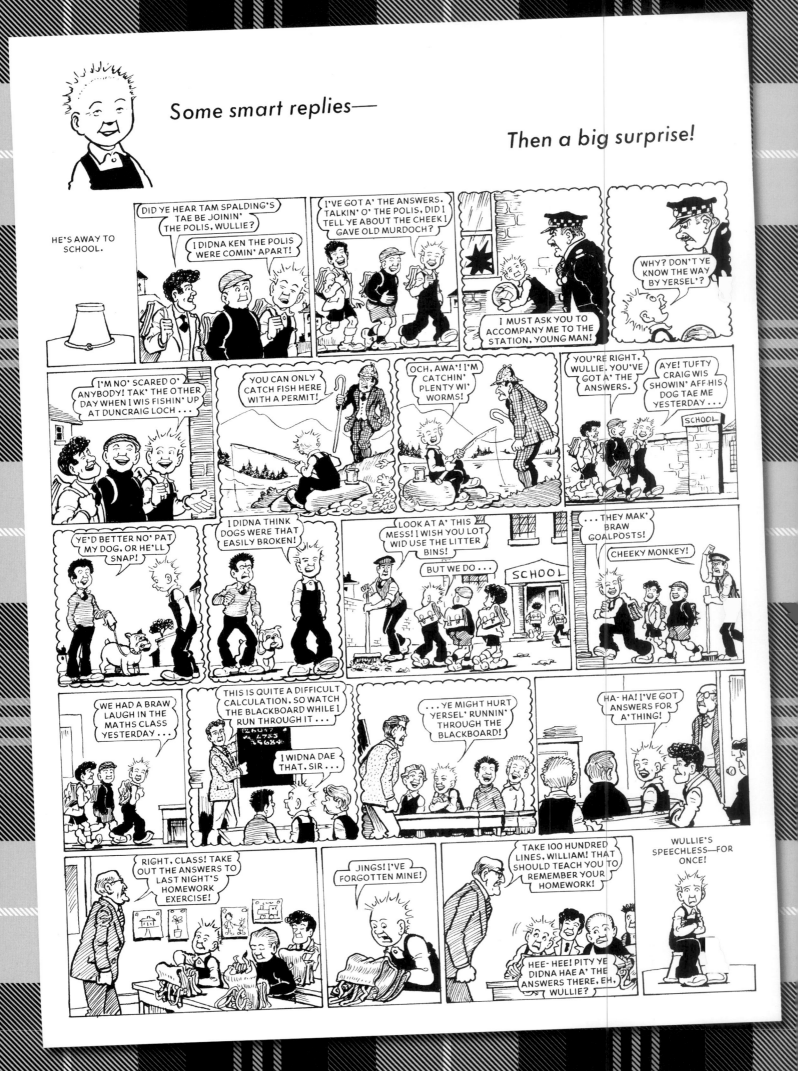

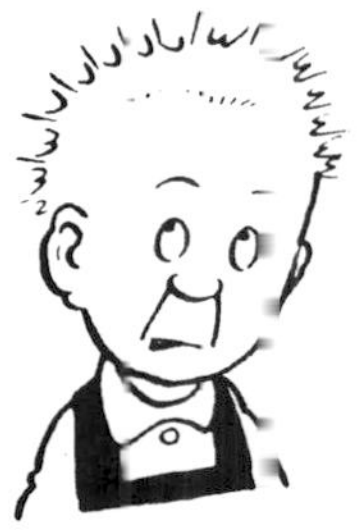

A box o' chalks—

Brings Wullie shocks!

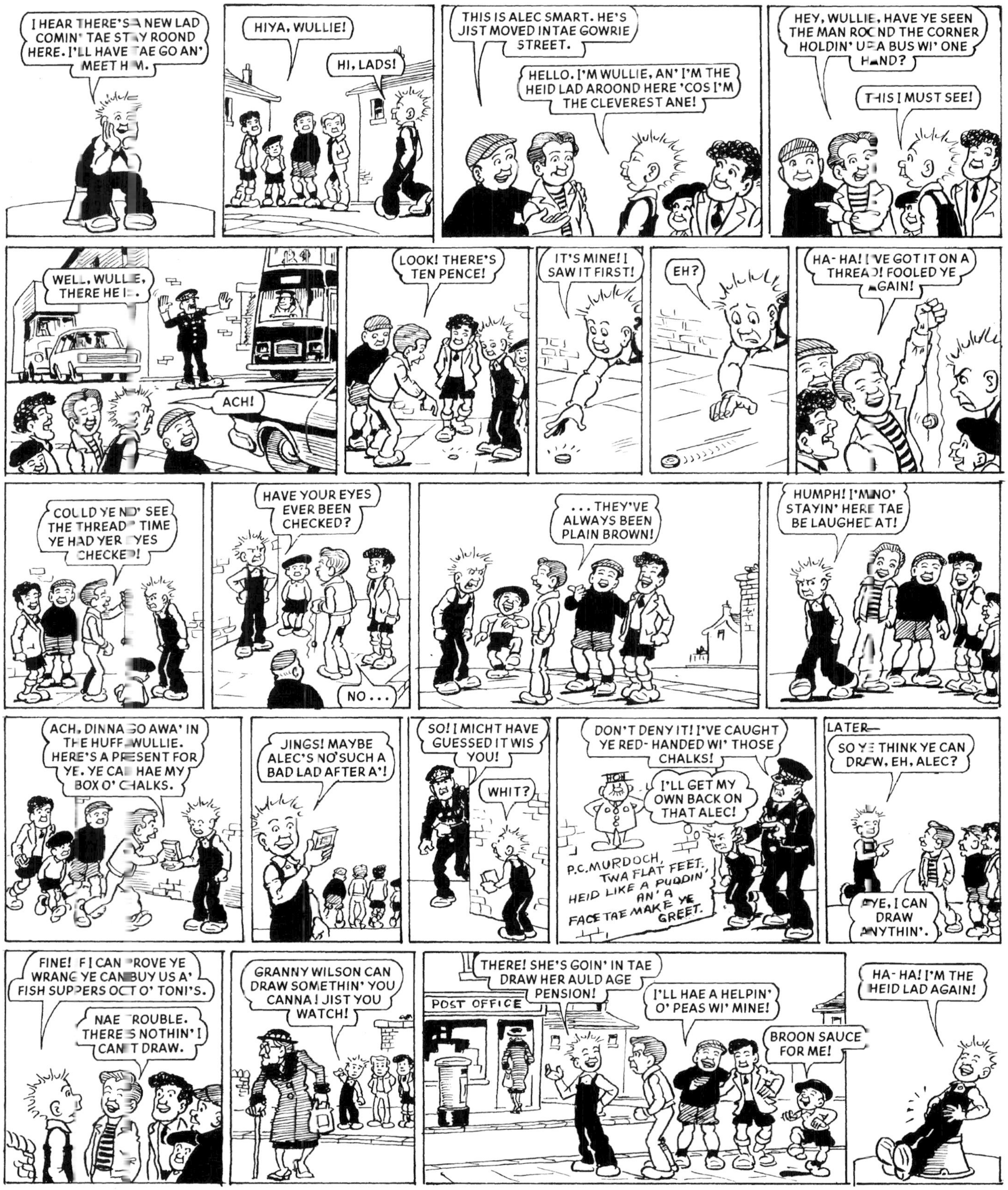

I HEAR THERE'S A NEW LAD COMIN' TAE STAY ROOND HERE. I'LL HAVE TAE GO AN' MEET HIM.
HIYA, WULLIE!
HI, LADS!
THIS IS ALEC SMART. HE'S JIST MOVED INTAE GOWRIE STREET.
HELLO. I'M WULLIE, AN' I'M THE HEID LAD AROOND HERE 'COS I'M THE CLEVEREST ANE!
HEY, WULLIE, HAVE YE SEEN THE MAN ROOND THE CORNER HOLDIN' UP A BUS WI' ONE HAND?
THIS I MUST SEE!
WELL, WULLIE, THERE HE IS.
ACH!
LOOK! THERE'S TEN PENCE!
IT'S MINE! I SAW IT FIRST!
EH?
HA-HA! I'VE GOT IT ON A THREAD! FOOLED YE AGAIN!
COULD YE NO' SEE THE THREAD? TIME YE HAD YER EYES CHECKED!
HAVE YOUR EYES EVER BEEN CHECKED?
NO . . .
. . . THEY'VE ALWAYS BEEN PLAIN BROWN!
HUMPH! I'M NO' STAYIN' HERE TAE BE LAUGHED AT!
ACH, DINNA GO AWA' IN THE HUFF, WULLIE. HERE'S A PRESENT FOR YE. YE CAN HAE MY BOX O' CHALKS.
JINGS! MAYBE ALEC'S NO' SUCH A BAD LAD AFTER A'!
SO! I MICHT HAVE GUESSED IT WIS YOU!
WHIT?
DON'T DENY IT! I'VE CAUGHT YE RED-HANDED WI' THOSE CHALKS!
I'LL GET MY OWN BACK ON THAT ALEC!
P.C. MURDOCH, TWA FLAT FEET, HEID LIKE A PUDDIN', AN' A FACE TAE MAKE YE GREET.
LATER—
SO YE THINK YE CAN DRAW, EH, ALEC?
AYE, I CAN DRAW ANYTHIN'.
FINE! IF I CAN PROVE YE WRANG YE CAN BUY US A' FISH SUPPERS OOT O' TONI'S.
NAE TROUBLE. THERE'S NOTHIN' I CAN'T DRAW.
GRANNY WILSON CAN DRAW SOMETHIN' YOU CANNA! JIST YOU WATCH!
POST OFFICE
THERE! SHE'S GOIN' IN TAE DRAW HER AULD AGE PENSION!
I'LL HAE A HELPIN' O' PEAS WI' MINE!
BROON SAUCE FOR ME!
HA-HA! I'M THE HEID LAD AGAIN!

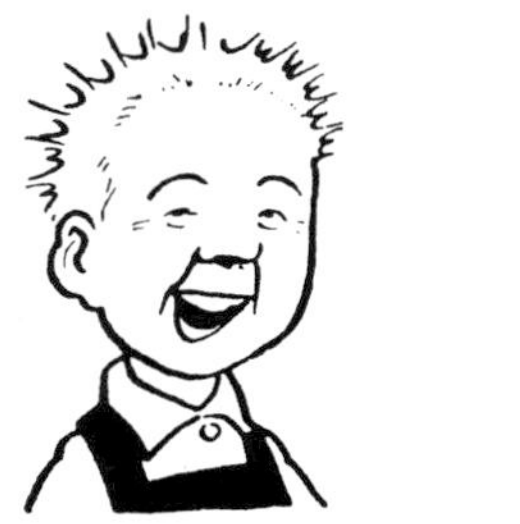

See that big smile on Ma's face—

She's got the perfect hiding-place!

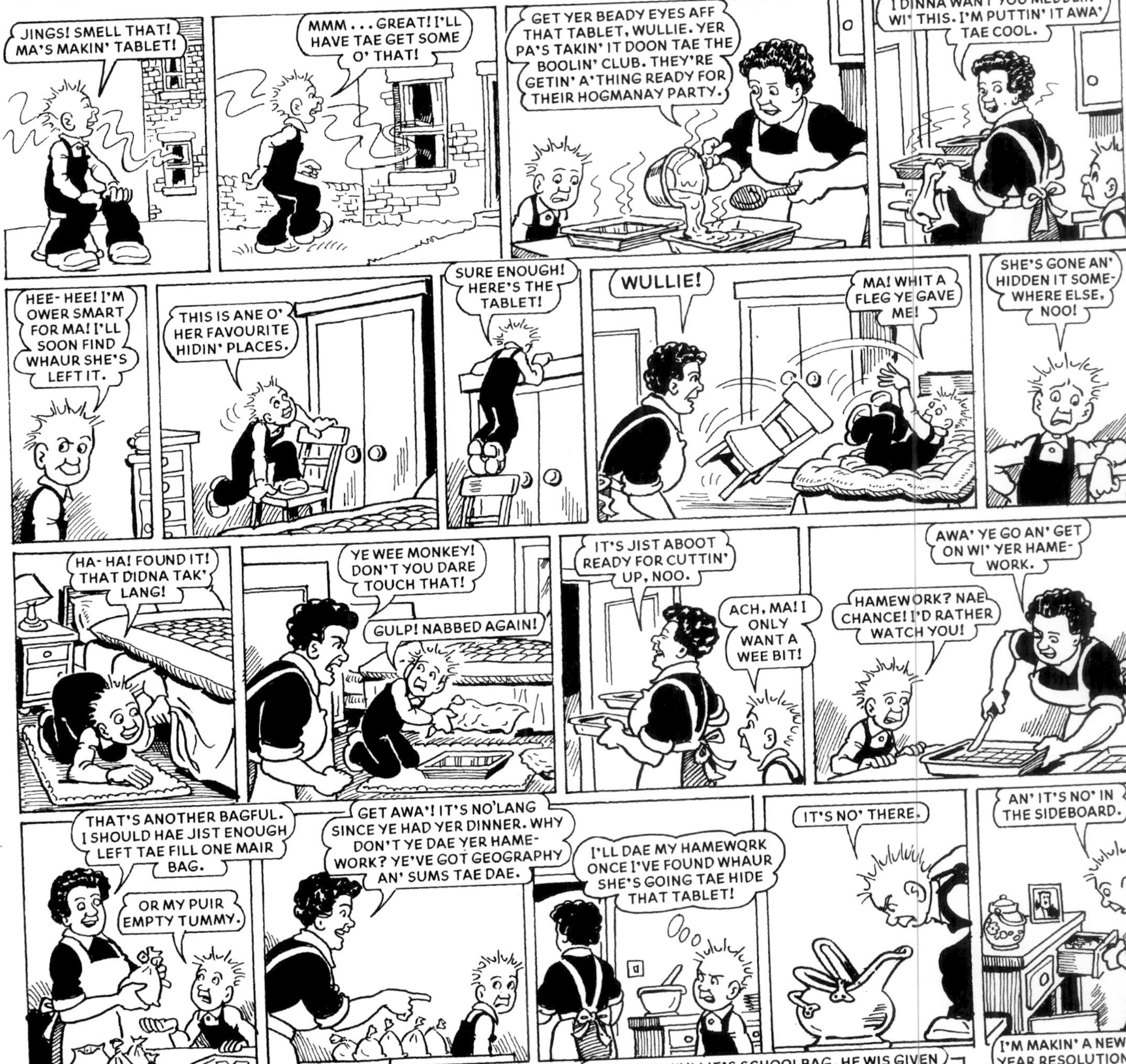

JINGS! SMELL THAT! MA'S MAKIN' TABLET!
MMM . . . GREAT! I'LL HAVE TAE GET SOME O' THAT!
GET YER BEADY EYES AFF THAT TABLET, WULLIE. YER PA'S TAKIN' IT DOON TAE THE BOOLIN' CLUB. THEY'RE GETIN' A' THING READY FOR THEIR HOGMANAY PARTY.
I DINNA WANT YOU MEDDLIN' WI' THIS. I'M PUTTIN' IT AWA' TAE COOL.
HEE-HEE! I'M OWER SMART FOR MA! I'LL SOON FIND WHAUR SHE'S LEFT IT.
THIS IS ANE O' HER FAVOURITE HIDIN' PLACES.
SURE ENOUGH! HERE'S THE TABLET!
WULLIE!
MA! WHIT A FLEG YE GAVE ME!
SHE'S GONE AN' HIDDEN IT SOMEWHERE ELSE, NOO!
HA-HA! FOUND IT! THAT DIDNA TAK' LANG!
YE WEE MONKEY! DON'T YOU DARE TOUCH THAT!
GULP! NABBED AGAIN!
IT'S JIST ABOOT READY FOR CUTTIN' UP, NOO.
ACH, MA! I ONLY WANT A WEE BIT!
AWA' YE GO AN' GET ON WI' YER HAMEWORK.
HAMEWORK? NAE CHANCE! I'D RATHER WATCH YOU!
THAT'S ANOTHER BAGFUL. I SHOULD HAE JIST ENOUGH LEFT TAE FILL ONE MAIR BAG.
OR MY PUIR EMPTY TUMMY.
GET AWA'! IT'S NO'LANG SINCE YE HAD YER DINNER. WHY DON'T YE DAE YER HAMEWORK? YE'VE GOT GEOGRAPHY AN' SUMS TAE DAE.
I'LL DAE MY HAMEWORK ONCE I'VE FOUND WHAUR SHE'S GOING TAE HIDE THAT TABLET!
IT'S NO' THERE.
AN' IT'S NO' IN THE SIDEBOARD.
NO' UP THE LUM, EITHER.
I'M AWA' DOON TAE THE BOOLIN' CLUB NOO, MA. CAN YE GIVE ME THAT TABLET YE MADE?
AYE.
I HID IT IN WULLIE'S SCHOOLBAG. HE WIS GIVEN HAMEWORK TAE DAE OWER THE HOLIDAYS, AN' I KENT HE WID NEVER GO NEAR THE BOOKS IN HIS BAG.
I'M MAKIN' A NEW YEAR RESOLUTION TAE AYE DAE MY HAMEWORK AS SOON AS POSSIBLE!

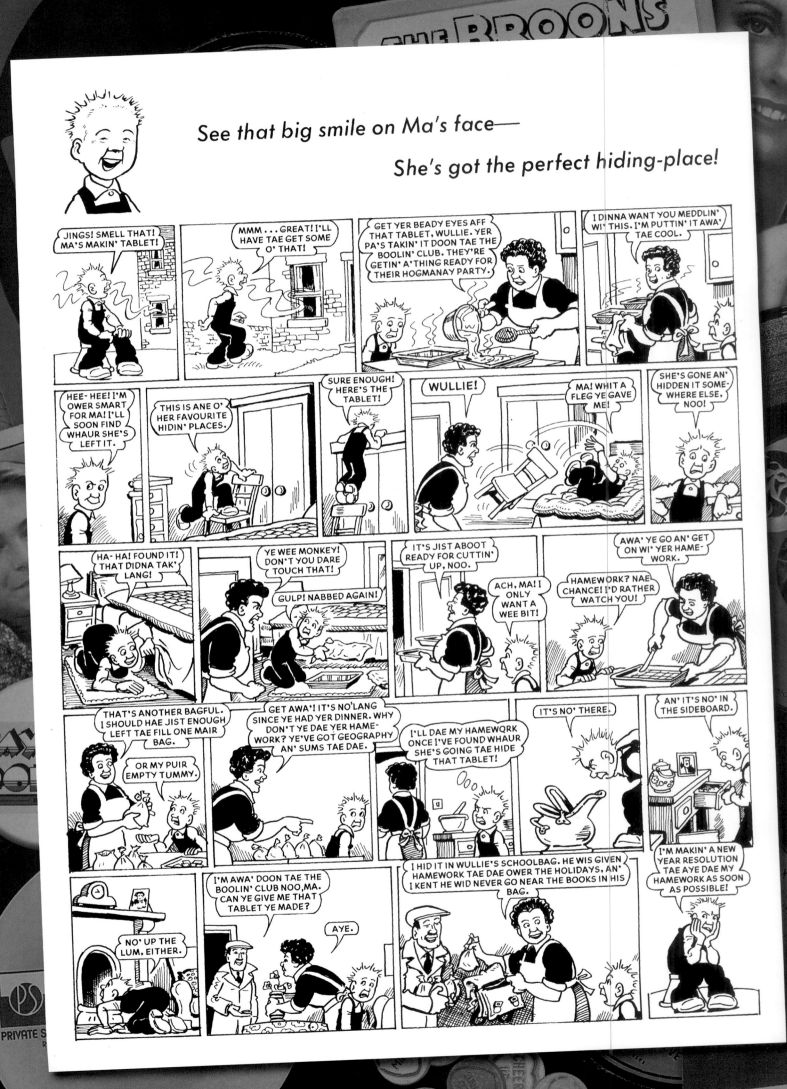

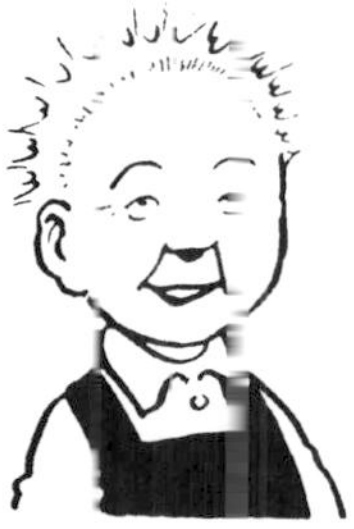

Now Oor Wullie's gone and done it—

He's put on the wrong-sized bunnet!

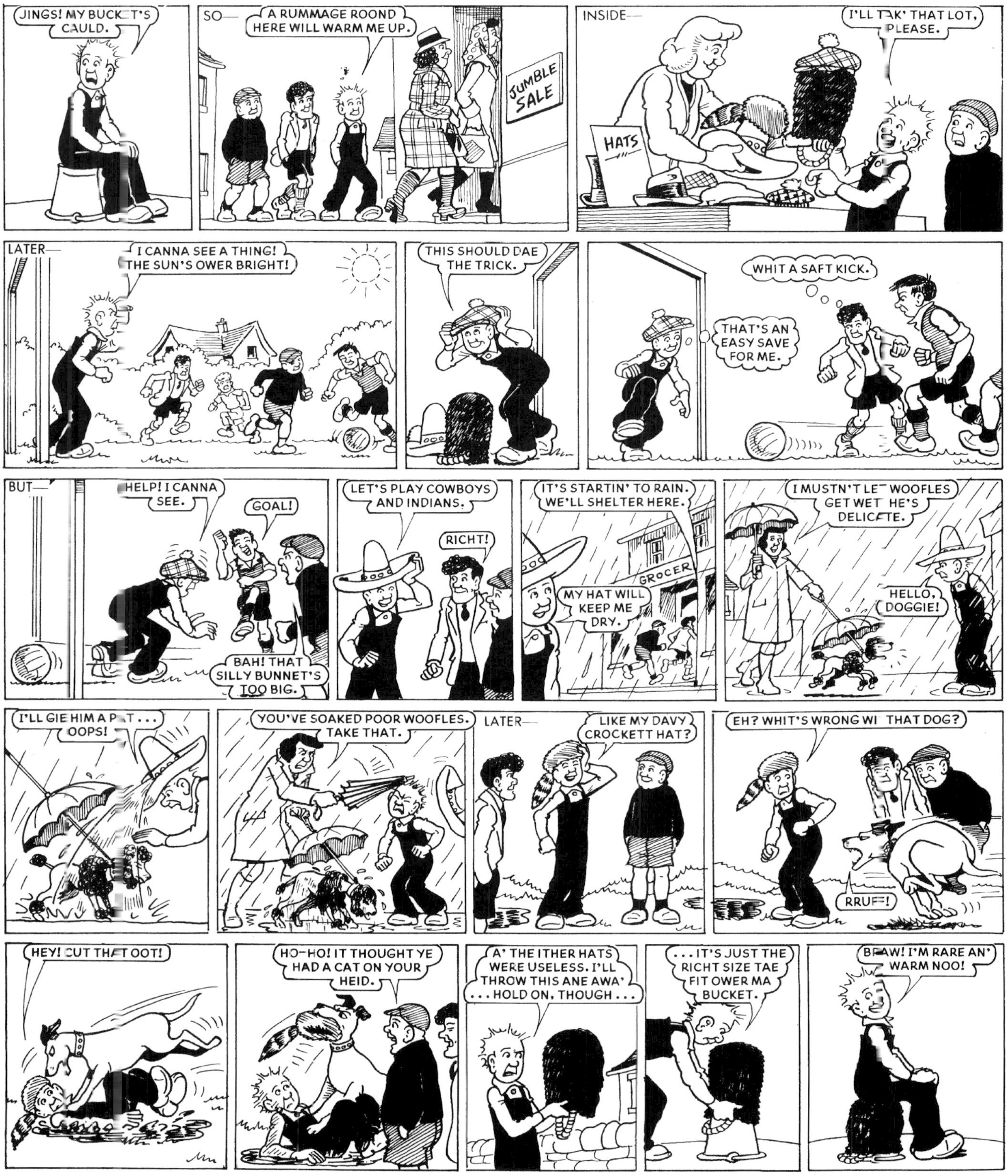
JINGS! MY BUCKET'S CAULD.
SO—
A RUMMAGE ROOND HERE WILL WARM ME UP.
JUMBLE SALE
INSIDE—
I'LL TAK' THAT LOT, PLEASE.
HATS
LATER—
I CANNA SEE A THING! THE SUN'S OWER BRIGHT!
THIS SHOULD DAE THE TRICK.
WHIT A SAFT KICK.
THAT'S AN EASY SAVE FOR ME.
BUT—
HELP! I CANNA SEE.
GOAL!
BAH! THAT SILLY BUNNET'S TOO BIG.
LET'S PLAY COWBOYS AND INDIANS.
RICHT!
IT'S STARTIN' TO RAIN. WE'LL SHELTER HERE.
MY HAT WILL KEEP ME DRY.
GROCER
I MUSTN'T LET WOOFLES GET WET. HE'S DELICATE.
HELLO, DOGGIE!
I'LL GIE HIM A PAT . . . OOPS!
YOU'VE SOAKED POOR WOOFLES. TAKE THAT.
LATER—
LIKE MY DAVY CROCKETT HAT?
EH? WHIT'S WRONG WI' THAT DOG?
RRUFF!
HEY! CUT THAT OOT!
HO-HO! IT THOUGHT YE HAD A CAT ON YOUR HEID.
A' THE ITHER HATS WERE USELESS. I'LL THROW THIS ANE AWA' . . . HOLD ON, THOUGH . . .
. . . IT'S JUST THE RICHT SIZE TAE FIT OWER MA BUCKET.
BRAW! I'M RARE AN' WARM NOO!

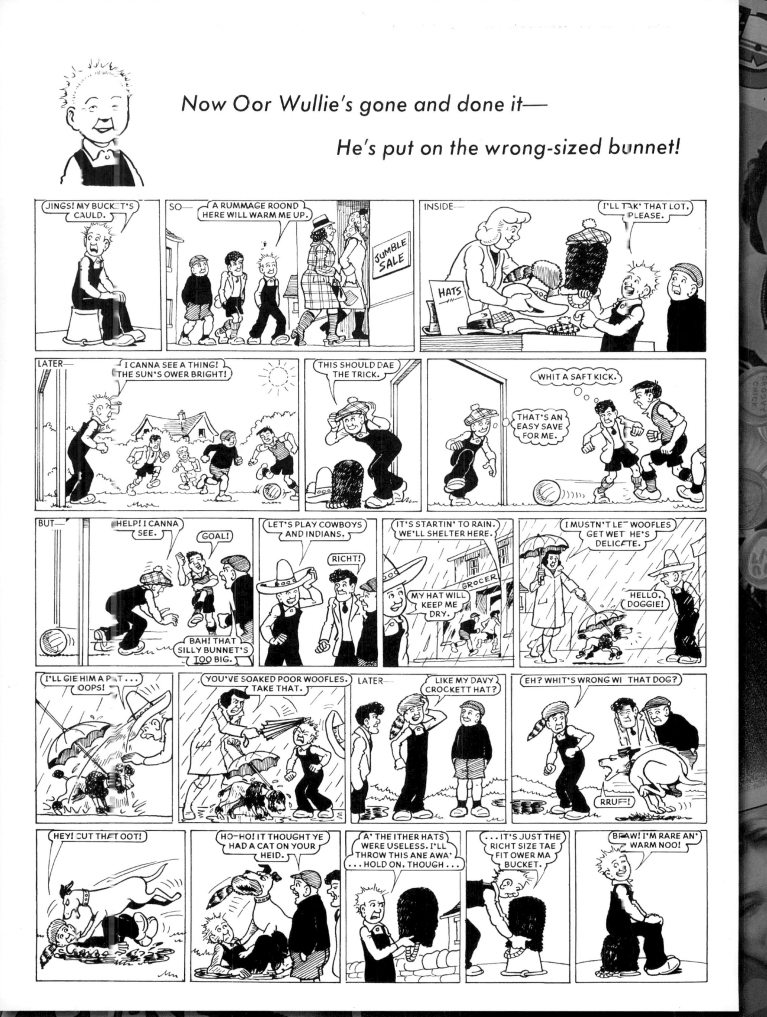

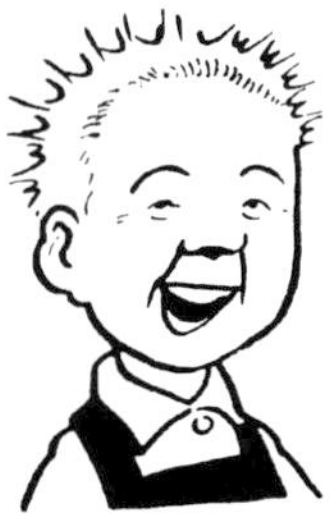

Bad luck wi' this, bad luck wi' that—

Nae wonder Wullie's feelin' FLAT!

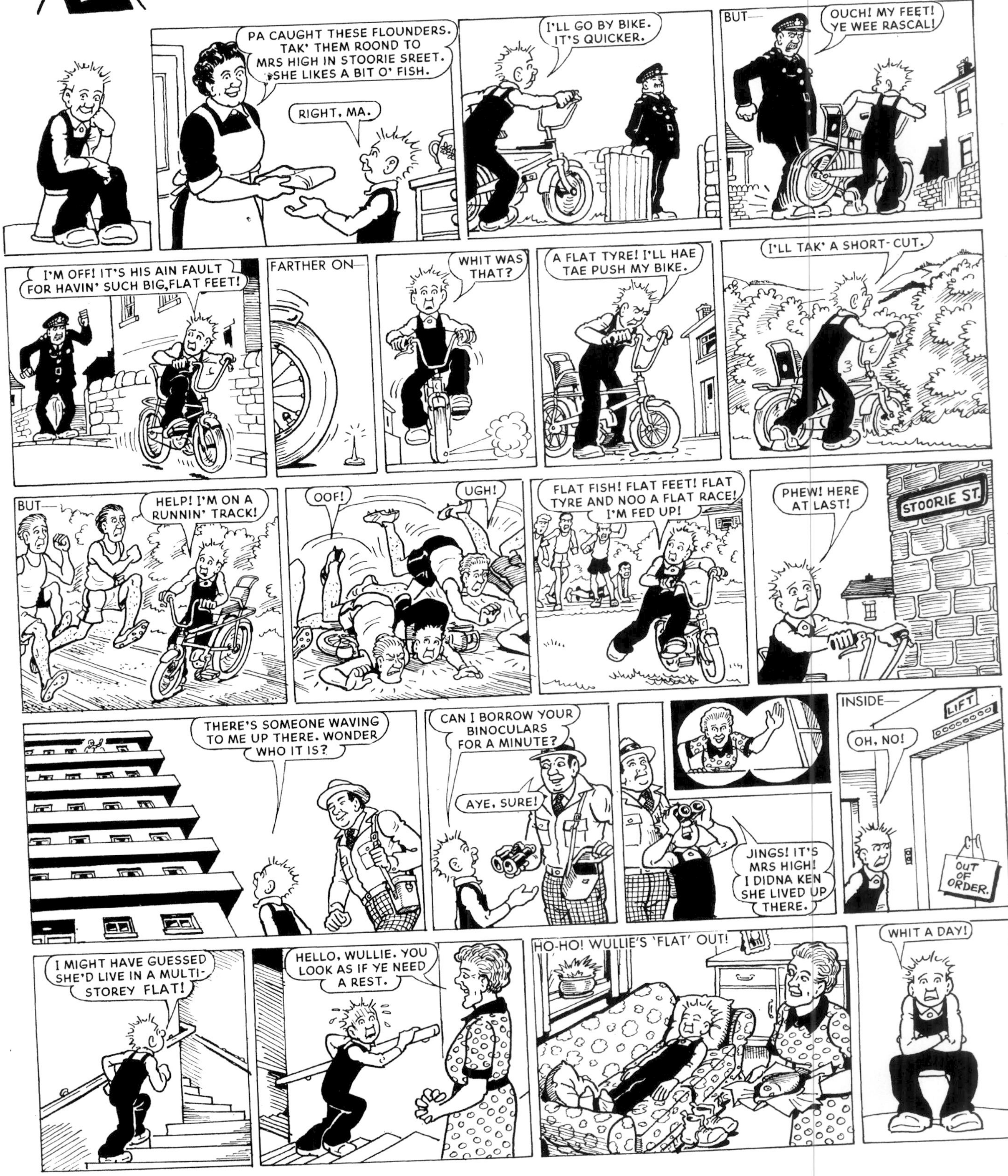

PA CAUGHT THESE FLOUNDERS. TAK' THEM ROOND TO MRS HIGH IN STOORIE SREET. SHE LIKES A BIT O' FISH.
RIGHT, MA.
I'LL GO BY BIKE. IT'S QUICKER.
BUT—
OUCH! MY FEET! YE WEE RASCAL!
I'M OFF! IT'S HIS AIN FAULT FOR HAVIN' SUCH BIG, FLAT FEET!
FARTHER ON—
WHIT WAS THAT?
A FLAT TYRE! I'LL HAE TAE PUSH MY BIKE.
I'LL TAK' A SHORT-CUT.
BUT—
HELP! I'M ON A RUNNIN' TRACK!
OOF!
UGH!
FLAT FISH! FLAT FEET! FLAT TYRE AND NOO A FLAT RACE! I'M FED UP!
PHEW! HERE AT LAST!
STOORIE ST.
THERE'S SOMEONE WAVING TO ME UP THERE. WONDER WHO IT IS?
CAN I BORROW YOUR BINOCULARS FOR A MINUTE?
AYE, SURE!
JINGS! IT'S MRS HIGH! I DIDNA KEN SHE LIVED UP THERE.
INSIDE—
LIFT
OH, NO!
OUT OF ORDER.
I MIGHT HAVE GUESSED SHE'D LIVE IN A MULTI-STOREY FLAT!
HELLO, WULLIE. YOU LOOK AS IF YE NEED A REST.
HO-HO! WULLIE'S 'FLAT' OUT!
WHIT A DAY!

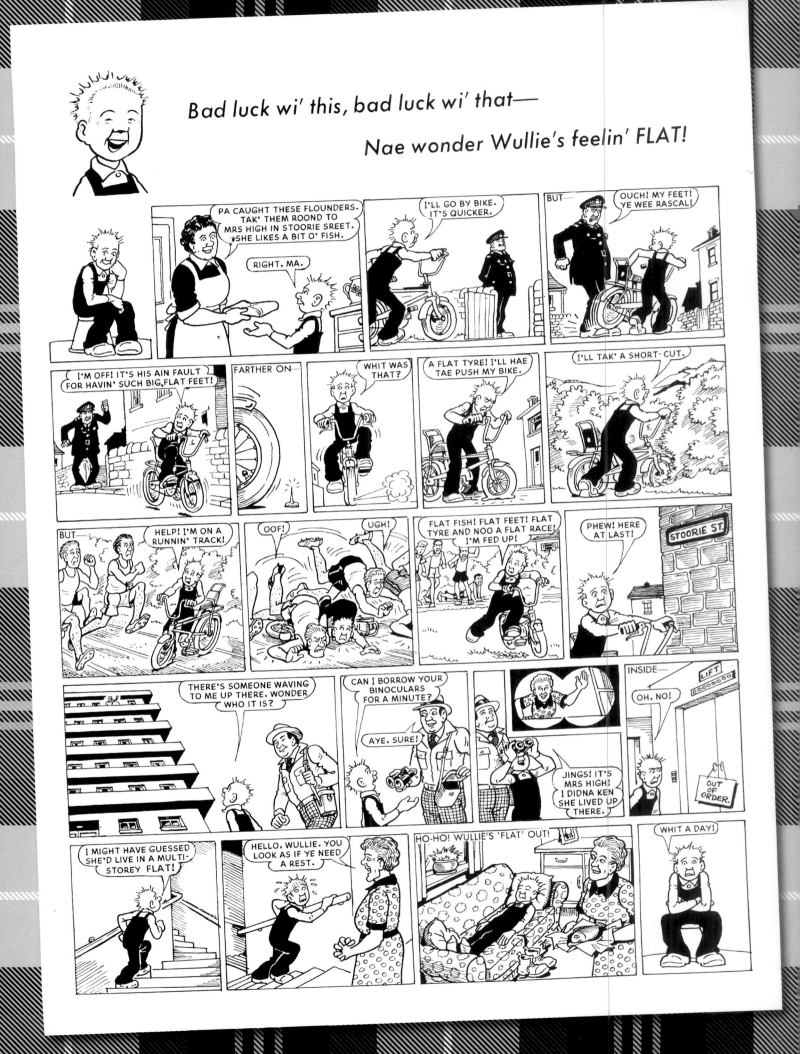

Wullie sure feels " sheepish " when—

Aunty Jean sees him again!

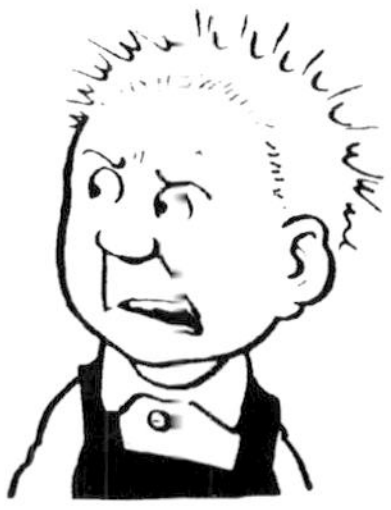

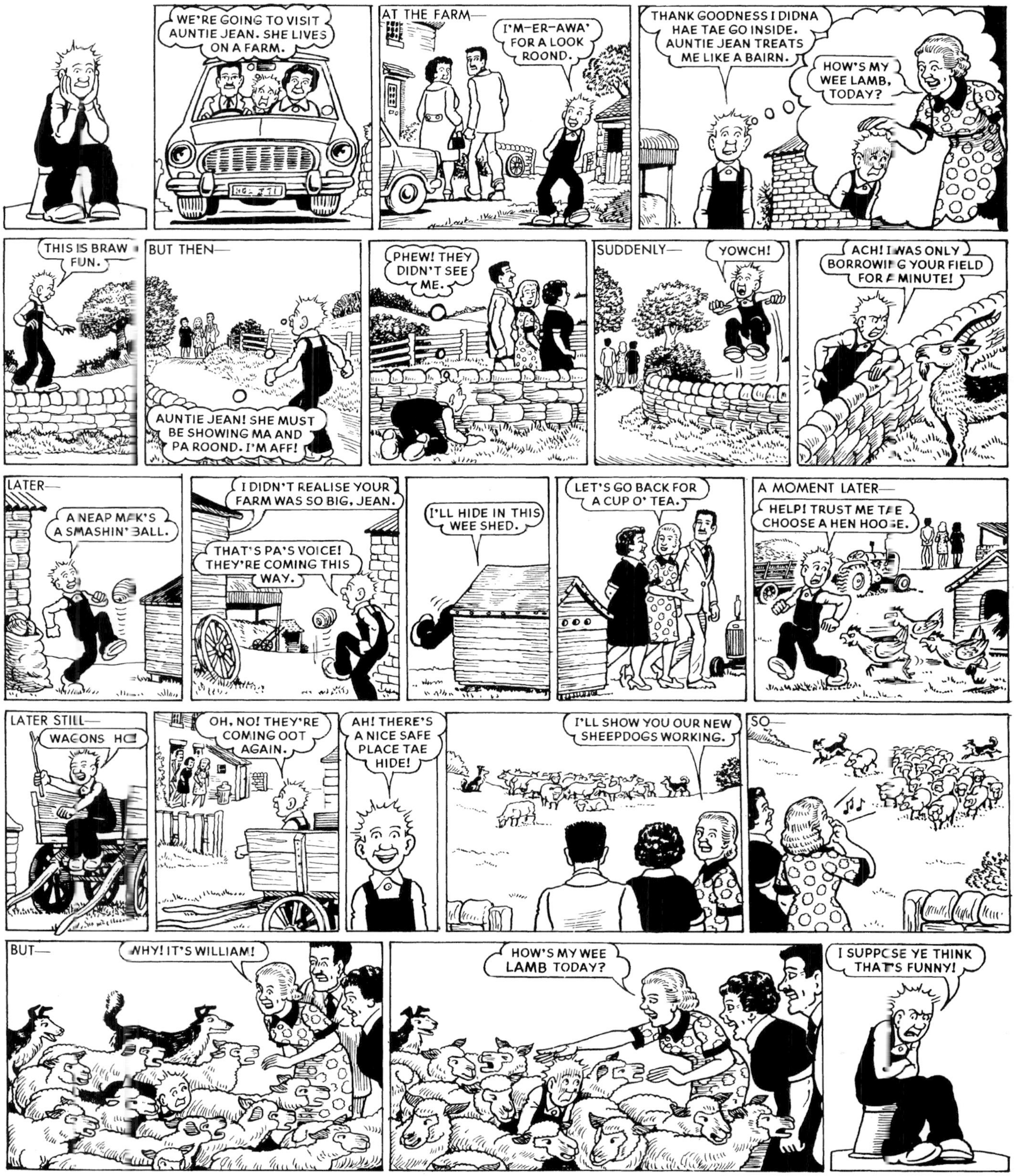
WE'RE GOING TO VISIT AUNTIE JEAN. SHE LIVES ON A FARM.
AT THE FARM—
I'M—ER—AWA' FOR A LOOK ROOND.
THANK GOODNESS I DIDNA HAE TAE GO INSIDE. AUNTIE JEAN TREATS ME LIKE A BAIRN.
HOW'S MY WEE LAMB, TODAY?
THIS IS BRAW FUN.
BUT THEN—
AUNTIE JEAN! SHE MUST BE SHOWING MA AND PA ROOND. I'M AFF!
PHEW! THEY DIDN'T SEE ME.
SUDDENLY—
YOWCH!
ACH! I WAS ONLY BORROWING YOUR FIELD FOR A MINUTE!
LATER—
A NEAP MAK'S A SMASHIN' BALL.
I DIDN'T REALISE YOUR FARM WAS SO BIG, JEAN.
THAT'S PA'S VOICE! THEY'RE COMING THIS WAY.
I'LL HIDE IN THIS WEE SHED.
LET'S GO BACK FOR A CUP O' TEA.
A MOMENT LATER—
HELP! TRUST ME TAE CHOOSE A HEN HOOSE.
LATER STILL—
WAGONS HO!
OH, NO! THEY'RE COMING OOT AGAIN.
AH! THERE'S A NICE SAFE PLACE TAE HIDE!
I'LL SHOW YOU OUR NEW SHEEPDOGS WORKING.
SO—
BUT—
WHY! IT'S WILLIAM!
HOW'S MY WEE LAMB TODAY?
I SUPPOSE YE THINK THAT'S FUNNY!

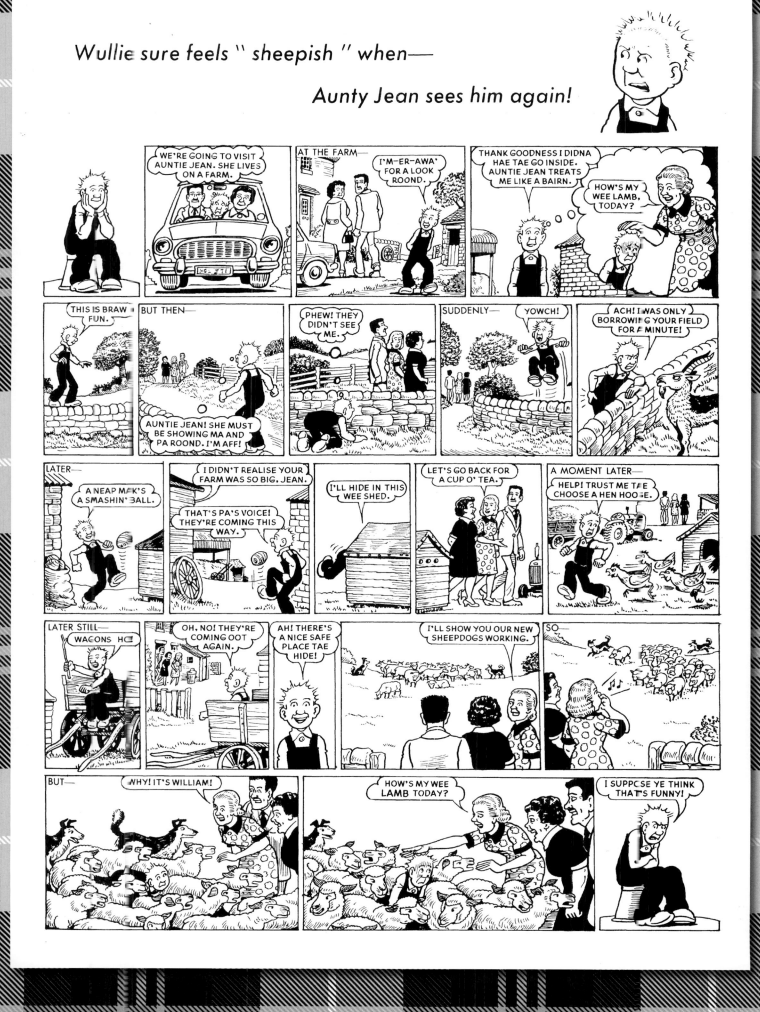

"There are times when it pays—

To be young!" Wullie says.

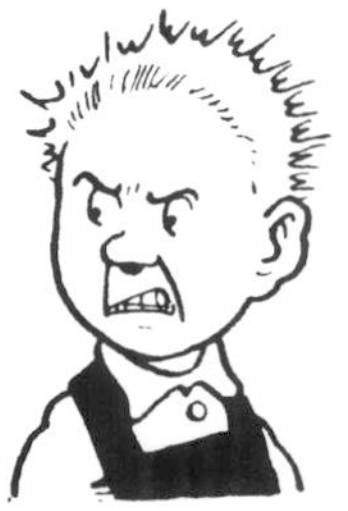

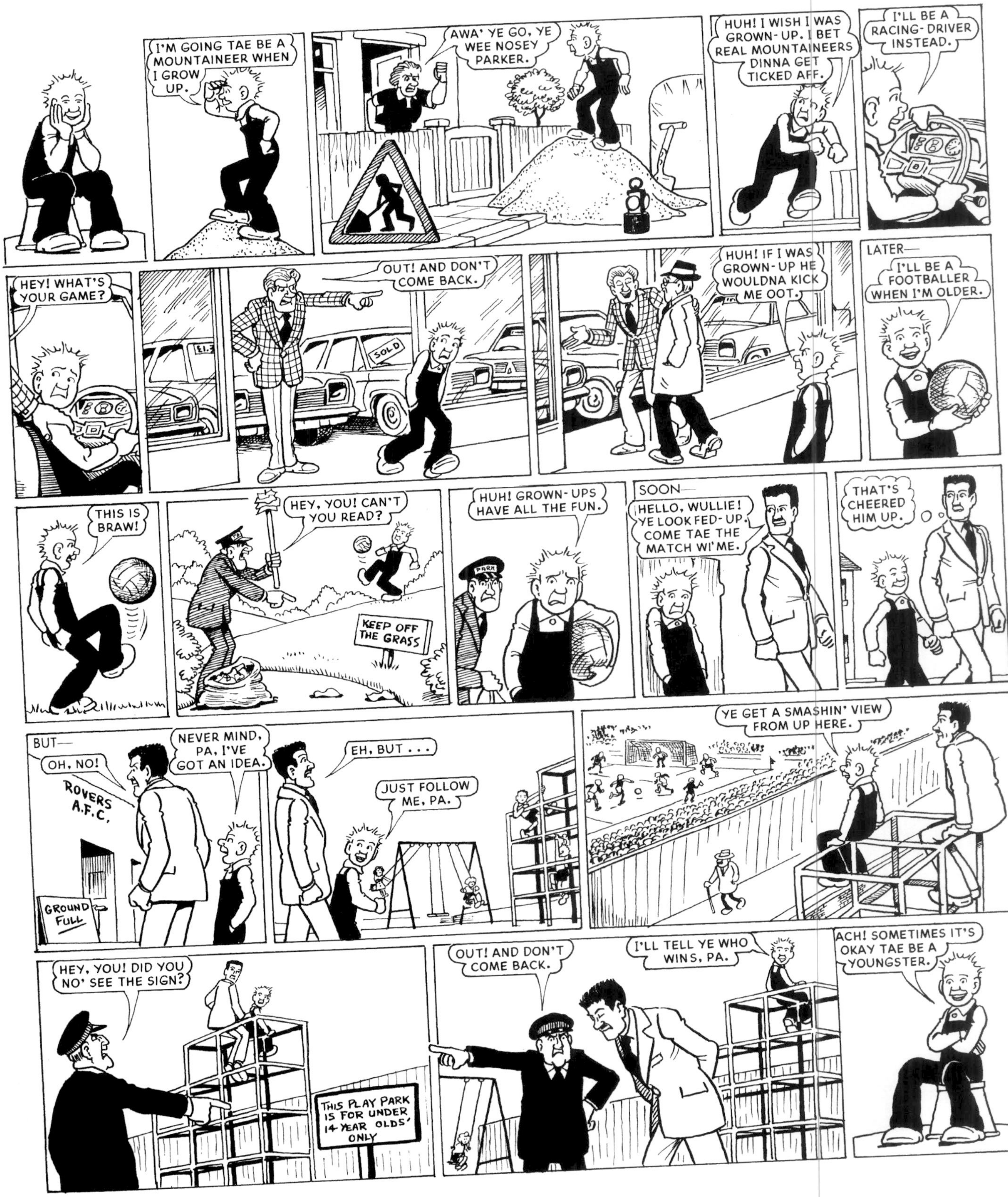
I'M GOING TAE BE A MOUNTAINEER WHEN I GROW UP.
AWA' YE GO, YE WEE NOSEY PARKER.
HUH! I WISH I WAS GROWN-UP. I BET REAL MOUNTAINEERS DINNA GET TICKED AFF.
I'LL BE A RACING-DRIVER INSTEAD.
HEY! WHAT'S YOUR GAME?
OUT! AND DON'T COME BACK.
SOLD
HUH! IF I WAS GROWN-UP HE WOULDNA KICK ME OOT.
LATER—
I'LL BE A FOOTBALLER WHEN I'M OLDER.
THIS IS BRAW!
HEY, YOU! CAN'T YOU READ?
KEEP OFF THE GRASS
HUH! GROWN-UPS HAVE ALL THE FUN.
PARK
SOON—
HELLO, WULLIE! YE LOOK FED-UP. COME TAE THE MATCH WI' ME.
THAT'S CHEERED HIM UP.
BUT—
OH, NO!
ROVERS A.F.C.
GROUND FULL
NEVER MIND, PA, I'VE GOT AN IDEA.
EH, BUT . . .
JUST FOLLOW ME, PA.
YE GET A SMASHIN' VIEW FROM UP HERE.
HEY, YOU! DID YOU NO' SEE THE SIGN?
THIS PLAY PARK IS FOR UNDER 14 YEAR OLDS' ONLY
OUT! AND DON'T COME BACK.
I'LL TELL YE WHO WINS, PA.
ACH! SOMETIMES IT'S OKAY TAE BE A YOUNGSTER.

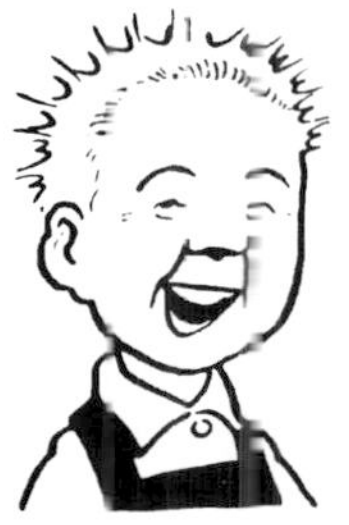

Wullie's in a proper tizzy—

He's doing his best tae look real busy.

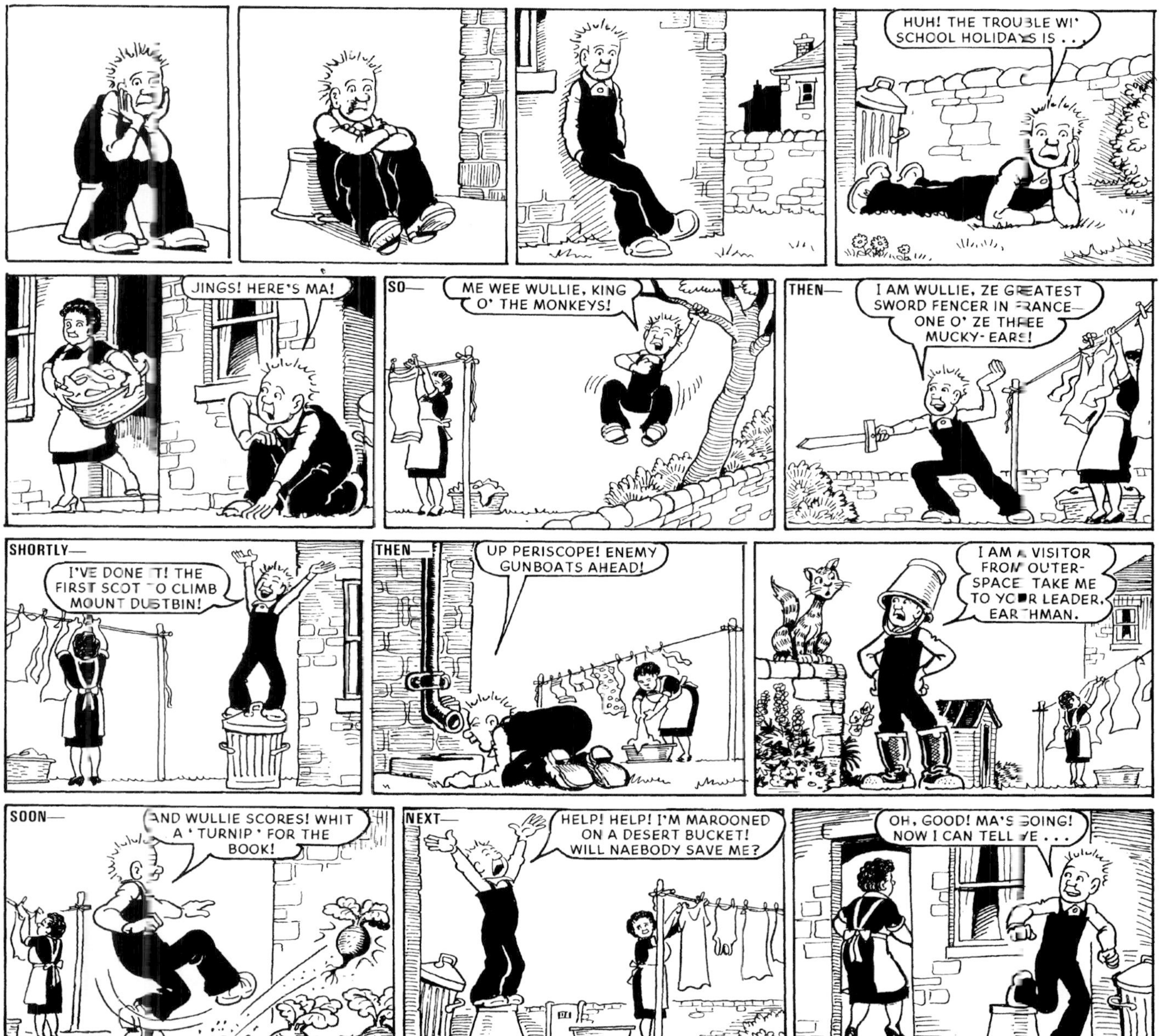

HUH! THE TROUBLE WI' SCHOOL HOLIDAYS IS . . .
JINGS! HERE'S MA!
SO—
ME WEE WULLIE, KING O' THE MONKEYS!
THEN—
I AM WULLIE, ZE GREATEST SWORD FENCER IN FRANCE— ONE O' ZE THREE MUCKY-EARS!
SHORTLY—
I'VE DONE IT! THE FIRST SCOT TO CLIMB MOUNT DUSTBIN!
THEN—
UP PERISCOPE! ENEMY GUNBOATS AHEAD!
I AM A VISITOR FROM OUTER-SPACE. TAKE ME TO YOUR LEADER, EARTHMAN.
SOON—
AND WULLIE SCORES! WHIT A 'TURNIP' FOR THE BOOK!
NEXT—
HELP! HELP! I'M MAROONED ON A DESERT BUCKET! WILL NAEBODY SAVE ME?
OH, GOOD! MA'S GOING! NOW I CAN TELL YE . . .
. . . THE TROUBLE WI' SCHOOL HOLIDAYS IS, YE GET BORED WI' NOTHIN' TAE DAE!
I HEARD THAT! NOTHIN' TAE DAE, EH? WE'LL SOON FIX THAT!
AW!
SOON—
I KENT IF SHE HEARD ME, SHE'D MAK' ME WORK!
THERE'S NAE JUSTICE!

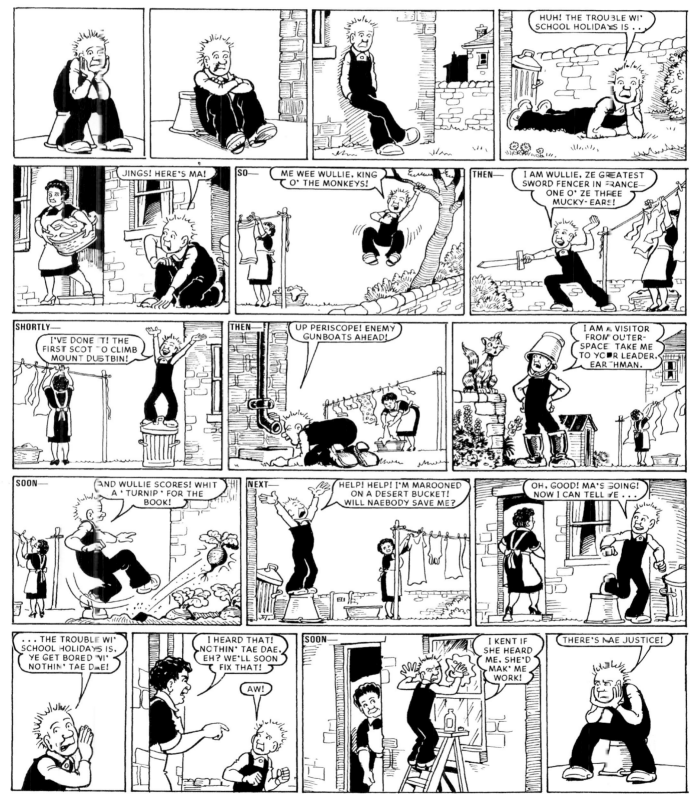

Oor Wullie finds a lot of hitches—

Tryin' tae turn rags intae riches!

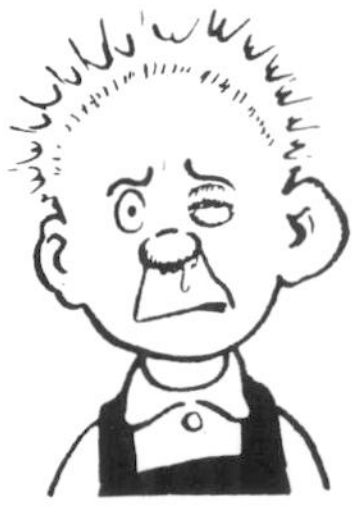

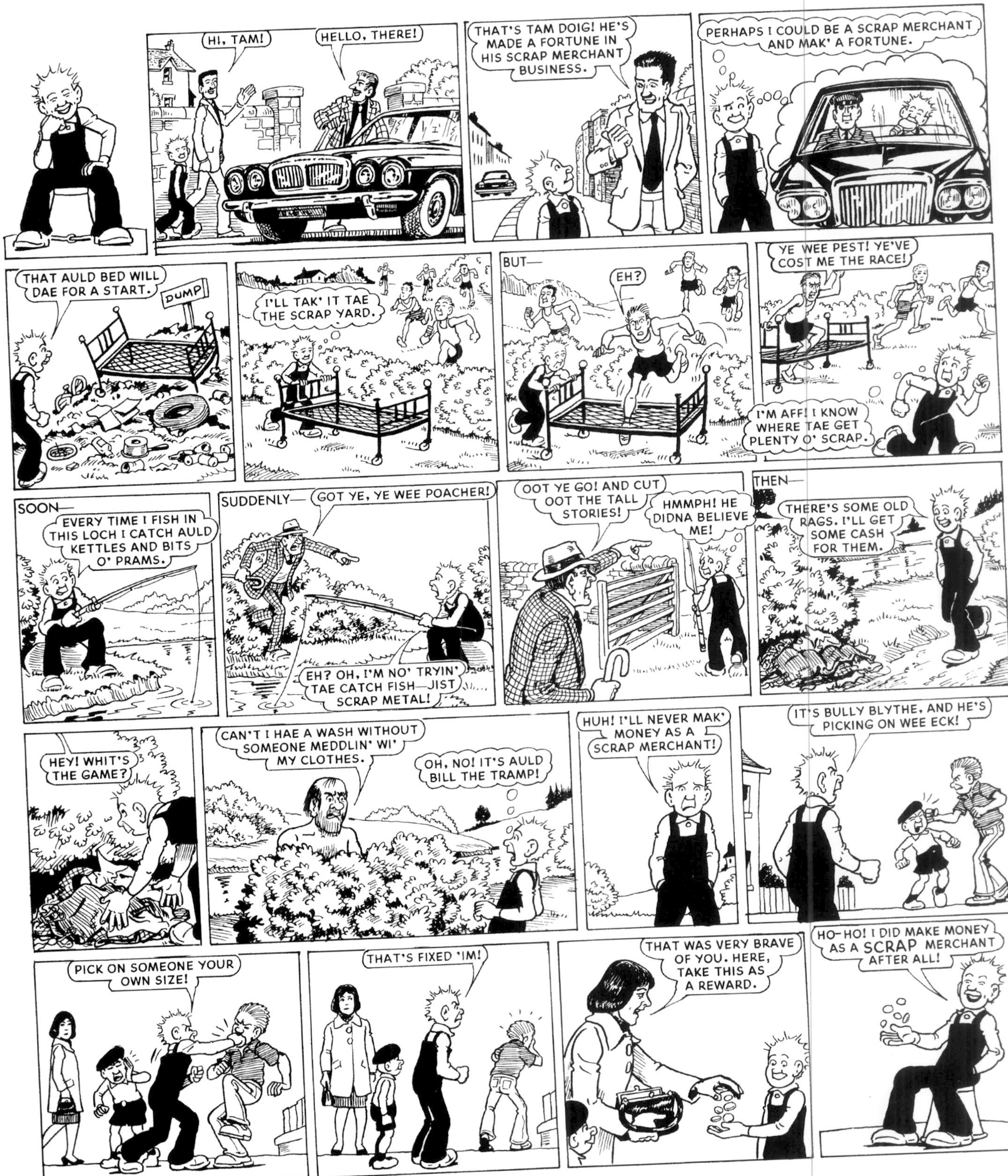
HI, TAM!
HELLO, THERE!
THAT'S TAM DOIG! HE'S MADE A FORTUNE IN HIS SCRAP MERCHANT BUSINESS.
PERHAPS I COULD BE A SCRAP MERCHANT AND MAK' A FORTUNE.
THAT AULD BED WILL DAE FOR A START.
DUMP
I'LL TAK' IT TAE THE SCRAP YARD.
BUT—
EH?
YE WEE PEST! YE'VE COST ME THE RACE!
I'M AFF! I KNOW WHERE TAE GET PLENTY O' SCRAP.
SOON—
EVERY TIME I FISH IN THIS LOCH I CATCH AULD KETTLES AND BITS O' PRAMS.
SUDDENLY—
GOT YE, YE WEE POACHER!
EH? OH, I'M NO' TRYIN' TAE CATCH FISH—JIST SCRAP METAL!
OOT YE GO! AND CUT OOT THE TALL STORIES!
HMMPH! HE DIDNA BELIEVE ME!
THEN—
THERE'S SOME OLD RAGS. I'LL GET SOME CASH FOR THEM.
HEY! WHIT'S THE GAME?
CAN'T I HAE A WASH WITHOUT SOMEONE MEDDLIN' WI' MY CLOTHES.
OH, NO! IT'S AULD BILL THE TRAMP!
HUH! I'LL NEVER MAK' MONEY AS A SCRAP MERCHANT!
IT'S BULLY BLYTHE, AND HE'S PICKING ON WEE ECK!
PICK ON SOMEONE YOUR OWN SIZE!
THAT'S FIXED 'IM!
THAT WAS VERY BRAVE OF YOU. HERE, TAKE THIS AS A REWARD.
HO-HO! I DID MAKE MONEY AS A SCRAP MERCHANT AFTER ALL!

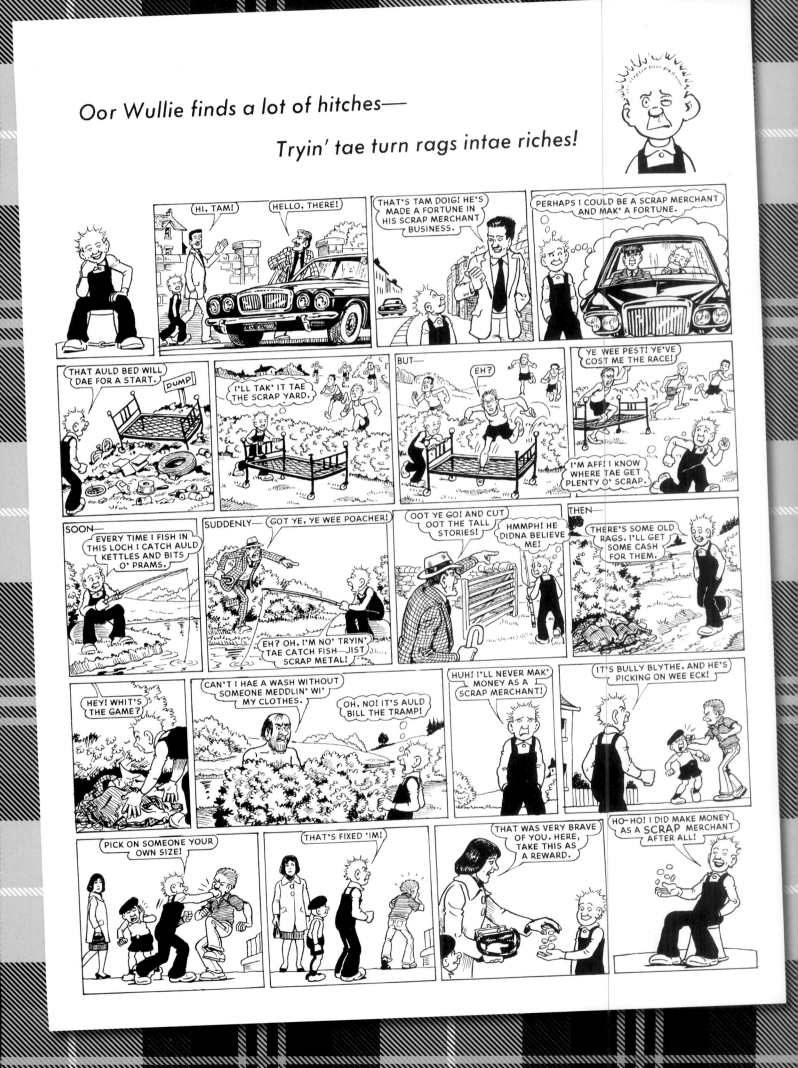

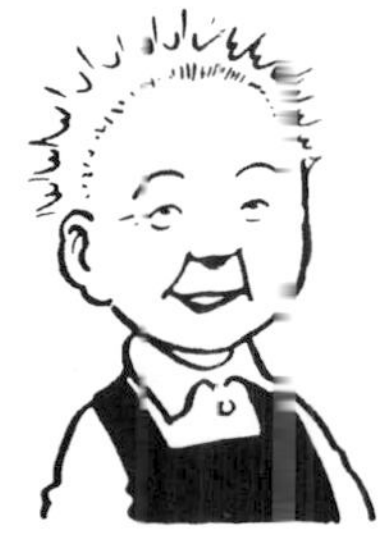

Horse-shoes bring good luck, it's said—

But no' when they land on your head!

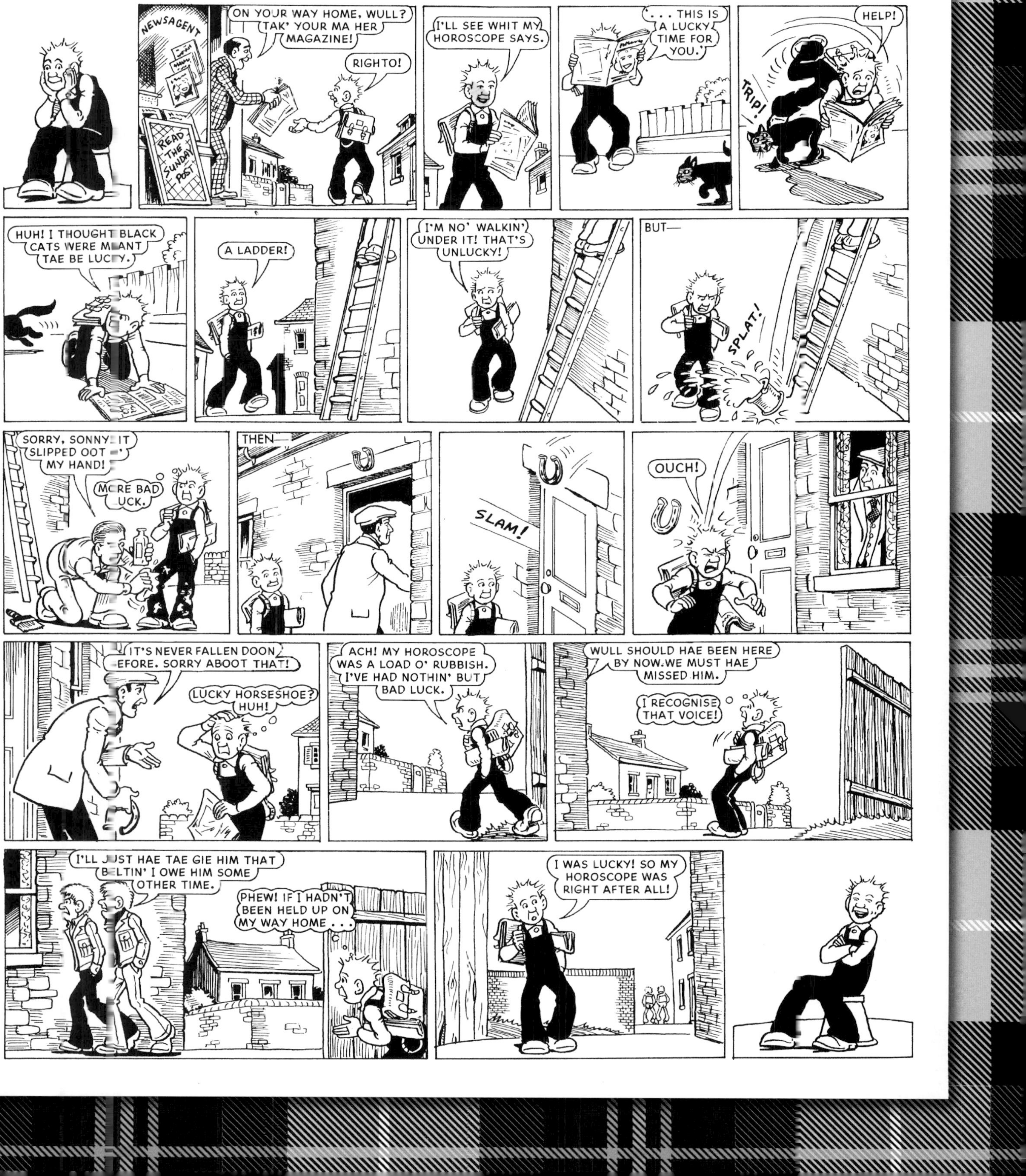

NEWSAGENT
ON YOUR WAY HOME, WULL? TAK' YOUR MA HER MAGAZINE!
RIGHTO!
READ THE SUNDAY POST
I'LL SEE WHIT MY HOROSCOPE SAYS.
'. . . THIS IS A LUCKY TIME FOR YOU.'
HELP!
TRIP!
HUH! I THOUGHT BLACK CATS WERE MEANT TAE BE LUCKY.
A LADDER!
I'M NO' WALKIN' UNDER IT! THAT'S UNLUCKY!
BUT—
SPLAT!
SORRY, SONNY! IT SLIPPED OOT O' MY HAND!
MORE BAD LUCK.
THEN—
SLAM!
OUCH!
IT'S NEVER FALLEN DOON BEFORE. SORRY ABOOT THAT!
LUCKY HORSESHOE? HUH!
ACH! MY HOROSCOPE WAS A LOAD O' RUBBISH. I'VE HAD NOTHIN' BUT BAD LUCK.
WULL SHOULD HAE BEEN HERE BY NOW. WE MUST HAE MISSED HIM.
I RECOGNISE THAT VOICE!
I'LL JUST HAE TAE GIE HIM THAT BELTIN' I OWE HIM SOME OTHER TIME.
PHEW! IF I HADN'T BEEN HELD UP ON MY WAY HOME . . .
I WAS LUCKY! SO MY HOROSCOPE WAS RIGHT AFTER ALL!

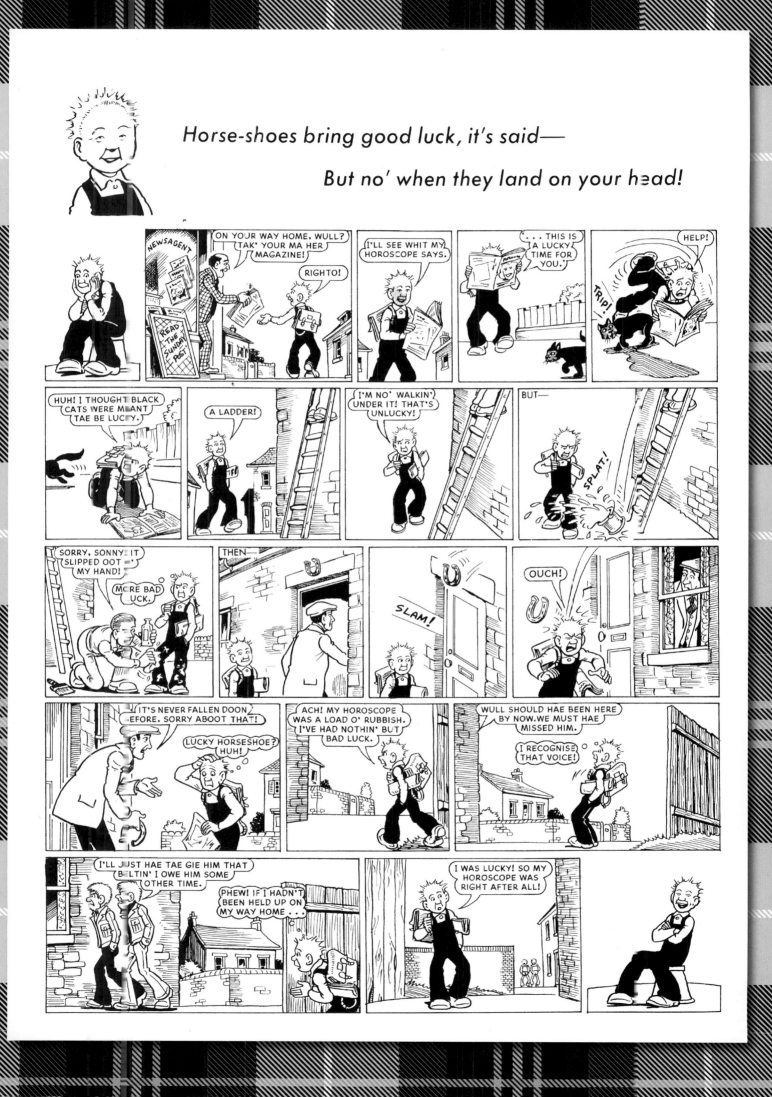

T-shirts are handy things for some—

But Wull's T-BREEKS mak' his chums glum!

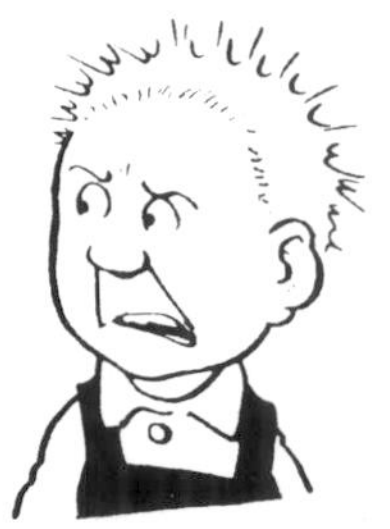

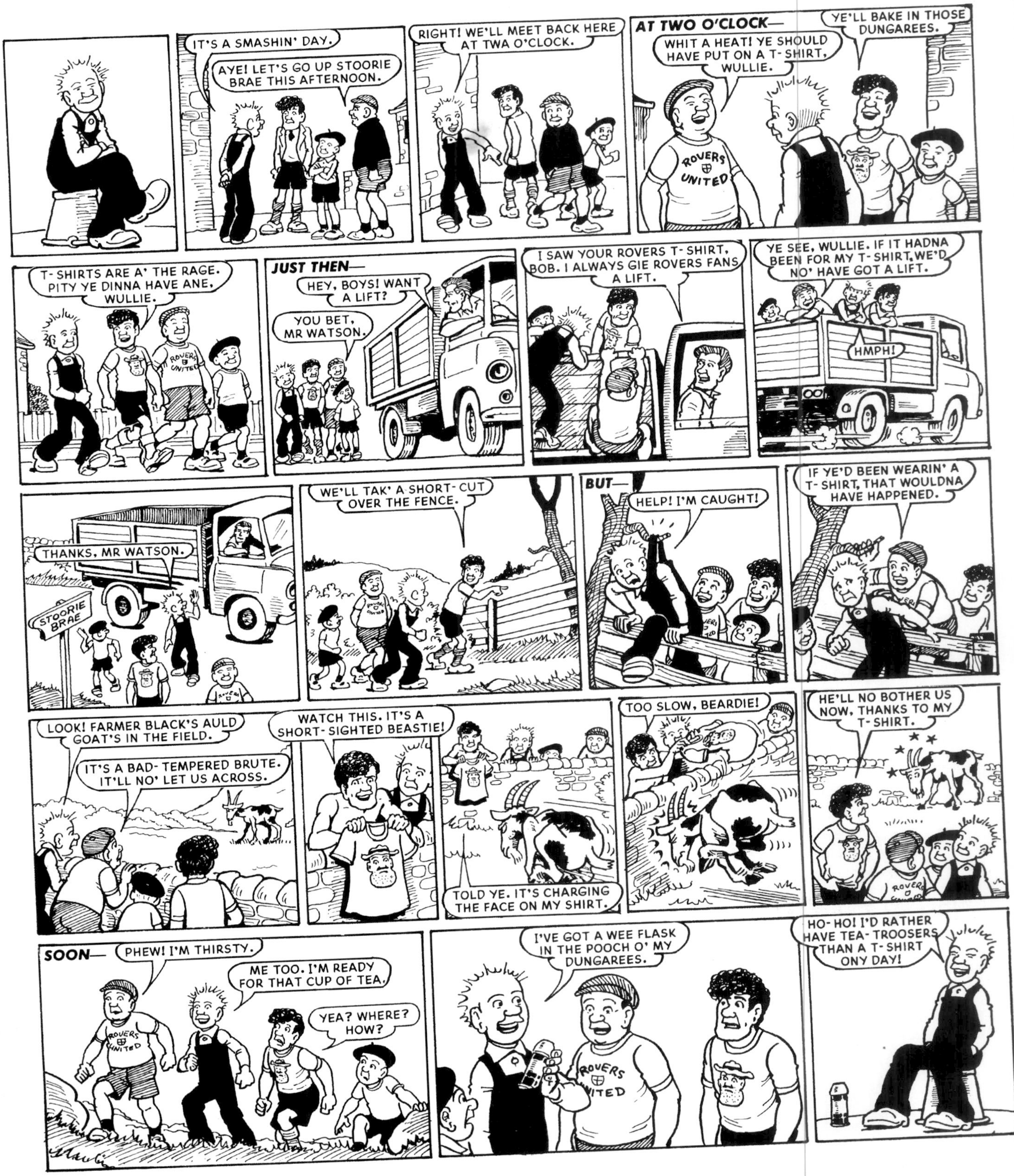
IT'S A SMASHIN' DAY.
AYE! LET'S GO UP STOORIE BRAE THIS AFTERNOON.
RIGHT! WE'LL MEET BACK HERE AT TWA O'CLOCK.
AT TWO O'CLOCK—
WHIT A HEAT! YE SHOULD HAVE PUT ON A T-SHIRT, WULLIE.
YE'LL BAKE IN THOSE DUNGAREES.
ROVERS UNITED
T-SHIRTS ARE A' THE RAGE. PITY YE DINNA HAVE ANE, WULLIE.
JUST THEN—
HEY, BOYS! WANT A LIFT?
YOU BET, MR WATSON.
I SAW YOUR ROVERS T-SHIRT, BOB. I ALWAYS GIE ROVERS FANS A LIFT.
YE SEE, WULLIE. IF IT HADNA BEEN FOR MY T-SHIRT, WE'D NO' HAVE GOT A LIFT.
HMPH!
THANKS, MR WATSON.
STOORIE BRAE
WE'LL TAK' A SHORT-CUT OVER THE FENCE.
BUT—
HELP! I'M CAUGHT!
IF YE'D BEEN WEARIN' A T-SHIRT, THAT WOULDNA HAVE HAPPENED.
LOOK! FARMER BLACK'S AULD GOAT'S IN THE FIELD.
IT'S A BAD-TEMPERED BRUTE. IT'LL NO' LET US ACROSS.
WATCH THIS. IT'S A SHORT-SIGHTED BEASTIE!
TOLD YE. IT'S CHARGING THE FACE ON MY SHIRT.
TOO SLOW, BEARDIE!
HE'LL NO BOTHER US NOW, THANKS TO MY T-SHIRT.
SOON—
PHEW! I'M THIRSTY.
ME TOO. I'M READY FOR THAT CUP OF TEA.
YEA? WHERE? HOW?
I'VE GOT A WEE FLASK IN THE POOCH O' MY DUNGAREES.
ROVERS UNITED
HO-HO! I'D RATHER HAVE TEA-TROOSERS THAN A T-SHIRT ONY DAY!

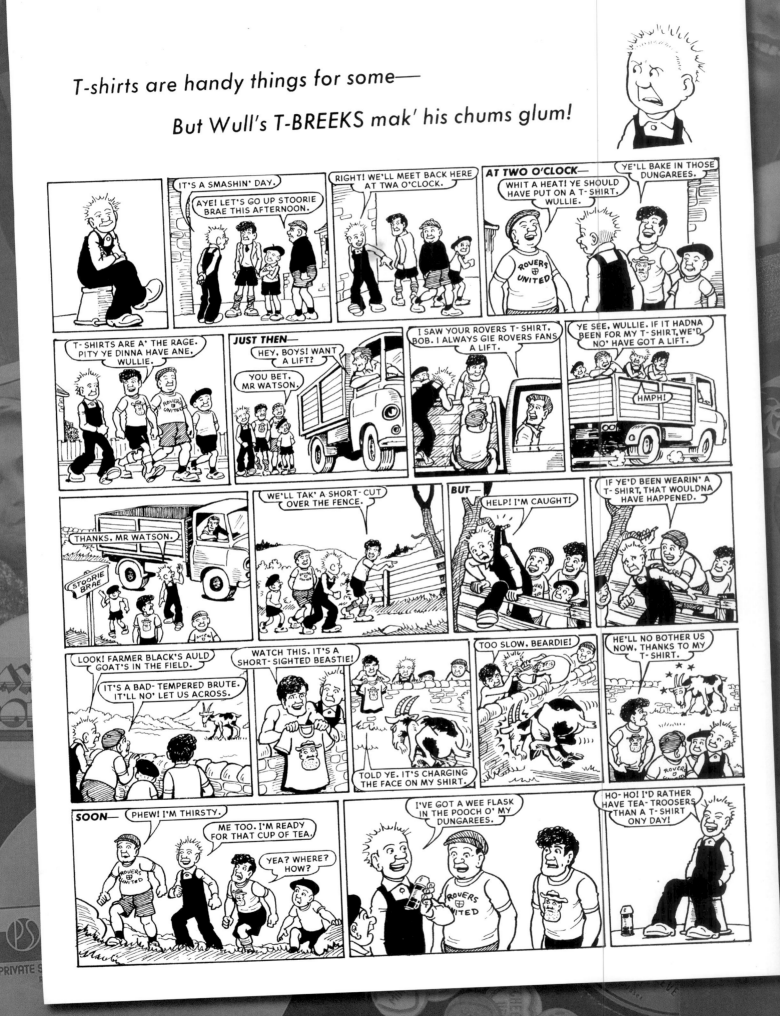

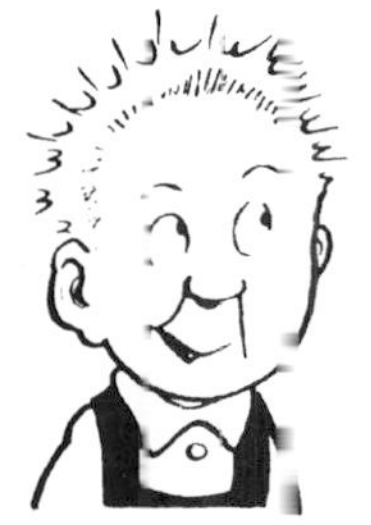

It's just one big surprise—

Wi' Wullie's bargain buys!

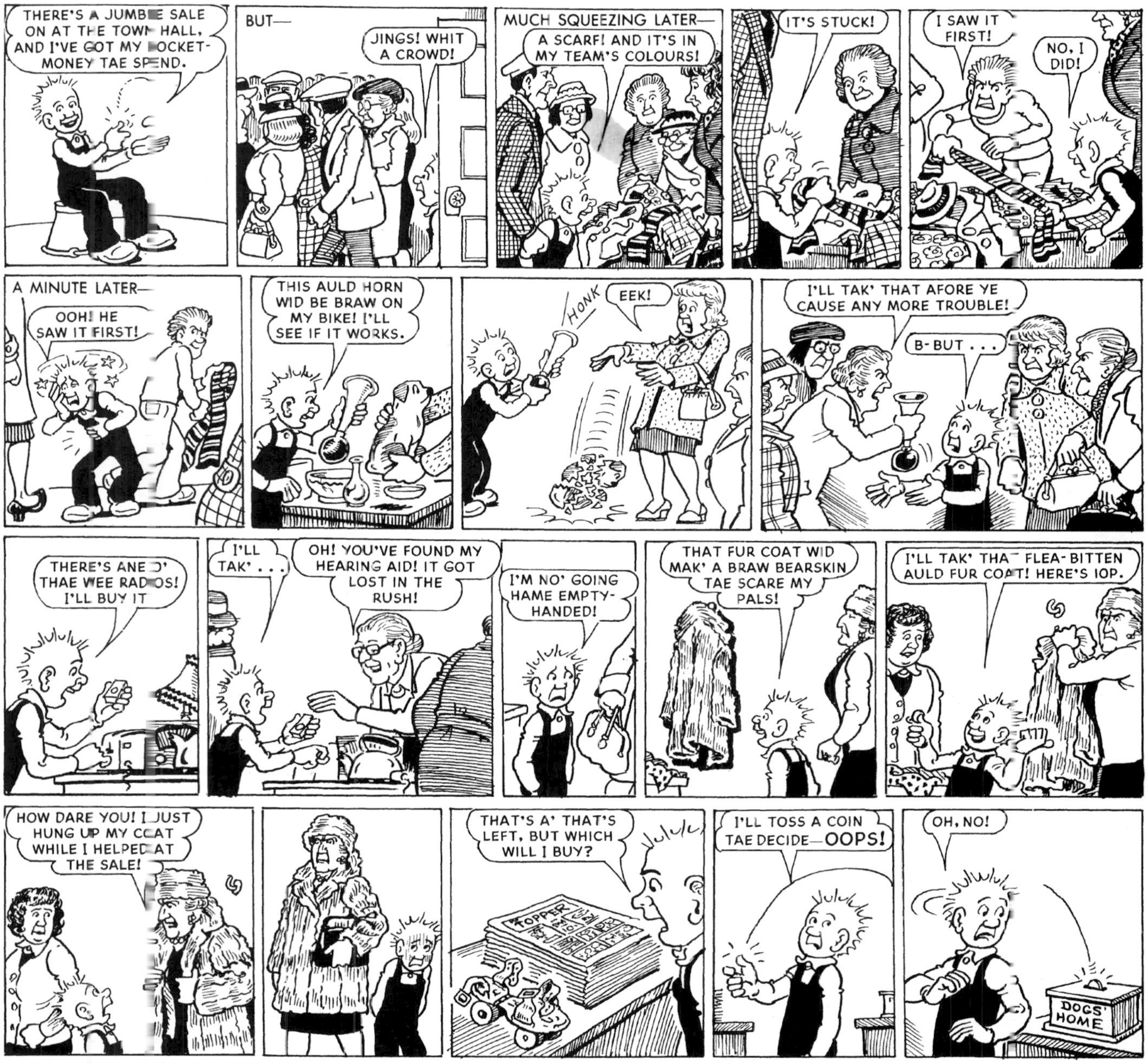

THERE'S A JUMBLE SALE ON AT THE TOWN HALL, AND I'VE GOT MY POCKET-MONEY TAE SPEND.
BUT—
JINGS! WHIT A CROWD!
MUCH SQUEEZING LATER—
A SCARF! AND IT'S IN MY TEAM'S COLOURS!
IT'S STUCK!
I SAW IT FIRST!
NO, I DID!
A MINUTE LATER—
OOH! HE SAW IT FIRST!
THIS AULD HORN WID BE BRAW ON MY BIKE! I'LL SEE IF IT WORKS.
HONK
EEK!
I'LL TAK' THAT AFORE YE CAUSE ANY MORE TROUBLE!
B-BUT . . .
THERE'S ANE O' THAE WEE RADIOS! I'LL BUY IT
I'LL TAK' . . .
OH! YOU'VE FOUND MY HEARING AID! IT GOT LOST IN THE RUSH!
I'M NO' GOING HAME EMPTY-HANDED!
THAT FUR COAT WID MAK' A BRAW BEARSKIN TAE SCARE MY PALS!
I'LL TAK' THAT FLEA-BITTEN AULD FUR COAT! HERE'S 10P.
HOW DARE YOU! I JUST HUNG UP MY COAT WHILE I HELPED AT THE SALE!
THAT'S A' THAT'S LEFT, BUT WHICH WILL I BUY?
TOPPER
I'LL TOSS A COIN TAE DECIDE—OOPS!
OH, NO!
DOGS' HOME
HOLD ON, SONNY
TOWN HALL
EVERYONE'S GONE HOME AND THESE HAVE BEEN LEFT. YOU CAN HAVE THEM.
THANKS!
HO-HO! I'VE GOT A PILE O' COMICS WI' THEIR AIN TRANSPORTER!
BEEZER

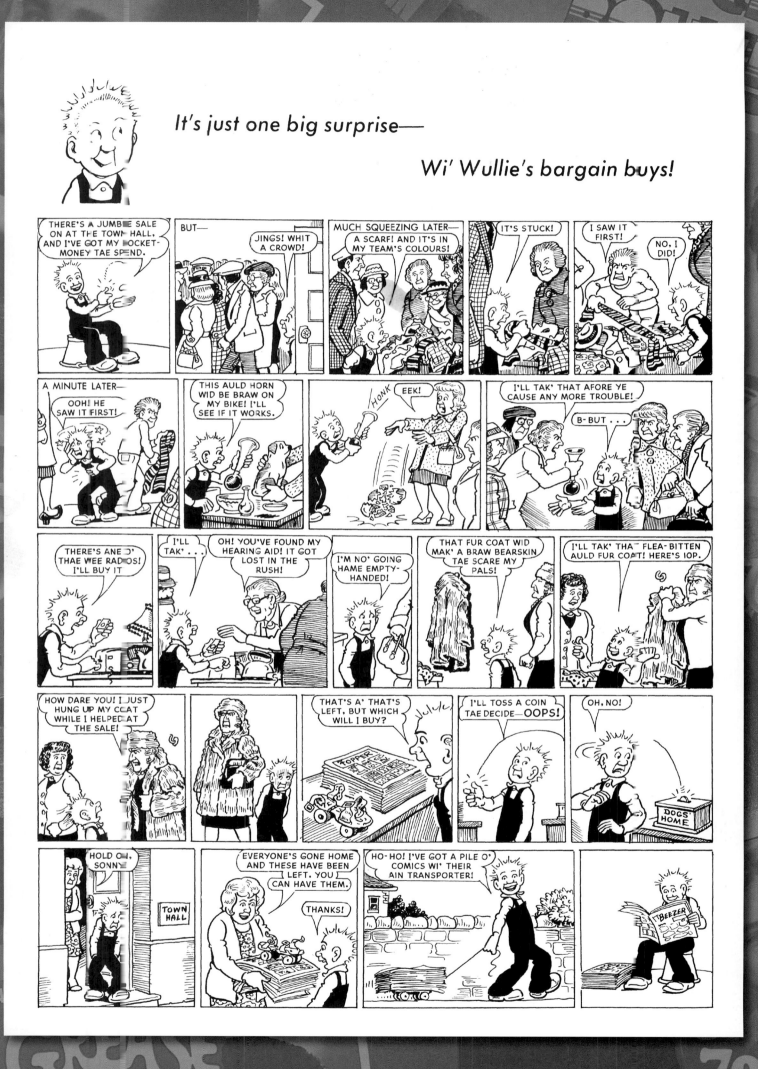

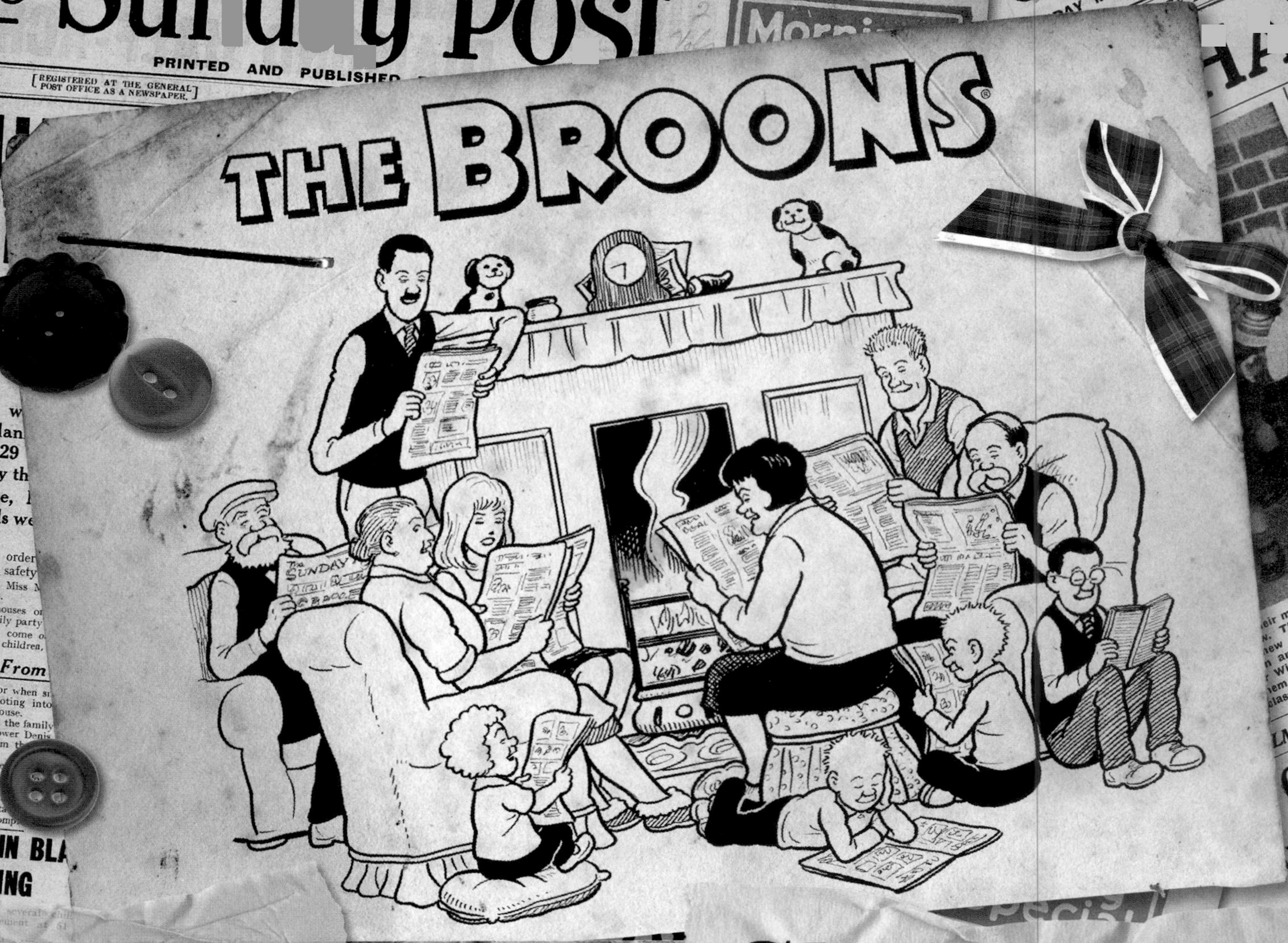
THE BROONS

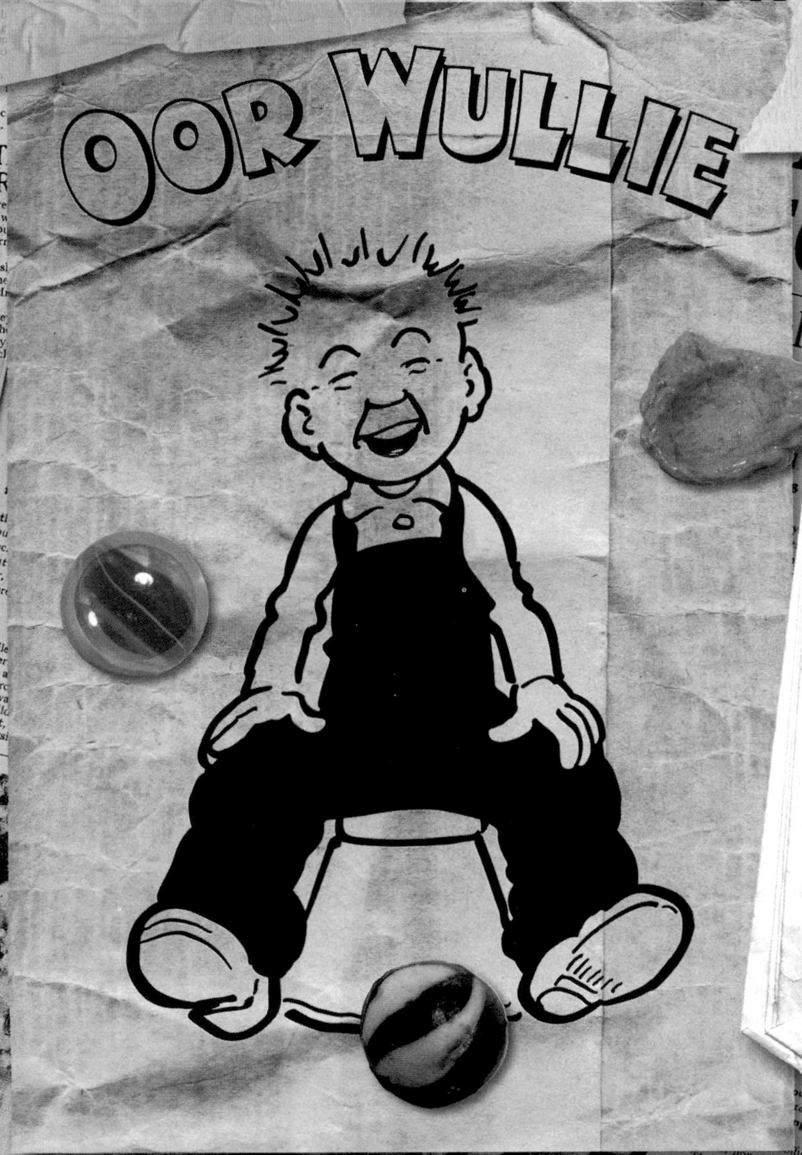
OOR WULLIE

The SUNDAY POST

Well, that's oor
tales frae the
seventies done,
We a' hope they
brought you fun,
And if its mair such
tales ye seek,
find us in
The Sunday Post
each week.

Published 2012 by DC Thomson Annuals Ltd,
Courier Buildings, 2 Albert Square, Dundee DD1 9QJ
ISBN 978-1-84535-494-7

www.dcthomson.co.uk
Printed in China
Please retain this information for future reference.

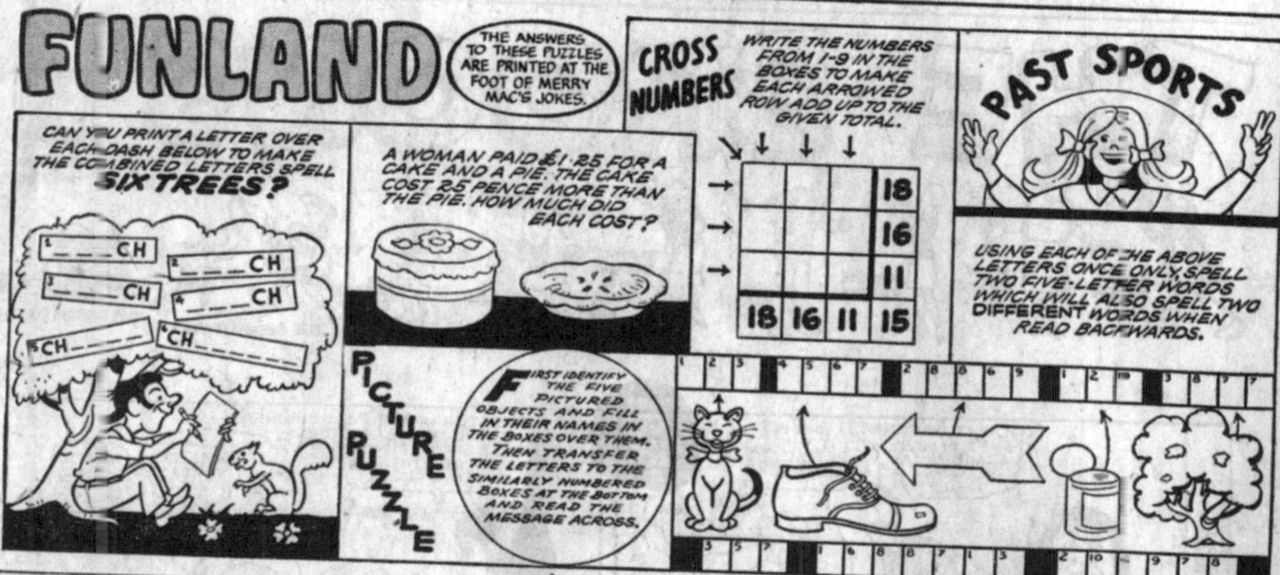
FUNLAND
THE ANSWERS TO THESE PUZZLES ARE PRINTED AT THE FOOT OF MERRY MAC'S JOKES.
CROSS NUMBERS
WRITE THE NUMBERS FROM 1-9 IN THE BOXES TO MAKE EACH ARROWED ROW ADD UP TO THE GIVEN TOTAL.
18
16
11
18 16 11 15
PAST SPORTS
USING EACH OF THE ABOVE LETTERS ONCE ONLY, SPELL TWO FIVE-LETTER WORDS WHICH WILL ALSO SPELL TWO DIFFERENT WORDS WHEN READ BACKWARDS.
CAN YOU PRINT A LETTER OVER EACH DASH BELOW TO MAKE THE COMBINED LETTERS SPELL SIX TREES?
1 _ _ _ CH
2 _ _ _ CH
3 _ _ _ CH
4 _ _ _ CH
5 CH _ _ _
6 CH _ _ _
A WOMAN PAID £1·25 FOR A CAKE AND A PIE. THE CAKE COST 25 PENCE MORE THAN THE PIE. HOW MUCH DID EACH COST?
PICTURE PUZZLE
FIRST IDENTIFY THE FIVE PICTURED OBJECTS AND FILL IN THEIR NAMES IN THE BOXES OVER THEM. THEN TRANSFER THE LETTERS TO THE SIMILARLY NUMBERED BOXES AT THE BOTTOM AND READ THE MESSAGE ACROSS.

CURIOUS CUSTOMS

UP AN' DOON AN' ROON' THE TOON!

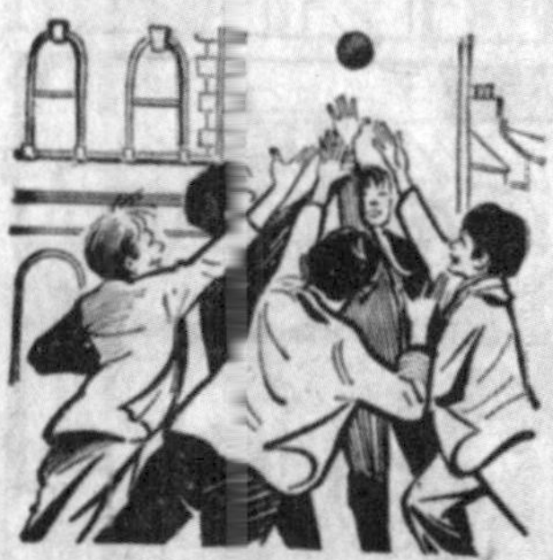

"COME away the Doonies!" "Up with the Uppies!"

The battle-cries ring out, and up go the shutters in the border town of Jedburgh! Windows are boarded, street lamps caged in — for it's time for Candlemas Ba', the roughest, toughest ball game in all Scotland!

The game takes place on a Thursday in February. There are 70-odd players — the Uppies, who were born south of the town's Mercat Cross, and the Doonies, who were born north of the Cross.

The balls, or ba's, as they are called, are made of leather, packed with hay, and are donated by local firms and organisations.

The game starts at noon, and depending on how many ba's are donated, can last for seven hours or more!

Dead on midday, the first ba' is thrown high into the air, and from then on, anything goes!

The opposing teams try to get the ba' to their respective "goals", or marks, at each end of the town. The ba' can be kicked or carried, and the chase can — and does — go through houses, gardens, and even into the icy-cold Jed Water!

FUN in VERSE

ECK McCOLL—HIS TALES ARE TALL.

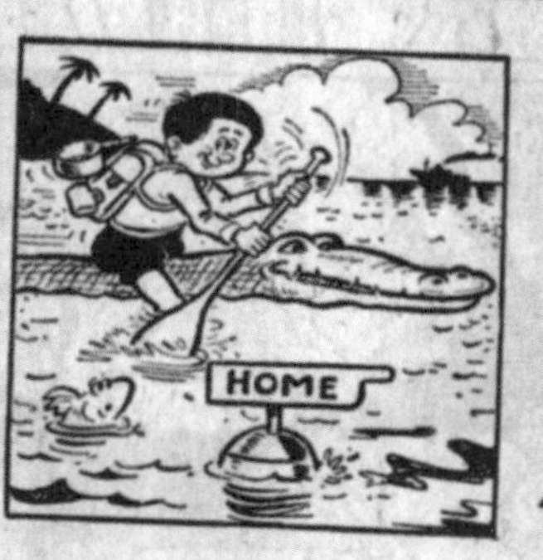
HOME

I like a visit to the zoo
Like any other child.
But once I went to jungle-land
To see them in the wild!

Loaded with my camping gear,
To Africa I went.
I caught six snakes and used them all
As guy-ropes for my tent.

A rhino charged at me one day—
I never turned a hair.
I bent my head and tossed the brute
A mile into the air.

I made friends with a tall giraffe
Which helped to keep me fit!
You'll maybe not believe this,
But I played leapfrog with it!

A herd of elephants came near—
I grabbed them with one hand,
And taught them to play music—
Now they've got a great brass band!

I paddled home aboard a croc—
It didn't take a trice.
Soon I went hunting once again—
Mum set me catching mice!

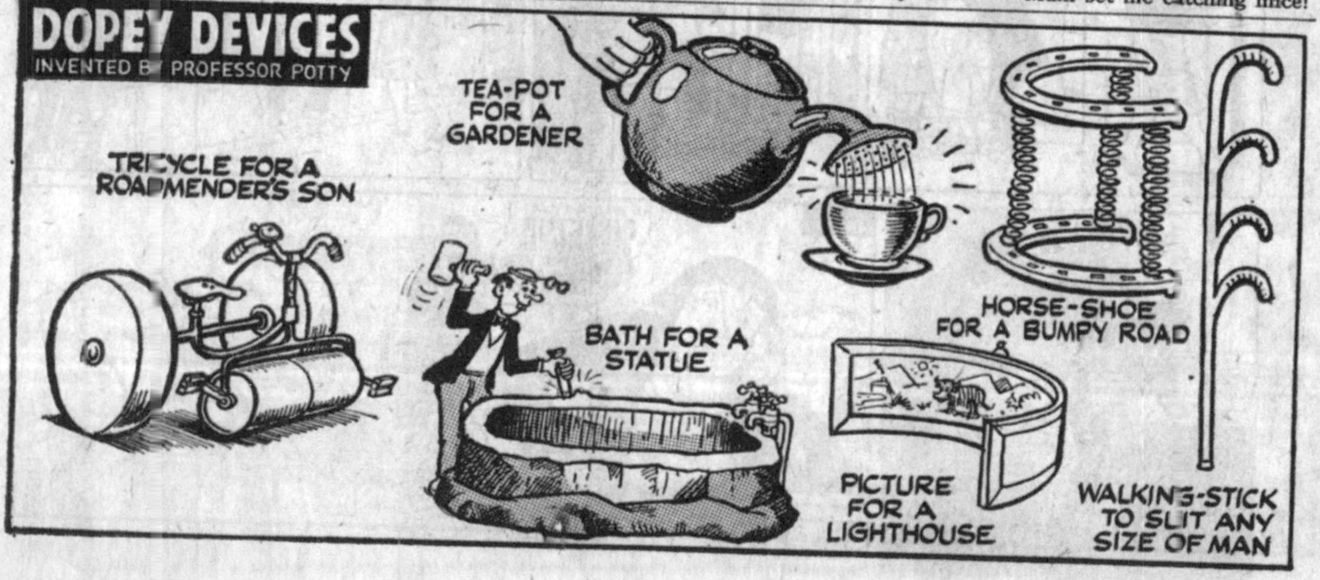
DOPEY DEVICES
INVENTED BY PROFESSOR POTTY
TEA-POT FOR A GARDENER
TRICYCLE FOR A ROADMENDER'S SON
BATH FOR A STATUE
HORSE-SHOE FOR A BUMPY ROAD
PICTURE FOR A LIGHTHOUSE
WALKING-STICK TO SUIT ANY SIZE OF MAN

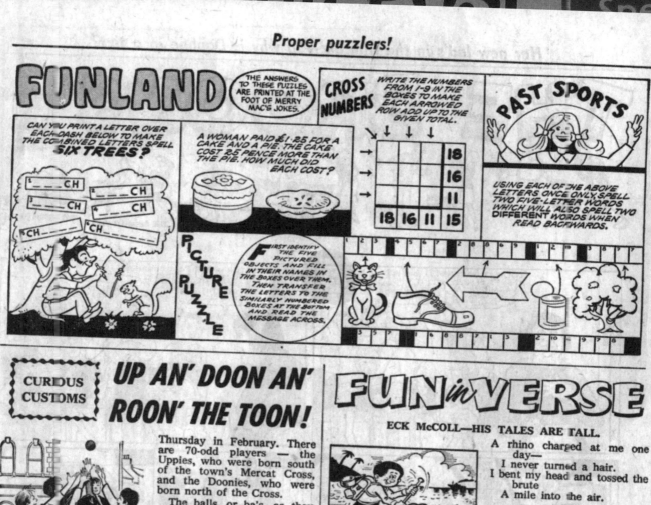

Funland's latest are the greatest!

FUNLAND

The answers to these puzzles are printed at the foot of Merry Mac's Jokes.

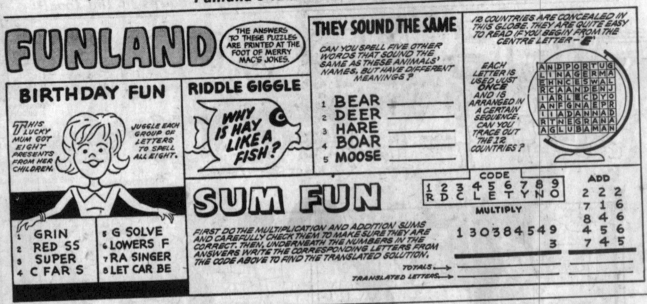

BIRTHDAY FUN

This lucky mum got eight presents from her children.

Juggle each group of letters to spell all eight.

1 GRIN
2 RED SS
3 SUPER
4 C FAR S
5 G SOLVE
6 LOWERS F
7 RA SINGER
8 LET CAR BE

RIDDLE GIGGLE

WHY IS HAY LIKE A FISH?

THEY SOUND THE SAME

Can you spell five other words that sound the same as these animals' names, but have different meanings?

1 BEAR ______
2 DEER ______
3 HARE ______
4 BOAR ______
5 MOOSE ______

12 countries are concealed in this globe. They are quite easy to read if you begin from the centre letter—'E'

Each letter is used just **once** and is arranged in a certain sequence. Can you trace out the 12 countries?

A	N	D	P	O	R	T	U	G
L	I	N	A	G	E	R	M	A
E	H	N	C	E	S	W	A	L
R	C	A	A	N	D	E	N	J
I	A	R	L	E	C	D	Y	O
A	N	F	G	N	A	E	P	R
I	I	A	D	A	N	N	A	D
R	T	N	E	G	R	A	N	A
A	G	L	U	B	A	M	A	N

SUM FUN

CODE

1	2	3	4	5	6	7	8	9
R	D	C	L	E	T	Y	N	O

First do the multiplication and addition sums and carefully check them to make sure they are correct. Then, underneath the numbers in the answers write the corresponding letters from the code above to find the translated solution.

MULTIPLY

130384549
× 3

ADD

222
716
846
456
745

TOTALS → ______
TRANSLATED LETTERS → ______

HE'S A ONE-SHOT WINNER!

CURIOUS CUSTOMS

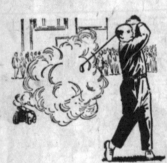

HERE is the strangest golf competition in all the world! There is only one competitor, he plays only one shot — and he always wins the trophy!

The trophy is the Silver Club of the Royal and Ancient Golf Club of St Andrews. By tradition, it is held by the captain of the club and only he plays for it. At one time, proper competitions were played for the trophy and the winner automatically became captain of the club.

The captain's single-shot victory takes place on the morning of the first day of the Autumn Meeting. At eight o'clock he drives off the first tee of the famous Old Course, and at the same time, a cannon booms out. As soon as his ball comes to earth, it is chased by the caddies of the district, who have positioned themselves on the first fairway.

They scramble for the ball and the winner then takes it back to the new captain, who presents him with a shining gold sovereign.

FUN in VERSE

A SHOCKER ROCKER!

!!!!!!!
PEONG!

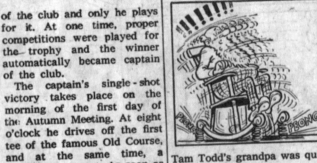

Tam Todd's grandpa was quite old,
With beard and snowy hair.
He spent his days a-resting in
His favourite rocking-chair.

But, lately, poor old Grandpa
Had been feeling rather blue.
He'd lost the knack of rocking—
Now what was he to do?

Wee Tammie had a brainwave!
Thought he, "It can't go wrong!
Old springs beneath the rockers—
They'll help Grandpa along!"

Tam found four springs and tied them on,
Then gave the chair a push.
It started rocking slowly,
But got faster . . . faster . . .
WHOOSH!

Poor Grandpa Todd was just a blur,
As he rocked to and fro.
The air was filled with anguished cries—
He sure was filled with woe!

Then—TWANG!—the springs broke. He nose-dived
On to an old settee.
Wee Tam soon took a nose-dive, too—
Across his father's knee!

DOPEY DEVICES

INVENTED BY PROFESSOR POTTY

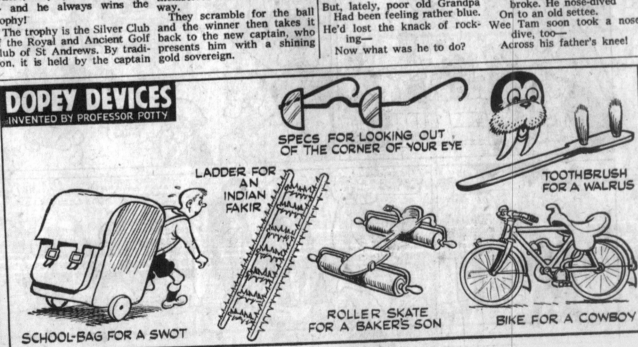

SPECS FOR LOOKING OUT OF THE CORNER OF YOUR EYE
TOOTHBRUSH FOR A WALRUS
LADDER FOR AN INDIAN FAKIR
SCHOOL-BAG FOR A SWOT
ROLLER SKATE FOR A BAKER'S SON
BIKE FOR A COWBOY